ILLINOIS
CENSUS RETURNS

1810 and 1818

Edited with Introduction and Notes by

MARGARET CROSS NORTON

ILLINOIS STATE LIBRARY

CLEARFIELD

Originally Published As
Collections of the Illinois State Historical Library
Volume XXIV
Statistical Series, Volume II
Springfield, 1935

Reprinted With Permission
Genealogical Publishing Company
Baltimore, 1969

Reprinted for
Clearfield Company, Inc. by
Genealogical Publishing Co., Inc.
Baltimore, Maryland
1993, 1996, 2002

Library of Congress Catalogue Card Number 70-75351
International Standard Book Number: 0-8063-0261-5

Made in the United States of America

COLLECTIONS OF THE ILLINOIS STATE HISTORICAL LIBRARY

VOLUME XXIV

———

STATISTICAL SERIES, VOLUME II

ILLINOIS
CENSUS RETURNS
1810, 1818

Edited with Introduction and Notes by
MARGARET CROSS NORTON
ILLINOIS STATE LIBRARY

———

Published by the Trustees of the
ILLINOIS STATE HISTORICAL LIBRARY
SPRINGFIELD, ILLINOIS

ACKNOWLEDGMENT

The editor wishes to thank the following for assistance in compiling this volume: Dr. Theodore C. Pease for placing notes for a previously planned edition at my disposal, also for providing the copy of the 1810 census from his files, and for many helpful suggestions and advice; to Miss Georgia L. Osborne, late librarian of the Illinois State Historical Library, and her assistants for reference material freely supplied; and to present and former assistants in the State Archives Division, particularly to Miss Helen R. Thompson, Mrs. Edith D. Strain and Mrs. Helen J. Hanson, typists.

TABLE OF CONTENTS

ILLINOIS CENSUS RETURNS
1810, 1818

SPECIAL INTRODUCTION

INTRODUCTION

From the time the French settlements in the Illinois country can be said to have existed as such, various estimates of their population, more or less accurate, were made. Two such censuses, one for the year 1732, and one for 1752, quite detailed in their classification of persons and property, are reproduced herewith.[1] Under the British régime an enumeration was made in 1767 for Major General Gage, apparently for military purposes. This document, printed in volume 11 of the *Collections* of the Illinois State Historical Library,[2] summarizes the number of inhabitants, white and black, their live stock, number of bushels of Indian corn and wheat in storage and number of mills at Kaskaskia, and the number of families at Cahokia, Prairie du Rocher, St. Philip and Fort Chartres, respectively. The first census listing names of heads of families appears to have been prepared in 1787 for the use of Barthélemi Tardiveau, an agent sent to Washington in that year to petition Congress for land grants for French and American settlers in Illinois. These schedules, with biographical annotations by C. W. Alvord, are to be found in the *Illinois Historical Collections*, volumes 2 and 5.[3] These list inhabitants in Cahokia, Kaskaskia, and Prairie du Rocher, and Americans in Illinois in August

---

[1] See *post*, XXII-XXVII. For a still earlier enumeration that is scarcely a detailed census, see *post*, XXI.
[2] C. W. Alvord and C. E. Carter, *The New Régime 1765-1767* (*Illinois Historical Collections*, 11), 469:
At Kaskaskias in 1767.
Inhabitants, Men, Women and Children: 600
Negro Men: 142
Negro Women: 81
Negro Boys: 80
....
N. B. Number of Familys, at Kahokia: 60
Prairie de Rocher: 25
St. Philip: 3
Fort Chartres: 3

[3] Alvord, *Cahokia Records 1778-1790* (*I. H. C.*, 2), 624-632: Total of 239 [240?] "male persons residents and inhabitants in the two villages [Cahokia and Prairie du Pont], all French, both men and male children." Certified September 9, 1787. Alvord, *Kaskaskia Records 1778-1790* (*I. H. C.*, 5), 414-423: 191 French inhabitants at Kaskaskia; 22 French families at Prairie du Rocher; 62 American men and 35 American children in Illinois.

and September of 1787. Although not intended for a census, the reports of the commissioners appointed by the United States government to settle the Cahokia and Kaskaskia land claims, printed in the *American State Papers,*[1] contain the most reliable information concerning the population of Illinois, especially the French inhabitants, prior to 1800. Petitions and memorials to the territorial legislatures and to Congress contain many names, but are unreliable because of numerous forgeries, faked names, and names of minors and nonresidents.

The earliest American censuses were those taken by the federal government in 1800, while Illinois was still a part of Indiana Territory, and in 1810, one year after Illinois became a separate territory. Except for summaries these two censuses have never been published. A transcript of a portion of the 1810 census for Illinois has been found in the files of the Illinois State Historical Survey, and has been reproduced in this volume. In addition to these federal censuses, the territorial legislature of Indiana ordered two census enumerations. The revenue act of 1805 ordered the sheriffs to take an "exact account of all free male inhabitants" at the time of taking the list of taxable property and to transmit the same to the secretary of the territory by April 1, 1806 on penalty of a $500 fine; three cents per name was allowed as compensation.[2] The sheriffs failed in some cases to make these returns, which were desired as a basis of apportionment of representation, and at the 1806 session of the General Assembly, they were warned by a joint resolution[3] to return lists of all free males of the ages of twenty-one years and upwards by June 1, 1807, subject to the same penalty and for the same fee. Early tax lists, poll books, marriage and probate records in the various county archives, as yet uncompiled, will eventually yield much of the data now missing for the record of territorial population.

By 1800 much of the original French population had disappeared from Illinois by emigration to the Louisiana coun-

[1] *American State Papers: Public Lands,* vol. 2.
[2] *Laws . . . of the Indiana Territory, . . . 1805,* p. 83 (F. S. Philbrick ed. [*I. H. C.,* 21], 152; compare next note).
[3] *Laws . . . of the Indiana Territory, . . . 1806,* p. 6 (Philbrick ed. [*I. H. C.,* 21], 177).

try, partly due to the activities of American land speculators who pointed out to them the probable discouragement by the Americans of slaveholding in the territory and the difficulties in proving title to their lands, because of the absence of records. The story of this migration can be pieced out from the testimony taken before the United States commissioners to settle the Kaskaskia and Cahokia land claims, in the volume of *American State Papers* referred to above.[1] A second dwindling of population in Illinois came as the result of the War of 1812 which kept the Indians so restless from 1811 to 1815 that the pioneers were forced to abandon their claims and congregate in the few towns and forts. Many left the territory and never returned. The story of this migration awaits further exploration in local records.

From 1816 on, the population of Illinois grew by leaps and bounds. For the period from 1818 to and including 1865, the federal census records are supplemented by census schedules taken by the territory and state of Illinois. The first of these censuses was taken in 1818 to substantiate the claim that Illinois had sufficient population to be given statehood. Although the Ordinance of 1787 indicated that admission was mandatory with a population of 60,000, it suggested possible admission with a less number. The memorial to Congress asking statehood claimed a population of 40,000 and that number was accepted as sufficient.[2] The original census act[3] provided that the enumeration should be taken between April 1 and June 1, 1818, and a supplementary act[4] provided for the listing of all new persons settling in Illinois between June 1 and December 1. The state constitution of 1818[5] required that a state census should be taken every five years beginning in 1820, and the state constitution of 1848[6] required that censuses be taken every ten years commencing in 1855. The last state census for Illinois was taken in 1865. Unfortunately many of these early census

[1] See *ante*, X, n. 1.
[2] S. J. Buck, *Illinois in 1818* (*Centennial History of Illinois,* introductory volume), chapter 8: The movement for admission.
[3] *Laws of Illinois Territory, 1817-1818* (1898 reprint), 42-44.
[4] *Ibid.,* 44-45.
[5] Constitution of 1818, article II, section 31.
[6] Constitution of 1848, article III, section 8.

records are missing from the state archives, particularly most of those for the 1818 supplementary census, all for the 1825 and 1830 censuses, and most of the 1835 and 1845 census returns.[1] The General Assembly of 1824-1825 passed a law[2] giving detailed instructions for taking the census. Commissioners were to be appointed by the county commissioners; the enumeration was to be taken in the three months following the first Monday in September of 1825 and in the corresponding periods every five years; the rate of compensation was fixed, based on the number of names turned in; and the commissioners, after exposing their lists for correction at their respective court houses, were to report to the secretary of state who was in turn to file the schedules with the speaker of the house at the next General Assembly. The governor transmitted schedules for the 1825 census to a special session[3] called January 26, 1826 to reapportion representation. The returns indicated a population of 72,817 inhabitants. "The tide of emigration, which had been for several years checked by various causes, both general and local, has again set in, and has afforded a greater accession of population to the state during the past, than it had for the three preceding years." No copies of these returns are in the state archives, but returns for Randolph County are in the court house of that county.[4]

The census law was revised in 1829[5] and provided for payment of the census from any otherwise unappropriated moneys in the state treasury. The returns were to give further information concerning ages, manufactures, mills, etc., and were to be accompanied by certified lists of persons subject to militia duty for the use of the adjutant general. No census returns for 1830 are now in the state archives, though the bills for the apportionment of representation in 1830-1831 were introduced by the joint committee[6] to whom the census

---

[1] See list of extant state census schedules, *post*, XIX-XXI.
[2] *Laws of 1825*, p. 32: An Act to provide for taking the Census or enumeration of the Inhabitants of the State of Illinois. Approved December 27, 1824.
[3] *Journal of the House of Representatives*, special session, 1826, p. 11.
[4] T. C. Pease, *County Archives of the State of Illinois* (*I. H. C.*, 12), 559.
[5] *Revised Code of 1829*, p. 18: An act to provide for the taking of the census, or enumeration of the inhabitants of the state.
[6] *Journal of the House of Representatives*, 1830-1831, pp. 7, 125, etc.

returns were turned over, and the secretary of state[1] transmitted the schedules for Hancock County after the committee was appointed. Copies of an 1830 census, either state or federal, for Bond County, are in the court house for that county.[2] Subsequent state censuses, namely 1835, 1840, 1845, 1855, and 1865 were taken under the provisions of the 1829 law, which, with minor revisions, was reënacted as chapter 19 of the revised laws of 1845[3] and amended in minor details in 1855.[4] Under the constitution of 1848[5] the federal and state censuses were to be used as bases for apportionment of representation, and under the constitution of 1870[6] only the federal census was to be used for that purpose. Returns for 1835 are tabulated in the House Journal for 1835-1836,[7] but only the original schedules for Fulton and Jasper counties were found in the archives, supplemented by the Fayette County schedules deposited a few years ago by the supervisors of that county. The 1840 census schedules for about half the counties are in the files, while the respective county archives have schedules for Alexander, Crawford, Gallatin, Monroe, Perry, Pope and Rock Island counties.[8] Tabular statements for the 1840 and 1845 censuses are to be found in the Senate reports for 1840 and 1846 respectively.[9] All the 1845 schedules except for Cass, Macoupin, and Tazewell counties are missing from the files, though Stephenson County has a copy of its returns.[10] The 1855 returns are complete. A supplemental volume for that year contains a census of the deaf, blind, and insane, giving their names, ages, names of heads of families, and addresses. Although no state census was taken in 1860, three counties, Alexander, Bond, and Clark, made returns. Returns

[1] *Ibid.*, 198.
[2] Pease, *County Archives of the State of Illinois* (I. H. C., 12), 59.
[3] *Revised Laws of 1845*, chapter 19. Approved March 3, 1845.
[4] *Laws of 1855*, p. 151: An Act to provide for taking the census. Approved February 15, 1855.
[5] Constitution of 1848, article III, section 8.
[6] Constitution of 1870, article IV, section 6.
[7] *Journal of the House of Representatives*, 1835-1836, p. 372.
[8] Pease, *County Archives of the State of Illinois* (I. H. C., 12), 47, 148, 240, 472, 511, 536, 571. Returns for Monroe, Perry, and Pope counties are federal census returns.
[9] *Senate Reports:* 12 General Assembly, 2 session, 1840, pp. 181-183, 403-414; 15 General Assembly, 1 session, 1846, pp. 65-71.
[10] Pease, *County Archives of the State of Illinois* (I. H. C., 12), 621.

for the last state census, taken in 1865, are complete. A list of state census returns is appended.

Until the publication of the present volume there has been no compilation of early census schedules for Illinois. Although disappointing in that biographical and genealogical data concerning the early settlers are not given in these census records, they are valuable not only for the sentimental reason that they preserve the names of hundreds of pioneers otherwise forgotten, but also as providing the basis for studies in population movement in the United States. That these state census enumerations were taken more frequently than those by the federal government make them particularly useful for such studies. This point is illustrated by the fact that the population of Illinois increased between forty and fifty per cent in the two and a half years between taking the first census in June, 1818, and the enumeration returned in December, 1820. In June, 1818, the secretary reported the population as 34,610;[1] if the census commissioner's estimate of 980 souls at the frontier forts be deducted, the net figure will be 33,630. An additional census taken in part of the counties added 1948 by December 1, 1818, and by December, 1820, it had reached 51,159, a gain of over 15,000. The federal census for 1820, certified to on March 22, 1821, but for the most part taken at the same time as the state census, gives the population as 55,211.

Incidentally, the discrepancies between the state and the federal census of 1820 show vividly the mobility of the settlers. As is shown in notes appended to the volume of 1820 census returns, which is to follow this volume, the returns for the various counties show decided differences both in numbers and in the names of families, only partly to be explained by occasional padding (as in the case of Madison County) or inaccuracies on the part of the census takers. These census returns were being compiled in 1820 at just that season of the year when, the crops having been harvested, people began coming into the state or moving about in the state seeking new home sites. This is particularly shown in those counties along the highways to the west, notably in Gallatin County, where

[1] See tables, *post*, XXX.

large numbers of single men are listed—presumably men who
had left their families behind while they scouted for new loca-
tions. Also there is found a considerable repetition of names,
often a mere coincidence of common names, but occasionally
of names sufficiently distinctive to warrant the assumption
that they are the same persons. The early settler seldom
purchased his homestead inside of two or three years. Thus
a comparison between the 1818 and 1820 returns shows that
though a large number of families remained in the same county, the neighborhoods and number of persons in the various
families shifted considerably. To what extent the returns were
padded by listing families merely in transit through the state
is difficult to determine, but as very few immigrants had a
fixed location in view and might choose a site close to where
they might be found temporarily encamped, the census
enumerator was justified in listing them. This constant shift-
ing about makes all population statistics very unreliable, but
it adds interest to a study of the names themselves.

County histories list some persons who tradition says had
settled in the state before 1820 whose names do not appear in
these records, sometimes because the census taker did not find
them, often because two families living together more or less
temporarily, were listed as one family. On the other hand,
hundreds of pioneers whose names appear, sometimes in both
the 1818 and 1820 returns, have been forgotten by the com-
pilers of county histories. This is particularly true of those
pioneers who removed from the county or who left no descendants there.

The exact location of the various families is not given in
the schedules, but this can be approximated from the fact that
the names of families were generally listed in the order enu-
merated. A map showing the principal settlements in Illinois
is reproduced here from S. J. Buck, *Illinois in 1818,* in which
volume he devotes a chapter to a study of "The Extent of
Settlement."[1] A map for 1820 would look much the same. It
would show a denser population in southern Illinois and a
spreading of settlement into the region west of the third prin-

[1] Buck, *Illinois in 1818*, chapter 8.

cipal meridian and northward to the Sangamon River, the furthest north being a settlement in what is now Logan County. Between the Illinois and the Mississippi rivers the outlying settlement was near what is now Atlas, in Pike County. By 1820 there were also settlements at Chicago and in the Fever River lead mine country in the present Jo Daviess County, neither of which were visited when the census was taken.

The original census law of 1818[1] provided in detail the method for taking the enumeration. The governor was to appoint "some fit person in each county" to take the returns. The census enumerator took his oath before a justice of the peace or a judge of the county court and was subject to a penalty of $200 for dereliction of duty. The county was to pay him a specified lump sum ranging from $40 each for Bond, Franklin, and Pope counties to $80 for Crawford County. Any person over sixteen years of age was to be fined $20 for failure or refusal to answer the questions correctly. The censor was to make the enumeration by "actual enquiry at the dwelling house, or of the head of every family in their respective counties." In gathering this data, however, he must have been somewhat handicapped by the further provision that he was to combine with his duties of census taker that of tax assessor. Another temptation to falsify statements to him must have been the fear that this was another device for listing persons subject to militia duty. The law specified the following form:

Names of heads of families,
Free white males, twenty-one years and upwards,
All other white inhabitants,
Free people of colour,
Servants or slaves.

The law of 1819[2] providing for taking the census of 1820 makes similar provisions. The commissioners to take this census were appointed by the county commissioners, and their compensation was paid from the state treasury. The additional duty of acting as assessor was omitted from this law. The enumeration was to begin the first of August, and returns

[1] *Laws . . . of Illinois Territory . . . 1817-1818* (1898 reprint), 42-45.
[2] *Laws of 1819*, pp. 197-198.

were to be made to the secretary of state on or before the first Monday in December, 1820. The form to be used was similar to that for the 1818 census, though some of the census takers interpreted their instructions as calling for more detailed information as to ages and sex.

When the State Archives Division found the 1818 and 1820 census returns, they were bound in one large volume. At some time prior to binding they had gone through a fire, and part of the returns for St. Clair County for 1818 were missing and the rest charred. All papers in the volume were badly water soaked and stained. The paper was so soft and discolored that immediate repair and rebinding were necessary. These records are now bound in three volumes, the sheets having been covered on both sides with silk gauze and enclosed in paper frames. In their present condition they can be handled freely and are protected from further disintegration. For the most part the writing is clear and legible, though without authorization or knowledge of the Archives Division the binder undertook to retouch the writing in places with the inaccurate results to have been expected. In editing this volume, however, the spelling as shown on a photostatic copy made before binding has been followed. Often, particularly in the spelling of the French names, the census taker spelled names phonetically, and this spelling has been preserved in the printed copy even when obviously the result of carelessness. The 1820 state census has been compared with the 1820 federal census records in Washington, and important discrepancies cited in footnotes appended to the second volume containing the 1820 census.

The chief purpose of these volumes is to present as accurately as possible a list of settlers in Illinois in 1818 and 1820 as found in census records. The names found in the 1818 and 1820 state census have been compared with each other and with the federal census of 1820, and discrepancies noted where they occur within the same counties. The federal census of 1820 gives much fuller information as to ages, occupations and township residence than either of the state returns. Since this federal census will eventually be printed no attempt has been made to compare anything but the actual names of families.

For the most part, of course, such a comparison of names yields little more than a list of minor discrepancies in spelling, but where the returns were taken by more than one person there are often found wide differences not only as to the spelling of names but as to what the names actually were. This is notably true for Gallatin County, where as between a list of 554 families in the state census for 1820 and a list of 451 families in the federal census taken two months later there is a discrepancy of 343 names which cannot be matched. There are several probable reasons for these disagreements. In the first place, brothers or several unrelated families frequently lived together temporarily and might not name the same man as head of the family to the different enumerators. There were, of course, some deaths between 1818 and 1820, and widows or other persons of the family are named as heads of families. In many cases the enumerators visited different communities in the more sparsely settled areas. There was also some vagueness as to county boundary lines. Again, rather frequently the census takers misunderstood names of similar sound, especially among French settlers whose names they spelled phonetically. All such differences are noted where the location and numerical data given show that such dissimilar names really referred to the same family. Evidences of padding or other items of special interest are noted in the footnotes to the returns of each county. No attempt has been made to trace families removing to another county between 1818 and 1820 since it is difficult to determine identities accurately in such cases.

Footnotes giving supplementary biographical data concerning the various settlers would have been desirable, but such a presentation was found impracticable for this volume, partly because of space limitations but largely because such data as is at present available is sketchy and unreliable, based largely on commercial county histories and not on research in state and county records. The State Historical Library and the State Archives Division are collecting such data which it is hoped can be incorporated in a later volume.

EXTANT CENSUS RETURNS TAKEN BY THE
STATE OF ILLINOIS

1818

Bond
Crawford
Franklin
Gallatin
Jackson
Jefferson
Johnson
Madison
Monroe
Pope
St. Clair
Union
Washington
White

1820

Alexander
Bond
Clark
Crawford
Edwards (Summary)
Franklin
Gallatin
Jackson
Jefferson
Johnson
Madison
Monroe
Pope
Randolph
St. Clair
Union
Washington
Wayne
White

1825

*Randolph

1830

*Bond

1835

Cook (Summary)
*Crawford
*Edwards
†Fayette
Fulton
*Hamilton
Jasper
*Knox
For tabular statement see *House Journal*, 1835-1836, p. 372.

1840

Adams
‡Alexander
Bond
Boone (Summary)
Calhoun
Carroll (Summary)
Champaign
Christian (Summary)
Clark
Clay
Clinton
Coles
Cook
‡Crawford
DeKalb (Summary)
DeWitt (Summary)
Edgar
Effingham
Fayette (Summary)
Franklin
Fulton
*Gallatin
Greene (Summary)

* In records at county court house. See Pease, *County Archives of the State of Illinois* (*I. H. C.*, 12).
† Deposited in State Archives Division by Fayette County Board of Supervisors.
‡ Returns in both state and county archives.

1840

Hamilton (Mostly illegible)
Hancock (Summary)
Henry (Summary)
Hardin
Iroquois (Summary)
Jackson
Jasper
Jefferson (Summary)
Jersey (Summary)
Jo Daviess
Johnson
Kane (Summary)
Knox
LaSalle
Lawrence
Lee (Summary)
Livingston
Logan (Summary)
‡Monroe
*Perry (U. S.)
*Pope (U. S.)
Randolph
‡Rock Island
St. Clair (Summary)
Sangamon (Summary)
Schuyler
Scott (Summary)
Shelby (Summary)
Stark
Tazewell
Union
Vermilion
Wabash (Summary)
Washington (Summary)
Warren (Summary)
Wayne (Summary)
White
Whiteside
Will (Summary)
Williamson (Summary)
Winnebago (Summary)
For tabular statements see *Senate Reports,* 12 General Assembly, 2 session, 1840, pp. 181-183, 403-414.

1845

Cass
Kendall (Summary)
Macoupin
Morgan (Summary)
*Stephenson
Tazewell
For tabular statement see *Senate Reports,* 15 General Assembly, 1 session, 1846, pp. 65-71.

1850

(None taken)

1855

Adams
Alexander
Bond
Boone
Brown
Bureau
Calhoun
Cass
Champaign
Christian
Clark
Clay
Clinton
Coles
Cook
Crawford
Cumberland
DeKalb
DeWitt
DuPage
Edgar
Edwards
Effingham
Fayette
Fulton
Greene
Grundy
Hamilton

CENSUS OF ILLINOIS, 1723[1]

1724, Juillet

Memoire concernant les postes des Illinois.

M. Diron a fait au mois de Juin 1723,
un Recensement des habitans Establis dans ces
differents postes
Suivant lequel il y a,

	habitans	Ouvriers blancs	femmes	Enfants
Aux Kaskassias	64	41	37	54
Au Fort de Chartres dont un detachment de Maramek	39	42	28	17
Aux Koakias ou Tamarois	7	1	1	3
	110	84	66	74

[*Translation*]

1724, July

Memoir relating to the posts of the Illinois.

Monsieur Diron has made, to the month
of June 1723, a census of the inhabitants
residing in these various posts.
Following that, there are:

	Inhabitants	White laborers	Women	Children
At Kaskaskia	64	41	37	54
At Fort Chartres which is a detachment from Maramek	39	42	28	17
At Cahokia or Tamaroa.	7	1	1	3
	110	84	66	74

[1] Archives Nationales, Colonies, C¹³A, 8:226.

CENSUS OF ILLINOIS 1732[1]

Recensement general des habitans de la Prairie du Fort de Chartres des Illinois et de leur etat au premièr de Janvier 1732

. . . .

Enfans legitimes	66
Enfans bastardes	6
Arpents de terre de face	140
Terres en valleur	827
Negres Piece d'Indes	13
Negresses " " "	6
Negrillons ou negrettes	18
Esclaves Indiens	19m et 20fem
Boeufs	116
Vaches	122
Cochons	376
Chevaux	59
Moulins	5
Maisons	41
Granges	19

Recensement general des habitans des Cascassias aux Illinois et leur etat au 1er Janvier 1732

[*Translation*]

General census of the inhabitants of the Prairie of Fort de Chartres of Illinois and of their condition on the first of January, 1732

. . . .

Legitimate children	66
Illegitimate children	6
Arpents in frontage	140
Lands in good condition	827
Negroes	13
Negresses	6
Little negroes or negresses	18
Indian slaves	19 men 20 women
Oxen	116
Cows	122
Pigs	376
Horses	59
Mills	5
Houses	41
Barns	19

General census of the inhabitants of the Kaskaskia of the Illinois and their state on the first of January, 1732

[1] Archives Nationales, Ministère des Colonies, G[1] vol. 464.

Enfans legitimes 87
Enfans batards 14
Arpents de terre de face......... 126
Terres en valleur..............2054
Negres Piece d'Indes.......... 38
Negresses " " " 23
Negrillon ou negrittes.......... 41
Esclaves Indiene .... 30 m—38 fem
Boeufs 256
Vaches 237
Cochons 894
Chevaux 108
Moulins 11
Maisons 52
Granges 28
Mission des Cahoquias et son etat
Terres en valleur.............. 39
Negres Piece d'Indes.......... 3
Negresses " " " 1
Esclaves Indiene 5
Esclaves Indiennes 3

[*Translation*]

Legitimate children 87
Illegitimate children 14
Arpents of frontage............ 126
Land in good condition........2054
Negroes 38
Negresses 23
Little negroes or negresses...... 41
Indian slaves .... 30 men 38 women
Oxen 256
Cows 237
Pigs 894
Horses 108
Mills 11
Houses 52
Barns 28
Mission at Cahokia and its condition
Lands in good condition........ 39
Negroes 3
Negresses 1
Indian slaves 5
Indian women slaves.......... 3

Boeufs 7
Vaches 30
Chevaux 10
Cochons 30
Maisons 2
Granges 1
Concession de M. Renault et des habitans dud. Lieu
Enfans Legitimes 17
Arpents de terre de face........ 250
Terres en valleur 471
Negres piece d'Indes 14
Negresses " " " 3
Negrillons et nigrettes......... 5
Esclaves Indien 1
" Indienne 1
Boeufs 28
Vaches 42
Chevaux 25
Cochons 163
Maisons 9
Moulins 2

[*Translation*]

Oxen 7
Cows 30
Horses 10
Pigs 30
Houses 2
Barns 1
Concession of M. Renault and the inhabitants of the said place
Legitimate children 17
Arpents of frontage........... 250
Lands in good condition....... 471
Negroes 14
Negresses 3
Little negroes and negresses..... 5
Indian slaves 1
Indian women slaves........... 1
Oxen 28
Cows 42
Horses 25
Pigs 163
Houses 9
Mills 2

Granges 7
Ecuries 5
Recapitulation general de tout le pays des Illinois
Hommes 159
Femme 39
Orphelins ou batards........... 20
Arpents de terre de face........ 266
Terres en valleur...............3391
Negres Piece d'Indes........... 68
Negresses " " " 33
Negrillons et negrittes.......... 64
Esclaves Indien 57
Esclaves Indienne 62
Boeufs 407
Vaches 431
Chevaux 202
Cochons 1463
Maisons 104
Moulins 18
Granges 55
Ecuries 5

[*Translation*]

Barns 7
Stables 5
General recapitulation of all the country of the Illinois
Men 159
Women 39
Orphans or illegitimate children.. 20
Arpents of frontage............ 266
Lands in good condition........3391
Negroes 68
Negresses 33
Little negroes and negresses..... 64
Indian slaves 57
Indian women slaves........... 62
Oxen 407
Cows 431
Horses 202
Pigs 1463
Houses 104
Mills 18
Barns 55
Stables 5

RECENCEMENT GENERAL

	Hommes [*Men*]	Femmes [*Women*]	Veuve [*Widows*]	Garçon portant armes [*Youth of Military Age*]	Garçon² audessus 12 ans [*Youth above 12 years*]	Filles Nubiles [*Marriageable Girls*]	Filles² audess. 12 ans [*Girls above 12 years*]	Voluntaires [*Volunteers*]	Negroes [*Negroes*]	Negrisses [*Negresses*]
Village de Caskaskias	58	50	8	36	64	11	46	77	102	67
Fort de Chartre	26	24	7	27	20	10	36	35	34	25
Village de St Philip	15	12	2	9	6	8	12	6	20	7
Praire de Rocher	10	9	2	6	6	1	5	14	18	8
Caodskias³	18	13	1	3	16	6	17	15	11	6
Vilage de st Jeune Vieve⁴	7	4	0	3			4	3	2	
Total general	134	112	20	84	36⁵	36	120	156⁵	187	113

[1] Chatham MSS., Public Record Office, Bundle 95. This appears in the Chatham Papers and is apparently a piece of intelligence of about the year 1752 which had found its way into the hands of William Pitt. The English copy apparently leaves something to be desired.

[2] Ordinarily these columns would read "under twelve years" but the word for "above" is used.

DU PAIS DES ILLINOIS 1752[1]

Negritton [Little Negroes]	Negrittes [Little Negresses]	Sauvage [Indians]	Sauvagess [Indian Women]	Beuf [Oxen]	Vache [Cows]	Genisse [Heifers]	Cheveau [Horses]	Jument [Mares]	Cochon [Pigs]	Fusil [Guns]	Poudre [Powder]	Plomb & Balle [Lead and Ball]	Arpent de Terre [Arpents of Land]	Arpent de Terre et value [Arpents of Land in Condition]	Carreau [Plows]
45	32	31	44	320	331	145	346	75	841	155	61	1771	128	2232	147
16	13	13	23	172	131	78	72	30	198	101	97	276	131	1800	80
10	8	1	4	96	63	32	35	27	184	27	13	159	62	874	51
8	6	4	4	87	80	37	29	19	174	37	9	30	74	1205	54
4	3	11	12	84	90	45	13	25	100	29	67	68	33	350	53
				18	19	12	24	4	85	14	3	7	34	797	23
83	62	60	87	757[5]	714	349	519	180	1582	363	250	2311	462	6658[5]	408

[3] Cahokia.
[4] Ste. Genevieve.
[5] The totals for these columns should be 112, 150, 777, and 7258 respectively.

FEDERAL CENSUS FOR 1800[1]

Schedule of the whole number of Persons in the Territory of Indiana

NAMES OF COUNTIES.	NAMES OF Towns, or other civil Divisions.	FREE WHITE MALES.					FREE WHITE FEMALES.					All other Free Persons except Indians, not taxed.	Slaves.
		Under 10 Years of Age.	Of 10 and under 16.	Of 16 and under 26, including Heads of Families.	Of 26 and under 45, including Heads of Families.	Of 45 and upwards, including Heads of Families.	Under 10 Years of Age.	Of 10 and under 16.	Of 16 and under 26, including Heads of Families.	Of 26 and under 45, including Heads of Families.	Of 45 and upwards, including Heads of Families.		
County of Knox.	Town of St. Vincennes.	104	55	79	90	45	112	58	72	50	25	16	8
	Neighborhood of St. Vincennes.	144	65	78	80	40	134	50	78	58	22	55	15
	Traders on the Wabash river.	4	—	17	22	5	1	—	1	—	—	—	5
	Illinois Grant.	184	75	61	108	33	191	55	83	106	17	16	—
Randolph county.	Kaskaskias Town and Township.	99	18	40	63	23	66	14	30	35	10	22	47

	Praire de Roche township.	33	5	20	26	4	30	1	7	16	6	4	60
	Mitchel Township.	53	38	33	43	22	49	26	28	28	8	6	—
	Massac.	20	3	14	13	11	9	4	7	5	2	2	—
St. Clair county.	Eahokia Town and Township.	135	47	64	119	49	106	32	60	55	10	42	—
	Belle Fountaine.	44	24	35	44	14	46	18	28	26	7	—	—
	L'Aigle Township.	34	17	25	37	16	47	22	30	14	8	—	—
	TOTAL,	854	347	466	645	262	791	280	424	393	115	163	135

The whole number of persons in the Indiana Territory allotted to JOHN GIBSON, Secretary of the same, amounts to four thousand eight hundred and seventy-five, as appears by the annexed Schedule.

St. Vincennes, July 4th, 1801.

JOHN GIBSON,
Secretary, Indiana Territory.

At Machilamakanac on the 1st August 1800, there were	- - -	251 souls.
Boatmen from Canada, &c.	- - - - -	300
At Praire du Chien on the Mississippi,	- - -	65
Green Bay on Lake Michigan,	- - -	50
Opee² on the Illinois river,	- - - -	100

TOTAL, 766 souls.

¹ This is printed in the *United States Second and Third Censuses 1800-1810.*
² Peoria.

RECAPITULATION FOR FEDERAL CENSUS FOR 1810

Free White Males.............3665
Free White Females...........2973
Indented servants 500
Slaves 129

TOTAL...........7267

SUMMARY OF CENSUS RETURNS
1818

County	Free white males 21 & upwards	All other white inhabitants	Free persons of color	Servants or slaves	Total	Report of Secretary in June	Report to Convention
Bond	264	1107	0	15	1386	1382	1398
Crawford	422	1558	78	20	2078	2074	2839
Edwards	...	....	....	....	....	1948	2243
Franklin	219	1043	52	15	1329	....	1281
Gallatin	742	2290	80	236	3348	3256	3849
Jackson	250	986	0	49	1285	1295	1619
Johnson	118	535	1	24	678	678	767
Madison	1012	3386	34	77	4509	5456	6303
Monroe	316	1008	6	41	1371	1358	1517
Pope	399	1481	....	64	1944	1975	2069
Randolph	...	....	....	....	....	2939	2974
St. Clair	*676*	*2393*	*39*	*88*	*3196*[1]	4519	5039
Union	439	2007	0	39	2485	2484	2709
Washington	281	1382	16	26	1705	1707	1819
White	720	2751	11	57	3539	3539	3832
TOTAL	5858	21927	317	751	28853	34610	40258

ADDITIONAL CENSUS

County	Free white males 21 & upwards	All other white inhabitants	Free persons of color	Servants or slaves	Total	Report of Secretary in June	Report to Convention
Crawford	179	698	0	0	877		
Edwards	38	104	0	0	142		
Gallatin	167	247	9	85	508		
Jackson	75	28	0	4	107		
Randolph	23	20	0	2	45		
Washington	59	205	0	5	269		
TOTAL	541	1302	9	96	1948	30801	

[1] See paragraph on St. Clair County in the discussion of the Census of 1818, *post*, XXXI

NOTES ON 1818 CENSUS

An abstract of the census for 1818 is given in Buck, *Illinois in 1818*, pp. 318-319, but as those figures do not in all cases agree with the ones found in rechecking the schedules, they are ignored here. The differences are minor. Most of the census commissioners made mistakes in footing the columns so only the totals have been listed in printing the schedules. The figures for the report of the secretary of the territory are copied here from Mr. Buck's list. The "Report to the Convention" is taken from the Journal of the Constitutional Convention reprinted in the Illinois State Historical Society, *Journal*, 6: 359.

Edwards County. No returns for 1818 are extant except that the supplementary census for Washington County contains also that "from the detached parts of Edwards Co. on the maridian line joining Washington."

Madison County. At the end of the enumeration of families the census commissioner adds a note to the effect that there are 980 souls at Forts Crawford, Armstrong, Edwards and Clark. As this is obviously an estimate, if not frankly padding, this figure 980 has not been added in, though included in the secretary's report. Fort Crawford was located at the mouth of the Wisconsin River, north of the Illinois boundary as set by the enabling act.

Pope County. Sixty-four "blacks" are added to the total without indication of family connections or status as slave or free.

Randolph County. Only the "additional census" schedules are extant.

St. Clair County. The manuscript for this county has been partly destroyed by fire. The names beginning with A to E and part of those beginning with F are entirely missing; also about thirty-one names and many figures from the bottoms of the pages as indicated. The total of the extant figures in the first four columns is 3196, and of the extant figures in the "totals" column, 3110. The figures for St. Clair County are in italics to indicate that they are incomplete.

RECAPITULATION FOR STATE CENSUS FOR 1820[1]

Name of county	Free white males of 21 years and upwards	All other white inhabitants	Free persons of color	Servants or slaves	Total
Alexander	180	589	0	4	773
Bond	641	2241	22	27	2931
Clark	207	724	0	1	932
Crawford	732	2344	71	24	3171
Edwards	775	2570	17	6	3368
Franklin	314	1376	63	7	1760
Gallatin	784	2335	98	239	3456
Jackson	363[2]	1170	1	38	1572
Jefferson	176	603	0	1	780
Johnson	177	682	1	13	873
Madison	2064	6317	45	96	8522
Monroe	393	1111	10	34	1548
Pope	635	2083	16	21	2755
Randolph	776	2415	Blacks 342		3533
St. Clair	1261	3880	108	80	5329
Union	474	1888	0	22	2384
Washington	336	1178	Blacks 33		1547
Wayne	254	888	2	3	1147
White	1005	3706	15	52	4778
TOTAL	11547	38100	469 668 375	668	51159
			1512		

[1] The recapitulation of the federal and state censuses of 1820 is included in this volume for purposes of comparison.

[2] This number is an estimate only. A part of the Jackson County enumeration included a column of free white males 16-26. In this case the arbitrary assumption was made that the number of persons above and under 21 was equal, and the total was divided by two to arrive at those persons included over 21.

RECAPITULATION FOR FEDERAL CENSUS OF 1820

County	Free White Males						Free White Females					Foreigners not naturalized	Employment			Slaves								Free people of color								All other persons except Indians not taxed	Total
																Males				Females				Males				Females					
	Under 10 yrs.	10-16 yrs.	16-18 yrs.	16-26 yrs. including heads of families	26-45 yrs. including heads of families	45 yrs. plus including heads of families	Under 10 yrs.	10-16 yrs.	16-26 yrs. including heads of families	26-45 yrs. including heads of families	45 yrs. plus including heads of families		Agriculture	Commerce	Manufacture	Under 14 yrs.	14-26 yrs.	26-45 yrs.	45 yrs. plus	Under 14 yrs.	14-26 yrs.	26-45 yrs.	45 yrs. plus	Under 14 yrs.	14-26 yrs.	26-45 yrs.	45 yrs. plus	Under 14 yrs.	14-26 yrs.	26-45 yrs.	45 yrs. plus		
Alexander	65	47	17	68	87	26	131	54	68	61	19	2	116	8	104	5	7	3	1	4	6	1											626
Bond	528	211	61	381	292	134	505	224	288	215	104	6	283		13					1						2							2931
Clark	164	76	21	109	94	47	158	77	87	83	35		204		21									4	4			4	4				931
Crawford	553	218	66	303	322	139	543	212	296	251	90	5	975	5	87		1				1	1		14	6	9	4	15	12	4	5	23	3022
Edwards	690	236	82	347	426	162	668	215	279	301	98	387[1]	767	21		2	1	2		2	1	1		17	2	5	4	3	2	2	3		3444
Franklin	339	133	49	175	154	72	345	129	155	133	56	19	441		286	38	70	69	24	26	22	13	5	8	7	4	1	17	10		1		1763
Gallatin	522	224	67	381	363	119	478	197	274	219	83	18	620	29	30	11	7	4	2	4	7	15	3		3	7	1	3	1		1		3155
Jackson	294	112	28	93	58	32	267	105	135	114	38	2	234	20	5		1			3	3		1		5	1	1	4	6		1		1542
Jefferson	137	50	18	75	75	35	112	49	65	51	25		191			4	1	1						8	12	1	1	11	3				691
Johnson	154	68	19	99	76		157	60	91	62	27		178												8	1		23		4			843
Madison	2682	1140	291	1509	1519	704	2206	1085	1037	1080	461	60	4133	9	101	19	15	9	13	22	16	15	5	4	5	1	1	20		1		13550
Monroe	251	111	28	183	196	87	252	112	124	127	50		410	47	66	2	3			5	1			4	2	9	2					21	1537
Pope	594	213	140	290	127	100	545	273	240	107	87	7	419	11										4	8	1	1		1	1	1		2610
Randolph	589	237	76	408	358	159	546	214	306	242	116	34	944	20	128	49	39	25	13	41	39	20	7	24	12	9	3	11	6	8	6		3492
St. Clair	971	412	113	602	554	322	830	364	456	385	172	19	608	12	64	18	17	10	13	8	16	9	7	8	8	13	5	23	3	8	6	5	5253
Union	531	162	47	253	218	90	435	161	238	173	77	5	599	8	41	6	4	4		6	2	2	3	8	14	9	1	20	8	8	6		2362
Washington	303	123	34	198	144	71	256	80	145	108	56	10	77	18	39	5	4	2		5	1	4	7	2	3	13	3	2	4	3	1		1517
Wayne	209	83	21	107	127	48	229	70	111	87	40		217	9		2	4			9					6	2	5						1114
White	978	371	135	530	431	236	895	337	447	367	169	13	979	20	17	9	10	3		7	13	3	3	1			1	2	4	3			4828
	10554	4227	1313	6224	5755	2641	9558	4018	4842	4166	1803	598	12395	233[*]	1007[*]	170	179	133	66	139	128	71	31	86	71	55	25	104	50	44	22	49	55211

[1]The number of foreigners not naturalized probably should be 2 instead of 387. The census taker inserted at this point an undesignated extra column totaling 387. Two foreigners would be more in line with average for the rest of the state. [2]Total should be 231.

ILLINOIS CENSUS RETURNS
1810, 1818

No. 5

JO DAVIESS | STEPHENSON | WINNEBAGO | BOONE | MC HENRY | LAKE

CARROLL | OGLE | KANE | DU PAGE

WHITESIDE | DE KALB | LEE

KENDALL

HENRY | BUREAU | LA SALLE | WILL

MERCER | GRUNDY

PUTNAM | KANKAKEE

STARK | MARSHALL

KNOX | LIVINGSTON

WARREN | HENDERSON | PEORIA | WOODFORD | IROQUOIS

HANCOCK | MC DONOUGH | FULTON | TAZEWELL | MC LEAN | FORD

MASON

DE WITT | CHAMPAIGN | VERMILION

SCHUYLER | MENARD | LOGAN

ADAMS | CASS | PIATT

BROWN | MACON | DOUGLAS | EDGAR

MORGAN | SANGAMON

PIKE | SCOTT | CHRISTIAN | MOULTRIE | COLES

GREENE | MACOUPIN | MONTGOMERY | SHELBY | CUMBERLAND | CLARK

CALHOUN | JERSEY

FAYETTE | EFFINGHAM | JASPER | CRAWFORD

MADISON | BOND

LAWRENCE

CLAY | RICHLAND

ST. CLAIR | CLINTON | MARION | WABASH | EDWARDS

MONROE | WASHINGTON | JEFFERSON | WAYNE

RANDOLPH | PERRY | WHITE

FRANKLIN | HAMILTON

JACKSON | WILLIAMSON | SALINE | GALLATIN

UNION | JOHNSON | POPE | HARDIN

ALEXANDER | PULASKI | MASSAC

ST. CLAIR COUNTY

RANDOLPH COUNTY

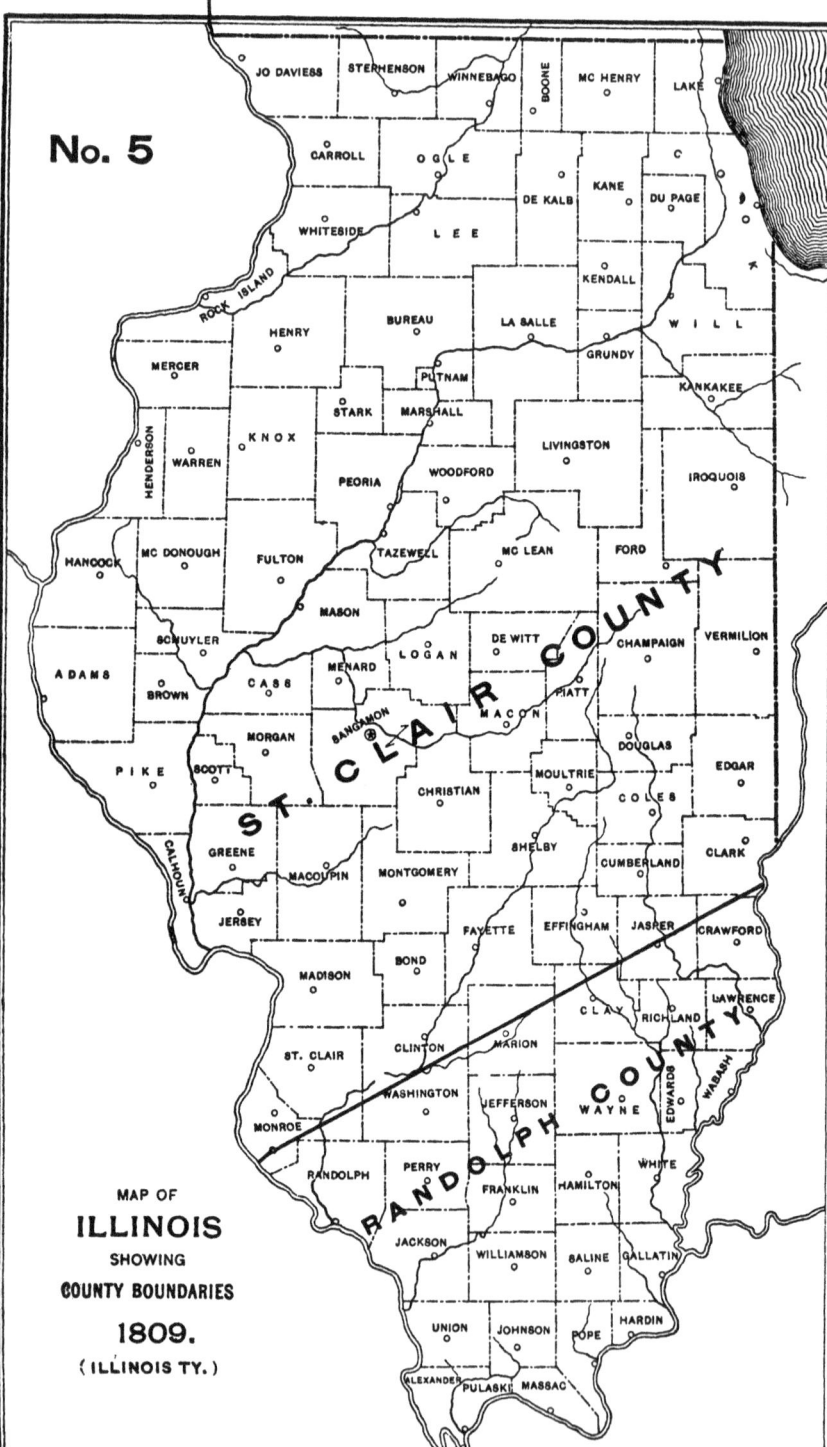

MAP OF
ILLINOIS
SHOWING
COUNTY BOUNDARIES
1809.
(ILLINOIS TY.)

FRANK LINDE, DEL.

No. 11

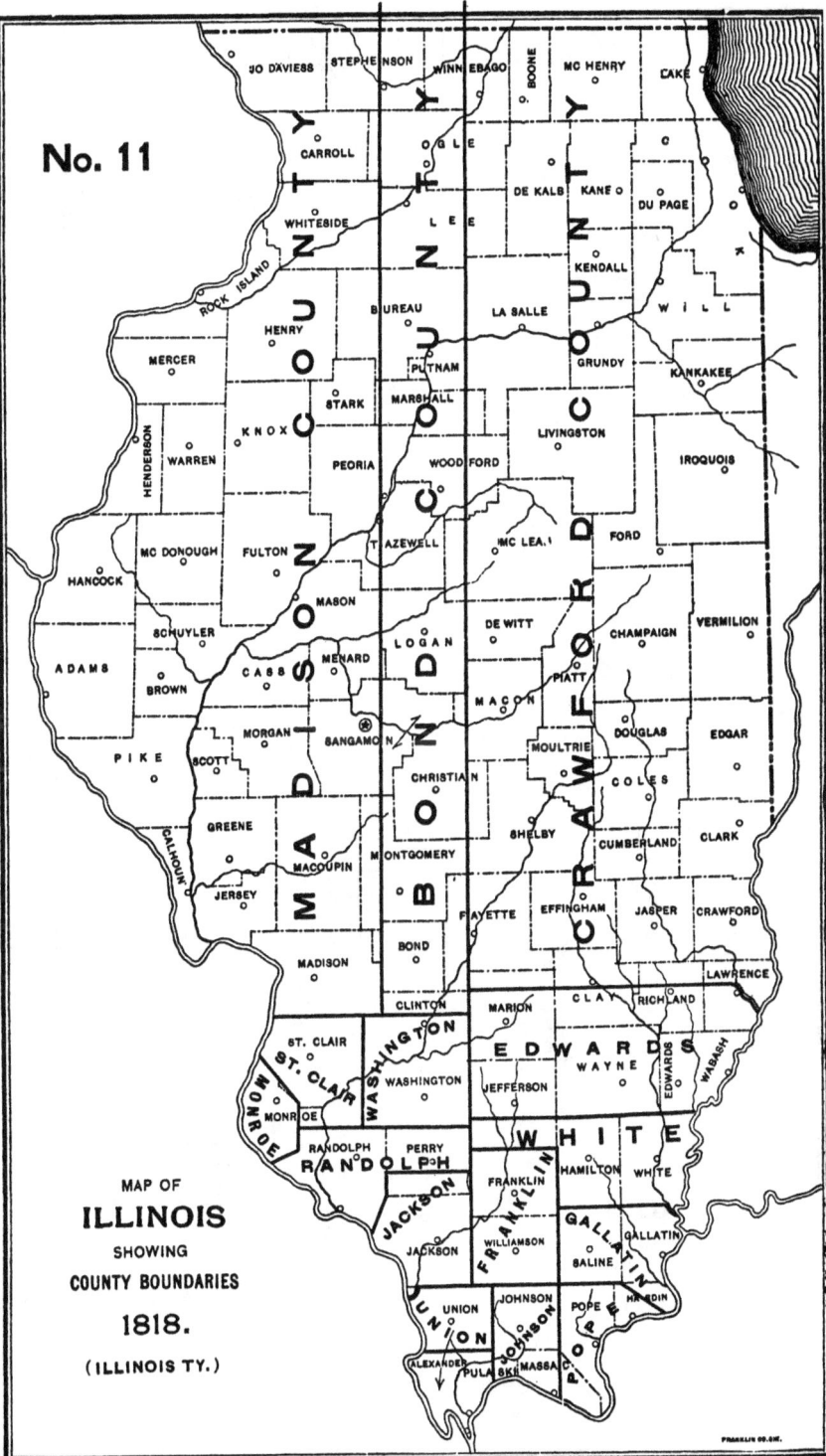

MAP OF
ILLINOIS
SHOWING
COUNTY BOUNDARIES
1818.
(ILLINOIS TY.)

JO DAVIESS
STEPHENSON
WINNEBAGO
BOONE
MC HENRY
LAKE
CARROLL
OGLE
DE KALB
KANE
DU PAGE
WHITESIDE
LEE
KENDALL
COUNTY
BUREAU
LA SALLE
WILL
HENRY
PUTNAM
GRUNDY
MERCER
STARK
MARSHALL
KANKAKEE
KNOX
LIVINGSTON
PEORIA
WOODFORD
IROQUOIS
HENDERSON
WARREN
COUNTY
MC DONOUGH
FULTON
TAZEWELL
MC LEAN
FORD
HANCOCK
MASON
DE WITT
CHAMPAIGN
VERMILION
SCHUYLER
LOGAN
CRAWFORD
ADAMS
CASS
MENARD
PIATT
BROWN
MACON
DOUGLAS
EDGAR
MORGAN
SANGAMON
MOULTRIE
PIKE
SCOTT
CHRISTIAN
COLES
GREENE
SHELBY
CUMBERLAND
CLARK
CALHOUN
MACOUPIN
MONTGOMERY
JERSEY
BOND
FAYETTE
EFFINGHAM
JASPER
CRAWFORD
MADISON
LAWRENCE
CLINTON
MARION
CLAY
RICHLAND
ST. CLAIR
WASHINGTON
EDWARDS
WAYNE
MONROE
ST. CLAIR
WABASH
MONROE
WASHINGTON
JEFFERSON
EDWARDS
RANDOLPH
PERRY
WHITE
RANDOLPH
HAMILTON
WHITE
JACKSON
FRANKLIN
GALLATIN
JACKSON
WILLIAMSON
GALLATIN
FRANKLIN
SALINE
UNION
JOHNSON
POPE
HARDIN
ALEXANDER
PULASKI
MASSAC
JOHNSON
POPE

ROCK ISLAND

FRANKLIN CO. ENG.

No. 12

JO DAVIESS STEPHENSON WINNEBAGO BOONE MC HENRY LAKE

CARROLL OGLE KANE DE KALB DU PAGE KENDALL

WHITESIDE LEE

B UREAU LA SALLE WILL

HENRY PUTNAM GRUNDY KANKAKEE

MERCER STARK MARSHALL LIVINGSTON IROQUOIS

KNOX PEORIA WOOD FORD

WARREN HENDERSON

MC DONOUGH FULTON TAZEWELL MC LEAN FORD

HANCOCK MASON DE WITT CHAMPAIGN VERMILION

SCHUYLER MENARD LOGAN PIATT DOUGLAS EDGAR

ADAMS BROWN CASS MORGAN SANGAMON MACON MOULTRIE COLES

PIKE SCOTT CHRISTIAN SHELBY CLARK

GREENE MACOUPIN MONTGOMERY CUMBERLAND

CALHOUN JERSEY FAYETTE EFFINGHAM JASPER CRAWFORD

MADISON BOND CRAWFORD LAWRENCE

CLINTON MARION CLAY RICHLAND

ST. CLAIR WASHINGTON WAYNE EDWARDS WABASH

MONROE MONROE JEFFERSON EDWARDS

RANDOLPH PERRY HAMILTON WHITE

JACKSON FRANKLIN SALINE GALLATIN

JACKSON WILLIAMSON GALLATIN

UNION JOHNSON POPE HARDIN

ALEXANDER PULASKI MASSAC JOHNSON POPE

ALEXANDER

COUNTY COUNTY COUNTY MADISON BOND CLARK

ROCK ISLAND

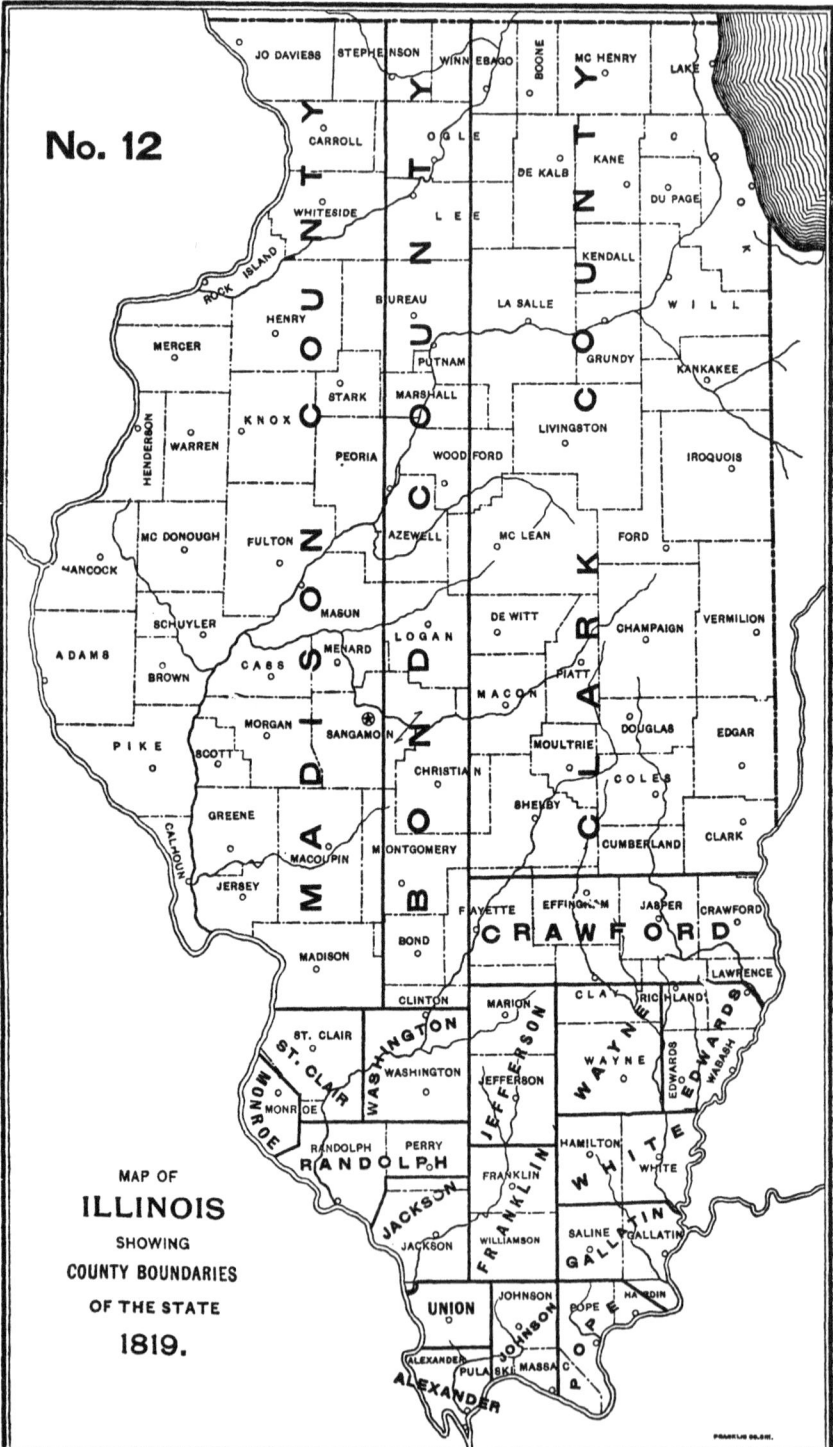

MAP OF
ILLINOIS
SHOWING
COUNTY BOUNDARIES
OF THE STATE
1819.

Illinois in 1818

Extent of settlement, counties, general location of Indian tribes,
and principal roads

Counties in 1818 ....**BOND**	
Modern counties........... BOND	
County lines in 1818......... ▬▬▬	
Modern county lines......... ▬▬	
Roads in 1818.............. ▬▬▬	
County seats in 1818......... ○	
Populations of 50 or major fractions thereof and smaller distinct settlements .... ●	

Maps showing county boundary lines in 1809, 1818, and 1819 are reprinted
from L. L. Emmerson, *Counties of Illinois.* The one indicating the extent of
settlement in 1818 is from S. J. Buck, *Illinois in 1818.*

CENSUS OF 1810[1]

(A.)

Schedule of the whole number of Persons within the division allotted to Thomas C. Patterson

NAME OF Town, City, or county.	NAMES OF Heads of families.	FREE WHITE MALES.					FREE WHITE FEMALES.					All other free persons, except Indians, not taxed.	Slaves.
		Under ten years of age. to 10.	Of ten years, and under sixteen. to 16.	Of sixteen, and under twenty-six, including heads of families. to 26.	Of twenty-six, and under forty-five, including heads of families. to 45.	Of forty-five and upwards, including heads of families. 45 &c.	Under ten years of age. to 10.	Of ten years, and under sixteen. to 16.	Of sixteen, and under twenty-six, including heads of families. to 26.	Of twenty-six, and under forty-five, including heads of families. to 45.	Of forty-five and upwards, including heads of families. 45 &c.		
Kaskaskias	[1] Tho. Swearingen	1		1	7		2		3			5	
	[2] B. Stephenson	1		9	11		2		1	1		8	
	[3] N: Edwards Govr					1		2	2	1		2	
	[4] Jnᵒ R. Jones	3	1	3									1

[1] The portion of the 1810 census here reproduced (see ante, X) seems to be for Randolph County alone. Numbers in brackets preceding names have been added for purpose of indexing. Figures in the tables that were corrected, according to a transcript in the Illinois Historical Survey, either by erasure or writing over, are reproduced thus: 4 — 1 has been rubbed out and 2 written over it. Cancelled figure alone means that number was rubbed out and nothing added. Corrected letters in names are similarly treated.

Town or County	Heads of families	FREE WHITE MALES to 10	to 16	to 26	to 45	45 &c.	FREE WHITE FEMALES to 10	to 16	to 26	to 45	45 &c.	Other Free, etc.	Slaves
	[5] Jos. Arshambo			2		1			1	1	1	1	
	[6] Elijah Backus					1						3	2
	[7] Nathl Pope				1		1	1	1			1	
	[8] Jacob Funk		1	3	2		4		2				
	[9] Micl Jones		1	1	1	1	2	1	1		1	1	
	[10] Robt Robinson	1		1	1	1							
	[11] Clemt C. Conway				1								
	[12] Danl Dice												
	[13] Philip Fouke	2		4	1		2		1			6	
	[14] Lewis Saguin	2	1	1		1	3	2	1	1		3	
	[15] Solo. Thom	2			2			2	2				
	[16] A Peltion	2		1	2	1	3	1	1	1	1		
	[17] Rob Morrison	1		3	1			1	1			4	
	[18] James Gilbreath	2	3	3	3		1			1		1	
	[19] G. Storm	1	1	3	1		3		2	1			
	[20] Geo: Baker					1				1			
	[21] M Brewer					1							
	[22] John Edgar					1						9	2
	[23] Jesse B Thomas		2		1		1			1		1	2
	[24] Jas Edgar				1								
	[25] Jno McFerrin	2		2	2		2	1	1				
	[26] S. Davis	1		1					1				
	[27] Bapt Lashapell	4			2					1			

Town or County	Heads of families	FREE WHITE MALES					FREE WHITE FEMALES					Other Free, etc.	Slaves
		to 10	to 16	to 26	to 45	45 &c.	to 10	to 16	to 26	to 45	45 &c.		
	[28] A. Lashapell	1		2	1	1				1	1		
	[29] John Dix	2	3	5					3			1	7
	[30] Wᵐ Morrison	1		2	2	1	1			1		1	
	[31] B. M. Piatt	1			1		2			1			
	[32] J. Doyle	1	1			1	1		2		1	3	
	[33] M. Donis	1				1		1	2		1		
	[34] J. Page				1				2	1			
	[35] L Lemieux	2			1	1		1			1	1	1
	[36] Chaˢ Donis			2								8	
	[37] Eliz: Labuche			1		1							
	[38] J. Derousse	5	1	1				1		1		1	
	[39] B. Dorousse	4	3			1		1		1		1	
	[40] M. Degagnez	1								1	1		
	[41] M. Deruse	2	1	1		1	2	1	1		1		
	[42] J. Donis		1	2		1	1	1	1		1		
		45	20	50¹	45	20	34	15	33	17	10	59	15
	[43] Luys Buyatt	1			1		2		1				
	[44] Batˢ Seguin	2	1	2	1	2	2	2	1		1		
	[45] Elexis Doza	2		1		1	1	2		1			
	[46] J Barutel	3	2			1	3	1	1		1		
	[47] M Bienvenu				2	1				1			7
	[48] M. Buyatt	1	1	4			1				4		

2

¹ Correct total 51.

Town or County	Heads of families	FREE WHITE MALES					FREE WHITE FEMALES					Other Free, etc.	Slaves
		to 10	to 16	to 26	to 45	45 &c.	to 10	to 16	to 26	to 45	45 &c.		
	[49] A. Casson	3	1	1		1	2	2	1	1			1
	[50] C Donis	1		1	1			1	1				
	[51] L. Chamberlin		3	2	2	1		1	1		1		7
	[52] A Bienvenu	2	1	1	1			3	1			1	6
	[53] B Jondro	1	1								1	1	
	[54] Md Pera	3	1				1			1			
	[55] Md Godin										1		10
	[56] Jos. Devegne	2			1		2	1	1	1			
	[57] A Ravell	1				1	2	1	1				
	[58] A Labruyer	1			1			1	1				
	[59] A Montreaille			1		1	1		1		1		
	[60] M Peltier	1		1		1	2			1			
	[61] J Barutell				1				1				
	[62] M. Charleville			4							1		
	[63] Jno Bakey										1		
	[64] A. Bienvenue		1	1	1		1		2	1	1	1	
	[65] E Rovey	1			1					1	1		
	[66] J. Garsce	2			1	1	1		1	1			1
	[67] B. Chamberlin	1	2	1	1		1		1				1
	[68] Jno Wootan	3		1	1		1		1				
	[69] B Montreuille				1		2		1				
	[70] P. Lasource						2						
	[71] N. Etace			1		1					2		

Town or County	Heads of families	FREE WHITE MALES					FREE WHITE FEMALES					Other Free, etc.	Slaves
		to 10	to 16	to 26	to 45	45 &c.	to 10	to 16	to 26	to 45	45 &c.		
	[72] N. Buyatt	3			1	1	1			1			
	[73] J. Lonval	2	1		1		1	2		1			
	[74] J. Fulton	3	1	2		1		1	1	1	1		
	[75] J Luzador	1			1		3	2		1			
	[76] E. Carperter	2	1	1	1		1	1	1	1			
	[77] A Donis												
	[78] L Wakely												
	[79] H. F. Greenwood				1								
	[80] D. C. Knox			1									
	[81] Jno Manard	3			1		1			1			
Springfield Township	[82] Wm Haley				1					3			
	[83] Peter Laflore	4	1	2		1		1	1	1	1		
	[84] F. Gardner					1							
		49	19	26	23	16	31	21	20	18	17	3	33
3 Springfield Township	[85] Peire Manard	1			1	1	2		1	1			
	[86] A Longloy	1			1	1	2		2[1]	1			7
	[87] J Daniels			3	1				2				
	[88] A. Postlewait			3	1						1		
	[89] J.Inks	1	1		1		3			1			
	[90] J. B. Montruil		1		2	1							
	[91] W. Rosin				1		1			1			
	[92] PeterWolrick		2			1	1	1			1		

[1] Figure 2 erased but apparently included in total, which should be 22 instead of 24 given for this column.

Town or County	Heads of families	FREE WHITE MALES					FREE WHITE FEMALES					Other Free, etc.	Slaves
		to 10	to 16	to 26	to 45	45 &c.	to 10	to 16	to 26	to 45	45 &c.		
	[93] J. Crawfort	1			2		1			1			
	[94] A. Lovett	2		1	1		2		1	1			
	[95] E. Stapleton	1			1		3		1				
	[96] F. Touluse	2	1	1	1		1			1			
	[97] Wᵐ Roberts	2		1	1	1	3		1				
	[98] D. Holly	3		1	1		2			1			
	[99] S. Jones	1			1		1			1			
	[100] J Bilderback	2	1		1	1	1						
Horse Creek	[101] I. Hickes					1							
	[102] N. Been	1		1						1			
Springfield Township	[103] J. Liveley	2	2			1	2			1			
	[104] Rob. Robinson	3	3	3		1	2			1		3	
	[105] J. Adkins	3	1		1		1	1		1			
	[106] B. Allen	1	1	2	1		2	2	1	1			
	[107] Geo. Wilson	1			1		2		1				
	[108] N. Hill	2		1	1		1	1	1				
	[109] J. Hill	1		1			1		1		1		
	[110] J. Clark	1		1					1				
	[111] B. Claxton			1		1			1				
	[112] Tho. Stublefield	1					2			1			
	[113] A.Gastion		1				1			1			
Marys River	[114] J Hurd	1	1				1		1	1	1	1	
	[115] J. Clendennen	1		3			1			1	1		

Town or County	Heads of families	FREE WHITE MALES					FREE WHITE FEMALES					Other Free, etc.	Slaves
		to 10	to 16	to 26	to 45	45 &c.	to 10	to 16	to 26	to 45	45 &c.		
	[116] R. Lacey			2		1			1	1			
	[117] J Philips			1					1	1			
	[118] J. Gill	1			1				1			1	
	[119] G. Engram		1		1		3	1	1		1		
	[120] J. Crane	2		3			1	1	1		1		
	[121] B Crane	3			1	1	2					1	
	[122] J Patton	2								1	1	1	
	[123] J. Henderson	2			1		1		1				
	[124] Wm McRoberts	2			1				1				
	[125] Jos McCortney	1				1	1			1			
	[126] R. Pritchard	46	17	30	25	17	46	11	24	22	7	7	7
	[127] J. Gastion	1	1	1	1	1	1		3		1		4
	[128] J. Crane	3	1		1	1	1			1			
	[129] J Lower	2	1	2	1				1	1	1		
	[130] R. Tindle	1	1			1	1	1		1			
	[131] J. Brithart	1		1		2	1	1		1			
	[132] J. Ray				1		3	1					
	[133] Wm Kelly		2			1	1	2		1			
	[134] Jnº Grosvernor			3	2	1	1	2			1		
	[135] Able Duey	1			1		2	1	1				
	[136] J. Kelly	1		1			1	1	1				

Town or County	Heads of families	\(FREE WHITE MALES\) to 10	to 16	to 26	to 45	45 &c.	\(FREE WHITE FEMALES\) to 10	to 16	to 26	to 45	45 &c.	Other Free, etc.	Slaves
	[137] E Rooker			1									
	[138] Wm Keston		2	1	1				1	1			
	[139] J. Mamco	3	1		1		1	1		1			
	[140] A. Stewart	3	1	1		1				1			
	[141] B. McGlacy, Sr [?]	1		2	1			1					
	[142] T. Allen	1			1		2			1			
	[143] H. Laughlin	1			1		1		1				
	[144] Wm Moss	2			1		3			1			
	[145] J. Gittar		1		1				1				
	[146] G. Drodrick	3	3		1		1			1		1	
	[147] Sam Cochrin	1	2	2		1	1	1			1		
	[148] Wm Cochrin	1		1				1					
	[149] T. Tolor	2	1		1	1	2	1		2			
	[150] G. Crith	2	1		1	1	2	2		1			
	[151] R. Glim	1	1	1			2				1		
	[152] J. Bailey	1		1	1				1	1			
	[153] G Franklin				1		1		1				
	[154] H. Noble			1		1					1		
	[155] J. Griggs	3							1				
	[156] H McMullen	1	2	2				2			1		
	[157] G. Cochrin	3	2			1	2	1		1		1	
	[158] J. Lewis	2	1			1	2	1		1		1	
	[159] J. West			1					1				

Town or County	Heads of families	FREE WHITE MALES					FREE WHITE FEMALES					Other Free, etc.	Slaves
		to 10	to 16	to 26	to 45	45 &c.	to 10	to 16	to 26	to 45	45 &c.		
	[160] A West	2		2					2				
	[161] Jas Davis				1		1		1				
	[162] Jno Davis				1		3		1	1			
	[163] J. Patterson	2		1			1	1		1			
	[164] J. Irwin	2		1					1				
	[165] B McDaniel					1	1	2	2		1	1	
	[166] T. Fulton	2			1		2		1				
		49	24	27	24	16	40	21	25	19	8	4	4
5	[167] J. Lard	2	1	1				2	1				
	[168] A Ross	2	1	1			2		1				
	[169] J Miller	2	1	1	1		1			1			
	[170] A Burba	3		1	1		1		1				
	[171] J. Lee	1		1			3		2				
	[172] S Lard	1		4					1				
	[173] J. Fulton	1	1	1						1		1	
	[174] A. Eadens	1	1	1							1	2	
	[175] S. Allen	3	3	1	1		1	1		1			
	[176] S. Hill	1	2				1		1				
	[177] J Johnson	3			1		1			1			
	[178] P. Howard	2	2		1			1		1			
	[179] P. Harelston							1			1		
	[180] Wm Fisher	3			1					1			

Town or County	Heads of families	Free White Males to 10	to 16	to 26	to 45	45 &c.	Free White Females to 10	to 16	to 26	to 45	45 &c.	Other Free, etc.	Slaves
	[181] Jas Slater	3	1		1		3	2	1		1		
	[182] J. Fulten	1		1		2					1	5	
	[183] T. Roberts	1		2					1				
	[184] E. Bilderback	4	2	2		1	2	1	1	1			
	[185] Wm Wilson	1	1		1			1	1	1			
	[186] D. Bilderback	2		1					1				
	[187] N. Preston	1		1					1		1		
	[188] J. Alcorn	2	1		1		2			1			
	[189] Aguslau Davy	1			1				1				
	[190] Jas Hux	1	1		1		2	1		1			
	[191] S. Liveley	3			1				1		1		
	[192] J. Pillers			1					1				
	[193] Wm Lemins	2	2		1		4			1	1		
	[194] J. McDonough				1				1	1			
	[195] J. Robinson	1		1									
	[196] J. Pettite	3	2	2		1	2	1		2			
	[197] J. McFerlen	3			1		3			1			
	[198] A. Thompson		1	3		1	1	1	1	1			
	[199] S Chrozier	4	1		1		1	1		1			
	[200] J Campbell	2	1		1		2			1			
	[201] J Tolwiyh							1					
	[202] E. Crofard	1				1				1			
	[203] S. Lard				1		1		1				

Town or County	Heads of families	FREE WHITE MALES					FREE WHITE FEMALES					Other Free, etc.	Slaves
		to 10	to 16	to 26	to 45	45 &c.	to 10	to 16	to 26	to 45	45 &c.		
		59	23	28	17	9	33¹	17	20	19	10	12	
6	[204] Wm Barnett			2		1		1	1		2	4	
	[205] T Patten	2	1		1		4		2				
	[206] J. Patton	1			1		2		1				
	[207] A White	1		1	1				1				
	[208] R. Dees	1		1			1		1				
	[209] D Fulton	1					1		1				
	[210] R. Hill	1	1		1		2		1				
	[211] M. Hill	3		2	1	1	2	2	1		1		
	[212] T. McBride	3	2						1				
	[213] W. Anderson	3						1		1			
	[214] Wm Smith		1				1	2	1	1	1		
	[215] R. Thompson	1		1			3	4	1		1		
	[216] J. Batey			2					1		1		
	[217] J. Thompson			1	1	1			1		1		
	[218] J. Couch	2			1	1	5		1	1	1		
	[219] Dad Anderson	1		1	1		2			1			
	[220] J. Anderson		1				1						
	[221] W McBride	1		1					1				
	[222] Wm McBride		1			1	1		1		1		
	[223] A. Cox	3			1		1	2		1			
	[224] Tho Wideman	2		1	1		1	1	1	1			

¹ Correct total 32.

Town or County	Heads of families	FREE WHITE MALES					FREE WHITE FEMALES					Other Free, etc.	Slaves
		to 10	to 16	to 26	to 45	45 &c.	to 10	to 16	to 26	to 45	45 &c.		
	[225] R. Foster	1		1				1	1				
	[226] J Dees	3			1			3	1	1			
	[227] J. Liveley	2	2	2		1	1	1	1		1		
	[228] A. McCormack	1	2	1		1	1	1		1	1		
	[229] J Liveley	2		1	1		2	1		1			
	[230] Jas. Lively	1					1		1				
	[231] R. Heyens	2	1		1		1	1	1	1			
	[232] D. Dees	1			1		1		1				
	[233] A Jones	1		2					1				
	[234] D. Hugans	2	2	2	1	1	2		2	1	1		
Grand Tower	[235] J. Dent		2		1		3	2		1			
	[236] B. Smith	2	1		1		1						
	[237] R. Alexander			1									
	[238] J. Blocker	1			1				1				
	[239] Jno May	1			1		2		1				
	[240] B. Walker	2	1		1					1			
	[241] J. Wimete		2		1					1			
	[242] J. Fisher	1		1	1		2	1	1				
	[243] G. Henson							1	1				
		50	20	22	21	7	44	23	26	15	8		
	[244] Wm Boon	2			1		2			1			
	[245] R. Marshall	1			1		4			1		1	

7

Town or County	Heads of families	FREE WHITE MALES					FREE WHITE FEMALES					Other Free, etc.	Slaves
		to 10	to 16	to 26	to 45	45 &c.	to 10	to 16	to 26	to 45	45 &c.		
	[246] J Marshall	2					2		1				
	[247] F. Blau			1							1		
	[248] J. Worthen	4	1			1		1		1	1	2	
	[249] C Davis	1				1				1	1		
	[250] M. Davis			1					1				
	[251] J. Davis	2	1		1		2	1		1		2	
	[252] J. Chandler	2			1		3	2		1		3	
	[253] E Wells			1	2		2		1			2	
	[254] N. Davis	1	1		1		4		1	1			
	[255] J. Bires	2	2				2		1				
	[256] J. Sipiss	1		1			2		1			2	
	[257] T. Black	1		1					1				
	[258] T. Roberts	3		1	1	1[1]	2	3		1		8	
	[259] D Black		1	1	1		1		1	1			
	[260] J. Piles	1				1	1						
	[261] W. Piles	4		1	1		1			1			
	[262] A Piles	1			1		1		1	1			
	[263] W Acken	3	1		1		3		1	1			
	[264] J Davis	1	2	2			2	2	1		1		
	[265] T. Manson		2	2	2		1		1				
	[266] A Thompson		2	2		1			1	1	1	4	
	[267] E. Thompson	1			1		3		1				

¹ Figure 1 written over 2. Apparently latter used in total, which should be 9.

Town or County	Heads of families	FREE WHITE MALES					FREE WHITE FEMALES					Other Free, etc.	Slaves
		to 10	to 16	to 26	to 45	45 &c.	to 10	to 16	to 26	to 45	45 &c.		
	[268] E. W. Glune	1		1			3		1				
	[269] W. Welch	2			1			1		1			
	[270] J. Phelpes	2		1	2		1	2		1			
	[271] J Manue	2	1	1	1		1			1			
	[272] J. Griffith	3			1		1			1			
	[273] J. East					1					1		
	[274] D. Ellems	2		1	1		2	1		1			
	[275] J. Griffith	1		1					1				
	[276] W. Griffith			1	1				2		1		
	[277] W. Daniels	1	2	1	1		2		1	1			
	[278] W. Daniels			2		1			1				
	[279] D. Gilmore				1								
	[280] A. Noble	1	2		1		2			1			
	[281] E. Owens	4		2	1		1	2		1			
	[282] G. Fisher			2	1		2	3		1			
	[283] T. Levins	1		1			1			1			
	[284] S. Taylor	1	2	3		1	2	1	1	1	1	1	
	[285] D. Wager	2				1					1		
		56	18	28	28	10	55	21	19	22	10	25	
	[286] M. Smith	1			1		1			1			
	[287] E. Taylor	2		1					1		1		
	[288] A. Barbeu				1		3		1				
													4

8

Town or County	Heads of families	FREE WHITE MALES					FREE WHITE FEMALES					Other Free, etc.	Slaves
		to 10	to 16	to 26	to 45	45 &c.	to 10	to 16	to 26	to 45	45 &c.		
	[289] P. Lawunt	2	1	1	1	1		1		1			9
	[290] P. Lawson				1								5
	[291] M. Barbeu		3	1				2	1		1		12
	[292] F. Tebou	1	2		1		1	1					1
	[293] B. Godar				1		3		1	1	1		2
	[294] Madam Blau	1		1			3	3	1		1		3
	[295] O Perya	1	1		1		1		1	1			5
	[296] A. Blau	1	1		1		1						
	[297] J. Lemar	2				1		2			1		
	[298] A Laschoimu	2			1		3			1	1		6
	[299] A. Lavise		1	1	1		1	1		1			4
	[300] G. Nelmar	2	1	1	1	1	3	1		1			
	[301] C. Drury	1		1	1		1	1	1	1			
	[302] J. Longloy			1		1	1						
	[303] J. Gronduru	2		1			1		2				1
	[304] Mam Coteleve		1	3			3				1		
	[305] P. Penar	1	3	1		1	1	1	1		1		
	[306] F. Tongo	1		1			1		1				
	[307] J Penar		1	1	1				1				
	[308] P. Pener	3			2		1	1	1				
	[309] J. Belcore	1		2	1	1	2	1	1		1		
	[310] J. B. Paner		2	2	1	1	3	1		1			
	[311] B. Declue		1		1		1	1	1				

Town or County	Heads of families	FREE WHITE MALES					FREE WHITE FEMALES					Other Free, etc.	Slaves
		to 10	to 16	to 26	to 45	45 &c.	to 10	to 16	to 26	to 45	45 &c.		
	[312] J. Lover	2				1							
	[313] O Doratison					1							
	[314] C. Blau	2	2						1	1			
	[315] L Pargue	2	2	1	1		1	1	2				
	[316] A Cotino	1		1			1		1				
	[317] J. Blau	2	2		1		1	2		1			
	[318] J. Trokey	1					1		1				
	[319] P. Gadar	1		1			1		1				7
	[320] Maᵐ Damon						1		1		1		
	[321] M. Degarnu		1	2			1	1	1		1		
	[322] A. McNabb	4			1					1			
	[323] R. Drury				3				1				3
	[324] W McGlacy	3			2	1			1			1	
	[325] R. Kid	1					3						
	[326] R. Jurden	1	1	1				1					
	[327] W. Everett	1	1				1	1	1		1		
	[328] J. Everett	41	20	22	26	9	45	19	25	12	11	1	62
	[329] Henry Conner	1	1		1	1	1		1		1		
	[330] Wm Winn			3		1	1		1		1		
	[331] J Mitchel	2	1			1	3			1		1	
	[332] M. Martinon	1				1	1					1	

Town or County	Heads of families	FREE WHITE MALES					FREE WHITE FEMALES					Other Free, etc.	Slaves
		to 10	to 16	to 26	to 45	45 &c.	to 10	to 16	to 26	to 45	45 &c.		
	[333] J. Noland	3		2		1		1	1		1		
	[334] J. Riner	1		2		1	1	1	1				
	[335] Wm Alexander		1	1	1		2			1			
	[336] J. Mansfield	1		1	1			1	1				
	[337] E. Clark	1					1	1	1			1	
	[338] J. Levins	1			1		1						
	[339] W. Chaffin			3		3	2			1	1		
	[340] J. Worley			2			1	1	1				
	[341] J. Worley	3		1	1			1	1	1			
	[342] Wm Bradley			1									
	[343] R. Miller	2	2	2		1	1	1		1			
	[344] J. Carter	1			1		2			1			
	[345] S. Cropper	1			1		2			1			
	[346] J. Henderson	3	2	1	1				1				
	[347] Widow Ford	4	1	1					2		1		
	[348] H Bolston	1		1	1		1	1	2				
	[349] A Kinney	2		1			1	1		1			
	[350] J. McRoberts	2	1	1		1	2	1	1	1			
	[351] A. Traler	3			1	1		2		1	1		
	[352] B. Jurden		1		1		1	2					
	[353] J. Eberman	2			2		1	1		1		1	
	[354] S Doddg				1		1		1				
	[355] A. Eaden			1					1				

Town or County	Heads of families	FREE WHITE MALES					FREE WHITE FEMALES					Other Free, etc.	Slaves
		to 10	to 16	to 26	to 45	45 &c.	to 10	to 16	to 26	to 45	45 &c.		
	[356] J Stubblefield			1					1			1	
	[357] R. Roller		2			1	2	1	2		1		
	[358] B. Vermition			2		1	2		2		1		
	[359] J. Thompson	1	1	2			1	2		1			
	[360] S. McBride	1	1		1	5	1		1				
	[361] G. Brikey	2	1	1	1		2	1		1			
	[362] WmMcDaniels	1		1					1				
	[363] H. Levins			1		1	1		1		1		
	[364] O Levins				2		1		1				
	[365] J. Fisher				1		1		1				
	[366] A Henderson	3	2			1	2	2		1	1		
	[367] A. Fifer	3	1		1	1	2	2				2	
	[368] C. McNabb	1	1		1	1	3	1			1		
	[369] Wm Hamilton	1		1	1		1		1	1			
	[370] D Dick	1		1	1		3		1				
	[371] J. Pellem	2	1			1	1			1			
	[372] T. Pellem			1			1		1				
		49	20	35	24	23	45	25	29	17	11	7	
	[373] J Griffin	3		1					1				
	[374] W Ratliff		1	2						1			
	[375] W. Shuck							1	2		1		
	[376] J. McKenney	4	3		1		1	2	1				

10

Town or County	Heads of families	FREE WHITE MALES					FREE WHITE FEMALES					Other Free, etc.	Slaves
		to 10	to 16	to 26	to 45	45 &c.	to 10	to 16	to 26	to 45	45 &c.		
	[377] J Shane	3			1		3			1			
	[378] A Teeters		2		1		4	1		1			
	[379] S Shuck	1		2					2				
	[380] J Anderson		4	1		1			1	1	1		
	[381] W. Going		1	1						1	1		
	[382] J Going			1			1						
	[383] P. Mitchel	4	1		1		4	1		1			
	[384] J. Mason	1	2		1		3	2		1			
	[385] J. Steel		3			1	2	1		1			
	[386] F. Longloy	2	1		1				1	1			1
	[387] A Dulo	3			1				1				
	[388] P. Cassee	1		1			4						
	[389] J Fersceto	4	1		1		2	1		1			1
	[390] J. White	2			2		2			1	1		1
	[391] E Clerk	2	1	1	1		3	1		1			
	[392] S Bowerman	2	2	2		1	4		1	1	1		
	[393] J Steel Snr	1	2	1	1			1	1	1			
	[394] J Steel Jnr	3			1		4			1			
	[395] R. Woods		2		1					1			
	[396] J Smith			1			4		1				
	[397] A May	3	2	2	1			1		1			
	[398] J. Lucas			1			4		1				1
	[399] A Flack	2		1	1			1	1	1			

Town or County	Heads of families	FREE WHITE MALES					FREE WHITE FEMALES					Other Free, etc.	Slaves
		to 10	to 16	to 26	to 45	45 &c.	to 10	to 16	to 26	to 45	45 &c.		
	[400] R. Cox	1			3		1	1	1	1			1
	[401] N. Devers	2			1		3	1		1			1
	[402] W. Biers			1					1	1			
	[403] S. Gaston	1		1	1	1	3				1		
	[404] J C Slokem		2	2					2				
	[405] S Slokem	1		1	1		2		2				
	[406] J Ratliff	1			1		2	2					
	[407] J Jordan			1	1		1		1				
	[408] F Jourdon	3			1		1	1		1			
	[409] E Brownen			1				1	1				
	[410] J Smith		1		1					1			
	[411] G Darneal	1	1		1					1			
	[412] R Bankston	3			1		1						
	[413] R. Waller	1		1			1		1				
	[414] R. Smith					1					1		1
	[415] R. Henson	2	1	2		1	1	2	2		1		
	[416] R. Robb			1									
U. S. Saline	[417] J. Young	3		1	1		1	2		1			
	[418] J Pumroy	4		1	6			1		1			
	[419] Taylor Wilkens &c		18	18	24	3						176	
	[420] Henry Carson	1			1		1		1	1			
	[421] W. Banford	1	3	3	3				1				
		64	33	52	62	10	58	21	27	26	8	176	7

Town or County	Heads of families	FREE WHITE MALES					FREE WHITE FEMALES					Other Free, etc.	Slaves
		to 10	to 16	to 26	to 45	45 &c.	to 10	to 16	to 26	to 45	45 &c.		
11	[422] J Wilson				1				1			1	
	[423] C White				1								
	[424] J. Carter			1									
	[425] J. Watker			1									
	[426] J. Allen	2			1					1		10	
	[427] W Cochrin	2		2	6	3	1	1		1		11	
	[428] A Eury												
	[429] L Parres	2	1		1		2			1			
	[430] J Madcalf	3			1		3			1			
	[431] J. Glasbuff			1	1				1				
	[432] W Wofard		1	1									
	[433] A. Colwell											9	
	[434] T. Jester		1		1		2		1				
	[435] B Commins	1	2		1		2			1			
	[436] J Young			2	1	1					1		
	[437] T. Hubbard				1		1			1			
	[438] F. Check	1								1			
	[439] W Harper	2	1		1		2	1		1			
	[440] J Shearer	2					2	1		1			
	[441] J Berry	2							1				
	[442] G Masterson						2		1		1		
	[443] H. Simmons	2					1		1				

Town or County	Heads of families	FREE WHITE MALES					FREE WHITE FEMALES					Other Free, etc.	Slaves
		to 10	to 16	to 26	to 45	45 &c.	to 10	to 16	to 26	to 45	45 &c.		
	[444] J. Hargrave	1	1				1	1		1			
	[445] J White	2	2		1		3	1	2	1		15	
	[446] G C Hart				2		1		1				
	[447] P. Trampbile	2	1	1	1		1	2		1	1	11	
	[448] P. Monlis			1		1		1	1				
	[449] B. May	1	2	1	1		2	1	1				
	[450] J Saxton				4	1						5	
	[451] W. Gordan	1		2	1		1	2	1				
	[452] J. Trousdal	1			1		1	1	1	1			
	[453] G Robinson	4	2			1	1	1	1		1		
	[454] D. Saxton	4			2			1	1				
	[455] J. Lon				1	1	1				1		
	[456] El Emminger	1		1			1		2				1¹
	[457] J. Saxton			2					2				
	[458] J Willis	1	1	1					3		1		
	[459] H Morland	1	2	3	1	1	2			1	1		
	[460] N Morland	2		1		1				1	1	2	
12		39	17	21	31	10	32	12	20	15	7	64	
	[461] J. Gibson	1		1			1						
	[462] S. McClure		1	1		1			1	1			
	[463] W. Dune	2			1		1		1	1		1	
	[464] A Davenport	1	3	3	1	1	1		1	1		1	

¹ Not carried into totals row.

Town or County	Heads of families	FWM to 10	FWM to 16	FWM to 26	FWM to 45	FWM 45 &c.	FWF to 10	FWF to 16	FWF to 26	FWF to 45	FWF 45 &c.	Other Free, etc.	Slaves
	[465] M. S. Davenport			1			1		1			1	
	[466] W. Thornberry				1				1				
	[467] J B. Levins			1	1								
	[468] E Hovard	4			2		1	1		1		2	
	[469] H. Oldam	1			1				1			3	
	[470] J Flim	1			1							2	
	[471] W. Piles												
	[472] Ben & Betty												
	[473] W Sellers	3		1	1	1	1		1	1			
	[474] B. Brisland		1	3	1								
	[475] H Kenyon							1		1			
	[476] J. Leathern					1		1		1			
	[477] B. Hensley			1			1	1	1	1		5	
	[478] J Campbell	4		7	2				1				
	[479] E Brown		1	1					1				
	[480] B. Colvert	3	1	2	1		1		-	1		4	
	[481] A Wilson	4	1	4	1		3	1	1	1			
	[482] S Birks							1			1		
	[483] J Young	3	1	1	1			2		1			
	[484] W Acers	1		1	1			1	1				
	[485] J Reed	3	1	1	1		1			1		4	
	[486] J Loden		1					1		1			
	[487] J. Craw			2	3		1			1		1	

Heads of families	FREE WHITE MALES to 10	to 16	to 26	to 45	45 &c.	FREE WHITE FEMALES to 10	to 16	to 26	to 45	45 &c.	Other Free, etc.	Slaves
[488] G Woodrin	3			2					1		1	
[489] J Rohr				1					1		2	
[490] M. Sprinkle		1	4	1			1		1		2	
[491] E Hubbard			1	2	1					1		
[492] J. Wilcox			2	1								
[493] J Sellers	1			1		1			1		1	
[494] J Damwood	1	1	1			1	1	1	1	1	1	
[495] J Donis	2			1		1						
[496] W Morrison	1		2		1	1	1	1	1	1	4	
[497] W Chick			2	5		1		1	1			
[498] T. Dorsen			3	1		1		1	1		2	
[499] T Foster			1	2				1				
[500] J Davis	3		1	2			1		1			
[501] J Morgan				1								
	43	10	47	40	6	17	13	13	21	4	36	
[502] A Roberts	1		1					1				
[503] J. Blevins	2	1	1	1			2		1		2	
[504] J Standley	1	1	2	2		2	1	1		1		
[505] W Wheeler	2	2	2	1		1						
[506] W Strong	1	1							1			
[507] M. Welles				1	2	2	1	1				

Town or County

13

Town or County	Heads of families	FREE WHITE MALES					FREE WHITE FEMALES					Other Free, etc.	Slaves
		to 10	to 16	to 26	to 45	45 &c.	to 10	to 16	to 26	to 45	45 &c.		
Shawnee Town	Hogan [508] A Davenport	2			1				1				
	[509] W Weles	1			1		1		1				
	[510] B Kirkendol			1	1		1						
	[511] J Williams	1	1		1			1	1	1	1		
	[512] J Gallen		2				2		1				
	[513] J. McCool	2	1	2		1	1		1		1		
	[514] G. Baker				1		2		1				
	[515] J Black	1			2		1		1				
	[516] Wm Jonston	2					3			2			
	[517] E Hall	2	1	1	1		3	1		2			
	[518] J. B. Slovall		2	2		1	3		2	1			
	[519] W Watson	1			1		1		1				
	[520] N Mayon			1			1						
	[521] J McAllester	2		3		1	3		1		1		
	[522] D. Stanley	1	2	1	1		1	1	1	1			
	[523] J Stanley	1		1			2		1	2			
	[524] J Darden		2	4	1		5	2	1	1			
	[525] J Harris	3	3	1				2	1	1			
	[526] J Grant	2	2	1	2	1	2		1	1			
	[527] G Cod	3		1	1		1						
	[528] J. Harris Jnr	1					2	1	1	1		1	
	[529] M. Whitford	1		1	1		2		1	1		7	

Town or County	Heads of families	FREE WHITE MALES					FREE WHITE FEMALES					Other Free, etc.	Slaves
		to 10	to 16	to 26	to 45	45 &c.	to 10	to 16	to 26	to 45	45 &c.		
	[530] W Riggs	1			1		1	1	1				
	[531] S. Copper	1	1		1		1	1	1				
	[532] J. Pate	1		2	1		4	2	1	1			
	[533] A Cock		1		1	1	1	2		1			
	[534] S. Ingram		2			1							
	[535] M. Gutrey					1			2				
	[536] J. Whitford					1			1		1	1	
	[537] W Daniel	1			1	1	2						
	[538] J Philips	1			1		1		1	1			
	[539] J Copper	2	2		3		4	1	3				
	[540] M. Hancock	2		1			4	2	2	1	1		
	[541] W Baley	1		2		1			1				
	[542] J. Liveley	1		1	2			2		1			
	[543] J. Willis Jn	3			1			2		1			
	[544] J. Willis Snr		1	1		1		2			1		
		47	27	31	33	13	64	26	33	22	7	11	
	[545] W. Nash	2			1		1		1				
	[546] J. Wiatt	3	1	2		1	3						
	[547] J. Deprist	1			1		2			1			
	[548] J. Wisman	2	1	2	1		1	1		1			
	[549] F. Haney					1				1			
	[550] J. Bolding	1			1		2		1		1		

14

Town or County	Heads of families	FREE WHITE MALES					FREE WHITE FEMALES					Other Free, etc.	Slaves
		to 10	to 16	to 26	to 45	45 &c.	to 10	to 16	to 26	to 45	45 &c.		
	[551] J. Kenny	4			1		1		1				
	[552] J. Hamilton		2		1				2		1		
	[553] D. Haney	1	2	1		1			3		1	5	
	[554] J Robinson		1	4		1	3		1	1	1		
	[555] J Morris	1	1			1	2						
	[556] R. Hanen	1		1	1		1	1	2	1	1		
	[557] S Dodds	2	1			1	1						
	[558] T. McDaniel	1		1	1				1				
	[559] R. Casey		2	1	1				1				
	[560] J Casey			1	1		2	1	1	1	1¹		
	[561] R. Jaxson	1	2			1			1				
	[562] J Wallis	1		3	1		1		1				
	[563] T. Mangomery			1	1	1		2		1			
	[564] H. Ledbetter	5	1					1	1				
	[565] W. Childers	2			1		1		1				
	[566] G Scrodgins	2			1		1		1				
	[567] C Scrodgins			1					1				
	[568] L Barker	3	2		1			2		1		4	
	[569] H. Cup Snr			1							1		
	[570] H. Cup Jnr	2		1	1		2		1				
	[571] P. Coon			1	1				1				
	[572] M. Hethhorn	3	1	1			1				2	1	
	[573] J. Anderson	3	1	1	1		1	2		1			

¹ Figure 1 erased but included in total, which should be 13 instead of 14.

Town or County	Heads of families	FREE WHITE MALES					FREE WHITE FEMALES					Other Free, etc.	Slaves
		to 10	to 16	to 26	to 45	45 &c.	to 10	to 16	to 26	to 45	45 &c.		
	[574] M. Haner	1		1			1		1		1		
	[575] R. Kesterson			1		1			1				
	[576] W. Kesterson			1					1				
	[577] J. Hull			1					1				
	[578] E. Pirkens	2	2				3			1			
	[579] W Wookens	1				1			1				
	[580] C. Smock	4	1	1	1		2	1	2	1			
	[581] J Barten	1			1		1			1			
	[582] J Tilley		1	1		1			2		1		
	[583] S Stilley	3	1			1	2						
	[584] J Wilson			2	1		2		2				
	[585] D. Glass	2		1					1				
	[586] D. Glass	3	1		1		2	1		1			
	[587] J. Hamburd					1					1		
	[588] P. Bell	2	1				3	1		1			
	[589] J. Self			1		1					1		
	[590] M. Robinson	3	1	1	1		2	1		1			
		60	26	33	21	15	43	14	35	15	14	10	
	[591] D. Self	1	3	1	1		2		1				
	[592] G Gratehouse	2	2		1		2	2		1			
	[593] H Rose	2		1	1		1	1	1	1			
	[594] W Woodes	1	1	1	1			1	1	1			

15

Town or County	Heads of families	FREE WHITE MALES					FREE WHITE FEMALES					Other Free, etc.	Slaves
		to 10	to 16	to 26	to 45	45 &c.	to 10	to 16	to 26	to 45	45 &c.		
	[595] W Pankey	2		1		1	1	1	1	1			
	[596] J. Lee	1	1		1				1	1			
	[597] W Morris	2	4	2	1	1	1	1		1		2	
	[598] R. Lee				1		2		1	1			
	[599] B. Bennett	3				1	1		1				
	[600] J Vinard			1	1		2		1				
	[601] J. Adams	1	1	4	1			1					
	[602] J. Wilson	2	1	1			1		2	1			
	[603] B Lee	1	1	1	1		1		1				
	[604] J McFerlan	2		1	2		3	2		1		1	
	[605] H. Pankey	1	2		1		2		1	1			
	[606] B. Smith	2		1	1		1		1			1	
	[607] C Hudson	1	1		1		3		1	1			
	[608] R. Palmon	1			2				1	1			
	[609] D. Palmon	3	1	1			2		1	2			
	[610] P. Etter					1			1	1			
	[611] J. Vawn	3	1	1	1		1	3	1	1			
	[612] W Hudson	3			1			1	1	1			
	[613] J. Riley				1		2	1		1			
	[614] W Flimon	3		2	1		1	1	2	1			
	[615] E Jourdon	3			1		3	2		1			
	[616] J Russell		2		1		1	1	1	1			
	[617] D. Garrett	1	2		1					1			

Town or County	Heads of families	\<FREE WHITE MALES\> to 10	to 16	to 26	to 45	45 &c.	\<FREE WHITE FEMALES\> to 10	to 16	to 26	to 45	45 &c.	Other Free, etc.	Slaves
	[618] J Morrow	1		2		1			1		1		
	[619] J. Engram	1		1					1				
	[620] H Person	2		1					1				
	[621] R John	1		2			2		1				
	[622] P Hammon	1	1	1	1			2	1	1			
	[623] B Waldon	1			1		3		1				
	[624] A Madleaf	2	1		1		2		1				
	[625] D. Shelvy	1	1		1			1	3	1		1	
	[626] E Colbert	1	2		1		1	1		1			
	[627] E Rose	1		1					1				
	[628] P. Rose	1		1					1				
Grampear	[629] G Ritenous				1					1			
	[630] J. Storey		1		1				1	1			
	[631] J. Carter	1	1	1					1				
	[632] G Storey	1			1		1			1			
	[633] C Hox	2	1	1	1				1				
	[634] J. Shelby	2	2	3	1		1	1		1			
	[635] R. McRony						1		1				
		59	28	31	34	5	45	23	35	28	1	5	
	[636] J Shelby	2	2		1		1	1		1	1		
	[637] J Story	3			1		2	1		1			
16	[638] R Dischax				1		2		1			5	

Town or County	Heads of families	FREE WHITE MALES					FREE WHITE FEMALES					Other Free, etc.	Slaves
		to 10	to 16	to 26	to 45	45 &c.	to 10	to 16	to 26	to 45	45 &c.		
	[639] J Lackey			1		1			2		1		
	[640] O Aplace	1		1		1		1	1				
	[641] J Aplace			1			1	1					
	[642] J Johnson	1	1		1	1	1			1	1		
	[643] J Woodes	3	1		1		1	1		1			
	[644] S Readfern	2	2				1						
	[645] S Modglen	1		2	1	1	3	1	1	1	1		
	[646] S Roberts	2	1				2	2					
	[647] J. Neel			2			2	1	1	2			
	[648] A Neel	3	1	1		1	6	1	1		1		
	[649] D. Copper	1			2		2		1	1			
	[650] W. Pitsford	3			1		1			1			
	[651] R. Jourdon	2	1	1	1		2				1		
	[652] W. Andrew	1	2					2	1				
	[653] T Ross	3		1	1		1		1				
	[654] J Odle		1	1			2			1			
	[655] R Waller	1		1			1		1				
	[656] J Batv			1			1		1				
	[657] T Hayes			1	1				1				
	[658] J Riley	3			1				2				
	[659] W Jackson			2	1	1	1	1	1			2	
	[660] J Morris	2			1		1	1	1				
	[661] D Lade	1			1		4			1			

Town or County	Heads of families	FREE WHITE MALES					FREE WHITE FEMALES					Other Free, etc.	Slaves
		to 10	to 16	to 26	to 45	45 &c.	to 10	to 16	to 26	to 45	45 &c.		
	[662] W Reed	2	1	2			3		2			1	
	[663] J. Ford				1					1		10	
	[664] S Dunn		1	1	1		3	1		1		1	
	[665] T Johnson			1									
	[666] J Clay	5		1			1						
	[667] J Williams	1			1		2			1			
	[668] J Steel	2			1		2			1			
	[669] S Omvelvrany	1			1		2		1	1		1	
	[670] A Blair	2	1				3	2					
	[671] J Crofard	4	1	1		1	3	1	1	1			
	[672] D. Stanley	1	1	2		1	3	1	1	1			
	[673] C Meek	1	1	1	1			1	1	1	1		
	[674] J. Leeper	2	2	1	1		2	1		1			
		55	18	25	23	11	63	21	22	19	6	16	
17	[675] G: Clemens	1		1	1		2	1		1		1	
	[676] S Standley	3	3	1	1		2	2	3	1			
	[677] J Harper		2	1		1				1			
	[678] M Fell	1			1		1	1		1			
	[679] G Williamson	1	2	2	1	1	1	1		1			
	[680] T Forguson	1		1	1		2	2	2	1			
	[681] F. Haney	1		1	1		1		1				
	[682] C Ledumes	1			1			2				5	

Town or County	Heads of families	FWM to 10	FWM to 16	FWM to 26	FWM to 45	FWM 45 &c.	FWF to 10	FWF to 16	FWF to 26	FWF to 45	FWF 45 &c.	Other Free, etc.	Slaves
Big Bay	[683] C King	1			1		1			1			
	[684] C Vickrey	1	2		1		2			1			
	[685] Tho. Pritchell	2		1			2		2				
	[686] S Wolsey			1					1				
	[687] D Colier	1		1		1	4		1		1		
	[688] S Rise	1			1		2			1			
	[689] J Cohn			1					1				
	[690] J Linch	2		1	1		2		1	1			
	[691] W. Edwards	3	1		2		3	2	1	1		1	
	[692] J Flanery	3		1	1		2		1	1			
	[693] J. Flanery	1		1	1			1					
	[694] W. Alcorn	1	3	4	1					1			
	[695] S Walters				1		1	1	1				
	[696] H Forguson	4			1			1		1		6	
	[697] J Simpson	2			1		1		1	1			
	[698] J Simpson				1		1		1				
	[699] J Simpson			1					1				
	[700] D. Griffin	2		1					1				
	[701] J Lowrey					1							
	[702] J. Lowry				1		1						
	[703] J Solovin	2			1					1			
	[704] J. Hickes	1	1		1		4	1		1			
	[705] R. Smith	1			1					1			

Town or County	Heads of families	FREE WHITE MALES					FREE WHITE FEMALES					Other Free, etc.	Slaves
		to 10	to 16	to 26	to 45	45 &c.	to 10	to 16	to 26	to 45	45 &c.		
	[706] A Herrill	2		1		1	1		2		1		
	[707] J Wornak	1			1				2				
	[708] E Rolston	2			1		2	1		1			
	[709] J Miller	1		1			1		1				
	[710] N. Miller							2			1		
	[711] H. Barnett	4	2		1		1			1	1		
	[712] G Crandle				1					1			
18		47	16	21	26	5	36	17	24	20	4	13	
	[713] M. Blau	3		1	1			2	1	1			
	[714] J Brown	1			1				1				
	[715] D Blau			1					1				
	[716] G Titteswon			1									
	[717] W. Rolston	2		1			1		1			2	
	[718] J Wittenton	3		1			1		1				
	[719] J Tilford	1		1			1		1				
Fort Massack	[720] Butler &c	2		19	16	2	1		6		1	1	
	[721] J. Putiand	1	2	1	3		4		1	1			
	[722] J. Deen	2	1			1		1		1			
	[723] J Weaver	2			1	1	2			1			
	[724] C Pennen				1		2		1				
	[725] S Gaffen	2								1			
	[726] L Wilcox							1			1		

Town or County	Heads of families	FREE WHITE MALES					FREE WHITE FEMALES					Other Free, etc.	Slaves
		to 10	to 16	to 26	to 45	45 &c.	to 10	to 16	to 26	to 45	45 &c.		
Wilkenson-ville	[727] M. Lesourse	2			1		1			1	1		
	[728] S Logston	1		1					2	1	1		
	[729] D. Pritchard		1	1	1					1			
	[730] F. Grater	3	1		1	1							
	[731] W. Brewer		1	2	1		2		1				
	[732] J. Heter					1	3				1		
	[733] M Davis				1		2		1				
	[734] W McGomery			1					1			1	
	[735] N McGomery			1					1			1	
	[736] J Taylor	4	1	2	1	1		2	1	1			
	[737] W. James	1	1	1		1			1	1	1		
	[738] W Gossett	2		1		1		1	1				
	[739] W. McGomery	3			1		4		1			1	
	[740] J. Oneal		1		1				1				
	[741] J. Larence	4		1	1				2				
	[742] J. James	1		1	1				1	1			
	[743] R. Simes				1				1				
	[744] G. Hacker	1		1	1		1	1		1			
	[745] J. Stimpson				1		1	1		1			
	[746] L Crain	2	1		1	1	1			1			
	[747] W. Hiihouse	1	2				2			1			
	[748] J.L. Tindle			1					1			1	
	[749] B. Boise			1		1					1		

Town or County	Heads of families	FREE WHITE MALES					FREE WHITE FEMALES					Other Free, etc.	Slaves
		to 10	to 16	to 26	to 45	45 &c.	to 10	to 16	to 26	to 45	45 &c.		
19	[750] G Boise	1			1	1	1	1	1	1			
	[751] Wm Philips	2										7	
		47	13	41	38	12	32	9	31	15	7		
	[752] J Tenney	2		1		1	3		2		1		
	[753] L Hux	1			1					1			
	[754] R Groome	2			1		3	1		1			
	[755] C Carpenter			1		1	1		1	1			
	[756] J Coper				1		3			1			
	[757] D McMelmurry	3	1		1		2			1			
	[758] J Murry			2		1			2		1		
	[759] J Kirkendol		1	3				1	1	1	1		
	[760] W Langston	1	1	2		1	1				1		
	[761] J Parker	2	1		1		3	2		1			
	[762] J Cochrin	1			1		3		1				
	[763] J Davis	2		1	1		2						
	[764] M Fuiler			1	1					1			
	[765] W Ware	1	1	1	1		2	2	1	1	1		
	[766] J Young	1		1					1				
	[767] J Harman	2	2	2		1			1	1			
	[768] H Holcorn	2	1	1		1	2		1				
	[769] J Alcorn	2	1		1		3		2		1		
	[770] J. H. Langston	2	1	1	1		3		1	1			

Town or County	Heads of families	FREE WHITE MALES					FREE WHITE FEMALES					Other Free, etc.	Slaves
		to 10	to 16	to 26	to 45	45 &c.	to 10	to 16	to 26	to 45	45 &c.		
	[711] R. Ware	1	2	1			2		1	1			
	[772] E. Hagon			1		1	2	2	2	1			
	[773] J. Burns	2	1	2			2	2	2				
	[774] J Jefferry	2	1	1	1	1		2		2			
	[775] J. Chick							1	1				
	[776] C Bridley	3		1					2		1		
	[777] S Jiles			3		1							
	[778] R. Thompson	2		3	1	1	1		1				
	[779] J Weatherston				1			1	1		1		
	[780] S. Bradley					1	1	1	1				
	[781] W. Conner				1	1	1	1	1				
	[782] W. Walker		2		1		3	1		1			
	[783] G. Dennis		3	1					2	1			
	[784] S. Allens	3			2		3			1	1		
	[785] G. Allen			1		1							
	[786] W Laurence	3	1	1	1		2	2		1			
	[787] C. Windmiller	1			1		1			1			
	[788] J. Barnhart	2		1					1				
	[789] R. Henderson	1			1	1	3						
	[790] D. Fullerton	1			1								
	[791] F. Henderson			1	1		2	1	1	1			
	[792] W. Hamilton			1	1		2	1	1	1			
		43	18	32	22	17	55	17	30	21	9		

Town or County	Heads of families	FREE WHITE MALES					FREE WHITE FEMALES					Other Free, etc.	Slaves
		to 10	to 16	to 26	to 45	45 &c.	to 10	to 16	to 26	to 45	45 &c.		
	[793] F Henderson		2		1		2	1	1	1			
	[794] G Laurence	4			1			3		1			
	[795] S. Weathernton			1			1		1		1		
	[796] J.Weathernton					1					1		
	[797] J Godar				1		3		2				
	[798] D. Harris					1					1		
	[799] J. Highland	1		1	1		2			1			
	[800] O Russell	1		3		1	1	1	2		1		
	[801] J. Clark	2			1		3			1	1		
	[802] W McIntosh				2		1	1	1				
	[803] J. Sanders	2			1		3			1			
	[804] A Clapp	3		1		1	1	2			1		
	[805] A Blau	3			1		1	1		1			
	[806] A Clap			1					1				
	[807] J. Murry	3				1	1	2	2		1		
	[808] S Lunsford	1	1		1		1			1			
	[809] J Bradley			1			1		1				
	[810] J Wearthington	2			1		2	1		1			
	[811] J Murphy			2			1		1	1			
	[812] S Costley	2		1			1		1				
	[813] B McIntosh	1	1	1		1					1		
20	[814] J Bonn		1	1		1					1	4	

Town or County	Heads of families	FREE WHITE MALES					FREE WHITE FEMALES					Other Free, etc.	Slaves
		to 10	to 16	to 26	to 45	45 &c.	to 10	to 16	to 26	to 45	45 &c.		
	[815] H Bonn	2		1			3		1				
	[816] T. McIntosh	3	2		1		2		1				
	[817] J MIntosh	1	1	1	1		1			1			
	[818] S Bonn	1		1	1		2			1			
	[819] C MIntosh	2					1		1				
	[820] S. Gutry	2		1	1		1	1	1	1			
Clear Creek	[821] W Norton				1						1		
	[822] G Brown	1	1	2	1			3	1				
	[823] D Brown			1		1			1				
	[824] J Brown	3		1	1		2		1				
	[825] E Bags	3			1		2		1				
	[826] J Bags			1			2		1				
	[827] J. Hargrave		2	1		1		1	1		1		
	[828] J Parmer		1	1	1		1		1				
	[829] D Arneld			2					1				
	[830] J Huntsaker				1		1		1				
	[831] D. Cunble								1				
	[832] A Morgan	1		1	1				1			4	
21		42	13	25	22	9	42	18	27	12	10		
	[833] S Sprous	3			1		2		1				
	[834] B Sekes	2			1		1		1				
	[835] G Woolf	1			1		1			1			

Heads of families	FREE WHITE MALES					FREE WHITE FEMALES					Other Free, etc.	Slaves
	to 10	to 16	to 26	to 45	45 &c.	to 10	to 16	to 26	to 45	45 &c.		
[836] J Woolf	1	1		1		3			1			
[837] J Hansucker		1			1		1	1		1		
[838] G Davis	2			1		2			1		1	
[839] R Waller	3		2			1	1	1		1		
[840] J Robinson	2		1		1	1		1		1		
[841] J Gregery	2			1		1		1				
[842] J Ervin	1		1	1		1		1			1	
[843] W. Wilson		1				1		1		1		
[844] G. James	1			1		2		1	1			
[845] A Murphy			1		1	2			1			
[846] R. Twidey	2	1	2		1	3	1	1		1		
[847] N. Green	3			1		2		1			5	
[848] T. Green	3			1		1		1				
[849] T. Whiteker	1			1		1		1	1			
[850] E Wiles	3			1		1		1	1			
[851] J Huggins	1		1	1		2		2				
[852] J. Huggins	2		1					1				
[853] A Huggins			1					2				
[854] T. Roberts			1		1	3	2		1	1		
[855] W Robinson	2		1			2		1				
[856] J Parmely	1		1	1		2		1	1			
[857] J Maner	2	2	1	1		1	1		1			
[858] H Heten	1			1		2		2				

Town or County	Heads of families	FREE WHITE MALES					FREE WHITE FEMALES					Other Free, etc.	Slaves
		to 10	to 16	to 26	to 45	45 &c.	to 10	to 16	to 26	to 45	45 &c.		
	[859] J Ravell	1	1							1	1		
	[860] D Retter	1		2	2				1				
	[861] W Godwin	3	1	2	1				1	1			
	[862] T Godwin			1	1				1				
	[863] R. Ravel	4	1	1	1		1	1		1			
	[864] A Friend	1	1		1		1	1		1			
	[865] J Frunch	3	2		1		2	2		1			
	[866] P. Galeher	4			1		1			1		2	
	[867] J Vanxl				1		3		1				
	[868] E Vanxl	3		1	1		1			1			
	[869] J Bratcher			1	1				1				
	[870] W. Ingram			1					1				
	[871] D Holder	1		1						1			
	[872] J Messa				1						1		
	[873] S. Snider	3			1					1			
	[874] W. Blackford	1	1		1		1	2		1			
	[875] J Spivey	2			1		3		1				
	[876] N. Blackford			1					1				
	[877] J. Spann				1		4	1		1			
		66	13	23	30	5	57	12	32	21	7	9	
	[878] W Bird	2			1		1		1	1			
	[879] R. Sampson		1			1	1			1	1		

22

Town or County	Heads of families	FREE WHITE MALES					FREE WHITE FEMALES					Other Free, etc.	Slaves
		to 10	to 16	to 26	to 45	45 &c.	to 10	to 16	to 26	to 45	45 &c.		
	[880] J Griggs	1			1			1		1			
	[881] N Bird							2		1		1	
	[882] G. Evens		2		1		4			1		3	
	[883] P. Evens		3		1		3			1			
	[884] J Alkens	1				1	3			1			
	[885] W Lankens	1			1				1				
	[886] W. Hensley	1	1		1		3	1		1			
	[887] D. Brasel			1									
	[888] R. Brasell	2	1	1		1	1				1		
	[889] G Brasell	2			1		1		1				
	[890] W Stites	2	2	3	1		2	1	1	1			
	[891] J. Lare	2	1		1		3	1		1			
	[892] W Powel	1	2		1		2	1		1			
	[893] J Fisher	2	3			1		1	1	1			
	[894] J Haghbanks	1			1					1			
	[895] E Eslers	2	1	1	1	1		1	1	1			
	[896] W Boggs	1	1		1				1		1		
	[897] M. Mathews	3		1	1								
	[898] J Graves		1				1		1	1			
	[899] J Bridges	4			1					1	1		
	[900] J Cribens	2			1					1	1		
	[901] A Russell	1				1	1			1	1		
	[902] J Russell		1				1		1	1			

Town or County	Heads of families	FREE WHITE MALES					FREE WHITE FEMALES					Other Free, etc.	Slaves
		to 10	to 16	to 26	to 45	45 &c.	to 10	to 16	to 26	to 45	45 &c.		
	[903] G Bradley	3		1			1		1	1			
	[904] N. Hickson	1			1		1	1		1			
	[905] S Oxford	2			1		3			1			
	[906] J Bane	2			1		4			1			
	[907] J Hux				1		2			1			
	[908] J Husley				1		2			1			
	[909] C Hensley	1	1		1				2		1		
	[910] M. Hux						1		1	1			
	[911] W Gattaut	3		1									
	[912] J Hightele												
	[913] M. Lensey	3	1		1		1	1		1			
	[914] W. Fisher	2			1		3			1			
	[915] S. Sholtes	2			1			1	1	1			
	[916] K. Fisher	2			1		3		1			1	
	[917] D Johnson	1		1			1		1				
	[918] J Johnon	1			1				1	1			
	[919] H Johnson		1		1		1			1			
	[920] E Chaffen				1	1	5	1		1			
	[921] M. Johnson						1	1	2				
	[922] J Harwich		1	2	1		2	1	2				
	[923] F. Murphy		1	1		1	2	3	2	1	1		
Big Bay	[924] W McClunn	3	1	1									
	[925] D. Simpson		1	1					1	1		2	

Town or County	Heads of families	FREE WHITE MALES					FREE WHITE FEMALES					Other Free, etc.	Slaves
		to 10	to 16	to 26	to 45	45 &c.	to 10	to 16	to 26	to 45	45 &c.		
	[926] W. Simpson	1	3	3	1		1	2	1	1			
	[927] J. Hebbens	2			1		2	2	3	1			
		58	25	19	32	8	68	16	27	33	7	7	
	[928] J. Rolston	1				1							
	[929] J Reed												
	[930] T Reed	2		1	1		1						
	[931] W. Belfon	1	3	1	1				1		1		
	[932] D Shearer	2	1					1		1			
	[933] C Goodner	1	2	4	1	1	2		2				
	[934] J Wait	3		1	1		1		1				
	[935] J Canidy	1	1	2		1	1	1	1				
	[936] J Dieres	1	2	2		1			2		1		
	[937] W. Dieres	3	1		1		1			1			
	[938] G Shotts		2	1		1		1					
	[939] D. Shotts		2		1				1				
	[940] E Smith	2	1		1		1		1	1	1	1	
	[941] L Casey		2		1		2	1	1				
	[942] J Row	2	2		1					1			
	[943] H Skinner	1	1		1					1			
	[944] R. Reed	3	2		2	1			1				
	[945] M. Newel						3			1			
	[946] J Walsey		2			1		1		1	1		

23

Town or County	Heads of families	FREE WHITE MALES					FREE WHITE FEMALES					Other Free, etc.	Slaves
		to 10	to 16	to 26	to 45	45 &c.	to 10	to 16	to 26	to 45	45 &c.		
	[947] J Hays	2			1		1		1				
	[948] A Hayse	2			1		1		1	1		2	
	[949] G W ˙˙on	2	1				2	1		1			
	[950] A McClure					1					1		
	[951] R Penny				1		2		1	1			
	[952] W Baley		2		1		4	1	1	1			
	[953] D. Hagle				4¹	1	2				1		
	[954] R. Hagle	1		2					1	1		1	
	[955] G Nown	2			1		1			1	1		
	[956] W Modglin	2	2	2		1		2	1		1		
	[957] A Penny		2	3	1	1	1				1		
	[958] R. McCormick				1		3			1			
	[959] J Whitesides	1	1		1		2	2		1		1	
	[960] J Fisher	2	2	1		1		2		1	1		
	[961] J Daniels	2	2	2		1	2	1	1	1	1		
	[962] J Rutliff		3	3		1		1		1	1		
	[963] J Rutliff	2		1	1							1	
	[964] W Miller	1		1			1	1	2	1	1		
	[965] G Waddle	4	2		1		2	1		1	1		
	[966] M. Daniel	2	2		1		2	1		1	1		
	[967] C Estes	2			1		1	1		1	1		
	[968] J Jourdon		2		1		4	1		1	1		2
	[969] D Trampbile	2	2		1		1	1		1	1		

Figure erased but included in total, which should be 31 instead of 32.

Town or County	Heads of families	FREE WHITE MALES					FREE WHITE FEMALES					Other Free, etc.	Slaves
		to 10	to 16	to 26	to 45	45 &c.	to 10	to 16	to 26	to 45	45 &c.		
	[970] W Tampbile	2	1	2			1			1			
	[971] D. Tamel	2			1		1		1				
	[972] G Trampbile	2	2		1					1			
	[973] T Batrite	1	1	2	1			1	2	1		1	
	[974] P. Trampbile					1					1		
	[975] G. Green	2	3			1			1	1	1		
	[976] J. Sommers	2		1	1		1						
	[977] J Sommers	1			1				1	1			
		58	52	32	32	17	50	19	24	28	16	9	
	[978] W Maxwell	4	2		1					1		1	
	[979] H Taylor	4	2		1					1		2	
	[980] H Wood	2			1		1		1				
	[981] J Lon		1	1		1		1			1		
	[982] P Powel	2	1	1		1	2	2		1			
	[983] J. Murphy				1		2			1			
	[984] J Roburn	2	1		1		2	2	1	1		3	
	[985] J Hampton	1		1	1		1		1			2	
	[986] D Morgan			2	1				1				
	[987] N. Lacey				1					1			
	[988] J Lam	3	1	1	1		1	1	1	1			
	[989] S Comoke					1							
	[990] J Clark	1		1			1	1	1				

24

Town or County	Heads of families	FREE WHITE MALES					FREE WHITE FEMALES					Other Free, etc.	Slaves
		to 10	to 16	to 26	to 45	45 &c.	to 10	to 16	to 26	to 45	45 &c.		
	[991] R Polack	2			1		2			1			
	[992] T Max	2			1		4			1			
	[993] A Clark			3								4	
	[994] T Wilson	1			1		2			1			
	[995] C Sparkes				1								
	[996] C Lesenby	2			1		2		1				
	[997] G Patterson				1								
	[998] J Raglen			1						1			
	[999] R. Cates	2			1				1				
	[1000] P. Bons			2			1		1				
	[1001] W. Forkner			1		1					1		
	[1002] C Marten	2	2		2[1]		3	1		1			
	[1003] J Bradberry	2	2		2		2			1			
	[1004] E Rodgers	1	2	1	1		2	1		1			
	[1005] A Richey	2	1	1	1		3			1			
	[1006] R. Lane	2		1	1		2			1			
	[1007] J Harris	1			1		2		1				
	[1008] D Snotgrass	2		1	1		1		1				
	[1009] J Upton				1		3	2		1			
	[1010] A Hamilton		1	1	1				1				
	[1011] J Harris	1	1		1		3			1			
	[1012] P. Kirkendol	2	1	2	1	1	1	3	1				

[1] Cancelled figures in this row apparently those used in totals—which should be one less in each case.

Town or County	Heads of families	\[to 10,\]	\[to 16\]	\[to 26\]	\[to 45\]	\[45 &c.\]	\[to 10\]	\[to 16\]	\[to 26\]	\[to 45\]	\[45 &c.\]	Other Free, etc.	Slaves
		FREE WHITE MALES					**FREE WHITE FEMALES**						
	[1013] W Blackford	2		2					2		1		
	[1014] N. Young			1						1			
	[1015] E Blackford			1					1				
	[1016] W McHenrey	3	1		1		2						
	[1017] H Jones	3	1		1			1		1			
	[1018] D. McHenrry	3		1	2		1		1	1			
	[1019] J Gareson	2			1		1			1			
	[1020] J Boman			1	1		3	2		1			
	[1021] G Daniels	2			1		3			1			
	[1022] J Mott	1			1		1			1			
	[1023] J Miller	2			1		3			1	1		
	[1024] J Steapleton					1	1						
	[1025] J. Buckles	3	1		1		2	1	1	1			
	[1026] J Weakes	2		3	1		2		1	1			
25	[1027] J More	2			1		2		1	1		1	
		68	19	30	41	7	59	18	18	33	4	13	
	[1028] J Lucas	1			1		1		1				
	[1029] J Burway	2		1			1	1		1			
Coffee	[1030] B. Longloy	3	1				1			1			
Island	[1031] A Godar	2	1				1						
	[1032] W Lunte	3		1	1		1		1				
	[1033] H Launt	1			1		2		1				

Town or County	Heads of families	FREE WHITE MALES					FREE WHITE FEMALES					Other Free, etc.	Slaves
		to 10	to 16	to 26	to 45	45 &c.	to 10	to 16	to 26	to 45	45 &c.		
	[1034] J Sonser	1	1		1				1		1		
	[1035] J Gratehouse	2	1	1		1	3	1	1		1		
	[1036] J. Selby	1			1		1			1			
	[1037] W Monian	1	1		1			1	3		1		
	[1038] W Baeney			2		1	2		1				
	[1039] S Higgins			2					1			1	
	[1040] J Ingram	2	1		1		1	1	1				
	[1041] J Wood	1	1	2		1		1	1		1		
	[1042] M. Darker			2		1			1		1		
	[1043] J Dukes			1					1				
	[1044] J Drennum	1			1		1		1				
	[1045] J Wood			1			1		1				
	[1046] W Arnald			1					1				
	[1047] J Arnald	1			1		1	1		1			
	[1048] J Glover	1	1		1			1		1			
	[1049] T Thompson				1					1			
	[1050] C Campbell	2		1	1		1		1				
	[1051] W Hall	1			1		1						
	[1052] W Arnald	1		1			2	1	3				
	[1053] J. Esley	1		1					1		1		
	[1054] W Gardner			1			1		1				
	[1055] J Strate	2			1		1			1			
	[1056] J Wisey	2	1		1		3			1			

Town or County	Heads of families	FREE WHITE MALES					FREE WHITE FEMALES					Other Free, etc.	Slaves
		to 10	to 16	to 26	to 45	45 &c.	to 10	to 16	to 26	to 45	45 &c.		
	[1057] J Magas	1					2		1				
	d												
	[1058] J Jourgan	1	2		2		2	1		1			
	[1059] L Compton	2		1	1			1		1			
	[1060] J Morrison			4¹	1		1	1	1				
	[1061] A Buchanen	1	1				1		1				
	[1062] J Stillwell	2		2	1			1	1	1			
	[1063] B. Arnell			1					1				
	[1064] L Bosso			2		1				1	1		
	[1065] C Gremore	1			1				1	1			
	[1066] P. Gremore	2	2		1		3	1		1			
	[1067] T Togon	3	1		1		1			1			
	[1068] J Togon					1					1		
	[1069] F Tupon	2			1		1		1	1			
	[1070] C Gale	2			1		1	1		1			
	[1071] B. Sabott	1			1		1		1				
	[1072] N. Collow	1		1			1		1				
	[1073] Philipi Dejin	3	1			1	1	1		1			
	[1074] L Baney	1			1		1			1			1
	[1075] A. Conie	1			1		1			1		1	2
		56	16	25	32	7	41	14	32	19	7		
	[1076] J Amlaw	1	1								1		

¹ Figure erased but included in total, which should be 24 instead of 25.

26

Town or County	Heads of families	FREE WHITE MALES					FREE WHITE FEMALES					Other Free, etc.	Slaves
		to 10	to 16	to 26	to 45	45 &c.	to 10	to 16	to 26	to 45	45 &c.		
	[1077] J Mar	1			1		1		1				
	[1078] R Leplonk	1	2		1		1			1			
	[1079] E Romble	1	1		1		1		1				
	[1080] J Deblaw	2	1		1		1	1	1	1			
	[1081] G Loving				1		1	1					
	[1082] J Brooks		1	1		1							
	[1083] W. Spencer	1	1	6	1		2	1	1	1			
	[1084] N Dear	1	1		1		4	1	1	1			
	[1085] J Clow	1	2		1		1	1	1				
	[1086] D Throp	3		1	2					1			
	[1087] J. McColley			5									
	[1088] A Magafee			2									
	[1089] J Morten	2			2		2			1			
	[1090] [MS. illegible]	1			1					1			
	[1091] D. Vanrix					2					1		
		14	10	15	14	2	14	3	5	7	1		

Page No	FREE WHITE MALES to 10	to 16	to 26	to 45	45 &c.	FREE WHITE FEMALES to 10	to 16	to 26	to 45	45 &c.	Other Free, etc.	Slaves
No 1	45	20	50¹	45	20	34	15	33	17	10	59	15
" 2	49	19	26	23	16	31	21	21²	18	17	3	33
" 3	46	17	30	25	17	46	11	24³	22	7	7	7
" 4	49	24	27	24	16	40	21	25	19	8	4	•
" 5	59	23	28	17	9	33⁵	17	20	19	10	12	
" 6	50	20	22	21	7	44	23	26	15	8		
" 7	56	18	28	28	10⁹	55	21	19	22	10	25	62
" 8	41	20	22	26	9	45	19	25	12	11	1	7
" 9	49	20	35	24	23	45	25	29	17	11	7	•
" 10	64	33	52	62	10	58	21	27	26	8	176	
" 11	39	17	21	31	10	32	12	20	15	7	64	
" 12	43	10	47	40	6	17	13	13	21	4	36	
" 13	47	27	31	33	13	64	26	33	22	7	11	
" 14	60	26	33	21	15	43	14	35	15	14⁸	10	
" 15	59	28	31	34	5	45	23	35	28	1	5	
" 16	55	18	25	23	11	63	21	22	19	6	16	
" 17	47	16	21	26	5	36	17	24	20	4	13	
" 18	47	13	41	38	12	32	9	31	15	7	7	
" 19	43	18	32	22	17	55	17	30	21	9		
" 20	42	13	25	22	9	42	18	27	12	10	4	
" 21	66	13	23	30	5	57	12	32	21	7	9	
" 22	58	25	19	32	8	68	16	27	33	7	7	
" 23	58	52	32	32⁹	17	50	19	24	28	16	9	

Page	FREE WHITE MALES					FREE WHITE FEMALES					Other Free, etc.	Slaves
	to 10	to 16	to 26	to 45	45 &c.	to 10	to 16	to 26	to 45	45 &c.		
" 24	68	19	30	41[10]	7	59[11]	18	18	33	4	13	
" 25	56	16	25[12]	32	7	41	14	32	19	7	2	
" 26	14	10	15	14	2	14	3	5	7	1		
	1310	535	771	766[13]	286	1149	446	657	516	211	500	128

[1] Should be 51.
[2] Miscopied from schedule—should be 20.
[3] Should be 22.
[4] Figure 4 omitted.
[5] Incorrect total in schedule—should be 32.
[6] Should be 9.
[7] Figure 1 omitted.
[8] Should be 13.
[9] Should be 31.
[10] Should be 40.
[11] Should be 58.
[12] Should be 24.
[13] In this totals row the fourth column should total 764; the fifth, 285; the sixth, 1147; the eighth, 654; the tenth, 210; the twelfth, 129. This would change the total number of free males to 3665, females to 2973, and slaves 129, making the grand total 7267.

The number of persons within my division consisting of Seven thousand two hundred and Seventy five appears in a schedule hereto annexed. Subscribed by me this 24th day of November 1810.

THOS C PATTERSON

Free White Males	3668
Free White Females	2979
Indented Servants	500
Slaves	128
Total amount	7,275

CENSUS OF BOND COUNTY, 1818

Census of Bond County Illinois Terriory May 14th 1818

Names of heads of Famelies[1]	Free white males 21 yr. & upwards	All other white inhab- itants	Free people of colour	Servants or slaves
[1††] Inman Rufus	1	3		[MS.torn]
[2††] Haly John	1	5		[MS.torn]
[3††] Reavis Charles	2	8		[MS.torn]
[4] Johnson Samuel	1	6		
[5] Reavis Solamon	1	2		
[6††] Hickason William	1	5		
[7††] Stubblefield John	1	5		
[8††] Clary John	1	9		
[9††] Hill Robert	1	9		
[10††] Casey Levi	2	4		1
[11] Robertson William	1			
[12††] Reavis Harris	2	5		
[13††] Casey Aaron	2	3		
[14††] Lee John	1	7		
[15††] Hill John	1	4		
[16††] Hill Henry	1	5		
[17††] Wright Joseph	1	4		
[18††] Pyatt Henry	1	6		
[19††] Hill Thomas	1			
[20††] Coffe Newton	1	8		
[21††] Blair Colbin	1	5		
[22††] Daniel Martin	1	5		
[23] Hall Samuel	1	6		
[24] [F]inley Samuel	1	6		
[25††] Jones Martin	5	2		1
[26††] Steel John	1	8		
[27††] Kirkpatrick Thomas	1	14		
[28††] Smith Henry	1	4		
[29] Steel Adam	1	2		
[30††] Brown Francis	1	4		
[31] Willoughby Vincen	2	4		
[32††] Card James	1	3		
[33] Reavis Noah	1	3		1

[1] Figures and symbols preceding names have been supplied by the editor:
‡ Found also in the Federal Census for 1820.
† Found also in the State Census for 1820.

CENSUS OF BOND COUNTY, 1818 *(Continued)*

Names of heads of families	Free white males 21 yr. & upwards	All other white inhab- itants	Free persons of color	Servants or slaves
[34†‡] Hubbard Peter	1	5		
[35†‡] Henderson William	1	9		
[36†‡] Howel William	1	7		
[37†‡] Smith John	1	6		
[38†‡] Lee Loyd	1	4		
[39†‡] Whitley John	1	7		
[40†‡] Huff John	1	7		
[41†‡] Pusley William	1	9		
[42†‡] Whitley John, Junr	1	2		
[43†‡] Whitley Mills	1	4		
[44†‡] Little William	4	9		
[45†‡] Duncan Sarah		10		
[46†‡] Reavis Isham	1	9		
[47†‡] Bateman Abraham	1	10		
[48†‡] Wakefield John A	2	3		
[49†‡] Nichols Thomas	1	10		
[50†‡] Whatley Henry	1	7		
[51†‡] Hill Isaac	2	3		2
[52†‡] Burnside James	2	2		
[53†‡] Altom James	1	6		
[54] Miller John	1	5		
[55] Burton Gibbon	2	7		
[56] Griffin Jesse	1	2		
[57] Felps Jacob	1	4		
[58†‡] Harmon Francis	1	4		
[59†‡] Edington John	1	4		
[60†‡] Nichols William	1	3		1
[61†‡] Robertson Thomas	2	6		
[62†‡] Felps John	1	2		
[63†‡] Felps Zedoch	1	6		
[64†‡] Mires Stephen	1	6		
[65†‡] Dunn William	1	7		
[66] Hanon Sarah		5		
[67†‡] Hanon Jesse	1	5		
[68] Graig Jacob	2	6		
[69†‡] Anderson Ignatious	1	8		
[70†‡] Mires Joseph	1	5		

CENSUS OF BOND COUNTY, 1818 (*Continued*)

Names of heads of families	Free white males 21 yr. & upwards	All other white inhab- itants	Free persons of color	Servants or slaves
[71†‡] Inman Rufus	3	2		
[72†‡] Hanon Samuel	1	4		
[73†‡] Hanon James	1	4		
[74] Downing William	2	9		
[75] Morse Samuel G	1	5		
[76†‡] Baker Robert	1	5		
[77†‡] Harlin Bonham	1	6		
[78†‡] Boles James	1	6		
[79] White James	2	3		
[80†‡] White John	1			
[81†‡] Blizzard James	1	3		
[82†‡] Leeper John	2	8		
[83†‡] Dickson Samuel	1	9		
[84†‡] White Robert	1	5		
[85†‡] Stubblefield Wyatt	1	5		
[86†‡] Hussong Conrad	1	2		
[87†‡] Davison George	1	6		
[88†‡] Enloe Ashel	1	9		
[89] Davidson Samuel	1	1		
[90†‡] Beck Paul	1	8		
[91†‡] Kirkpatrick John	1	13		
[92†‡] White Thomas	4	5		
[93†‡] Kirkpatrick Francis	1	7		
[94] Lane William	1	4		
[95†‡] Gallispi Robert	1	9		
[96†‡] Davis Jonathan	2	6		
[97†‡] Scribner William	1	10		
[98] Price Isaac	1	5		
[99†‡] Young William	1	1		
[100] Spillars John	2	4		
[101†‡] Powers Thomas	1	5		
[102] Lewis Berry	1	5		
[103] Scribner Pleasant	1	6		
[104†‡] Lindley John	1	6		
[105] Riley Anderson	1	4		
[106] Cox Mary		9		
[107†‡] Hopton John	1	4		

CENSUS OF BOND COUNTY, 1818 (*Continued*)

Names of heads of families	Free white males 21 yr. & upwards	All other white inhab- itants	Free persons of color	Servants or slaves
[108†‡] White David	2	7		
[109] Roberts William	1	6		
[110†‡] Barker Joshua	1	1		
[111] Rule Henry	1	3		
[112] Bruce Walker	1	8		
[113] Barker William	1	4		
[114†‡] Stice Charles	1	3		
[115†‡] Henson Benjamin	1	8		
[116†‡] Green James	2	8		
[117†‡] Henson John	1	1		
[118†‡] Prewit Fields	2	9		
[119†‡] Powers Elijah	1	6		
[120†‡] Powers John	2	6		
[121†‡] Wakefield Dianna	1	10		
[122] Fagan William	1	4		
[123†‡] Orr Alexander	1	13		
[124] Moore Charles	1	5		
[125] Moore John A	1	1		
[126†‡] Barber Joseph	1	8		
[127†‡] Reed James	2	2		
[128] Kennady Archbald	1	4		
[129†‡] Jackson Hugh	2	12		
[130] Smith Joseph D	1	7		
[131†‡] Hill John	1	1		
[132†‡] King John	2	7		
[133†‡] Lorton John	3	3		
[134] Robertson Hardy	1	1		
[135] Bowling James	1	1		
[136†‡] Osmus Phillip	1	2		
[137] Matthews Cliburn	1	7		
[138] Boalton Benjamin	1	5		
[139†‡] Bowling Benjamin	1	4		
[140†‡] Burgess William	1	5		
[141] Holland John	1	4		
[142†‡] Samples John	1	2		1
[143†‡] Duff Phillip	1	9		
[144†‡] Johnson Charles	1	9		

CENSUS OF BOND COUNTY, 1818 (*Continued*)

Names of heads of families	Free white males 21 yr. & upwards	All other white inhab- itants	Free persons of color	Servants or slaves
[145††] Grisham Austin	1	4		
[146††] Volintine Hardy	1	2		1
[147] Ross Alexander	2	3		
[148††] Lee Samuel	8	7		
[149††] Coyle John	1	8		
[150††] Lewis John	1	6		
[151††] Wheelock E L R	3	2		
[152] Neel William	1	5		
[153††] James Benjamin	1	4		
[154††] Volintine William	1	5		1
[155††] Smith Joel	1	3		
[156††] Hill Samuel	2	6		
[157††] McCord Robert	1	11		
[158††] Robertson Alexander	1	7		
[159††] Berry Jonathan	1	6		
[160††] Parsley Robert	1	6		
[161††] Crisp William	1	4		
[162††] Briggs Robert	1	7		
[163††] Wilson James	1	3		
[164††] Kirkpatrick Hugh	2	4		6
[165] Matthew Absalom	1	5		
[166] Matthews Benjamin	1	4		
[167] McKee Thomas	1	5		
[168††] Bridgwater Zachariah	1	3		
[169] Tilley John	2	1		
[170] Randolph Elihu H	1	3		
[171††] Clerk William	1	5		
[172††] Forhand Jarvis	1	7		
[173] Lockerman Nicholas	1	6		
[174††] McWilliams Alexander	1	3		
[175] Yokem James	2	5		
[176] Yokem Martha	1	6		
[177††] Yokem John	1	8		
[178] Prewit Solomon	2	8		
[179] Shepherd Rowland	1	11		
[180††] Street James	1	8		
[181††] Corrandle Gordon B.	2	1		

CENSUS OF BOND COUNTY, 1818 (*Continued*)

Names of heads of families	Free white males 21 yr. & upwards	All other white inhab- itants	Free persons of color	Servants or slaves
[182] Coyle James	1	2		
[183††] Hinton Evans	1	7		
[184††] Estep Elijah	1	10		
[185††] Hunter John	1	4		
[186††] Hunter Samuel	1	1		
[187††] Hunter William	1	5		
[188††] Archer Hezekiah	1	1		
[189] Archer William	1	5		
[190] Hicks Job	1	1		
[191] Lindley Joseph	1	1		
[192††] Finley Andrew	1	5		
[193††] Lindley William	1	1		
[194††] Archer Israel	1	5		
[195] Hicks Jacob	1	5		
[196] David Edward	1	4		
[197††] Johnson James	1	8		
[198††] Comer Allen	1	1		
[199††] Brown William	1	7		
[200††] White Richard	1	5		
[201††] McKinney James	1	2		
[202††] Moody Andrew	1	5		
[203††] Robinson William	2	5		
[204††] Robinson Gideon	1	2		
[205] Beck Paul Junr	2	3		
[206††] Elles John	1	7		
[207] Beck Guy	1	2		
[208††] Massey Burwell	1	6		
[209††] Stubblefield William	1	10		
[210††] Diamond Robert	1	7		
[211††] McGinnis Abraham	1	6		
[212††] Daniel Robert	1	5		
Finis	264	1103	0	15

I do certify that this is a just and true
Enumeration as given to me by the Heads of Famelies of Bond county
according to Law

MARTIN JONES C. B. C.

CENSUS OF BOND COUNTY, 1818 (*Concluded*)

[*Recapitulation:*]¹

Free white males 21 years and upwards	264
All other whites	1107
Servants or slaves	15
Total	**1386**

¹ The recapitulations at the end of the county schedules are supplied by the editor. See these for correct totals of columns.

CENSUS OF CRAWFORD COUNTY, 1818

Census of Crawford Co. 1818

Date of receiving list	Names of heads of Families[1]	Free White Males Twenty-one & upwards	All other White Inhab-itants	Free people of colour	Serv-ants or Slaves
	6th				
[1] April	Alexander Hutton	1	8		
[2‡*]	Ashers Haskin	1	6		
[3‡*] 9th	Abram Bogard	1	7		
[4‡*] 11	Abram Taylor	1	5		
[5‡*]	Adam Lackey	1	6		
[6] 14	Andrew McMahhan	1	2		
[7‡*]	Abram Cairnes	1	9		
[8‡*]	Andrew MClewer	1	5		
[9]	Alexander Terner	1	7		
[10‡*] 20	Abram Coonrod	2	6		
[11‡†] 22	Abram Snider	1	9		
[12‡†]	Anthony Cocks	1	5		
[13‡†]	Amos Ashmore	1	8		
[14‡*] 29th	Aaron Guyer	1	1		
[15‡*]	Axim Guyer	1			
[16‡*]	Axim Spiqrey	1	5		
[17‡†]	Aloscous Brown	1	3		
[18‡†]	Anthony Sanders	1	3		
[19‡*]	Aaron Ball	1	5		
[20‡*]	Andrew Montgomery	1	9		
[21] May 12	Arthur Jones			1	
[22]	Abraham Camp			9	
[23]	Abraham Jones			1	
[24‡*]	Amos Phelps	1	4		
[25]	Boils Hew	1			
[26‡*] 6th	Benjamin Eaton	1	6		
[27‡*] April	Benjamin Wilson	1			
[28]	Benoni Middleton	1	9		
[29]	Bennit Mason	1	1		
[30]	Benjamin Parker	1	6		
[31]	Baldon Mattet	1			

[1] Figures and symbols preceding names have been supplied by the editor:
‡ Found also in the Federal Census for 1820.
† Found also in the State Census for Clark County, 1820.
* Found also in the State Census for Crawford County, 1820.

CENSUS OF CRAWFORD COUNTY, 1818 (*Continued*)

Date of receiving list	Names of heads of families	Free white males 21 yr. & upwards	All other white inhabitants	Free persons of color	Servants or slaves
[32‡*]	Barbary Lacy		5		
[33‡*]	Benjamin MCrary	1	3		
[34] 15	Benjamin Matthew	1	3		
[35] April	Benjamin Feeles	1	9		
[36‡*]	Benjamin Evins	1	13		
[37‡†]	Barnabas Runnels	1	5		
[38‡*] 6	Cristopher Morrs	1	7		
[39‡*]	Chester Fitch	5	4		
[40‡*] 7th	Charles Sudevoit	1	6		
[41‡†]	Charles Neely	1	9		
[42‡*]	Cornelious Taylor	1	12		
[43]	Cornelious Vanosdoll	1	4		
[44]	Charles St. Jervenue	1			
[45]	Charles Mills	1	4		
[46‡*] April 9	Chalkley Draper	1	9		
[47‡†]	Charles K Archer	1	2		
[48‡†]	Cyrus Sharp	1	8		
[49‡†]	David Caldwell	1	1		
[50‡*] 4	Daniel Funk	1	4		
[51‡*]	David MCgahey	1	7		
[52‡*]	Daniel Martin	1	6		
[53‡*]	Daniel Delap	1	7		
[54‡*]	David Vanwinkle	2	10		
[55‡†] 7	Daniel Parker	1	9		
[56‡*]	Daniel Travers	2	4		
[57‡*]	Daniel Alison	1	2		
[58‡*]	Daniel Kaykedall	1	2		
[59‡*]	Doctor Hill	1	3		
[60‡†]	Daniel Cornel	1	2		
[61‡†]	Daniel Brite	1	6		
[62‡†] 22	Daniel Lane	1	3		
[63]	Daniel Beckwourth	1			
[64‡†] 27	David Hogue	1	7		
[65‡*]	David Goss	1	5		
[66‡*]	Daniel Wilard	1	6		
[67‡*]	David Porter	1	5		
[68‡*] 14	Edward N Cullom	1	10		

CENSUS OF CRAWFORD COUNTY, 1818 (*Continued*)

Date of receiving list		Names of heads of families	Free white males 21 yr. & upwards	All other white inhabitants	Free persons of color	Servants or slaves
[69]		Etion Tromley	1	5		
[70‡*]		Edward H Piper	1			
[71]	15	Esaw Morrison	1	1		
[72‡*]		Edmond Hearn	1	3		
[73‡*]		Elias Driskell	1	4		
[74‡*]	17	Elisha Bradbury	1			
[75‡*]		Elizabeth Stockwell		8		
[76‡*]		Elizabeth Beard		5		5
[77]		Eli Adams	1			
[78*]	19	Eady Coal			3	
[79*]		Edward Goins			2	
[80*]		Enoch Jones			1	
[81‡*]		Edward Alison	1			
[82‡*]		Edward Mill	1	2		
[83]		Eliga Larnsfer	1	9		
[84‡†]	27	Edward Purcell	1	7		
[85‡*]		Elisha Crocker	1			
[86‡*]		Esir Heacock	1	4		
[87‡†]	28	Eliga Auston	1	9		
[88‡†]		Enoch Davis	1	4		
[89‡†]	29	Ezekel Perdew	1	7		
[90‡*]		Elezer Spawling	1	1		
[91‡*]	May	Francis Cullom	1	1		
[92‡*]	4th	Frederick Alison	1	6		
[93]		Francis Pealo	3	4		
[94‡*]		Frederick Markley	2	4		
[95‡*]		Frances Boggs	2	5		
[96]	April	George Farr			1	
[97‡*]	27	George Westnor	2	10		
[98‡*]		George W Kinkade	1	4		
[99‡†]		George W Catron	1	3		
[100‡*]		Gabril Funk	1	4		
[101‡*]		George W Bratton	1	8		
[102]		George Moor	1			
[103]		George Daugherty	1			
[104‡*]	30th	George Baugher	1	4		
[105*]		George Anderson			4	

CENSUS OF CRAWFORD COUNTY, 1818 *(Continued)*

Date of receiving list		Names of heads of families	Free white males 21 yr. & upwards	All other white inhab- itants	Free persons of color	Serv- ants or slaves
[106‡*]		George Pharris	1	3		
[107‡*]		George Parker	1	6		
[108]		Gabril Murfy	1	4		
[109]	May	George Beckwourth	1			
[110‡*]	6	George Smith	1	8		
[111‡*]		George Bayth	2	10		
[112‡*]		Hall Sims	1	4		
[113]		Henry Jons	1			
[114]	May	Henry B Palmer	2	9		2
[115*]	11th	Henry Jonson	1	8		
[116]		Henry Laymountain	1			
[117‡*]		Henry Price	1	4		
[118‡†]		Hew Henderson	1	9		
[119]		Hesakiah Ashmore	1	2		
[120‡†]		Henry Harrison	1	8		
[121‡*]	April	Henry Buckner	1			
[122‡†]	24	Hew Miller	2	4		
[123‡†]		Heli Cornel	1	5		
[124]		Heli Wils	1	4		
[125]		John Storey	1			
[126‡*]		Jonas Butterfield	[*No data given*]			
[127‡*]		John Lamb	1	5		
[128‡*]		Jeremiah Hogue	1	3		
[129‡*]		Joel Cheek	1	2		
[130‡*]		John Waldrop Junr	2	9		
[131‡*]		James Rhea	1	5		
[132‡*]		John Malcom	1	2		
[133‡*]		James Shaw	3	12		
[134]		John Cowan	2	3		
[135‡*]		Jonathan Wood	1	3		
[136‡*]		John Crews	1	7		
[137‡*]	April	John Waldrop	1	3		
[138‡*]	1	John Gill	1	4		
[139‡*]		John Eaton	1	2		
[140‡*]		John Barlow	1	6		
[141‡*]		John W Mills	1	4		
[142‡*]		James Caldwell	1	8		

CENSUS OF CRAWFORD COUNTY, 1818 (*Continued*)

Date of receiving list		Names of heads of families	Free white males 21 yr. & upwards	All other white inhab- itants	Free persons of color	Serv- ants or slaves
[143]		James Gillaspy	1	3		
[144]	3	James McDaniel	1	3		
[145‡*]		Joseph Person	1	7		
[146]		Jesse Low	1	1		
[147‡*]		Jefry Salsbury	1	1		
[148‡*]		Joseph P Jones	1			
[149]		James Martin	1	1		
[150]		Joseph Pendlton	1			
[151]		John Chandler	1			
[152]	April 9	James Overstreet	1	2		
[153‡*]		Joseph Shaw	3	5		
[154]		Jacob Morris	2	10		
[155‡*]		Isaac Brimberry	1	10		
[156‡*]		John Funk Senr	1	5		
[157]		John Dopher	1			
[158‡]		John White	1	2		
[159‡*]		John Martin	1	6		
[160‡*]	10	John Veach	1	7		
[161]		John Robins	1			
[162‡*]		Jacob Garrard Junr	1	5		
[163]		Isaac Galland	1	2		
[164‡*]	12	Jesse Page	1	4		
[165‡†]		John Parker	2	5		
[166‡*]		Joseph Eaton	1	3		
[167‡†]		James Martin	2	9		
[168]		John Morris [?]	1			
[169]	14	Jacob Laplont	1	7		
[170]		Isaac Alison	1	2		
[171‡*]	9	James Bryans	1	5		
[172‡*]		John Porter			5	
[173‡*]	2	Isaac Goins			8	
[174]	May	Joseph Anderson			3	
[175]		John Morris			3	
[176]		Jobe Haden	2	7		
[177]		Joshua Flinn	1			
[178]		Jerremiah Robinson	1			
[179‡*]	April	James Spensor	1			

CENSUS OF CRAWFORD COUNTY, 1818 (*Continued*)

Date of receiving list		Names of heads of families	Free white males 21 yr. & upwards	All other white inhab- itants	Free persons of color	Serv- ants or slaves
[180‡*]	14th	Jesse Spensor	2	2		
[181‡*]		James Deal	1			
[182‡*]		Isaac Goin	1			
[183]		John Matthew	2	4		
[184‡*]	14th	John Dunlap	1	7		
[185‡*]	April	John Berry	1	4		
[186]		Joseph A Addams	1			
[187‡*]		John R Addams	1			
[188]		John Ashbrook	2	4		
[189‡*]		Johnathan Alison	2	6		
[190‡*]		John Luster	1	9		
[191‡*]		Joseph Alison	1	7		
[192‡*]		Isaac Alison	1	10		
[193‡†]		John Richardson	2	6		
[194‡*]		John Goliher	1	6		
[195]	11	John Taylor	1	1		
[196]		Joseph Lamotte	1	1		
[197‡*]		Joshua Gilferd	1	5		
[198‡*]		James Gipson	1	3		
[199‡*]		John Goliher Junr	1	1		
[200]		Jerremiah Morreson	1	4		
[201‡*]		Jane Dubois	1	4		6
[202]	15	John Shelton			1	
[203*]		James Butler			7	
[204]		Jacob Garner	1	4		
[205‡*]		John Moor	1	7		
[206‡*]	17	John Hill	1	8		
[207‡†]		John Blake	1	8		
[208‡†]		Joseph Shaw	2	9		
[209‡†]		John Welch	1	2		
[210‡†]		John Chenowith	2	4		
[211‡†]	20th	Joseph Dunlap	1	5		
[212‡†]	April	James Taylor	1	8		
[213]		Jacob Taylor	1	7		
[214‡†]		John Baker	1	5		
[215‡†]		James Cocks	1	1		
[216‡†]		James Ashmore	1			

CENSUS OF CRAWFORD COUNTY, 1818 (*Continued*)

Date of receiving list		Names of heads of families	Free white males 21 yr. & upwards	All other white inhab- itants	Free persons of color	Serv- ants or slaves
[217‡†]		Jacob Long	1	4		
[218‡†]	19	James M. Love	1	4		
[219‡†]		John Struton	1	6		
[220‡†]		Johnathan Mayo	2	1		
[221‡*]		Jesse Guyer	1	6		
[222‡†]		Jacob Blaze	1	3		
[223‡†]		James Cocks	1	4		
[224‡]		Joseph Richardson	3	6		
[225‡†]		Joseph Oins	1	6		
[226‡†]		James Conaway	1	7		
[227‡]	22	James Dolson	1	9		
[228‡†]		Isaac Moor	2	6		
[229‡†]		James MCGerth	2	6		
[230‡†]		John M'Clewer	1	8		
[231‡†]		[James]¹ M'Cabe	1	6		
[232‡†]	20th	John Esry	1	4		
[233]	April	Joseph Parker	1			
[234‡†]		James Parker	1	2		
[235‡*]		Isaac Parker	1	2		
[236‡†]		John Handy	1	4		
[237‡*]		John Sackrider	1	4		
[238‡*]		John Snipes	1	3		
[239‡*]		Joseph Wels	1	4		
[240‡*]		Isral Harris	1	5		
[241‡*]	May 2	John Nealy	2	7		
[242‡†]		James Moor	1	3		
[243]		John Ridenour	1	4		
[244‡*]		Johnathan Persell	1			
[245‡*]		Jobe Harnis	1			
[246‡*]	3	Joseph Wood Senr	1	2		
[247‡*]		John S. Woodwourth	1	1		
[248‡*]		Lewis Lavelit	3	8		
[249‡*]		Lewis Goin	1			
[250‡†]		Laurence Holanback	1	10		
[251]		Lewis Bean	1	6		
[252]		Lemuel Derrence	1			
[253‡*]		Lewis Goodin	1	2		

¹ Name filled in from old copy in the Illinois Historical Survey.

CENSUS OF CRAWFORD COUNTY, 1818 (*Continued*)

Date of receiving list		Names of heads of families	Free white. males 21 yr. & upwards	All other white inhab- itants	Free persons of color	Serv- ants or slaves
[254‡*]		Lot Watts	1	1		
[255‡*]	April	Marthy Hatton		4		
[256]	6th	M Corpen T Hutson	1	4		
[257‡*]		Marvel Marcom	. 1	10		
[258‡*]		Mary Hearn		7		
[259]		Martin Funk	1			
[260‡†]	8	Moses Williams	1			
[261‡*]		Michael Rollins	1	2		
[262‡*]		Matthew Nealy	1	1		
[263]		Mary Jones			1	
[264]	May 9th	Nathaniel Brown	1			
[265‡*]		Nathan Rellens	2	5		
[266]		Niholass Leming	1			
[267]		Otious M Hart	1	1		
[268‡*]		Peter Price	2	6		
[269]	April	Peter Edilene	1	2		
[270‡†]	17	Peter Kaykendall	1	3		
[271‡*]		Peter Boon	2	2		
[272‡*]	6th	Robert McDowl	2	5		
[273]		Robert Gill	1	1		
[274‡*]		Robert Haskin	1	1		
[275‡*]	April	Richard Easton	2	10		
[276‡*]	6th	Richard Eaton	1	7		
[277‡*]		Rubin Norton	1	5		
[278]		Robert Terner	1	5		
[279‡*]		Ruth Terner		7		
[280‡*]		Richard Hismith	1	4		
[281‡*]		Richard Alison	1	4		
[282]	7	Robert Henderson	2	9		
[283‡†]		Rubin Crow	2	6		
[284‡*]		Robert Holedy	1	1		
[285‡†]		Remember Blackmon	1	2		
[286]		Robert Jerdon	1	1		
[287‡*]		Robert Montgomery	1	4		
[288‡*]	April	Smith Shaw	1	8		
[289‡*]	4th	Samuel Harris	1	4		7
[290‡*]	6th	S B A Carter	2	5		

CENSUS OF CRAWFORD COUNTY, 1818 (*Continued*)

Date of receiving list	Names of heads of families	Free white males 21 yr. & upwards	All other white inhab- itants	Free persons of color	Serv- ants or slaves
[291]	Susanna Anderson			1	
[292‡*]	Samuel Brimberry	1	3		
[293]	Samuel Freemon	1			
[294‡*]	Stephen Eaton	1	4		
[295‡*] 7	Samuel Alison	1	2		
[296‡*]	Samuel Drake	1	3		
[297*]	Sian Moris			5	
[298‡*]	Samuel Lemmons	1	6		
[299]	Samuel Gastin	1	8		
[300]	Sith King	1	6		
[301‡*] 9	Samuel MClewer	2	1		
[302]	Samuel MClewer Junr	1			
[303‡*]	Scot Riggs	1	8		
[304‡*]	Samuel Lanear	1	6		
[305]	Samuel Alison, Junr	1	1		
[306]	Sinnet Basye	1	6		
[307] 11	Sharlow Dubois	1	1		
[308‡†]	Samuel Ashmore	1	8		
[309‡†]	Samuel Jimerson	1	2		
[310‡†]	Samuel Prevo	1	9		
[311‡*]	Silus Harlin	1	1		
[312]	Simon Lotrip	1			
[313‡†] 13	Stephen Handy	1	3		
[314]	Samuel G Beckwourth	1			
[315‡*]	Samuel Lindly	2	5		
[316]	Samuel Martin	1	5		
[317‡†]	Samuel Pery	4	13		
[318‡*] April 6	Thomas Low	1	2		
[319‡*]	Thomas Kenady	1	7		
[320‡*]	Thomas Anderson	2	7		
[321‡*]	Thomas Dunlap	1	2		
[322‡*] April 9	Thomas Jones	1	8		
[323‡*]	Thomas Patton	1	2		
[324‡*]	Thomas Watts	1	6		
[325‡*]	Thomas Gill	1	7		
[326‡*]	Thomas Harden	1	5		
[327]	Thomas MCall	1			

CENSUS OF CRAWFORD COUNTY, 1818 (*Continued*)

Date of receiving list		Names of heads of families	Free white males 21 yr. & upwards	All other white inhabitants	Free persons of color	Servants or slaves
[328]	8	Thomas Spensor	1			
[329]		Thomas Flinn	1	5		
[330‡*]		Thomas Mills	1	2		
[331‡†]		Thomas Wilson	1	9		
[332‡†]		Thomas Handy	1	12		
[333‡*]		William Ryan	1			
[334‡*]	6	William Young	1	3		
[335‡*]		William Barbee	1			
[336‡*]		William Waldrop	1	9		
[337‡*]		William Hern	1	3		
[338‡†]		William Lockard	1	8		
[339‡*]	4	William Dunlap	1	2		
[340‡*]		William Flipper	1	5		
[341]		William Merkel	1			
[342‡*]		William Evermon	1	9		
[343‡*]		William Gerrard	1	1		
[344‡*]	2	William Gerrard Senr.	1	2		
[345‡*]		William Hix	1	9		
[346]		William Row	1	2		
[347‡†]		William D Cilbern[1]	1			
[348]		William Travers	1	6		
[349‡*]		William Westrope	1	7		
[350‡*]	16th	William Adams	1	11		
[351‡*]		William Parker	1	3		
[352‡*]		William Howard	1	8		
[353]	9	William Basadon			1	
[354]		William Man	1	8		
[355‡*]		William Hesmith	1			
[356]		William Miller	1	9		
[357]		William Hays	1			
[358‡†]	13	William Lewis	1	2		
[359]		William Mulley	1	3		
[360]		William Hogue	1	6		
[361‡†]		William B Archer	1	1		
[362]		William Lee	1			
[363‡*]		William Houston	1	8		

[1] Retouched by binder to read Dellbern. Probably originally William D. Cilbern.

CENSUS OF CRAWFORD COUNTY, 1818 (*Continued*)

Date of receiving list		Names of heads of families	Free white males 21 yr. & upwards	All other white inhab- itants	Free persons of color	Serv- ants or slaves
[364*]	14th	Ezekel Anderson			4	
[365‡*]		Ezekel Terner	1	1		
[366‡†]		Zachariah Archer	1	7		
[367‡†]		Zachaus Hastel	1	4		
[368]	May	Mary Jones			1	
[369‡*]	6th	Elizabeth Jones			3	
[370]		Wm Thoves	1			
[371‡*]		Wm Bradburry	1	6		
[372]		Ames Phelps	1	4		
[373]		Abram Jones			1	
[374]		Abram Camp			9	
[375]		George Farr			1	
[376]		David Porter			1	
[377‡*]		Jehu Harden	1	2		
[378‡*]		Daniel Vanwikle	1	6		
[379‡*]		David Reavell	1	2		
[380‡*]		David Ruby	1			
[381‡*]		William Wilson	1	2		
[382‡*]		Joseph Kitchell	1	7		
[383*]		Nancy Kitchell	2	2		
[384]		Joseph Wood Junr	1	4		
[385‡†]		James Knight	4	5		
[386‡*]		Samuel Henry	1	10		
[387]	11th	Solomon Eaton	1	5		
[388]		Stephen Terry	1			
[389‡*]		Barnabas Mavern	1	1		
[390]		Wm Cullom	1			
[391]		Lewis Jones	1			
[392‡*]		Benjamin Eaton Junr	1			
[393]		Wm Florough	1			
[394]		Abram Jones			1	
[395]	14	Adam Hogeboome	1			
[396‡*]		Philip Edwards	2	11		

CENSUS OF CRAWFORD COUNTY, 1818 (*Continued*)

Palastine Crawford County

I do certify on honour that the above is a true
correct list of the number of Inhabitants in Crawford County
Illinoi Territory, amounting to two thousand & twenty four
souls. Given under my hand this 15th day of May 1818

WILLIAM CULLOM C. C. C.

ADDITIONAL CENSUS OF CRAWFORD COUNTY, 1818

Date of receiving list	Names of heads of families	Free white males 21 yr. & upwards	All other white inhab- itants	Free persons of color	Serv- ants or slaves
July 10th 1818					
[397] 10	David Miller	1			
[398]	John S. Woodworth		2		
[399]	John Waldrop Sen	1			
[400‡*]	Benjamin Shook	1			
[401‡*]	George Miller	1	8		
[402]	Braxton Pollard	1	5		
[403]	Sam¹ King	2	3		
[404]	Thomas Boatright	1	6		
[405‡*] 11	Joseph Festler	1	3		
[406‡*]	Thomas Young	1	5		
[407‡*]	John Evens	1	6		
[408‡*]	Ralph Jeffers	1	8		
[409‡†]	James Johnson	1	7		
[410]	William Akify	1	4		
[411]	Zachariah Bolen	1	5		
[412]	James Right		3		
[413]	William Holly	1	4		
[414] 14	Wm Perkins	1	5		
[415‡†]	Newel Leonard	2	4		
[416]	James McDaniel	1	6		
[417]	William Wood	1	8		
[418]	James C. Mitchel	5	3		
[419]	Cushing Snow	1	8		
[420]	William Crow	1	2		
[421‡†]	Risen Ball	1	2		
[422]	Moses McCrane	1	3		
[423]	John M William	1	8		
[424‡*]	Bernard Goff	1	6		
[425‡*]	David Goff	1	4		
[426‡*]	James Hungerford	1	3		
[427]	Eterea Creker		8		
[428‡†]	James Bartlet	1	5		
[429]	Moses Dotston	1	14		
[430‡*]	Elisha Fitch	3	12		
[431]	Moses Pee	2	6		
[432‡*]	James B Bennet	1	5		

ADDITIONAL CENSUS OF CRAWFORD COUNTY, 1818 (*Continued*)

Date of receiving list		Names of heads of families	Free white males 21 yr. & upwards	All other white inhab- itants	Free persons of color	Serv- ants or slaves
[433]		Muryan Anderson	4	8		
[434‡*]		John B Richardson	1	8		
[435]		John L. McCoullough	1	3		
[436]		Wᵐ P. Bennet	2	9		
July 19th 1818						
[437]		William Brown	1	5		
[438‡*]		Andrew Rhea	1	8		
[439]		John Newton	1	5		
[440‡*]		Chᵃˢ Hill	1	4		
[441‡*]		James Newlin	1	6		
[442]		John Hill	1	8		
[443‡*]		John Newlin Junʳ	1	3		
[444]		Benjamin Chardy	1	6		
[445]		James Meed	1	8		
[446]		Adam Huff	1	6		
[447]		James Obannon	1	3		
[448]		Adam Galegar	1	5		
[449‡*]		Saml Shoulders	1	7		
[450‡*]		John Jackson	1	4		
[451]		Geo. Criles	1	4		
[452]		Coonrad Criles	1	7		
[453]		John Smith	5	6		
[454‡*]		Isaac Lamasters	1	3		
[455]	19	Michael Quin	1			
[456]		William Howard	2	8		
[457]		Henry Johnson	3	1		
[458]		John Jeffers	1	7		
[459]		John Ashbroock		4		
[460]		John Rollins	3	7		
[461]		Major Spencer	1	3		
[462‡*]	21	Camon Rathbourn	1	7		
[463‡*]		John Brigman	1	4		
[464‡*]		Thomas Fiffe	1	9		
[465]		Wm Baker	1	8		
[466]		Wm Blythe	1	2		
[467‡†]		James Anderson	1	4		
[468]		Wm. Anderson	1	4		

ADDITIONAL CENSUS OF CRAWFORD COUNTY, 1818 (*Continued*)

Date of receiving list	Names of heads of families	Free white males 21 yr. & upwards	All other white inhab- itants	Free persons of color	Serv- ants or slaves
[469]	John Brockelbank	1	5		
[470]	Cornelius Taylor	9	11		
[471]	Frederick Price	1	2		
[472]	Jonathan A Goss	1	2		
[473‡*]	John Johnson	1	8		
[474‡*]	John Asbel	1	2		
[475]	Saml Asbel	1	4		
[476‡*]	John Johnson Junr.	2	9		
[477‡*]	James Johnson	1	6		
[478]	Hoga Bolin	1	6		
[479]	James Walters	1	7		
July 22nd 1818					
[480‡*]	Jacob Walters	1	8		
[481‡*]	Abraham Walters	1	3		
[482‡*]	Stephen Lee	1	2		
[483‡*]	David Stewart	2	4		
[484]	Michael Shanks	1	7		
[485‡*]	James Lasters	1	3		
[486]	Elijah McNilley	1	3		
[487]	James Only	1	10		
[488]	Allen Cobb	1	8		
[489‡*]	Benjamin Parker	3	8		
[490]	James John	1	7		
[491]	Saml John	1	9		
[492]	Saml Rearch	2	8		
[493]	Saml Stephens	2	5		
[494]	John Pamberson	1	7		
[495]	Aaron Stout	3	10		
[496]	John Wiatt	2	7		
[497]	Peter Vangant	1	4		
[498]	James Gambert	3	7		
[499]	Aleson Henton	1	9		
[500]	Saml Galeworth	2	6		
[501]	Jeremiah Wires	2	9		
[502]	Zachariah Mesmore	1	3		
[503]	Thomas Morehead	3	8		
[504]	John Shenks	2	7		

ADDITIONAL CENSUS OF CRAWFORD COUNTY, 1818 (*Concluded*)

Date of receiving list	Names of heads of families	Free white males 21 yr. & upwards	All other white inhabitants	Free persons of color	Servants or slaves
[505]	Saml Commons	2	5		
[506]	Benjª Shanks	3	8		
[507]	Elenor Shanks		8		
[508]	James Murphy	3	5		
[509]	Aaron Welton	2	5		
[510]	John Welton	2	4		
[511]	Abraham Jones	3	9		
[512]	John Jones	1	7		
[513]	John Decant	2	11		
[514]	Wᵐ Shannon	1	9		
[515]	Lewis Shannon	2	3		
[516]	Peter Eutors	3	9		
[517]	John Shalor	2	6		
[518]	Aaron Vanlenberg	3	10		

[*Recapitulation:*]

Census of 1818

Free white males 21 years and upwards   422
All other white inhabitants   1558
Free people of color   78
Servants or slaves   20

Total   2078

Additional Census

Free white males 21 years and upwards   179
All other whites   698

Total   877
Grand total   2955

CENSUS OF FRANKLIN COUNTY, 1818

A list of the Census for Franklin Coty.
in the year 1818.

Cences Taken in by John Browning of The County of Franklin Illinois
Territory

Names of heads of families[1]	Free white males 21 yr. & upwards	All other white inhab- itants	Free people of colour	Serv- ants or slaves	Place of Residence
[1‡†] John Moore	2	8			Big Muddy
[2‡†] Simon M. Hubbard	4	7		2	Same
[3‡†] Francis Jourdan	1	12	1		Same
[4‡†] thos Moore	1	6			Same
[5‡†] Jnọ Kirkpatrick	1	7			Same
[6‡†] David Diment	1	10			Same
[7] Elizabeth Armstrong	1	8			Same
[8‡†] William Dunlap	1	6			Same
[9‡†] Wm Mceya	2	10			Same
[10‡†] Kinching odam	1	4			Same
[11] Arther owens	1	1			Same
[12‡†] Jnọ Robinson	1	3			Same
[13‡†] Martin A Duncan	1	3			Same
[14] Moses Ham	1	9			Same
[15] Miller Shelton	1	3			———
[16] James Shelton	1	3			———
[17‡†] Isaac Perkins	1	3			———
[18‡†] John Waddle	1	2			———
[19] Nichols Wiser	1	5			———
[20] Thos Jourdan	1	4			———
[21] Mathew kinsaid	1	1			———
[22‡†] Charles humphry	1	6			Same
[23] Reuben Rogers	1	5			Same
[24‡†] Crawford Burnes	1	10			Same
[25‡†] Jas Armstrong	1	5			Same
[26‡†] Coonrad Baker	1	6			Same
[27] fraces grham	1	5			Same
[28‡†] Isaac Herring	2	9			Same
[29‡†] Jonathan Herring	1	2			Muddey

[1] Figures and symbols preceding names have been supplied by the editor:
‡ Found also in the Federal Census for 1820.
† Found also in the State Census for 1820.

CENSUS OF FRANKLIN COUNTY, 1818 (*Continued*)

Names of heads of families	Free white males 21 yr. & upwards	All other white inhab- itants	Free persons of color	Serv- ants or slaves	Place of Residence
[30‡†] Philip Russel	1	7			Same
[31‡†] Nathan Arnett	1	8			Same
[32‡†] Abraham Pyott	1	2			
[33‡†] Joshua tiner	2	14			B.Mudey
[34‡†] John tippey	1	3			Same
[35] Edward H. Kees	2	7			Same
[36‡†] Willes tiner	1	4			Same
[37‡†] Wᵐ Campbell	1	7			Same
[38] Wᵐ Linsey	1	5			Same
[39‡†] Nelson McDowel	1	5			Same
[40] Jaˢ Arnett	1	3			Same
[41‡†] Jesper Crain	1	10			Crab orchard
[42‡†] John Roland	1	5			C..f.. Mudey
[43‡†] Ragsdale Roland	1	9			Same
[44‡†] Spencer Crain	1	11			Same
[45‡†] Elijah Spiller	1	7			Same
[46‡†] John Dunkin	1	8			Same
[47‡†] John Nelson	1	8			Same
[48‡†] Cudworth Harrison	1	5			Same
[49] James Menees	1	4			C..b or- chard s. Mudey
[50‡†] Richard Bankston	1	7			Same
[51‡†] Zachariah Wright	2	9			hon Creek
[52‡†] Abraham flanery	1	3			e of Mudey
[53‡†] Abraham tippey	1	12			Same
[54‡†] Elijah flanary	2	7			Same
[55] Peter Holeday	1	5			Same
[56‡†] Samuel froo	1	7			Same
[57‡†] Starling Hill	1	8			Same
[58‡†] thomas griffeth	1	7			Same
[59‡†] John Boles	1	3			Same
[60‡†] Solomon Snider	1	10			Same
[61] John Bittle	1	5			Same

CENSUS OF FRANKLIN COUNTY, 1818 (*Continued*)

Names of heads of families	Free white males 21 yr. & upwards	All other white inhab- itants	Free persons of color	Serv- ants or slaves	Place of Residence
[62‡†] John g. Simpkins	1	6			Same
[63‡†] John Shultz	1	5			Litle salene
[64‡†] Jacob Shultz	1	2			Same
[65‡†] John Shultz	1	1			Same
[66‡†] Susannah Shultz	1	9			Same
[67‡†] John Dammern, sr.	2	9			Same
[68‡†] John Damren, jur.	1	3			Same
[69‡†] Richard Ratcliff	1				
[70‡†] Jesse Aplen	1				Saline
[71] Richard ratliff	1	3			Same
[72‡†] Joseph Newten	1	7			Same
[73‡†] David trammel	1	6			Same
[74‡†] Joseph Suratt	1	9			Same
[75‡†] Samuel Deeson	3	6			Same
[76‡†] Elijah burnes			9		Same
[77] John grey			6		————
[78‡†] Magey Lockler	1		13		————
[79‡†] Stephen Burnes			11		Same
[80‡†] Wᵐ Burnes			8		Same
[81‡†] John Roberts	2	7			Same
[82] Dickeson garret	1	3			Same
[83‡†] Henrey parsons	1	6			Same
[84‡†] John hooker	1	6			Sm
[85‡†] Jabez hooker	1	3			Sm
[86‡†] Wᵐ green	2	7			Same
[87‡†] Robert armstrong	2	6			Same
[88‡†] Jas Rogers	1	2			Saline
[89] Matthew hall	1	5			Same
[90‡†] Mason Crawford	1	22			Same
[91‡†] Dempsey odam	2	4			B.Mudey
[92] Jno. M'Creerey	2	9		3	Saline
[93] thoˢ Whitesides	1	3			Same
[94‡†] Isaac Moberley	1	9			Same
[95‡†] Elias Jordan	1	7			Muddey
[96] Isham Houson	2	6		5	Same
[97] thomas adams	1	10			Same
[98‡†] Edmond baker	1	8			Same

CENSUS OF FRANKLIN COUNTY, 1818 (*Continued*)

Names of heads of families	Free white males 21 yr. & upwards	All other white inhab- itants	Free persons of color	Serv- ants or slaves	Place of Residence
[99‡†] thomas Smothers	1	4			Same
[100‡†] Edward suillevin	1	4			Sm
[101‡†] Jacob philips	2	9			Same
[102‡†] Nat hamerson	1	3			Same
[103‡†] John Kirk	1	7			———
[104] Jesse Parsons	1	12		1	Same
[105] John Parsons	1	3			———
[106] Zoah Parsons	1	3			Same
[107] thos Markim	1	8			Same
[108] James Markim	1	5			Same
[109‡†] John Cox	3	11			Same
[110] Wilson damron	1	6			Same
[111‡†] Joseph Estes	1	9			Muddey
[112‡†] Absalom Estes	1	9			Same
[113] John Hays	1	4			Same
[114‡†] Chamberlin hutson	1	6			Same
[115‡†] Wm frizell	1	6			Same
[116] Jos Mcfarling	3	9			Same
[117‡†] Mikel Rollens	1	9			Same
[118‡†] John Miller	1	9			Same
[119‡†] Charles Miller	1	4			Same
[120‡†] Lazerous Web	1	12			Same
[121‡†] Eli web	1	5			Same
[122‡†] John Sendusky	1	2			Same
[123‡†] Elgah taylor	1	2			Same
[124‡†] William king	1	9			Same
[125‡†] James Jordan	1	5			Same
[126‡†] Welden Manon	1	7			Same
[127‡†] Joseph Neal	1	2			Same
[128‡†] William Neal	1	3			Same
[129‡†] John lounius	1	3			Same
[130‡†] John Crawford	1	8			Same
[131‡†] William Ewbanks	1	10			Same
[132‡†] Elijah Ewing	2	6			Big Muddey
[133‡†] Davis stilley	1	10			Same
[134] Hua Moor	1	3			Same
[135‡†] Andrew cronk	1	8			Same

CENSUS OF FRANKLIN COUNTY, 1818 (*Continued*)

Names of heads of families	Free white males 21 yr. & upwards	All other white inhab- itants	Free persons of color	Serv- ants or slaves	Place of Residence
[136‡†] thos Dorres	16	25	1	2	Same
[137‡†] John farris	3	16			Same
[138‡†] Moses garret	5	13			Same
[139‡†] Rial Williams	1	3			Same
[140‡†] John tompson	2	6		1	————
[141‡†] Saml Yong	1	3			Same
[142‡†] Joseph thompson	1	7			Same
[143‡†] thos Roberts	1	3			Same
[144‡†] Wm faris	1	6			Same
[145‡†] Aaron yongblood	1	12			Same
[146‡†] hezekiah garret	1	3			Same
[147‡†] Speser watkins	1	1	3		Same
[148‡†] Richard Waler	1	8			Same
[149‡†] fanney Odle	1	4			Sam
[150‡†] Isaac galey	2	10			f Cty
[151‡†] thos Lampley	1	4			Sam
[152] John odle	1	2			Same
[153‡†] Nancey adams	1	7			Same
[154‡†] Robert Mcreerey	1	2			Same
[155‡†] Elexander Mcreerey	1	4			Sam
[156] Milley Jackson	1	5			Same
[157‡†] John Williams	1	5			Sal[ene?]
[158‡†] Williams Rogers	1	3			Same
[159] William pate	1	8			————
[160] pairet pate	1	7			————
[161‡†] John hall	1	5			Same
[162‡†] John wren	1	6		1	Same
[163] Mossbey owens	1	4			————
[164] Margret Nettles	1	6			————
[165‡†] James Smith	1	6			Muddey
[166‡†] Benj. Rogers	3	10			Same
[167] george Ward	2	7			Same
[168‡†] William Roberts	2	4			Same
[169‡†] Cassandra Jones	1	11			Same
[170] Samuel Biddick	1	6			————
[171‡†] John Browning Amount 1081	1	9			Salene

CENSUS OF FRANKLIN COUNTY, 1818 (*Concluded*)

I Do hereby Certify that the within Sheets
Contains a True Enumeration of the Inhabittants
of the County of Franklin in the Teritory of
Illenois Given under my hand this 11th July
1818

JOHN BROWNING Comr

[*Recapitulation*:]

Free white males 21 years and upwards	219
All other white inhabitants	1043
Free people of color	52
Servants or slaves	15
	1329

CENSUS OF GALLATIN COUNTY, 1818

Census of Gallatin County

1818

The census of the inhabitants of Gallatin, Illinois Territory, taken by William McCoy under a commission from the Governor, in conformity to a law of the Territory entitled "An act providing for taking the census of the inhabitants of the Illinois Territory & for other purposes passed 7th January 1818. And of the supplement thereto passed 10th January 1818 taken between 1st April and the 1st June 1818.

Names of heads of families[1]	Free white males 21 yr. & upwards	All other white inhab- itants	Free persons of colour	Servants or slaves
[1‡†] Joseph M. Street	1	7		3
[2] Christopher Robinson	3	1		
[3†] John Cook	1	9		
[4‡†] Jacob Sexton	1	4		
[5] Michael Robinson	1	8		
[6] Nicholas Egbert	1	7		
[7] [Agnes] Hatfield		6		
[8‡] [Sa]m! Hayes	2			
[9‡†] ——— Vanlandingham	2			
[10] [Pe]ter Goodnight	1	6		
[11] Richard Elliott	1			
[12] James Kirkpatrick	1			
[13‡] John C Rives	1			
[14] [Si]nah Killess			3	
[15] [E]dward T Pullom	1	3		
[16] [Arun?] Thompson	1	5		
[17] [Wm.] C. Vought	1			
[18] [Thomas] Shannon	1			
[19] [Elias] Hubbard	1			
[20] [Squire] Brown	2	9		
[21‡†] Martin Hitchcock	2	11		
[22] David Apperson	2			
[23‡] John Cowan	2			
[24‡†] John Marshall	2	6		2

[1] Figures and symbols preceding names have been supplied by the editor:
‡ Found also in the Federal Census for 1820.
† Found also in the State Census for 1820.
* Pope County State and Federal Census for 1820.

CENSUS OF GALLATIN COUNTY, 1818 (*Continued*)

Names of heads of families	Free white males 21 yr. & upwards	All other white inhab- itants	Free persons of color	Servants or slaves
[25‡] Peter C. Seaten	1	1		
[26] Charles B. Williams	1			
[27] Alexander M'Intosh	1			
[28] Henry Nickless	1	4		
[29] Asah Savery	1	2		
[30] May Tear		4		
[31] Clary Robinson			8	
[32] James Melten	1	2		
[33] James Jones	1	2		1
[34] Sarah Brunden		2		
[35] James B Humphris	1	2		
[36] James H. King	1			
[37] Juball Fuller	2	2		
[38‡†] Robert Peebles	1			
[39] Simon M. Hubbard	2	3		2
[40] David W. Maxwell	1			
[41] Elander Wilson	1	5		9
[42‡†] Joseph Reed	1	8		
[43] Daniel Dickins	1	3		
[44‡†] James Cain	[1]	[2]		
[45] Owen Reely	[2]			
[46‡†] Hubbard Dare	1	3		
[47‡†] Jacob Berger	1	5		3
[48] Saml Seaton	1	5		3
[49‡†] Saml R. Campble	1			3
[50‡†] Charles Cambple	12	6		2
[51] Parmenus Redman	1			
[52‡†] Thomas Barlow	1	2		
[53†] Nancy Witherow		2		
[54‡†] Simon Cade		1	3	
[55†] John Rohrer	3	4		
[56‡†] William Thomason	1	9		
[57] Benj Nickles	1	3		
[58] Thomas Mosby	1			
[59] Luuis [?] Guthman	1			
[60] William Bowls	1	1		1
[61] John M'Intire	1			

CENSUS OF GALLATIN COUNTY, 1818 (*Continued*)

Names of heads of families	Free white males 21 yr. & upwards	All other white inhab- itants	Free persons of color	Servants or slaves
[62‡†] John Caldwell	1	5		
[63‡†] Thomas Sloo, Sen	3		1	
[64] William Anderson	1			
[65] James Fealand	1	2		
[66‡†] James Wilson	17	9		4
[67] John Hambleton	1			
[68] David Nortel	1	12		
[69‡†] Robert Hardin	1	3		
[70] Stephen Beck	2	5		1
[71] Herod Wilson	1	1		
[72‡†] Thomas G. Wood	[1]	[7]		
[73] Sam Ford			3	
[74] Margaret Carry		7		
[75] John Waggener	1			
[76] Ebenezer Stewart	1	6		
[77] William Morris	1	3		
[78] John [Gather?]	1	1		
[79] Richard Feirs	1	3		
[80‡] William Thompson	2	6	1	
[81‡] Joseph Cooper	1	2		
[82] Thomas Gasten	1	5		
[83‡†] Brice Hannah	1	2		
[84] Joseph Bridger	1	3		
[85†] Stephen Boutwell	1	8		
[86†] James Dillard	1	7		
[87‡†] Phillip Henson	1	7		
[88] Walter White	1			
[89] Wm Wood	1	2		
[90] L. R. Harrison	1	2		
[91] Britton Bates	1	5		
[92] Lewis Watkins	1	9		
[93†] Wm Finch	1	2		
[94‡†] Joseph Clarke	2	6		
[95] Elisha Hall	1	5		
[96] Nancy Barnhill	1	5		
[97†] John Carter	1	3		
[98] James Clift	1	2		

CENSUS OF GALLATIN COUNTY, 1818 (*Continued*)

Names of heads of families	Free white males 21 yr. & upwards	All other white inhab- itants	Free persons of color	Servants or slaves
[99‡†] Wm Kelly	2	5		
[100‡†] John Robinson	1	2		
[101] James K Harris	1			
[102‡†] Wm Dart	1	4		
[103‡†] James M Pettygrew	1	6		
[104‡†] Thomas Akers	1	3		
[105‡†] Wm Duvall	1	6		
[106‡†] Leony Boutwell	2	4		
[107] James Hutchcrafft	1	2		
[108‡†] James Albin	2	5		
[109†] Joshua Sexton	1	2		
[110] Alphred Wood	1	4		
[111‡†] Haly Ragline	1	3		
[112] Allin Smith	1	3		
[113†] Isaac Riley	1	2		
[114‡†] Joseph Reily	1	8		
[115‡] [Willliam Moody	2	7		
[116] Joseph Reed	1	3		
[117‡†] John M'Lauflen	2	4		
[118] Elisha Baldin	1	6		
[119‡†] Armstord Smoot	1	9		
[120‡†] Judey Meeks	1	1		
[121‡†] John Reed	2	7		
[122‡†] Andrew Slack	1	3		1
[123‡†] Ames Wiley	1	4		
[124†] Bazel Dodge	1	2		
[125] Moses Overfield	1	5		
[126‡†] Moses M Rowlings	1	3		2
[127‡†] Warner Buck	3	2		
[128†] William Akers	1	4		
[129‡†] John Campbel	1	3		
[130] Benjamin Ellis	1	1		
[131†] John Murphey	1	6		
[132‡†] Joel Martin	1	6		
[133] William Thompson	1	8		
[134‡†] M. D. Devanpert	1	3		
[135] Andrew Furgeson	1	4		

CENSUS OF GALLATIN COUNTY, 1818 (*Continued*)

Names of heads of families	Free white males 21 yr. & upwards	All other white inhab- itants	Free persons of color	Servants or slaves
[136] Turner Edwards	1	4		
[137‡†] Elias Chaffen	1	1		
[138†] Alexander Barnhill	1	6		
[139] Will M'Laughlin	1			
[140‡†] Joseph Cozad	1	6		
[141] Baker Tyler	1			
[142] Robt A. Deacen	1	3		
[143] James Heaton	1	4		
[144] Seth Casen	1	3		
[145] Anthony Pate	1	9		
[146‡†] John Forrester	2	4		3
[147‡†] Benjamin Moseby	3	5		2
[148] Humphrey Leach	1	8		
[149‡†] Saml Clark	1	8		7
[150‡†] Robert Owens	1	8		
[151‡†] John Damewood	1	5		
[152] David Doolin	3	8		
[153] Oliver Ormsby	1	2		
[154] James Collins	1			
[155] Benj C Brown			2	
[156‡] Wm McGhee	1	4		
[157] James Trousdale	2	[8]		
[158] John Loon	[2]	2		
[159‡†] Townsen Tarlton	1	5		
[160] Merrel Willis	1	4		
[161] George Wildey	1	5		
[162] Enoch Tolbert	1	10		
[163†] Jeffrey Deprest			2	
[164†] James Hood			11	
[165] Thomas Rossen	1	4		
[166†] Nimrod Scott	1	3		
[167] Will Willis	1	5		
[168‡†] Otho Devanport	1	7		
[169] Thornten Tally	1	4		
[170] Robt K Bridges	1			
[171‡†] James Fields	1	2		
[172‡†] Stephen Fields	1	4		

CENSUS OF GALLATIN COUNTY, 1818 (*Continued*)

Names of heads of families	Free white males 21 yr. & upwards	All other white inhab- itants	Free persons of color	Servants or slaves
[173‡†] James Drake	1	2		
[174] Sussanah Willis		2		
[175] Thomas Coxe	2	6		
[176] Nathaniel Armstrong	1	7		
[177‡†] Henry Medlock	1	5		
[178] George Ragsdale	1			
[179] John W. Ormsby	2	6		
[180] Wm Hedges	1			
[181] Wm Roark	1	6		
[182‡†] Cornelus Lafferty	2	8		
[183] Robt Craig	1			
[184‡†] Hazel Moreland [Senr?]	3	6		2
[185‡†] Hazel Moreland [Junr?]	2	5		
[186‡†] Abriham M'Cool	1	[4]		
[187] Rachel M'Gee	1	2		
[188†] Daniel Norante			9	
[189†] James Willis, Jun	1	2		
[190] James Ellis	1	3		
[191†] James Willis	1	4		
[192‡†] Joseph Scott	2	5		
[193] Hiram Hutchcrafft	1	1		
[194] Squir Young	1			
[195†] James Pantus	1	5		
[196†] Mason Wood	1	4		
[197†] John Hutchcrafft	1	7		
[198†] David Hany	1	5		
[199] Natly Duvall	1	3		
[200] Nancy Barnhill	1	5		
[201] David Tade	1	7		
[202] Thomas Hunt	1	1		
[203] Thomas Jent	2	3		
[204] Ruben Bellah	1	4		
[205] James Michaels	2	5		
[206] George [?] Michaels	2	6		
[207‡†] Eli Gaston	1	7		
[208] Abriham Merrill	1	5		
[209†] Wm Young	1	9		

CENSUS OF GALLATIN COUNTY, 1818 (*Continued*)

Names of heads of families	Free white males 21 yr. & upwards	All other white inhab- itants	Free persons of color	Servants or slaves
[210] John Perry	1	2		
[211] John Carter	1	3		
[212‡†] Anesly Clarke	1	7		
[213] Elijah Frost	1	9		
[214] John Dunn	2	7		
[215] Beder Wood	1	8		
[216‡†] Stephen Perkins	1	6		
[217‡†] Nicholas Powell	1	5		
[218‡†] Green Powell	1	4		
[219‡†] John Newell	1	6		
[220†] Mary Hatchel		4		
[221‡†] George Ragline	2	2		
[222‡] John Black	1	2		
[223] Nathaniel Lacy	1	1		
[224‡†] John Wilson	1	3		
[225] John Watts	1	6		
[226] John Ambars	1	2		
[227] Wyatt Adkin Jun	1	2		
[228] Wm Harrison	1	1		
[229] Darkis Dawson		7		
[230†] John Wilson	3	3		
[231‡†] Ephrim Hubbard	2			8
[232] Martin Herrel	2	6		
[233] John Lewis	2	5		
[234‡†] Peggy Logston	1	6		
[235] Mark Cheach	1	3		
[236] Benjamin M'Cary	1	2		
[237] Absolem Wilcox	1			
[238] Morrison Wilcox	1			
[239‡†] Thomas Thompson	4	5		
[240] Roady Young		5		
[241‡†] Michael Sprinkle	1	4		3
[242] James Cheach	1	7		
[243] Ezekiel Smith	2	9		
[244†] Saml Underwood	1	7		
[245†] Nicholas Powell	1	2		
[246] Thomas Wilson	1	6		

CENSUS OF GALLATIN COUNTY, 1818 (*Continued*)

Names of heads of families	Free white males 21 yr. & upwards	All other white inhab- itants	Free persons of color	Servants or slaves
[247] Stephen Landers	1	3		
[248] John M'Intire	1	2		
[249] Edward Roberts	1	3		
[250] John Hopkins	1	3		
[251] Daniel Duff	1	3		
[252] Wm Blizard	1	5		
[253] Esa Webb	2	9		
[254] Isaac Wilson	1	4		
[255] Jonathan D Munn	1	1		
[256] Owen Adkin	1	8		
[257] Wyatt Adkin	3	4		
[258] James Hobbs	1	1		
[259] Will Hobbs	1			
[260] John Goodman	1	6		
[261] Moses Michaels	2	2		
[262†] Edward Mobley	1	2		
[263] Saml Bratton	1			
[264‡†] Richard Folly	1			
[265] Paton Montrow	1	4		
[266] David Martin	1	4		
[267] Eliza Dunkin		7		
[268] Rody Young		5		
[269‡†] John Freazer	1	6		1
[270‡†] Wm Ellis	1	8		1
[271] Stephen Farmer	[1]	[6]		
[272] Wm Somall	1	3		
[273‡†] Thomas Johnston	1	6		1
[274‡] Jessee Cravens	1	8		
[275] Daniel M'Fain	1	3		
[276] Fanny Stephens		6		
[277] Peggy Hutson		6		
[278‡†] Ezekiel Freazer	1	5		
[279] David Kimsey	3	10		
[280‡†] George Bond	1	11		
[281‡†] Robt. M Tarlton	1	4		
[282†] Benjamin Tolly	1	6		
[283†] Willis Owen	1			

CENSUS OF GALLATIN COUNTY, 1818 (*Continued*)

Names of heads of families	Free white males 21 yr. & upwards	All other white inhab- itants	Free persons of color	Servants or slaves
[284‡†] Jeter Baker	2	5		
[285‡] Wm Berry	1	8		
[286] John Jones	1			
[287†] Wm C Petters	1	4		
[288‡†] Isaac Hogan	2	7		
[289] Josiah Duglass	1	7		
[290] Elisha Hall	1	9		
[291] Jeremiah Hall	1	5		
[292‡†] Harrison Wilson	5	3		2
[293] John G Finny	2			2
[294] Th. C Pattersen	6	1		3
[295] Wm Cheake	[3]	4	7	1
[296] James Bird	2	3		
[297‡†] Nicholas Cassy	3	2		4
[298‡†] Neal Thompson	[1]	7		
[299] Hosea King	[6?]	7		
[300‡†] Robt Watson	1			
[301‡†] Thomas Dawsen	10	6		6
[302] Cornelus M'Laughlin	1	5		
[303‡†] Wm Moore	1	7		
[304†] Giles Taylor	1	3		
[305‡] Thomas Addison	1	4		
[306‡†] Thornton Cummins	1	4		
[307‡†] Wm Cummins	1	4		
[308‡†] Edward Matney	1	3		
[309] Elizabeth Grenshaw	1	4		
[310‡†] Jacob Prowitt	1	8		
[311†] John Smith	1	7		
[312‡†] Humphrey Scroggins	2	11		
[313‡] Benj Rice	1	3		
[314‡†] James Colbert	1	2		
[315] George Idolett	2	10		
[316†] Isaac Hide	1	3		
[317] George Davis	1	6		
[318†] Malacah Willis	1	1		
[319‡†] Lewis Kuykendoll	2	4		
[320] Lindsey Campble	2	4		

CENSUS OF GALLATIN COUNTY, 1818 (*Continued*)

Names of heads of families	Free white males 21 yr. & upwards	All other white inhabitants	Free persons of color	Servants or slaves
[321] Jane Carby		3		
[322‡†] Thomas Barlow	2	6		
[323] Abner Pearce	1	2		
[324‡†] John Duvall	1	3		1
[325‡] Jephath Hardin	1	3		5
[326‡†] William Robinson	1	5		
[327] Jacob Whitson	1	4		
[328‡†] Wm Wagner	1	5		
[329] John Jones	2	2		
[330] Andrew Bratton	1	1		
[331] Thomas C Alsep	7	7		25
[332] Robt Baily	1			
[333] John Funkhouser	11	10		10
[334†] Richard Riddle	1	10		
[335‡†] Emanuel Ensminger	1	6		3
[336] John Collins	1	3		
[337‡†] Saml Watkins	9	6	1	11
[338] George Logan	1	5	3	
[339] John Boldin	1	5		
[340†] Charles Micks	1	9		
[341‡†] Elizabeth Koetah	1	1		1
[342] John Leitner	3	7		
[343] Hugh Lambert	1			
[344] Matthew Caldwell	2	5		2
[345] Archabald Harris	1	9		
[346‡†] Hankersen Rude	2	6		
[347‡†] Chism Este	1	8		1
[348] Edman Russle	1	8		
[349] Herren Taylor	1	8		
[350] John Barker	2	1		
[351‡†] Bird Stafford	1	3		
[352†] Charles M'Clain	2	11		
[353†] Joseph Atkinson	1	7		
[354†] John Atkinson	1	2		
[355] Saml Larimore	1	1		4
[356†] Hugh Robertson	2	7		
[357] James Allen	2	5		

CENSUS OF GALLATIN COUNTY, 1818 (*Continued*)

Names of heads of families	Free white males 21 yr. & upwards	All other white inhab- itants	Free persons of color	Servants or slaves
[358] Elizabeth Trammel	2	2		
[359‡†] Reuben Birdon	2	1		
[360] James Talbert	1	5		
[361‡†] Isaac N Baker	1	4		
[362‡†] James M. D. Russell	2	13		
[363] James Russell	2	3		
[364‡†] Jessee Michael			5	
[365‡†] William Strickland	1	2		
[366‡†] Henry Cox	3	9		
[367] Phillip Henderson	2	5		
[368‡†] James Henderson	1	5		
[369‡†] John Hall	1	3		
[370‡†] Parrett Pate	2	7		
[371‡†] Wm Pate	1	6		
[372‡†] Ths Gassaway	1	4		
[373‡†] Chester Bethel	2	7		
[374‡†] James Reives	1	3		
[375] Wm Gassaway	2	2		
[376‡†] John Gassaway	1	2		
[377‡†] James Hampton	2	1		
[378‡†] Elijah Butler	1	7		
[379‡†] Coleman Brown	2	7		
[380‡†] Marvel Brown	1	1		
[381‡†] Henry Bramlett	1	4		
[382‡†] Benj Bramlett	1	2		
[383‡†] John Bery	3	[10]		
[384‡†] Thomas Smith	[1]	4		
[385‡†] Simpson Newman	1	8		
[386†] Wm Dillingham	1	5		
[387†] Mich Dillingham	1	1		1
[388‡†] Eli Adams	1	3		
[389] John Bramblett	2			
[390‡†] John Brown	1	3		
[391‡†] Thomas Brown	1	2		
[392‡†] Wm Sutton	2	5		
[393] Isaac Brackin	1	9		8
[394‡†] John Gaskins	2	6		

CENSUS OF GALLATIN COUNTY, 1818 (*Continued*)

Names of heads of families	Free white males 21 yr. & upwards	All other white inhab- itants	Free persons of color	Servants or slaves
[395‡†] Smith Hampton	1	9		1
[396‡†] Jonathan Strickland	1	4		
[397‡†] Hamton Panky	1	10		
[398‡†] Shadric Dunn	1	10		
[399‡†] Elisha Cooke	2	9		
[400†] Joseph Tayler	1	2		
[401‡†] Joseph T Attchasen	1	2		
[402‡†] Absolom Abney	1	3		
[403†] Wm Abney	1	4		
[404‡†] Wm Cox	1	1		
[405] David Rage	1	8		
[406‡†] John Williams	1	7		
[407] Martin Cooper	3	6		
[408†] Isaac Hall	[1]	6		
[409] James Reives	[1]	[3]		
[410†] Nathan Bridgman	[1]	[6?]		
[411†] Saml Little	[2]	10		
[412] David Bridgman	1			
[413] Nicholas Choplin	1	10	[*missing*]	
[414†] Danl L Miner	1	6		
[415‡†] Timothy Gaurd	3	8	4	20
[416†] Isem Cheach			3	
[417‡†] John Hubbard	1	4		
[418] John Grenshaw	1	4		
[419] Abriham Grenshaw	2	3		1
[420] James Harrison	1			
[421‡] John Glaspy	1	5		
[422†] James Ledbetter	1	8		
[423] John Robertson	14	18	3	21
[424] James Crabbtree	1	7		
[425‡†] James M'Caslin	4	8		
[426‡†] Will Burnett	1	7		
[427‡†] Benjamin Cummins	1	9		
[428] Leonard White	1	4		2
[429] Joseph Bridgman	1	1		
[430†] Joseph Owens	4	2		4
[431] Rowland Allen	1	2		

CENSUS OF GALLATIN COUNTY, 1818 (*Continued*)

Names of heads of families	Free white males 21 yr. & upwards	All other white inhabitants	Free persons of color	Servants or slaves
[432] David Whimsey			5	
[433‡†] Saml Caldwell			5	
[434‡] John Spencer	1	7		
[435‡†] David Barnett	2	7		
[436‡†] James Barnett	1	3		
[437] Thomas Galard	1	5		
[438†] Wm Runnels	1	3		
[439] Gerge King	1	1		
[440†] Joseph Baker	1	9		
[441] Simon Wemble	1	8		
[442] Wm Aterson	1	8		
[443] Isaac Reeder	1	9		
[444†] John Scroggins	1	5		
[445†] Saml Morriss	1	3		
[446] Wm Christem	1	4		
[447] John Huschun	1	8		
[448] Wm Huchen	1	8		
[449] Robt Fields	1	4		
[450] James Hicks	1	1		
[451†] Charles Williams	1	5		
[452‡†] Hugh M'Connell	2	8		
[453] Jeremiah Hambleton	1	6		
[454] Aaren Goin	1	1		
[455] Jessee Adams	1	2		
[456] Hubbard Dare	1	3		
[457†] Obadiah Flinn	1	2		3
[458] Stephen Hans	1	5		
[459†] John Brown	3	3		
[460] John Blakeky	2	4		
[461] Filbert Hern	1	1		
[462‡] Matthew Willhite	1	2		
[463] Saml Reed	1	7		
[464] Danl Dederich	1	8		
[465] Peter Etter	1	3		
[466‡*] Morris Realy	1	1		
[467] Abriham Smith	1	6		
[468‡†] Henry Dunkin	1	7		

CENSUS OF GALLATIN COUNTY, 1818 (*Continued*)

Names of heads of families	Free white males 21 yr. & upwards	All other white inhab- itants	Free persons of color	Servants or slaves
[469] James Colbert	1	3		
[470] Jessee Green	1	2		
[471] Robt Holt	1	3		
[472†] Benj Walden	1	8		
[473] Giles Stewart	1			3
[474†] Green Wormack	1	3		
[475] Wm Walace	3	4		
[476†] Wm Wormack	2	8		
[477†] Chattin Croggins	1	4		
[478†] Henry Ledbetter	1	9		
[479] James Haly	1	5		
[480†] Asa Ledbetter	1	4		
[481] Susanah Hase		5		
[482] Wm Hicks	1	7		
[483] Francis Hany	1	2		
[484‡†] Joseph Ferdin	1	3		
[485‡†] Andrew Wilkins	1	7		
[486‡†] Wm Daniel	1	6		
[487†] Isaac Baldin	1	5		
[488] James Greer	1	3		9
[489] David Potts	1	6		
[490] John Hutson	1	3		1
[491] Hosea Adams	1	2		
[492] Benjamin Hayes	1	9		
[493] Ths Williams	1	7		
[494] John Hady	1	9		
[495] Adam Funk	1	[7]		
[496] Andrew Hutson	[2]	[missing]		
[497†] Luess Parris	[1]	2		
[498] Starling Kindrich	1	2		
[499] Thomas Jones	[1]	[10]		
[500] Able Cox	2	1		
[501] Benj Aarnet	1	1		
[502] Isaac Cox	1	1		
[503] Charles Ross	1	1		
[504] Wm Arnett	1	2		
[505] Flanders Shoemaker	2	9		

98   *ILLINOIS HISTORICAL COLLECTIONS*

CENSUS OF GALLATIN COUNTY, 1818 (*Continued*)

Names of heads of families	Free white males 21 yr. & upwards	All other white inhab- itants	Free persons of color	Servants or slaves
[506] Saml Cerbow	1	5		
[507‡†] Alexander M['1Koy	1	5		
[508†] Isaac Potts	3	2		1
[509] Peter Lyle	1	4		
[510] Turner Edwards	1	5		
[511‡†] Moses Sherewood	2	6		
[512] Daniel Mosby	1	1		
[513‡†] David Gill	1	5		
[514‡†] Wm M'Coy	1	5		3
[515] John Wyatt	1	4		
[516] Daniel Doolin	3	6		
[517] John Mertin	2	3		
[518‡†] Abner Rosen	1	5		
[519] Macen Wood	1	4		
[520] Saml Lee	6	6		
[521] Caberger Lee	1	3		
[522†] Wm Black	1	6		
[523†] Moses Odrien	1	8		
[524] Benjamin Baker	1	6		
[525†] Henry Blalocke	1	9		
[526†] Robt Patton	1	7		
[527†] John Herod	1	6		
[528†] Jacob Boier	1	8		
[529†] Joseph M['1Cool	2	1		
[530‡†] Harlande Carrel	2	3		
[531] Jeremiah Pool	1	3		
[532] Asa Williams	1	4		
[533] Joseph Merrl	1	7		
[534] John Black	2	4		
[535] Henry Needam	1	1		
[536‡†] Michael Jones	3	3	1	12
[537] Joel Pace	1			
[538‡†] Boston Daimwood	1	1		
[539†] Sampson Dun	2	7		
[540] Joseph Windle	1			

CENSUS OF GALLATIN COUNTY, 1818 *(Continued)*

Names of heads of families	Free white males 21 yr. & upwards	All other white inhab- itants	Free persons of color	Servants or slaves
[541] William Gardner	1			
[542] Luck Barber		3		
Total amt of souls	3256			

I do Certify that the foregoing List of
Cences was taken in by me and
Thr are three thousand
Two hundred & fifty six Souls in all
Given under my hand this 30th May
1818

     W^M M'COY

ADDITIONAL CENSUS OF GALLATIN COUNTY, 1818

A Census of the inhabitants of Gallatin County in the Illinois Territory taken by William M'Coy under a Commission from the Governor, in Conformity to a law of the Territory entitled "An act providing for taking the Census of the inhabitants of the Illinois Territory and for other purposes" passed January 7 1818 and of the Suplement thereto passed 10th January 1818 taken between the first of June & the 28th of July 1818

Names of heads of families	Free white males 21 yr. & upwards	All other white inhab- itants	Free persons of colour	Servants or slaves
[543‡†] John Hambleton	1			
[544] Washington A. G. Posey	1			
[545] Thomas Blarney	1			
[546] James A. Porter	1			
[547] Saml Larimere	1	1		1
[548] Oliver Williams	1	3		
[549] Saml Right	5	8		
[550] John C Woodall	1	3		
[551] John Levallam	1	6		
[552] Elijah Mayfield	1	6		
[553] Lucy Anderson			2	
[554‡] Saml White	1			
[555] Ths Linn	3	3		
[556‡] John M'Clane	1			
[557] John Sexton		1		
[558] Charles Cochren	3			
[559‡] Henry Eddy	1	1		
[560] Wm Harderster	1	3		
[561] Frederic Marberry	4	8		
[562] Wm Kellum	1	4		
[563] Wm Ashban	1	1		
[564] John Barnhart	1	6		
[565] Thomas M'Kinsey	1	6		
[566] David Brown			7	
[567] Joseph Brown	1			
[568] James M'Intire	1			
[569] John Allen	1			
[570] Ths. Dawson				5
[571‡†] John Kinsall	2	4		
[572] James Baly	1	8		

ADDITIONAL CENSUS OF GALLATIN COUNTY, 1818 (*Continued*)

Names of heads of families	Free white males 21 yr. & upwards	All other white inhab- itants	Free persons of color	Servants or slaves
[573] Ths Simpsen	1	7		
[574] John Jones	1			
[575] Elender Jivens		5		
[576] Ritman House	1			
[577] Henry Cooper	1			
[578] John Brown	10	2		3
[579] Elijah Jordin	1			
[580‡†] Webster MCassahan	3	7		
[581] John Robinson	12	18		14
[582] Richard Woodson	1	4		5
[583] Ths. C Alsop	4			7
[584] Bernard Stiner	9	19		
[585] Jonathan Cook	2	8		
[586] John O Ragan	1			
[587] R. Larana	8			
[588] C. Trimmer	30	20		
[589] Robert Ormsby	1			
[590] Jacob Hite	1			
[591†] [Josep]h Owens	2	3		33
[592] Timothy Gaurd	12	4		11
[593] Allen More	1	2		
[594] Isaac Meiers	1	8		
[595] George Mikles	1	4		
[596] John Sebolt	1			
[597] James Moffet	3	4		
[598‡†] Robert Funkhouser	1	6		
[599] Wm. Fitzgerald	1	1		
[600] Young Funkhouser	1	3		
[601] James M. Jones	2	5		1
[602] Saml Scofield	1	1		
[603] James Hutcheson	1			
[604] John D. Tinmon	1			
[605] C Snedley	1	8		
[606] Joseph Blakely	1	3		
[607] Jonathan Robinson	1			
[608] John Baker	1			
[609] E. B. Clemson	[1]	3		3

ADDITIONAL CENSUS OF GALLATIN COUNTY, 1818 (*Concluded*)

Names of heads of families	Free white males 21 yr. & upwards	All other white inhab- itants	Free persons of color	Servants or slaves
[610] John Posey	1	6		2
[611†] John Marton	2	3		
[612] Jacob Blauer	1	1		
[613‡†] Saml Turner	1	2		
[614] John D. Rutan	1	2		
[615] Hesekiah Meirs	1	10		
[616] Ths. Freazer	1	6		
first Colm	111	148	00	76
2nd do	56	93	9	9
Total Amt	167	241	9	85
	241			
	9			
	85			
Total Amt of Souls	502			

I do Certify that the above is a true Copy

Wᴹ M'Cᴏʏ

[*Recapitulation:*]

Census of 1818

Free white males 21 years and upwards	742
All other white inhabitants	2290
Free persons of color	80
Servants or slaves	236
	3348

Additional census

Free white males 21 years and upwards	167
All other white inhabitants	247
Free persons of color	9
Servants or slaves	85
	508
Grand total	3856

CENSUS OF JACKSON COUNTY, 1818[1]

Names of heads of families[2]	Free white males 21 yr. & upwards	All other white inhab- itants	Free persons of colour	Serv- ants or slaves	Total
[1] James Tumelson, Junr	1	7			8
[2‡†] Conrad Will	11	5			16
[3‡†] John Byars	2	9			11
[4‡†] George Butcher	2	5			7
[5†] John Lastley	1				1
[6‡†] Thomas Taylor	1	10			11
[7‡†] Lewis Wells, Senr	2	5			7
[8‡†] Benjamin F. Conner	1	4			5
[9‡†] Drewry Harrington	1	8			9
[10‡†] Jacob Lusadder	1	9			10
[11‡†] Jas. Gill (Bucoup)	1	10			11
[12‡†] Robert Henderson	1	5			6
[13‡†] Hezekiah Davis	1	4			5
[14‡†] Henry Noble, Senr	1	3		1	5
[15‡†] Matthew Duncan	2	2		4	8
[16‡†] Francis Garner	1	5			6
[17‡†] William Boon	3	12		1	[16]
[18] Nathan Davis	1	5		1	[7]
[19] Daniel Reese	1	4			5
[20‡†] James Smith	1	9			10
[21] William E. Glenn	1	9			10
[22] John Tinnan	1	2			3
[23‡†] Thomas Wadley	1	3			4
[24] Moses Wooten	1	1			2
[25‡†] James West	1	6			7
[26‡] Samuel Davis	1	7			8
[27‡†] Stephen Jones	1	9			10
[28] James Gill	1	8		1	10
[29‡†] John Span	1	9		1	11
[30] Joshua Davis	2	10		2	14
[31] Jacob Prilhart	1	3		1	5
[32‡†] Jacob Butcher	1	7			8
[33‡†] John Flack	3	7			10

[1] This census was taken by Conrad Will. Executive Record, 1809-1818, Vol. B, p. 79 (State Archives).

[2] Figures and symbols preceding names have been supplied by the editor:
‡ Found also in the Federal Census for 1820.
† Found also in the State Census for 1820.

CENSUS OF JACKSON COUNTY, 1818 (*Continued*)

Names of heads of families	Free white males 21 yr. & upwards	All other white inhab- itants	Free persons of color	Serv- ants or slaves	Total
[34‡†] Joseph French	4	3		5	12
[35‡†] William Davis	1	3			4
[36‡†] David Holliday	1	8			9
[37‡†] James Davis	1	6			7
[38‡†] Benjamin Henderson	1	2			3
[39‡†] Nancy Worthen		7			7
[40‡†] Marvin Fuller	5	6			11
[41] John Martial	1	9			10
[42‡†] Elias Ford	[1]	1			2
[43] Jeremiah Davis	1	8			9
[44‡†] Thomas Burns	1	9		3	13
[45‡†] James Hall, Senr.	1	1		2	4
[46] William Simpson	1	3			4
[47] Jaral Jackson	1	7		6	14
[48‡†] Parker Grovenor	1	5			6
[49‡†] John Phelps	1	11		2	14
[50] Sincler Manson	1	6		1	8
[51] John Akins	1	2		1	4
[52‡†] Jesse Rasco	1	8			9
[53‡†] Jesse Griggs	6	8			14
[54] John Brown	1	4			5
[55‡†] Terry Williams	1	9			10
[56] John Reynolds	1	5			6
[57‡†] Valentine Dillinger	1	10			11
[58] Joseph Robinson	1				1
[59‡†] Catherine Swartz		8			8
[60‡†] George Creath	1	11			12
[61‡] John Thornton	1				1
[62] George Saddler	2	5			7
[63] Fielding Paine	1				1
[64] David McWilliams	1	10			11
[65‡†] Waters Cocthrin	1	5			6
[66‡†] Daniel Wooten	2	3			5
[67] James Haley	1				1
[68‡†] John Ankeney	1	5		1	7
[69‡†] John Shannan	1	4			5
[70‡†] Charles McKinney	1	5			6

CENSUS OF JACKSON COUNTY, 1818 (*Continued*)

Names of heads of families	Free white males 21 yr. & upwards	All other white inhab- itants	Free persons of color	Serv- ants or slaves	Total
[71‡†] Peter Kimmel	3	1			4
[72‡†] Danl De Chein	1	10			11
[73‡†] Benjn Ripley	2	6		1	9
[74] Thomas Whitson	1	7			8
[75‡†] William F. Garner	1	3			4
[76‡†] Ralph Davis	1	2			3
[77†] Peter Wolerick	2	4			6
[78‡] Abner Thompson	1	3			4
[79] Charles C. Humphreys	1	5			6
[80‡†] James Quarles	1	4			5
[81‡†] David Woods	1	3			4
[82] Wiley Hooker	1	6			7
[83] Samuel Atherton	1	5			6
[84‡†] William Osburn	1	7			8
[85] James Swafort	1	6			7
[86] Abraham Couchenour	1	4			5
[87] George Laile	1	4			5
[88] Henry Laile	1	3			4
[89] John Laile	1	3			4
[90‡†] Thomas Arnold	1	2			3
[91] Ezekiel Wells	1	5			6
[92] David Miller	1	8			9
[93‡†] John Campbell, Sen.	1	9			10
[94‡†] John Bowles	2	5			7
[95‡†] William Baker	1	6			7
[96‡†] Robert Johnston	1	4			5
[97‡†] William Johnston	1	3			4
[98] David Milligan	1	3			4
[99] Abraham Brotherton	1	3			4
[100‡†] James White	1				1
[101‡†] Lewis Wells, Junr.	1	2			3
[102] Reeden Crisp	1	7			8
[103‡†] Eden Thompson	1	6			7
[104‡†] Samuel Piatt	1	3			4
[105‡†] Alexander Clark	1	9		1	11
[106‡†] Rachel Pyle		8			8
[107‡†] Elijah Witworth	1	9			10

CENSUS OF JACKSON COUNTY, 1818 (*Continued*)

Names of heads of families	Free white males 21 yr. & upwards	All other white inhab- itants	Free persons of color	Serv- ants or slaves	Total
[108‡†] William Taylor	2				2
[109‡†] Thomas Jenkens	1	6			7
[110‡†] Thomas Wells	1	7			8
[111‡†] Abner Pyle	1	8			9
[112‡†] John Pyle	1	6			7
[113‡†] Elisha Wells	1	6			7
[114‡†] Ebenezer Piatt	1	4			5
[115‡†] Robt. Muckelvane	1	4			5
[116‡†] Clement Davis	1	4		5	10
[117‡†] Eliphaz Davis	1	5			6
[118‡] Jesse Davis	1	3			4
[119‡†] Adam Fifer	2	7			9
[120‡] Hezekiah Davis, Jr.	1	3			4
[121] William Gragg	1	4			5
[122] Jacob Wolsey	1	10			11
[123] Thomas Lewis	1	10			11
[124] Andrew Thompson	1	5		4	10
[125‡†] Isaac Thompson	1	4			5
[126‡†] Hugh McMillen	2	5			7
[127] Mary McGowen		4			4
[128‡†] William Grubb	1	3			4
[129] John Flemming	1	6			7
[130‡†] Polly Tumelson		6			6
[131‡†] Francis Thornsberry	1	7		1	9
[132‡†] Richᵈ Brown, Sen.	1	1			2
[133] Joseph Davis	1	7			8
[134‡†] James Hall, Junr	1	9		1	11
[135‡†] Richᵈ Sorrels	2	10			12
[136] Moses Wooten, Senr.	1	1			2
[137] Geo. W. Wooten	1	2			3
[138] Nathaniel Davis	2	5			7
[139] Russell E. Heacock	3	6			9
[140‡†] William D. Fuquay	1	6			7
[141‡†] James S. Dorris	1	3			4
[142‡†] James Herreld	1	1			2
[143‡†] James Taylor	1				1
[144] Henry Leeder	1				1

CENSUS OF JACKSON COUNTY, 1818 (*Continued*)

Names of heads of families	Free white males 21 yr. & upwards	All other white inhab- itants	Free persons of color	Serv- ants or slaves	Total
[145‡†] John Lucas	1	3			4
[146‡†] Allen Henson	1	5		1	7
[147‡†] William Gastin	1	4			5
[148‡†] Green Henson	1	6			7
[149‡†] Peter Hammond	1	6			7
[150‡†] William Hiars	2	5			7
[151‡†] Benja. Henson	1	6			7
[152‡†] Joseph Goodbread	1	1			2
[153‡†] Giles Henson	1	7			8
[154‡†] Benjn Walker	1	6			7
[155‡†] John Morrow	2	4			6
[156‡†] Thos. Morrow	1	3			4
[157] Alexander Gastin	1	1			2
[158‡†] Thomas Glenn	1				1
[159‡†] John Robinson	1	4			5
[160‡†] William Fox	1	8			9
[161‡†] John Glenn	1	6			7
[162‡†] Robt. Glenn	1	2			3
[163‡†] James Wooten	1	3			4
[164‡†] Henry Noble, Jr.	1	3			4
[165‡†] Isaac Jarret	1	10			11
[166‡†] Kinian Edwards	1	2			3
[167‡†] Shadrach Massey	1	4			5
[168] Hugh Lewis	1	1			2
[169‡†] William Brewer	1	6			7
[170‡†] Isaac Gleenn	2	3			5
[171‡†] William McRoberts	1	6			7
[172] John Ingram	1	6			7
[173‡†] George Cline	2	1			3
[174‡†] John Henn	1	5			6
[175‡†] Thomas Crain	1	6			7
[176‡†] Squire Crain	1	1			2
[177‡†] Aaron Davis	1	6			7
[178] James Davis, Senr	1	2			3
[179] George Cochran	2	9			11
[180‡†] John Aaron	1	3			4
[181] ———— Atherton	1	1			2

CENSUS OF JACKSON COUNTY, 1818 (*Continued*)

Names of heads of families	Free white males 21 yr. & upwards	All other white inhab- itants	Free persons of color	Serv- ants or slaves	Total
[182‡†] S. Neip & Co.	3	4		2	9
[183] Stephen Statcup	1				1
[184‡†] John Deason	1	8			9
[185] Charels Thomson	1	2			3
[186‡†] William Dotey	1	4			5
[187‡†] Charels Gernor	1	6			7
[188] William Ingrum	1	7			8
[189] John Hinson	1	1			2
[190‡†] Robert Gilliham	1	1			2
in the Bottom					
[191] William McRoberts	1	5			6
[192] Thomes Hindricks	1	6			7
[193] James Henson	2	1			3
[194†] George Ingrum	1	5			6
[195‡†] ——— Brucks	1	2			3
[196‡†] Daniel Beldeback	1	4			5
[197‡†] William Roberts	1	6			7
[198] Bartlett Henson	1	4			5
[199‡†] John Roberts	1	1			2
[200‡†] William McMellen	1	4			5
[201] Louis McMellen	1	5			6
[202] John Morrow	1				1

ADDITIONAL CENSUS OF JACKSON COUNTY, 1818

Jackson

Names of heads of families	Free white males 21 yr. & upwards	All other white inhab- itants	Free persons of colour	Serv- ants or slaves	Total
[203] Joseph Page	1				1
[204] Charles Bowers	1				1
[205] Joseph Norten	1				1
[206] Richard Cummins	1	2			3
[207] Geoarge Steadman	2				2
[208] Mr. White	1				1
[209] John Triplet	2			1	3
[210] M^{r.} moore	2				2
[211] John Adams	1			1	2
[212] James Grawsham	2				2
[213] Thomas Mcqueen	2	7			9
[214] Joseph Andrews	6				6
[215] Joseph Scroggs	2				2
[216‡†] Mr Chapman	1				1
[217] Robert Brown	1			1	2
[218] Mr Mountgommery	2			1	3
[219] Damon Prossnite	6				6
[220] J H Jaacob	1				1
[221] Jos. Little	2				2
[222] James E Fog	1	2			3
[223] Samuel Burnside	1				1
[224] Bengeman Crow	1				1
[225] Cristifer Cains	1				1
[226] Robert Rowley	2	5			7
[227] Thomas English	3	1			4
[228] James Moffets	8	5			13
[229] Geoarge Swartz	1				1
[230] John Reid	1				1
[231] William Kinsella	1				1
[232] George Jones	3				3
[233] William White	1				1
[234] Thomas Dutton	1				1
[235] Widow		5			5
[236] Thomas Randel	3				3
[237] one woman		1			1
[238] William Watterson	3				3

ADDITIONAL CENSUS OF JACKSON COUNTY (*Concluded*)

Names of heads of families	Free white males 21 yr. & upwards	All other white inhab- itants	Free persons of color	Serv- ants or slaves	Total
[239] Edward Hard	2				2
[240] Jeacob Malvin	5				5

Census of Jackson Co
June st 1818

[*Recapitulation* :]

Census of 1818

Free white males 21 years and upwards	250
All other white inhabitants	986
Free people of color	0
Servants or slaves	49
Total	1285

Additional Census

Free white males 21 years and upwards	75
All other white inhabitants	28
Free people of color	0
Servants or slaves	4
Total	107

CENSUS OF JOHNSON COUNTY, 1818

The following Pages Contains the Numbers of
the inhabitants of Johnson County I.T.
as taken between the first day of April & June 1818
Certified to the Secretary of Illinois teritory this
26th day of May 1818 by me

HEZEKIAH WEST   C of C

	free males over 21	No. of whites	free of colour	Servants or Slaves
Page the first contains as followeth[1]				
first page	18	73	0	2
second Do	27	110	1	12
third Do	26	129	0	10
fourth Do	23	84	0	0
fifth Do	19	102	0	0
sixth Do	5	17	0	0
total is	117	535	1	24

or thus free Mails	118
No of families of white	535
free of coulour	1
Servants or Slaves	24
	678

the Number of free white Mails in Johnson County
as taken April & May 1818 is   118 free Mails
other White persons is   535 other whites
free of Colour is   1 free of Colour
Servants of Colour is   24 Negroes

HEZ. WEST   C. of C.   678 total

---

[1] Pages of this volume do not correspond with those of the manuscript.
See recapitulation, *post*, 116.
Figures and symbols preceding names have been supplied by the editor:
    ‡ Found also in the Federal Census for 1820.
    † Found also in the State Census for 1820.

CENSUS OF JOHNSON COUNTY, 1818 (*Continued*)

the No. of Negroes taxable are	9
No. of Horse for tax are	229
hath no ferries	
3 taverns at $5.00 each	$ 15.00
the 9 Negroes at $1.00 each	9.00
the 229 horses at $0.50 each	114.50

Anual Revenue will be	138.50
take out the Sherriffs anual fee of	$ 50.00
the Clerks fee of	30.00

	makes	80.00
take $80 from $138.50 and there remains		$ 58.00

of an Anal Revenue

Johnson County oweth at present $2000.
which at an Average will take some more than thirty six
years to Discharge the old Debt
Poor Little Johnson   But is not yet on
the Parish
the teritorial tax in Johnson County this year is near
about 48 or 50 Dollars from the Lands Returned to me
for tax as will be seen more correct when I draw
off my Book in alphabetical order.
the following List is for Johnson County. It
Contains the Numbers agreeable to Each Column
1st of free white Mails   2 No of whites   3d free of Colour   4th
servants or Slaves

Names of heads of families	Free white males of 21 & upwards	All other white inhab-itants	Free persons of colour	Servants or slaves
[1] Irvin Morriss	1			
[2] Jane Morriss a widow		2		1
[3‡†] James Finney	1			1
[4‡†] Andrew Coghren	1	8		
[5‡†] James Bain	1	7		
[6‡†] Samuel S. Simpson	1	3		
[7‡†] Adam Harvick	1	3		
[8] James Price	1	5		
[9‡†] Jacob Harvick	2	5		
[10] Barbary Price—a widow		9		
[11] Jesse Kenedy	1	3		
[12‡†] David Shearer	1	7		

CENSUS OF JOHNSON COUNTY, 1818 *(Continued)*

Names of heads of families	Free white males 21 yr. & upwards	All other white inhab- itants	Free persons of color	Servants or slaves
[13‡†] John Gressham	1	11		
[14] Simon Price	1	3		
[15] Jonathan Price	1	1		
[16‡†] Hardy Johnson	1	7		
[17‡†] Matthew Johnson	1	7		
[18‡†] Joel Johnson	1	5		
[19] Richard Burk	1	7		
[20] Charles Burk	1	4		
[21‡†] Jesse Allen		5		
[22] Jonathan Price	1	1		
[23‡†] Wheeler Bivens	1	2		
[24‡†] Samuel Wiot	1			
[25‡†] Isaac D. Wilcox	3	3		5
[26] Wm. Cherry	1	5		6
[27] Balas Wilcox	1	4		
[28] Soloman Wrathman	1	3		
[29‡†] Aron B. Brown	1	1		1
[30‡†] Moses Cochran	1	5		
[31] John Johnson			1	
[32‡†] John Heeter	1	5		
[33] John Kurry	1	3		
[34] John Humphries	1	9		
[35‡†] John C. Smith	2	6		
[36‡†] Hezekiah West	1	7		
[37] Asa West	1	2		
[38‡†] Willis Boren	1	7		
[39‡†] Wm Mc norten	1	4		
[40‡†] Wm. Standard	2	7		
[41‡†] Ricks Carter	1	6		
[42‡†] James Lizenby	1	4		
[43‡†] John Bridges	1	8		
[44] Absalom Heddy	1	9		
[45‡†] Milliton Smith	1	10		
[46‡†] Richard Mcginness	2	10		
[47‡†] Isaac Worldley	3	4		
[48] Jacob Littleton	1	6		4
[49‡†] Wm Godthard	1	7		

CENSUS OF JOHNSON COUNTY, 1818 (*Continued*)

Names of heads of families	Free white males 21 yr. & upwards	All other white inhab- itants	Free persons of color	Servants or slaves
[50] James Coghorn, Sner	1	4		
[51‡†] Joshua Elkins	1	7		
[52‡†] John Elkins	1	4		
[53‡†] Bennet Hancock	1	9		
[54‡†] George Brasele	1	8		
[55‡†] James Hawkins	1	3		
[56] John Pruwit	1	1		
[57‡†] John W. Gore	1	7		
[58‡†] Thomas Doyle	1	1		
[59] Wm Porter	1	3		
[60] John Cooper	1	11		
[61‡†] Jeremiah Lizenby	1	2		
[62‡†] John Peterson	1	7		
[63‡†] Henry Mangram	1	7		
[64‡†] John Copeland	1	8		6
[65] Isaac Reaves	1	3		
[66‡†] John Reaves	1	1		
[67‡†] Matthew Matthews	1	6		
[68‡†] Randolph Kasey	1	3		
[69‡†] Alexander Megowen	1	5		
[70‡†] Samuel Megowen	1	5		
[71‡†] Abraham Russel	1	3		
[72‡†] John O. Russel	1	6		
[73‡†] Jesse Fane		2		
[74‡†] John Olever		3		
[75‡†] Benjamin Gurley	1	1		
[76‡†] John Meginness	1	4		
[77] Wm Townsend	1	10		
[78‡†] Wm Elkins	1	2		
[79‡†] John L. Cooper	1	1		
[80‡†] Robert Little	1	8		
[81‡†] Wm Copeland	1	8		
[82‡†] Wm Russel	1			
[83] Robert Hancock	1			
[84] Anderson Standerford	1	4		
[85‡†] James Sutton	1	3		
[86] Robert Rogers	1	2		

CENSUS OF JOHNSON COUNTY, 1818 (*Continued*)

Names of heads of families	Free white males 21 yr. & upwards	All other white inhab-itants	Free persons of color	Servants or slaves
[87‡†] Fredrick Graves	1	1		
[88] John York	1			
[89] John Hancock	1	1		
[90‡†] Jeptha Wise	1	7		
[91] Adam Hibargus	1	3		
[92] James Tolbey	1	2		
[93‡†] David Elems	1	12		
[94‡†] Spencer Grogan	1	7		
[95‡†] Joshua Gore, sener	1	2		
[96] Wm R. Jones	1			
[97] James Lowry	1			
[98] John Bowman	1	5		
[99‡†] Squire Choat	1	8		
[100‡†] Wm Mcfatridge	1	10		
[101‡†] Reubin Wilson	1	9		
[102‡†] Samuel Reed	1	5		
[103‡†] Lewis Simpson	1	3		
[104‡†] Wm Simpson, Senr	1	4		
[105] Joseph Kuykendall	1	6		
[106] Wm Taylor	1	4		
[107] Thomas H. Dugless	1	2		
[108‡†] Elizabeth Mount widow		8		
[109‡†] Wᵐ Shelby	1	4		
[110] Obediah Johnson	1	4		
[111] Elijah Baker	1	2		
[112] Daniel Simpson	1	7		
[113] James Baker	1	1		
[114] Thomas Long	1	2		
[115‡†] Levi Kasey	1	5		
[116‡†] John S. Graves	1	5		
[117‡†] James Crunk	1	4		

CENSUS OF JOHNSON COUNTY, 1818 (*Concluded*)

Page the first[1]	18	73	0	2
Page the second	27	110	1	12
Page the third	26	129	0	10
Page the fourth	23	84	0	0
Page the fifth	18	102	0	0
Page the sixth	5	17	0	0
total of Johnson County	118	535	1	24

total of souls 678   HEZ. WEST Comisioner of Johnson County

May yᵉ 22ᵈ 1818

This Book Contains the Census of
Johnson County in Illinois teritory as
taken April & May 1818 ──────
Directed to the HONOURABLE J. PHILLIPS
Secretary of sᵈ teritory at Kaskaskia
from ─────── HEZEKIAH WEST C. of C.

May 26ᵗʰ 1818
by favour of the Revᵈ
Pleasant Axley ──── Post Rider &c

[*Recapitulation*:]

Free white males 21 years and upwards	118
All other white inhabitants	535
Free persons of color	1
Servants or slaves	24
Total	678

[1] Pages of this volume do not correspond with those of the manuscript. See recapitulation following.

CENSUS OF MADISON COUNTY, 1818

Census of Madison Co. 1818

Census of the Inhabitants of Madison County

Names of heads of families[1]	Free white males 21 yr. & upwards	All other white inhabitants	Free persons of colour	Servants or slaves
[1†] Samuel Woods	1	7		
[2‡†] Titus Gregg	1	11		
[3†] Henry Beck	1	3		
[4] William Leonard	2	1		
[5‡†] John Jarvice	1	6		
[6‡†] Joseph Everman	1	5		
[7] Jane Nesbet	1	7		
[8] Daniel Reece	1	8		
[9‡†] James Watt	1	6		
[10] Andrew Stice	1	7		
[11‡†] Hesse Conley		9		
[12‡†] Isaac Conley	1	3		
[13] William Howard	1	1		
[14‡†] Abraham Vanhooser, Jnr	1	6		
[15‡†] Anderson Smith	1	10		
[16‡†] Isaac Clark	2	4		
[17] James Newell	1	6		
[18‡†] Whitmill Herrington	1	6		
[19‡†] William Baird	1	10		
[20‡†] John Riggin	1	6		
[21‡] William Norman	1	3		
[22‡†] Simon Lindley	2	7		
[23‡†] John Brisco	1	9		
[24‡†] Richard Wood	1	9		
[25‡†] Allen Bridges	1	1		
[26‡†] Thomas Armstrong	1	1		
[27] Abraham Prickett	4	3		
[28‡†] John Springer	1	5		
[29‡†] George Teas	1	9		
[30‡†] Solomon Pearce	1	4		
[31‡†] Samuel Seybold	1	1		

[1] Figures and symbols preceding names have been supplied by the editor:
‡ Found also in the Federal Census for 1820.
† Found also in the State Census for 1820.

CENSUS OF MADISON COUNTY, 1818 (*Continued*)

Names of heads of families	Free white males 21 yr. & upwards	All other white inhab- itants	Free persons of color	Servants or slaves
[32‡†] Sylvanus Gaskill	2	5		
[33‡†] Joseph Snotgrass	1	7		
[34‡†] William Parviance	2	4		
[35†] Henry Taylor	1	7		
[36] Mary Allard		7		
[37‡†] David Gaskill	1	10		
[38‡†] Robert McMahan	1	7		
[39‡†] Robert McMahan	1	1		
[40‡†] Alexander Conly	1	5		
[41‡†] Absolam Baker	2	1		
[42‡†] Elijah Renshaw	1	8		
[43] Absalom Baker	1	1		
[44‡†] Nutter Piper	2	1		
[45] ——— Seemore	1	1		
[46‡] Richard William	1	5		
[47‡†] John Herrington	1	4		
[48] Absolam Baker	1	5		
[49] Louis Renfro	1	4		
[50] Joshua Renfro	1	5		
[51‡†] Margerett Renfro	1	5		
[52‡†] Andrew Turner	2	5		
[53‡†] John Turner	2	4		
[54‡†] Israel Turner	1	2		
[55‡†] Evan Smith	1	1		
[56‡†] William Hall	2	3		
[57‡†] John Hall	1	8		
[58‡†] John Cook	1	3		
[59‡†] David Moore	1	5		
[60] James Smith	1	3		
[61] Alexander W. Anderson	1	9		
[62‡†] James Downing	1	7		
[63] Jeremiah Cook	1	4		
[64] Jessee Holder	1	8		
[65‡†] Rivers Cormack	1	7		
[66‡†] George Armstrong	1	5		
[67‡†] Bennett Nowling	1	3		
[68‡†] William B. Penny	1	3		

CENSUS OF MADISON COUNTY, 1818 (*Continued*)

Names of heads of families	Free white males 21 yr. & upwards	All other white inhab- itants	Free persons of color	Servants or slaves
[69‡†] Philip Teeter	1	4		
[70‡†] George Debond	1	7		
[71†] Seth Hodges	1	4		
[72] Josiah Brown	1	9		
[73‡] John Robinson	1	4		
[74‡†] Robert Seybold	1	4		
[75‡†] Henry Reavis	1	2		
[76‡†] Jessee Conoway	2	6		
[77‡†] Abner Right	1	3		
[78] Augustus Collins	2	7		
[79‡†] John Blackburn	1	4		
[80] Markus Pelham	1	3		
[81‡†] Michael Squires	1	5		
[82] Katy Holkum	1	5		
[83‡†] Thomas Mannen	1	8		
[84‡†] John Waggoner	1	3	1	
[85‡†] Jonathan Casterline	1	6		
[86‡†] Abisha Pritchard	1	1		
[87‡†] Hanna Smith	1	4		
[88] Jeremiah Claypole	2	5		1
[89‡†] William Whitehead	1	5		
[90‡†] Sarah Groats		8	4	
[91‡†] Thomas More	1			
[92] Zachariah Holkum	1	1		
[93‡†] Robert Reynold	1	2		
[94] Lydia Moore		3		
[95‡†] Henry Cook	1	5		1
[96‡] Charles McCance	2	4		
[97] Joshua Vaughn	1	12		4
[98‡†] Samuel Judy	1	8	1	3
[99†] Isaac Taylor	1	6		
[100‡†] Ambrose Nix	2	2		
[101†] Benjamin Allen	1	2		
[102‡†] John Barnett	1	8		
[103‡†] Micajah Cox	1	6		1
[104‡†] John Nix	1	4		
[105‡†] James Reynolds	1	2		

CENSUS OF MADISON COUNTY, 1818 (*Continued*)

Names of heads of families	Free white males 21 yr. & upwards	All other white inhabitants	Free persons of color	Servants or slaves
[106‡†] Robert Reynolds, sr	1	2		4
[107‡†] Thomas Reynolds	2	2		2
[108‡] George Belsha	1	2		2
[109‡†] Jacob Hagler	2	7		
[110‡†] William B. Whitesides	3	9	4	1
[111‡†] Uel Whitesides	2	8		
[112‡†] David Nix	1	2		1
[113†] Cleveland Hagler	1	5		
[114‡†] Jonas Bradshaw	1	1		
[115‡†] Ann Bradshaw	2	10		
[116] Polly Collins		4		
[117] Peter Prow	1	3		
[118‡†] Jessee Belle	1	7		
[119‡†] William Lawless	1	1		
[120†‡] Matthew Torance	2	7		
[121†‡] Joseph Robinson	1	4		
[122†‡] John Delaplane	1	1		
[123†‡] Henry Bonner	1	4		
[124†] Alexander Bonner	1	2		
[125†‡] William Ottwell	1	6		
[126†‡] Benj Delaplane	1	3		
[127†‡] Samuel Delaplane	1	8		
[128‡] John Taylor	3	5		
[129†‡] John Delaplane	1	1		
[130†‡] Joshua Delaplane	1	10		
[131†‡] James Right	2	3		
[132] James Kirpatrick	1	6		
[133] James Randle	3	6		
[134] Jonas Right	2	4		
[135†‡] William R. Hagler	1	4		
[136†‡] Isham Randle	1	2		
[137‡] Thomas Randle	2	5		
[138†‡] John McKinny	1	8		1
[139] William T. McCance	1	2		
[140‡] William Courtney	1	8		
[141] John Vanderpool	1	7		
[142‡†] James Lard	1	5		

CENSUS OF MADISON COUNTY, 1818 (*Continued*)

Names of heads of families	Free white males 21 yr. & upwards	All other white inhab- itants	Free persons of color	Servants or slaves
[143†‡] Beverly Guthrie	1	7		
[144†‡] John Barbour	1	6		
[145‡] James Robinson	1	6		
[146‡] Robert McKee	1	2		
[147†‡] Benj. J. Hagler	1	4		
[148‡] Ransom Milan	1	4		
[149†‡] Benj. Stedman	2	7		
[150] William Holland	4	4		
[151‡†] Abnor O Kelly	1	6		
[152‡†] William L. May	1	2		2
[153‡†] James Snotgrass	1	3		
[154‡†] James Snotgrass	3	7		
[155‡†] Jessee Rountree	1	6		
[156] Gabriel Wott	1	7		
[157‡†] James Simmons	1	4		
[158‡†] Robert Stice	1	3		
[159‡†] Jessee Renfro	1	1		
[160‡†] Isaac West	3	7		
[161] Louis Nowling	1	3		
[162] Abraham Casteel	1	3		
[163] Isaac Casteel	1	1		
[164] Felly Vanhooser	1	10		
[165‡†] Abraham Vanhooser, Snr.	1	1		
[166] John Warren	1	3		
[167†] John McKee	1	2		
[168‡†] Harden Warren	1	5		
[169‡†] David Samples	2	8		
[170‡†] Robert Armstrong	1	6		
[171‡†] Joshua Armstrong	1	4		
[172‡†] George Bridges	1	5		
[173‡†] Richard Kingston	1	1		
[174] Lubon Smart	2	3		
[175‡†] John Lindley	1	1		
[176‡†] John Howard	1	7		
[177‡†] John Wood	1	6		
[178‡†] William Parkerson	2	9		

CENSUS OF MADISON COUNTY, 1818 (*Continued*)

Names of heads of families	Free white males 21 yr. & upwards	All other white inhab- itants	Free persons of color	Servants or slaves
[179†] William Shelton	1	10		
[180‡†] Thomas Shelton	2	1		
[181‡†] James Shelton	2	2		1
[182‡†] John Herron	2	8		
[183‡†] Daniel Parkison	1	6		
[184‡†] John Reed	1	1		
[185‡†] Abraham Howard	1	11		
[186‡†] John Taylor	1	3		
[187‡†] Nelson Alexander	1	3		
[188‡†] John E. Davis	1	5		
[189] Reuben Padly	1	2		
[190] John Guiger	3	7		
[191‡†] Moses Miller	1	8		
[192‡†] David Miller	1	2		
[193‡†] John Furguson	1	4		
[194‡†] Christopher Paine	1	4		
[195] Thomas Breeze	1	3		
[196] Sarah Johnson		4		
[197‡†] Isaac Furguson	2	6		
[198‡†] John Warwick	1	4		
[199‡†] William McAdams	1	8		
[200] Wm McAdams	1	2		
[201] William Lee	1	6		
[202‡†] Robert Hines	1	3		
[203‡] John Wood	1	5		
[204‡†] Hiram Robbins	1	1		
[205‡†] John Lard	1	4		
[206‡†] Adam Kile	1	5		
[207‡†] Joshua Deen	1	10		
[208†] Jacob Varner	2	2		
[209] Elijah Allison	2	5		
[210‡†] John Campbell	1	1		
[211‡] John Scott	1	7		
[212‡†] Daniel G. Moore	1	3		
[213] Phillis Furguson		2		
[214†] John C. Wood	1	5		
[215‡†] James Simms	1	10		

CENSUS OF MADISON COUNTY, 1818 (*Continued*)

Names of heads of families	Free white males 21 yr. & upwards	All other white inhab- itants	Free persons of color	Servants or slaves
[216‡†] Alston Furguson	1	1		
[217†] Aaron Rule	1	2		
[218‡†] John Shinn, Jnr	1	4		
[219] Whaley Moore	1	2		1
[220‡†] Jacob Hoosong	2	4		
[221†] William Armstrong	1	2		
[222] Abner T Henson	1	1		
[223‡†] Andrew St. John	1	9		
[224] Jacob Ceely	1	5		
[225‡†] John White	1	10		
[226‡†] Robert White	1	6		1
[227‡†] Thomas Flanigin	1	2		
[228] Elizabeth White		4		
[229‡†] Robert Brassell	1	8		
[230‡†] Moses Archer	1	2		
[231] Jacob Huttson	1	4		
[232] John Hutson	1	5		
[233‡†] Matthias Shelton	1	3		
[234] Jane Shelton		5		
[235] Isaac Scroggins	1	7		
[236‡†] Robert G. Anderson	2	8		
[237] Jessee Hasting	1	2		
[238‡†] Jarrot Dugger	1	5		
[239] Elizabeth Dugger		5		
[240‡†] Jordan Uzzel	1	6	1	
[241‡†] Wesley Dugger	2	2		
[242‡†] John Wallace	2	6		1
[243] Josiah Wallace	1	1		
[244] Andrew Wallace	1	1		
[245] Jacob Landers	1	5		
[246] Peggy Johnson		3		
[247‡†] Henry Landers	1	2		
[248] William Mitchel	1	9		
[249] Nancy Mitchel	1	6		
[250‡] William Clark	5	6		
[251‡†] John McCullum	2	1		
[252‡†] Robert Coulter	1	11		

CENSUS OF MADISON COUNTY, 1818 (*Continued*)

Names of heads of families	Free white males 21 yr. & upwards	All other white inhab- itants	Free persons of color	Servants or slaves
[253‡†] James East	1	8		
[254‡†] Philip Penn	1	3		
[255‡†] Thomas Johnson	1	3		
[256‡] John Johnson	1	3		
[257‡†] James Pearce	1	5		
[258] Thomas Allison	1	2		
[259‡†] Henry East	1	4		
[260‡†] Gilbert Watson	1	8		
[261‡†] James Ramsey	3	2		
[262‡†] John Berry	1	2		
[263‡†] Robert Craig	1	6		
[264‡†] Beniah Gullick	1	1		
[265‡†] Elizabeth Jingles		6		1
[266‡†] Matthew Holland	2	1		
[267‡†] Joseph Smith	2	3		
[268‡†] Jonathan L. Harris	1	8		
[269‡] Eli G. Harris	1	2		
[270‡†] Adley Harris	3	1		
[271‡†] Joseph Duncan	1	6		
[272] John Morgan	1	3		
[273‡†] Francis Coleen	1	3		
[274‡†] John Vickory	1	6		
[275‡†] Thomas Davidson	2	9		
[276‡†] Benj. Wood	1	3		
[277‡†] Christopher Stubbins	2	6		
[278‡†] John Stout	1	4		
[279‡†] Christopher Stout	1	5		
[280‡†] John Hewit	3	2		
[281‡†] Josiah Vaughn	2	9		
[282‡†] Abram Pruitt	1	8		
[283‡†] Hauston V. Gibbs	1	1		
[284‡†] James Stockton	2	3		
[285‡†] James Pruitt	1	7		
[286†] William Pruitt	2	6		
[287] Thomas Shockley	1	3		
[288‡†] William Haskins	2	3		
[289‡†] James G. Swinerton	2	5		

CENSUS OF MADISON COUNTY, 1818 (*Continued*)

Names of heads of families	Free white males 21 yr. & upwards	All other white inhab- itants	Free persons of color	Servants or slaves
[290‡†] Daniel Dunsmore	3	1		
[291‡†] Walter J. Seely	8	2		1
[292] Eunice Meacham	2	1		
[293†] Andrew V. Patton	1	3		
[294] John Bates	1	2		
[295] William Bates	1	4		
[296] Samuel P. Hibberd	2	8		
[297‡†] William Morris	1	8		
[298†] Reodolphus Lang- worthy	6	2		
[299] Elisha Dodge	2			
[300‡†] Zachariah Allen	2	12		2
[301‡†] Thomas Allen	2	5		
[302‡†] Francis Belle	2	7		
[303‡†] John Allen	2	3		
[304] Benj Tungate	3	4		
[305‡†] Jonathan Brown	3	6		
[306‡†] Ebenezer Hodges	3	6		
[307] Edmund Hodges	1	6		
[308‡†] Chad Brown	2			
[309‡†] Thomas Carland	2	2		
[310‡] John B. Teoboc	1	3		
[311‡†] William Morrow	1	8		
[312‡†] Rebecca Wauson		3		
[313‡†] James Beeman	1	7		1
[314†] Thomas Hall	1	1		
[315] William Savage	1	3		
[316†] James Carland	1	3		
[317‡†] Samuel Beeman	1	3		
[318] M. W. Lovelin	2	3		
[319‡†] James Gribbin	2	1		
[320‡†] Davis Stockton	1	10		
[321‡†] Isham Gilham	4	6		1
[322‡†] Thomas Cox	1	4		
[323] George Coventry	4	4		
[324‡†] John Gilham	2	4		
[325‡†] Ann Dunagan		7		

CENSUS OF MADISON COUNTY, 1818 (*Continued*)

Names of heads of families	Free white males 21 yr. & upwards	All other white inhab- itants	Free persons of color	Servants or slaves
[326‡†] George Saunders	2	6		
[327‡†] James Gilham	1	4		
[328‡] Rydus C. Gilham	2	6		
[329] Michael Dodd	2	5		
[330] Susanah Brown	1	1		
[331‡†] Daniel Brown	1	3		
[332‡†] Marian Black	1	2		
[333‡†] William Savage	6	5		2
[334] Eli Savage	1	1		
[335‡†] William Thompson	2	5		
[336‡†] Samuel Gilham	1	8		
[337‡†] James Steen	3	1		
[338†] Clement Gilham	1	6		
[339] Lorenzo Edwards	1	1		
[340] Saml Vanderburgh			6	
[341] Charles Barton			6	
[342] Priscilla Dennis	2	1		
[343‡†] George Coonrad	1	10		
[344‡†] Samuel Brown	1	11		
[345‡†] Isaac Gilham	1	5		
[346‡†] Charles Dezurley	1	2		
[347‡†] Louis Mars	1	10		
[348‡†] Antoine Dezurley	2	7		
[349] Jack Labarb	1	2		
[350‡†] Rachel Runbolt	2	3		
[351] ——— Doyan	1	6		
[352] Wiley Wilbanks	1	3		
[353] Milly Dunbar		7		
[354‡†] Daniel Petingill	2			
[355‡†] John Stallings	1	1		
[356‡†] Samuel Stallings	1	2		
[357‡†] Blackston Howard	1	7		
[358‡†] Edward Larkins	2	5		
[359‡†] Joseph Buck	1	6		
[360‡†] John Smith	1	3		
[361‡†] John Adkins	7	6		
[362†] Jessee Waddle	1	11		

CENSUS OF MADISON COUNTY, 1818 (*Continued*)

Names of heads of families	Free white males 21 yr. & upwards	All other white inhab-itants	Free persons of color	Servants or slaves
[363‡†] Matthew Dair	1	3		
[364‡] John Jones	1	4		
[365‡] James Watson	1	4		
[366] Timothy Lumberson	1	3		
[367‡†] Thomas Furguson	1	1		
[368‡†] Jacob Segar	1	3		
[369‡†] Joseph Williams	2	3		
[370] John Hammond	1	7		
[371‡†] George Cadwell	1	8		
[372] Abraham Welsh	1	7		
[373‡†] Benj Merritt	1	6		
[374] Richard Ackles	2	5		
[375] [He]nry Smith	1	1		
[376‡†] William Blair	3	7		
[377] Thomas Osburn	1	5		
[378‡†] Moses Batterton	1	11		
[379] Saml Jeffres	2	7		
[380‡†] Charles Simms	3	6		
[381‡†] George Hewitt	4	2		
[382‡] Henry Haze	2	8		2
[383] Jacob Haze	1	3		
[384‡†] Reuben Walker	1	7		
[385‡†] John Clark	3	6		
[386‡†] Jacob Kinder	1	5		
[387‡†] Alex^n Laughlin	1	9		
[388] Charles Gilham	1	3		
[389‡†] James Gilham	1	1		
[390‡†] John Davidson	2	2		
[391‡] Jane Gilham	1	5		
[392‡†] William Gilham	1	2		
[393‡†] William Davidson	1	1		
[394‡†] John G. Lofton	1	8		
[395‡] Esther Lofton		5		
[396‡†] William Gilham	2	5		
[397‡†] Charles Davis	1	4		
[398‡†] John Hawks	1	4		
[399‡†] Philip Hawks	3	5		

CENSUS OF MADISON COUNTY, 1818 (*Continued*)

Names of heads of families	Free white males 21 yr. & upwards	All other white inhab-itants	Free persons of color	Servants or slaves
[400] Colby Waddle	2	4		
[401†] Amos Squires	2	7		
[402‡†] William Adkin	2	2		
[403‡†] John Medford	1	10		
[404‡†] William Astin	1	2		
[405‡†] John Singleton	1	4		
[406] William Bridges	2	5		
[407‡] Abiram McKiney	1	6		
[408‡†] Andrew Emmett	1	8		
[409‡†] Henry Emmertt	2	1		
[410] Daniel Harklerod	1	12		
[411‡†] Jacob Snider	1	5		
[412] Charles Billingsly	1	2		
[413‡†] John Gilham	1	2		
[414] Margerett Thompson		8		
[415] John Griffin	2	1		
[416‡†] Abraham Sippi	1	1		
[417†] Nathan Carpenter	2	3		
[418‡†] Thomas Gilham	2	5		
[419‡†] Isaac Gilham	1	4		
[420‡†] Robert Whitesides	3	7		1
[421‡†] Rhody Bishop	1	9		
[422] John Satterfield	1	1		
[423‡†] William Goings	1	1		
[424†] Joel Whitesides	1	10		
[425‡†] Susanah Armstrong		4		
[426‡†] Aron Armstrong	1	10		
[427‡†] David Roach	1	4		
[428‡†] Edward Taylor	2	5		
[429‡†] Augustin Simms	1	3		
[430‡†] Peter Yoakum	1	3		
[431‡†] Joseph Bartlett	1	7		
[432] Samuel Carter	1	10		
[433] John Downs	1	2		
[434‡†] William Hinch	2	4		
[435†] James Dunn	1	7		
[436‡†] James Pharis	1	3		

CENSUS OF MADISON COUNTY, 1818 (*Continued*)

Names of heads of families	Free white males 21 yr. & upwards	All other white inhab- itants	Free persons of color	Servants or slaves
[437‡] James Pharis	1	1		
[438‡†] George W. Pharis	1	1		
[439‡†] James Gray	2	12		5
[440‡†] David Aikman	1	5		
[441‡†] William Hocksey	3	10		1
[442‡†] Isham Vincent	1	5		
[443] James Carlock	1	6		
[444‡] James Keown	1	3		
[445‡†] Wiley Smart	1	4		
[446‡†] David Hendershot	1	9		
[447‡†] Samuel Vials	1	9		
[448] James McKee	1	4		
[449] Mary West		5		
[450‡†] Levi Deeze	1	4		
[451‡†] Samuel A. Walker	1	8		
[452‡†] Saml. Allen	1	4		
[453‡†] Solomon Keltner	1	2		
[454] Alexander Wilson	2	4		
[455] William Kemp	1	3		
[456‡†] Abraham Hayter	3	4		
[457‡] Benett Jones	3	6		
[458‡†] Henry Kelly	4	4		
[459‡] Thomas Barnett	1	3		
[460‡†] Caleb Shinn	1	1		
[461‡†] Thomas Wall	1	8		
[462‡†] Jacob Guntryman	1	12		
[463‡†] Jonathan Stark	1	9		
[464†] Jubilee Posey	2	2		
[465†] Milicent Holliday	1	2		
[466‡] John Paint	1	9		
[467] George Mayho	2	3		
[468] Robert Crockett	1	1		1
[469] James Carson	3	5		
[470‡†] George Kinder	2	5		
[471‡†] George Barnsback	1	6		
[472‡†] John Owings	1	2		
[473‡†] Simms Owings	1	5		

CENSUS OF MADISON COUNTY, 1818 (*Continued*)

Names of heads of families	Free white males 21 yr. & upwards	All other white inhab- itants	Free persons of color	Servants or slaves
[474‡†] Andrew Lockhart	1	13		
[475] Thomas Tindal	1	5		
[476] Thomas C. Hall	1	4		
[477‡†] Charles Tindal	1	1		
[478‡†] Edward Fountain	12	8		
[479‡†] Benjamin Stephenson	1	6		8
[480‡] Ninian Edwards	1	5		4
[481] Simon Ray	3	3		
[482] Edmund Dana	3	2		
[483‡†] Paris Mason	4	4	2	
[484‡†] Rowland P. Allen	1	3	2	
[485‡†] Hail Mason	1	2		
[486‡†] James Metta	1	3		
[487‡†] John T. Lusk	4	3		
[488‡†] William Green	2	1		
[489‡†] Aaron Sutton	14	8		1
[490‡†] Jopthah Lampkins	2	3		
[491‡†] Joshua Atwater	16	5		
[492] Nathaniel Buckmaster	3			2
[493] Isaac Brown	2	2		
[494‡†] John McKee	3	7		1
[495‡†] John Todd	1	6		1
[496] William Cox	1	5		
[497‡†] James Haines	2	3		
[498‡†] Matthew Cowen	1	2		
[499] John White	1	7		
[500] William Robinson	1	4		
[501‡] David Robinson	1	6		
[502‡†] John Green	1	4		
[503‡†] John Drumm	1	3		
[504‡] James McFadgin	1	2		
[505‡†] William Ryan	1	4		
[506‡†] William Jones	1	7		
[507‡†] Sampson Wood	1	1		
[508‡†] Young Wood	1	2		
[509‡†] Jacob Linder	1	7		
[510‡†] John Cooper	1	5		

CENSUS OF MADISON COUNTY, 1818 (*Continued*)

Names of heads of families	Free white males 21 yr. & upwards	All other white inhabitants	Free persons of color	Servants or slaves
[511] Isaac Jones	1	5		
[512‡†] Low Jackson	1	12		
[513‡†] William Jones	1	8		
[514‡†] Moses Findley	1	1		
[515‡†] John Rattan	3	2		
[516‡†] Wm Montgomery	2	5		
[517‡†] John Rose	1	7		
[518‡†] Richard Rattan	1	8		
[519‡†] Thomas Rattan	1	11		1
[520] Robert Cannon	1	7		
[521‡†] Joseph Reynolds	1	6		
[522‡†] William Vaughn	2	7		
[523‡†] George Moore	1	3		
[524‡†] Walter McFarland	1	2		
[525‡†] John Collins	1	4		
[526‡†] Petter Waggoner	2	6		
[527‡†] William Wiatt	1	2		
[528‡†] Charles Kitchens	1	4		
[529†] John Hunter	2	3		
[530‡†] George Hunter	1	3		
[531‡†] Isaac Chandler	1	2		
[532‡†] Thomas Chandler	1	3		
[533‡†] James Parks	1	3		
[534‡†] David Barrow	1	8		
[535‡†] William Right	1	2		
[536‡†] James Right	1	2		
[537] Roland Bramscomb	1	4		
[538] William Blackburn	1	5		
[539] Absolem Wullums	1	6		
[540‡†] Carry happy Mc Afee		3		
[541‡†] John Moore	2	12		
[542‡†] Jacob Deeds	1	7		
[543‡†] William Wiatt	1	6		
[544] Michael Deeds	1	2		
[545‡] Jessee Ennis	2	5		
[546‡†] Levi Scott	1	2		
[547‡†] John Quigley	1	5		

CENSUS OF MADISON COUNTY, 1818 (*Continued*)

Names of heads of families	Free white males 21 yr. & upwards	All other white inhab- itants	Free persons of color	Servants or slaves
[548‡†] William Quigley	1	5		
[549] Elisha Fowler	1	4		
[550‡†] Dennis Davis	1	3		
[551‡†] Saml Thomas	1	2		
[552‡†] William Watson	1	7		
[553†] William York	1	2		
[554‡†] Martin Wood	1	5		
[555‡†] Orman Beeman	1	2		
[556‡†] Isaac Moore	1	2		
[557‡†] Samuel Williams	1	5		
[558‡†] Hartwell Honeycut	1	10		
[559‡†] Abel Moore	1	6		
[560‡†] Jehue George	1	4		
[561†] Thomas Hamilton	1	1		
[562‡†] William Moore	2	5		
[563‡†] William Barton			7	
[564] John Brunk	1	7		
[565‡†] Jacob Deck	1	2		
[566†] John Stone	2	5		
[567†] James Caldwell	1	6		
[568‡†] Saml Vann	1	1		
[569‡†] Alexnr Byran	1	1		
[570‡] James New	1	7		
[571] Job Day	1	1		
[572] Isham Shockley	1	4		
[573‡†] William Woods	1	3		
[574‡†] John Louis	2	6		
[575‡†] Adit Meacham	1	1		
[576‡] Simon Wheelock	2	3		
[577‡†] Andrew Dunagun	1	7		
[578‡†] James Thompson	1	2		
[579‡†] James Smith	1	6		
[580‡†] James Bates	1	4		
[581‡†] Thomas Piper	1	5		
[582‡†] John Evelin	1	12		
[583†] Moses Evelin	1	6		
[584‡†] Levi Roberts	2	5		

CENSUS OF MADISON COUNTY, 1818 (*Continued*)

Names of heads of families	Free white males 21 yr. & upwards	All other white inhab- itants	Free persons of color	Servants or slaves
[585] Samuel Touns	1	5		
[586‡†] John Powel	1	9		
[587‡†] James Willson	1	5		
[588] Thomas Dutton	1	9		
[589] Henry Gates	3	7		
[590] James Moorning	1	9		
[591] John Hinkley	1	6		
[592] Robert Church	1	9		
[593‡†] Thomas Cowhill	1	1		
[594] Louis Belfort	1	4		
[595] Samuel Lindly	1	5		
[596†] John Shaw	10	5		
[597] George Wise	5	4		
[598] Alfred Pope	1	6		
[599‡] Samuel Stockton	1	2		
[600‡†] George Richardson	2	9		
[601‡] John Richardson	1	1		
[602‡†] Obadiah Waddle	1	2		
[603‡†] William Griffin	1	4		
[604†] Joseph White	3	9		
[605‡†] John Findley	2	7		
[606‡†] John Wilkins	1	2		1
[607‡†] Josiah Cummons	3	6		
[608‡†] Saml Kinkaid	2	6		
[609‡] John Gilham	1	6		
[610‡†] Jacob Lurton	1	9		3
[611] Martin Jackson	1	3		
[612‡†] William Rowden	2	4		
[613‡†] Daniel Allen	3	5		
[614‡†] John Allen	1	1		
[615] Joseph King	1	2		
[616‡†] John Thomas	1	2		
[617‡†] Walker Daund	2	6		
[618‡†] Philip Grimes	1	6		
[619‡†] William Johnson	1	4		
[620‡†] William Costly	3	10		
[621‡†] Davis Carter	1	4		

CENSUS OF MADISON COUNTY, 1818 (*Continued*)

Names of heads of families	Free white males 21 yr. & upwards	All other white inhab- itants	Free persons of color	Servants or slaves
[622‡†] Willy Green	2	1		
[623‡†] John Johnson	1	7		
[624‡†] Philemon Higgins	2	6		
[625‡†] James Johnson	2	3		
[626‡†] Willis Cheek	2	2		
[627] George Carrol	3	5		
[628‡†] Thomas Dannel	1	4		
[629‡†] Stephen Pool	1	7		
[630‡†] Elijah Kelly	2	3		
[631†] David Coop	3	6		
[632‡†] William Scott	2	11		1
[633‡†] Jessee Starky·	1	9		2
[634] Aron Hammer	1	11		
[635‡†] John Starky	1	3		
[636‡†] Alsa Pulliem	1	8		
[637‡†] John Findley	2	6		
[638‡] Charles Hunter	1	3		
[639] Jarvice Starky	1	4		
[640] Joel Starky	1	5		3
[641] Abram Derrybury	1	2		
[642] Isaac Hammer	1	2		
[643‡†] William Ogle	2	4		
[644] Saml Lockhart	1	4		
[645] Sarah Lockhart		6		
[646‡†] Edmund Fruitt	1	6		
[647‡] John Walker	1	2		
[648] John Hunt	1	8		
[649‡†] William Gilham	4	10		
[650] James Wilson	1	7		
[651] Edmund Randle	2	6		
[652] John Rhea	1	7		
[653] James Dolton	1	6		
[654‡†] Saml Scott	1	9		
[655‡] Joseph Newman	2	3		
[656‡†] Henry Brown	1	5		
[657‡†] Zadock Newman	1	3		
[658] David Alley	1	2		

CENSUS OF MADISON COUNTY, 1818 (*Continued*)

Names of heads of families	Free white males 21 yr. & upwards	All other white inhab- itants	Free persons of color	Servants or slaves
[659‡†] John Barrow	1	2		
[660†] Nancy Barrow		8		
[661‡†] Martin Jones	1	4		
[662‡†] John Jones	1	2		
[663‡†] Vynes Hicks	1	7		
[664‡†] Ephraim Wood	1	11		
[665‡†] James Tunnel	1	2		
[666‡†] Elizabeth Higgins		3		
[667‡†] William Webb	2	2		
[668‡†] Isaac Pruitt	1	6		
[669] Martin Pruitt	2	3		
[670‡†] Solomon Pruitt	2	5		
[671‡†] Robert Means	1	6		
[672] Matthew Means	1	6		
[673‡†] Calvin Tunnell	1	4		
[674] Polly Hunter		8		
[675] William Thoman	2	4		
[676‡†] John Robinson	2	3		2
[677‡†] John Robinson	1	4		
[678] Mark Foster	1	1		
[679] Joseph J. [?] Wode	1	2		
[680†] Charles Gilham	1	5		
[681‡†] Thomas Good	2	4		2
[682‡†] James Good	1	1		
[683‡†] John Good	1	2		
[684‡] Parham Randle	1	9		
[685] Saml. Drunnen	1	7		
[686] John Drunen	1	8		
[687‡] John Cox	1	7		
[688] James Drunen	1	10		
[689] Louis Baptiste	4	11		
[690‡†] Pascal P. Enos	6	7		
[691‡†] John Franklin	1	4		
[692] Alfred Judd	4			
[693‡†] Thomas Smith	2	2		
[694‡†] Dempsey Guthrie	1	10		
[695] John Adley	1	10		

CENSUS OF MADISON COUNTY, 1818 (*Continued*)

Names of heads of families	Free white males 21 yr. & upwards	All other white inhab- itants	Free persons of color	Servants or slaves
[696‡†] John Hawker	3	1		
[697] John Ware	1	3		
[698‡†] John Williamson	7	1		
[699‡†] Elihue Matthers	1	6		
[700‡†] Peter Martin	1	5		
[701‡†] William Kerns	1	7		
[702] Piere L. Mcenry	1			
[703‡†] Baptiste Janderow	1	7		
[704] Baptiste Beckett	1	7		
[705†] John Bolgar	1	1		
[706] Joseph Brigham	2	1		
[707‡†] Benj Eves	1	4		
[708‡] Hampton Mc Keney	1	1		
[709‡†] Cornelius Tolly	1	4		
[710‡†] Saml Whiteside	1	9		
[711‡†] Joseph Borough	2	5		
[712] Peter Fountain	1	7		
[713] Jack Avery	1	13		
[714‡†] James Palmer	1	9		
[715] Jeremiah Pierce	[*no data given*]			
[716] John Kain	2	6		
	1012	3364	33	77

4486 Total

I the undersigned being duly qualified as com
missioner of Madison County Illinois Territory
for the purpose of takeing the census of the inhabitants of said County do Certify that the
foregoing statement is correct as given to me
by heads of families

JOSEPH BOROUGH Commissioner

I beg leave further to state from good
information that there are at Fort Craw-
ford,   680 souls
Fort Armstrong   150 souls
Fort Edwards   70 "
do Clark   80 "

CENSUS OF MADISON COUNTY, 1818 (*Concluded*)

Makeing in the whole 5466 souls
within the boundary of Madison County.

J. B.

[*Recapitulation*:]

Free white males 21 years and upwards	1012
All other white inhabitants	3386
Free persons of color	34
Servants or slaves	77
Total	4509
Forts Crawford, Armstrong, Edwards, and Clark	980
	5489

138   *ILLINOIS HISTORICAL COLLECTIONS*

CENSUS OF MONROE COUNTY, 1818

Names of heads of families[1]	Free white males 21 yr. & upwards	All other white inhab- itants	Free persons of colour	Servants or slaves
[1‡†] J Milton Moore		5		
[2‡†] Henry Fields		2		
[3] Rolley Mc Kinzie		3		
[4] Levi Taylor		5		
[5‡†] Michael Miller	1	6		
[6] Nathan Brewer		2		
[7‡†] Felix Clark		6		
[8] Abraham Eastwood		6		
[9‡†] Jacob Eastwood		8		
[10‡†] Daniel Bryan		2		
[11‡†] Joseph Kinney		2		
[12‡†] Jacob Clark		7		
[13‡†] George McMurtry		6		
[14‡†] John Tolin		5		
[15] Widow McMurtry		1		
[16‡†] William Lemen		4		
[17] John Tolin, Ser	1	2		
[18‡†] Isaac Tolin		6		
[19‡†] Joshua Cary		4		
[20‡†] Moses Varnum	1	4		
[21‡†] Daniel Barker		3		
[22‡†] Zopher Williams	1	9		
[23‡†] Moses Lemen	1	3		
[24‡†] Josiah Lemen		5		
[25‡†] James McDonald		4		
[26‡†] Thomas Sterrit		6		
[27‡†] Absalum Bradshaw	1	7		
[28‡†] Robert Kidd		8		
[29‡†] John Mc David		5		
[30‡†] William Everitt	2	6		
[31‡†] Raphael Drury	1	4		
[32‡†] Alexander Mc Nabb		7		
[33] Jacob Skeen		6		
[34] John Brimberry	2	5		

[1] Figures and symbols preceding names have been supplied by the editor:
‡ Found also in the Federal Census for 1820.
† Found also in the State Census for 1820.

CENSUS OF MONROE COUNTY, 1818 (*Continued*)

Names of heads of families	Free white males 21 yr. & upwards	All other white inhab- itants	Free persons of color	Servants or slaves
[35‡†] Joseph Worley		6		
[36] Stephen Ayers		1		
[37‡] Samuel Raner	1			
[38‡†] Ezekiel Preston		7		
[39‡†] William Alexander		6		
[40] John M Wilson		4		
[41] John Wilson		2		
[42] John Jeffress	1	2		
[43‡†] Edward Clark		6		
[44‡†] William Chalfin		2		
[45‡†] Seth Chalfin		3		
[46‡†] Elis Chalfin		1		
[47‡†] Amos Chalfin		3		
[48‡†] Thomas Marrs		7		
[49‡†] William Worley	1	7		
[50‡†] John Worley		5		
[51‡†] Benjamin Scovel		6		
[52‡†] Isaiah Levens	2	4		
[53] Henry Scovel		1		
[54‡†] Prince Bryant		7		
[55‡†] Andey Kinney	2	8		
[56‡†] Daniel Sink	1	8		
[57] Ichabod Badgley		7		
[58‡†] Benjamin Marney	1	6		
[59‡†] William Howard	2	5		
[60‡†] Adams Payne	1	3		
[61‡†] John Mitchel		6		
[62‡†] William Chance	3	3		
[63‡†] Philip Rader	1	4		2
[64] John Winters		3		
[65] Noah Blankinship		4		
[66‡†] Richard Mattingly	1	2		2
[67] John Woodrome		6		
[68] Elijah Davis		5		
[69‡†] Jacob Trout	1	4		1
[70‡†] Gerardis Lock		9		
[71‡†] Daniel Starr		6		

140   *ILLINOIS HISTORICAL COLLECTIONS*

CENSUS OF MONROE COUNTY, 1818 (*Continued*)

Names of heads of families	Free white males 21 yr. & upwards	All other white inhab- itants	Free persons of color	Servants or slaves
[72] Andrew Hettick		6		
[73‡†] John Sheehen		2		
[74] George Vallentine	1	4		
[75‡†] William Arundel		1		
[76] Jehu Estes		3		
[77] James Smith		1		
[78‡†] Ishmael Dillard		4		
[79‡†] Francis Baldwin	1	4		
[80‡†] Adam Smith		8		
[81‡†] David Bagley		10		
[82] Levi Gilbert		3		
[83‡†] William Lemmon		7		
[84] Joseph Miller	[*No data given*]			
[85‡†] Reuben Miller		7		
[86] Silas Crawford	1	4		
[87‡†] Michael Dace		6		
[88‡†] Daniel Raport		3		
[89‡†] James Henderson		9		
[90‡†] Jesse W. Cooper	1		1	
[91] William Rogers		1		
[92] Edward Crouch		4		
[93‡†] Alexander Jameson	1	5		
[94‡†] John Miller		2		
[95] Jacob Borer		4		
[96‡†] Francis Orsborn	1	5		
[97‡†] James McRoberts		8		1
[98‡†] Thomas Porter		2		
[99‡†] John Jameson	1	5		1
[100‡†] Joseph A. Beaird		5		10
[101] Alexander Wells		4		
[102‡†] John McClure	2	2		
[103] John Warnock		3		
[104‡†] John Cooper	1	2		
[105‡†] Thomas Lusby	2	3		
[106] Edward Smith		6		
[107‡†] James Whaley	3	8		
[108‡†] Henry Wadderman		1		

CENSUS OF MONROE COUNTY, 1818 (*Continued*)

Names of heads of families	Free white males 21 yr. & upwards	All other white inhab- itants	Free persons of color	Servants or slaves
[109‡†] Baker Whaley		5		
[110‡†] William Hogan	1	5		
[111‡†] Christian Halderman	1	5		
[112] Peter Stroud	1	2		
[113‡†] Joseph Hogan				4
[114] Amos Chandlor		3		
[115‡†] Jonathan Shepherd		2		
[116‡†] John James	3	2		
[117‡†] Samuel Nolin		5		
[118‡†] John Roach	1	8		
[119‡†] Michael Hammon	1	6		
[120] William Robins		7		
[121‡] John Summers	1	4		
[122‡†] Ichabod Volentine	1	4		
[123‡†] Thomas James	2	4		
[124‡†] George Estes		4		
[125‡†] Solomon Shook	3	5		4
[126] John Myers		3		1
[127‡†] George Dickason		5		
[128‡] Widow Todd		1		
[129‡†] William Grote	1	2		
[130‡†] Michael Crossen		2		
[131‡†] Samuel Turner	1			
[132‡†] Reuben Bradley		1		
[133] Samuel Stephens		2		
[134‡†] Wm Barrick	1	3	4	5
[135] Daniel Thompson		1		
[136‡] William Thompson		2		
[137‡†] Jehu Scott	2	6		
[138‡†] George Atcheson		4		
[139] Laurance Yannie		1		
[140‡†] Solomon Stong		4		
[141‡†] James Garetson	1	9		
[142‡†] Daniel Shook		3		
[143‡†] Henry Miller		8		
[144‡†] John Moredock	1	5		
[145‡†] Abraham Amos		5		

CENSUS OF MONROE COUNTY, 1818 (*Continued*)

Names of heads of families	Free white males 21 yr. & upwards	All other white inhabitants	Free persons of color	Servants or slaves
[146‡†] John Moore	1	9		
[147‡†] William Sterrett		2		
[148‡†] James Woodrome		4		
[149‡†] Elijah Talbott		8 ·		
[150‡†] Thomas Talbott		1		
[151‡†] Thomas Taylor, ser		8		
[152‡†] James Sheepherd		4		
[153‡†] David Woodrome		1		
[154‡†] Joseph McMeen		3		
[155‡†] Levi Piggott		7		
[156‡†] Joshua Talbott		7		
[157‡†] William Riggs		1		
[158†] Thomas Nelson	2	5		
[159] George Brock	3	6		
[160‡†] John Robins		3		
[161‡†] Joel Woodrome		4		
[162‡†] Henry Modglin		7		
[163‡†] David Robison	1	9		
[164‡†] James Bradshaw		7		
[165‡†] ——— Herren	1	4		2
[166‡†] Wᵐ Johnson		9		
[167] Joseph Dowling		3		
[168] Elijah Ladd		4		
[169] Jacob Bradley		5		
[170‡†] Daniel Vaughan	2	6		
[171‡†] Davis Whiteside		9		
[172‡†] James Fowler		1		
[173‡†] Wᵐ Woodrome		4		
[174] Mary Whiteside	1	3	1	2
[175‡†] Luke Patterson		7		
[176‡†] Charles Patterson		2		
[177‡†] Solomon Goss	2	5		
[178‡†] Elisha Axley		4		
[179] John C. Triplitt		5		
[180] Prior Hogan	[*No data given*]			
[181‡†] George Wallis		3		
[182‡†] Robert Hawk		5		

CENSUS OF MONROE COUNTY, 1818 (*Continued*)

Names of heads of families	Free white males 21 yr. & upwards	All other white inhab- itants	Free persons of color	Servants or slaves
[183‡†] John Hogan		4		1
[184‡] Avington Sherill	1	4		
[185] Samuel Smith		3		
[186‡†] John Modglin, Sr		9		
[187‡†] Francis Kirkpatrick		4		
[188] James Corwin		1		
[189] Wm Brown		1		
[190‡†] Linville McDanold	1	8		
[191] James Nowlin		8		
[192] Jacob Casteel		1		
[193] Otho Wilson		3		
[194] George Barney	3	9		1
[195] John Atcheson		3		
[196] Edward Welsh		4		
[197] William Atcheson		3		
[198‡] Joseph Try		5		
[199] John Primm		6		
[200‡†] John Alexander		6		
[201] Ann Calhoun		3		
[202] John Sullivan	1	5		
[203] Thomas Sullivan		2		
[204‡†] John Divers		3		
[205] John Johnson		6		
[206] Francis Scott		2		
[207‡†] Leonard Carr		10		
[208] James Hendricks	1	5		
[209‡†] Jacob Clover		7		
[210‡†] Enoch Moore	1	8		
[211‡†] Caldwell Cairns	1	4		2
[212‡†] Richard Brownfield	1	9		
[213] Wm Ayers		8		
[214‡†] Theron Brownfield	1	5		
[215‡†] Arthur Eberman		6		
[216] Jas. Belloow	2	9		2
[217‡†] Jas Taylor		3		
[218‡†] Thomas Taylor ju		2		
[219‡†] Elizabeth Ford	1	4		

CENSUS OF MONROE COUNTY, 1818 (*Concluded*)

Names of heads of families	Free white males 21 yr. & upwards	All other white inhab- itants	Free persons of color	Servants or slaves
[220‡†] William Forquer		4		
[221‡†] James Lemen		1		
[222] Thos. Winstanley		4		
[223‡†] Naṭ Hambleton		3		
[224‡†] Thoꝰ M. Hambleton		4		
[225‡†] Daꝟ H. Hambleton		3		
[226‡†] Zebediah Barker	2	1		
[227] Widow Phillips		1		
217	95	999	6	41

Heads of Families	217
Free white males over 21 years	95
All other white Inhabitants	999
Free People of Colour	6
Servants or Slaves	41
Total of all	1358

I do hereby Certify that this a just and true
Enumeration of Monroe County in Illinois Teritory
to the best of my Skill and Ability;   JOHN MOORE
                    Commissioner of Said County

[*Recapitulation:*]

Heads of families	227
Free white males 21 years and upwards	95
All other white inhabitants	1002
Free persons of color	6
Servants or slaves	41
Total	1371

CENSUS OF POPE COUNTY, 1818

Names of heads of families[1]	Free white males 21 yr. & upwards	All other white inhab- itants	
[1‡†] Molten Eubanks	1	4	
[2‡†] Richard Lee	1	10	
[3‡†] George Von	1	7	
[4‡†] Willice Stucker	5	7	
[5] Charels Mc Cloud	2	6	
[6‡†] John Robarts	3	2	
[7] John Anderson	1	3	
[8] Isaac Smyth	1	2	
[9] Bengeman Jonston	1	2	
[10‡†] Frances Glass	3	5	
[11‡†] John Glass	1		
[12] James Alcorn	1	2	
[13] Widow Harington		3	
[14‡†] James Lard	5	1	
[15] Henery Slankard	1	4	
[16] Frances Glass	1	5	
[17‡†] David Glass	1	3	
[18] Robart Hemphill	3	4	
[19] Celib E Irven	1	3	
[20] Erastes Willard	2	3	
[21] Simon Willard	2	6	
[22‡†] Daniel Fields	2	5	
[23] Ephram Cowan	1	2	
[24] George Loren	2	4	
[25] Jacob Sevely	2	3	
[26] Green B. Fields	1	4	
[27] Milton Ladd	1		
[28] Samuel Hamely	1	6	
[29‡†] Thomas Reed	1	6	
[30] William Fishback	2	5	
[31‡†] Shedrick Waters	1	2	
[32‡†] Frances Moor	1	5	
[33‡†] David S. Taylor	1	9	
[34‡†] James E Willis	3	4	

[1] Figures and symbols preceding names have been supplied by the editor:
‡ Found also in the Federal Census for 1820.
† Found also in the State Census for 1820.

CENSUS OF POPE COUNTY, 1818 (*Continued*)

Names of heads of families	Free white males 21 yr. & upwards	All other white inhab- itants	
[35‡†] Robert Scott	2	8	
[36‡†] Allen Robison	1	8	
[37‡†] Isaac B. Scott	1	1	
[38] John Faires	1	1	
[39‡†] Samuel Smyth	2	4	
[40‡†] Robert Faires	1	4	
[41‡†] David Cowan	2	2	
[42‡†] John Crocket	1	3	
[43‡†] William Dyer	2	3	
[44‡†] Abiga Dyer	2	7	
[45‡†] Charels Dyer	1	10	
[46‡†] William S Redkin	1	5	
[47] Abenezer Keeler	1	3	
[48‡†] Solomon Lamar	1	1	
[49] William Sams	3	3	
[50‡†] John Henley	1	8	
[51] Widow Codall		6	
[52‡†] Ruben Glover	1	4	
[53] Widow Heston	1	4	
[54‡†] Owen S. Clark	1	1	
[55‡†] John Glover	1	2	
[56] Joshua Cross	1	2	
[57‡†] John Wood	3		
[58] Hamlet Fergison	1		
[59] William Wells	1	2	
[60‡†] Henery Lues	1	3	
[61] John Weaver	1	2·	
[62] Jacob Lues	2	6	
[63] John Lues	1		
[64‡†] John p. Gelespy	1	6	
[65] Daniel Gray	1	10	
[66‡†] George Lues	1	6	
[67] John Smyth	1	4	
[68‡†] John Neely	1	3	
[69‡†] William Neely	1	2	
[70‡†] thomas thompson	1	9	
[71‡†] John Edwards	1	6	

CENSUS OF POPE COUNTY, 1818 (*Continued*)

Names of heads of families	Free white males 21 yr. & upwards	All other white inhabitants	
[72‡†] Joseph Brown	1	6	
[73] John B. Brown	1	6	
[74] Isaac Flanery	1	3	
[75‡†] John Diterline	1	7	
[76] John Jones	3	3	
[77] Charley Ray	2	6	
[78] Robart Faires	1	4	
[79‡†] Joshua Williams	1	7	
[80‡†] John Clavert, senr	1	5	
[81‡†] John Clavert, Junr	1	1	
[82‡†] Herman Slankard	1	4	
[83‡†] Bengman McCool	1	2	
[84] Jessey McCool	1	2	
[85‡†] Jessey McCool, senr	2	6	
[86] James titsworth	1	7	
[87] Isaac titsworth	3	4	
[88] Joshua taugue	1	4	
[89‡†] Eliga Flanery	1	3	
[90] Isham F Alcorn	1	3	
[91] Andrew Kidd	1	4	
[92‡†] James N. Fox	1	4	
[93] Samuel A Givens	3	3	
[94‡†] John Maning	1	2	
[95‡†] James Richey	1	8	
[96] Samuel Langdon	2	3	
[97‡] Ezekel Clay	1	3	
[98] Nicoles Edwards	3	9	
[99‡†] Benegar thompson	1	8	
[100] thomas thompson	1	10	
[101‡†] George Slankard, snr	1	3	
[102‡†] Georg Slankard junr	1	5	
[103‡†] Joshua Slankard	1		
[104‡†] Charels Shelvey	1	1	
[105‡†] Jacob Shelvery	2	6	
[106‡†] Reece Shelvey	1	3	
[107‡†] Even Shelvey	2	3	
[108] George Evets	1	3	

CENSUS OF POPE COUNTY, 1818 (*Continued*)

Names of heads of families	Free white males 21 yr. & upwards	All other white inhab- itants	
[109‡†] James A Whitsids	1	7	
[110] William Goodman	1	2	
[111‡†] frenklen penny	2	4	
[112‡†] Robart Hays	1	6	
[113‡†] Widow Jonston		2	
[114] William John	2	5	
[115] James Hazelwood	1	1	
[116‡†] thomas Roas	1	6	
[117‡†] Abel Richison	1	9	
[118‡†] William Hays	1	2	
[119] John Arnut	1	3	
[120‡†] Bengamin Belford	1	4	
[121‡†] George Storey	1	7	
[122‡†] John Witt	1	12	
[123] Robart penny	1	8	
[124‡†] Hiram penny	1	6	
[125] Enough penny	2	4	
[126] William thomas	1	3	
[127] Charels Hudelston	1		
[128] Daniel shipman	1	7	
[129] John Stanley	1	6	
[130] Jacob Slankard	1	1	
[131‡†] Lincolen Harper	1	9	
[132‡†] King Hazel	1	5	
[133] Isrel Bageth	2	6	
[134‡†] John Hays	1	4	
[135‡†] Josia Leech	1	7	
[136] thomas McCroney	1	10	
[137‡†] Jacob Robison	3	6	
[138‡†] Widow frost		4	
[139] Allen Green	2	7	
[140] Henery Davis	2	4	
[141‡†] Amos Chipps	2	4	
[142‡†] John Mattison	1	2	
[143‡†] Frances Hogg	1	6	
[144‡†] John Wilson	1	4	
[145‡†] William Huston	1	7	

CENSUS OF POPE COUNTY, 1818 (*Continued*)

Names of heads of families	Free white males 21 yr. & upwards	All other white inhab-itants	
146‡†] John Glass	1	4	
147‡†] Robert Adkison	1	5	
148‡†] Richard Bennett	1	4	
149‡†] Isam Clay	1	7	
150‡†] Mark Whitiker	1	7	
151] James Hazelwood	1	1	
152] Absolem Joiner	1	5	
153‡†] David Dees	1	8	
154‡†] Lot Joiner	1	5	
155‡†] Samuel M. Morow	2	5	
156‡†] thomas Brown	1	8	
157‡†] Hugh Robison	2	8	
158] thomas Ragsdale	1	8	
159] William Jackson	1	3	
160‡†] John Jackson	1	3	
161‡†] George Jackson	1	4	
162‡†] John Morice	1	7	
163] Miss trusdale		2	
164] William Burdsill	1	7	
165] Waren Burdsill	1	2	
166‡†] James D Scott	3		
167‡†] James Lee, senr	2	2	
168‡†] James Hill	1	7	
169] James Lee, Junr	2	4	
170] John Litey	1	1	
[171‡†] William pankey	2	8	
[172‡†] Lues pankey	1	1	
[173‡†] Achilles McFarlen	1	5	
[174‡†] Dudly Glass	2	12	
[175] Samuel Basset	1		
[176‡†] Benoni Lee	1	9	
[177‡†] Straingman Modglen	1	7	
[178‡†] George Lackey	1	5	
[179‡†] Linsey Modglen	1	3	
[180‡†] Henery Roas	3	7	
[181] John Henery	1	1	

CENSUS OF POPE COUNTY, 1818 (*Continued*)

Names of heads of families	Free white males 21 yr. & upwards	All other white inhab- itants	
[182] Hawkins Lues & Company	3		
[183‡†] John palmor	1	8	
[184‡†] Widow Smock	2	7	
[185] Steven Stilley	1	3	
[186‡†] Robert Kesterson	2	2	
[187‡†] John Leeper	2	6	
[188‡†] John Daniel	1	1	
[189‡†] Lues Barker	1	8	
[190] Widow Coon		6	
[191] James Wallace	1	3	
[192‡†] James Hull	2	4	
[193‡†] John Von	2	7	
[194] John Stilley	1	5	
[195‡†] Larken Kesterson	1	1	
[196‡†] Alexander Blair	1	7	
[197‡†] James Steel	1	8	
[198‡†] George Hamilton	1	3	
[199‡†] Samuel Omelveny	1	7	
[200‡†] James Cousart	1	8	
[201‡†] thomas Cousart	1	3	
[202‡†] Robart Cousart	1	3	
[203‡†] Alexander parkison	1	7	
[204‡†] John Crawford	1	11	
[205‡†] John Braner	1	4	
[206] Samuel B. Glass	1	4	
[207‡†] Jacob Storm	2	6	
[208] Robart Shields	1	1	
[209‡†] William Belford	1	4	
[210‡†] Jas King	1	3	
[211] Alexander Glass	1	1	
[212‡†] John Howard	1	7	
[213] Reece price	1	6	
[214‡†] Richart Robenet	1	2	
[215‡†] Abram G. fisk	2	3	
[216‡†] Richard D Robison	2	2	
[217] John Johnston	1	5	

CENSUS OF POPE COUNTY, 1818 (*Continued*)

Names of heads of families	Free white males 21 yr. & upwards	All other white inhab- itants	
[218‡†] Robart fisk	2	5	
[219] Abram Miller	1	7	
[220] Vincen Cook	1	3	
[221‡†] Willice Barklet	1	5	
[222‡†] Moses Stubs	1	6	
[223] Victor Edwards	1	1	
[224‡†] Bengeman titsworth	1	1	
[225] William Richey	1	3	
[226‡†] John Stubs	1	8	
[227] Isom Safold	1	5	
[228] James Sanders	1	4	
[229] Widow Mc Coy		4	
[230‡†] Julies Warick	1	3	
[231] Widow Anderson		4	
[232] David Anderson	1		
[233] James Givens	2	3	
[234] Robart Givens	1	2	
[235] John Simpson	1	6	
[236] thomas Larison	2	5	
[237] James Hall	1	6	
[238‡†] Lues Drurey	3	9	
[239] Jessey Everet	1	5	
[240‡†] John Cross	1	4	
[241‡†] George Simkens	1	7	
[242‡†] James young Blood	1	7	
[243‡†] William Wilson	1	7	
[244‡†] Jonathan Ethridge	1	5	
[245‡†] Hizekia Hail	1	5	
[246] thomas Cribens	1		
[247‡†] James Craford	1	3	
[248] Wᵐ Morice	1	5	
[249] James Wilson	1	9	
[250‡†] William Wilson	1	2	
[251‡†] Robart Hamilton	2	8	
[252‡†] William Hannah	2	2	
[253‡†] James Hannah	2	4	
[254] Antony Ward	1	8	

CENSUS OF POPE COUNTY, 1818 (*Continued*)

Names of heads of families	Free white males 21 yr. & upwards	All other white inhab- itants	
[255] John Reed	1	3	
[256‡†] Bengeman Bowman	1	5	
[257‡†] John Bruington	1	8	
[258‡†] Josaph Dilard	2	6	
[259‡†] John Mc Henery	1	3	
[260‡†] William Modglen	1	2	
[261] Gramer Fisher	1	2	
[262‡†] John Modglen	1	3	
[263] John Stanley	1	6	
[264‡†] Jacob McColam	1	2	
[265‡†] Joseph Mc Henery	1	6	
[266‡†] Isaac Ralston	1	3	
[267] John Ginkens	1	8	
[268] Mathew Ginkens	1	1	
[269‡†] Alexander Murphy	2	11	
[270] Mathew Moss	2	6	
[271‡†] James Buckner	1	2	
[272] John penny	1	6	
[273] Mathew Brown	1	3	
[274] Jacob Canady	1	3	
[275] Solomon Redfern	1	9	
[276‡†] John Redfern	1	1	
[277] Right Modglen	1	1	
[278‡†] William Modglen	1	4	
[279‡†] Daniel Wadkens	1	8	
[280‡†] Henery Skinner	1	4	
[281‡†] Isaac Harper	1	8	
[282‡†] Daniel Hazel	1	8	
[283‡†] John Colier	1	9	
[284] William Dees	1	2	
[285‡†] John Joiner	1	3	
[286‡†] thomas Wallace	1	8	
[287‡†] Colman Haws	1	7	
[288‡†] John Haws	1	7	
[289‡†] Nethan Storey	1	5	
[290‡†] John Storey	1	2	
[291] Widow Neel		10	

CENSUS OF POPE COUNTY, 1818 (*Continued*)

Names of heads of families	Free white males 21 yr. & upwards	All other white inhab- itants	
[292] Jeremia Neel	1	4	
[293] William John	1	3	
[294‡†] Widow Lisenbay		9	
[295‡†] William Joiner, senr	1	4	
[296‡†] Abram Joiner	1	2	
[297‡†] William Joiner, Junr	1	3	
[298‡†] John Armstrong	1	3	
[299‡†] Jessey Green	1	8	
[300‡†] Richard Green	1	4	
[301] thomas Kelton	1	2	
[302‡†] Isaac peteet	1	5	
[303‡†] Jessey Green	1	6	
[304‡†] Squire Shingelton	1	7	
[305‡†] Ezekel McCoy	1	12	
[306‡†] Daniel Vinyard	1	6	
[307‡†] John Ginger	1	1	
[308‡†] Abram Warnick	1	5	
[309‡†] Nethan Warnick	1	2	
[310] Jessey King	1	7	
[311‡†] Jonas Ingram	1	7	
[312] Steven Stilley	1	7	
[313] philip Luster	1		
[314‡†] George vinyard	1	5	
[315‡†] John turnar	1	3	
[316‡†] Ruben Green	1	3	
[317] Nethan Clampet	1	7	
[318] William Eubanks	2	8	
[319] John Robarts	1	7	
[320] John Cedon	2	5	
[321] John Cedon	1	2	

White Males over 21 years of age
411
All other white Inhabitants

1500
411
64 Blacks

1975 Total

SAMUEL OMELVENY Com^r
Pope County

Census of Pope County 1818

CENSUS OF POPE COUNTY, 1818 (*Concluded*)

[*Recapitulation*:]

Free white males 21 years and upwards	399
All other whites	1481
	1880
Blacks	64
Total	1944

ADDITIONAL CENSUS OF RANDOLPH COUNTY, 1818

A return of the additional census

Names of heads of families[1]	Free white males 21 yr. & upwards	All other white inhab- itants	Free persons of colour	Serv- ants or slaves	Total
[1‡†] Joseph Sprigg	2	10			12
[2] Richard D. Hamilton	3				3
[3] John Moore	1				1
[4] Alansing Barr	1				1
[5‡†] Curtis Conn	1	5		1	7
[6] Jacob Placing	1				1
[7‡] Joshua Davis	1				1
[8] Elisha E. Hickcox	2	2			4
[9] John W. Mix	1				1
[10] Thomas Mather	1				1
[11‡†] Edward Cowles				1	1
[12] John C. Dunlavy	1				1
[13‡†] William Berry		1			1
[14] Rudolph Bauman	6	1			7
[15‡†] Norton Hull	1	1			2
[16] Solomon Harness	1				1

Total   45

[*Recapitulation*:]

Free white males 21 years and upwards	23
All other white inhabitants	20
Servants or slaves	2
Total	45

[1] Figures and symbols preceding names have been supplied by the editor:
‡ Found also in the Federal Census for 1820.
† Found also in the State Census for 1820.

CENSUS OF ST. CLAIR COUNTY, 1818

Names of heads of families[1]	Free white males 21 yr. & upwards	All other white inhab- itants	Free persons of colour	Serv- ants or slaves	Total
[1] Fulton, James	2	4			6
[2] Fanning, John	1	4			5
[3‡†] Free, Absolam P.	1	1			2
[4‡†] Free, Andrew	1	7			8
[5‡†] Fowler, William	1	3			4
[6] Feppe, Pear	1	6		1	8
[7] Fadette, Pillipp	2	1		3	6
[8‡†] Farriree, Franey	1	4			5
[9] Foster, Thomas	2	6			8
[10] Funderburk, Henry	1	8			9
[11] Gossett, Elijah	2	5			7
[12‡†] Gilham, Thomas	1	6			7
[13] Grogan, Abdon	2	12			14
[14] Gilbreath, John, Junr	1	1			2
[15‡†] Gaskill, Jonathan	1	8			9
[16‡†] Gaskill, Paul	1	8			9
[17†] Gilbreath, Hugh	1	6			7
[18] Gilbreath, John Senr	1	5			6
[19] Gilbreath, James	1	7			8
[20‡†] Griffin, Isaac	1	7			8
[21‡†] Griffith, Daniel	2	7			9
[22‡†] Guiler, William	1	6		1	8
[23] Gover, John	1	4			5
[24] Goings, Pleasant	2	4			6
[25] Griffin, William	1	1			2
[26] Gash, John	1	1			2
[27‡†] Goodner, Benjamin	1	2			3
[28‡†] Glass, James	1	6			7
[29‡†] Goodner, Cornelius	1	4			5
[30‡†] Goodin, Robert	1	4			5
[31‡†] Goodner, Conrad	1	5			6
[32] Gimer, Pear	1	4			5
[33] Gonvell, Joseph	1	4			5
[34] Grenyer, Joseph	1	4			5

[1] Figures and symbols preceding names have been supplied by the editor:
‡ Found also in the Federal Census for 1820.
† Found also in the State Census for 1820.

CENSUS OF ST. CLAIR COUNTY, 1818 (*Continued*)

Names of heads of families	Free white males 21 yr. & upwards	All other white inhab- itants	Free persons of color	Serv- ants or slaves	Total
[35] Graves, Thomas H.	2	3			5
[36] Greneus, Francis	1	4			5
[37] Garret, Joseph	1	5			6
[38‡†] Godan, Louis	1	4			5
[39‡†] Gambla, Michael	1	4			5
[40‡†] Gambla, Pear	1	8			9
[41] Goda, John	1	4			5
[42‡†] Goda, Pear	4	5			9
[43‡†] Glass, John	2	5			7
[44‡†] Hughes, Robert	1	3			4
[45‡†] Herren, Lewis	1	1			2
[46‡†] Halcomb, William	1	3			4
[47‡] Halcomb, Zacabiah	1	3			4
[48] Hale, Benjamin	1	9			10
[49‡†] Hale, Enoch	1	3			4
[50‡†] Henry, Samuel	1	1			2
[51] Herns, William	1	10			11
[52‡†] Hill, Peter	1	9			10
[53‡†] Herin, Moses	1	6			7
[54‡†] Hill, Burrell	1	4			5
[55] Herin, Major	1	9			10
[56‡†] Hutton, Henry	1	7			8
[57‡†] Howel, Thomas	1	1			2
[58‡†] Howel, David	1	5			6
[59‡†] Hawkins, Marshal	1	1			2
[60] Holt, Harman	2	11			13
[61] Horner Nicholas[1]	1	4	1		
[62‡†] Horner, Nathan	1	1			
[63‡†] Higgins, John	1	5			
[64] Huffman, Michael	1				
[65‡†] Hays, John	1				
[66‡†] Hays, Zachariah					
[67] Hill, John					
[68‡†] Hicman, Is[aac]					
[69‡†] Hale, [Robert?]					
[70] Huff, Samuel	1	9			10

[1] Manuscript partly burned opposite names 61 to 69.

CENSUS OF ST. CLAIR COUNTY, 1818 (*Continued*)

Names of heads of families	Free white males 21 yr. & upwards	All other white inhab- itants	Free persons of color	Serv- ants or slaves	Total
[71‡†] Hill, Nathaniel	1	4			5
[72‡†] Huggins, Patrick	1	4			5
[73] Hendrick, William	1	1			2
[74‡†] Hogshead, James	1	5			6
[75‡†] Hill, William	1	3			4
[76‡†] Hand, Jeremiah	1	8			9
[77‡†] Hook, William	1	5			6
[78‡†] Heath, William	1	5			6
[79] Hufman, Robert	1	2			3
[80‡†] Hill, David	1	2			3
[81] Hook, Elijah	1	7			8
[82‡†] Harrison, Thomas	1	8			9
[83‡†] Hinton, Samuel	1	4			5
[84] Haley, Mrs.		5			5
[85] Holzer, Samuel	1	5			6
[86‡†] Hendricks, John	2	8			10
[87‡†] Hart, James	1	4			5
[88‡†] Eli Hart	1	5			6
[89] Hatfield, John	1	7			8
[90] Hays, John	2	6		6	14
[91‡†] Howzer, Jacob, Sr	1	5			6
[92‡†] Hay, John	1	11			12
[93] Hill, Mr.	2	2			4
[94] Ivey, George	1	1			2
[95‡] Jarvis, Franklin	1	6			7
[96‡†] Johnson, Malcomb	1	7			8
[97] Inman, Henry	1	8			9
[98] Johnson, William	1	1			2
[99‡†] Journey, Elizabeth		8		1	9
[100] James, David	1	7			8
[101‡†] Jamesson, George	1	1			2
[102‡†] Jackson, Joel	1	9			10
[103‡†] Johnson, Abraham	1	7			8
[104] Ivey, James	1	6			7
[105‡†] James, William	1	8			9
[106] Johnson, George W.	1	4			5
[107‡†] Jarver, Lous	2	5			7

CENSUS OF ST. CLAIR COUNTY, 1818 (*Continued*)

Names of heads of families	Free white males 21 yr. & upwards	All other white inhabitants	Free persons of color	Servants or slaves	Total
[108‡†] Jarver, Enos	1	3			4
[109‡†] Jarrot, Nicholas	4	8		10	22
[110] Jousamurt, Touisant	1	1			2
[111‡†] Jarvis, Parker	6	2			8
[112] Jenkins, Thomas	1	6			7
[113] Kimberling, James	2	7			9
[114‡†] Knighton, Thomas	1	2			3
[115‡†] Kinkand, William T	1	3			4
[116‡†] Kinney, William	2	8			10
[117‡†] Kingston, Paul	3	6	2		11
[118] Koen, David	1	7			8
[119] Kelly, Thomas	1	8			9
[120‡†] Kingston, John	2	6			8
[121‡†] King, William	1	8			9
[122‡†] Knight, David	1	1			2
[123‡†] Kenada, George F.	1	4			5
[124] Kenada, Mr.	1	2			3
[125] Lindsey, John	1	7			8
[126‡†] Land, Joseph[1]	1	7			8
	1	7			8
	2	7			9
	1	2			3
	1	4			5
	1	5			6
	1	1			[2]
[127‡†] Low, David	1	4			5
[128] Linck, David, Jnr	1	5			6
[129] Lynn, Thomas	3	3			6
[130] Linck, David	1	3			4
[131‡†] Linck, Solomon	1	5			6
[132] Langston, Samuel	1	2			3
[133] Langston, Nathan	1	4			5
[134] Langston, John	1	6			7
[135‡†] Lively, John	1	4			5
[136] Lively, Reuben	1	3			4
[137‡†] Leach, John	1	7			8
[138‡†] Laremore, Louis	1	2			3

[1] Manuscript partly burned between names 126 and 127.

CENSUS OF ST. CLAIR COUNTY, 1818 (*Continued*)

Names of heads of families	Free white males 21 yr. & upwards	All other white inhabitants	Free persons of color	Servants or slaves	Total
[139‡†] Lacey, Stephen	1	2			3
[140‡†] Lacey, Ann	2	5			7
[141] Lott, George	2	5			7
[142] Love, Mr.	1	3			4
[143‡†] Lacours, Batise	1	2		1	4
[144‡†] Laremire, Louis	1	3			4
[145] Langway, Joseph	1	7			8
[146] Labra, Batise	1	2			3
[147] Lachane, Joseph	3				3
[148‡†] Lacounpt, Batise	1	5			6
[149‡†] Lacompt, Brazil	1	2			3
[150‡†] Laparsu, Francis	1	2			3
[151‡†] Lafranbroo, John B	2	3			5
[152‡†] Lacompt, Julian	1	5			6
[153] Lagrais, Louis	1				1
[154] Lacompt, Mrs.	1	2			3
[155] Labraze, John B	1	1			2
[156‡†] Lacompt, Louis	2	2			4
[157] Lafrarcu, Anthony	1	3			4
[158‡†] Labasere, Louis	1	7			8
[159] Larelu, Francis	1	3			4
[160] Lamott, Swashin	1	4			5
[161] Louis Laparsu	2	6			8
[162‡†] Luncford, Jacob	2				2
[163‡†] Moore, William D	1	3		1	5
[164†] Million, Bennett	1	10			11
[165] Mace, John	2	6			8
[166] Myers, Samuel C.	1	2			3
[167‡†] Marney, James	1	5			6
[168‡†] Million, Benjamin	1	4			5
[169‡†] Mitchell, Samuel	4	8	4		16
[170‡†] McLamore, John H.	1	1			2
[171‡†] Moore, Risdon, Junr	1	8		3	12
[172‡] Moore, Curtis	2	6			8
[173] Morris, Thomas	1	3			4
[174‡†] Moore, Robert	1	6			7
[175] McMurtry, William	1	1			2

CENSUS OF ST. CLAIR COUNTY, 1818 (*Continued*)

Names of heads of families	Free white males 21 yr. & upwards	All other white inhabitants	Free persons of color	Servants or slaves	Total
[176‡††] McNail, Abel A	1	5			6
[177‡††] McNail, William	1	4			5
[178‡††] Moore, Risdon, Sen⁰	1	7		8	16
[179‡††] Matheny, Noah	1	2			3
[180‡††] Mace, Henry	1	8			9
[181] Matthias, Jeremiah	1	9			10
[182] Matheny, George	1	4			5
[183‡††] McDonald, Samuel	1	7			8
[184] Moore, Bryant	1	4			5
[185] McNabb, William	1	3			4
[186‡††] Moore, James	1	6			7
[187‡††] Moore, William, Jn⁰.¹	1	2			
[188] McCrary, Andrew	1	2			
[189] Morris, Zachariah	2	8			
[190‡††] Moody, Benjamin	1	9			
[191‡††] McC[an]n, James	1	10			
	1				
[192‡††] McMilliom, Paul	1	8			9
[193‡††] Moore, William, Sr.	2	3		1	6
[194‡††] Mears, William	1	1			2
[195] Miller, Jacob	1	5			6
[196‡††] Middleton, Robert	1	5			6
[197] McKinny, John	1	2			3
[198‡††] Manvill, Ira	2	4	1		7
[199] Matthew, David	1	3			4
[200‡††] McMurtry, Abraham	1	7			8
[201‡††] Matheny, Charls R	2	6			8
[202] McGehee, Stephn	1	3			4
[203] McRunnols, William	1	6			7
[204‡††] Moore, Jane		4			4
[205‡††] Morgan, Arthur	1	11			12
[206‡††] Million, Daniel	1	7			8
[207‡††] Messenger, John	1	10			11
[208‡††] Myre, Luois W	2	5			7
[209] Muray, Daniel	1	9			10
[210‡††] Merril, Sylvester	1	2			3
[211‡††] Mauzy, Silas	1	2			3

¹ Manuscript partly burned between names 187 and 192.

CENSUS OF ST. CLAIR COUNTY, 1818 (*Continued*)

Names of heads of families	Free white males 21 yr. & upwards	All other white inhab- itants	Free persons of color	Serv- ants or slaves	Total
[212‡†] Miller, William	2	8			10
[213] McNary, Samuel	1	1			2
[214] Montgomery, William	1	4			5
[215] Meo, Pear	1	5			6
[216‡†] Marlo, Gabrele	2	6			8
[217] Mc Carty, William	1	5			6
[218‡†] Maxey, Francis	1	6			7
[219‡†] Moreson, Guy	1			2	3
[220] Moreson [?], Julian	2	1			3
[221] Moreson [?], ——	1	7			8
[222†] McLaughlin, R. K.	5	1		3	9
[223] Matheny, Ch	[*no data given*]				
[224‡†] Null, Bolser	2	5			7
[225‡†] Null, Henry, Jnr	1	1			2
[226‡†] Nichols, Theophilus M	1	7			8
[227] Nichols, Thomas	1	7			8
[228] Nichols, John	1	7			8
[229] Nichols, Julius	1	11			12
[230] Neill, Henry, Senr	1	1			2
[231] Nelson, William	1	7			8
[232] Neeley, Joseph	1	8			9
[233†] Ogle, Joseph, Jnr	2	5			7
[234‡†] Ogle, Jacob, Jnr	2	7			9
[235‡†] Ogle, Benjamin	2	5			7
[236‡†] Ogle, Joseph, Sr	1	3			4
[237‡†] Ogle, Joseph, 3r	2	2			4
[238] Osmus, John	1	6			7
[239‡†] Ogle, Jacob, Sr	1	5			6
[240] Orendeff, Christopher	1	12			13
[241] Ogle, Benjamin	1	4			5
[242‡†] Oglesby, Joshua	2	4			6
[243‡†] Osmus, Peter	1	8			9
[244‡†] Prentice, John O.	1	6			7
[245‡†] Peirce, Daniel	3	6			9
[246‡†] Perkins, Joshua	1	2			3
[247‡†] Philips, William	1	7			8
[248‡†] Pea, John	1	5			6

CENSUS OF ST. CLAIR COUNTY, 1818 (*Continued*)

Names of heads of families	Free white males 21 yr. & upwards	All other white inhabitants	Free persons of color	Servants or slaves	Total
[249‡†] Peoples, Thorton	1	4			5
[250‡†] Penn, Joseph	1	1			2
[251‡†] Pyle, Samuel	2	3		1	6
[252‡†] Padfeld, William Jr	1	3			4
[253] [Pulliam?] Robert¹	3	10			13
[254†‡] [Prickett?] George	1	4		1	6
	1	4		1	6
	1	3			4
	1	5			6
	1	3		1	5
		4			5
					7
					6
				6	17
					5
[255] Chesley²	1	6			
[256] [Po]stleweight, John	1	5			
[257] [P]adfield Lydia		3			
[258‡†] Philips James	1	5			
[259] Pulham Thomas	2	8		2	
[260‡†] Pulham David	1	2			3
[261‡†] Pennington Absolom	1	1			2
[262‡†] Perkins Jessee	1	2			3
[263‡†] Perkens Ephraim	1	2			3
[264‡†] Porter Rebecca		8			8
[265‡†] Penn William	1	1			2
[266] Pulham John	1	4			5
[267‡†] Pulham James	1	5			6
[268‡†] Philips David	1	4			5
[269‡†] Phillips Jeremiah	1	3			4
[270] Patterson Joseph	1	2			3
[271‡†] Primm John	2	4			6
[272] Patten John	1	11			12
[273] Pincinnoau Etinni	2	3		2	7
[274‡†] Peradee Batese	1	2			3
[275‡†] Pincinneau Louis	2	7			9

¹ Manuscript partly burned between names 253 and 259.
² 1818 Census has a Chesley Allen.

CENSUS OF ST. CLAIR COUNTY, 1818 (*Continued*)

Names of heads of families	Free white males 21 yr. & upwards	All other white inhabitants	Free persons of color	Servants or slaves	Total
[276‡†] Pincinnsau Louision	2	10		1	13
[277‡†] Petitte Louis	1	1			2
[278‡†] Petitte Michael	1	2			3
[279] Petka Louis	3	2			5
[280] Parspal Joseph	1	5			6
[281‡†] Paupa Joseph	3	2			5
[282‡†] Paupa Paul	2	5			7
[283] Peripe Joseph	1	6			7
[284] Punninial Augustin	2	9		2	13
[285‡†] Primm Thomas	3	6			9
[286‡†] Quick Isaac	1	2			3
[287] Quick Moses	2	3			5
[288‡†] Quick Aaron	1	9			10
[289] Roweling Nathanial	1	5			6
[290] Raney John	1	2			3
[291] Randolph Eligah	1	4			5
[292‡†] Rutherford William	2	4			6
[293] Rutherford John	1	1			2
[294] Riggs Joseph	1	1			2
[295‡†] Robinson Israel	1	2			3
[296‡†] Ray Thomas	1	4			5
[297‡†] Riggs Clemment	1	2			3
[298] Rice Eligah	1	4			5
[299] Reaves Isaac	2	9			11
[300] Rodgers James	1	6			7
[301] Rawles Edward	1	5			6
[302‡†] Rawles Raleigh	1	5		1	7
[303‡†] Ratcliff Charles	1	3			4
[304‡†] Ratcliff Michel	1	3			4
[305‡†] Rettenhouse William	2	4			6
[306‡†] Redmond Samuel	1	2			3
[307‡†] Roach Mathew	1	8			9
[308‡†] Riggs Hosea	2	3			5
[309‡†] Rettonhouse Peter	1	8			9
[310†] Robertson John	1	4			5
[311‡†] Randleman Jacob	1	4			5
[312‡†] Randleman Henry	2	1			3
[313‡†] Rian William	2	6			8

CENSUS OF ST. CLAIR COUNTY, 1818 (*Continued*)

Names of heads of families	Free white males 21 yr. & upwards	All other white inhab- itants	Free persons of color	Serv- ants or slaves	Total
[314] Russel John	1	1			2
[315‡†] Rittenhouse Eligah	1	6			7
[316‡†] Ratcliff William	4	4			8
[317] Rector Enoch	2	11		2	15
[318] Revi Joseph	1	1			2
[319] Revi Mr.	1	4			5
[320‡†] Reeder Isaac	1	2			3
[321‡†] Roach Thomas	1	3			4
[322‡†] Reynoalds John	1	2		2	5
[323‡†] Rows James	1	4			5
[324] Reevere Louis	1	6			7
[325] Roeall Joseph	1	6			7
[326‡†] Rider John	1	5			6
[327‡†] Rittenhouse Mary		10			10
[328‡†] Rittenhouse William	1	5			6
[329] Rachel, a blak			3		3
[330‡†] Scott William Sen	1	8			9
[331‡†] Stout Henry	2	2		1	5
[332‡†] Stout Daniel	1	4			5
[333‡†] Stout William	1	3			4
[334] Simmons Jessee	1	10			11
[335] Stuart Alphonso C.	1	4			5
[336‡†] Shook Aaron[1]	1	5			6
	2	3	1		6
	1	3			4
	1	9			10
[337] [St. Jean, J]oseph	1	3			4
[338‡†] Sim[m]on[s] John	5	1			6
[339‡†] Scott Samuel	3	5			8
[340‡†] Swan Frances	1	7			8
[341] Scott William Jn^r	1	10			11
[342] Strickland Redmon	1	2			3
[343] Stroud Asa	1	6			7
[344‡†] Stanley John	2	6			8
[345] Sharp Jonathan	1	1			2
[346] Sharp Samul	1	3			4
[347] Simpson William H	1	3			4

[1] Manuscript partly burned between names 336 and 337.

CENSUS OF ST. CLAIR COUNTY, 1818 (*Continued*)

Names of heads of families	Free white males 21 yr. & upwards	All other white inhab- itants	Free persons of color	Serv- ants or slaves	Total
[348] Simpson Ann		5			5
[349] Silir William	1	4			5
[350] Silir Jacob	2	9			11
[351] Silir Adam	1	1			2
[352] Short William	1	2			3
[353†] Smith Philip	3	5			8
[354‡†] Slaton George	1	7			8
[355] Stanford Shelton	1	8			9
[356] Stanford Ruth		7			7
[357] Smith David	1	1		1	3
[358‡†] Steel John	2	5			7
[359‡†] Shook Samuel Jnr	1	6			7
[360‡†] Stogdon Robert	2	4			6
[361] Stuart Peter	2	8			10
[362‡†] Stroud Levi	1	5			6
[363‡†] Stubblefield Thomas	1	6			7
[364‡†] Straigh Israel	1	7			8
[365‡†] Smith Robert	2	9			11
[366†] Smily Hugh	1	3			4
[367‡†] Scott John Jnr.	1	1			2
[368] Sam Burdet	1	1		2	4
[369] Skidmore Thomas	1	6			7
[370‡†] Shook Jonas	3	2			5
[371‡†] Scott John Snr.	2	6			8
[372‡†] Summers Edward D.	2	2			4
[373] Small Samuel	3	10			13
[374‡†] Scott Alexander	1	8	1		10
[375] Short Hubbard	1	5			6
[376‡†] Scott Samuel	1	8			9
[377‡†] Stookey Daniel	2	9			11
[378] Swaggert John	1	7			8
[379‡†] Swaggert George	4	5			9
[380‡] Schenbarger Lawrence	2	3			5
[381‡†] Schenbarger Batise	2	4			6
[382] St. John Pear	1	3			4
[383‡†] St. John Louis	1	3			4
[384‡†] St. Garnaw Louis	1	1			2

CENSUS OF ST. CLAIR COUNTY, 1818 (*Continued*)

Names of heads of families	Free white males 21 yr. & upwards	All other white inhabitants	Free persons of color	Servants or slaves	Total
[385] St. John Mrs		6			6
[386‡†] Sosha Michael	1	3			4
[387] Stallion Margret		4			4
[388‡†] Stuntz John	1	8			9
[389‡†] Shook Samuel Senr	3	8			9
[390‡†] Short Jacob	1	10		3	14
[391‡†] Scott Joseph	1	8			9
[392‡†] Sparks David	1	9			10
[393] Tozer Samul	1	2			3
[394‡†] Tannehill James	3	6			9
[395‡†] Thomas Robert	1	6			7
[396‡†] Thomas Anthony M	2	6			8
[397‡†] Thomas James D.	3	2			5
[398‡†] Thomas John D.	1	9			10
[399] Thomson John	1	6			7
[400‡†] Tetricks, Peter	1	3			4
[401] Titus Samul (a black)				4	4
[402] Townzen Edmond	1	2			3
[403‡†] Townzen Whitfield	1	4			5
[404] Tilford William	1	3			4
[405] Tetricks Abraham	1	1			2
[406] Tetricks Jacob	1	3			4
[407] Tetricks George	1	2			3
[408‡†] Thompson William	1	3			4
[409] Travis Francis	1	2			3
[410] Thompson James	1	2			3
[411] Thompson John	1	4			5
[412] Talent David	1	7			8
[413] Teter Mary		9			9
[414‡†] Teter Solomon	1	2			3
[415‡] Taylor Joseph	1	2			3
[416] Thompson Abel	1	7			8
[417] Tryon William	1				1
[418‡†] Talbott Thomas W.¹	1				
[419‡†] Taylor Henry	1	5			
[420] Taylor Bellington	1	8			
[421‡†] Teter John	2	6			

¹ Manuscript partly burned opposite names 418 to 421.

CENSUS OF ST. CLAIR COUNTY, 1818 (*Continued*)

Names of heads of families	Free white males 21 yr. & upwards	All other white inhab- itants	Free persons of color	Serv- ants or slaves	Total
[422‡†] Terry Stephen	1	5			6
[423‡†] Titus Nan (A black)			10		10
[424] Turner Isaiah	1	1		1	3
[425‡†] Trotier Augestine	1	5			6
[426‡†] Trusoo Nicholas	2	6			8
[427‡†] Trotier Francis	1	4			5
[428] Tiffin Clayton	18	4		3	25
[429‡†] Trotier Joseph	1	3		1	5
[430‡†] Tarcourt Francis	3	7			10
[431] Trotier, Mrs		4			4
[432] Troubler Touisant	1	2			3
[433] Thomas Jessee B	1	3		3	7
[434] Thomas Mr	2	8			10
[435] Tolman Nathan	1	9			10
[436‡†] Updike Gilbert	1	1			2
[437‡†] Vineyard Philip	1	5			6
[438‡†] Vanwinkle Job	1	7			8
[439‡†] Vanosdole Richard	1	8			9
[440] Vineyard William	1	2			3
[441‡†] Vanosdol Simon	14	5		5	24
[442] Ventura Asa	1	5			6
[443‡†] Virgin Brice	2	5			7
[444‡†] Virgin William	1	3			4
[445] Valuntine Franceway	1	8			9
[446] Vaudry Dunn	2	3			5
[447] Vaudry Margerit		9			9
[448‡†] Vaudry Louis	2	2			4
[449‡†] Varner Abraham	1	5			6
[450‡†] Woods Benjamin	1	7			8
[451] Weigh William	2	3			5
[452‡†] Wright Richard	1	1		1	3
[453] Welch Thoma	1	7			8
[454‡†] Watts James	1	2	1		4
[455‡†] Walker John	1	4			5
[456‡†] Watts Benjamin	1	7			8
[457] Wilkerson John	1	7			8
[458‡†] Whiteside Stephen	2	6			8

CENSUS OF ST. CLAIR COUNTY, 1818 (*Continued*)

Names of heads of families	Free white males 21 yr. & upwards	All other white inhab- itants	Free persons of color	Serv- ants or slaves	Total
[459] Wakefield Enoch	1	4			5
[460‡†] Walker William	1	6			7
[461] Wakefield Charles	1	7			8
[462‡] Walker, Jessee Sr.	1	2			3
[463‡†] Winson Samuel (A black)			4		4
[464‡†] West David L.	1	5			6
[465‡†] Wilks Paul	1	1			2
[466] Walker Samuel	1	7			8
[467‡†] Walker Henry	1	5			6
[468] Williams Thomas	1	4			5
[469] White Robert	1	8			9
[470] White David S.	1	7			8
[471] Charles Wakefield	1	3			4
[472] Wallace Francis	1	5			6
[473‡†] Walker James Junr	1	1			2
[474] Winters Nathan	1	2			3
[475‡†] [Walker]¹ James Sr.	1	10			11
[476‡†] [Walk]er Henry	1	3			4
[477] [W]etherford William	2	5			7
[478‡†] Ward Eli	1	8			9
[479] Whooberry Jessee B	1	2			3
[480‡†] Walker David	1	8			9
[481] Woolseye Nehemiah	2	9			11
[482‡†] Ward John	1	1			2
[483‡†] Ward Mark	1	8			9
[484] Wilcox John	1	10			11
[485] Walker John	1	5			6
[486‡†] Whitesides William L	4	8			12
[487] Whitesides Johnson J	3	6			9
[488‡†] Whitesides Jacob	1	4			5
[489] Wise Daniel	5	3			8
[490‡†] Woods John	2	6			8
[491‡†] Walker Charles	1	4			5
[492‡] Walker Jessee Jr	1	1			2
[493‡†] Whitesides John L	3	3			6
[494] Williams Benjamin	1	9			10

¹ Manuscript burned. Portions of names in brackets supplied by the editor.

CENSUS OF ST. CLAIR COUNTY, 1818 (*Concluded*)

Names of heads of families	Free white males 21 yr. & upwards	All other white inhab- itants	Free persons of color	Serv- ants or slaves	Total
[495‡†] Walton Joseph	1	5			6
[496‡†] Wilderman Dossey	1	4			5
[497] Wood James	1	8			9
[498‡†] Wilderman George	3	6			9
[499‡†] Wilderman James	1	5			6
[500] Wilderman George J.	1	5			6
[501‡†] Worrick (A black)			6		6
[502] Antigo (a black)			5		5

The above is a tru return of the inhabitants
of St Clear County as rendred to me

WM. MOORE   com.

1 June 1818.

[*Recapitulation of extant schedules*:]

Free white males 21 years and upwards   676
All other white inhabitants   2393
Free persons of color   39
Servants or slaves   88

Total   3196

Adding extant figures in "Totals" column gives

3110

CENSUS OF UNION COUNTY, 1818

Census of Union Co. 1818

To Union County
Ilinois Teritory
March 27th day 1818
Ilinois Teretorry
Union County
April the 10th Day 1818
DAVID BROWN
JEREMIAH BROWN

Names of heads of families¹	Free white males 21 yr. & upwards	All other white inhab- itants	Free persons of colour	Servants or slaves
[1‡†] Joel Boges	1	9		
[2‡†] Jeremiah Brown	1	4		
[3‡†] John Brown	1	9		
[4‡†] Abraham hunsaker	1	5		
[5‡†] Daniel lingle	1	4		
[6‡†] wilkson godwin	1	5		
[7‡†] John burden	1	5+		
[8‡†] Jacob hunsaker Junur	1			
[9‡†] emanuel penrod	1	9		
[10] william pitsford	1	4		
[A.11‡†] Samuel etherton	1	8		
[12‡†] James willes		6		
[13‡†] John huse	1	2+		
[14‡†] Jacob willes	1	6		
[15] Thomas ellems	1	6		
[16] John woters	1	6		
[17‡†] Anthony lingle	1	7		
[18‡†] John mowry	1	4		
[19‡†] michel Delo	1	7		
[20‡†] John tope	1	2		
[21‡†] fedrick tope	1	7+		
[A.22‡†] Stephen mckinsy	1	3		
[23] ralph auston	1	5		
[24‡†] Joseph lamer	1	1		
[25‡†] David penrod	1	5		

¹ Figures and symbols preceding names have been supplied by the editor:
‡ Found also in the Federal Census for 1820.
A† Found also in the State Census for Alexander County, 1820.
† Found also in the State Census for Union County, 1820.

CENSUS OF UNION COUNTY, 1818 (*Continued*)

Names of heads of families	Free white males 21 yr. & upwards	All other white inhab- itants	Free persons of color	Servants or slaves
[26‡†] Henry lamer	1	7		
[27‡†] abner keith	1	6		
[28‡†] Peter portmess	1	4		
[29†] Patrick Corgen	1	6		
[30] Jacob butcher	1	8		
[A 31‡†] Richard Brown	1	6		
[32‡†] william morgen, seinor	1	8		
[33‡†] John Crips	1	5		
[34] John tilor	1	6		
[35] Jacob tilor	1	4		
[36] James tilor	1	7		
[37‡†] Samuel butcher	1	4		
[38] mathew Sparks	1	4		
[39] nathaniel arnett	1	1		
[40‡†] John Daly	1	5		
[41] Edmond Sawyers	1	4		
[42‡†] Gils parmerly	1	8		
[43‡†] andrew irvin	1	3		
[44] anthony wells	1	1		
[45] James swaferd	1	6		
[46] Thomas roberds	2	7		
[47‡†] Robert fryatt	1	1		
[48] henry bug	1	2		
[49] Ezekel wells	2	4		
[50] Samuel latherm	1	6		
[51] Jeremiah latherm	1	3		
[52] John weldon	1	10		
[53] Robert twedy	1	8		
[54‡†] hugh Irvin	1	6+		
[55‡†] aron howard	1	2		
[56‡†] Robert H. lloyd	1	3		
[57‡†] Mary boon		4		
[58‡†] Thomas Cox, junr	1	5		
[59] George gemes	1	6		
[60] Washington abernathy	2	4		
[61‡†] Benjamin hall	1	8		
[62‡†] Samuel lewis	1	7		

CENSUS OF UNION COUNTY, 1818 (*Continued*)

Names of heads of families	Free white males 21 yr. & upwards	All other white inhab- itants	Free persons of color	Servants or slaves
[63‡†] Squire boon	1	6		
[64] Richard mc bride	1	3		1
[65†] Thomas green	1	8		
[66‡†] Christopher houser	1	3		
[67] william galerher	2	5		
[68‡†] francies furphy¹	1	7		
[69‡†] John roberson	1	7		
[70] Washington edwards	1	4		
[71‡†] John twedy	1	3		
[72] george lilses	1	1		
[73] Jacob knely		1		
[74‡†] Thomas Craft	1	3		
[75‡†] George lemmons	1	5		
[76] Joseph abro	1	4		
[77] John latherm	1	9		
[78] John mury	1	1		
[79] James latherm	1	2		
[80‡†] John rupe	1	3		
[81‡†] Davd Brown	1	7		
[82‡†] David miller	1	4		
[83‡†] William Craglo	1	6		
[84] henry mc elmurrey	1	6		
[85‡†] george Crite	1	6		
[86‡†] Rice Sams	1	6		
[87‡†] William shelton	1	6		
[A 88‡†] James tash	1	2		
[89] Siph Standly	1	8		
[90] William habifield	1	5		
[91] thomas watson	1	5+		
[92] william piles	1	10		
[93‡†] Benjamin menees	2	4		
[94] ann Snotgrass		5		
[95] James howington	1	2		
[96] John ellems	1	2		
[97] John pels	1	9		
[98] John huston	2	8		
[99‡] peeter Johnson	1	3		

¹ i. e., Murphy.

CENSUS OF UNION COUNTY, 1818 (*Continued*)

Names of heads of families	Free white males 21 yr. & upwards	All other white inhab-itants	Free persons of color	Servants or slaves
[100‡†] James abernathy	1	4		
[101‡†] william welch	1	2		
[102‡†] John jinkens	1	6+		
[103‡†] Elijah bryant	3	1		
[104‡†] James ellems	1	6		
[105‡†] Bazzel billingsly	2	6		
[106‡†] Jinny tripe	3	5		
[107] James Cohenn	1	2		
[108‡†] John trip	1	9		
[109‡†] walter tedford	1	7		
[110‡†] James tingly	1	4		
[111] James pritchart	1	4		
[112] thomas Pritchart	1	5		
[113] Isaac Canada	1	6		
[114] John tedford	1	3+		
[115] John fisher	1	5		
[116‡†] John Smith	1	5		
[117] Jonas achard	1	5		
[118‡†] William Davidson	1	5		
[119] Samuel hosly	1	7		
[120‡†] william thornto[n] junr	1	2		
[121‡†] hugh Crag	1	13		
[122‡†] John hopkins	1	4		
[123] andrew hopkins	1	1		
[124‡†] oen evenas	1	15		1
[125‡†] elijha evans	1	1		
[126‡†] George evens	2	6		1
[127‡†] masias Davidson	1	9+		
[128‡†] hyly murphy		8		
[129] James ward senior	1	1		
[130] James ward junr	1	7		
[131†] Isaac Williams	1	3		
[132††] thomas Deen	1	2		
[133†‡] John Crise	1	4		
[134‡†] Isaac beggs	1	7		
[135‡] John Yost	1	2		

CENSUS OF UNION COUNTY, 1818 (*Continued*)

Names of heads of families	Free white males 21 yr. & upwards	All other white inhab- itants	Free persons of color	Servants or slaves
[136‡†] George Davis	1	7		
[137] oran Jones	1	9		
[138‡†] thomas Sams	1	8		
[A 139‡†] moses etherton	1	8		
[140‡†] alexandria whitaker	1	4		
[141‡†] David Sams	1	3		
[142‡†] Jane fisher	1	3		
[143] king fisher	1	1		
[144] Elisha Delany	1	5		
[145] george ward	1	2		
[A 146‡†] Nicholas wilson	1	6		
[147] Rachel fisher		4		
[148‡†] Joshua morgain	1	5		
[149‡†] Robert beggs	1	5		
[150] george godwin	1	5		
[151] John godwin	1	2		
[152] David minterf	1	4		
[153] James Delany	2	5		
[154‡†] william mcgines	1	4+		
[155‡†] Joshua throgmorton	1	2		
[156‡†] Patrick mc gines	1	1		
[157‡†] John Stokes	2	7		
[158‡†] Charles mcintosh	1	8		
[159] Samy Standerd	1	3		
[160‡†] James roberson	1	4		
[161‡†] Thomas Standerd	2	7		
[162‡†] thomas gore	1	6		
[163] Jane peterson		4		
[164‡†] william barten	1	6+		
[165] Jones Stokes	1			
[166‡†] william Durham	1	6		
[167‡†] Joshua gore	1	3		
[168] Elizabeth bradshaw		3		
[169] Richard Merien	1	6		
[170‡†] John west	1	5		
[171‡†] Levy paterson	1	6		
[172‡†] Louis penrod	1	4		

CENSUS OF UNION COUNTY, 1818 (*Continued*)

Names of heads of families	Free white males 21 yr. & upwards	All other white inhab- itants	Free persons of color	Servants or slaves
[A 173‡†] Alexandria beggs	2	6		
[174‡†] John Mcintosh	1	6		
[175‡†] Thomas adams	1	5		
[176] Margain boren	1	3		
[177] Susanna boren		5		
[178‡†] John Boren	1	6		2
[179] thomas Delany	1	6		
[180‡†] Leonard morgen	1	6		
[181‡†] John hunsaker junr	1	1		
[182‡†] Arichibel beggs	1	8		
[183‡†] hoza boren	1	8		2
[184‡†] Thomas mc intosh	1	7		
[A 185‡†] William Smith	1	2		
[A 186‡†] william mc intosh	1	3+		
[A 187‡†] James mu[r]phy	1	4		
[188] Johnathan Clark	1	6		
[A 189‡†] Edmond Sutten	1	5		
[A 190‡†] John lanahan	1	8		
[191] Darius Canns		4		
[192] Obediah russel	1	4		
[A 193‡†] Nathan russel	1	3		
[194] Sion Clanton	1	9		
[A 195‡†] Edmond russel	1	2		
[A 196‡†] William Daniel	2	10		
[197] James lee	1	3		
[A 198‡†] william m alexandria	1			
[A 199‡†] Leroy Smith	2	6		
[200] francies hollenhead	1	11		
[201] Nathaniel bostel	1	7		
[202] francies harvy	1	5		
[203] Rosanna brown		5		
[A 204‡†] John Coniers	1	4		
[205] Zimmy Carney	2	3		
[206] Banaja baney	1	1		
[207] Polly Sarvis		2		
[A 208‡†] fitz hutchings	2	1		
[A 209‡†] Thomas howard	1	2		

CENSUS OF UNION COUNTY, 1818 (*Continued*)

Names of heads of families	Free white males 21 yr. & upwards	All other white inhab- itants	Free persons of color	Servants or slaves
[A 210‡†] aron etherton	1	6		
[A 211‡†] william bigerstaff	1	3		
[A 212‡†] John etherton	1	4		
[A 213‡†] William wafferd	1	2		
[A 214‡†] Levi huse	2	6		
[215] Benjamin Dextr	2	6+		
[A 216‡†] James Mcclain	1	5		
[A 217‡†] mathew gasten	1	7		
[A 218‡†] mark pervo	1	7		
[219] Erasmes nally	3	2		
[220] Benjamin w atherton	1	5		
[221‡†] william worthington	1	3		
[222‡†] James worthington seinor	1	2		
[223‡†] Nathaniel huse	1	9		
[224‡†] Easter leawrance		4		
[225‡†] Daniel ritter	1	5		
[226‡†] henry baringer	2	7		
[227] harrey Croswit	1	3		
[228‡†] william Eachols	2	2		
[229‡†] Joseph hunsaker	1	6		
[230‡] John Eachols	2	7		
[231‡†] James Brown	1	4		
[232‡†] Jinny graham		3		
[233‡†] John whitaker	1	4		
[234‡†] andrew penrod	1	2		
[235‡†] Jacob tope	1	2		
[236‡†] Joseph palmer	1	5		
[237‡†] John penrod	1	2		
[238‡†] John langly	1	5		
[A 239‡†] Car allen	2	5		
[240‡†] John Barker	1	6		
[241‡†] Ephrem noel	1	4		
[242‡†] Samuel Sprous	1	8		
[243‡†] Jacob snider	1	5		
[244‡†] Daniel kimmel	3	3		
[245‡†] James ells	1	6		

CENSUS OF UNION COUNTY, 1818 (*Continued*)

Names of heads of families	Free white males 21 yr. & upwards	All other white inhab- itants	Free persons of color	Servants or slaves
[246‡†] David cotner	2	6+		
[247‡†] John grammer	1	8		
[248‡†] Joseph mclehanny	1	1		
[249‡†] thomas Cox seiner	1	4		5
[250] John mcintosh	1	3		
[251‡†] John hunsaker	1	4		
[252†] Robert hargrave	1	4		
[253‡†] anthony morgan	1	5		
[254†‡] fedrick tolbert	1	2		
[255] David arndell	1	3		
[256‡†] John B roberds	1			
[257] william hickem	1	10		
[258‡†] Samul penrod junr	1	9		
[259] David Salyers	1	8		
[260‡†] Elijha P woodoll	1	1		
[261] abraham Comer	1	4		
[262‡†] George smily	2	4		
[263] James westbrooke	1	7		
[264‡†] Jacob wigle	1	4		
[265] James Jackson	1	6		
[266‡†] Jacob trees	1	5		
[267‡†] Robert Casa	1	6		
[268‡†] John hargrave junr	1	1		
[269‡†] William thornton seinor	1	8		
[270] William Waker	1	7		
[A 271‡†] Samuel Philips	1	5		
[A 272‡†] James Philips	1	4		
[273] John kilor	1	3		
[274] Joel wit	2	7		
[275] Jesse blanks	1			8
[A 276‡†] Chals bradley	1	3		
[277] Benjamin hammon	1	4		
[A 278‡†] John Shaver	1	6		
[279] William goldsmith	1	5		
[280] arther mc comel	1	9		
[A 281‡†] John Smith	1	5		

CENSUS OF UNION COUNTY, 1818 (*Continued*)

Names of heads of families	Free white males 21 yr. & upwards	All other white inhabitants	Free persons of color	Servants or slaves
[A 282‡†] Maryan Smith	1	4		
[283] Josiah Cambert	1	5		
[A 284‡†] thomas B Paten	1	5+		
[285] thomas whitaker	1	7		
[A 286†] Samuel fowuler	1	5		
[A 287‡†] william f holley	1	2		
[288] Robert wier	1	7		
[A 289‡†] george oller	1	2		
[290] Lewis tash	1	6		
[A 291‡†] absolem hacker	1	4		
[292] gabril woodry	1	4		
[293] James powers	1	2		
[A 294‡†] George hacker	3	7		6
[A 295‡†] Alexandria milligen	1	3		
[296‡†] John hacker	1	2		
[297] george watson	1	6		
[A 298‡†] nezebe allen	1	8		
[299] Richard marten	1	5		
[300] william turpen	1	4		
[301] David Johnson	1	7		
[A 302‡†] nathen turpen	1	7		
[A 303‡†] James Stephenson	1	3		
[304] joseph panter	1	3		
[305] George allen	1	2		
[306] arther allen		2		
[307] Leonard allen	1	5		
[A 308‡†] Allen mckinsy	1	6		
[309] mathew allen	1	4		
[310] James r allen	1	2		
[311] william Brown	1	8		
[A 312‡†] thomas williams	1	6		
[313] John parker	1	9		
[A 314‡†] meret harvel	1	8		
[315†] william parker	1	1		
[316†] Alexandria beggs	1	9		
[A 317‡†] greenberry brown	1	2		
[318] Jesse Stripling	1	6		

CENSUS OF UNION COUNTY, 1818 (*Continued*)

Names of heads of families	Free white males 21 yr. & upwards	All other white inhab-itants	Free persons of color	Servants or slaves
[A 319‡†] Levy grham	1	6		
[320] Edward graham	1	4		
[321] Charles Campbell	1	9		
[322‡†] Clif hazzelwood	2	11		
[323‡†] William hudson	1	3		
[324] peter Click	1	6		
[325] moses macen	1	3		
[326] James pritchet	1	1		
[327] fanny hill		4		
[328] Sary Snider		5		
[329‡†] Solomon penrod	1	3		
[330‡†] Leven L hollen	2	1		
[331‡†] Ezekel Staten	1	5		
[332] John goset	1	6		
[333‡†] Robert Craften	1	7		2
[334] Silas risley	1	6		
[335] william morgen Junr	1	5		
[336] william leatherm	1	6		
[337‡†] william Dod	1	9		
[338‡†] Samuel hunsaker Seinor	1	9		
[339‡†] Jacob hunsaker Seinor	3	2		
[340‡†] george Brown junr	1	5		
[341†] george Brown Seinor	1	2		
[342‡†] Jonas Vancel	1	9		
[343‡†] Jacob Wolf	2	6		
[344‡†] John hargrave Seinor	1	3		
[345‡†] David hunsaker	1	1		
[346‡†] Jesse eachols	1	5		
[347] plesant axly	1	11		
[348‡†] george woolf	2	8		
[349‡†] John thornton	1	4		1
[350‡†] John vinyard	1	7		
[351‡†] Christian miller	2	7		
[352†] John wigle	1	11		

CENSUS OF UNION COUNTY, 1818 (*Continued*)

Names of heads of families	Free white males 21 yr. & upwards	All other white inhab- itants	Free persons of color	Servants or slaves
[353‡†] george hunsaker seinor	1	4		
[354‡†] Jacob wagner	1	6		
[355‡†] John Bradshaw	2	7		3
[356‡†] Samuel hunsak juner	1	5		
[357‡†] george hunsaker junr	1	3		
[358‡†] John husky	1	3		1
[359‡†] william grammer	1	9		
[360‡] John miller	1	9		
[361‡†] Jonathan husky	1	5		2
[362‡†] Edmond vancel	1	5		
[363‡†] Adam Clap Junr	1	1		
[364] Benjamin a Parsons	1			
[365] Joseph taylor	1			
[366‡†] Daniel T. Coleman	1			
[367‡†] michel limbaugh	1	4		
[368‡†] John harsten	1	3		
[369‡†] John garner	1	6		
[370‡†] John B. murray	2	11		
[371‡†] adam Clap seinor	2	5		
[372] Sousanna reyonalds		2		
[373‡†] John landers	1	7		
[374] John Bradley	1	3		
[375] george marten	1	1		
[376] Oliver armor	1	4		
[377] Sousanna price		4		
[378] James worthington Junr	1	4		
[379‡†] George vinyard	2	4		
[380‡†] Lee Cude	1	4		
[381‡†] Jesse suttler	1	7		
[382] Katharina Crise	1	6		
[383‡†] John Kimmel	1	5		
[384‡†] Zachariah mcDaniel	1	13		
[385‡†] Joseph waller	1	3		
[386‡†] Henry Cluts	1	5+		
[387‡†] Robert Axley	1	5		

CENSUS OF UNION COUNTY, 1818 (*Concluded*)

Names of heads of families	Free white males 21 yr. & upwards	All other white inhab- itants	Free persons of color	Servants or slaves
[388‡†] Jacob Brown	1	5		
[389‡†] Benjamin mccravens	1	6		
[390‡†] James write	1	5		
[391] James underwood	1	7		
[392‡] Elizabeth Doerty		3		
[393‡†] Jacob rentelman	2	7		
[394] Peeter gaspen	1	6		
[395] Iseral tomson	1	11		
[396‡†] Samuel penrod Seinor	2	8		
[397] Adam vancel	2	2		
[398‡†] thomas sumers	1	6		
[399‡†] Isaac vancel	1	4		
[400‡†] Robert W. Craften	1	2		
[401] John wever	1	2		
[402‡†] Jacob Littleton	1	6		4
[403‡†] William huse	1	4		
[404] Jonas Vancel Junr.	1	2		
[405] Jude Coalmen		2		
[406‡†] Oen huse	1	5		
[407‡†] Davoult Lense	1	6		
[408‡†] John Lense Junr.	1	2		
[409‡†] John Lense Seinor	1	2		
[410‡†] Boysten Lense	1	2		
[411] Matte mccool		3		
[412] Abner Eastwood	1	5		

[*Recapitulation*:]

Free white males of 21 years and upwards	**439**
All other white inhabitants	2007
Free persons of color	0
Servants or slaves	39
Total	2485

CENSUS OF WASHINGTON COUNTY, 1818

Names of heads of families[1]	Free white males 21 yr. & upwards	All other white inhab- itants	Free persons of colour	Serv- ants or slaves	Total number
[1] Daniel Dikes	1	6			7
[2] David S. White	1	9			10
[3‡†] Philip Martin	5				5
[4] David Lester	1	3			4
[5] Archibald Lester	1	6			7
[6] Henry Lester	1	5			6
[7] Henry Ginger	1	3			4
[8] David Roarch	1	3			4
[9] Nancy Atkins		5			5
[10] Samuel Seward	2	3			5
[11] Peter Branstetter	2	12		1	15
[12] Isaac Conger	2	8			10
[13‡†] Samuel Brown	1	2			3
[14‡†] George Brown	1	1		9	11
[15‡†] John Brown	1	3			4
[16‡†] Colier Brown	1	3			4
[17‡†] Charles Stephens	1	6			7
[18] Ephraim Walker	1	8			9
[19] John Martin	1	4			5
[20] John Padon	1	3			4
[21‡†] Leonard Maddux	1	7			8
[22‡†] Leven Maddux	1	8			9
[23] Abraham Baker	1	11			12
[24‡†] Alexander Maddux	1	10			11
[25‡†] John Nichols	1	8			9
[26] Parker Dike	1	9			10
[27] Thomas Isbell	1	3			4
[28] Joseph Isbell	1	6			7
[29] Henry Isbell	1	7			8
[30‡†] Alexander Chesney	1	3			4
[31‡†] Alexander Maddux, Junr.	1	7			8
[32‡†] David White	1	9			10

[1] Figures and symbols preceding names have been supplied by the editor:
‡ Found also in the Federal Census for 1820.
† Found also in the State Census for 1820.

CENSUS OF WASHINGTON COUNTY, 1818 (*Continued*)

Names of heads of families	Free white males 21 yr. & upwards	All other white inhab- itants	Free persons of color	Serv- ants or slaves	Total number
[33‡] Asahel Smith	1				1
[34‡†] Wingate Maddux	1	10			11
[35‡†] Zachariah Maddux	1	6			7
[36] James Bankson	2	4	1		7
[37] Frances Petty		6			6
[38] Elijah Bankson	1	5			6
[39‡†] Leeaiden Posey	1	4			5
[40] Whitmill Ryal	1	9			10
[41‡†] William Steel	2	6			8
[42] George Shipman	1	6			7
[43] William Wakefield	1	7			8
[44‡†] John Creal	1	12			13
[45‡†] Absalem Yarbrough	3	8			11
[46‡†] Richard Thomason	1	15			16
[47‡†] Jonathan Hill	1	7			8
[48‡†] Caton Usher	1	3			4
[49‡†] Isaac Darnal	1	9			10
[50‡†] Lemuel Hackins	1	4			5
[51‡†] Gilless Maddux	1	9			10
[52‡†] John Carter	1	3			4
[53] Simeon Wakefield	1	5			6
[54] John Wakefield	1	4			5
[55] James Crocker	1	7			8
[56] Nimrod Hambrick	1	5			6
[57‡†] John Wadsworth	1	6		1	8
[58‡†] Thomas Wadsworth	1	5			6
[59‡†] Robert Mc Iver	1	7			8
[60††] Haden Walls	1	7			8
[61‡†] Jacob Crocker	1	5			6
[62] Thomas Crocker	1	9			10
[63‡†] Elizabeth Allen	1	10			11
[64‡] Harry Wilton	1	1			2
[65] John Margrave	1	4			5
[66] James Wafer	2	5			7
[67] Lester Fish	2	3			5

CENSUS OF WASHINGTON COUNTY, 1818 (*Continued*)

Names of heads of families	Free white males 21 yr. & upwards	All other white inhab-itants	Free persons of color	Serv-ants or slaves	Total number
[68] Hedly Smith	2	10			12
[69‡†] Edward Cole	3	10		1	14
[70‡†] John Lewis Laughlin	1	8			9
[71] Henry McDonald	2	4			6
[72] George Roper, Senr·	1	4			5
[73] George Roper, Junr·	1	5			6
[74‡†] William Taylor	1	6			7
[75] William Renfrow	3	6			9
[76] Peter Renfrow	1	5			6
[77] William Umphrey	1	9			10
[78‡†] John Carigan	1	7		2	10
[79‡†] Archibald Andrus	1	9			10
[80] Benjamin Moody	1	10			11
[81] John Faning	1	5			6
[82] Jeremiah Daniel	1	5			6
[83] Barton Daniel	1	6			7
[84] Martin Daniel	1	5			6
[85] Robert Daniel	1	3			4
[86] Samuel Danley	1	7			8
[87] Isaac Myers	1	3			4
[88] Robert Gibson	1	6			7
[89‡†] Thomas Wadkins	1	4			5
[90‡†] Daniel S. Swearingen	1	7		2	10
[91‡] Benjamin Brasilton	1	3			4
[92] Samuel Lear	1	1			2
[93] Thomas Motley	1				1
[94] Jobe Harris	1	2			3
[95] Nathaniel Scroggin	1	4			5
[96‡†] Bowling Green	1	6			7
[97‡†] David & Caleb Peirce	2				2
[98] Abraham Thompson	1	10			11
[99] Robert Armstrong	1	7			8
[100] Royal Potter	2	5			7
[101] Abraham Starnes	1	2			3
[102] Stephen French	1	2			3

CENSUS OF WASHINGTON COUNTY, 1818 (*Continued*)

Names of heads of families	Free white males 21 yr. & upwards	All other white inhab- itants	Free persons of color	Serv- ants or slaves	Total number
[103] Joseph Wadkins	1				1
[104] Abner Eades	1	5			6
[105] Nathaniel Lowe	1				1
[106‡†] Benjamin Jones	1	14			15
[107] Thomas Little	1	12			13
[108] William Read	1	3			4
[109] George Green	1	7			8
[110] Cyrus Kerby	1	7			8
[111] John Clary	1	4			5
[112‡†] Andrew Bankson	1	6			7
[113] Matthias Eades	1	3			4
[114‡†] William Crocker	1	4			5
[115‡†] Arthur Crocker	2	7			9
[116‡†] Samuel Stewart	1	4			5
[117‡†] Archibald Taylor	2	6			8
[118‡†] John Bitto	1	3			4
[119‡†] James Edon	1	5			6
[120‡†] William Darnall	1	3			4
[121‡†] Abraham Minson	1	9			10
[122] George Harrison	1	4			5
[123] James Hooper	1	8			9
[124‡†] John Huey	1	4			5
[125] Thomas Williams	1	7			8
[126] Loyd Lee	1	5			6
[127‡†] John Smith	1	7			8
[128‡†] Theophilus Harrel	1	3			4
[129] Edmund Taylor	1	6			7
[130‡†] Collins Matheny	1	5			6
[131‡†] Thomas Huey	2	6			8
[132‡†] Daniel Cymons	1	8			9
[133] Moses Pharrer	1	3			4
[134] Daniel White	1	11			12
[135†] Hosea Rollins	1	5			6
[136] Adam Smith	1	7			8
[137] Henry Smith	1	5			6
[138] Adam Smith, Sen.ʳ	1	4			5

CENSUS OF WASHINGTON COUNTY, 1818 (*Continued*)

Names of heads of families	Free white males 21 yr. & upwards	All other white inhabitants	Free persons of color	Servants or slaves	Total number
[139] William Howel	1	8			9
[140] William Daniel	1	4			5
[141] Robert Daniel	1	3			4
[142‡†] William Roundtree	1	11			12
[143‡†] Briton Jordan	1	3			4
[144] William Speaks	1	5			6
[145‡†] James Orton	2	7			9
[146‡†] John Welch	1	6			7
[147] Archibald Izel	1	5			6
[148‡†] William Johnston	1	7			8
[149‡†] John Orton	1	3			4
[150] Neal Kenedy	1	5			6
[151‡†] John Starnatur	1	8			9
[152‡†] James Mc Reaken	1	7			8
[153‡†] Charles Cox	1	7			8
[154] William Tilley	1	4			5
[155‡†] Jacob Turman	1	4			5
[156‡†] Jonathan Browder	1	5			6
[157] Phinehas Hill	1	7			8
[158] Clemuel Jones	1	4			5
[159‡†] William Sims	1	9			10
[160] Joseph Billue	1	10			11
[161] Nancy Journey		10			10
[162] Valentine Brazil	1	4			5
[163] John Savage	1	10			11
[164‡†] Beverly Wadkins	1	7			8
[165] Caleb Odell	1	9			10
[166] Solomon Odell	1	9			10
[167] Thomas Higgens	1	6			7
[168] William Journey	1	4			5
[169] Alexander Ore	1	14			15
[170] Delilah Dannel	1	7			8
[171] William Bugg	1	2			3
[172] William Fagan	1	5			6
[173] Henry Webb	1	9			10
[174] Barnett Bone	1	6			7

CENSUS OF WASHINGTON COUNTY, 1818 (*Continued*)

Names of heads of families	Free white males 21 yr. & upwards	All other white inhab- itants	Free persons of color	Serv- ants or slaves	Total number
[175] John Robbins	1	4			5
[176†] Joseph Robbins	1	4			5
[177‡†] Ellis Chaffin	2	8			10
[178‡†] Robert Davis	1	5			[6]
[179‡†] John Johnston	1	6			7
[180] Charles Beaty	1	5			6
[181‡†] Hugh Johnston	1	2			3
[182‡†] William Johnston, Junr.	1	3			4
[183‡†] Benjamin Cox	1	10			11
[184‡†] William Middleton	1	4			5
[185] Elisha Givvens	1	2			3
[186‡†] Solomon Silkwood	3	8			11
[187] James Silkwood	1	7			8
[188†] Charles Butler	1	8			9
[189] Obadiah Silkwood	1	6			7
[190] Harmon Lick	1	4			5
[191] Jacob Carnes	1	4			5
[192‡†] Benjamin Hagerman	1	8			9
[193‡†] Joseph Kinyon	1	6			7
[194‡†] Brazilla Silkwood	1	3			4
[195‡] Hyram Silkwood	1	3			4
[196‡†] John Woodrum	1	8			9
[197] Nicholas Edwards	1	7			8
[198‡†] James Thompson	1	6			7
[199‡†] Reuben Middleton	2	5			7
[200‡†] Ruth Washburn		7			7
[201] Joseph Cox	1	3			4
[202‡†] Aron Williams	1	7			8
[203‡†] Pleasant Apling	1	6			7
[204] John Ratliff	1	5			6
[205] William Ratliff	1	3			4
[206] Jobe Ratliff	1	7			8
[207] James Ratliff	1	8			9
[208] Joseph Fisher	1	7	1		9
[209] Ephraim Stewart			10		10
[210] William Stewart			4		4

CENSUS OF WASHINGTON COUNTY, 1818 (*Continued*)

Names of heads of families	Free white males 21 yr. & upwards	All other white inhab- itants	Free persons of color	Serv- ants or slaves	Total number
[211] Joshua Fisher	2	3			5
[212] George Stamps	1	6			7
[213] George Damron	1	3			4
[214] Harmon Hatfield	1	3			4
[215] James Fisher	1	4			5
[216] Robert Waddle	1	2			3
[217] William Elston	1	2			3
[218‡†] John Handy	1	6			7
[219] John Lizenby	1	2			3
[220] Thomas Allen	1	8			9
[221‡†] John Evans	1	3			4
[222] Benjamin Wheeless	1	4			5
[223] Jessee Henson	1	6			7
[224] William Henson	1	5			6
[225] Philip Henson	1	7			8
[226‡†] William Wheeless	1	2			3
[227] Reubin Wheeless	1	4		3	8
[228] Daniel Rizley	1	10			11
[229‡†] Lewis Huggins	1	2			3
[230‡†] David Huggins	1	4			5
[231‡†] William Huggins	1	4			5
[232] Henry Darter	1	9			10
[233‡†] John Deas	1	7			8
[234‡†] Alexander White	1	5			6
[235‡†] William Johnston	1	1			2
[236‡†] John Lard	1	4			5
[237‡] Hartshorn White	2			5	7
[238] Rufus Ricker	2				2
[239] Thomas McKnight	1	4			5
[240] Mederith Roberson	1	7			8
[241‡†] John S. Johnston	1	4			5
[242‡†] David Mc Cord	1	5			6
[243] John Ridgway	1	6			7
[244] Robert Carter	6	4			10
[245‡†] Richard Carter	1	8			9
[246‡†] Patsey Short		7			7

CENSUS OF WASHINGTON COUNTY, 1818 (*Continued*)

Names of heads of families	Free white males 21 yr. & upwards	All other white inhab- itants	Free persons of color	Serv- ants or slaves	Total number
[247] George Boxley	2	8		1	11
[248‡†] William H. Bradsby	1			1	2
[249] John K. Maugham	2	7			9
				93	
				249	
				282	
				193	
		Brot forward		201	
				253	
				245	
				191	
		Total			1707

The above is a true
return of the ennu-
meration of the
inhabitants in
Washington County
Ilinois Teritory as
rendered to me on
application

JOHN K. MAUGHAM
June the 1st 1818

ADDITIONAL CENSUS OF WASHINGTON COUNTY, 1818

Names of heads of families	Free white males 21 yr. & upwards	All other white inhabitants	Blacks	Totals
[250] Thomas Jordan	3	6		9
[251] William Hynds	2	8		10
[252] Joseph Jordan	2	7		9
[253] James Jordan	1	6		7
[254] Thomas Jordan, Junr	1	5		6
[255] Isaac Casey	2	8		10
[256] Lemuel Casey	1	4		5
[257] William Caysey Junr	1	4		5
[258] William Casey sen^r	2	7		9
[259] Leonard Casey	1	6		7
[260] George Casey	1	5		6
[261] Samuel Casey	1	3		4
[262] Thomas Sayles	2	6		8
[263] Joseph Sayles	2	6		8
[264] Henry Sayles	1	2		3
[265] Samuel Sayles	1	2		3
[266] David Starke	1	4		5
[267] Henry Starke	1	6		7
[268] William Starke	1	4		5
[269] John Bunch	2	6		8
[270] James Bunch	1	4		5
[271] Joseph Rowlin	1	6		7
[272] Britan Baily	1	5		6
[273] John Bailey	1	3		4
[274‡†] Thomas F. Herbert	7		2	9
[275‡†] John Hutchings	1	5	3	9
[276] William Hutchings	1	8		9
[277] Rufus Lee	2	6		8
[278] John Coles	1	4		5
[279] Thomas Coles	1	6		7
[280] Robert Anderson	1	8		9
[281] John Craig	1	4		5
[282] Jessee Y. Wellbourne	1	5		6
[283] Thomas Crabtree	1	7		8
[284] Thomas Head	1	6		7
[285‡†] Christopher Richerfuse	2	3		5
[286] Abraham Romine	1	4		5

ADDITIONAL CENSUS OF WASHINGTON COUNTY, 1818
(*Continued*)

Names of heads of families	Free white males 21 yr. & upwards	All other white inhab- itants	Blacks	Totals
[287] Isaac Romine	1	2		3
[288] Charles Moore	2	8		10
[289] George Jones	2	6		8
this is from the de- tached parts of Ed- wards County on the maridian line Joining Washington				
[290] Joseph McKinney	5	8		13
[291] Joshua Pyles	2	10		12
[292] Jeremiah McKinney	2	4		6
[293] Philip McBride	2	6		8
[294] Robert McBride	3	8		1
[295] John Going	1	4		5
[296] William Going	3	8		11
[297] Robert Hensley	2	3		5
[298] John Hensley	3	7		10
[299] Hugh Shearwood	3	10		13
[300] Jacob Brimbury	2	6		8
[301] Samuel Young	2	5		7
[302] James Young	1	5		6
[303] Jacob Albert	1	3		4
[304] William Albert	1	4		5
[305] Robert Snodgrass	1	3		4
[306] John Snodgrass	2	7		9
[307] John Rutherford	2	3		5

[*Recapitulation*:]

1818

Free white males 21 years and upwards	281
All other white inhabitants	1382
Free people of color	16
Servants or slaves	26
	1705

ADDITIONAL CENSUS OF WASHINGTON COUNTY, 1818
(*Concluded*)

Additional census

Free white males 21 years and upwards	59
All other whites	205
Negroes	5
	269

Additional census for Edwards County

Free white males 21 years and upwards	38
All other white inhabitants	104
	142

CENSUS OF WHITE COUNTY, 1818

I cirtify that this and the inclosed list is
a just and true ennumeration of the inhabitants of
White county Illinois Territory given under my
hand this third day of June 1818

DANIEL HAY, Commissioner

Total Aggregate 3539

Names of heads of families[1]	Free white males 21 yr. & upwards	All other white inhab-itants	Free persons of colour	Servants or slaves
[1‡†] John Craig	1	5		
[2‡†] Griffin Sowerd	1	8		
[3‡†] Samuel Dagley	1	1		
[4‡†] Thomas Dagley	1	5		
[5‡†] Joshua Albin	1	2		
[6‡†] William Tombs	1	4		
[7‡†] Joshua Dewey	1	5		
[8] Jonathan Coburn	1	3		
[9] Edmon Stokes	1	5		
[10‡†] William Hargate	1	2		
[11‡†] John Lankford	1	6		
[12‡†] Benjn Smith	2	9		
[13] Abner Owings	1	6		
[14‡†] Josiah Carter	1	7		
[15‡†] Saml Spilman	1	1		
[16] George Jackson	1	4		
[17‡†] Isaac Shelby	1	5		
[18‡†] Adam Crouch	2	1		1
[19] William Hadden	1	5		
[20] William Elledge	1	2		
[21] John Elledge	1	2		
[22] Isaac Elledge	3	6		
[23] Whitnell Harrington	1	3		
[24‡†] Vincent Moreland	1	4		
[25‡†] ———— Young	1	4		
[26‡†] Peter Widdows	1	8		

[1] Figures and symbols preceding names have been supplied by the editor:
‡ Found also in the Federal Census for 1820.
† Found also in the State Census for White County for 1820.
* Found also in the State Census for Jefferson County for 1820.

CENSUS OF WHITE COUNTY, 1818 (*Continued*)

Names of heads of families	Free white males 21 yr. & upwards	All other white inhab- itants	Free persons of color	Servants or slaves
[27] Clarender Hooper	1	2		1
[28‡†] John Ridgway	3	10		
[29‡†] William Cain	2	5		
[30] Isaiah Humphrey	1	7		
[31] Thomas Griffy	1	3		
[32‡†] John B Compton	1	8		
[33‡†] William Ellis	1	4		
[34‡†] Arch^d Standefore	1	10		
[35‡†] Joseph Waller	2	9		
[36] Jacob Weldon	1	4		
[37‡*] William Maxy	1	8		
[38] Nathl Parker	1	3		
[39‡†] Edward M^ccallister	1	4		
[40] Isaac Brown	1	3		
[41‡†] Simon M^ccallister	1	3		
[42‡†] Thomas Thornsberry	1	4		
[43] Richd Adams	1	3		
[44] Mallaci Weir	1	6		
[45‡†] Ruth Smith	2	6		
[46‡†] James Mccallister	1	5		
[47‡†] James Voris	1	4		
[48‡†] John Read	3	6		
[49‡†] Isaac Johnson	1	6		
[50‡†] Comstock Chappel	1			
[51‡†] Edward Farley	4	9		
[52‡†] William Robertson	8	5		
[53‡†] William McKee	1	5		
[54] Zacheriah Downs	1	2		
[55‡†] Elam Stewert	2	5		
[56‡†] John Wilson	1	3		
[57] Binjn Young	1	6		
[58] Emela Groves		7		
[59‡†] Halyard Dorsey	3	1		
[60‡†] Mary Walbert		3		
[61] Robert Stafford	1	3		
[62‡†] Elijah Goodwin	1	10		
[63] John Lastly	1	6		

CENSUS OF WHITE COUNTY, 1818 (*Continued*)

Names of heads of families	Free white males 21 yr. & upwards	All other white inhab- itants	Free persons of color	Servants or slaves
[64‡†] Arvin Wilson	1	5		
[65‡†] Joseph Culberson	1	6		
[66‡†] John Stevens	1	10		
[67] Peter Wilkerson	2	6		
[68] Lewis Dickerson	1	12		
[69] Ellender Webster		8		
[70‡†] Joseph Burrell	1	4		
[71] William Frazer	1	3		
[72] George Russell	1	3		
[73] Mary Snodgrass		6		
[74‡†] Adam Miller	1	6		
[75‡†] Joel Berry	1	2		
[76‡†] Saml Hargrave	1	2		3
[77‡†] Hosea Pearce	1	1		
[78‡†] John Townsand	1	5		
[79‡†] Jorden Vance	1	5		
[80‡†] John Dale	2	5		
[81] Joseph Lowrey	2	5		
[82] Nathan Jackson	1	5		
[83‡†] William Allen	3	4		
[84] Daniel Gains	1	3		
[85‡†] Edward Badger	3	5		
[86‡†] Thomas Williams	1	4		
[87] Betsey Medcalf		8		
[88‡†] Daniel McHenry	1	7		
[89‡†] William McHenry	2	9		
[90‡†] Isaac Blagg	1	3		
[91‡†] Thomas Rutledge	1	10		
[92‡†] Enoch Berry	1	7		
[93‡†] William McGehee	1	6		
[94‡†] James Fips	1	6		
[95‡†] Abraham Auxier	2	6		
[96‡†] David Shelby	2	2		2
[97] Eli York	1	5		
[98] Edmon York	1	5		
[99‡†] Lewis Green	1	3		

CENSUS OF WHITE COUNTY, 1818 (*Continued*)

Names of heads of families	Free white males 21 yr. & upwards	All other white inhab- itants	Free persons of color	Servants or slaves
[100‡†] Thomas Wickers	1	7		
[101‡†] Young Funkhouser	1	4		
[102] Elijah Cravens	1	3		
[103‡†] Isaac Funkhouser	1	6		
[104‡†] Henry Morgan	1	8		
[105] Benjn Spilman	2	9		
[106‡†] George McKinsey	1	5		
[107‡†] Peter Steel	1	5		
[108‡†] John Snider	1	7		
[109‡†] George Knott	1	5		
[110‡†] Isaac Knott	1	3		
[111‡†] John Lamb	2	5		
[112‡†] Solomon Brill	1	7		
[113‡†] William McGehee	1	3		
[114] John Groves	1	4		
[115] Robert Torrea	1	3		
[116] Thomas Torrea	1	3		
[117‡†] George Saturfield	1	1	3	
[118‡†] Isaac Saturfield	1	5		
[119‡†] Robert Davis	1	5		
[120‡†] William Davis	1	6		
[121‡†] Walter McCoy	2	1		
[122‡†] John Vinyard	1	4		
[123‡†] William Jorden	1	4		
[124] Andrew Mclenehen	2	4		
[125‡†] Henry McMurtry	1	5		
[126‡†] John McMurtry	1	4		
[127‡†] Jacob Forrester	1	1		
[128] William Potts	1	4		
[129‡†] Alexd Trousdale	1	10		
[130] John Trousdale	1	2		
[131‡†] James Trousdale	1	2		
[132] James Pearce	1	6		
[133‡†] John S. Patillo	1	4		
[134‡†] Robert Bruce	1	5		
[135] Ruben Walden	1	3		
[136‡†] Jesse Pearce	1	7		

CENSUS OF WHITE COUNTY, 1818 (*Continued*)

Names of heads of families	Free white males 21 yr. & upwards	All other white inhab- itants	Free persons of color	Servants or slaves
[137‡†] Zepheniah Johns	1	4		
[138] Richmond Green	1	3		
[139‡†] James Flemming	1	5		
[140‡†] Even Johns	1	2		
[141‡†] Elisha Hall	1	5		
[142‡†] Moses Pearce	1	3		
[143] Paul Abney	2	7		
[144] Simon Leakey	1	7		
[145‡†] Saml Chapman	1	4		
[146‡†] Hezekiah ONeill	2	4		
[147] Joseph Newkum	1	3		
[148‡†] James Watson	1	2		
[149] John Watson	1	7		
[150‡†] Robert Watson, Jr	1	3		
[151] John B Stovall	2	3		
[152] Squire Stovall	1	4		
[153] Abraham Stovall	1	2		
[154‡†] George Nicols	1	5		
[155] John Woodall	1	3		
[156] Jonathan Luallen	1	5		
[157‡†] Frederick Mayberry	1	2		
[158‡†] Jesse Mayberry	1	2		
[159‡†] William Hardisty	2	2		
[160‡†] Charles Cook	2	7		
[161] Robert Watson	1	2		
[162‡†] John Stone	1	3		
[163‡†] David Mayberry	1	3		
[164] Valuntine Nicols	2	7		
[165] John Drew	1	4		
[166‡†] Thomas Garrison	2	5		
[167‡†] Absolum Garrison	1	7		
[168‡†] John B Wilson	1	6		
[169] Ruben S Spencer	2	1		
[170] James Ramesey	1	4		
[171] Alexd Nesbit	1	3		
[172] Alexander Ramsey	1	5		
[173‡†] James Mays	1	3		

CENSUS OF WHITE COUNTY, 1818 (*Continued*)

Names of heads of families	Free white males 21 yr. & upwards	All other white inhab-itants	Free persons of color	Servants or slaves
[174‡†] James Rutledge	2	8		
[175‡*] Robert Maxwell	1	2		
[176] Samuel Davidson	2	10		
[177‡†] William Rutledge	2	5		
[178‡†] James Miller	1	7		
[179‡†] James Veach	1	2		
[180‡†] John Veach	1	2		
[181‡†] Isaac Logan	1	4		
[182‡†] Thomas Camron	2	9		
[183‡†] Mathew Park	1	2		
[184‡*] Saml Martin	1	3		
[185‡†] Elias Veach	1	8		
[186‡†] Absolum Hurt	2	9		1
[187] Daniel Bain, jr	1	9		
[188] Anthony Richy	1	6		
[189‡†] George McCown	1	2		
[190‡†] Emanuel Metcalf	1	7		
[191] John C Bains	1	3		
[192] Elisabeth Counsil	1	5		
[193] James Taylor	1	2		
[194‡†] John Lane	1	3		
[195‡†] William Hurt	1	9		
[196] Rebekah Jones	1	3		
[197‡†] Charles Cato	1	4		
[198] Mark Duncan	1	5		
[199‡†] John Starkey	1	3		
[200‡†] Walter Garner	2	4		
[201] Robert McLelland	2	3		
[202‡†] Thomas Mays	1	7		
[203‡†] Henry Jones	1	6		
[204‡†] William Files	1	3		
[205‡†] John Files	2	5		
[206] Enoch Nevel	1	3		
[207‡†] John Chism	1	4		1
[208‡†] Archibald Brown	2	2		
[209‡†] David Hanks	1	7		
[210‡†] Hamlet Underwood	1	1		

CENSUS OF WHITE COUNTY, 1818 (*Continued*)

Names of heads of families	Free white males 21 yr. & upwards	All other white inhab- itants	Free persons of color	Servants or slaves
[211‡†] Young Stokes	1	4		
[212‡†] Wiley Hilyard	1	5		
[213‡†] Philip Underwood	1	4		
[214‡†] Richd Graves	2	6		
[215] Samuel Lunsford	1	3		
[216‡†] Francis Nash	1	4		
[217‡†] James B. Martin	1	8		
[218‡†] Thomas Harper	1	6		
[219] William Corder	1	1		
[220] Stephen Michel	1	3		
[221‡†] John Ewing	1	6		
[222‡†] William Nash	1	4		
[223‡†] James Conn	1	8		
[224‡†] William Lock	1	3		
[225‡†] James McNeal	1	2		
[226‡†] William Counsil	1			
[227‡†] James Jaggers	2	7		
[228‡†] Arch^d Farr	1	4		
[229] Rufus Farmer	1	6		
[230] Nathan Farmer	1	1		
[231‡†] William Cross	3	3		
[232] John Hawkins	1	5		
[233‡†] William Whitnell	1	6		
[234‡†] Eli Stewert	1	6		
[235‡†] John Elliott	2	8		
[236‡†] James Devenport	1	1		
[237‡†] George Graham	3	5		
[238‡†] William Gilston	3	3		
[239‡†] Henry Vansicle	1	2		
[240‡†] Burnside Philips	1	1		
[241‡†] Betsey Thrash		6		
[242] Polly Gallant		5		
[243] William Hughs	1	9		
[244] David Hughs	1	5		
[245‡†] John Kenneday	1	6		
[246‡†] James Meredith	2	11		
[247] Thomas Cohoon	1	5		

CENSUS OF WHITE COUNTY, 1818 (*Continued*)

Names of heads of families	Free white males 21 yr. & upwards	All other white inhab- itants	Free persons of color	Servants or slaves
[248‡†] James Dunlap	1	8		
[249‡†] Jonathan Williams	1	5		
[250] Jonathan Shelby	1	6		
[251] Thomas Carna	1	3		
[252‡†] Walter Jacobs	1	9		
[253‡†] Moses Thompson	1	10		1
[254] Betsy Hughs		9		
[255‡†] Thomas Gray	1	3		
[256‡†] James Hambleton	1	7		
[257] William Whitford	1	4		
[258] Jesse Hendricks	1	2		
[259‡†] Amos Howell	2	8		
[260] Barney Chambers	1	1		
[261‡†] James Potter	1	7		
[262] David Robertson	2	10		
[263‡†] John Taylor	1	9		2
[264] John Curry	1	2		
[265] William Harris	1	7		
[266‡†] Stephen Stanley	2	6		
[267] James C Williams	1	3		
[268‡†] Samuel Hencely	1	2		
[269‡†] Nelly Read		6		
[270‡†] Bazil Daniel	1	8		
[271‡†] Jesse Hearing	1	3		
[272‡†] Thomas Forsythe	1	3		
[273] John Buckils	1	12		
[274‡†] Aron Williams	1	11		
[275‡†] John Lucas	3	5		
[276‡†] George Sturn	1	3		
[277] George Steel	1	4		
[278‡†] Green Baker	1	5		
[279] Andrew Read	1	3		
[280‡†] Moses Carlock	2	9		
[281‡†] Benjn Bryon	1	6		
[282‡†] John Graham	1	6		
[283‡†] Joseph Patton	2	3		
[284] James Gregory	1	7		

CENSUS OF WHITE COUNTY, 1818 (*Continued*)

Names of heads of families	Free white males 21 yr. & upwards	All other white inhabitants	Free persons of color	Servants or slaves
[285‡*] John Jorden	1	5		
[286] Benjn White	5	4	2	2
[287] Lowrey Hay	10	8		2
[288] Benjn Bloomer	1	3		
[289‡†] Willis Hargrave	3	6		14
[290] Mathew Moss	1	1		
[291‡†] Mordica Hambleton	1	5		
[292‡†] Pearce Hawley	1	2		
[293‡†] John Hanna	3	9		
[294] John Hay	4	1		1
[295‡†] Alexd Hammelton	1	5		
[296] Peter Simpson	1	5		
[297‡†] William Brown	1	2		
[298] Stacy McDaniel	1	8		
[299‡†] Jerremiah Hargrave	2	2		
[300‡†] Jerremiah More	1	13		
[301‡†] Robert More	1	1		
[302‡†] Isaac Hill	1	7		
[303*] Joel Page	1	9		
[304‡†] John Manus	1	2		
[305‡†] Thos Mccallister	1	2		
[306] Robert Elder	2	3		
[307‡†] Saml Hogg	2	4		1
[308‡†] George Long	2	2		
[309‡†] John Carter	1	4		
[310] Robert Whitaker	1	7		
[311] Isaac Jones	1	3		
[312] Susanna Mcrary		7		
[313] Abraham Groce	1	7		
[314‡†] James Hanna	2	1		
[315‡†] Willis Cherry	1	8		2
[316‡†] John Clark	1	7		
[317‡†] Francis Miller	2	6		
[318‡†] Aron Williams	1	1		
[319‡†] Joseph Pumroy	1	8		
[320‡†] Charles Mobley	1	4		
[321] Robert Lane	1	6		

CENSUS OF WHITE COUNTY, 1818 (*Continued*)

Names of heads of families	Free white males 21 yr. & upwards	All other white inhabitants	Free persons of color	Servants or slaves
[322‡†] Edward D Hart	1	2		
[323] Ersilla Davis		6		
[324‡†] William Merrill	1	5		
[325‡†] Abraham Griffith	1	5		
[326‡†] James McCoy	1	9		
[327‡†] Thomas Southerd	1	3		
[328] Mary Estes		2		
[329‡†] Thomas Logan	1	1		
[330‡†] Alexᵈ Logan	1	3		
[331‡†] John Mathews	1	6		
[332‡†] Balaam May	2	6		
[333] Alanson Dawdy	1	7		
[334] Saml Garrison	1	2		
[335‡†] James Garrison	2	9		
[336‡†] Anna Bowie		2		
[337‡†] Morgan Wallis	1	4		
[338‡†] Saml Slocumb	1	5		
[339‡†] John C Slocumb	3	9		1
[340] Isham Blankinship	1	3		
[341‡†] John Baker	1	1		
[342‡†] Jacob Baker	1	4		
[343] James Graham	4	5		2
[344] James A. Richerdson	3	3		
[345] James Carlile	1	3		
[346‡†] Francis Smith		2		
[347‡†] John Craw	7	5		1
[348‡†] Charles Williams	2	2		
[349] Evins Brock	1	3		
[350‡†] Daniel Hay	1	5		
[351] Samuel Kimberly	3	6		
[352‡†] James Garrison	1	6		
[353‡†] Christopher Funkhouser	1	4		
[354‡†] John Funkhouser	1	4		
[355] Robert Funkhouser	1	4		1
[356] James Fitzjereld	1	1		
[357‡†] James Gray	2	5		4
[358‡†] James Ratcliff	1	6	1	5

CENSUS OF WHITE COUNTY, 1818 (*Continued*)

Names of heads of families	Free white males 21 yr. & upwards	All other white inhab- itants	Free persons of color	Servants or slaves
[359] James E. Throckmorton	2	1		
[360] Luke Vaughn	1	6		
[361‡†] Robert Carlile	1	2		
[362] William Mc entire	1	6		
[363‡†] James Shipley	1	6		
[364‡†] Joshua Riggan	1	5		
[365] Benjamin Sumpter	1	3		
[366] Lydna North	1	5		
[367] Arthur Fowler	1	7		
[368‡†] Robert Shipley	1	7		
[369] Daniel Bain	3			
[370‡†] Thomas Ezell	2	7		
[371] Enoch Berry, Jn	1	6		
[372] David Wooley Jr	4	3		
[373‡†] Henry Wooley	2	4		
[374] William Stephenson	1			
[375‡†] George Berry	2	6		
[376‡†] John Sumpter	2	4		
[377] David Wooley	1	2		
[378‡†] Carnaby Stevens	1	7		
[379‡†] Noah Stevens	1	2		
[380‡†] Adam Dosier	2	7		
[381‡†] John Barbra	1	4		
[382] Henry Harris	1			
[383‡†] John Armstrong	1	12		1
[384‡†] John Mires	1	2		
[385] John Mires jr	1	6		
[386‡†] Henry Mires	1	5		
[387‡†] William Hosick	1	9		
[388‡†] Alexd Mahan	1	4		
[389‡†] Achelus Pearson	1	3		
[390‡†] Seth Hargrave	1	1		1
[391] Peggy Lyons	1	7		
[392‡†] Robert Story	1	8		
[393‡†] George Story	2	4		
[394‡†] John McLelland	1	3		
[395‡†] George Story, Jr	1	3		

CENSUS OF WHITE COUNTY, 1818 (*Continued*)

Names of heads of families	Free white males 21 yr. & upwards	All other white inhab- itants	Free persons of color	Servants or slaves
[396‡†] Andrew Story	1	5		
[397‡†] John Ferguson	1	4		
[398‡†] William Fields	1	2		
[399‡†] William Davidson	1	8		
[400‡†] Saml Craig	1	10		
[401‡†] David Upton	1	7		
[402‡†] David Calvert	2	6		
[403‡†] Frederick Farmer	2	7		1
[404‡†] William Farmer	2	2		
[405‡†] Elijah Mayfield	1	5		
[406‡†] William Watson	1	6		
[407‡†] Jacob Barker	1	9		
[408‡†] John Wilson	1	5		
[409] Jacob Conner	2	4		
[410‡†] Randolph Smith	1	7		
[411‡†] Thomas Smith	1	2		
[412‡†] Elijah Parker	2	4		
[413] James Claybrook	1	5		
[414‡†] John Hardesty	1	4		
[415‡†] John Haynes	2	6		
[416‡†] William Wheeler	1	9		
[417‡†] Wm Wheeler Jr	3	4		
[418‡†] Willis Wheeler	2	7		
[419] James Gaston	2	5		
[420] William Claybrook	1	5		
[421] Saml Ernsparger	1	3		
[422‡†] Elisha Gorden	1	3		
[423‡†] Edward Gatland	1	7		
[424] Fisher Rice	1	3		
[425‡†] Elijah Kimsey	2	2		
[426‡†] Jesse Hiatt	1	6		
[427‡†] John C Gore	3	3		
[428] Saml Stanfield	2	8		
[429] Anthony Street	1	9		
[430‡†] Isaac Veach	1	4		
[431‡†] Peter Miller	2	9		
[432‡†] Mathew Wilson	1	5		

CENSUS OF WHITE COUNTY, 1818 (*Continued*)

Names of heads of families	Free white males 21 yr. & upwards	All other white inhab-itants	Free persons of color	Servants or slaves
[433‡†] Christopher Nation	1	11		
[434‡†] Robert Hawthorn	1	5		
[435‡†] Simon Newman	2	4		2
[436‡†] Asa Ross	2	4		
[437‡†] John Gillison	1	5		
[438] Hiram Jones	1	1		
[439‡†] Levi Morgan			3	
[440‡†] Noah Kuykendall	1	5		
[441] Oliver Simpson	1	3		
[442] John Nixon	1	2		
[443‡†] Jacob Bozeman	1	9		
[444] Moses Page	1	2		
[445‡†] George McCown	2	9		
[446‡†] Solloman Mayberry	1	4		
[447] James Warren	1	7		
[448‡†] William Lucas	1	4		
[449‡†] George Hoover	1	14		
[450] Daniel Hoover	1	2		
[451‡†] James Philips	1	6		
[452‡†] John More	2	5		
[453‡†] David Daniel	2	10		
[454‡†] William Stanley		6		
[455‡†] Julas Driggers	1	8		
[456‡†] Isaac Driggers	1	1		
[457‡†] Absolam Driggins	1	2		
[458] John Price	1	1		
[459] Rebekah Corl		7		
[460] Saml Yandle	1	5		
[461] Eliazer Cohoon	1	8		
[462] John Cannada	1	4		
[463] John Pea	1	2		
[464‡†] James Bryant	1	6		
[465] John Vickery	1	2		
[466] Nathan Harris	3	6		
[467‡†] Edmon Covington	1	9		
[468‡†] Richd Davis	1	3		
[469‡†] Daniel Boltinghouse	3	11		

CENSUS OF WHITE COUNTY, 1818 (*Continued*)

Names of heads of families	Free white males 21 yr. & upwards	All other white inhab- itants	Free persons of color	Servants or slaves
[470] John Mothrall	1	11		
[471‡†] Richd Haynes	2	4		
[472] Susan Hahn		9		
[473‡†] Daniel Brown	1	6		
[474‡†] Jonathan Stewert	1	6		
[475‡†] Daniel Brown, Jr	1	2		
[476‡†] James Hodkins	1	5		
[477] George Jameson	1	6		
[478‡†] William Long	1	3		
[479] William Warren	2	4		
[480] Samuel Huntsinger	1	2		
[481‡†] Alexd Philips	2	4		
[482‡†] John Brown	1	1		
[483] Elisabeth Fields		4		
[484‡†] Josiah Daniels	1	6		
[485‡†] Thomas Pool	1	4		
[486‡†] William Hood	1	2		
[487] John Sturn	1	1		
[488‡†] James Hood	2	6		
[489‡†] James Boyd	2	3		
[490‡†] John McIntire	2	6		
[491‡†] Philip Patton	2	6		
[492‡†] John Short	1	8		
[493‡†] George Morris	1	1		
[494‡†] Sarah Hood		6		
[495] John Sturn	1	4		
[496] Joseph Dixon	1	1	1	
[497‡†] Henry Sturn	1	3		
[498‡†] Arthur Pool	1	6		
[499] William Baldwin	1	4		
[500] Moses Sweeton	1	3		
[501‡†] John Dennis	3	9		
[502‡†] John Robeson	1	3		
[503‡†] James Finly	1	2		
[504] Edmon Fears	2	6		
[505] Susan Clark		4		
[506‡†] Jesse Hubbard	1	7		

CENSUS OF WHITE COUNTY, 1818 (*Continued*)

Names of heads of families	Free white males 21 yr. & upwards	All other white inhab- itants	Free persons of color	Servants or slaves
[507‡†] John Holland	1	2		
[508‡†] Michael Collins	1	4		
[509‡†] Roley Williams	1	2		
[510‡†] Nathl Blackford	1	3		
[511‡†] Henry Grimes	1	3		
[512‡†] Mary Blackford		6		
[513] Mary Randolph		6		
[514] Robert Gaston	1	3		
[515‡†] William Barnes	1	6		
[516‡†] William Vines	1	6		
[517‡†] John Anderson	3	2		
[518] John Hinch	1			
[519] John Sanford	1	6		
[520] George Sanford	1	5		
[521] William Simpson	1	7		
[522] Luke Holmes	1	4		
[523] William Nash	2	9		
[524‡†] Merret Tayler	1	4		
[525] John Culbeth	1	9		
[526] Asa Benton	1	3		
[527] Joseph Boon	1	5		
[528] Robert Stewart	1	5		
[529] William Clark	1	5		
[530‡†] William Withro	1	5		
[531] James Barlow	1	5		
[532] Hugh McCammon	1	5		
[533‡*] Henry B Maxy	1	2		
[534‡*] John Wilkerson	1	8		
[535*] James Johnson	1	6		
[536‡*] Lucy Robertson	1	6		
[537‡*] Peter Fannon	2	3		
[538‡*] Maxwell Wilkey	1	4		
[539‡*] Saml Bradford	1	4		
[540‡*] Abner Bradford	1	1		
[541‡*] Barton Atcheson	1	2		
[542‡*] Joseph Read	1	3		
[543‡*] Demps Hood	2	5		

CENSUS OF WHITE COUNTY, 1818 (*Continued*)

Names of heads of families	Free white males 21 yr. & upwards	All other white inhab- itants	Free persons of color	Servants or slaves
[544‡*] Daniel Crenshaw	1	8	1	
[545‡†] Thomas Thompson	1	4		
[546‡†] Hiram				
William Hodge	2	6		
[547‡†] James Davis	1	5		
[548‡†] William Hungate	1	9		
[549‡†] John Bishop	1	6		
[550‡†] Andrew Vance	1	8		
[551‡†] Wᵐ Veach	1	1		
[552*] Benjn Bishop	1	3		
[553‡†] Nimrod Shirley	1	7		
[554‡†] Ambrose Maulding	1	9		2
[555‡†] John Anderson	1	6		
[556‡†] Ennes Maulding	1	5		
[557‡†] James Maulding	2	5		
[558] Richᵈ Maulding	1	3		
[559‡†] George Crisle	2	9		
[560] Henry Crisle	1	6		
[561‡†] Jarrot Trammel	1	10		2
[562‡†] John Griffith	1	3		
[563‡†] Malleki Hubbard	1	4		
[564] Guilford Parrish	1	4		
[565] John King	1	6		
[566] James Addams	1	3		
[567‡†] Carter Smith	1	1		
[568‡†] Joseph gooden	1	1		
[569‡†] George Saturfield	1	3		
[570] John Stovall	1	4		
[571‡†] Saml Smith	1	4		
[572‡†] Charls Herd	1	6		
Total	720	2752	11	56

List of Souls in
White County Ill T.
Total *3539*

CENSUS OF WHITE COUNTY, 1818 (*Concluded*)

[*Recapitulation*:]

Free white males 21 years and upwards	720
All other white inhabitants	2751
Free persons of color	11
Servants or slaves	57
Total	3539

INDEX

cers, W., 484[1]
cken, W., 263
dams, J., 601
dkins, J., 105
lcorn, J., 188, 769
lcorn, W., 694
lcorn, *see also* Holcorn
lexander, R., 237
lexander, Wm., 335
lkens, J., 884
llen, B., 106
llen, G., 785
llen, J., 426
llen, S., 175
llen, T., 142
llens, S., 784
mlaw, J., 1076
nderson, Dad., 219
nderson, J., 220, 380, 573
nderson, W., 213
ndrew, W., 652
place, J., 641
place, O., 640
rnald, J., 1047
rnald, W., 1046, 1052
rneld, D., 829
rnell, B., 1063
rshambo, Jos., 5

ackus, Elijah, 6
aeney, W., 1038
ags, E., 825
ags, J., 826
ailey, J., 152
aker, G., 514
aker, Geo., 20
akey, Jno., 63
aley, W., 541, 952

Bane, J., 906
Baney, L., 1074
Banford, W., 421
Bankston, R., 412
Barbeu, A., 288
Barbeu, M., 291
Barker, L., 568
Barnett, H., 711
Barnett, Wm., 204
Barnhart, J., 788
Barten, J., 581
Barutel, J., 46
Barutell, J., 61
Batey, J., 216
Batrite, T., 973
Baty, J., 656
Been, N., 102
Belcore, J., 309
Belfon, W., 931
Bell, P., 588
Ben & Betty, 472
Bennett, B., 599
Berry, J., 441
Bienvenu, A., 52
Bienvenu, M., 47
Bienvenue, A., 64
Biers, W., 402
Bilderback, D., 186
Bilderback, E., 184
Bilderback, J., 100
Bird, N., 881
Bird, W., 878
Bires, J., 255
Birks, S., 482
Black, D., 259
Black, J., 515
Black, T., 257
Blackford, E., 1015

[1] This and succeeding numbers refer, not to pages, but to numbers assigned l the county lists.

Blackford, N., 876
Blackford, W., 874, 1013
Blair, A., 670
Blau, *Madam,* 294
Blau, A., 296, 805
Blau, C., 314
Blau, D., 715
Blau, F., 247
Blau, J., 317
Blau, M., 713
Blevins, J., 503
Blocker, J., 238
Boggs, W., 896
Boise, B., 749
Boise, G., 750
Bolding, J., 550
Bolston, H., 348
Boman, J., 1020
Bonn, H., 815
Bonn, J., 814
Bonn, S., 818
Bons, P., 1000
Boon, Wm., 244
Bosso, L., 1064
Bowerman, S., 392
Bradberry, J., 1003
Bradley, G., 903
Bradley, J., 809
Bradley, S., 780
Bradley, Wm., 342
Brasel, D., 887
Brasell, G., 889
Brasell, R., 888
Bratcher, J., 869
Brewer, M., 21
Brewer, W., 731
Bridges, J., 899
Bridley, C., 776
Brikey, G., 361
Brisland, B., 474
Brithart, J., 131
Brooks, J., 1082
Brown, D., 823
Brown, E., 479
Brown, G., 822

Brown, J., 714, 824
Brownen, E., 409
Buchanen, A., 1061
Buckles, J., 1025
Burba, A., 170
Burns, J., 773
Burway, J., 1029
Butler &c., 720
Buyatt, Luys, 43
Buyatt, M., 48
Buyatt, N., 72

Campbell, C., 1050
Campbell, J., 200, 478
Campbell, *see also* Tampbile, Trampbile
Canidy, J., 935
Carpenter, C., 755
Carperter, E., 76
Carson, Henry, 420
Carter, J., 344, 424, 631
Casey, J., 560
Casey, L., 941
Casey, R., 559
Cassee, P., 388
Casson, A., 49
Cates, R., 999
Chaffen, E., 920
Chaffin, W., 339
Chamberlin, B., 67
Chamberlin, L., 51
Chandler, J., 252
Charleville, M., 62
Check, F., 438
Chick, J., 775
Chick, W., 497
Childers, W., 565
Chrozier, S., 199
Clap, A., 806
Clapp, A., 804
Clark, A., 993
Clark, E., 337
Clark, J., 110, 801, 990
Claxton, B., 111
Clay, J., 666

Clemens, G., 675
Clendennen, J., 115
Clerk, E., 391
Clow, J., 1085
Cochrin, G., 157
Cochrin, J., 762
Cochrin, Sam., 147
Cochrin, W., 427
Cochrin, Wm., 148
Cock, A., 533
Cod, G., 527
Cohn, J., 689
Colbert, E., 626
Colier, D., 687
Collow, N., 1072
Colvert, B., 480
Colwell, A., 433
Commins, B., 435
Comoke, S., 989
Compton, L., 1059
Conie, A., 1075
Conner, Henry, 329
Conner, W., 781
Conway, Clemt. C., 11
Coon, P., 571
Coper, J., 756
Copper, D., 649
Copper, J., 539
Copper, S., 531
Costley, S., 812
Coteleve, Mam, 304
Cotino, A., 316
Couch, J., 218
Cox, A., 223
Cox, R., 400
Crain, L., 746
Crandle, G., 712
Crane, B., 121
Crane, J., 120, 128
Craw, J., 487
Crawfort, J., 93
Cribens, J., 900
Crith, G., 150
Crofard, E., 202
Crofard, J., 671

Cropper, S., 345
Cunble, D., 831
Cup, H., Jr., 570
Cup, H., Sr., 569

Damon, Mam, 320
Damwood, J., 494
Daniel, M., 966
Daniel, W., 537
Daniels, G., 1021
Daniels, J., 87, 961
Daniels, W., 277, 278
Darden, J., 524
Darker, M., 1042
Darneal, G., 411
Davenport, A., 464
Davenport, M. S., 465
Davis, C., 249
Davis, G., 838
Davis, J., 251, 264, 500, 763
Davis, Jas., 161
Davis, Jno., 162
Davis, M., 250, 733
Davis, N., 254
Davis, S., 26
Davy, Aguslau, 189
Dear, N., 1084
Deblaw, J., 1080
Declue, B., 311
Dees, D., 232
Dees, J., 226
Dees, R., 208
Degagnez, M., 40
Degamu, M., 321
Deen, J., 722
Dejin, Philipi, 1073
Dennis, G., 783
Dent, J., 235
Deprist, J., 547
Derousse, J., 38
Deruse, M., 41
Devegne, Jos., 56
Devers, N., 401
Dice, Danl., 12
Dick, D., 370

Steel, J., Jr., 394
Steel, J., Sr., 393
Stephenson, B., 2
Stewart, A., 140
Stilley, S., 583
Stillwell, J., 1062
Stimpson, J., 745
Stites, W., 890
Storey, G., 632
Storey, J., 630
Storm, G., 19
Story, J., 637
Strate, J., 1055
Strong, W., 506
Stubblefield, J., 356
Stublefield, Tho., 112
Swearingen, Tho., 1

Tamel, D., 971
Tampbile, W., 970
Taylor, E., 287
Taylor, H., 979
Taylor, J., 736
Taylor, S., 284
Taylor, Wilkens & Co., 419
Tebou, F., 292
Teeters, A., 378
Tenney, J., 752
Thom, Solo, 15
Thomas, Jesse B., 23
Thompson, A., 198, 266
Thompson, E., 267
Thompson, J., 217, 359
Thompson, R., 215, 778
Thompson, T., 1049
Thornberry, W., 466
Throp, D., 1086
Tilford, J., 719
Tilley, J., 582
Tindle, J. L., 748
Tindle, R., 130
Titteswon, G., 716
Togon, J., 1068
Togon, T., 1067
Tolor, T., 149

Tolwiyh, J., 201
Tongo, F., 306
Touluse, F., 96
Traler, A., 351
Trampbile, D., 969
Trampbile, G., 972
Trampbile, P., 447, 974
Trokey, J., 318
Trousdal, J., 452
Tupon, F., 1069
Twidey, R., 846

Upton, J., 1009

Vanrix, D., 1091
Vanxl, E., 868
Vanxl, J., 867
Vawn, J., 611
Vermition, B., 358
Vickrey, C., 684
Vinard, J., 600

Waddle, G., 965
Wager, D., 285
Wait, J., 934
Wakely, L., 78
Waldon, B., 623
Walker, B., 240
Walker, W., 782
Waller, R., 413, 655, 839
Wallis, J., 562
Walsey, J., 946
Walters, S., 695
Ware, R., 771
Ware, W., 765
Watker, J., 425
Watson, W., 519
Weakes, J., 1026
Wearthington, J., 810
Weathernton, J., 796
Weathernton, S., 795
Weatherston, J., 779
Weaver, J., 723
Welch, W., 269
Weles, W., 509

[1]This and succeeding numbers refer, not to pages, but to numbers assigned in the county lists.

Anderson, Alexander W.
Madison, 61
Anderson, David
Pope, 232
Anderson, Ezekel
Crawford, 364
Anderson, George
Crawford, 105
Anderson, Ignatious
Bond, 69
Anderson, James
Crawford, 467
Anderson, John
Pope, 7
White, 517, 555
Anderson, Joseph
Crawford, 174
Anderson, Lucy
Gallatin, 553
Anderson, Muryan
Crawford, 433
Anderson, Robert
Washington, 280
Anderson, Robert G.
Madison, 236
Anderson, Susanna
Crawford, 291
Anderson, Thomas
Crawford, 320
Anderson, William
Crawford, 468
Gallatin, 64
Andrews, Joseph
Jackson, 214
Andrus, Archibald
Washington, 79
Ankeney, John
Jackson, 68
Antigo
St. Clair, 502
Aplen, Jesse
Franklin, 70
Apling, Pleasant
Washington, 203
Apperson, David
Gallatin, 22

Archer, Charles K.
Crawford, 47
Archer, Hezekiah
Bond, 188
Archer, Israel
Bond, 194
Archer, Moses
Madison, 230
Archer, William
Bond, 189
Archer, William B.
Crawford, 361
Archer, Zachariah
Crawford, 366
Armor, Oliver
Union, 376
Armstrong, Aron
Madison, 426
Armstrong, Elizabeth
Franklin, 7
Armstrong, George
Madison, 66
Armstrong, Jas.
Franklin, 25
Armstrong, John
Pope, 298
White, 383
Armstrong, Joshua
Madison, 171
Armstrong, Nathaniel
Gallatin, 176
Armstrong, Robert
Franklin, 87
Madison, 170
Washington, 99
Armstrong, Susanah
Madison, 425
Armstrong, Thomas
Madison, 26
Armstrong, William
Madison, 221
Arndell, David
Union, 255
Arnett, Jas.
Franklin, 40

Bain, Daniel
  White, 369
Bain, Daniel, Jr.
  White, 187
Bain, James
  Johnson, 5
Bains, John C.
  White, 191
Baird, William
  Madison, 19
Baker, Abraham
  Washington, 23
Baker, Absalom
  Madison, 43
Baker, Absolam
  Madison, 41, 48
Baker, Benjamin
  Gallatin, 524
Baker, Coonrad
  Franklin, 26
Baker, Edmond
  Franklin, 98
Baker, Elijah
  Johnson, 111
Baker, Green
  White, 278
Baker, Isaac N.
  Gallatin, 361
Baker, Jacob
  White, 342
Baker, James
  Johnson, 113
Baker, Jeter
  Gallatin, 284
Baker, John
  Crawford, 214
  Gallatin, 608
  White, 341
Baker, Joseph
  Gallatin, 440
Baker, Robert
  Bond, 76
Baker, William
  Crawford, 465
  Jackson, 95

Baldin, Elisha
  Gallatin, 118
Baldin, Isaac
  Gallatin, 487
Baldwin, Francis
  Monroe, 79
Baldwin, William
  White, 499
Ball, Aaron
  Crawford, 19
Ball, Risen
  Crawford, 421
Baly, James
  Gallatin, 572
Baney, Banaja
  Union, 206
Bankson, Andrew
  Washington, 112
Bankson, Elijah
  Washington, 38
Bankson, James
  Washington, 36
Bankston, Richard
  Franklin, 50
Baptiste, Louis
  Madison, 689
Barbee, William
  Crawford, 335
Barber, Joseph
  Bond, 126
Barber, Luck
  Gallatin, 542
Barbour, John
  Madison, 144
Barbra, John
  White, 381
Baringer, Henry
  Union, 226
Barker, Daniel
  Monroe, 21
Barker, Jacob
  White, 407
Barker, John
  Gallatin, 350
  Union, 240

Beck, Paul
  Bond, 90
Beck, Paul, Jr.
  Bond, 205
Beck, Stephen
  Gallatin, 70
Beckett, Baptiste
  Madison, 704
Beckwourth, Daniel
  Crawford, 63
Beckwourth, George
  Crawford, 109
Beckwourth, Samuel G.
  Crawford, 314
Beeman, James
  Madison, 313
Beeman, Orman
  Madison, 555
Beeman, Samuel
  Madison, 317
Beggs, Alexandria
  Union, 173, 316
Beggs, Arichibel
  Union, 182
Beggs, Isaac
  Union, 134
Beggs, Robert
  Union, 149
Beldeback, Daniel
  Jackson, 196
Belford, Bengamin
  Pope, 120
Belford, William
  Pope, 209
Belfort, Louis
  Madison, 594
Bellah, Ruben
  Gallatin, 204
Belle, Francis
  Madison, 302
Belle, Jessee
  Madison, 118
Belloow, Jas.
  Monroe, 216
Belsha, George
  Madison, 108

Bennet, James B.
  Crawford, 432
Bennet, Wm. P.
  Crawford, 436
Bennett, Richard
  Pope, 148
Benton, Asa
  White, 526
Berger, Jacob
  Gallatin, 47
Berry, Enoch
  White, 92
Berry, Enoch, Jr.
  White, 371
Berry, George
  White, 375
Berry, Joel
  White, 75
Berry, John
  Crawford, 185
  Madison, 262
Berry, Jonathan
  Bond, 159
Berry, William
  Gallatin, 285
  Randolph, 13
Bery, John
  Gallatin, 383
Bethel, Chester
  Gallatin, 373
Biddick, Samuel
  Franklin, 170
Bigerstaff, William
  Union, 211
Billingsly, Bazzel
  Union, 105
Billingsly, Charles
  Madison, 412
Billue, Joseph
  Washington, 160
Bird, James
  Gallatin, 296
Birdon, Reuben
  Gallatin, 359
Bishop, Benjn.
  White, 552

Bonner, Alexander
Madison, 124
Bonner, Henry
Madison, 123
Boon, Joseph
White, 527
Boon, Mary
Union, 57
Boon, Peter
Crawford, 271
Boon, Squire
Union, 63
Boon, William
Jackson, 17
Boren, Hoza
Union, 183
Boren, John
Union, 178
Boren, Margain
Union, 176
Boren, Susanna
Union, 177
Boren, Willis
Johnson, 38
Borer, Jacob
Monroe, 95
Borough, Joseph
Madison, 711
Bostel, Nathaniel
Union, 201
Boutwell, Leony
Gallatin, 106
Boutwell, Stephen
Gallatin, 85
Bowers, Charles
Jackson, 204
Bowie, Anna
White, 336
Bowles, John
Jackson, 94
Bowling, Benjamin
Bond, 139
Bowling, James
Bond, 135
Bowls, William
Gallatin, 60

Bowman, Bengeman
Pope, 256
Bowman, John
Johnson, 98
Boxley, George
Washington, 247
Boyd, James
White, 489
Bozeman, Jacob
White, 443
Brackin, Isaac
Gallatin, 393
Bradburry, Wm.
Crawford, 371
Bradbury, Elisha
Crawford, 74
Bradford, Abner
White, 540
Bradford, Saml.
White, 539
Bradley, Chals.
Union, 276
Bradley, Jacob
Monroe, 169
Bradley, John
Union, 374
Bradley, Reuben
Monroe, 132
Bradsby, William H.
Washington, 248
Bradshaw, Absalum
Monroe, 27
Bradshaw, Ann
Madison, 115
Bradshaw, Elizabeth
Union, 168
Bradshaw, James
Monroe, 164
Bradshaw, John
Union, 355
Bradshaw, Jonas
Madison, 114
Bramblett, John
Gallatin, 389
Bramlett, Benj.
Gallatin, 382

Bramlett, Henry
  Gallatin, 381
Bramscomb, Roland
  Madison, 537
Braner, John
  Pope, 205
Branstetter, Peter
  Washington, 11
Brasele, George
  Johnson, 54
Brasilton, Benjamin
  Washington, 91
Brassell, Robert
  Madison, 229
Bratton, Andrew
  Gallatin, 330
Bratton, George W.
  Crawford, 101
Bratton, Saml.
  Gallatin, 263
Brazil, Valentine
  Washington, 162
Breeze, Thomas
  Madison, 195
Brewer, Nathan
  Monroe, 6
Brewer, William
  Jackson, 169
Bridger, Joseph
  Gallatin, 84
Bridges, Allen
  Madison, 25
Bridges, George
  Madison, 172
Bridges, John
  Johnson, 43
Bridges, Robt. K.
  Gallatin, 170
Bridges, William
  Madison, 406
Bridgman, David
  Gallatin, 412
Bridgman, Joseph
  Gallatin, 429
Bridgman, Nathan
  Gallatin, 410

Bridgwater, Zachariah
  Bond, 168
Briggs, Robert
  Bond, 162
Brigham, Joseph
  Madison, 706
Brigman, John
  Crawford, 463
Brill, Solomon
  White, 112
Brimberry, Isaac
  Crawford, 155
Brimberry, John
  Monroe, 34
Brimberry, Samuel
  Crawford, 292
Brimbury, Jacob
  Washington, 300
Brisco, John
  Madison, 23
Brite, Daniel
  Crawford, 61
Brock, Evins
  White, 349
Brock, George
  Monroe, 159
Brockelbank, John
  Crawford, 469
Brotherton, Abraham
  Jackson, 99
Browder, Jonathan
  Washington, 156
Brown, Aloscous
  Crawford, 17
Brown, Archibald
  White, 208
Brown, Aron B.
  Johnson, 29
Brown, Benj. C.
  Gallatin, 155
Brown, Chad
  Madison, 308
Brown, Coleman
  Gallatin, 379
Brown, Colier
  Washington, 16

Brunk, John
  Madison, 564
Bryan, Daniel
  Monroe, 10
Bryans, James
  Crawford, 171
Bryant, Elijah
  Union, 103
Bryant, James
  White, 464
Bryant, Prince
  Monroe, 54
Bryon, Benjn.
  White, 281
Buck, Joseph
  Madison, 359
Buck, Warner
  Gallatin, 127
Buckils, John
  White, 273
Buckmaster, Nathaniel
  Madison, 492
Buckner, Henry
  Crawford, 121
Buckner, James
  Pope, 271
Bug, Henry
  Union, 48
Bugg, William
  Washington, 171
Bunch, James
  Washington, 270
Bunch, John
  Washington, 269
Burden, John
  Union, 7
Burdsill, Waren
  Pope, 165
Burdsill, William
  Pope, 164
Burgess, William
  Bond, 140
Burk, Charles
  Johnson, 20
Burk, Richard
  Johnson, 19

Burnes, Crawford
  Franklin, 24
Burnes, Elijah
  Franklin, 76
Burnes, Stephen
  Franklin, 79
Burnes, Wm.
  Franklin, 80
Burnett, Will
  Gallatin, 426
Burns, Thomas
  Jackson, 44
Burnside, James
  Bond, 52
Burnside, Samuel
  Jackson, 223
Burrell, Joseph
  White, 70
Burton, Gibbon
  Bond, 55
Butcher, George
  Jackson, 4
Butcher, Jacob
  Jackson, 32
  Union, 30
Butcher, Samuel
  Union, 37
Butler, Charles
  Washington, 188
Butler, Elijah
  Gallatin, 378
Butler, James
  Crawford, 203
Butterfield, Jonas
  Crawford, 126
Byars, John
  Jackson, 3
Byran, Alexnr.
  Madison, 569

Cade, Simon
  Gallatin, 54
Cadwell, George
  Madison, 371
Cain, James
  Gallatin, 44

Chapman, Saml.
White, 145
Chappel, Comstock
White, 50
Chardy, Benjamin
Crawford, 444
Cheach, Isem
Gallatin, 416
Cheach, James
Gallatin, 242
Cheach, Mark
Gallatin, 235
Cheake, Wm.
Gallatin, 295
Cheek, Joel
Crawford, 129
Cheek, Willis
Madison, 626
Chenowith, John
Crawford, 210
Cherry, Wm.
Johnson, 26
Cherry, Willis
White, 315
Chesney, Alexander
Washington, 30
Chipps, Amos
Pope, 141
Chism, John
White, 207
Choat, Squire
Johnson, 99
Choplin, Nicholas
Gallatin, 413
Christem, Wm.
Gallatin, 446
Church, Robert
Madison, 592
Cilbern, William D.
Crawford, 347
Clampet, Nethan
Pope, 317
Clanton, Sion
Union, 194
Clap, Adam, Sr.
Union, 371

Clap, Adam, Jr.
Union, 363
Clark, Alexander
Jackson, 105
Clark, Edward
Monroe, 43
Clark, Felix
Monroe, 7
Clark, Isaac
Madison, 16
Clark, Jacob
Monroe, 12
Clark, John
Madison, 385
White, 316
Clark, Johnathan
Union, 188
Clark, Owen S.
Pope, 54
Clark, Saml.
Gallatin, 149
Clark, Susan
White, 505
Clark, William
Madison, 250
White, 529
Clarke, Anesly
Gallatin, 212
Clarke, Joseph
Gallatin, 94
Clary, John
Bond, 8
Washington, 111
Clavert, John, Sr.
Pope, 80
Clavert, John, Jr.
Pope, 81
Clay, Ezekel
Pope, 97
Clay, Isam
Pope, 149
Claybrook, James
White, 413
Claybrook, William
White, 420

Claypole, Jeremiah
  Madison, 88
Clemson, E. B.
  Gallatin, 609
Clerk, William
  Bond, 171
Click, Peter
  Union, 324
Clift, James
  Gallatin, 98
Cline, George
  Jackson, 173
Clover, Jacob
  Monroe, 209
Cluts, Henry
  Union, 386
Coal, Eady
  Crawford, 78
Coalmen, Jude
  Union, 405
Cobb, Allen
  Crawford, 488
Coburn, Jonathan
  White, 8
Cochran, George
  Jackson, 179
Cochran, Moses
  Johnson, 30
Cochren, Charles
  Gallatin, 558
Cocks, Anthony
  Crawford, 12
Cocks, James
  Crawford, 215, 223
Cocthrin, Waters
  Jackson, 65
Codall, *Widow*
  Pope, 51
Coffe, Newton
  Bond, 20
Coghorn, James, Sr.
  Johnson, 50
Coghren, Andrew
  Johnson, 4
Cohenn, James
  Union, 107

Cohoon, Eliazer
  White, 461
Cohoon, Thomas
  White, 247
Colbert, James
  Gallatin, 314, 469
Cole, Edward
  Washington, 69
Coleen, Francis
  Madison, 273
Coleman, Daniel T.
  Union, 366
Coles, John
  Washington, 278
Coles, Thomas
  Washington, 279
Colier, John
  Pope, 283
Collins, Augustus
  Madison, 78
Collins, James
  Gallatin, 154
Collins, John
  Gallatin, 336
  Madison, 525
Collins, Michael
  White, 508
Collins, Polly
  Madison, 116
Comer, Abraham
  Union, 261
Comer, Allen
  Bond, 198
Commons, Saml.
  Crawford, 505
Compton, John B.
  White, 32
Conaway, James
  Crawford, 226
Conger, Isaac
  Washington, 12
Coniers, John
  Union, 204
Conley, Hesse
  Madison, 11

Coventry, George
Madison, 323
Covington, Edmon
White, 467
Cowan, David
Pope, 41
Cowan, Ephram
Pope, 23
Cowan, John
Crawford, 134
Gallatin, 23
Cowen, Matthew
Madison, 498
Cowhill, Thomas
Madison, 593
Cowles, Edward
Randolph, 11
Cox, Able
Gallatin, 500
Cox, Benjamin
Washington, 183
Cox, Charles
Washington, 153
Cox, Henry
Gallatin, 366
Cox, Isaac
Gallatin, 502
Cox, John
Franklin, 109
Madison, 687
Cox, Joseph
Washington, 201
Cox, Mary
Bond, 106
Cox, Micajah
Madison, 103
Cox, Thomas
Madison, 322
Cox, Thomas, Sr.
Union, 249
Cox, Thomas, Jr.
Union, 58
Cox, William
Gallatin, 404
Madison, 496

Coxe, Thomas
Gallatin, 175
Coyle, James
Bond, 182
Coyle, John
Bond, 149
Cozad, Joseph
Gallatin, 140
Crabbtree, James
Gallatin, 424
Crabtree, Thomas
Washington, 283
Craford, James
Pope, 247
Craft, Thomas
Union, 74
Craften, Robert
Union, 333
Craften, Robert W.
Union, 400
Crag, Hugh
Union, 121
Craglo, William
Union, 83
Craig, John
Washington, 281
White, 1
Craig, Robert
Gallatin, 183
Madison, 263
Craig, Saml.
White, 400
Crain, Jesper
Franklin, 41
Crain, Spencer
Franklin, 44
Crain, Squire
Jackson, 176
Crain, Thomas
Jackson, 175
Crandle, see Corrandle
Cravens, Elijah
White, 102
Cravens, Jessee
Gallatin, 274

Craw, John
White, 347
Crawford, John
Franklin, 130
Pope, 204
Crawford, Mason
Franklin, 90
Crawford, Silas
Monroe, 86
Creal, John
Washington, 44
Creath, George
Jackson, 60
Creker, Eterea
Crawford, 427
Crenshaw, Daniel
White, 544
Crews, John
Crawford, 136
Cribens, Thomas
Pope, 246
Criles, Coonrad
Crawford, 452
Criles, Geo.
Crawford, 451
Crips, John
Union, 33
Crise, John
Union, 133
Crise, Katharina
Union, 382
Crisle, George
White, 559
Crisle, Henry
White, 560
Crisp, Reeden
Jackson, 102
Crisp, William
Bond, 161
Crite, George
Union, 85
Crocker, Arthur
Washington, 115
Crocker, Elisha
Crawford, 85

Crocker, Jacob
Washington, 61
Crocker, James
Washington, 55
Crocker, Thomas
Washington, 62
Crocker, William
Washington, 114
Crocket, John
Pope, 42
Crockett, Robert
Madison, 468
Croggins, Chattin
Gallatin, 477
Cronk, Andrew
Franklin, 135
Cross, John
Pope, 240
Cross, Joshua
Pope, 56
Cross, William
White, 231
Crossen, Michael
Monroe, 130
Croswit, Harrey
Union, 227
Crouch, Adam
White, 18
Crouch, Edward
Monroe, 92
Crow, Bengeman
Jackson, 224
Crow, Rubin
Crawford, 283
Crow, William
Crawford, 420
Crunk, James
Johnson, 117
Cude, Lee
Union, 380
Culberson, Joseph
White, 65
Culbeth, John
White, 525
Cullom, Edward N.
Crawford, 68

Dillingham, Mich.
Gallatin, 387
Dillingham, Wm.
Gallatin, 386
Diment, David
Franklin, 6
Diterline, John
Pope, 75
Divers, John
Monroe, 204
Dixon, Joseph
White, 496
Dod, William
Union, 337
Dodd, Michael
Madison, 329
Dodge, Bazel
Gallatin, 124
Dodge, Elisha
Madison, 299
Doerty, Elizabeth
Union, 392
Dolson, James
Crawford, 227
Dolton, James
Madison, 653
Doolin, Daniel
Gallatin, 516
Doolin, David
Gallatin, 152
Dopher, John
Crawford, 157
Dorres, Thos.
Franklin, 136
Dorris, James S.
Jackson, 141
Dorsey, Halyard
White, 59
Dosier, Adam
White, 380
Dotey, William
Jackson, 186
Dotston, Moses
Crawford, 429
Dowling, Joseph
Monroe, 167

Downing, James
Madison, 62
Downing, William
Bond, 74
Downs, John
Madison, 433
Downs, Zacheriah
White, 54
Doyan, ———
Madison, 351
Doyle, Thomas
Johnson, 58
Drake, James
Gallatin, 173
Drake, Samuel
Crawford, 296
Draper, Chalkley
Crawford, 46
Drew, John
White, 165
Driggers, Isaac
White, 456
Driggers, Julas
White, 455
Driggins, Absolam
White, 457
Driskell, Elias
Crawford, 73
Drumm, John
Madison, 503
Drunen, James
Madison, 688
Drunen, John
Madison, 686
Drunnen, Saml.
Madison, 685
Drurey, Lues
Pope, 238
Drury, Raphael
Monroe, 31
Dubois, Jane
Crawford, 201
Dubois, Sharlow
Crawford, 307
Duff, Daniel
Gallatin, 251

East, Henry
  Madison, 259
East, James
  Madison, 253
Easton, Richard
  Crawford, 275
Eastwood, Abner
  Union, 412
Eastwood, Abraham
  Monroe, 8
Eastwood, Jacob
  Monroe, 9
Eaton, Benjamin
  Crawford, 26
Eaton, Benjamin, Jr.
  Crawford, 392
Eaton, John
  Crawford, 139
Eaton, Joseph
  Crawford, 166
Eaton, Richard
  Crawford, 276
Eaton, Solomon
  Crawford, 387
Eaton, Stephen
  Crawford, 294
Eberman, Arthur
  Monroe, 215
Eddy, Henry
  Gallatin, 559
Edilene, Peter
  Crawford, 269
Edington, John
  Bond, 59
Edon, James
  Washington, 119
Edwards, John
  Pope, 71
Edwards, Kinian
  Jackson, 166
Edwards, Lorenzo
  Madison, 339
Edwards, Nicholas
  Washington, 197
Edwards, Nicoles
  Pope, 98

Edwards, Ninian
  Madison, 480
Edwards, Philip
  Crawford, 396
Edwards, Turner
  Gallatin, 136, 510
Edwards, Victor
  Pope, 223
Edwards, Washington
  Union, 70
Egbert, Nicholas
  Gallatin, 6
Elder, Robert
  White, 306
Elems, David
  Johnson, 93
Elkins, John
  Johnson, 52
Elkins, Joshua
  Johnson, 51
Elkins, Wm.
  Johnson, 78
Elledge, Isaac
  White, 22
Elledge, John
  White, 21
Elledge, William
  White, 20
Ellems, James
  Union, 104
Ellems, John
  Union, 96
Ellems, Thomas
  Union, 15
Elles, John
  Bond, 206
Elliott, John
  White, 235
Elliott, Richard
  Gallatin, 11
Ellis, Benjamin
  Gallatin, 130
Ellis, James
  Gallatin, 190

Gassaway, Ths.
Gallatin, 372
Gassaway, Wm.
Gallatin, 375
Gasten, Mathew
Union, 217
Gasten, Thomas
Gallatin, 82
Gastin, Alexander
Jackson, 157
Gastin, Samuel
Crawford, 299
Gastin, William
Jackson, 147
Gaston, Eli
Gallatin, 207
Gaston, James
White, 419
Gaston, Robert
White, 514
Gates, Henry
Madison, 589
[Gather ?], John
Gallatin, 78
Gatland, Edward
White, 423
Gaurd, Timothy
Gallatin, 415, 592
Gelespy, John P.
Pope, 64
Gemes, George
Union, 59
George, Jehue
Madison, 560
Gernor, Charels
Jackson, 187
Gerrard, William
Crawford, 343
Gerrard, William, Sr.
Crawford, 344
Gibbs, Hauston V.
Madison, 283
Gibson, Robert
Washington, 88
Gilbert, Levi
Monroe, 82

Gilbreath, Hugh
St. Clair, 17
Gilbreath, James
St. Clair, 19
Gilbreath, John, Sr.
St. Clair, 18
Gilbreath, John, Jr.
St. Clair, 14
Gilferd, Joshua
Crawford, 197
Gilham, Charles
Madison, 388, 680
Gilham, Clement
Madison, 338
Gilham, Isaac
Madison, 345, 419
Gilham, Isham
Madison, 321
Gilham, James
Madison, 327, 389
Gilham, Jane
Madison, 391
Gilham, John
Madison, 324, 413, 609
Gilham, Rydus C.
Madison, 328
Gilham, Samuel
Madison, 336
Gilham, Thomas
Madison, 418
St. Clair, 12
Gilham, William
Madison, 392, 396, 649
Gill, David
Gallatin, 513
Gill, James
Jackson, 28
Gill (Bucoup), Jas.
Jackson, 11
Gill, John
Crawford, 138
Gill, Robert
Crawford, 273
Gill, Thomas
Crawford, 325

Goings, William
  Madison, 423
Goins, Edward
  Crawford, 79
Goins, Isaac
  Crawford, 173
Goldsmith, William
  Union, 279
Goliher, John
  Crawford, 194
Goliher, John, Jr.
  Crawford, 199
Gonvell, Joseph
  St. Clair, 33
Good, James
  Madison, 682
Good, John
  Madison, 683
Good, Thomas
  Madison, 681
Goodbread, Joseph
  Jackson, 152
Gooden, Joseph
  White, 568
Goodin, Lewis
  Crawford, 253
Goodin, Robert
  St. Clair, 30
Goodman, John
  Gallatin, 260
Goodman, William
  Pope, 110
Goodner, Benjamin
  St. Clair, 27
Goodner, Conrad
  St. Clair, 31
Goodner, Cornelius
  St. Clair, 29
Goodnight, [Pe]ter
  Gallatin, 10
Goodwin, Elijah
  White, 62
Gorden, Elisha
  White, 422
Gore, John C.
  White, 427

Gore, John W.
  Johnson, 57
Gore, Joshua
  Union, 167
Gore, Joshua, Sr.
  Johnson, 95
Gore, Thomas
  Union, 162
Goset, John
  Union, 332
Goss, David
  Crawford, 65
Goss, Jonathan A.
  Crawford, 472
Goss, Solomon
  Monroe, 177
Gossett, Elijah
  St. Clair, 11
Gover, John
  St. Clair, 23
Gragg, William
  Jackson, 121
Graham, Edward
  Union, 320
Graham, George
  White, 237
Graham, James
  White, 343
Graham, Jinny
  Union, 232
Graham, John
  White, 282
Graham, *see also* Grham
Graig, Jacob
  Bond, 68
Grammer, John
  Union, 247
Grammer, William
  Union, 359
Graves, Fredrick
  Johnson, 87
Graves, John S.
  Johnson, 116
Graves, Richd.
  White, 214

Grisham, Austin
Bond, 145
Groats, Sarah
Madison, 90
Groce, Abraham
White, 313
Grogan, Abdon
St. Clair, 13
Grogan, Spencer
Johnson, 94
Grote, William
Monroe, 129
Grovenor, Parker
Jackson, 48
Groves, Emela
White, 58
Groves, John
White, 114
Grubb, William
Jackson, 128
Guard, *see* Gaurd
Guiger, John
Madison, 190
Guiler, William
St. Clair, 22
Gullick, Beniah
Madison, 264
Guntryman, Jacob
Madison, 462
Gurley, Benjamin
Johnson, 75
Guthman, Luuis[?]
Gallatin, 59
Guthrie, Beverly
Madison, 143
Guthrie, Dempsey
Madison, 694
Guyer, Aaron
Crawford, 14
Guyer, Axim
Crawford, 15
Guyer, Jesse
Crawford, 221

Habifield, William
Union, 90

Hacker, Absolem
Union, 291
Hacker, George
Union, 294
Hacker, John
Union, 296
Hackins, Lemuel
Washington, 50
Hadden, William
White, 19
Haden, Jobe
Crawford, 176
Hady, John
Gallatin, 494
Hagerman, Benjamin
Washington, 192
Hagler, Benj. J.
Madison, 147
Hagler, Cleveland
Madison, 113
Hagler, Jacob
Madison, 109
Hagler, William R.
Madison, 135
Hahn, Susan
White, 472
Hail, Hizekia
Pope, 245
Haines, James
Madison, 497
Halcomb, William
St. Clair, 46
Halcomb, Zacabiah
St. Clair, 47
Halderman, Christian
Monroe, 111
Hale, Benjamin
St. Clair, 48
Hale, Enoch
St. Clair, 49
Hale, [Robert?]
St. Clair, 69
Haley, *Mrs.*
St. Clair, 84
Haley, James
Jackson, 67

Handy, John
Crawford, 236
Washington, 218
Handy, Stephen
Crawford, 313
Handy, Thomas
Crawford, 332
Hanks, David
White, 209
Hanna, James
White, 314
Hanna, John
White, 293
Hannah, Brice
Gallatin, 83
Hannah, James
Pope, 253
Hannah, William
Pope, 252
Hanon, James
Bond, 73
Hanon, Jesse
Bond, 67
Hanon, Samuel
Bond, 72
Hanon, Sarah
Bond, 66
Hans, Stephen
Gallatin, 458
Hany, David
Gallatin, 198
Hany, Francis
Gallatin, 483
Hard, Edward
Jackson, 239
Harden, Jehu
Crawford, 377
Harden, Thomas
Crawford, 326
Harderster, Wm.
Gallatin, 560
Hardesty, John
White, 414
Hardin, Jephath
Gallatin, 325

Hardin, Robert
Gallatin, 69
Hardisty, William
White, 159
Hargate, William
White, 10
Hargrave, Jerremiah
White, 299
Hargrave, John, Sr.
Union, 344
Hargrave, John, Jr.
Union, 268
Hargrave, Robert
Union, 252
Hargrave, Saml.
White, 76
Hargrave, Seth
White, 390
Hargrave, Willis
White, 289
Harington, *Widow*
Pope, 13
Harklerod, Daniel
Madison, 410
Harlin, Bonham
Bond, 77
Harlin, Silus
Crawford, 311
Harmon, Francis
Bond, 58
Harness, Solomon
Randolph, 16
Harnis, Jobe
Crawford, 245
Harper, Isaac
Pope, 281
Harper, Lincolen
Pope, 131
Harper, Thomas
White, 218
Harrel, Theophilus
Washington, 128
Harrington, Drewry
Jackson, 9
Harrington, Whitnell
White, 23

Hawley, Pearce
White, 292
Haws, Colman
Pope, 287
Haws, John
Pope, 288
Hawthorn, Robert
White, 434
Hay, Daniel
White, 350
Hay, John
St. Clair, 92
White, 294
Hay, Lowrey
White, 287
Hayes, Benjamin
Gallatin, 492
Hayes, [Sa]ml.
Gallatin, 8
Haynes, John
White, 415
Haynes, Richd.
White, 471
Hays, John
Franklin, 113
Pope, 134
St. Clair, 65, 90
Hays, Robart
Pope, 112
Hays, William
Crawford, 357
Pope, 118
Hays, Zachariah
St. Clair, 66
Hayter, Abraham
Madison, 456
Haze, Henry
Madison, 382
Haze, Jacob
Madison, 383
Hazel, Daniel
Pope, 282
Hazel, King
Pope, 132
Hazelwood, James
Pope, 115, 151

Hazzelwood, Clif
Union, 322
Heacock, Esir
Crawford, 86
Heacock, Russell E.
Jackson, 139
Head, Thomas
Washington, 284
Hearing, Jesse
White, 271
Hearn, Edmond
Crawford, 72
Hearn, Mary
Crawford, 258
Heath, William
St. Clair, 78
Heaton, James
Gallatin, 143
Heddy, Absalom
Johnson, 44
Hedges, Wm.
Gallatin, 180
Heeter, John
Johnson, 32
Hemphill, Robart
Pope, 18
Hencely, Samuel
White, 268
Hendershot, David
Madison, 446
Henderson, Benjamin
Jackson, 38
Henderson, Hew
Crawford, 118
Henderson, James
Gallatin, 368
Monroe, 89
Henderson, Phillip
Gallatin, 367
Henderson, Robert
Crawford, 282
Jackson, 12
Henderson, William
Bond, 35
Hendrick, William
St. Clair, 73

Hendricks, James
Monroe, 208
Hendricks, Jesse
White, 258
Hendricks, John
St. Clair, 86
Henery, John
Pope, 181
Henley, John
Pope, 50
Henn, John
Jackson, 174
Henry, Samuel
Crawford, 386
St. Clair, 50
Hensley, John
Washington, 298
Hensley, Robert
Washington, 297
Henson, Abner T.
Madison, 222
Henson, Allen
Jackson, 146
Henson, Bartlett
Jackson, 198
Henson, Benjamin
Bond, 115
Jackson, 151
Henson, Giles
Jackson, 153
Henson, Green
Jackson, 148
Henson, James
Jackson, 193
Henson, Jessee
Washington, 223
Henson, John
Bond, 117
Henson, Philip
Washington, 225
Henson, Phillip
Gallatin, 87
Henson, William
Washington, 224
Henton, Aleson
Crawford, 499

Herbert, Thomas F.
Washington, 274
Herd, Charls
White, 572
Herin, *Major*
St. Clair, 55
Herin, Moses
St. Clair, 53
Hern, Filbert
Gallatin, 461
Hern, William
Crawford, 337
Herns, William
St. Clair, 51
Herod, John
Gallatin, 527
Herrel, Martin
Gallatin, 232
Herreld, James
Jackson, 142
Herren, ———
Monroe, 165
Herren, Lewis
St. Clair, 45
Herring, Isaac
Franklin, 28
Herring, Jonathan
Franklin, 29
Herrington, John
Madison, 47
Herrington, Whitmill
Madison, 18
Herron, John
Madison, 182
Hesmith, William
Crawford, 355
Heston, *Widow*
Pope, 53
Hettick, Andrew
Monroe, 72
Hew, Boils
Crawford, 25
Hewit, John
Madison, 280
Hewitt, George
Madison, 381

Hiars, William
Jackson, 150
Hiatt, Jesse
White, 426
Hibargus, Adam
Johnson, 91
Hibberd, Samuel P.
Madison, 296
Hickason, William
Bond, 6
Hickcox, Elisha E.
Randolph, 8
Hickem, William
Union, 257
Hicks, Jacob
Bond, 195
Hicks, James
Gallatin, 450
Hicks, Job
Bond, 190
Hicks, Vynes
Madison, 663
Hicks, Wm.
Gallatin, 482
Hicman, Is[aac]
St. Clair, 68
Hide, Isaac
Gallatin, 316
Higgens, Thomas
Washington, 167
Higgins, Elizabeth
Madison, 666
Higgins, John
St. Clair, 63
Higgins, Philemon
Madison, 624
Hill, *Doctor*
Crawford, 59
Hill, *Mr.*
St. Clair, 93
Hill, Burrell
St. Clair, 54
Hill, Chas.
Crawford, 440
Hill, David
St. Clair, 80

Hill, Fanny
Union, 327
Hill, Henry
Bond, 16
Hill, Isaac
Bond, 51
White, 302
Hill, James
Pope, 168
Hill, John ı
Bond, 15, 131
Crawford, 206, 442
St. Clair, 67
Hill, Jonathan
Washington, 47
Hill, Nathaniel
St. Clair, 71
Hill, Peter
St. Clair, 52
Hill, Phinehas
Washington, 157
Hill, Robert
Bond, 9
Hill, Samuel
Bond, 156
Hill, Starling
Franklin, 57
Hill, Thomas
Bond, 19
Hill, William
St. Clair, 75
Hilyard, Wiley
White, 212
Hinch, John
White, 518
Hinch, William
Madison, 434
Hindricks, Thomes
Jackson, 192
Hines, Robert
Madison, 202
Hinkley, John
Madison, 591
Hinson, John
Jackson, 189

Hinton, Evans
Bond, 183
Hinton, Samuel
St. Clair, 83
Hismith, Richard
Crawford, 280
Hitchcock, Martin
Gallatin, 21
Hite, Jacob
Gallatin, 590
Hix, William
Crawford, 345
Hobbs, James
Gallatin, 258
Hobbs, Will
Gallatin, 259
Hocksey, William
Madison, 441
Hodge, Hiram
White, 546
Hodge, William
White, 546
Hodges, Ebenezer
Madison, 306
Hodges, Edmund
Madison, 307
Hodges, Seth
Madison, 71
Hodkins, James
White, 476
Hogan, Isaac
Gallatin, 288
Hogan, John
Monroe, 183
Hogan, Joseph
Monroe, 113
Hogan, Prior
Monroe, 180
Hogan, William
Monroe, 110
Hogeboome, Adam
Crawford, 395
Hogg, Frances
Pope, 143
Hogg, Saml.
White, 307

Hogshead, James
St. Clair, 74
Hogue, David
Crawford, 64
Hogue, Jeremiah
Crawford, 128
Hogue, William
Crawford, 360
Holanback, Laurence
Crawford, 250
Holder, Jessee
Madison, 64
Holeday, Peter
Franklin, 55
Holedy, Robert
Crawford, 284
Holkum, Katy
Madison, 82
Holkum, Zachariah
Madison, 92
Holland, John
Bond, 141
White, 507
Holland, Matthew
Madison, 266
Holland, William
Madison, 150
Hollen, Leven L.
Union, 330
Hollenhead, Francies
Union, 200
Holley, William F.
Union, 287
Holliday, David
Jackson, 36
Holliday, Milicent
Madison, 465
Holly, William
Crawford, 413
Holmes, Luke
White, 522
Holt, Harman
St. Clair, 60
Holt, Robt.
Gallatin, 471

Holzer, Samuel
St. Clair, 85
Honeycut, Hartwell
Madison, 558
Hood, Demps
White, 543
Hood, James
Gallatin, 164
White, 488
Hood, Sarah
White, 494
Hood, William
White, 486
Hook, Elijah
St. Clair, 81
Hook, William
St. Clair, 77
Hooker, Jabez
Franklin, 85
Hooker, John
Franklin, 84
Hooker, Wiley
Jackson, 82
Hooper, Clarender
White, 27
Hooper, James
Washington, 123
Hoosong, Jacob
Madison, 220
Hoover, Daniel
White, 450
Hoover, George
White, 449
Hopkins, Andrew
Union, 123
Hopkins, John
Gallatin, 250
Union, 122
Hopton, John
Bond, 107
Horner, Nathan
St. Clair, 62
Horner, Nicholas
St. Clair, 61
Hosick, William
White, 387

Hosly, Samuel
Union, 119
House, Ritman
Gallatin, 576
Houser, Christopher
Union, 66
Houson, Isham
Franklin, 96
Houston, William
Crawford, 363
Howard, Abraham
Madison, 185
Howard, Aron
Union, 55
Howard, Blackston
Madison, 357
Howard, John
Madison, 176
Pope, 212
Howard, Thomas
Union, 209
Howard, William
Crawford, 352, 456
Madison, 13
Monroe, 59
Howel, David
St. Clair, 58
Howel, Thomas
St. Clair, 57
Howel, William
Bond, 36
Washington, 139
Howell, Amos
White, 259
Howington, James
Union, 95
Howzer, Jacob, Sr.
St. Clair, 91
Hubbard, [Elias]
Gallatin, 19
Hubbard, Ephrim
Gallatin, 231
Hubbard, Jesse
White, 506
Hubbard, John
Gallatin, 417

Hunter, George
  Madison, 530
Hunter, John
  Bond, 185
  Madison, 529
Hunter, Polly
  Madison, 674
Hunter, Samuel
  Bond, 186
Hunter, William
  Bond, 187
Huntsinger, Samuel
  White, 480
Hurt, Absolum
  White, 186
Hurt, William
  White, 195
Huschun, John
  Gallatin, 447
Huse, John
  Union, 13
Huse, Levi
  Union, 214
Huse, Nathaniel
  Union, 223
Huse, Oen
  Union, 406
Huse, William
  Union, 403
Husky, John
  Union, 358
Husky, Jonathan
  Union, 361
Hussong, Conrad
  Bond, 86
Huston, John
  Gallatin, 490
  Union, 98
Huston, William
  Pope, 145
Hutchcrafft, Hiram
  Gallatin, 193
Hutchcrafft, James
  Gallatin, 107
Hutchcrafft, John
  Gallatin, 197

Hutcheson, James
  Gallatin, 603
Hutchings, Fitz
  Union, 208
Hutchings, John
  Washington, 275
Hutchings, William
  Washington, 276
Hutson, Andrew
  Gallatin, 496
Hutson, Chamberlin
  Franklin, 114
Hutson, John
  Gallatin, 490
  Madison, 232
Hutson, M'Corpen T.
  Crawford, 256
Hutson, Peggy
  Gallatin, 277
Hutton, Alexander
  Crawford, 1
Hutton, Henry
  St. Clair, 56
Huttson, Jacob
  Madison, 231
Hynds, William
  Washington, 251

Idolett, George
  Gallatin, 315
Ingram, John
  Jackson, 172
Ingram, Jonas
  Pope, 311
Ingrum, George
  Jackson, 194
Ingrum, William
  Jackson, 188
Inman, Henry
  St. Clair, 97
Inman, Rufus
  Bond, 1, 71
Irven, Celib E.
  Pope, 19
Irvin, Andrew
  Union, 43

Jordan, Thomas, Jr.
Washington, 254
Jorden, John
White, 285
Jorden, William
White, 123
Jordin, Elijah
Gallatin, 579
Jourdan, Francis
Franklin, 3
Jourdan, Thos.
Franklin, 20
Journey, Elizabeth
St. Clair, 99
Journey, Nancy
Washington, 161
Journey, William
Washington, 168
Jousamurt, Touisant
St. Clair, 110
Judd, Alfred
Madison, 692
Judy, Samuel
Madison, 98

Kain, John
Madison, 716
Kasey, Levi
Johnson, 115
Kasey, Randolph
Johnson, 68
Kaykedall, Daniel
Crawford, 58
Kaykendall, Peter
Crawford, 270
Keeler, Abenezer
Pope, 47
Kees, Edward H.
Franklin, 35
Keith, Abner
Union, 27
Kellum, Wm.
Gallatin, 562
Kelly, Abnor O.
Madison, 151

Kelly, Elijah
Madison, 630
Kelly, Henry
Madison, 458
Kelly, Thomas
St. Clair, 119
Kelly, Wm.
Gallatin, 99
Keltner, Solomon
Madison, 453
Kelton, Thomas
Pope, 301
Kemp, William
Madison, 455
Kenada, Mr.
St. Clair, 124
Kenada, George F.
St. Clair, 123
Kenady, Thomas
Crawford, 319
Kenedy, Jesse
Johnson, 11
Kenedy, Neal
Washington, 150
Kennady, Archbald
Bond, 128
Kenneday, John
White, 245
Keown, James
Madison, 444
Kerby, Cyrus
Washington, 110
Kerns, William
Madison, 701
Kesterson, Larken
Pope, 195
Kesterson, Robert
Pope, 186
Kidd, Andrew
Pope, 91
Kidd, Robert
Monroe, 28
Kile, Adam
Madison, 206
Killess, [Si]nah
Gallatin, 14

Kilor, John
Union, 273
Kimberling, James
St. Clair, 113
Kimberly, Samuel
White, 351
Kimmel, Daniel
Union, 244
Kimmel, John
Union, 383
Kimmel, Peter
Jackson, 71
Kimsey, David
Gallatin, 279
Kimsey, Elijah
White, 425
Kinder, George
Madison, 470
Kinder, Jacob
Madison, 386
Kindrich, Starling
Gallatin, 498
King, Gerge
Gallatin, 439
King, Hosea
Gallatin, 299
King, James H.
Gallatin, 36
King, Jas.
Pope, 210
King, Jessey
Pope, 310
King, John
Bond, 132
White, 565
King, Joseph
Madison, 615
King, Saml.
Crawford, 403
King, Sith
Crawford, 300
King, William
Franklin, 124
St. Clair, 121
Kingston, John
St. Clair, 120

Kingston, Paul
St. Clair, 117
Kingston, Richard
Madison, 173
Kinkade, George W.
Crawford, 98
Kinkaid, Saml.
Madison, 608
Kinkand, William T.
St. Clair, 115
Kinney, Andey
Monroe, 55
Kinney, Joseph
Monroe, 11
Kinney, William
St. Clair, 116
Kinsaid, Mathew
Franklin, 21
Kinsall, John
Gallatin, 571
Kinsella, William
Jackson, 231
Kinyon, Joseph
Washington, 193
Kirk, John
Franklin, 103
Kirkpatrick, Francis
Bond, 93
Monroe, 187
Kirkpatrick, Hugh
Bond, 164
Kirkpatrick, James
Gallatin, 12
Kirkpatrick, John
Bond, 91
Franklin, 5
Kirkpatrick, Thomas
Bond, 27
Kirpatrick, James
Madison, 132
Kitchell, Joseph
Crawford, 382
Kitchell, Nancy
Crawford, 383
Kitchens, Charles
Madison, 528

Knely, Jacob
Union, 73
Knight, David
St. Clair, 122
Knight, James
Crawford, 385
Knighton, Thomas
St. Clair, 114
Knott, George
White, 109
Knott, Isaac
White, 110
Koen, David
St. Clair, 118
Koetah, Elizabeth
Gallatin, 341
Kurry, John
Johnson, 33
Kuykendall, Joseph
Johnson, 105
Kuykendall, Noah
White, 440
Kuykendoll, Lewis
Gallatin, 319

Labarb, Jack
Madison, 349
Labasere, Louis
St. Clair, 158
Labra, Batise
St. Clair, 146
Labraze, John B.
St. Clair, 155
Lacey, Ann
St. Clair, 140
Lacey, Stephen
St. Clair, 139
Lachane, Joseph
St. Clair, 147
Lackey, Adam
Crawford, 5
Lackey, George
Pope, 178
Lacompt, *Mrs.*
St. Clair, 154

Lacompt, Brazil
St. Clair, 149
Lacompt, Julian
St. Clair, 152
Lacompt, Louis
St. Clair, 156
Lacounpt, Batise
St. Clair, 148
Lacours, Batise
St. Clair, 143
Lacy, Barbary
Crawford, 32
Lacy, Nathaniel
Gallatin, 223
Ladd, Elijah
Monroe, 168
Ladd, Milton
Pope, 27
Lafferty, Cornelus
Gallatin, 182
Lafranbroo, John B.
St. Clair, 151
Lafrarcu, Anthony
St. Clair, 157
Lagrais, Louis
St. Clair, 153
Laile, George
Jackson, 87
Laile, Henry
Jackson, 88
Laile, John
Jackson, 89
Lamar, Solomon
Pope, 48
Lamasters, Isaac
Crawford, 454
Lamb, John
Crawford, 127
White, 111
Lambert, Hugh
Gallatin, 343
Lamer, Henry
Union, 26
Lamer, Joseph
Union, 24

Lamott, Swashin
St. Clair, 160
Lamotte, Joseph
Crawford, 196
Lampkins, Jopthah
Madison, 490
Lampley, Thos.
Franklin, 151
Lanahan, John
Union, 190
Land, Joseph
St. Clair, 126
Landers, Henry
Madison, 247
Landers, Jacob
Madison, 245
Landers, John
Union, 373
Landers, Stephen
Gallatin, 247
Lane, Daniel
Crawford, 62
Lane, John
White, 194
Lane, Robert
White, 321
Lane, William
Bond, 94
Lanear, Samuel
Crawford, 304
Langdon, Samuel
Pope, 96
Langly, John
Union, 238
Langston, John
St. Clair, 134
Langston, Nathan
St. Clair, 133
Langston, Samuel
St. Clair, 132
Langway, Joseph
St. Clair, 145
Langworthy, Reodolphus
Madison, 298
Lankford, John
White, 11

Laparsu, Francis
St. Clair, 150
Laparsu, Louis
St. Clair, 161
Laplont, Jacob
Crawford, 169
Larana, R.
Gallatin, 587
Lard, James
Madison, 142
Pope, 14
Lard, John
Madison, 205
Washington, 236
Larelu, Francis
St. Clair, 159
Laremire, Louis
St. Clair, 144
Laremore, Louis
St. Clair, 138
Larimere, Saml.
Gallatin, 547
Larimore, Saml.
Gallatin, 355
Larison, Thomas
Pope, 236
Larkins, Edward
Madison, 358
Larnsfer, Eliga
Crawford, 83
Lasters, James
Crawford, 485
Lastley, John
Jackson, 5
Lastly, John
White, 63
Latherm, James
Union, 79
Latherm, Jeremiah
Union, 51
Latherm, John
Union, 77
Latherm, Samuel
Union, 50
Laughlin, Alexn.
Madison, 387

Laughlin, John Lewis
Washington, 70
Lavelit, Lewis
Crawford, 248
Lawless, William
Madison, 119
Laymountain, Henry
Crawford, 116
Leach, Humphrey
Gallatin, 148
Leach, John
St. Clair, 137
Leakey, Simon
White, 144
Lear, Samuel
Washington, 92
Leatherm, William
Union, 336
Leawrance, Easter
Union, 224
Ledbetter, Asa
Gallatin, 480
Ledbetter, Henry
Gallatin, 478
Ledbetter, James
Gallatin, 422
Lee, Benoni
Pope, 176
Lee, Caberger
Gallatin, 521
Lee, James
Union, 197
Lee, James, Sr.
Pope, 167
Lee, James, Jr.
Pope, 169
Lee, John
Bond, 14
Lee, Loyd
Bond, 38
Washington, 126
Lee, Richard
Pope, 2
Lee, Rufus
Washington, 277

Lee, Samuel
Bond, 148
Gallatin, 520
Lee, Stephen
Crawford, 482
Lee, William
Crawford, 362
Madison, 201
Leech, Josia
Pope, 135
Leeder, Henry
Jackson, 144
Leeper, John
Bond, 82
Pope, 187
Leitner, John
Gallatin, 342
Lemen, James
Monroe, 221
Lemen, Josiah
Monroe, 24
Lemen, Moses
Monroe, 23
Lemen, William
Monroe, 16
Leming, Niholass
Crawford, 266
Lemmon, William
Monroe, 83
Lemmons, George
Union, 75
Lemmons, Samuel
Crawford, 298
Lense, Boysten
Union, 410
Lense, Davoult
Union, 407
Lense, John, Sr.
Union, 409
Lense, John, Jr.
Union, 408
Leonard, Newel
Crawford, 415
Leonard, William
Madison, 4

Lusadder, Jacob
  Jackson, 10
Lusby, Thomas
  Monroe, 105
Lusk, John T.
  Madison, 487
Luster, John
  Crawford, 190
Luster, Philip
  Pope, 313
Lyle, Peter
  Gallatin, 509
Lynn, Thomas
  St. Clair, 129
Lyons, Peggy
  White, 391

McAdams, William
  Madison, 199, 200
McAfee, Carry Happy
  Madison, 540
McBride, Philip
  Washington, 293
McBride, Richard
  Union, 64
McBride, Robert
  Washington, 294
M'Cabe, [James]
  Crawford, 231
M'Call, Thomas
  Crawford, 327
McCallister, Edward
  White, 39
McCallister, James
  White, 46
McCallister, Simon
  White, 41
McCallister, Thos.
  White, 305
McCammon, Hugh
  White, 532
McCance, Charles
  Madison, 96
McCance, William T.
  Madison, 139

McC[an]n, James
  St. Clair, 191
McCarty, William
  St. Clair, 217
M'Cary, Benjamin
  Gallatin, 236
M'Caslin, James
  Gallatin, 425
M'Cassahan, Webster
  Gallatin, 580
M'Clain, Charles
  Gallatin, 352
Mcclain, James
  Union, 216
M'Clane, John
  Gallatin, 556
M'Clewer, Andrew
  Crawford, 8
M'Clewer, John
  Crawford, 230
M'Clewer, Samuel
  Crawford, 301
M'Clewer, Samuel, Jr.
  Crawford, 302
McCloud, Charels
  Pope, 5
McClure, John
  Monroe, 102
McColam, Jacob
  Pope, 264
McComel, Arther
  Union, 280
M'Connell, Hugh
  Gallatin, 452
M'Cool, Abriham
  Gallatin, 186
McCool, Bengman
  Pope, 83
McCool, Jessey
  Pope, 84
McCool, Jessey, Sr.
  Pope, 85
M'Cool, Joseph
  Gallatin, 529

Mccool, Matte
Union, 411
McCord, David
Washington, 242
McCord, Robert
Bond, 157
McCoullough, John L.
Crawford, 435
McCown, George
White, 189, 445
McCoy, *Widow*
Pope, 229
McCoy, Ezekel
Pope, 305
McCoy, James
White, 326
McCoy, Walter
White, 121
M'Coy, Wm.
Gallatin, 514
McCrane, Moses
Crawford, 422
McCrary, Andrew
St. Clair, 188
M'Crary, Benjamin
Crawford, 33
Mcrary, Susanna
White, 312
Mccravens, Benjamin
Union, 389
M'Creerey, Jno.
Franklin, 92
McCroney, Thomas
Pope, 136
McCullum, John
Madison, 251
McDaniel, James
Crawford, 144, 416
McDaniel, Stacy
White, 298
McDaniel, Zachariah
Union, 384
McDanold, Linville
Monroe, 190

McDavid, John
Monroe, 29
McDonald, Henry
Washington, 71
McDonald, James
Monroe, 25
McDonald, Samuel
St. Clair, 183
McDowel, Nelson
Franklin, 39
McDowl, Robert
Crawford, 272
Mace, Henry
St. Clair, 180
Mace, John
St. Clair, 165
Mcelmurrey, Henry
Union, 84
Macen, Moses
Union, 325
Mcenry, Piere L.
Madison, 702
Mcentire, William
White, 362
Mceya, Wm.
Franklin, 9
McFadgin, James
Madison, 504
M'Fain, Daniel
Gallatin, 275
McFarland, Walter
Madison, 524
McFarlen, Achilles
Pope, 173
McFarling, Jos.
Franklin, 116
Mcfatridge, Wm.
Johnson, 100
MCgahey, David
Crawford, 51
M'Gee, Rachel
Gallatin, 187
McGehee, Stephn
St. Clair, 202

Mather, Thomas
Randolph, 10
Mathews, John
White, 331
Matney, Edward
Gallatin, 308
Mattet, Baldon
Crawford, 31
Matthers, Elihue
Madison, 699
Matthew, Absalom
Bond, 165
Matthew, Benjamin
Crawford, 34
Matthew, David
St. Clair, 199
Matthew, John
Crawford, 183
Matthews, Benjamin
Bond, 166
Matthews, Cliburn
Bond, 137
Matthews, Matthew
Johnson, 67
Matthias, Jeremiah
St. Clair, 181
Mattingly, Richard
Monroe, 66
Mattison, John
Pope, 142
Maugham, John K.
Washington, 249
Maulding, Ambrose
White, 554
Maulding, Ennes
White, 556
Maulding, James
White, 557
Maulding, Richd.
White, 558
Mauzy, Silas
St. Clair, 211
Mavern, Barnabas
Crawford, 389

Maxey, Francis
St. Clair, 218
Maxwell, David W.
Gallatin, 40
Maxwell, Robert
White, 175
Maxy, Henry B.
White, 533
Maxy, William
White, 37
May, Balaam
White, 332
May, William L.
Madison, 152
Mayberry, David
White, 163
Mayberry, Frederick
White, 157
Mayberry, Jesse
White, 158
Mayberry, Solloman
White, 446
Mayfield, Elijah
Gallatin, 552
White, 405
Mayho, George
Madison, 467
Mayo, Johnathan
Crawford, 220
Mays, James
White, 173
Mays, Thomas
White, 202
Meacham, Adit
Madison, 575
Meacham, Eunice
Madison, 292
Means, Matthew
Madison, 672
Means, Robert
Madison, 671
Mears, William
St. Clair, 194
Medcalf, Betsey
White, 87

Medford, John
  Madison, 403
Medlock, Henry
  Gallatin, 177
Meed, James
  Crawford, 445
Meeks, Judey
  Gallatin, 120
Meginness, John
  Johnson, 76
Megowen, Alexander
  Johnson, 69
Megowen, Samuel
  Johnson, 70
Meiers, Isaac
  Gallatin, 594
Meirs, Hesekiah
  Gallatin, 615
Melten, James
  Gallatin, 32
Menees, Benjamin
  Union, 93
Menees, James
  Franklin, 49
Meo, Pear
  St. Clair, 215
Meredith, James
  White, 246
Merien, Richard
  Union, 169
Merkel, William
  Crawford, 341
Merril, Sylvester
  St. Clair, 210
Merrill, Abriham
  Gallatin, 208
Merrill, William
  White, 324
Merritt, Benj.
  Madison, 373
Merrl, Joseph
  Gallatin, 533
Mertin, John
  Gallatin, 517

Mesmore, Zachariah
  Crawford, 502
Messenger, John
  St. Clair, 207
Metcalf, Emanuel
  White, 190
Metta, James
  Madison, 486
Michael, Jessee
  Gallatin, 364
Michaels, George [?]
  Gallatin, 206
Michaels, James
  Gallatin, 205
Michaels, Moses
  Gallatin, 261
Michel, Stephen
  White, 220
Micks, Charles
  Gallatin, 340
Middleton, Benoni
  Crawford, 28
Middleton, Reuben
  Washington, 199
Middleton, Robert
  St. Clair, 196
Middleton, William
  Washington, 184
Mikles, George
  Gallatin, 595
Milan, Ransom
  Madison, 148
Mill, Edward
  Crawford, 82
Miller, Abram
  Pope, 219
Miller, Adam
  White, 74
Miller, Charles
  Franklin, 119
Miller, Christian
  Union, 351

Miller, David
  Crawford, 397
  Jackson, 92
  Madison, 192
  Union, 82
Miller, Francis
  White, 317
Miller, George
  Crawford, 401
Miller, Henry
  Monroe, 143
Miller, Hew
  Crawford, 122
Miller, Jacob
  St. Clair, 195
Miller, James
  White, 178
Miller, John
  Bond, 54
  Franklin, 118
  Monroe, 94
  Union, 360
Miller, Joseph
  Monroe, 84
Miller, Michael
  Monroe, 5
Miller, Moses
  Madison, 191
Miller, Peter
  White, 431
Miller, Reuben
  Monroe, 85
Miller, William
  Crawford, 356
  St. Clair, 212
Milligan, David
  Jackson, 98
Milligen, Alexandria
  Union, 295
Million, Benjamin
  St. Clair, 168
Million, Bennett
  St. Clair, 164
Million, Daniel
  St. Clair, 206

Mills, Charles
  Crawford, 45
Mills, John W.
  Crawford, 141
Mills, Thomas
  Crawford, 330
Miner, Danl. L.
  Gallatin, 414
Minson, Abraham
  Washington, 121
Minterf, David
  Union, 152
Mires, Henry
  White, 386
Mires, John
  White, 384
Mires, John, Jr.
  White, 385
Mires, Joseph
  Bond, 70
Mires, Stephen
  Bond, 64
Mitchel, James C.
  Crawford, 418
Mitchel, John
  Monroe, 61
Mitchel, Nancy
  Madison, 249
Mitchel, William
  Madison, 248
Mitchell, Samuel
  St. Clair, 169
Mix, John W.
  Randolph, 9
Moberley, Isaac
  Franklin, 94
Mobley, Charles
  White, 320
Mobley, Edward
  Gallatin, 262
Modglen, John
  Pope, 262
Modglen, Linsey
  Pope, 179

Modglen, Right
Pope, 277
Modglen, Straingman
Pope, 177
Modglen, William
Pope, 260, 278
Modglin, Henry
Monroe, 162
Modglin, John, Sr.
Monroe, 186
Moffet, James
Gallatin, 597
Moffets, James
Jackson, 228
Montgomery, Andrew
Crawford, 20
Montgomery, Robert
Crawford, 287
Montgomery, William
Madison, 516
St. Clair, 214
Montrow, Paton
Gallatin, 265
Moody, Andrew
Bond, 202
Moody, Benjamin
St. Clair, 190
Washington, 80
Moody, [Wil]lliam
Gallatin, 115
Moor, Frances
Pope, 32
Moor, George
Crawford, 102
Moor, Hua
Franklin, 134
Moor, Isaac
Crawford, 228
Moor, James
Crawford, 242
Moor, John
Crawford, 205
Moore, *Mr.*
Jackson, 210

Moore, Abel
Madison, 559
Moore, Bryant
St. Clair, 184
Moore, Charles
Bond, 124
Washington, 288
Moore, Curtis
St. Clair, 172
Moore, Daniel G.
Madison, 212
Moore, David
Madison, 59
Moore, Enoch
Monroe, 210
Moore, George
Madison, 523
Moore, Isaac
Madison, 556
Moore, J. Milton
Monroe, 1
Moore, James
St. Clair, 186
Moore, Jane
St. Clair, 204
Moore, John
Franklin, 1
Madison, 541
Monroe, 146
Randolph, 3
Moore, John A.
Bond, 125
Moore, Lydia
Madison, 94
Moore, Risdon, Sr.
St. Clair, 178
Moore, Risdon, Jr.
St. Clair, 171
Moore, Robert
St. Clair, 174
Moore, Thos.
Franklin, 4
Moore, Whaley
Madison, 219

Moore, William
Gallatin, 303
Madison, 562
Moore, William, Sr.
St. Clair, 193
Moore, William, Jr.
St. Clair, 187
Moore, William D.
St. Clair, 163
Moorning, James
Madison, 590
More, Allen
Gallatin, 593
More, Jerremiah
White, 300
More, John
White, 452
More, Robert
White, 301
More, Thomas
Madison, 91
Moredock, John
Monroe, 144
Morehead, Thomas
Crawford, 503
Moreland, Hazel [Sr. ?]
Gallatin, 184
Moreland, Hazel [Jr. ?]
Gallatin, 185
Moreland, Vincent
White, 24
Moreson [?], ———
St. Clair, 221
Moreson, Guy
St. Clair, 219
Moreson [?], Julian
St. Clair, 220
Morgain, Joshua
Union, 148
Morgan, Anthony
Union, 253
Morgan, Arthur
St. Clair, 205
Morgan, Henry
White, 104

Morgan, John
Madison, 272
Morgan, Levi
White, 439
Morgen, Leonard
Union, 180
Morgen, William, Sr.
Union, 32
Morgen, William, Jr.
Union, 335
Morice, John
Pope, 162
Morice, Wm.
Pope, 248
Moris, Sian
Crawford, 297
Morow, Samuel M.
Pope, 155
Morreson, Jerremiah
Crawford, 200
Morris, George
White, 493
Morris, Jacob
Crawford, 154
Morris, John
Crawford, 168 [?], 175
Morris, Thomas
St. Clair, 173
Morris, William
Gallatin, 77
Madison, 297
Morris, Zachariah
St. Clair, 189
Morrison, Esaw
Crawford, 71
Morriss, Irvin
Johnson, 1
Morriss, Jane
Johnson, 2
Morriss, Saml.
Gallatin, 445
Morrow, John
Jackson, 155, 202
Morrow, Thos.
Jackson, 156

Neill, Henry, Sr.
St. Clair, 230
Neip, S. & Co.
Jackson, 182
Nelson, John
Franklin, 47
Nelson, Thomas
Monroe, 158
Nelson, William
St. Clair, 231
Nesbet, Jane
Madison, 7
Nesbit, Alexd.
White, 171
Nettles, Margret
Franklin, 164
Nevel, Enoch
White, 206
New, James
Madison, 570
Newell, James
Madison, 17
Newell, John
Gallatin, 219
Newkum, Joseph
White, 147
Newlin, James
Crawford, 441
Newlin, John, Jr.
Crawford, 443
Newman, Joseph
Madison, 655
Newman, Simon
White, 435
Newman, Simpson
Gallatin, 385
Newman, Zadock
Madison, 657
Newten, Joseph
Franklin, 72
Newton, John
Crawford, 439
Nichols, John
St. Clair, 228
Washington, 25

Nichols, Julius
St. Clair, 229
Nichols, Theophilus M.
St. Clair, 226
Nichols, Thomas
Bond, 49
St. Clair, 227
Nichols, William
Bond, 60
Nickles, Benj.
Gallatin, 57
Nickless, Henry
Gallatin, 28
Nicols, George
White, 154
Nicols, Valuntine
White, 164
Nix, Ambrose
Madison, 100
Nix, David
Madison, 112
Nix, John
Madison, 104
Nixon, John
White, 442
Noble, Henry, Sr.
Jackson, 14
Noble, Henry, Jr.
Jackson, 164
Noel, Ephrem
Union, 241
Nolin, Samuel
Monroe, 117
Norante, Daniel
Gallatin, 188
Norman, William
Madison, 21
Nortel, David
Gallatin, 68
Norten, Joseph
Jackson, 205
North, Lydna
White, 366
Norton, Rubin
Crawford, 277

Owen, Willis
Gallatin, 283
Owens, Arther
Franklin, 11
Owens, Joseph
Gallatin, 430, 591
Owens, Mossbey
Franklin, 163
Owens, Robert
Gallatin, 150
Owings, Abner
White, 13
Owings, John
Madison, 472
Owings, Simms
Madison, 473

[P]————, Chesley
St. Clair, 255
Pace, Joel
Gallatin, 537
Padfeld, William, Jr.
St. Clair, 252
[P]adfield, Lydia
St. Clair, 257
Padly, Reuben
Madison, 189
Padon, John
Washington, 20
Page, Jesse
Crawford, 164
Page, Joel
White, 303
Page, Joseph
Jackson, 203
Page, Moses
White, 444
Paine, Christopher
Madison, 194
Paine, Fielding
Jackson, 63
Paint, John
Madison, 466
Palmer, Henry B.
Crawford, 114

Palmer, James
Madison, 714
Palmer, Joseph
Union, 236
Palmor, John
Pope, 183
Pamberson, John
Crawford, 494
Pankey, Lues
Pope, 172
Pankey, William
Pope, 171
Panky, Hamton
Gallatin, 397
Panter, Joseph
Union, 304
Pantus, James
Gallatin, 195
Park, Mathew
White, 183
Parker, Benjamin
Crawford, 30, 489
Parker, Daniel
Crawford, 55
Parker, Elijah
White, 412
Parker, George
Crawford, 107
Parker, Isaac
Crawford, 235
Parker, James
Crawford, 234
Parker, John
Crawford, 165
Union, 313
Parker, Joseph
Crawford, 233
Parker, Nathl.
White, 38
Parker, William
Crawford, 351
Union, 315
Parkerson, William
Madison, 178

Parkison, Alexander
Pope, 203
Parkison, Daniel
Madison, 183
Parks, James
Madison, 533
Parmerly, Gils
Union, 42
Parris, Luess
Gallatin, 497
Parrish, Guilford
White, 564
Parsley, Robert
Bond, 160
Parsons, Benjamin A.
Union, 364
Parsons, Henrey
Franklin, 83
Parsons, Jesse
Franklin, 104
Parsons, John
Franklin, 105
Parsons, Zoah
Franklin, 106
Parspal, Joseph
St. Clair, 280
Parviance, William
Madison, 34
Pate, Anthony
Gallatin, 145
Pate, Pairet
Franklin, 160
Pate, Parrett
Gallatin, 370
Pate, William
Franklin, 159
Gallatin, 371
Paten, Thomas B.
Union, 284
Paterson, Levy
Union, 171
Patillo, John S.
White, 133
Patten, John
St. Clair, 272

Pattersen, Th. C.
Gallatin, 294
Patterson, Charles
Monroe, 176
Patterson, Joseph
St. Clair, 270
Patterson, Luke
Monroe, 175
Patton, Andrew V.
Madison, 293
Patton, Joseph
White, 283
Patton, Philip
White, 491
Patton, Robt.
Gallatin, 526
Patton, Thomas
Crawford, 323
Paupa, Joseph
St. Clair, 281
Paupa, Paul
St. Clair, 282
Payne, Adams
Monroe, 60
Pea, John
St. Clair, 248
White, 463
Pealo, Francis
Crawford, 93
Pearce, Abner
Gallatin, 323
Pearce, Hosea
White, 77
Pearce, James
Madison, 257
White, 132
Pearce, Jesse
White, 136
Pearce, Moses
White, 142
Pearce, Solomon
Madison, 30
Pearson, Achelus
White, 389

Porter, David
Crawford, 67, 376
Porter, James A.
Gallatin, 546
Porter, John
Crawford, 172
Porter, Rebecca
St. Clair, 264
Porter, Thomas
Monroe, 98
Porter, Wm.
Johnson, 59
Portmess, Peter
Union, 28
Posey, John
Gallatin, 610
Posey, Jubilee
Madison, 464
Posey, Leeaiden
Washington, 39
Posey, Washington A. G.
Gallatin, 544
[Po]stleweight, John
St. Clair, 256
Potter, James
White, 261
Potter, Royal
Washington, 100
Potts, David
Gallatin, 489
Potts, Isaac
Gallatin, 508
Potts, William
White, 128
Powel, John
Madison, 586
Powell, Green
Gallatin, 218
Powell, Nicholas
Gallatin, 217, 245
Powers, Elijah
Bond, 119
Powers, James
Union, 293

Powers, John
Bond, 120
Powers, Thomas
Bond, 101
Prentice, John O.
St. Clair, 244
Preston, Ezekiel
Monroe, 38
Prevo, Samuel
Crawford, 310
Prewit, Fields
Bond, 118
Prewit, Solomon
Bond, 178
Price, Barbary
Johnson, 10
Price, Frederick
Crawford, 471
Price, Henry
Crawford, 117
Price, Isaac
Bond, 98
Price, James
Johnson, 8
Price, John
White, 458
Price, Jonathan
Johnson, 15, 22
Price, Peter
Crawford, 268
Price, Reece
Pope, 213
Price, Simon
Johnson, 14
Price, Sousanna
Union, 377
Prickett, Abraham
Madison, 27
[Prickett ?], George
St. Clair, 254
Prilhart, Jacob
Jackson, 31
Primm, John
Monroe, 199
St. Clair, 271

Ragline, Haly
Gallatin, 111
Ragsdale, George
Gallatin, 178
Ragsdale, Thomas
Pope, 158
Ralston, Isaac
Pope, 266
Ramesey, James
White, 170
Ramsey, Alexander
White, 172
Ramsey, James
Madison, 261
Randel, Thomas
Jackson, 236
Randle, Edmund
Madison, 651
Randle, Isham
Madison, 136
Randle, James
Madison, 133
Randle, Parham
Madison, 684
Randle, Thomas
Madison, 137
Randleman, Henry
St. Clair, 312
Randleman, Jacob
St. Clair, 311
Randolph, Eligah
St. Clair, 291
Randolph, Elihu H.
Bond, 170
Randolph, Mary
White, 513
Raner, Samuel
Monroe, 37
Raney, John
St. Clair, 290
Raport, Daniel
Monroe, 88
Rasco, Jesse
Jackson, 52
Ratcliff, Charles
St. Clair, 303

Ratcliff, James
White, 358
Ratcliff, Michel
St. Clair, 304
Ratcliff, Richard
Franklin, 69
Ratcliff, William
St. Clair, 316
Rathbourn, Camon
Crawford, 462
Ratliff, James
Washington, 207
Ratliff, Jobe
Washington, 206
Ratliff, John
Washington, 204
Ratliff, Richard
Franklin, 71
Ratliff, William
Washington, 205
Rattan, John
Madison, 515
Rattan, Richard
Madison, 518
Rattan, Thomas
Madison, 519
Rawles, Edward
St. Clair, 301
Rawles, Raleigh
St. Clair, 302
Ray, Charley
Pope, 77
Ray, Simon
Madison, 481
Ray, Thomas
St. Clair, 296
Read, Andrew
White, 279
Read, John
White, 48
Read, Joseph
White, 542
Read, Nelly
White, 269
Read, William
Washington, 108

Realy, Morris
  Gallatin, 466
Rearch, Saml.
  Crawford, 492
Reavell, David
  Crawford, 379
Reaves, Isaac
  Johnson, 65
  St. Clair, 299
Reaves, John
  Johnson, 66
Reavis, Charles
  Bond, 3
Reavis, Harris
  Bond, 12
Reavis, Henry
  Madison, 75
Reavis, Isham
  Bond, 46
Reavis, Noah
  Bond, 33
Reavis, Solamon
  Bond, 5
Rector, Enoch
  St. Clair, 317
Redfern, John
  Pope, 276
Redfern, Solomon
  Pope, 275
Redkin, William S.
  Pope, 46
Redman, Parmenus
  Gallatin, 51
Redmond, Samuel
  St. Clair, 306
Reece, Daniel
  Madison, 8
Reed, James
  Bond, 127
Reed, John
  Gallatin, 121
  Madison, 184
  Pope, 255
Reed, Joseph
  Gallatin, 42, 116

Reed, Samuel
  Gallatin, 463
  Johnson, 102
Reed, Thomas
  Pope, 29
Reeder, Isaac
  Gallatin, 443
  St. Clair, 320
Reely, Owen
  Gallatin, 45
Reese, Daniel
  Jackson, 19
Reevere, Louis
  St. Clair, 324
Reid, John
  Jackson, 230
Reily, Joseph
  Gallatin, 114
Reives, James
  Gallatin, 374, 409
Rellens, Nathan
  Crawford, 265
Renfro, Jessee
  Madison, 159
Renfro, Joshua
  Madison, 50
Renfro, Louis
  Madison, 49
Renfro, Margerett
  Madison, 51
Renfrow, Peter
  Washington, 76
Renfrow, William
  Washington, 75
Renshaw, Elijah
  Madison, 42
Rentelman, Jacob
  Union, 393
Rettenhouse, William
  St. Clair, 305
Rettonhouse, Peter
  St. Clair, 309
Revi, *Mr.*
  St. Clair, 319
Revi, Joseph
  St. Clair, 318

Reynoalds, John
St. Clair, 322

Reynold, Robert
Madison, 93

Reynolds, James
Madison, 105

Reynolds, John
Jackson, 56

Reynolds, Joseph
Madison, 521

Reynolds, Robert, Sr.
Madison, 106

Reynolds, Thomas
Madison, 107

Reyonalds, Sousanna
Union, 372

Rhea, Andrew
Crawford, 438

Rhea, James
Crawford, 131

Rhea, John
Madison, 652

Rian, William
St. Clair, 313

Rice, Benj.
Gallatin, 313

Rice, Eligah
St. Clair, 298

Rice, Fisher
White, 424

Richardson, George
Madison, 600

Richardson, John
Crawford, 193
Madison, 601

Richardson, John B.
Crawford, 434

Richardson, Joseph
Crawford, 224

Richerdson, James A.
White, 344

Richerfuse, Christopher
Washington, 285

Richey, James
Pope, 95

Richey, William
Pope, 225

Richison, Abel
Pope, 117

Richy, Anthony
White, 188

Ricker, Rufus
Washington, 238

Riddle, Richard
Gallatin, 334

Ridenour, John
Crawford, 243

Rider, John
St. Clair, 326

Ridgway, John
Washington, 243
White, 28

Riggan, Joshua
White, 364

Riggin, John
Madison, 20

Riggs, Clemment
St. Clair, 297

Riggs, Hosea
St. Clair, 308

Riggs, Joseph
St. Clair, 294

Riggs, Scot
Crawford, 303

Riggs, William
Monroe, 157

Right, Abner
Madison, 77

Right, James
Crawford, 412
Madison, 131, 536

Right, Jonas
Madison, 134

Right, Saml.
Gallatin, 549

Right, William
Madison, 535

Riley, Anderson
Bond, 105

Riley, Isaac
Gallatin, 113

Robinson, Clary
Gallatin, 31
Robinson, David
Madison, 501
Robinson, Gideon
Bond, 204
Robinson, Israel
St. Clair, 295
Robinson, James
Madison, 145
Robinson, Jerremiah
Crawford, 178
Robinson, John
Franklin, 12
Gallatin, 100, 581
Jackson, 159
Madison, 73, 676, 677
Robinson, Jonathan
Gallatin, 607
Robinson, Joseph
Jackson, 58
Madison, 121
Robinson, Michael
Gallatin, 5
Robinson, William
Bond, 203
Gallatin, 326
Madison, 500
Robison, Allen
Pope, 36
Robison, David
Monroe, 163
Robison, Hugh
Pope, 157
Robison, Jacob
Pope, 137
Robison, Richard D.
Pope, 216
Rodgers, James
St. Clair, 300
Roeall, Joseph
St. Clair, 325
Rogers, Benj.
Franklin, 166
Rogers, Jas.
Franklin, 88

Rogers, Reuben
Franklin, 23
Rogers, Robert
Johnson, 86
Rogers, William
Monroe, 91
Rogers, Williams
Franklin, 158
Rohrer, John
Gallatin, 55
Roland, John
Franklin, 42
Roland, Ragsdale
Franklin, 43
Rollens, Mikel
Franklin, 117
Rollins, Hosea
Washington, 135
Rollins, John
Crawford, 460
Rollins, Michael
Crawford, 261
Romine, Abraham
Washington, 286
Romine, Isaac
Washington, 287
Roper, George, Sr.
Washington, 72
Roper, George, Jr.
Washington, 73
Rose, John
Madison, 517
Rosen, Abner
Gallatin, 518
Ross, Alexander
Bond, 147
Ross, Asa
White, 436
Ross, Charles
Gallatin, 503
Rossen, Thomas
Gallatin, 165
Roundtree, William
Washington, 142
Rountree, Jessee
Madison, 155

St. John, Pear
St. Clair, 382
Salsbury, Jefry
Crawford, 147
Salyers, David
Union, 259
Sam, Burdet
St. Clair, 368
Samples, David
Madison, 169
Samples, John
Bond, 142
Sams, David
Union, 141
Sams, Rice
Union, 86
Sams, Thomas
Union, 138
Sams, William
Pope, 49
Sanders, Anthony
Crawford, 18
Sanders, James
Pope, 228
Sanford, George
White, 520
Sanford, John
White, 519
Sarvis, Polly
Union, 207
Satterfield, John
Madison, 422
Saturfield, George
White, 117, 569
Saturfield, Isaac
White, 118
Saunders, George
Madison, 326
Savage, Eli
Madison, 334
Savage, John
Washington, 163
Savage, William
Madison, 315, 333
Savery, Asah
Gallatin, 29

Sawyers, Edmond
Union, 41
Sayles, Henry
Washington, 264
Sayles, Joseph
Washington, 263
Sayles, Samuel
Washington, 265
Sayles, Thomas
Washington, 262
Schenbarger, Batise
St. Clair, 381
Schenbarger, Lawrence
St. Clair, 380
Scofield, Saml.
Gallatin, 602
Scott, Alexander
St. Clair, 374
Scott, Francis
Monroe, 206
Scott, Isaac B.
Pope, 37
Scott, James D.
Pope, 166
Scott, Jehu
Monroe, 137
Scott, John
Madison, 211
Scott, John, Sr.
St. Clair, 371
Scott, John, Jr.
St. Clair, 367
Scott, Joseph
Gallatin, 192
St. Clair, 391
Scott, Levi
Madison, 546
Scott, Nimrod
Gallatin, 166
Scott, Robert
Pope, 35
Scott, Samuel
Madison, 654
St. Clair, 339, 376
Scott, William
Madison, 632

Scott, William, Sr.
St. Clair, 330
Scott, William, Jr.
St. Clair, 341
Scovel, Benjamin
Monroe, 51
Scovel, Henry
Monroe, 53
Scribner, Pleasant
Bond, 103
Scribner, William
Bond, 97
Scroggin, Nathaniel
Washington, 95
Scroggins, Humphrey
Gallatin, 312
Scroggins, Isaac
Madison, 235
Scroggins, John
Gallatin, 444
Scroggins, *see also* Croggins
Scroggs, Joseph
Jackson, 215
Seaten, Peter C.
Gallatin, 25
Seaton, Saml.
Gallatin, 48
Sebolt, John
Gallatin, 596
Seely, Walter J.
Madison, 291
Seemore, ———
Madison, 45
Segar, Jacob
Madison, 368
Sendusky, John
Franklin, 122
Sevely, Jacob
Pope, 25
Seward, Samuel
Washington, 10
Sexton, Jacob
Gallatin, 4
Sexton, John
Gallatin, 557

Sexton, Joshua
Gallatin, 109
Seybold, Robert
Madison, 74
Seybold, Samuel
Madison, 31
Shalor, John
Crawford, 517
Shanks, Benja.
Crawford, 506
Shanks, Elenor
Crawford, 507
Shanks, Michael
Crawford, 484
Shannan, John
Jackson, 69
Shannon, Lewis
Crawford, 515
Shannon, [Thomas]
Gallatin, 18
Shannon, Wm.
Crawford, 514
Sharp, Cyrus
Crawford, 48
Sharp, Jonathan
St. Clair, 345
Sharp, Samul
St. Clair, 346
Shaver, John
Union, 278
Shaw, James
Crawford, 133
Shaw, John
Madison, 596
Shaw, Joseph
Crawford, 153, 208
Shaw, Smith
Crawford, 288
Shearer, David
Johnson, 12
Shearwood, Hugh
Washington, 299
Sheehen, John
Monroe, 73
Sheepherd, James
Monroe, 152

Shelby, David
White, 96
Shelby, Isaac
White, 17
Shelby, Jonathan
White, 250
Shelby, Wm.
Johnson, 109
Shelby, *see also* Shelvey
Shelton, James
Franklin, 16
Madison, 181
Shelton, Jane
Madison, 234
Shelton, John
Crawford, 202
Shelton, Matthias
Madison, 233
Shelton, Miller
Franklin, 15
Shelton, Thomas
Madison, 180
Shelton, William
Madison, 179
Union, 87
Shelvery, Jacob
Pope, 105
Shelvey, Charels
Pope, 104
Shelvey, Even
Pope, 107
Shelvey, Reece
Pope, 106
Shenks, John
Crawford, 504
Shepherd, Jonathan
Monroe, 115
Shepherd, Rowland
Bond, 179
Sherewood, Moses
Gallatin, 511
Sherill, Avington
Monroe, 184
Shields, Robart
Pope, 208

Shingelton, Squire
Pope, 304
Shinn, Caleb
Madison, 460
Shinn, John, Jr.
Madison, 218
Shipley, James
White, 363
Shipley, Robert
White, 368
Shipman, Daniel
Pope, 128
Shipman, George
Washington, 42
Shirley, Nimrod
White, 553
Shockley, Isham
Madison, 572
Shockley, Thomas
Madison, 287
Shoemaker, Flanders
Gallatin, 505
Shook, Aaron
St. Clair, 336
Shook, Benjamin
Crawford, 400
Shook, Daniel
Monroe, 142
Shook, Jonas
St. Clair, 370
Shook, Samuel, Sr.
St. Clair, 389
Shook, Samuel, Jr.
St. Clair, 359
Shook, Solomon
Monroe, 125
Short, Hubbard
St. Clair, 375
Short, Jacob
St. Clair, 390
Short, John
White, 492
Short, Patsey
Washington, 246
Short, William
St. Clair, 352

Smith, Ruth
    White, 45
Smith, Samuel
    Monroe, 185
    White, 571
Smith, Thomas
    Gallatin, 384
    Madison, 693
    White, 411
Smith, William
    Union, 185
Smock, *Widow*
    Pope, 184
Smoot, Armstord
    Gallatin, 119
Smothers, Thomas
    Franklin, 99
Smyth, Isaac
    Pope, 8
Smyth, John
    Pope, 67
Smyth, Samuel
    Pope, 39
Snedley, C.
    Gallatin, 605
Snider, Abram
    Crawford, 11
Snider, Jacob
    Madison, 411
    Union, 243
Snider, John
    White, 108
Snider, Sary
    Union, 328
Snider, Solomon
    Franklin, 60
Snipes, John
    Crawford, 238
Snodgrass, John
    Washington, 306
Snodgrass, Mary
    White, 73
Snodgrass, Robert
    Washington, 305
Snotgrass, Ann
    Union, 94

Snotgrass, James
    Madison, 153, 154
Snotgrass, Joseph
    Madison, 33
Snow, Cushing
    Crawford, 419
Somall, Wm.
    Gallatin, 272
Sorrels, Richd.
    Jackson, 135
Sosha, Michael
    St. Clair, 386
Southerd, Thomas
    White, 327
Sowerd, Griffin
    White, 2
Span, John
    Jackson, 29
Sparks, David
    St. Clair, 392
Sparks, Mathew
    Union, 38
Spawling, Elezer
    Crawford, 90
Speaks, William
    Washington, 144
Spencer, John
    Gallatin, 434
Spencer, Major
    Crawford, 461
Spencer, Ruben S.
    White, 169
Spensor, James
    Crawford, 179
Spensor, Jesse
    Crawford, 180
Spensor, Thomas
    Crawford, 328
Spillars, John
    Bond, 100
Spiller, Elijah
    Franklin, 45
Spilman, Benjn.
    White, 105
Spilman, Saml.
    White, 15

Stookey, Daniel
St. Clair, 377
Storey, George
Pope, 121
Storey, John
Crawford, 125
Pope, 290
Storey, Nethan
Pope, 289
Storm, Jacob
Pope, 207
Story, Andrew
White, 396
Story, George
White, 393
Story, George, Jr.
White, 395
Story, Robert
White, 392
Stout, Aaron
Crawford, 495
Stout, Christopher
Madison, 279
Stout, Daniel
St. Clair, 332
Stout, Henry
St. Clair, 331
Stout, John
Madison, 278
Stout, William
St. Clair, 333
Stovall, Abraham
White, 153
Stovall, John
White, 570
Stovall, John B.
White, 151
Stovall, Squire
White, 152
Straigh, Israel
St. Clair, 364
Street, Anthony
White, 429
Street, James
Bond, 180

Street, Joseph M.
Gallatin, 1
Strickland, Jonathan
Gallatin, 396
Strickland, Redmon
St. Clair, 342
Strickland, William
Gallatin, 365
Stripling, Jesse
Union, 318
Stroud, Asa
St. Clair, 343
Stroud, Levi
St. Clair, 362
Stroud, Peter
Monroe, 112
Struton, John
Crawford, 219
Stuart, Alphonso C.
St. Clair, 335
Stuart, Peter
St. Clair, 361
Stubbins, Christopher
Madison, 277
Stubblefield, John
Bond, 7
Stubblefield, Thomas
St. Clair, 363
Stubblefield, William
Bond, 209
Stubblefield, Wyatt
Bond, 85
Stubs, John
Pope, 226
Stubs, Moses
Pope, 222
Stucker, Willice
Pope, 4
Stuntz, John
St. Clair, 388
Sturn, George
White, 276
Sturn, Henry
White, 497
Sturn, John
White, 487, 495

Sudevoit, Charles
Crawford, 40
Suillevin, Edward
Franklin, 100
Sullivan, John
Monroe, 202
Sullivan, Thomas
Monroe, 203
Sumers, Thomas
Union, 398
Summers, Edward D.
St. Clair, 372
Summers, John
Monroe, 121
Sumpter, Benjamin
White, 365
Sumpter, John
White, 376
Suratt, Joseph
Franklin, 74
Sutten, Edmond
Union, 189
Suttler, Jesse
Union, 381
Sutton, Aaron
Madison, 489
Sutton, James
Johnson, 85
Sutton, Wm.
Gallatin, 392
Swaferd, James
Union, 45
Swafort, James
Jackson, 85
Swaggert, George
St. Clair, 379
Swaggert, John
St. Clair, 378
Swan, Frances
St. Clair, 340
Swartz, Catherine
Jackson, 59
Swartz, Geoarge
Jackson, 229
Swearingen, Daniel S.
Washington, 90

Sweeton, Moses
White, 500
Swinerton, James G.
Madison, 289
Symmond, *see* Cymons

Tade, David
Gallatin, 201
Talbert, James
Gallatin, 360
Talbott, Elijah
Monroe, 149
Talbott, Joshua
Monroe, 156
Talbott, Thomas
Monroe, 150
Talbott, Thomas W.
St. Clair, 418
Talent, David
St. Clair, 412
Tally, Thornten
Gallatin, 169
Tannehill, James
St. Clair, 394
Tarcourt, Francis
St. Clair, 430
Tarlton, Robt. M.
Gallatin, 281
Tarlton, Townsen
Gallatin, 159
Tash, James
Union, 88
Tash, Lewis
Union, 290
Taugue, Joshua
Pope, 88
Tayler, Joseph
Gallatin, 400
Tayler, Merret
White, 524
Taylor, Abram
Crawford, 4
Taylor, Archibald
Washington, 117
Taylor, Bellington
St. Clair, 420

Taylor, Cornelious
Crawford, 42
Taylor, Cornelius
Crawford, 470
Taylor, David S.
Pope, 33
Taylor, Edmund
Washington, 129
Taylor, Edward
Madison, 428
Taylor, Elgah
Franklin, 123
Taylor, Giles
Gallatin, 304
Taylor, Henry
Madison, 35
St. Clair, 419
Taylor, Herren
Gallatin, 349
Taylor, Isaac
Madison, 99
Taylor, Jacob
Crawford, 213
Taylor, James
Crawford, 212
Jackson, 143
Monroe, 217
White, 193
Taylor, John
Crawford, 195
Madison, 128, 186
White, 263
Taylor, Joseph
St. Clair, 415
Union, 365
Taylor, Levi
Monroe, 4
Taylor, Thomas
Jackson, 6
Taylor, Thomas, Sr.
Monroe, 151
Taylor, Thomas, Jr.
Monroe, 218

Taylor, William
Jackson, 108
Johnson, 106
Washington, 74
Tear, May
Gallatin, 30
Teas, George
Madison, 29
Tedford, John
Union, 114
Tedford, Walter
Union, 109
Teeter, Philip
Madison, 69
Teoboc, John B.
Madison, 310
Terner, Alexander
Crawford, 9
Terner, Ezekel
Crawford, 365
Terner, Robert
Crawford, 278
Terner, Ruth
Crawford, 279
Terry, Stephen
Crawford, 388
St. Clair, 422
Teter, John
St. Clair, 421
Teter, Mary
St. Clair, 413
Teter, Solomon
St. Clair, 414
Tetricks, Abraham
St. Clair, 405
Tetricks, George
St. Clair, 407
Tetricks, Jacob
St. Clair, 406
Tetricks, Peter
St. Clair, 400
Thoman, William
Madison, 675
Thomas, Mr.
St. Clair, 434

Tilor, Jacob
Union, 35
Tilor, James
Union, 36
Tilor, John
Union, 34
Tindal, Charles
Madison, 477
Tindal, Thomas
Madison, 475
Tiner, Joshua
Franklin, 33
Tiner, Willes
Franklin, 36
Tingly, James
Union, 110
Tinmon, John D.
Gallatin, 604
Tinnan, John
Jackson, 22
Tippey, Abraham
Franklin, 53
Tippey, John
Franklin, 34
Titsworth, Bengeman
Pope, 224
Titsworth, Isaac
Pope, 87
Titsworth, James
Pope, 86
Titus, Nan
St. Clair, 423
Titus, Samul
St. Clair, 401
Todd, *Widow*
Monroe, 128
Todd, John
Madison, 495
Tolbert, Enoch
Gallatin, 162
Tolbert, Fedrick
Union, 254
Tolbey, James
Johnson, 92

Tolin, Isaac
Monroe, 18
Tolin, John
Monroe, 14
Tolin, John, Sr.
Monroe, 17
Tolly, Benjamin
Gallatin, 282
Tolly, Cornelius
Madison, 709
Tolman, Nathan
St. Clair, 435
Tombs, William
White, 6
Tompson, John
Franklin, 140
Tomson, Iseral
Union, 395
Tope, Fedrick
Union, 21
Tope, Jacob
Union, 235
Tope, John
Union, 20
Torance, Matthew
Madison, 120
Torrea, Robert
White, 115
Torrea, Thomas
White, 116
Touns, Samuel
Madison, 585
Townsand, John
White, 78
Townsend, Wm.
Johnson, 77
Townzen, Edmond
St. Clair, 402
Townzen, Whitfield
St. Clair, 403
Tozer, Samul
St. Clair, 393
Trammel, David
Franklin, 73

Vaughn, *see also* Von
Veach, Elias
  White, 185
Veach, Isaac
  White, 430
Veach, James
  White, 179
Veach, John
  Crawford, 160
  White, 180
Veach, Wm.
  White, 551
Venturs, Asa
  St. Clair, 442
Vials, Samuel
  Madison, 447
Vickery, John
  White, 465
Vickory, John
  Madison, 274
Vincent, Isham
  Madison, 442
Vines, William
  White, 516
Vineyard, Philip
  St. Clair, 437
Vineyard, William
  St. Clair, 440
Vinyard, Daniel
  Pope, 306
Vinyard, George
  Pope, 314
  Union, 379
Vinyard, John
  Union, 350
  White, 122
Virgin, Brice
  St. Clair, 443
Virgin, William
  St. Clair, 444
Volentine, Ichabod
  Monroe, 122
Volintine, Hardy
  Bond, 146
Volintine, William
  Bond, 154

Von, George
  Pope, 3
Von, John
  Pope, 193
Voris, James
  White, 47
Vought, [Wm.] C.
  Gallatin, 17

Wadderman, Henry
  Monroe, 108
Waddle, Colby
  Madison, 400
Waddle, Jessee
  Madison, 362
Waddle, John
  Franklin, 18
Waddle, Obadiah
  Madison, 602
Waddle, Robert
  Washington, 216
Wadkens, Daniel
  Pope, 279
Wadkins, Beverly
  Washington, 164
Wadkins, Joseph
  Washington, 103
Wadkins, Thomas
  Washington, 89
Wadley, Thomas
  Jackson, 23
Wadsworth, John
  Washington, 57
Wadsworth, Thomas
  Washington, 58
Wafer, James
  Washington, 66
Wafferd, William
  Union, 213
Waggener, John
  Gallatin, 75
Waggoner, John
  Madison, 84
Waggoner, Petter
  Madison, 526

Wagner, Jacob
  Union, 354
Wagner, Wm.
  Gallatin, 328
Wakefield, Charles
  St. Clair, 461, 471
Wakefield, Dianna
  Bond, 121
Wakefield, Enoch
  St. Clair, 459
Wakefield, John
  Washington, 54
Wakefield, John A.
  Bond, 48
Wakefield, Simeon
  Washington, 53
Wakefield, William
  Washington, 43
Waker, William
  Union, 270
Walace, Wm.
  Gallatin, 475
Walbert, Mary
  White, 60
Walden, Benj.
  Gallatin, 472
Walden, Ruben
  White, 135
Waldrop, John
  Crawford, 137
Waldrop, John, Sr.
  Crawford, 399
Waldrop, John, Jr.
  Crawford, 130
Waldrop, William
  Crawford, 336
Waler, Richard
  Franklin, 148
Walker, Benjn.
  Jackson, 154
Walker, Charles
  St. Clair, 491
Walker, David
  St. Clair, 480
Walker, Ephraim
  Washington, 18

Walker, Henry
  St. Clair, 467, 476
[Walker], James, Sr.
  St. Clair, 475
Walker, James, Jr.
  St. Clair, 473
Walker, Jessee, Sr.
  St. Clair, 462
Walker, Jessee, Jr.
  St. Clair, 492
Walker, John
  Madison, 647
  St. Clair, 455, 485
Walker, Reuben
  Madison, 384
Walker, Samuel
  St. Clair, 466
Walker, Samuel A.
  Madison, 451
Walker, William
  St. Clair, 460
Wall, Thomas
  Madison, 461
Wallace, Andrew
  Madison, 244
Wallace, Francis
  St. Clair, 472
Wallace, James
  Pope, 191
Wallace, John
  Madison, 242
Wallace, Josiah
  Madison, 243
Wallace, Thomas
  Pope, 286
Waller, Joseph
  Union, 385
  White, 35
Wallis, George
  Monroe, 181
Wallis, Morgan
  White, 337
Walters, Abraham
  Crawford, 481
Walters, Jacob
  Crawford, 480

Web, Lazerous
Franklin, 120
Webb, Esa
Gallatin, 253
Webb, Henry
Washington, 173
Webb, William
Madison, 667
Webster, Ellender
White, 69
Weigh, William
St. Clair, 451
Weir, Mallaci
White, 44
Welch, John
Crawford, 209
Washington, 146
Welch, Thoma
St. Clair, 453
Welch, William
Union, 101
Weldon, Jacob
White, 36
Weldon, John
Union, 52
Wellbourne, Jessee Y.
Washington, 282
Wells, Alexander
Monroe, 101
Wells, Anthony
Union, 44
Wells, Elisha
Jackson, 113
Wells, Ezekel
Union, 49
Wells, Ezekiel
Jackson, 91
Wells, Lewis, Sr.
Jackson, 7
Wells, Lewis, Jr.
Jackson, 101
Wells, Thomas
Jackson, 110
Wells, William
Pope, 59

Wels, Joseph
Crawford, 239
Welsh, Abraham
Madison, 372
Welsh, Edward
Monroe, 196
Welton, Aaron
Crawford, 509
Welton, John
Crawford, 510
Wemble, Simon
Gallatin, 441
West, Asa
Johnson, 37
West, David L.
St. Clair, 464
West, Hezekiah
Johnson, 36
West, Isaac
Madison, 160
West, James
Jackson, 25
West, John
Union, 170
West, Mary
Madison, 449
Westbrooke, James
Union, 263
Westnor, George
Crawford, 97
Westrope, William
Crawford, 349
[W]etherford, William
St. Clair, 477
Wever, John
Union, 401
Whaley, Baker
Monroe, 109
Whaley, James
Monroe, 107
Whatley, Henry
Bond, 50
Wheeler, William
White, 416
Wheeler, Wm., Jr.
White, 417

Whitesides, Uel
Madison, 111
Whitesides, William B.
Madison, 110
Whitesides, William L.
St. Clair, 486
Whitford, William
White, 257
Whitiker, Mark
Pope, 150
Whitley, John
Bond, 39
Whitley, John, Jr.
Bond, 42
Whitley, Mills
Bond, 43
Whitmill, Ryal
Washington, 40
Whitnell, William
White, 233
Whitsids, James A.
Pope, 109
Whitson, Jacob
Gallatin, 327
Whitson, Thomas
Jackson, 74
Whooberry, Jessee B.
St. Clair, 479
Wiatt, John
Crawford, 496
Wiatt, William
Madison, 527, 543
Wickers, Thomas
White, 100
Widdows, Peter
White, 26
Wier, Robert
Union, 288
Wigle, Jacob
Union, 264
Wigle, John
Union, 352
Wilard, Daniel
Crawford, 66

Wilbanks, Wiley
Madison, 352
Wilcox, Absolem
Gallatin, 237
Wilcox, Balas
Johnson, 27
Wilcox, Isaac D.
Johnson, 25
Wilcox, John
St. Clair, 484
Wilcox, Morrison
Gallatin, 238
Wilderman, Dossey
St. Clair, 496
Wilderman, George
St. Clair, 498
Wilderman, George J.
St. Clair, 500
Wilderman, James
St. Clair, 499
Wildey, George
Gallatin, 161
Wiley, Ames
Gallatin, 123
Wilkerson, John
St. Clair, 457
White, 534
Wilkerson, Peter
White, 67
Wilkey, Maxwell
White, 538
Wilkins, Andrew
Gallatin, 485
Wilkins, John
Madison, 606
Wilks, Paul
St. Clair, 465
Will, Conrad
Jackson, 2
Willard, Erastes
Pope, 20
Willard, Simon
Pope, 21
Willes, Jacob
Union, 14

Wood, John C.
Madison, 214
Wood, Jonathan
Crawford, 135
Wood, Joseph, Sr.
Crawford, 246
Wood, Joseph, Jr.
Crawford, 384
Wood, Macen
Gallatin, 519
Wood, Martin
Madison, 554
Wood, Mason
Gallatin, 196
Wood, Richard
Madison, 24
Wood, Sampson
Madison, 507
Wood, Thomas G.
Gallatin, 72
Wood, William
Crawford, 417
Gallatin, 89
Wood, Young
Madison, 508
Woodall, John
White, 155
Woodall, John C.
Gallatin, 550
Woodoll, Elijha P.
Union, 260
Woodrome, David
Monroe, 153
Woodrome, James
Monroe, 148
Woodrome, Joel
Monroe, 161
Woodrome, John
Monroe, 67
Woodrome, Wm.
Monroe, 173
Woodrum, John
Washington, 196
Woodry, Gabril
Union, 292

Woods, Benjamin
St. Clair, 450
Woods, David
Jackson, 81
Woods, John
St. Clair, 490
Woods, Samuel
Madison, 1
Woods, William
Madison, 573
Woodson, Richard
Gallatin, 582
Woodworth, John S.
Crawford, 398
Woodwourth, John S.
Crawford, 247
Wooley, David
White, 377
Wooley, David, Jr.
White, 372
Wooley, Henry
White, 373
Woolf, George
Union, 348
Woolseye, Nehemiah
St. Clair, 481
Wooten, Daniel
Jackson, 66
Wooten, Geo. W.
Jackson, 137
Wooten, James
Jackson, 163
Wooten, Moses
Jackson, 24
Wooten, Moses, Sr.
Jackson, 136
Worldley, Isaac
Johnson, 47
Worley, John
Monroe, 50
Worley, Joseph
Monroe, 35
Worley, William
Monroe, 49

Wormack, Green
  Gallatin, 474
Wormack, Wm.
  Gallatin, 476
Worrick
  St. Clair, 501
Worthen, Nancy
  Jackson, 39
Worthington, James, Sr.
  Union, 222
Worthington, James, Jr.
  Union, 378
Worthington, William
  Union, 221
Woters, John
  Union, 16
Wott, Gabriel
  Madison, 156
Wrathman, Soloman
  Johnson, 28
Wren, John
  Franklin, 162
Wright, Joseph
  Bond, 17
Wright, Richard
  St. Clair, 452
Wright, Zachariah
  Franklin, 51
Wright, *see also* Right
Write, James
  Union 390
Wullums, Absolem
  Madison, 539
Wyatt, John
  Gallatin, 515

Yandle, Saml.
  White, 460
Yannie, Laurance
  Monroe, 139
Yarbrough, Absalem
  Washington, 45
Yoakum, Peter
  Madison, 430

Yokem, James
  Bond, 175
Yokem, John
  Bond, 177
Yokem, Martha
  Bond, 176
Yong, Saml.
  Franklin, 141
Yongblood, Aaron
  Franklin, 145
York, Edmon
  White, 98
York, Eli
  White, 97
York, John
  Johnson, 88
York, William
  Madison, 553
Yost, John
  Union, 135
Young, ———
  White, 25
Young, Binjn.
  White, 57
Young, James
  Washington, 302
Young, Roady
  Gallatin, 240
Young, **Rody**
  Gallatin, 268
Young, Samuel
  Washington, 301
Young, Squir
  Gallatin, 194
Young, Thomas
  Crawford, 406
Young, William
  Bond, 99
  Crawford, 334
  Gallatin, 209
Young Blood, James
  Pope, 242

A
GENEALOGICAL RECORD
OF THE DESCENDANTS OF

Henry
Rosenberger

OF
FRANCONIA, MONTGOMERY COUNTY,
PENNSYLVANIA

TOGETHER WITH HISTORICAL AND BIOGRAPHICAL
SKETCHES, AND ILLUSTRATED WITH
PORTRAITS AND OTHER
ILLUSTRATIONS

Rev. A. J. Fretz

With an Introduction by
Prof. Seward M. Rosenberger
of Quakertown, Pa.

HERITAGE BOOKS
2025

HERITAGE BOOKS

AN IMPRINT OF HERITAGE BOOKS, INC.

Books, CDs, and more—Worldwide

For our listing of thousands of titles see our website
at
www.HeritageBooks.com

A Facsimile Reprint
Published 2025 by
HERITAGE BOOKS, INC.
Publishing Division
5810 Ruatan Street
Berwyn Heights, MD 20740

Originally published 1906

International Standard Book Number
Paperbound: 978-0-7884-3095-4

PREFACE.

A short account of the Rosenberger family was prepared by Edward Mathews, of Lansdale, Pa., and published in a local paper in the beginning of 1888. This, however, pertained to only two branches of the family in Hatfield.

A more extended account was written by Mr. Mathews at the instigation of the publisher, I. R. Haldeman, himself related to the family both by birth and marriage, and which was published by him in book form in 1892. The work, however, while giving considerable valuable and interesting history of the pioneers of the family, their emigration to America, their settlement in Montgomery county, accounts of the homesteads, occupations, religion, and immediate descendants of these pioneers it does not give a complete history of the various lines or branches of the families in genealogical form to the present generation.

A more complete history of the family being desired by some of the connections arrangements were accordingly made to revise the work and compile a complete history of the family to the present date and generation. In the preparation of the work much labor and research has been required. The official records and registry of deeds and wills at Norristown, Doylestown and Philadelphia have been searched, various persons connected with the family by ties of relationship interviewed, and a large correspondence

5

carried on with the entire connections in Montgomery and Bucks counties and elsewhere in Pennsylvania, the far West and Canada.

The work will be of more or less interest to the public generally, but more especially to those bearing the name of Rosenberger and their descendants. The family of Rosenberger has been much extended in Montgomery and adjacent counties, and also in distant portions of the United States and Canada. In presenting this volume the writer has endeavored to give the history of the family together with other matter of interest to the descendants that would otherwise have been lost.

The author also acknowledges himself indebted to the many friends for kind favors received during the compilation of this work in the form of data, etc. Among those who have furnished us with considerable data, to whom we express our sincere gratitude, are: David Rosenberger, of Hatfield, Pa.; Enos L. Rosenberger, of Hiawatha, Kan.; Henry H. Rosenberger, of Quakertown, Pa.; A. A. Delp, of Lansdale, Pa.; Edward Mathews, of Lansdale, Pa. ("History of the Rosenberger Family of Montgomery County"); Rev. Henry A. Hunsicker, of Philadelphia, Pa., and others.   AUTHOR.

MILTON, N. J., Sept. 8, 1899.

Yours truly,
Rev. A. J. Fretz.

INTRODUCTION.

The present age is one distinctively of research. There is an intellectual restlessness and curiousness manifested which impels to a seeking of more knowledge in all departments of human affairs. Some of this activity is spent for practical ends, some for ends not so plainly practical. The physicist and the chemist in their labratories make discoveries that may greatly affect industrial and economic problems. The historian, groping his way through partly mutilated records of the misty past, adds to the sum total of human knowledge; but his labors may to a very limited degree, if at all, affect human affairs at the present time. Yet the labors of the latter in bringing to light and putting on record what was in part or altogether forgotten are not without interest and value, although, as it may be, a value founded in large part on sentiment.

Local history is receiving a large share of attention in our present era. It is probably this that has given stimulus to the compilation of family histories and genealogical records. By many Rosenberger descendants the appearance of a work which will give a wider knowledge of the different branches of the family to which they belong, and which will also serve to preserve the history of the family, will be hailed with delight. The writer must acknowledge that previous to his becoming interested in the first reunion of the family he knew very little of its

7

history. That he does not stand alone in this lack is
evidenced by these words from another member of the
family coming to notice through a communication :
"I should like to know something more of the
Rosenberger family ; I know all too little of them."

Preservation of and interest in family records
with us, where primogeniture and aristocracy do not
obtain, is, no doubt, largely a matter of sentiment,
but it is sentiment that is not to be despised. The
matter flavors also to a large degree of duty, and, in
this measure, it becomes an incumbency upon us.
There are two extremes into which the human family
may fall with respect to the attitude toward ancestry—
the one that of veneration amounting to worship ; the
other that of neglect amounting to dishonor. The
Chinee is a type of the first extreme ; the American
people, it is feared, are rapidly drifting into the
other. As we fulfill the divine command to honor
our parents we must needs become possessed of a
lively interest in those who have gone before and
through our parents have handed down to us those
qualities which are priceless legacies. While we
might desire a family history to contain fuller accounts
of the characteristics, traits and deeds of our ancestors
than this work does, we shall remember that there is
no clue known to this desirable knowledge. It is
gratifying, however, to have at hand a few bits of
data which may be used as a framework upon which
the fancy can build a structure. Among such facts
we find that they left the mother country for the sake
of liberty of conscience, that they helped to subdue
the rugged wilderness of the new world, and that
theirs was a religion that taught simplicity of life,
consistency of deeds and profession, and peace with all
men. Building upon these facts the imagination can-

not go far wrong. We look back with our minds and
eyes and see our father, the emigrant, with his
family bidding farewell to home surroundings and
friends and embarking for a foreign shore. We see
him select a site for his home in the new country and
then begin the erection of rude buildings for shelter.
We see him pursue from day to day his primitive
occupation, but with all finding time for higher
duties as he ministers to the little flock entrusted to
his care ; and along with all we conceive how he
fervently blesses God for the priceless boon of liberty
vouch-safed to him in this "Land of the Free."

As we picture these scenes we are made aware
that the lesson which these sturdy tillers of the soil,
our forefathers, teaches us is not without grave import.
In our time there is a tendency to measure success by
the degree of refinement and luxury, possible of
attainment. Of these they knew very little, but times
have changed, and we rejoice that they have. We
freely admit that it shows a commendable spirit to
keep abreast of the times. It remains, however, that
present conditions as contrasted with the past do not
necessarily determine the comparative value of our
lives. Personal worth is the truest crown of any life,
whenever and under whatever condition it may be
lived.

A large part of this work is simply a record of
names and to one outside of the family might appear
uninteresting, but to members of the family it will be
far from meaningless. Following up this record they
will be enabled to trace out the relations of the
various branches of the family, and they will, no
doubt, often be surprised to find that persons with
whom they have had a passing acquaintance are
bound to them by ties of kinship. Most of the fuller

biographical sketches are of those still living or
recently deceased. These will be of interest, as they
reveal the many different walks in life chosen by the
many descendants. In the light of the fact that at
first only a few vocations were represented by the
family these will have still more interest. When it is
noted that at first the family was limited to one
locality and now is spread over the whole extent of
the United States and quite largely represented in
Canada added interest will follow. But this part will
be of still more value and interest to coming generations, and we can do them a good service by giving
our assistance in making and preserving these records
and handing them over to posterity.

To Rev. A. J. Fretz, the author, every one connected with the family owes a debt of gratitude.
The preparation of a work of this character involves
the expenditure of much time and labor, besides the
accompaniment of many vexatious experiences. To
the members of the family who have assisted in
furnishing the necessary data and have helped in this
and other ways in kindling an interest in the history
of the family, especially to I. R. Haldeman, the
publisher, who was the prime mover in securing the
revision of the Rosenberger history, also acknowledge-
ment is due. It is hoped that the work will be widely
circulated and accomplish the end in view in its
preparation.

SEWARD M. ROSENBERGER.

QUAKERTOWN, Pa., Sept. 20, 1899.

EXPLANATIONS.

In the preparation of this work it will be observed that all descendants are recorded in the regular order of birth, from the oldest down to the youngest throughout the entire connection, each generation being marked consecutively from first to last. The Roman numerals placed before each name are used to designate the generation to which they belong, as :—

    I. Henry Rosenberger (First Generation).
    II. Benjamin Rosenberger (Second Generation).
    III. Yelles Rosenberger (Third Generation).
    IV. Benjamin Rosenberger (Fourth Generation).
    V. Elias Rosenberger (Fifth Generation), etc.

Beginning with the first (I) ancestor, Henry Rosenberger, his children as far as known are named. Then follows Benjamin Rosenberger (II Generation), and his children (III Generation) next. Yelles, probably the oldest, is followed down to the last of his descendants, then the second in order of birth of the III Generation, and so on until the end of the entire branch of Benjamin Rosenberger, of the II Generation, is reached. Then the descendants of Daniel Rosenberger, II Generation, is taken up and carried down in like manner to the last of his descendants, and so on throughout the entire connections.

Where marriages occur between members of the connection the husband carries the record. In all such cases a numbered reference is placed after the name and marriage of the wife, as for example (See Index of References No. 1). In the list of Index of References will be found No. 1, Mary A. Dennstedt, married Aaron R. Bock, Page —. On the page given in the body of the book the family record is given.

In the General Index will be found the names of all males of 18 years and over, and the maiden names of all females of 18 years and over ; also the pages on which their family record is given in the body of the book.

To find family records see Index of Branches, where names of all that had issue of the first, second and third generations are given.

ABBREVIATIONS :—D signifies died or deceased ; b born ; s single ; m married ; ch church ; Montg co Montgomery county ; twp township ; Ev Ass'n Evangelical Association ; Pres Presbyterian ; Luth Lutheran ; Menn Mennonite ; Ger Bap German Baptist ; Ger Ref German Reformed (Reformed church in the United States); Cong Congregational ; M E Methodist Episcopal.

THE ROSENBERGER FAMILY OF MONT-GOMERY COUNTY, PA.

The name of Rosenberger is of ancient origin in Germany, signifying Rosemount or Rose Castle. The first Rosenbergers in America probably came from the Palatinate, once a province of western Germany, bordering on the Rhine. September 20, 1738, Hans Peter Rosenberger arrived in Philadelphia on a ship from Rotterdam, containing a number of emigrants from that country. John F. Rauchenberger arrived a week later, and Erasmus Rosenberger on September 26, 1749. The first settler of the name of Rosenberger in Montgomery county was Henry Rosenberger, who came to the Indian Creek valley, in Franconia township, in 1729. In 1739 Benjamin Rosenberger settled in Hatfield township, where in that year he purchased 125 acres of land bordering the County Line at Line Lexington, which he held for five years. Daniel Rosenberger purchased another tract in Hatfield lying along the County Line near the hamlet called Hockertown in 1740. In the year 1745 Henry Rosenberger, Jr., came in possession by deed of his father's plantation in Franconia township. John Rosenberger settled in Hatfield township and first bought land around where is now the borough of Hatfield about 1749-50.

It is a tradition of the family that the Rosenbergers of Montgomery county, Pa., came from Germany, from a place called "Zweibrucken" (two bridges).

13

It is supposed that these families that settled in
Franconia and Hatfield townships were all related,
and while it is certain that Daniel and John were
brothers, it is quite evident that the four above
mentioned were all brothers and sons of Henry
Rosenberger, Sr. John Shutt Rosenberger, a great-
great-grandson of Benjamin Rosenberger, previous to
his death is said to have related that one of his
ancestors reached the great age of 96 years. It is not
now certain which one of his ancestors he named as
having reached that age. He also said that one of
his ancestors was born on board ship or soon after
the landing in America. It is quite certain that
neither Benjamin or his eldest son, Yelles, reached
the age of 96 years, therefore it must have been
Benjamin's father, the emigrant, who was 96 years
old at his death. This would also indicate that
Benjamin was the son of a pioneer. It is quite likely
that Henry Rosenberger, Sr., the pioneer, lived to be
96 years old, but it is not clear that any of the
ancestors were born on the voyage over. Benjamin,
who no doubt was the eldest, was in all probability
born in Germany, and was a lad of from 11 to 15
years old when he came with his father to America.
He was born as early as about 1714 and died about
1777, aged 63 years or more. His eldest son, Yelles,
was born before 1735 and died 1808, aged 73 or more.
The time of the emigration of Henry Rosenberger, Sr.,
is not known, but was in all probability between the
years of 1720 and 1729. The descendants of Benjamin
are now largely settled in Bucks county, Pa., and a
considerable number also reside in Waterloo county,
Ontario, Can.

All the earlier members of these families belonged

to the religious sect called Mennonites and worshipped
at Franconia and Line Lexington meetinghouses.

Since writing the above we have received a communication from Dr. M. Elizabeth Rosenberg, of
Omaha, Neb., which may throw some light on the
early history of the Rosenberger family in Europe.
The letter reads as follows :

OMAHA, NEB., Sept. 19, 1899.

REV. A. J. FRETZ,

Dear Sir :—Forgive me for plunging right into the subject.
My time is limited, the story is a long one, the pater's mind
is not so strong as it used to be.   I have obtained my side of
the tree by devious ways.

First, I will tell the story as I think it is ; then I will give
you proofs as near as I can.

I think we must start with Bohemia in Austria.   A family
of Rosenberg lived northwest of Vienna on a large estate.
History mixes them up with the Hohenzollern family and the
religious wars of Austria.   Between 1611 and 1660 they were
driven out to Switzerland, Holland, England, and lastly they
took ship with William Penn.   There must have been a father
and nine sons.   The pater (my father) is the eighth generation from the one coming on the ship.

PROOF I.   I have heard my father say (when I was small)
"my father was of a princely family.   There was Von to the
name ; but he, the original Von Rosenberg, had to drop it
because no Von could travel without a permit from his king."

PROOF II.   A Rosenberg living near Washingtonville, O.,
sent for father about the year 1851 to see what their relationship might be, and this cousin said that they (he and my
father) were the eighth generation, that the original emigrant
was a man with nine sons, that one son went to Virginia and
that he was from that branch.

PROOF III.   My father often heard his father tell that his
ancestors were driven out by religious persecution, that they
hid in Switzerland in caves, thence fled to Holland and England, that the name was changed during the flight, and the
Von never resumed, that a fierce battle was fought before
their flight.

PROOF IV.   There was an article in the "Boston Monthly

Scientific " on farming from a traveler in Austria describing
the Schwartzenberger estate.   These obtained the estate after
the flight of the Rosenberg family.   Wintergan is the central
village.   The fish pond still retains its original name, Rosenberg "Teuch."   I do not know the date of the article.   We
and Uncle Dave Rosenberg, of Bettsville, O., have copies of it.
The estate consists of 99 villages and 30,000 people, and about
75,000 acres under the control of this Prince.

Very respectfully,   M. E. ROSENBERG.

The article above referred to and furnished by
Miss Rosenberg reads as follows :

A PRINCELY ESTATE.

The domain of the Schwartzenbergs' estate consists of
99 cities and villages and 30,000 people on one farm.   The
extensive and interesting collection of products of the famous
estate of the Prince John Adolph Von Schwartzenberg's
pavillion in the National Exposition has led to a general
desire among those interested in agriculture to see for themselves the rich fields and perfect appointed farm establishment
that has brought forth such a wealth of various products.
Consequently the second excursion of a committee or jury that
visited the farm estate yesterday was a very popular one.   The
excursionists counted to be 150 persons, and they took for
themselves a special train at 6 a. m.   In four hours' ride we
landed there through hills and rich plains of Bohemia.   The
views, landscapes and sceneries before our sight while enroute
was interesting and instructive.   The Schwartzenbergs' domain
lieth towards the northwest from Vienna in the direction of
the Prague, and comprises about 75,000 acres, of which about
40,000 acres is woodland and 20,000 acres are under cultivation,
while 14,000 acres are covered with water, lakes, etc., the
remainder farm yards, streets, etc.   This domain has been in
the possession of the Schwartzenbergs' since A. D. 1660, having been formerly in the possession of the Rosenberg family.
The domain reverted to the Crown on the death of the last one
of the Rosenbergs', A. D. 1611, and was presented by the
Crown to John Adolph Schwartzenberg at the time of A. D.
1660.   The population of the domain is in the neighborhood
of about 30,000 people, who inhabit 99 villages, of which
Wintergan is the residence of the Prince.   The details of the

direction of affairs of the domain would occupy too much space to be given at length. The prince is assisted by the hereditary Prince Adolph Joseph in the management of the estate and there is an army of officials from all directions of this domain. The entire domain, exclusive of the sugar mills, brings a yearly product of the value of 6,000,000 florins, or about 3 per cent. of the capital represented. There is hardly a limit to the variety of substance of food produced on the estate. Fish culture has been for 300 hundred years a great specialty.

The Rosenberg family in the end of the fifteenth century stocked with fish the largest ponds for the first time. The large pond is still called today the Rosenberg "Teuch."

NOTE.—There is no doubt that Henry Rosenberger, Sr., of Franconia, was the pioneer emigrant, and that he in common with other Mennonites fled from Germany on account of religious persecution. Of the earlier history of the family and their connection with the " princely family," the original spelling of the name, as suggested in the foregoing, the number of children the pioneer had, and whether one of the sons emigrated to Virginia or not, we know nothing. We have seen Rosenberger's direct from Austria and Germany and one Rosenberg from Prussia. One of the former from Austria claimed to be of an old Austrian Rosenberger stock, and were Jews. The last mentioned Rosenberg, from Prussia, was also a Jew.   AUTHOR.

HENRY ROSENBERGER, OF FRANCONIA.

I. Henry Rosenberger is believed to have been the first of the name who came to Montgomery county as an emigrant from Germany, and was a Mennonite. He purchased land in Franconia on November 14, 1729, of James Steele, of Philadelphia. For £30 he obtained 150 acres. This was situated about two and one-half miles west of Souderton. It covered an area through which flows the Indian Creek. The greater part was the slope toward the northwest from the present Souderton and Harleysville turnpike to that stream, and including the site of the Mennonite burying ground. Within these boundaries are now the farm of Jacob S. Alderfer, Schueck's mill and the farm of Michael Swartley. The latter is the fifth in descent from Henry Rosenberger and owns the homestead. Here down in the valley of the Indian Creek and on its southeast side is a stone farm house of unusual size. It bears the date of 1809 and the name of John "Schwardle" in German, who was the grandfather of the present owner. To the north is a modern barn and close to hand an older one. The latter is the oldest building about the premises. On the wooden beam over the door is inscribed the name of Henry Rosenberger and Barbara, his wife, with the date of 1755. The first barn of all, in existence between 1730 and 1755, stood more closely adjacent to the banks of the stream, which was thought handy to wash away the manure at a time this was thought

of little value. A stone springhouse stands 70 yards
west of the house near the creek and bears the date of
1793. For this distance the water for household
purposes was carried for three or four generations.
In the present garden, just west of the house, stood
the humble log.dwelling which sheltered the old
Mennonite emigrant and his family. It was only one
and one-half stories high and existed for 80 years.

The bounderies of the wilderness tract purchased
of Steele in 1729 were : " Beginning at corner in line
of Christian Haldeman ; thence by same northeast
100 perches to line of Francis Daniel Pastorias ;
thence by same northwest 254 perches by marked
trees ; thence by marked trees southeast 254 perches
to beginning." This was part of 1000 acres which
Penn's commissioners of property, Isaac Norris, James
Logan and Thomas Griffith, had sold to Steele in
1728. The deed was witnessed by James Robinson
and Abraham Reiff. The Christian Haldeman here
mentioned held a tract on the south side of the turnpike, where is now the Jonas Moyer estate.

In the list of taxables of Franconia in 1734 is
found the name of Henry Rosenberger. In the old
records Franconia is styled " The Dutch Township,"
and to the present day its population is almost wholly
of German or Dutch origin.

Nothing is known of the personality of Henry
Rosenberger. He built a house and barn and cleared
some land, enduring the hardships of a first settler.
In the year 1745 he conveyed his plantation in Franconia to his son Henry. The bounderies of the deed
of 1745 are copied from the first deed and Henry Funk
and Christian Meyer, two Mennonites, were the
witnesses. The son Henry paid his father £200.
It is not known what became of the father after con-

veying his plantation to his son, but he probably remained with Henry.

It is not known when Henry Rosenberger died. He was a Mennonite and one of the original worshippers at Franconia, where he was also buried.

The Franconia Mennonite meetinghouse is one of the typical places of worship found in many localities of eastern Pennsylvania. A church was organized and a house of worship built here as early as 1730. The recent structure was succeeded by another in 1892. Like all others of this people it is plain to austerity. Many horse sheds encompass it about. It is built upon an elevation from which a splendid view of hill and valley to the north and west may be obtained. This overlooks a densely populated farming country, extending to the distant hills of Berks and the highlands beyond the Schuylkill. In the near view are the pleasant vales of the Indian Creek and the North Branch of the Perkiomen. On the northwest side of the meetinghouse lies the extensive burying ground, thickly dotted with marble tombstones, where repose the dead of many generations. This congregation is one of the strongest in number, having over 700 members. A communion service in the Spring brings out a very large attendance, and the services have a quaint interest for the stranger. The service, beginning at 8 o'clock in the morning, lasts over three hours. The women are seated within the two aisles, while the men occupy the side pews, their hats being hung on long rows of pegs over the aisles. In the rear vestibule, entered by a side door, is the women's room, where are hung their bonnets and extra clothing. The Scriptures are read in German and several preachers in turn exhort the congregation. The elements of the communion are handed to each member by the bishop, who has an assistant, meanwhile constantly exhorting. In time of prayer is seen a kneeling throng. The preacher from a hymn book reads one verse at a time in a sing-song tone. This is sung to an old-fashioned tune, sounding sweetly to the ear as it comes from the white-capped throng. Thus is conducted the worship of the followers of Menno Simons.

We name as the children of Henry Rosenberger, Sr., Benjamin, Daniel, John, Henry, Jr. If there were daughters we have not learned of them.

BENJAMIN ROSENBERGER, OF HATFIELD.

II. Benjamin Rosenberger, born in Germany ; died during the Revolution about 1777 ; married Helena ———. She died in 1799. Benjamin Rosenberger settled in Hatfield township, Montgomery county, Pa., where, as early as 1739, he purchased 125 acres on the County Line, comprising the present Oliver G. Morris and Frick farms at Line Lexington, of Ebenezer Kinnersley. This property he held until 1744, and it is probable that he made the first improvements there. He sold it to his son John, who only retained possession one year.

Benjamin Rosenberger was of a dealing, trading, speculative disposition, and we find him buying and selling various properties in different townships all his life. His next purchase was a tract of land of 112 acres in Hatfield, lying further southwest. This was 86 perches by 210 in dimensions. The neighboring landholders were James Dunn on the southeast, Jacob Weirman on the southwest, John Shooter on the northeast, and Edward Warner on the northwest. This place was bought of David Thomas for £120. It had belonged to a grant of 1210 acres made to Jonathan Hayes in 1705, who made the first improvements. His only son, Jonathan, had two sisters, Elizabeth, wife of Richard Maris, and Mary, wife of Evan Lewis. The daughters were the heirs after the death of their brother. They sold to John Williams in 1723, who conveyed to David Thomas in 1731.

We next find him the owner of the late Server farm, just north of Lansdale, a large part of which is now included in that borough. This he bought at a date now unknown, but which Rosenberger sold to Solomon Sell in 1760. It comprised 106 acres and in later times belonged to Edward Jenkins and his son Philip. A little later, before 1766, he came into possession of a farm in Gwynedd, near Friends' Corner, later owned by Jonathan Lukens. This he sold in 1776 to Cadwallader Foulke. In 1772 he bought a lot in Upper Gwynedd, comprising 50 acres, of Jonathan Clayton, near the present Kneedler hotel. Probably this had no building on it. It was sold by his heirs in 1781 to Jacob Heisler, the tavern keeper, for £400. It is supposed that he also owned a farm in Franconia, as his widow Helena died in that township. In the old deeds of Benjamin Rosenberger he is mentioned as a carpenter. At one time he also owned the present Beaver farm, near North Wales.

The death of Benjamin Rosenberger took place during the Revolution, near or in 1777, after an active life of over 50 years in this county. Helena, widow of Benjamin Rosenberger, Sr, died in Franconia during the Summer of 1799. In her will mention is made of her grandchild Helena, wife of Michael Wireman, and great-grandchild, Anna Weirman. From her daughter Elizabeth, who married John Alderfer, have sprung many descendants in Lower Salford. The surviving children of Benjamin Rosenberger were five in number, viz: Elias (or Yellis), John, Gertrude, Elizabeth, Henry.

DESCENDANTS OF YELLIS, SON OF
BENJAMIN ROSENBERGER, SR.

III. Yellis Rosenberger, born at Hatfield, Montgomery county, Pa., before 1735 ; died near Perkasie or Sellersville, in Rockhill township, Bucks county, in the early Fall of 1808. His will was registered October 3 of that year. In this he bequeathed to his son Benjamin the " plantation where I now live " containing 130 acres, then bounded by lands of Andrew Schlichter and Abraham Stroud. He also owned fourteen acres of woodland. His daughter Ann received £1000 and the other daughter, Rebecca, a farm in Springfield, where John Bissey lived. The son Henry had already received his portion. Yellis, or Julius Rosenberger, as he is often called in the old deeds, inherited the trading, money-making disposition of his father, and the records of Bucks county show that he bought and sold many different properties in that county. In 1760 he bought of Henry Funk a plantation in Hilltown of 166 acres for £400, which he sold in 1765. Before 1773 he lived in Springfield, on the Saucon line, a portion of his farm being in Northampton county. In that year he bought a farm in Bedminster, on the Hilltown border, of George Rothrock. In 1774 a farm of 106 acres was bought of Valentine Kramer, in Hilltown. In 1795 he bought 70 acres in Rockhill of Christian Dotterer, which just before his death, in 1808, he sold to his son Henry. He had also acquired a farm of 130 acres in that township.

24

Franconia Mennonite Meeting House.

The Springfield farm was inherited by his son Benjamin, as well as the one in Rockhill. There is a tradition concerning a large tract of land in Rockhill, which, in those days, was held by non-resident owners. It comprised, along with arable land, much of the Rockhills. Several squatters had settled on this land, among whom was a Rosenberger. They were ordered to vacate, but refused, and were only dispossessed by a Sheriff's posse. The latter came "with a band of soldiers," as the story goes, in the absence of Rosenberger. The women folks at home were very belligerent and prepared to scald the intruders. The Sheriff finally broke down the door and got possession. The writer has no dates as to the time of this transaction or which family were engaged. The children of Yellis Rosenberger were Benjamin, Henry, Anna, Rebecca.

IV. Benjamin Rosenberger, born probably in Hatfield about 1758 ; died in 1824 ; married Margaret Nash. He lived in Saucon in his early youth, and before his majority was teamster in the American army of the Revolution. The latter part of his life he lived in Rockhill, Bucks county. He also owned a grist, saw and oil mills in Haycock and 27 acres of land. He reached the age of 66, his will being registered April 24, 1824. In this document mention is made of his children, as follows : Elias, Abraham, William, John, Jacob, Joseph, Benjamin, Elizabeth, Rachel, Margaret.

V. Elias Rosenberger, b Dec 22, 1787 ; d Dec 14, 1829 ; m Barbara Fretz, dau of *Joseph and Maria (Krout) Fretz, April 4, 1809. She was b Sept 12, 1786 ; d Sept 18, 1816. C : Joseph, Rebecca, Maria, Benjamin, Jacob. Elias married second wife Elizabeth

* "Fuller Joe."

Hunsberger. She was b Oct 29, 1790 ; died Jan 24, 1835. C : Isaac and Henry (twins), Elias.

VI. Joseph Rosenberger, b Dec 27, 1809. He went to Canada.

VI. Rebecca Rosenberger, b Mar 4, 1812 ; m Solomon Bigley. C : William, Sarah, Lizzie.

VI. Mary Rosenberger, b in Pa Sept 30, 1813 ; d in Clinton twp, Lincoln co, Ont, Can, April 21, 1892 ; m William High. He was born in Lincoln co, Ont, Can, Oct 1, 1807 ; d May 23, 1893. Farmer ; Men. C : Sarah, Annie, infant, Margaret.

VII. Sarah High, b in Lincoln co, Ont, Feb 17, 1845 ; m David Sievenpiper Jan 23, 1865. He was born in Haldimand co, Ont, Apr 15, 1842. P O Jordon, Ont. Farmer ; Ev Ass'n. C : Milton, William, Harvey, Lillie, Stephen.

VIII. Milton Sievenpiper, b in Campden, Ont, May 11, 1866 ; died Aug 3, 1896, at St Luke's Hospital, Florida, where he went for the benefit of his health. He was buried in the Evergreen Cemetery, Jacksonville, Fla. Journalist ; Bap. S.

VIII. William E Sievenpiper, born July 8, 1871 ; m Minnie M Hamilton Oct 6, 1897. R 94 Leeming st, Hamilton, Ont. Employed by Electric Light Co; M E. C : (**IX**) Harry Sievenpiper, b August 11, 1898 ; d Sept 8, 1898.

VIII. Harvey Sievenpiper, born Aug 8, 1875. P O Campden, Ont. Farmer ; Ev Ass'n. S.

VIII. Lillie Sievenpiper, b Aug 31, 1880. Ev Ass'n.

VIII. Stephen Sievenpiper, b July 12, 1882. Ev Ass'n.

VII. Annie High, born in Lincoln co, Ont, Feb 16, 1849 ; m Edward O'Loughlin March 31, 1877. He died April 14, 1882. P O Campden, Ont. Farmer ; Ev Ass'n. C : (**VIII**) Maggie May O'Loughlin, born June 16, 1878. Ev Ass'n. (**VIII**) William Clayton O'Loughlin, b Mar 16, 1880. Ev Ass'n. (**VIII**) Norris Clare O'Loughlin, born June 16, 1884. (**VIII**) Mary Ellen O'Loughlin, b July 2, 1886.

VII. Infant son, b and d Oct 9, 1854.

VII. Margaret High, born March 17, 1856 ; m Simon Houser July 20, 1880. P O Campden, Ont. Ev Ass'n.

VI. Benjamin Rosenberger, b Dec 16, 1814. Lived in Canada.

VI. Jacob Rosenberger, b Sept 11, 1816. Lived in Ohio.

VI. Isaac Rosenberger, b June 10, 1818 ; d in 1886 ; m Susanna Bishop Sept 25, 1842. She was b Aug 10, 1820 ; died in 1888. Farmer ; Mens. C: Henry, Jacob, Elias, Isaac, Abraham, Anna, Mary.

VII. Rev Henry Rosenberger, born in Bucks co, Pa, July 22, 1844 ; married Mary Ann, dau of Jacob L Shattinger, December 19, 1868. P O Dublin, Pa. Farmer and minister. Mr Rosenberger was ordained to the ministry of the Mennonite church at Blooming Glen, Bucks co, Pa, Oct 27, 1885. where he has since served as one of the ministers of that congregation. No issue.

VII. Jacob B Rosenberger, b about 1846 ; m Sarah Myers in 1873. P O Dublin, Pa. Merchant ; Mens. C: (**VIII**) William M Rosenberger, b in 1875 ; Allen M, b 1881 ; Susie May, b 1886.

VII. Elias Rosenberger, b Aug 3, 1849 ; died Oct 29, 1849.

VII. Isaac Rosenberger, Jr, born Sept 25, 1851 ; died May 26, 1856.

VII. Abraham B Rosenberger, b March 27, 1853 ; m Mary Godshalk Jan 10, 1880. Farmer ; Mens. C: (**VIII**) Isaac G Rosenberger, born December 20, 1880. (**VIII**) Anna G Rosenberger, b September 19, 1882. (**VIII**) Mary Emma Rosenberger, b November 2, 1884. (**VIII**) Edward G Rosenberger, b Apr 6, 1888 ; died December 28, 1888.

VII. Anna Rosenberger, by Dec 19, 1855 ; d Nov 6, 1888 ; m Edwin Shaddinger Nov 22, 1879. He died Oct 29, 1884. Farmer ; Men. C: (**VIII**) Henry R Shaddinger, b Aug 4, 1881. (**VIII**) Susan Shaddinger, b Aug 4, 1883 ; d Feb 23, 1885.

VII. Mary Rosenberger, b December 6, 1858 ; died April 6, 1880. Single.

VI. Henry Rosenberger, b June 10, 1818 ; m Mary Gotwals. Merchant ; Men. No issue.

VI. Elias Rosenberger, born August 19, 1820 ; died March 5, 1842. He was subject to convulsions and

unable to take care of himself. After the death of
his parents he was put in the Industrial Home, where
he died. Single.

V. Abraham N Rosenberger, born in Bucks co, Pa,
April 26, 1792 ; d in 1861 ; m Elizabeth Haldeman
Oct 27, 1814. She was b in Montgomery co Oct 17,
1797 ; died Dec 23, 1846. Miller, millwright and
farmer ; Menn. C : Susanna, Henry, Samuel,
Hannah, Israel, Abraham, Mary, Enos, William,
Joseph, Levi, Mahlon.

VI. Susanna Rosenberger, b Jan 24, 1816 ; d infant.

VI. Henry Rosenberger, b Aug 13, 1818 ; d infant.

VI. Samuel Rosenberger, b Oct 16, 1819 ; d about
1879. Single.

VI. Hannah Rosenberger, born in Upper Providence
twp, Montg co, Dec 15, 1820 ; died Dec 10, 1885 ;
m Israel T Place March 27, 1842. He was born in
Montg co July 5, 1819 ; d in Hatfield twp, Montg co,
August 22, 1895. His parents were of German
ancestry and descended from old families well known
in eastern Pennsylvania, having resided for several
generations in the United States. His father, Henry
G Place, was a prominent citizen of Montg co, and a
personal acquaintance of Governor Francis R Shunk,
who occupied the Executive Chair of Pennsylvania
from 1845 until his death in 1848. Israel Place
received a common school education, after which he
learned the carpenter trade, which occupation he
followed successfully for many years. He resided
last in Hatfield twp with his oldest daughter, Sarah A
Gotwals, where he died. He was a Whig in early
life, but became a Republican upon the organization of
the party. He always took an interest in political
matters, though he never aspired to or held any
important office. In religion he was a member of the
Reformed Church. C : Sarah, Louise, Warren, Isabella, Hannah, Albert, Mary.

VII. Sarah Ann Place, b June 10, 1843 ; d Oct 13,
1896 ; m Jacob C Gotwals Dec 19, 1863. He was
born in Montg co, Pa, Aug 14, 1838 ; d Mar 9, 1897.
P O Phœnixville, Pa. Farmer and carpenter. C :
(**VIII**) Laura Gotwals, m —— Anson. P O Lansdale,

Pa. (**VIII**) John P Gotwals. P O Phœnixville, Pa.
(**VIII**) Samuel, Warren, Albert, Edwin, Lizzie, Charles,
Sadie.

VII. Louisa Place, b April 6, 1846 ; died April 1883.

VII. J Warren Place, b Dec 13, 1848 ; m Mary F
Dauber Feb 10, 1881. P O Lansdale, Pa. No issue.

VII. Isabella Place, b July 4, 1851 ; d Sept 28, 1853.

VII. Hannah Place, b in Montg co, Pa, August 26,
1854 ; married Anthony B Schultz March 13, 1875.
P O Worcester, Pa. Hotelkeeper ; Mrs S, Schwenk-
felder. C : (**VIII**) Mary Ella Schultz, b Feb 5, 1876.
(**VIII**) Idella P Schultz, b June 28, 1878 ; d Feb 2,
1891. (**VIII**) Emma P Schultz, b August 21, 1880.
Dressmaker. (**VIII**) Alice Minerva Schultz, b Dec 2,
1882. (**VIII**) Beckie Irene Schultz, b Jan 29, 1885.
(**VIII**) Norman P Schultz, born December 28, 1886.
(**VIII**) Stanley P Schultz, b June 3, 1889. (**VIII**) Cora
P Schultz, b May 28, 1892. (**VIII**) Ethel P Schultz,
born July 31, 1894.

VII. Albert R Place, Esq, born in Upper Providence
twp, Montg co, Pa, June 1, 1857 ; m Mary Alice
Frederick April 11, 1883. Mr Place received his
education in the academic department of Ursinus
College, Collegeville, Pa, and at Washington Hall
Collegiate Institute, Trappe, Pa. After completing
his studies he engaged in teaching, which he followed
continually until July 1885, at which time he commenced to read law in the office of Judge Aaron S
Swartz at Norristown. During the time he devoted
to teaching he was principal of the Lansdale public
schools for a period of four years and held a like
position in the Hatboro schools for three years. He
received at the hands of E E Higbee, State Superintendent, a permanent teacher's certificate for the State
of Pennsylvania. He was admitted to the Bar in
October 1887 and during the Winter following taught
commercial law at Pierce College of Business, Philadelphia. He then began the practice of law in
Montgomery county, Pa, having his office at Lansdale.
In April 1889 he formed a law partnership with
E L Hallman, of Royersford, Pa, and these gentlemen
have practiced together up to the year 1900. They

have conducted and still enjoy a prosperous general
law business, and practice in all the courts of Montgomery and Chester counties and also in the Supreme
Court of the State of Pennsylvania.

Politically Mr Place is a staunch Republican, but
has refrained from participation in politics, preferring
to strictly devote himself to business in the line of his
profession. He has served as a member of the School
Board of Lansdale for a number of years, is counsel
for the boroughs of Lansdale and Souderton, and also
solicitor of the North Wales bank, of which he was
one of the founders and first directors. He was also
one of the organizers of the North Penn Building and
Loan Association of Lansdale and was its first president. Possessed of ability and judgment his management of these enterprises has proved successful. He
was also vice president and one of the founders of
Schissler College of Business, located at Norristown.
In religion Mr Place was for a number of years connected with the Abington Presbyterian church, but
later became a member of the Reformed church of
Lansdale. He is a member of the Masonic Order,
with which he has been connected since 1893. His
business and professional career has been successful,
and being founded on the corner-stones of honesty,
integrity, ability and a determination to do thorough-
ly whatever he undertook, his career furnishes an example for the emulation of young men. P O Lansdale, Pa. C : (**VIII**) Kate Helen Place, b Feb 7,
1886.

VII. Mary Place, b in Montg co, Pa, June 1, 1861 ;
m Wilson Schultz Jan 3, 1880. P O Lansdale, Pa.
C : (**VIII**) Scelina Schultz, b Dec 4, 1880.

VI. Israel Rosenberger, b May 31, 1822; d at Eagle-
ville, Montg co, Pa, June 19, 1891 ; m Elizabeth
Reiff Dec 6, 1846. She was born in Montg co, Pa,
July 5, 1824. Stone mason; Trinity Ref. C : Sallie.

VII. Sallie C Rosenberger, b in Upper Providence
twp, Montg co, Dec 14, 1847 ; m Horace Place
Sept 30, 1876. P O Eagleville, Pa. Farmer. Trinity Reformed. C : (**VIII**) Lizzie R Place, b Aug 6,
1878. (**VIII**) Howard R Place, born June 16, 1879.

(**VIII**) Ira Place, born May 24, 1880; died September 6, 1880. (**VIII**) Clarence G Place, born Oct 13, 1882. (**VIII**) Cora Place, b Sept 6, 1885; d July 3, 1886. (**VIII**) Anna Florence Place, b Nov 23, 1888.
VI. Abraham Rosenberger, b Jan 11, 1825; d Oct 5, 1853; m Mary, daughter of Anthony Vanderslice, Feb 14, 1850. She was b Mar 1, 1825; d Feb 24, 1888. Shoemaker; Christian ch. C : Benjamin, Frank.
VII Benjamin H Rosenberger, born Apr 10, 1851 ; d Aug 4, 1853.
VII. Frank A Rosenberger, b at Trappe, Montg co, Pa ; m Ella K Geisinger June 27, 1878. R 2145 N 21st st, Phila. Salesman. C : (**VIII**) Laura May Rosenberger, b Mar 21, 1880 ; Marguerite G, b July 20, 1889.
VI. Mary Rosenberger, b Sept 17, 1827; d in 1855; m John O Zimmerman. He was b in Montg co; d Sept 1898. Carpenter, later music teacher in Philadelphia. Mr Z, Luth; Mrs Z, Bap. C : Son, Frank.
VII. —— Zimmerman, d aged about 4 years.
VII. Frank R Zimmerman, b in Montg co Nov 10, 1852 ; m Clara L Fauske Oct 23, 1881. R 223 First ave, West Cedar Rapids, Ia. After the death of his parents he was left with a family by name of Bergey, near Telford, Montg co, until nearly 12 years of age. Carpenter and hard wood finisher; U Ev. C : (**VIII**) Mabel Lulu Zimmerman, b at Belle Plains, Ia, in 1882; Irene Mildred, b at Kenesaw, Neb, in 1886; Ethel Viola, b at Cedar Rapids, Ia, in 1894.
VI. Enos H Rosenberger, b in Montg co June 16, 1830; m Elizabeth S Raudenbush in 1853. P O Kutztown, Pa. Teacher ; Ref. C : Mary, Horace.
VII. Mary Marcella Rosenberger, b in Montg co Jan 27, 1854 ; m Dr Cyrus Wanner June 13, 1878. He died Feb 27, 1890. Physician ; Ger Ref. C: (**VIII**) Charles R Wanner, b June 24, 1879. Ger Ref. (**VIII**) Elizabeth R Wanner, b July 7, 1883 ; died Dec 21, 1883. (**VIII**) Howard R Wanner, b Nov 26, 1884. (**VIII**) Jesse R Wanner, b Nov 28, 1888.
VII. Horace A Rosenberger, b 1856 ; d in 1858.
VI. William Rosenberger, b Nov 2, 1832 ; d 1834.

VI. Joseph H Rosenberger, b Oct 4, 1835 ; d about 1885; m Sophia T Lynch. Farmer ; Pres. No issue.
VI. Levi H Rosenberger, b Nov 22, 1839 ; m Vituria Schrack. She d Mar 1881. C : Elizabeth, Frank. Levi m second wife Mary Mull. P O Spring City, Pa. Teacher, scrivener and notary public ; Luth.
VII. Elizabeth Rosenberger, b May 9, 1869 ; m John H Godshall June 12, 1890. P O Spring City, Pa. Luth. C : (**VIII**) Mary R Godshall, b Apr 25, 1891 ; Anna R, b May 26, 1893.
VII. Frank S Rosenberger, b at Spring City, Pa, Dec 4, 1871. P O Spring City, Pa. Laborer ; Ger Ref. S.
VI. Mahlon Rosenberger, b Sept 23, 1842 ; d 1844.
V. William Rosenberger, b in Saucon twp, Lehigh co, Pa, in 1794 ; d in Rockhill twp, Bucks co, in 1877 ; m Susanna Button in 1817. She was b in 1791 ; d 1866. Farmer ; Menn. C : Amos, Aaron, Joel, William, Elias, Jacob, John, Isaac.
VI. Amos Rosenberger, b 1818 ; d infant.
VI. Aaron B Rosenberger, b in Rockhill twp, Bucks co, in 1819 ; d Dec 28, 1898 ; m Catharine Dill 1844. R 2236 Fairhill st, Phila. Mr Rosenberger was Clerk of the Orphans' Court of Bucks county from 1861 to 1864, elected on the Republican ticket. He is now a clerk and resides in Philadelphia. Ev. C : (**VII**) James Rosenberger, b 1845 ; d 1866. S. (**VII**) Susanna Rosenberger, b 1849. S. (**VII**) Lizzie Rosenberger, b in Bucks co 1852 ; m Joel C Van Cleve. R 2236 Fairhill st, Phila. Blacksmith ; M E. C : Myra ; James, William, both deceased.
VI. Rev Joel Rosenberger, b in Bucks co Aug 22, 1821 ; m Mary Kindig in 1850. She was b in Hatfield, Pa, Dec 10, 1830. P O South Hatfield, Pa. Mason, bricklayer and farmer. At one time he was an ordained minister of the "Johnson" Menn church and where he preached for about seven years. He then began preaching for and later connected himself with the Evangelical Mennonites (now Mennonite Brethren in Christ), in which connection he preached for about 25 years and to which church he still belongs. C : (**VII**) Milton Rosenberger, b 1853; d aged

3 mos. (**VII**) Oliver Rosenberger, b Aug 9, 1855;
m Lizzie, dau of Eli Kratz.   P O Lansdale, Pa.
Plasterer.   C: Harry, Dwight, Naaman, Joel, son (d
unnamed). (**VII**) Susanna Rosenberger, b Jan 11,
1859; d Aug 18, 1859. (**VII**) Ellamina Rosenberger, b Oct 22, 1861; d Aug 11, 1862. (**VII**) William Rosenberger, b Oct 17, 1865; d Oct 28, 1865.
VI. William Rosenberger, b in Bucks co in 1823; d
Aug 28, 1894; m Eliza Fox.   Farmer; Menn.   C:
(**VII**) Susanna Rosenberger; m Jacob Johnson.   P O
Perkasie, Pa.   Laborer; Luth.   No issue.
VI. Elias B Rosenberger, b in Rockhill twp, Bucks
co, Mar 5, 1826; m Matilda Weinberger Nov 23,
1850.   She was born in Milford, Bucks co, Mar 29,
1831.   P O Powder Valley, Pa.   Carpenter; Menn.
C: Harrison, Samuel, Enos, Adeline, Lucinda, son
(d unnamed).
VII. Harrison Rosenberger, b July 26, 1855; m Lilly
Crawford.   P O Slatedale, Pa.   Merchant.   No issue.
VII. Samuel Rosenberger, b Mar 13, 1857; m Cin-
derella Williams.   P O Slatington, Pa.   Yeoman;
Menn.   C: (**VIII**) David S Rosenberger, b in 1899.
VII. Enos Rosenberger, b Feb 24, 1859.   P O Bow-
manstown, Pa.   Potter; Menn.   S.
VII. Adeline Rosenberger, b Jan 22, 1861; m Daniel
Meyer.   P O Ziousville, Pa.   Yeoman.   Mrs M,
Menn; Mr M, Ref.   C: Adelaide, Blanche.
VII. Lucinda Rosenberger, b Mar 18, 1863; married
Harvey Schall (d).   He conducted a grocery store at
York, Pa.   R Astor st, Norristown, Pa.   C: John E.
VI. Jacob B Rosenberger, b in Rockhill twp, Bucks
co, Pa, Jan 19, 1828; d at Benjamin, Pa, Aug 19,
1897; m Mary Groff Nov 6, 1852.   She was born iu
Bucks co Jan 20, 1830.   P O Benjamin, Pa.   Farmer;
Menn.   C: Susan, Amanda, Mamie.
VII. Susan G Rosenberger, b Sept 28, 1857; died
Feb 6, 1863.
VII. Amanda G Rosenberger, b in Rockhill twp May 4,
1865; m Ephraim S Leister Nov 30, 1882.   P O
Benjamin, Pa.   Farmer; U Ev.   C: (**VIII**) Jacob
Warren Leister, b Oct 12, 1884; John Franklin, b
Jan 11, 1887; George R, b Oct 14, 1895.

VII. Mamie Rosenberger, b at Benjamin Mar 22, 1869. P O Benjamin, Pa. U Ev. S.

VI. John B Rosenberger, b in Rockhill twp, Bucks co, Dec 23, 1830; died Mar 28, 1883; m Lucy Ann Walter in 1867. She was b in Rockhill twp Dec 13, 1840; d Nov 22, 1881. Plasterer. Mr R, Menn; Mrs R, Ger Ref. C: **(VII)** Harvey W Rosenberger, b near Perkasie, Bucks co, Feb 22, 1870; m Minerva E Henry Mar 21, 1895. P O Perkasie, Pa. Cigarmaker; Luth. No issue.

VI. Isaac B Rosenberger, b in Rockhill twp, Bucks co, Aug 17, 1833; m Elizabeth Fluck Apr 26, 1856. She was b Nov 12, 1836. P O Perkasie, Pa. Carpenter; U Ev. C: Irwin, Mary, Maggie, William, Susan, James, Lizzie, Frank, Nora.

VII. Irwin Rosenberger, b Nov 6, 1856; d Jan 22, 1865.

VII. Mary Ann Rosenberger, b in Bucks co Nov 12, 1858; m Rev Joseph K Freed Feb 8, 1879. R 424 Locust st, Lebanon, Pa. Minister U Ev. C: **(VIII)** Mary Jane Freed, b Oct 20, 1879; d Oct 23, 1879. **(VIII)** Irwin R Freed, b Jan 20, 1881. **(VIII)** Ellsworth W Freed, b Sept 7, 1883. **(VIII)** Chester R Freed, b Aug 29, 1889.

VII Maggie Rosenberger, born in Bucks co Aug 9, 1860. P O Perkasie, Pa. S.

VII. William Rosenberger, b in Bucks co July 15, 1863; m Ida Hockman. R 1020 Willow st, Norristown, Pa. Mr Rosenberger was a fireman in the employ of the Reading Railway Co. On Wednesday evening, July 15, 1897, while his train was speeding near Westfield, N J, and just as he was shoveling coal into the furnace a water bar blew out in the boiler, and a cloud of steam and boiling water gushed upon him, frightfully scalding him. The train was checked and Mr. Rosenberger was carried to the caboose, where his body was covered with oil. The train was run on to Elizabeth, where he was taken to the hospital. He lived until Friday noon. Mrs R, U Ev. C: Raymond (d), Irene, Margaret.

VII. Susan Rosenberger, b Sept 30, 1865; d Oct 8, 1865.

VII. James Rosenberger, b in Bucks co Oct 8, 1867 ;
m Lizzie Moyer. P O Perkasie, Pa. Green grocer ;
Ref. No issue.

VII. Lizzie Rosenberger, b Apr 17, 1870. S.

VI. Frank F Rosenberger, b Aug 20, 1875 ; married
Mamie Rotzell Dec 1897. P O Perkasie, Pa. Cigarmaker ; Ref. No issue (1899).

VII. Nora Mae Rosenberger, b Nov 7, 1879. S.

V. John Rosenberger, b in Skippack twp, Montg co,
Nov 28, 1796 ; d Nov 26, 1855 ; m Nancy Shutt.
Farmer ; Menn. C : Abraham, Elizabeth, John.
John m second wife Mary Underkuffler. She was b
Aug 11, 1811 ; d Oct 17, 1894. Mrs R, Luth. C :
Lena, Margaret, Henry. Isaac, Emanuel, Horace,
Susanna, Franklin.

VI. Abraham S Rosenberger (d), b at Trappe, Montg
co, Oct 16, 1819 ; m Elizabeth, daughter of Rev Jos
Cassel. School teacher and farmer ; Menn. C :
Noah. Mary, Joseph, Catharine, Elizabeth, Barbara,
Abraham.

VII. Noah C Rosenberger, born at Skippack, Pa,
Aug 1, 1841 ; m Sarah Ann Kinsey July 18, 1869.
P O Souderton, Pa. Tailor ; Lutheran. Children :
(**VIII**) Samuel Rosenberger, b Aug 11, 1870 ; married
Mary Benner, of Souderton, Pa. (**VIII**) Elizabeth
Rosenberger, b in 1872 ; m Leidy Frankenfield. P O
Lansdale, Pa. C : Preston, Irenia. (**VIII**) Leidy
Rosenberger ; m Maggie Christman. C : Mary.
(**VIII**) Ida Rosenberger, died small. (**VIII**) William
Henry Rosenberger, b Jan 16, 1877 ; died in 1894.
(**VIII**) John Rosenberger, born February 16, 1879.
(**VIII**) Amanda Rosenberger, b September 25, 1881.
(**VIII**) Sallie Rosenberger, born Nov 1, 1883 ; died
infant. (**VIII**) Annie Rosenberger, born Feb 8, 1885 ;
d infant. (**VIII**) Horace Rosenberger, b Jan 8, 1887.
(**VIII**) Albanus Rosenberger, born November 8, 1889.
(**VIII**) Bertha Rosenberger, b May 11, 1893.

VII. Mary Rosenberger, m Joseph Wisler (d). P O
Souderton, Pa. C : Flora.

VII. Joseph C Rosenberry, born in Montg co, Pa,
Sept 18, 1852 ; died March 1, 1899 ; m Kate Cassel
Nov 21, 1874. P O Lansdale, Pa. Early in life

he learned the carpenter trade with Benjamin F
Frederick, of Lansdale. About 26 years ago he
entered the employ of Heebner & Sons in the wood-
work department, which position he retained for
years. Later he was promoted to the position of
superintendent of the works, which he resigned to
engage in the coal and feed business in partnership
with Amos Rosenberger. Three years later he re-
entered the employ of Heebner & Sons as a salesman,
which position he retained up to the time of his
death, and was a valued and trusted employe. During his many years residence in Lansdale he won and
retained the highest esteem of his fellow-citizens.
He was a member of the Borough Council for several
years, retiring in the Spring of 1896. He was re-
elected to that office at the Spring election of 1899 by
a handsome vote. He was also a director of the
North Penn Building and Loan Association. C :
(**VIII**) David C Rosenberry, b Sept 20, 1875. He is
a graduate of the Williamsport Business College and
now clerk in the First National Bank of Lansdale.
(**VIII**) Lillian Rosenberry, b Aug 25, 1877. R Germantown, Phila. (**VIII**) Emma Rosenberry, b Dec 29,
1878.

VII. Catharine Rosenberger, died Mar 27, 1898 ; m
Henry Goshow in 1876. He was born Dec 16, 1850.
Plasterer ; Menn. C : Lizzie, Leander, Mary.

VIII. Lizzie Goshow, born at Creamery, Pa, Jan 24,
1879 ; married William B Scheid Sept 10, 1896. P O
Souderton, Pa. Tobacconist ; Luth. C : (**IX**) R
Jordan Scheid, b Apr 5, 1897.

VIII. Leander Goshow, b Feb 27, 1881 ; d Aug 16,
1898.

VIII. Mary Goshow, b June 15, 1886.

VII. Elizabeth Rosenberger, m Jacob H Tyson. P O
Creamery, Pa. C : Two daughters.

VII. Barbara Rosenberger, b Feb 23, 1860 ; married
William H Nice in 1879. P O Steinsburg, Pa.
Miller ; Ger Bap. C : (**VIII**) Sallie Nice, b Aug 14,
1879. (**VIII**) Elizabeth Nice, b April 18, 1882 ; died
March 9, 1883. (**VIII**) Elmer Nice, born Jan 6, 1885.
(**VIII**) Melvin Nice, b May 20, 1886. (**VIII**) Harrison

Nice, born June 13, 1888. *(VIII)* Vincent Nice, born
Dec 23, 1891. **(VIII)** Ella Nice, born Oct 19, 1892.
(VIII) John Nice, b .Apr 4, 1896.
VII. Abraham Rosenberger, d aged 17 years.
VI. Elizabeth Rosenberger, m Zephenia Gross (d).
C : Mary, Kate, William.   Elizabeth married second
husband Omer Rees.   P O Montgomery Square, Pa.
C : Clara.
VI. John Shutt Rosenberger, b at Trappe, Montg co,
Pa, May 2, 1828 ; d Jan 27, 1891 ; married Hannah
Adeline Williams August 25, 1853.   She was born at
Brier Creek, near Mauch Chunk, Pa, Jan 7, 1839.

When a young man he learned the cabinetmak-
ing trade, and is said to have been one of the best.
He enlisted in the Rebellion September 1, 1864, in
Philadelphia, in the 203rd Regiment, Company D,
Pennsylvania, and was a volunteer in the 10th corps.
He was in the war about one year, when it broke up.
He was on detached services at Corps' Headquarters.
His duties were to build and to level off the ground
around the officers tents, and for this work he had as
many as 300 negroes in his employ.   At the second
battle of Chapman's farm, the Rebels discovering
General Birney and staff, began firing in that direction,
the bullets coming thick and fast about where Mr
Rosenberger was standing,causing him to tremble.   It
was an old saying "that whoever trembles will be the
next to be killed.   A piece of shell flew past without
hitting him but with such force that his head was
turned half way round and so suddenly that it
cracked, and he had to take both hands to put his
head in the right position again.   In this battle he
was on the reserve force and was stationed where he
saw the whole battle.   He was at another time
detailed to make a coffin for a deserter, who, when
taken to the grave to be shot, sitting on his coffin,
bared his breast and pointing to the spot said, "boys,
shoot me here," and when shot, fell stone dead in his
coffin.

It is related that when Mr Rosenberger was a
creeping baby that his sister took him up in the third
story of the mill in which they lived, and while she

was sweeping the floor he crept to the door and fell
down three stories, fortunately falling in a pile of
shavings, and bounced like a rubber ball. The millwright, who was standing there at his work, caught
him up and ran in the mill, and on examining him
found him unhurt.

Mr Rosenberger was superintendent of L W
Drake's sawing and planing mill at Hazleton, Pa, for
20 years. In August 1877 he moved his family to
Philadelphia, where he took charge of Boweby &
Larish's sawing and planing factory in that city.
In April 1878 he went to Bloomsbury, N J, to work
for the same firm, who had built a factory along the
banks of the Musconnteong. November 30, 1880, he
moved to Washington, N J, and worked in Daniel F
Beatty's large organ works, but owing to the condition of his health he was forced to leave his work and
he again moved to Bloomsbury in 1885. Having
somewhat regained his health and receiving an urgent
invitation to resume his position he again moved to
Washington February 24, 1887. After holding his
position for a short time he was advised by his
physician to quit work. He again moved to Bloomsbury April 27, 1888, and resided there until his
death. He was a member of John F Reynold's Post,
No 66, Dept of N J, G A R, of Washington, organized
April 26, 1882. He was a member of the M E church
and a class leader for many years in the German M E
church, of Hazelton, Pa. He was also a leader of
schools. C : William, Rosalia, John, Samson, Anna,
Mary, Jennie, Cassie, Lillian, Elizabeth.

VII. William A Rosenberger, b Sept 25, 1854; died
February 25, 1855.

VII. Rosalia Rosenberger, b at Hazelton, Pa, Mar 25,
1857 ; m Edward Caugle Oct 23, 1880. P O Bloomsbury, N J. M E. C : (**VIII**) Harry B Caugle, born
Apr 16, 1882 ; James C, b Oct 16, 1886 ; Lizzie W,
b Sept 30, 1890 ; Lillian E, b May 3, 1893.

VII. John B Rosenberger, b in Philadelphia Sept 25,
1860 ; m Jennie Louisa Young, of Orange, N J,
Feb 16, 1882. Mr Rosenberger is a barber and has
worked at his trade at Bloomsbury and elsewhere for

a number of years. After his conversion he united
with the church, but his business required him to
work on Sundays and which was not consistent with
his religious sentiment in the matter. However, in
considering the matter he thought that if he closed
his shop on Sunday his business would be ruined, but
being fully persuaded that it was his duty to close
he resolved to do so. He then moved to Easton, Pa,
but here he did not succeed. One Saturday night
he took the matter to the Lord in prayer, whom he
told he could not make a living in Easton with his
shop closed on the Sabbath and that he must have a
position given to him the Monday following. He
asked the Lord to direct his feet, for he knew not
where to go. The Lord graciously heard his prayer
and on Monday morning his wife came to the shop
and handed him a telegram from his sister, which ran
thus : '' John, come down at once ; important business.—Rose.'' He took the first train for Bloomsbury and in the afternoon returned to Easton with the
key of the Bloomsbury barber shop in his pocket, to
which place he removed and now conducts a successful business. He served as class leader, assistant
Sunday school superintendent and trustee of the
church. M E. C : (**VIII**) Hannah Adeline Rosenberger, born Feb 14, 1883 ; George N Young, born
Sept 9, 1888.

VII. Samson S Rosenberger, b at Hazelton, Luzerne
co, Pa, Feb 26, 1863 ; m Lillie V Abel Oct 3, 1889.
P O Bloomsbury, N J. Barber. C : (**VIII**) Bertha
A Rosenberger, b May 27, 1891 : d Aug 13, 1891.

VII. Anna M Rosenberger, b at Hazelton April 10,
1866 ; m John Morrison, of Philadelphia, Nov 29,
1882. P O Washington, N J. Organ and piano
finisher ; M E. C : (**VIII**) Daniel Williams Morrison,
born Sept 4, 1883 ; Joseph Samson, b Oct 19, 1885 ;
John William, b Jan 25, 1888 ; Anna Adeline, born
July 24, 1897.

VII. Mary L Rosenberger, b at Hazelton, Pa, Feb 1,
1868 ; m S A D Vliet Feb 11, 1890. P O Bloomsbury. M E. C : (**VIII**) Frank Vliet, born May 15,
1891 ; Hannah A, b Apr 9, 1893.

VII. Jennie Rosenberger, born at Hazelton Dec 26, 1870 ; m Chester P Huff Aug 4, 1894. P O Blooms-bury, N J. M E. No issue.

VII. Cassie L Rosenberger, born June 8, 1873 ; died July 6, 1873.

VII. Lillian Rosenberger, born July 12, 1874 ; died April 13, 1878.

VII. Elizabeth Rosenberger, b Feb 28, 1879 ; died March 17, 1880.

VI. Lena Rosenberger, b November 9, 1834 ; died March 24, 1848.

VI. Margaret Rosenberger, born in Montg co, Pa, Dec 26, 1836 ; m Henry S Landis Apr 19, 1856. He was born in Franconia twp, Montg co, Sept 30, 1832. P O Morwood, Pa. Blacksmith ; Menn. C : Josiah, Mary, Annie.

VII. Josiah Landis, b Apr 30, 1857 ; m Mary Moyer Jan 11, 1879. P O Morwood, Pa. Farmer ; Menn. C : Menno, Maggie, Henry, B Harrison.

VII. Mary Landis, born March 4, 1862 ; m Gideon Gehman. P O Morwood, Pa.

VII. Annie Landis, born Feb 11, 1864 ; m Samuel Keller. P O Morwood, Pa.

VI. Henry U Rosenberger, born May 3, 1839 ; died next day.

VI. Isaac U Rosenberger, b in Northumberland co, Pa, Oct 6, 1840 ; m Catharine H Wasser Jan 16, 1864. P O Mainland, Pa. Farmer ; Ref. Children : Mary, William, James, Annie, Sallie, Isaac, Maggie.

VII. Mary W Rosenberger, b Nov 26, 1864. Ref. S.

VII. William W Rosenberger, born Feb 11, 1866. Painter ; Ref. P O Mainland, Pa. S.

VII. James W Rosenberger, b April 22, 1868. P O Franconia, Pa. Farmer ; Ref. S.

VII. Annie W Rosenberger, b Dec 5, 1869 ; d May 3, 1872.

VII. Sallie W Rosenberger, b Oct 6, 1871 ; m Horace Z Kerr. P O Skippack, Pa. Farmer ; Mrs K, Ref. No issue.

VII. Isaac W Rosenberger, born Mar 6, 1874. P O West Point, Pa. Tinsmith ; Ref. S.

VII. Maggie W Rosenberger, born Oct 21, 1876 ; m

Fred H Bower Nov 6, 1897. Farmer ; Luth. C :
(**VIII**) Alverda R Bower, b May 25, 1898.

VI. Emanuel Rosenberger, b at Trappe, Montg co,
Pa, Sept 10, 1843 ; m Hannah Weidenmoyer Jan 16,
1867. R 2828 N 8th st, Phila. Plasterer and cigarmaker ; German Ref. C : Harry, Franklin, Anna,
Jennie, Edwin.

VII. Harry Rosenberger, b Feb 17, 1868. S.

VII. Franklin Rosenberger (d), b Aug 4, 1873.

VII. Anna Rosenberger, b June 26, 1874 ; m Reuben
Solliday June 1893. C : (**VIII**) Susanna Solliday,
b Mar 24, 1894 ; Walter, b July 4, 1896.

VII. Jennie Rosenberger, b Mar 28, 1876 ; m Irwin
Godshall Aug 10, 1897.

VII. Edwin Rosenberger, b Apr 22, 1878.

VI. Horace U Rosenberger, b Sept 24, 1846 ; died
Feb 18, 1890 ; m Mary Ann Gashow July 24, 1869.
She was born June 17, 1848 ; died Feb 22, 1890. C :
(**VII**) Harry G Rosenberger, b July 24, 1870 ; died
Sept 29, 1870. (**VII**) John G Rosenberger, b Mar 15,
1873. (**VII**) Horace G Rosenberger, b Feb 18, 1875.
(**VII**) Franklin G Rosenberger, b Apr 15, 1882 ; died
July 18, 1884. (**VII**) William G Rosenberger, born
Feb 11, 1886.

VI. Susanna U Rosenberger, born Dec 4, 1849 : died
Sept 9, 1891 ; m Franklin Beam Jan 20, 1872. He
was born September 30, 1836. Farmer ; Luth. C :
(**VII**) Emma Beam, born at Gwynedd Square, Pa,
May 24, 1878. P O North Wales, Pa. Bap. S.

VI. Frank U Rosenberger, b at Skippack, Pa, July 26,
1852 · m Tillie Gotwaltz Nov 1, 1873. P O Skippack, Pa. Blacksmith ; United Evan ch. C : Jacob.

VII. Rev Jacob G Rosenberger, b in Skippack, Pa,
Dec 25, 1875. P O Barnesville, Pa. At the age of
6½ years he was sent to the public schools, from
which he graduated in 1893 as valedictorian of the
class. Shortly after graduation he entered Schuylkill
Seminary, Fredericksburg, Schuylkill county, Pa,
for the purpose of receiving a thorough business
education, which he completed in the Spring of 1895.
After leaving school he entered J M Slifer's general
store at Lansdale, Pa, as clerk, remaining in the

store about six months, when he felt the need of a still higher education, and entered Albright Collegiate Institute, Myerstown, Lebanon county, Pa, where he remained two years, graduating in the Spring of 1897. When in his 16th year while attending campmeeting at Perkasie Park, Aug 1, 1891, he was converted to God, not of flesh and blood, but of water and the spirit. Soon after his conversion he was called of God to the ministry of the Gospel of Jesus Christ. In 1895, at Shamokin, Pa, he was licensed to preach according to the rules and regulations of the Eastern Pennsylvania Conference of the United Evangelical Church. During the last year of school at Albright Collegiate Institute (now Albright College), he was stationed as minister of the United Evangelical church at Barnesville, Schuylkill co, Pa, which charge he still serves, having three flourishing congregations to which he ministers, viz: Barnesville, Quakake and Locust Valley. On June 1, 1898, he was married to ... dau of Solomon Yerger, of Gratersford, Pa.

V   Jacob Rosenberger, b Feb 12, 1799; died in Bedminster twp, Bucks co, Pa, Mar 10, 1883; m Elizabeth Detweiler Mar 1824. She was b Aug 6, 1801, in New Britain twp; d Feb 22, 1839, in Tinicum twp. Farmer; Menn. C: Mary, John, Joseph, Jacob, Enos.

VI. Mary Rosenberger (d), b Jan 8, 1825; married Abraham Myers (d). Farmer; Mennonites. C: (VII) John Myers (d), m Mary Hockman. Farmer: Menn. C: Hannah (d), Aaron, Abraham.

VI. John D Rosenberger, born in Bucks co July 14, 1826; d Feb 21, 1891; m Catharine Stover May 14, 1848. She was b Sept 12, 1827; died Sept 15, 1882. Farmer; Ref. C: Mary, Gideon, Amanda, Jacob.

VII. Mary Lizzie Rosenberger, b in Hilltown twp, Bucks co, April 9, 1849; m Henry L Scholl Mar 20, 1877. P O Telford, Pa. Farmer; Ger Ref. C: (VIII) John Andrew R Scholl, b Oct 9, 1878. Cigarmaker; Ref. (VIII) Herbert Wallace R Scholl, born May 20, 1883.

VII. Gideon S Rosenberger, m Adeline Funk Jan 8, 1880. She was born Jan 28, 1859; d Sept 27, 1894.

P O Ridge, Pa. Farmer. Mr R, Luth ; Mrs R, Menn.
C : Joseph, Minnie.
VII. Amanda Rosenberger, born in Bucks co, Pa,
Nov 24, 1853 ; m Dr N C E Guth Sept 11, 1875. R
527 Liberty street, Allentown, Pa. Reformed. C :
(**VIII**) Herbert W Guth, b July 10, 1877. Doctor in
Pharmacy, Allentown, Pa. (**VIII**) Nevin H Guth,
b Mar 14, 1891.
VII. Jacob S Rosenberger, b in Hilltown twp May 11,
1856 ; m Ann Eliza Rosenberger Jan 15, 1878. They
own and occupy the Wireman farm in New Britain.
P O Chalfont, Pa. Farmer ; Ger Bap. Children :
(**VIII**) Paul Rosenberger, born and d June 17, 1879 ;
Elmer Wellington, b June 25, 1882 ; John Arthur,
b Aug 17, 1884 ; Jacob Wilmer, born Nov 25, 1886 ;
Leidy Herman, b May 30, 1892.
VI. Joseph D Rosenberger, born in New Britain twp,
Bucks co. Feb 11, 1830 ; m Mary Ann Bryan Sept 13,
1852. She died Dec 13. 1862. C : Eliza, Wilson,
Menno, Laura. Joseph m second wife Johanna K
Bryan October 1, 1864. P O Perkasie, Pa. Retired
farmer ; Menn. C : Reuben, David, Isaac, Jacob,
Edmond, Allen, Mary, Noah.
VII. Eliza Rosenberger, b in Bedminster twp Nov 7,
1853 ; m Joseph Tyson. P O Dublin, Pa. Laborer ;
Menn. No issue.
VII. Wilson Rosenberger, b in Bucks co, Pa, Jan 31,
1857 ; m Sue Sweigert. P O Perkasie, Pa. Shoe-
maker ; U Evan. C : Flora, Ammon.
VII. Menno Rosenberger, born in Bucks co May 24,
1859 ; m Kate Alderfer. She was b July 21, 1865.
P O Lederachville, Pa. Farmer. C : (**VIII**) Alice
Rosenberger, born July 14, 1883. Mr Rosenberger
adoped a child named Howard (Rosenberger) Landis.
VII. Laura Rosenberger, b in Bedminster twp, Bucks
co, May 11, 1861 ; m William Slight. P O North
Cramer's Hill, N J. Painter ; Meth. C : Raymond,
Verna, Irvin.
VII. Reuben Rosenberger, b in Bucks co, Pa, Oct 13,
1865 ; m Katie Moore. P O Perkasie, Pa. Painter ;
Ev Ass'n. C : Ezra Victor, Joseph Mervin, William
Russel, Anna Elizabeth.

VII. David Rosenberger, b in Bucks co Oct 13. 1867 ; m Sallie Gehman Nov 18, 1893. She was b Mar 13, 1865. P O Perkasie, Pa. Cigarmaker ; U Evan. C : (**VIII**) Daniel Elvin Rosenberger, born Feb 23, 1895 ; Chester Arthur, b Feb 1, 1897.

VII. Isaac Rosenberger, born in Bucks co, Pa, Dec 5, 1869 ; d Oct 13, 1896 ; married Laura Crouthamel. P O Perkasie, Pa. Cigarmaker. U Evan. C : Esther Rebecca.

VII. Jacob Rosenberger, b in Bucks co May 27, 1872. P O Perkasie, Pa. Cigarmaker. U Evan.

VII. Edmund Rosenberger, b Feb 5. 1875 ; d Feb 7, 1875.

VII. Allen Rosenberger, b in Bucks co, Pa. Apr 10, 1876 ; m Emma Wenhold in 1897. P O Perkasie, Pa. Cigarmaker. U Evan. No issue.

VII. Mary Ann Rosenberger, b in Bucks co Jan 26, 1879. P O Perkasie, Pa. Dressmaker. U Evan.

VII. Noah Rosenberger, born July 11, 1881. P O Perkasie, Pa. U Evan.

VI. Jacob D. Rosenberger, b in Tinicum twp, Bucks co, Dec 20. 1833 ; m Hannah G Barnes Oct 31, 1857. She was born Dec 3, 1838. P O Dublin, Pa. Dealer in farming implements. Menn. C : Daniel and Mary twins). Isaiah, Lizzie, Emma, John, Amanda, Fanny, William, Annetta.

VII. Daniel Rosenberger, b Dec 23, 1858 ; m Anna Godshalk. P O Fountainville, Pa. Farmer. C : Ella, Wilmer, Fannie, Oscar.

VII. Mary Rosenberger, born December 23, 1858 ; married Frank Snavely. P O Lake City, Iowa. C : Annetta, Agnes, J Warren, Lee, Naomi.

VII. Isaiah B Rosenberger, born Aug 25, 1860 ; m Rachel Lewis. P O Dublin, Pa. Blacksmith. No issue.

VII. Lizzie B Rosenberger, b Oct 23, 1862 ; married Jacob L Shelly February 9. 1888. P O Levin, Pa. Farmer ; Menn. C : (**VIII**) Edith R Shelly, born Oct 25, 1888. (**VIII**) Howard R Shelly, b Sept 6, 1890 ; died Nov 22, 1890. (**VIII**) Henry R Shelly, b Nov 1 1891. (**VIII**) Jacob Arthur Shelly, b Oct 19, 1894.

Albert R. Pike.

VII. Emma B Rosenberger, b Sept 7, 1865 ; m John A Guth Dec 24, 1888. R 38 N Spring st, Elizabeth, N J. Blacksmith ; Pres. C : (**VIII**) Mabel Gertrude Guth, b Feb 7, 1890. (**VIII**) Herbert Francis Guth, b Aug 21, 1892 ; d May 5, 1895.

VII. John H Rosenberger, b May 29, 1868 ; married Lizzie P Patten. R Haines and Chew sts, Germantown, Pa. Teamster. C : Eleanor.

VII. Amanda Magdalena Rosenberger, b Nov 6, 1870; m Hiram Anders. P O Perkasie, Pa. Hostler. C : Hannah, Blanche.

VII. Fanny B Rosenberger, b Apr 20, 1875 ; married Lamech F Myers, son of Jonas S Myers, of Bedminster, Pa, Feb 17, 1894. P O Perkasie, Pa. House painter ; Menn. C : (**VIII**) Roy R Myers, b Jan 4, 1895 ; Edith.

VII. William F Rosenberger, b May 20, 1876. S.

VII. Annetta B Rosenberger, b Sept 3. 1879. S.

VI. Enos Rosenberger, b Feb 13, 1839 ; d next day.

V. Joseph W Rosenberger, born Mar 20, 1801 ; died Aug 3, 1875 ; m Catharine Moyer, daughter of Henry and Salome (Stover) Moyer, of Bucks co, Pa. She was born Aug 29, 1796 ; d Aug 27, 1862. Farmer ; Menn. Deacon at Perkasie. C : Henry, Salome, John, Isaac.

VI. Henry Rosenberger, died single.

VI. Salome Rosenberger (d), married Samuel Seiple. Two sons lived in Pottstown, Pa.

VI. John Rosenberger, m Anna Yerger. Lived in Missouri. C : Charles (d), Edwin, ———.

VI. Isaac Rosenberger (d), m Elizabeth Crouthamel (d). C : Alten (d).

V. Benjamin Rosenberger, died single.

V. Elizabeth Rosenberger, m Henry Nonamaker. C : Aaron, Elias, Charles, Henry, Maria, Elizabeth.

VI. Aaron Nonamaker (d), m Anna Shutt (d). Farmer ; Luth. C : Deborah, Lizzie, Jacob, Noah.

VII. Deborah Nonamaker, m ——— Weiss. P O Perkasie, Pa.

VII. Lizzie Nonamaker, died young.

VII. Jacob Nonamaker, m Clementine Crouthamel.

P O Perkasie, Pa. Cigarmaker ; U Evan. C :
Washington, Irwin.

VIII. Washington Nonamaker, married ———. P O
Perkasie.

VIII. Irwin Nonamaker. P O Perkasie, Pa. Single.

VII. Dr Noah S Nonamaker, b in Bedminster, Bucks
co, Pa, Mar 23, 1854 ; m Lizzie Beau Mar 15, 1883.
P O Bedminster, Pa. Physician ; Luth. C : Annie
Lucretia (d), Edgar Vasco, Claudius Howard (d),
Bessie Gertrude (d), Mattie Pauline (d), Celia Helen.

VI. Elias Nonamaker (d), married ——— Keller.
Carpenter. No issue.

VI. Charles Nonamaker (d), m ——— Stout. One
child.

VI. Henry Nonamaker. m ——— Shive. No issue.

VI. Maria Nonamaker (d), m John Deiley (d). No
issue. Maria m second husband Peter Stout (d).
No issue.

VI. Elizabeth Nonamaker (d), m Samuel Stout (d).
C : (**VII**) Henry Stout. P O Doylestown, Pa. (**VII**)
Amos Stout. P O Hagersville, Pa. (**VII**) Maria
Stout (d).

V. Rachel Rosenberger, m Isaac Clemmer. C :
Jacob, Elizabeth, Kate.

VI. Jacob Clemmer, m Deborah Clemmer. C : Lucy,
Eliza, Kate.

VII. Lucy Clemmer (d), m ——— Clemmer. C :
(**VIII**) Lavina Clemmer, m James Savacool (d). C :
Raymond. Lavina m second husband William Sava-
cool. P O Newmansville, Pa. C : Raymond, Robert,
Hannah.

VII. Eliza Clemmer. Single.

VII. Kate Clemmer, m Levi O Biehn. P O Richland Centre, Pa. C : Flora, Deborah.

VI. Elizabeth Clemmer (d), m Philip Nace (d). No
issue.

VI. Kate Clemmer, m ———. Kate m second husband
Isaac Yokum. C : Debbie, Henry.

V. Margaret Rosenberger,* born in Bucks co, Pa,
April 13, 1805 ; d March 11, 1877 ; m George Lewis

*In her father's will her name is given as Rebecca. She
probably had a double name.

Sept 19, 1825.   He was b 1793; d 1828.   One child,
d in infancy.   Margaret m second husband Henry R
Alderfer (d), Aug 27, 1833.   He was b 1812.   One
child, d in infancy.   Margaret married third husband
Henry Harttle Oct 2, 1838.   He was b in Montg co,
Pa, Nov 24, 1791; d June 2, 1871.   Farmer; Pres.
C: Annie, Elizabeth.
   VI. Annie Harttle, b Sept 7, 1839; m John Brierley.
He was born in Lancashire, England, Oct 11, 1839.
P O Fairview Village, Pa.   Stone mason.   Children:
(**VII**) Sarah Brierley, died at birth, July 4, 1870.
(**VII**) Henry Harttle Brierley, b Dec 1, 1871; died
July 27, 1882.
   VI. Elizabeth Harttle, b July 15, 1841.   P O Fair-
view Village, Pa.   S.
   IV. Henry Rosenberry,* born probably in Hilltown
in 1761; died Jan 1834.   He was married twice, his
first wife being Mollie Holman, said to have been
from Milford, Lehigh county.   C: John, Betsey,
Kate, Susan, Mary.   His second wife was a widow,
Mrs Katie Kram, whose maiden name had been
Beam (or Boehm).   C: Abraham, Hannah, Nancy.
He was not a landholder in this county, but a renter.
Previous to his death he lived in a tenant house on
the farm of Paul Custer, Worcester.   This farm was
purchased from the Custer estate by Benjamin Brunner in 1864, and comprised 49 acres.   He left no will,
and the administrators of his estate were his son,
John H Rosenberry, of Skippack, and John Kratz, of
same township.
   V. John H Rosenberry, b Apr 1, 1799; d Sept 10,
1872; m Elizabeth Gotwals Nov 14, 1824.   She was
born July 17, 1804; d in 1858.   Lived in Skippack
township and was a stock dealer.   Mr Rosenberry,
Menn; Mrs Rosenberry, Ger Bap.   C: Charles,
Catharine, Mary, Christian, Christian, Abraham,
Elizabeth, John, Anna, Jesse, Elizabeth, Henry.
   VI. Charles G Rosenberry, b May 20, 1825; married

*Those now spelling the name Rosenberry instead of
Rosenberger are descended also from Benjamin Rosenberger,
of Hatfield   It is said that the present spelling is only a
modern change or variation.

Anna Hummel, who died, leaving two children. He then went to Illinois, where he married again and had several children. Lost all trace of him since 1874.

VI. Catharine Rosenberry, b Aug 4, 1826 ; d Jan 4, 1890 ; m John Hagey. He was b Aug 4, 1830 ; died Oct 3, 1857. Watchmaker ; Menn. C : Elizabeth, Anna. Catharine m second husband Joseph Kindig. C : John, Annie.

VII. Elizabeth Hagey, b in Montg co, May 8, 1853 ; m Frank W Dorn Sept 23, 1871. P O Telford, Pa. Farmer ; Ref. C : (**VIII**) Allen Dorn, born June 3, 1873 ; m Clara Metzger May 27, 1893. P O Telford, Pa. Bricklayer ; Ref. (**VIII**) Katie Dorn, b Dec 24, 1875. (**VIII**) Frank Dorn, born Apr 23, 1878. (**VIII**) Milton Dorn, born August 21, 1880 ; d aged 5 days. (**VIII**) Erwin Dorn, b Feb 2, 1882 ; d Aug 22, 1882. (**VIII**) Reinhart Dorn, b Mar 5, 1883. (**VIII**) Charles Dorn, b Mar 3, 1885. (**VIII**) Lizzie Dorn, b Nov 30, 1887. (**VIII**) Vernon Dorn, b June 29, 1892.

VII. Anna Hagey, b and d Apr 1, 1857.

VII. John R Kindig, born May 12, 1862 ; m Franie Rosenberger May 25, 1885. She was b Jan 3, 1866. P O Hatfield, Pa. C : (**VIII**) Harvey R Kindig, b June 4, 1886 ; died August 11, 1886. (**VIII**) Mary R Kindig, b March 23, 1889. (**VIII**) Harry R Kindig, b June 21, 1890 ; died Nov 22, 1890. (**VIII**) Emma R Kindig, b May 15, 1892. (**VIII**) Stella R Kindig, b Oct 2, 1893. (**VIII**) Frank R Kindig, born June 16, 1897 ; died July 3, 1898. Mr Kindig was elected Director of the Poor of Montgomery county in 1900.

VII. Annie R Kindig, b Dec 3, 1864 ; m Charles B Kratz May 23, 1883. P O Lansdale, Pa. C : (**VIII**) Wallace K Kratz, b Sept 10, 1884 ; C Quintin, born June 14, 1894.

VI. Mary Rosenberry, b in Montg co, Pa, Feb 14, 1828 ; d in Norristown, Pa, Mar 16, 1896 ; married Sylvester Lewis Oct 14, 1853. He was b in Montg co Sept 22, 1824 ; d in Norristown Jan 3, 1868. Mrs Lewis, Pres. C : (**VII**) James Irvin Lewis, b Feb 7, 1854 ; d Mar 29, 1862. (**VII**) Sallie Elizabeth Lewis, b Oct 7, 1855 ; d July 12, 1897. S. (**VII**) Mary Jane Lewis, b in Norristown Feb 20, 1858. R 541 Kohn

street, Norristown, Pa. Seamstress; Pres. S. (**VII**)
Ashton Lewis, born May 26, 1859; d Aug 23, 1859.
(**VII**) Elmira Lewis, born July 7, 1867; m William
Carnathan Dec 4, 1895. R 707 Astor st, Norristown, Pa. Milk dealer.
VI. Christian G Rosenberry, d in infancy.
VI. Christian G Rosenberry, b in Montg co, Feb 5,
1832; m Susanna, daughter of Peter B Hendricks,
December 15, 1860. P O Lansdale, Pa. He has
been in the stock business for 35 years, dealing in
horses, cattle and sheep. In 1880 he bought the
Broadway House and stock yards at Lansdale, Pa,
where he continued as proprietor for ten years, when
in 1890 he sold it for $16,000, being the principal
hotel in Lansdale. He now lives retired. C: Mary,
Elmer, Wellington, Lizzie, Anna, Sallie, Minerva,
Clayton.
VII. Mary Alice Rosenberry, born Apr 18, 1862; m
Charles P Woolfinger Oct 21, 1884. P O Lansdale,
Pa. Conductor on railroad. C: (**VIII**) Wellington
P Woolfinger, b July 30, 1886.
VII. Elmer E H Rosenberry, b Sept 27, 1863; was
drowned in stone quarry May 29, 1880.
VII. Wellington H Rosenberry, born in Skippack,
Montg co, Pa, Jan 8, 1866; married Tillie Hafler, of
Telford, in January 1901. P O Lansdale, Pa. He
is one of the largest and heaviest carriage dealers in
the State, and is also a dealer in live stock. He is
widely known as a business man, and is a rising
young politician. At the age of 24 years he was
elected Burgess of Lansdale, Pa, and at the general
election in Nov 1898 he was elected a member of the
State Legislature of Pennsylvania on the Democratic
ticket. He was again renominated by his party
in 1900 but was defeated. On April 1, 1901, he was
elected Chairman of the Montgomery County Democratic Committee.
VII. Lizzie Rosenberry, born March 1, 1868; m A R
Shepherd. P O Lansdale, Pa. C: Donald, Harold,
Richard, Ralph.
VII. Anna Rosenberry, b May 18, 1870; m Clayton
Alderfer. R Norristown, Pa.

VII. Sallie Rosenberry, born Aug 7, 1873. School-teacher. S.

VII. Minerva Rosenberry, b Mar 18, 1876. S.

VI. Abraham Rosenberry, d aged 10 years.

VI. Elizabeth Rosenberry, d in infancy.

VI. John G Rosenberry, b in Lower Providence twp, Montg co, Pa, June 30, 1836 ; m Elizabeth Flores, of Lower Milford twp, Lehigh co, Pa, August 27, 1859. P O Skippack, Pa. Veterinary surgeon ; Ger Ref. C : Mary, Anna, Peter, John, Emma, Katie.

VII. Mary Elizabeth Rosenberry, b Dec 21, 1859 ; d Mar 31, 1873.

VII. Annie Marie Rosenberry, born Dec 4, 1861 ; m Samuel D Kinsey. P O Mainland, Pa. Farmer ; Ger Ref. C : Paul Nevin, Bertha Viola, Russel.

VII. Peter Flores Rosenberry, b Apr 15, 1865 ; died April 15, 1883.

VII. John Henry Rosenberry, b Feb 10, 1867. P O San Mates, Cal. S.

VII. Emma Jane Rosenberry, born Nov 19, 1869 ; m John B Gottshall. P O Cedars, Pa. Farmer ; Ger Ref. C : Annie, d in infancy.

VII. Katie Martha Rosenberry, b Aug 2, 1879. S.

VI. Anna Rosenberry, married Joseph Rossiter (d). R 150 Third avenue, Pittsburg, Pa. No issue.

VI. Jesse Rosenberry, m Elizabeth Kauffman. P O Skippack, Pa. C : William, Anna.

VI. Elizabeth Rosenberry, m William Teany. C : (**VII**) Howard R Teany. R 1056 Cherry st, Norristown, Pa.

VI. Henry Rosenberry, b in 1844. He was a soldier in the Union Army and died while in service in 1863.

V. Betsey Rosenberry, d young.

V. Kate Rosenberry, d young.

V. Susan Rosenberry, d young.

V. Mary Rosenberry.

V. Abraham B Rosenberger, b Feb 9, 1807 ; died in Montg co, Pa, Sept 21, 1876 ; m Sarah Force Oct 30, 1834. She was b in Montg co March 13, 1814 ; died Sept 21, 1878. Farmer ; German Bap. C : Anna, Rebecca, Isaac, Hannah.

VI. Anna Rosenberger, b Aug 21, 1835 ; m David P

Horning Mar 12, 1856. P O Bridgeport, Kan. Ger Bap. C: Abraham, John, Sarah, Hannah, Anna, Emma, David, William.

VII. Abraham R Horning, b Feb 10, 1857 ; m Anna Numer (d). P O Redfield, Kan. Carpenter ; Ger Bap. C: Cora Anna, Henry Everett, Eddie (d), Freddie (d). Abraham m second wife Mary Ruth. C: Alice, Nelson.

VII. John U Horning, born Feb 17, 1859 ; m Maud Mackinson. P O Ocheltree, Kan. Carpenter ; M E. C: May Lena, Minnie Ola, Flossie Anna, Elva.

VII. Sarah R Horning, b June 6, 1861 ; m Jefferson Groom. P O Deepwater, Mo. Teacher ; Pres. C: Jesse, Bertha, Pearl, Emma.

VII. Hannah M Horning, b May 12, 1864 ; m Leroy B Stivers October 10, 1883. P O Fort Scott, Kan. Wheelwright ; United Br. C: (**VIII**) Bertha May Stivers (d), b July 15, 1884. (**VIII**) Morrison Leroy Stivers, born Oct 18, 1886 ; d July 14, 1887. (**VIII**) Frances Geneva Stivers, born November 25, 1889. (**VIII**) Claudia Lee Stivers, b Aug 2, 1891.

VII. Anna May Horning, b in Illinois May 20, 1868 ; m Richard P Sappington Dec 23, 1888. P O Windsor, Mo. Farmer ; Bap. C: (**VIII**) Roy Frederick Sappington, b July 9, 1890 ; Earl, born Feb 7, 1894 ; Claud, b Apr 1, 1899.

VII. Emma Horning (d), b July 1, 1871.

VII. David Henry Horning (d), b June 5, 1874.

VII. William W Horning, b June 30, 1875 ; m Lydia R Keller Feb 22, 1899. P O Ness City, Kan. Farmer ; Ger Bap.

VI. Rebecca Rosenberger, born in Port Providence, Montg co, Pa. Nov 2, 1837 ; m Thomas L Griffin Nov 4, 1860. P O Port Providence, Pa. Ger Bap. C: Tillie, Allen, Mary, Sadie, Hannah, Ida.

VII. Tillie Griffin, b Sept 19, 1861 ; married Horace Smith. P O Mont Clare, Pa. Farmer ; Ger Bap. C: Bertha, Mary, Raymond, Florence.

VII. Allen Griffin, b Sept 11, 1863 ; m Emma Kulp. P O Mont Clare, Pa. Employed in steel plant. No issue.

VII. Mary R Griffin, born March 5, 1866 ; m Horace

Kugler. R 1771 Newkirk st, Phila. Machinist. C :
Reba, Ora G.

VII. Sadie R Griffin, b Aug 25, 1871 ; m J B Root.
P O Port Providence, Pa.   Employed by Pennsylvania
Railroad Company.   One child.

VII. Hannah E Griffin, born Mar 30, 1874. R 1771
Newkirk st, Phila.   Stenographer ; Ger Bap.   S.

VII. Ida F Griffin, b Oct 10, 1877 ; d Oct 22, 1898.
Stenographer ; Ger Bap. S.

VI. Isaac F Rosenberger, b Sept 21, 1849 ; d Dec 2,
1849.

VI. Hannah Rosenberger, b Jan 13, 1852 ; m George
W March Mar 2, 1876.   R 501 Astor st. Norristown,
Pa.   Builder.   Mr M, Luth ; Mrs M, Bap.   C :
(**VII**) Eva March, b Jan 5, 1877.   Luth.   S.

V. Anna Rosenberger, b in 1810 ; m John Gotwals
Jan 29, 1843. He died about 1887.   Menns.   C :
Samuel, Catharine, David, John.

VI. Samuel Gotwals, born in Montg co, Pa, Apr 19,
1844 ; died Sept 20, 1895 ; m Kate Boyer, of Norristown, Pa.   C : (**VII**) George B Gotwals, died about
1897 ; aged 19 years.

VI. Catharine Gotwals, b at Port Providence, Montg
co, June 5, 1846 ; m George A Seidel Oct 26, 1880.
R 506 Kohn st, Norristown, Pa.   Cigar merchant ;
Ev ch.   C : (**VII**) Elmer Ellsworth Seidel, b July 30,
1881 ; Rosie, b Sept 13, 1883.

VI. David Gotwals, born in Montg co Dec 28, 1849 ;
m Ida Fields. She d in 1891.   R Phila. C : Ella ;
Katie, Alfred, William, Lafayette, all deceased.

VI. John Gotwals, b Mar 21, 1853 ; d Jan 17, 1871.

IV. Anna Rosenberger, m Joseph Naragary.

IV. Rebecca Rosenberger, m Jacob Bechtel.

DESCENDANTS OF JOHN, SON OF BENJAMIN ROSENBERGER, SR.

III. John Rosenberger was a resident of Hatfield; became the owner of the 112-acre farm in Hatfield, bought by his father in 1751. His eldest son Benjamin and grandson of Benjamin, Sr, became the owner in 1798. Farmer; Menn. C: Benjamin, Jacob, Anna, Susanna.

IV. Benjamin Rosenberger, born in Montgomery co, Pa, in 1769; m Elizabeth Biehn, dau of. John and Barbara (Fried) Biehn. She was b in 1775. They emigrated to Canada in 1801; lived a little north of Preston on the farm where the late Henry Hagey resided. Farmer; Menn. C: John, Abraham, Jacob, Barbara, Elizabeth, Nancy.

V. John Rosenberger, b in Montg co in 1797; d in Canada in .1863; m Margaret Pannebecker, dau of Cornelius Pannebecker. She was born Oct 12, 1805; d March 28, 1880. Farmer, and lived on his father's farm north of Preston, Ont; Menn. C: Magdalena, Joseph, Sarah, Rachel, Nancy, Elizabeth, Cyrus, Cyrus, Mary, John, Anne, George.

VI. Magdalena Rosenberger, b June 23, 1823; d in 1855; m Samuel Burkholder about 1840. He was b in Hamilton, Ont, in 1817; died 1890. Carpenter; Meth. C: Sarah, Elizabeth, Mary, Lemuel, John, Margaret, George, Rachel.

VII. Sarah Burkholder, b in Waterloo co, Ont, in 1842; married Jacob Beck in 1871. P O Doon, Ont. Gardener; Christadelphians. C: Emily, Sarah, John.

VIII. Emily Charlotte Beck, b in 1872 ; m William Marshall in 1892. P O Doon, Ont. Heckler. No issue.

VIII. Sarah Ann Beck, b 1875 ; d July 8, 1891.

VIII. John Frederick Beck, b 1877. P O Doon, Ont. Blacksmith. S.

VII. Elizabeth Burkholder, b June 29, 1844 ; m Jacob H Hunsperger Dec 24, 1866. P O Haysville, Ont. Farmer ; Church of God. C : **(VIII)** Joel Hunsperger, born October 13, 1867. P O Haysville, Ont. **(VIII)** Fannie Hunsperger, b Apr 23, 1870 ; d May 4, 1870. **(VIII)** Solomon Hunsperger, b Aug 12, 1871. **(VIII)** Isaiah Hunsperger, born July 18, 1873. **(VIII)** Samuel Hunsperger, b Feb 7, 1875. **(VIII)** Emeline Hunsperger, born Dec 9, 1878. **(VIII)** Laura Hunsperger, b Mar 15, 1888. **(VIII)** Sylvester Hunsperger, b June 25, 1890.

VII. Mary Burkholder, b in 1846 ; m Isaac Wismer. P O Preston, Ont.

VII. Lemuel Burkholder, b in Waterloo co, Ont, in 1848 ; m Rachel Ann Bock. She died May 20, 1889. P O Hensall, Ont. Farmer ; Meth. C : **(VIII)** Rosanna June Burkholder, m William B Smith. P O Preston, Ont. Cabinetmaker. **(VIII)** Sarah Alice Burkholder, died Feb 19, 1887. **(VIII)** Margaret Ida Burkholder, died Nov 17, 1886. **(VIII)** Annie Maud Burkholder.

VII. John Burkholder, b in 1850 ; married Barbara Smecker. P O Fife Lake, Mich.

VII. Margaret Burkholder, b in 1852 ; d in 1892. S.

VII. George Burkholder, b in Oxford co, Ont, Can, Aug 6, 1854 ; m Lydia Karcher Nov 4, 1879. P O Burnside, Mich. Laborer ; Menn Br in Christ. C : **(VIII)** Milton Burkholder, born Sept 21, 1880. **(VIII)** Elsie Maretta Burkholder, born August 25, 1882. **(VIII)** Bruce Aden Burkholder, b June 10, 1885 ; died Feb 5, 1887. **(VIII)** Hilda May Burkholder, b July 4, 1895.

VII. Rachel Burkholder, b in 1856 ; m Daniel Gearinger about 1880. P O New Dundee, Ont.

VI. Joseph Rosenberger, b in Preston, Ont, Jan 25, 1825 ; died Apr 10, 1893 ; m Hannah Sherk in 1847.

She was born Feb 2, 1828.   Lived in Preston, Ont.
Sawyer.   Mr R, Menn ; Mrs R, Meth.   C : Jacob,
Cyrus, Levi, Susanna, Mary, Sarah, Christian, Alice.

VII. Jacob Rosenberger, b 1847 ; d Sept 27, 1885. S.

VII. Cyrus Rosenberger, b 1849 ; d 1851.

VII. Levi Rosenberger, b Feb 27, 1851 ; m Georgiana
Winter in 1875.   P O Hamilton, Ont.   Moulder in
foundry ; Meth.   C : (**VIII**) William W Rosenberger,
born Sept 4, 1876.   R 94 Cannon st, Hamilton, Ont.
(**VIII**) George W Rosenberger, born May 30, 1879.
(**VIII**) Charles H Rosenberger, b Mar 25, 1882.

VII. Susanna Rosenberger, b in Waterloo co, Ont,
Aug 5, 1854 ; m John Linkert October 11, 1874.   R
Hamilton, Ont.   Shoemaker ; English church.   C :
(**VIII**) John J Linkert, b Dec 30, 1875.   Baker. S.
(**VIII**) Minnie M Linkert, born April 12, 1877. (**VIII**)
Edward R Linkert, born Apr 23, 1879.   Shoemaker.
(**VIII**) Henry W Linkert, born May 10, 1881 ; Alice
Gertrude, b June 30, 1883 ; Carl Albert, born Jan 29,
1886 ; Elton Percy, b July 14, 1893.

VII. Mary Rosenberger, b 1857 ; m John Cotterell.
R 10 Green st, Guelph, Ont.   Upholsterer.   C : John,
Henry, Mabel, Lillie.

VII. Sarah Rosenberger, b in Preston, Ont, Mar 28,
1859 ; m Wellington Shupe Dec 25, 1877.   P O Galt,
Ont.   Machinist ; Meth.   C : (**VIII**) Nellie Maudana
Shupe, b Dec 20, 1878 ; Albert Edwin, born Aug 27,
1880 ; Lillian Gertrude, b Sept 21, 1882.

VII. Christian Rosenberger, b 1862 ; m Mary Gibson.
P O Berlin, Ont.   Painter.   C : Louis Roy.

VII. Alice Rosenberger, born Aug 27, 1863 ; m Eli
Heinrich.   P O Waterloo, Ont.   C : Carl, Gordon.

VI. Sarah Rosenberger, b Aug 23, 1826 ; d in infancy.

VI. Rachel Rosenberger, b near Preston, Ont, June
16, 1828 ; m Levi Bock in 1843.   He was b May 20,
1815 ; died Nov 19, 1880.   Farmer ; Menns.   C :
Nancy, Isaac, Aaron, Hannah, Gideon, Jacob, Catharine, Margaret, Lena, Levi, Barbara, Elizabeth.

VII. Nancy Bock, born 1844 ; died 1890 ; m Charles
Spreeman about 1862.   He was born in Germany.
Teamster and sawyer ; Bap.   C : John, Matilda,

Isaac, Simeon, Samuel, Nancy, Aaron, Lizzie, Maggie, Charles, Allen, Levi, Menno.

VIII. John Spreeman, b in Waterloo co, Ont, Dec 26, 1862 ; m Geraldine Godbold January 26, 1888.   R 78 Lewis street, Toronto, Ont.   Carpenter ; Bap.   C : (**IX**) Orpha Spreeman, b Jan 16, 1889 ; Elma, born Feb 11, 1891 ; Chester, b Nov 22, 1893.

VIII. Matilda Spreeman, b 1864 ; d 1894 ; m Jacob Binkley.   P O New Hamburg, Ont.   C : Leslie, LeRoy, Philip.

VIII. Isaac Spreeman, b 1866 ; m Eliza Ann Bergey in 1893.   P O New Dundee, Ont.   Blacksmith ; Menn Br in Christ.   C : (**IX**) Viola Spreeman, born 1894 ; Herbert, b 1895 ; Cranston (d), born 1897 ; Michael, b 1898.

VIII. Nancy Spreeman.   P O New Hamburg, Ont.

VIII. Simeon Spreeman, b 1870.

VIII. Samuel Spreeman, b 1872 ; d 1874.

VIII. Aaron Spreeman, b 1874.

VIII. Lizzie Spreeman, b 1876.   P O Preston, Ont.

VIII. Maggie Spreeman, b 1878.   P O New Dundee, Ont.

VIII. Charles Spreeman, b 1879 ; d 1879.

VIII. Allen Spreeman, b 1881.

VIII. Levi Spreeman, b 1883.

VIII. Menno Spreeman, b 1885 ; d 1887.

VII. Isaac Bock, b July 24, 1846 ; m Mary Sararas Jan 29, 1878.   P O New Dundee, Ont.   Farmer ; Ger Bap.   C : (**VIII**) Nathaniel Bock, born July 22, 1879 ; Lucinda, b Mar 20, 1881 ; Eltruda, b July 11, 1883 ; Bernice, b May 21, 1885 ; Addison, b Sept 21, 1887 ; Maria, b Apr 9, 1890.

VII. Aaron R Bock, b Aug 17, 1848 ; m Mary Ann Dennstedt Dec 22, 1874.   P O New Dundee, Ont. Veterinary surgeon ; Bap.   C : (**VIII**) Sylva Bock, b June 6, 1877 ; Aggie, b Nov 28, 1880 ; Wellington, b Dec 21, 1882 ; Rachel, b July 4, 1894.

VII. Hannah Bock (d), b 1850.

VII. Gideon Bock, b in Waterloo co, Ont, in 1854 ; m Dianna Godbold Apr 22, 1884.   P O New Dundee, Ont.   Teamster ; Bap.   C : (**VIII**) Nora Bock, born Feb 21, 1885 ; Gertrude, b Apr 2, 1888.

VII. Jacob Bock (d), b 1856.

VII. Catharine Bock, b July 1, 1858 ; m George B Bechtel Dec 9, 1879. P O New Dundee, Ont. Bap. C : (**VIII**) Levi Bechtel, b Nov 19, 1880 ; d next day. (**VIII**) Gilbert Bechtel, b June 8, 1882. (**VIII**) Merven Bechtel, b Aug 21, 1884. (**VIII**) Sylvia Bechtel, born June 29, 1895 ; d Aug 14, 1895.

VII. Margaret Bock (d), b 1861 ; m Allan Bossenberry. P O New Hamburg, Ont. C : Arthur, Eldon.

VII. Lena Bock, born 1864 ; m Abram Willits. P O Roseville, Ont. C : Alvin, Lauretta (d), Archibald, Nora, Herbert, Ida.

VII. Levi Bock, b 1868 ; m Annie Reid. P O New Dundee, Ont. C : Thomas Russell.

VII. Barbara Bock, b at New Dundee, Ont, May 31, 1870 ; m William Buck June 4, 1889. P O New Hamburg, Ont. Tailor ; Ger Bap. C : (**VIII**) Percy Gideon Buck, b Nov 22, 1890 ; Lilly, b Aug 4, 1894.

VII. Elizabeth Bock, b 1862 ; m Wesley Erb. P O Plattsville, Ont. Bap. C : Lloyd, Laura.

VI. Nancy Rosenberger, b June 4, 1830 ; d in infancy.

VI. Elizabeth Rosenberger, b July 23, 1832 ; married Duncan McShannock. P O Muskegon, Mich. C : Daniel, Lizzie, John, Archibald (d), Joseph, Catharine, Thomas, Mary.

VI. Cyrus Rosenberger, born Nov 18, 1834 ; died in infancy.

VI. Cyrus Rosenberger, born Feb 26, 1837 ; died in infancy.

VI. Mary Rosenberger, b Dec 8, 1838 ; d in infancy.

VI. John Rosenberger, b Mar 24, 1843 ; m Susanna, dau of Jacob and Catharine (Shupe) Bock. b May 11, 1840. P O Preston, Ont. Engaged with Clare Bros in manufacturing furnaces and stoves. C : George, Jacob, Margaret, Joseph, Magdalena, Catharine, Elizabeth.

VII. George Rosenberger, b May 22, 1865 ; m Annie Killet. P O Creston, O. Stove polisher.

VII. Jacob Rosenberger, b Nov 30, 1867 ; m Polly Schoenan. P O Preston, Ont. Spinner in woolen mills. C : Laura, Norman.

VII. Margaret Rosenberger, b Jan 24, 1869 ; married Frederick Crosbie. P O Preston, Ont. Furnace mounter. C : Gladys, Maude.

VII. Joseph Rosenberger, born Sept 30, 1870. P O Preston, Ont. Engaged in Preston woolen mills as cloth finisher. S.

VII. Magdalena Rosenberger, b Oct 5, 1872 ; died Sept 8, 1873.

VII. Catharine Rosenberger, b May 15, 1875.

VII. Elizabeth Rosenberger, b April 22, 1884 ; died Aug 22, 1884.

VI. Annie Rosenberger, born Nov 18, 1845 ; died in infancy.

VI. George Rosenberger, born April 29, 1848 ; died in infancy.

V. Abraham Rosenberger, born in Montg co, Pa, Nov 15, 1799 ; d in Wilmot twp, Ont, Can, Jan 28, 1883 ; m Nancy, dau of Christian and Polly (Ruth) Strome, Nov 15, 1822. She was b in Lancaster co, Pa, Dec 31, 1807 ; d Sept 10, 1880. He was taken with his parents to Canada when he was 6 months old. Farmer ; Menn. C : Mary, Elizabeth, Samuel (d in infancy), Abraham, Christian, Sarah, Benjamin, Isaac, Susanna, Lydia.

VI. Mary Rosenberger, m Abram M Clemens. He was b May 26, 1820. P O Ravenswood, Ont. C : Sarah, Hannah, Nancy, Elizabeth, Mary, Hester, Lydia, Nathan, John, Benjamin, Julia.

VII. Sarah Clemens, b Aug 23, 1841 ; d April 1883 ; m Alfred Simpson. P O Waterloo, Ont. Retired farmer. No issue.

VII. Hannah Clemens, b Sept 11, 1843 ; d Feb 1870 ; m William Smith. Farmer. C : Alfred A, Samuel S, Jessie M.

VII. Nancy Clemens, b Nov 28, 1845. S.

VII. Elizabeth Clemens, b Jan 8, 1848 ; died Aug 2, 1863.

VII. Mary Ann Clemens, b June 5, 1850 ; d Aug 7, 1863.

VII. Hester Clemens, b Aug 3, 1852 ; d July 1, 1863.

VII. Lydia Clemens, b Sept 6, 1856 ; m Edward Sex-

smith. P O Victoria, B C.   C : Lena A, Clemens A,
Harvey C, Seda P, Maude.
VII. Nathan E Clemens, b June 8, 1859 ; m Catha-
rine German. P O Petrolia, Ont. Farmer. C :
Minnie G, Roy, Harry, Edna Grace.
VII. John H Clemens, born Feb 10, 1862 ; m Sophia
Ernst. P O Ravenswood, Ont. Farmer. C : Edwin
A, Martin E, John Abram, Ida May.
VII. Benjamin Clemens, b May 17, 1865 ; d Sept 17,
1868.
VII. Julia E Clemens, born Apr 6, 1868 ; m Herbert
Rawlings. P O Ravenswood, Ont. Farmer. C :
Walter C.
VI. Elizabeth Rosenberger, b in Waterloo co, Ont,
Apr 1829 ; d July 1878 ; m George Henry Dennstedt
Jan 1853. H was born at Muhlhausen, Prussia, Oct
1830 ; d at Blair, Ont, May 1890. Merchant ; Menn.
C : Mary, Abraham, Wilhelmina, Elizabeth, Elvina,
Isaac, George.
VII. Mary Ann Dennstedt, born in Blandford, Ont,
Dec 20, 1853 ; m Aaron R Bock. (See Index of
References No. 1.)
VII. Abram Dennstedt, b in Blenheim twp, Oxford
co, Ont, Jan 19, 1857 ; m Agnes Armstrong Oct 16,
1878. P O Carberry, Man. Farmer ; Meth. C :
(VIII) George James Dennstedt (d), b Sept 5, 1879.
(VIII) William Dennstedt, born Feb 7, 1881. (VIII)
Agnes Dennstedt, born Aug 17, 1882. (VIII) Ellie
Dennstedt, born Nov 22, 1884 ; died Oct 5, 1885.
(VIII) Chester Dennstedt, born Nov 22, 1886. (VIII)
Nellie Dennstedt, born Sept 24, 1888. (VIII) Lizzie
Dennstedt, b Aug 31, 1890.
VII. Wilhelmina Dennstedt, born in Wilmot twp,
Waterloo co, Ont, Oct 1857 ; m George Perry Mar 15,
1893. P O Deloraine, Man. Farmer ; Meth. No
issue by this marriage, but a dau by second marriage.
C : (VIII) Jennie Smiley, b Feb 17, 1880 ; m Leonard
M Sawyer October 13, 1897. P O Deloraine, Man.
Farmer ; Meth.
VII. Elizabeth Dennstedt, born in Ellis twp, Ont,
August 13, 1859 ; m James Armstrong July 1880. R
7th ave, Mt Pleasant, B C. Dairyman ; Meth. C :

(**VIII**) Olive Elizabeth Armstrong, b July 14, 1889 ;
Percy Calvin, b August 7, 1891 ; Muriel Agnes, born
Aug 24, 1895.

VII. Elvina Dennstedt, b in Perth co, Ont, May 13,
1861 ; m William John Carson July 15, 1890. R 10th
ave, Mt Pleasant, Vancouver, B C. Mechanic ; Meth.
C : (**VIII**) James Albert Carson, born May 24, 1891 ;
Margaret Elizabeth, b Nov 17, 1893 ; George Doug-
lass, b Sept 6, 1895.

VII. Isaac Dennstedt, born in Perth co, Ont, Aug 15,
1864. P O Carberry, Man. Small ware peddler ;
Meth. S.

VII. George Dennstedt, b in Perth co, Ont, March 4,
1866. P O Vancouver, B C. Engineer ; Meth. S.

VI. Abraham Rosenberger, b in Waterloo co, Ont,
Sept 3, 1831 ; m Catharine Moore Oct 18, 1853. She
was b in Waterloo co, Ont, Sept 29, 1836. When a
boy Mr Rosenberger moved with his parents to Wilmot
twp, Ont, where his parents were pioneer settlers and
had all the inconveniences and requisites of pioneer
life, such as living in a log cabin in the woods with
only a fireplace for cooking and a blanket for a door,
and hunting, horseback riding, fishing, etc. Abram
helped to clear many a new farm. Machinery being
almost unknown then and schools few and inferior,
boys were obliged to work hard, with but little
opportunity to get an education. Abram's schooling
consisted of about three Winter's of school. Though
a studious pupil he had little chance of learning anything besides reading, writing and arithmetic. His
mother taught him to read German, which he never
forgot.

In 1853 he bought a farm of his father, where he
lived until 1863, when he sold it and moved to Huron
co, Ont, where he had rented the Cober farm. In
1868 he moved to a farm of his own, where he lived
until 1876, when he sold and bought a farm nearer
school. In 1884 he again sold and bought a farm in
Tuscola co, Mich, where he still resides.

When Mrs Rosenberger was 11 years old her
parents moved near Antioch, Ill, where her father

died of a fever, and soon after the family returned to Canada.

Mr Rosenberger's whole family of eight children have musical talent inherited from their parents, and as long as a majority of them were at home they had a regular family choir. P O Unionville, Mich. Farmer; Menn. C: Nancy, Rachel, Lydia, Samuel, Aaron, Jesse, Mary, Sarah.

VII. Nancy A Rosenberger, b in Waterloo co, Ont, Aug 25, 1854; m Thomas A Tressler, of Waterloo co, Sept 16, 1885. P O Muskoka, Ont. Mr Tressler has enjoyed some traveling, having before marriage been on a trip to England and afterward to Virginia. Since his marriage he went to British Columbia with the intention of locating there, but soon after returned to Canada and located in Muskoka, near the village of Trout Creek. Farmer and carpenter; Christadelphian church. C : (**VIII**) Vida Catharine Tressler, born Feb 25, 1887 ; Charles Percival, born Aug 23, 1890.

VII. Rachel M Rosenberger, b in Waterloo co. Ont, Jan 9, 1856 ; m T G Page, of Halton co, Ont, Apr 11, 1895. P O Palermo, Ont. Farmer, and reside on the old page homestead in Halton co, Ont. Though a bright scholar Mrs Page's natural ability was sewing. At 12 years she made her own dresses and did much of the family sewing. At 13 she left home, going back to Waterloo, Ont, doing housework at the Uncle D Cole's and going to school, and later began sewing at 30 cents a day, until she opened up a dressmaking shop at New Hamburg, Ont, with only 30 cents in money. She bought a $65 sewing machine on time and gradually rose in her business, and after dressmaking in New Hamburg many years she sewed in Galt, New Dundee and Guelph. Three years before her marriage she was head mantle cutter in a large store in Hamilton, and some time in Dundas at $40 a month. Christadelphians.

VII. Lydia L Rosenberger, b in Waterloo co, Ont, June 6, 1857. P O Unionville, Mich. In 1884 she moved with her parents to Tuscola co. Mich. and still resides at home, and is engaged in dressmaking, her

chief delight being artistic work, in which she excels.
Before leaving Canada she united with the Evangelical church.

VII. Samuel Rosenberger, b in Waterloo co Oct 17,
1859 ; m Lucy Bingaman, of Oxford co, Ont, Jan 1,
1891. P O Pinconning, Bay co, Mich. In 1882 he
went to North Dakota intending to locate there, but
in 1884 returned and moved with his parents to
Michigan. He was something of a genius and
invented many articles in his boyhood, among them a
water wheel, thresher, windmill, etc. Carpenter by
trade, now farmer. Mrs Rosenberger, Men. C :
(**VIII**) Clayton Rosenberger, b Feb 19, 1892 ; Verian
John, b Mar 27, 1894 ; Vivian Jesse, b Oct 28, 1897.

VII. Rev Aaron Rosenberger, b in Waterloo co. Ont,
April 26, 1862 ; m Lizzie Bingaman, of Oxford co,
Ont, Jan 9, 1887. When first married he engaged in
farming for two years. In 1890 he moved to Tuscola
co, Mich, where he purchased a farm, but sold it in
1891, and later attended school at Dutton, Mich, to
prepare for the ministry of the New Mennonite church.
On leaving school he preached in Michigan and
Indiana as an evangelist for a year, then went to
Waterloo co, Ont, and took charge of the Bright
church congregation. He now resides in Berlin, Ont,
as local preacher. From boyhood his natural talents
were music and oratory. He had a beautiful clear
tenor voice, and at 13 years led the tenor in singing
school. C : (**VIII**) Lucy Rosenberger, born Aug 26,
1887 ; Elmore, b Oct 10, 1890 ; Roy, b May 6, 1894 ;
Ruth, b July 22, 1896.

VII. Jesse A Rosenberger, born in Huron co, Ont,
July 2, 1865 ; m Ella Daniels, of Waterloo co, Ont,
Dec 29, 1891. P O Pigeon, Huron co, Mich. In
1892 he moved to Michigan and rented his father's
farm. In 1895 he bought an 80-acre farm in Huron
county, where he now resides. In stature he is tall,
lacking not quite two inches of being as tall as his
Grandfather Rosenberger, whose height was 6 feet 2
inches. New Menn. C : (**VIII**) Vernon D Rosenberger, b Oct 31, 1893 ; Nina, b May 20, 1896.

VII. Mary J Rosenberger, born in Huron co, Ont,

July 6, 1868. Early in life she had strong inclinations for learning. She began going to school at 7 years. Soon after the family moved to Michigan, where she made efforts to earn means with which to gain a higher education than the district schools afforded. In August 1889 she passed the examination and received a third grade teachers' certificate, and in November following began teaching and taught four terms, then entered Caro High School in September 1891, remaining six months, after which she taught several terms. She took great interest in Sunday school work, in which she led the alto singing. Before leaving Canada she joined the Evangelical church. P O Unionville, Mich. S.

VII. Sarah J Rosenberger, b in Huron co, Ont, Dec 14, 1870. She began going to school at the age of 6 years, and at 10 she began to learn rapidly. In August 1889 she successfully passed the third grade teachers' examination. She then entered the Caro High school, where she remained six months, after which she taught five terms, then re-entered Caro High school for six months, and after leaving there again taught school. When quite young she took a course in penmanship and made a specimen of penwork that was the admiration of all. She has musical talents and is an accomplished musician. Her present address is South End, Ont.

VI. Christian S Rosenberger, b in Waterloo co, Ont, Nov 1, 1833; m Barbara Jones (d). C: Barbara, d in infancy. Christian married second wife Hannah Shantz May 13, 1856. She was born in Waterloo co, Ont, June 10, 1837; d Mar 1891. P O New Dundee, Ont. Retired farmer; Menn. C: Henry, Abraham, Maria, Rebecca, Hannah, Christian, Lucinda, Noah, Minerva.

VII. Henry Rosenberger, b Aug 23, 1857; d Apr 7, 1875.

VII. Abraham Rosenberger, b in Waterloo co Jan 11, 1859; m Lydia Tohman Sept 13, 1881. P O New Dundee, Ont. Farmer; Menn Br in Christ ch. C: **(VIII)** Elma Rosenberger, born Sept 30, 1884. **(VIII)** Son, b Mar 30, 1886; d Dec 20, 1887. **(VIII)** Myra

Rosenberger, b Sept 15, 1889. (**VIII**) Nora Rosenberger, b April 24, 1894.

VII. Maria Rosenberger, born in Waterloo co, Ont, May 9, 1861 ; m Rev Henry S Hallman Jan 18, 1881. P O Berlin, Ont. He was b in Waterloo co Aug 5, 1859. He attended the public school at New Dundee until old enough to assist on the farm. When in his "teens" he left the farm and engaged in the carpenter trade, and later entered the Berlin High school and studied at other places of education until he passed his examination for the teaching profession. After teaching two and a half years in Bruce co, Ont, he retired from the profession and moved to Berlin, where he still resides. When a young man he joined the River Brethren church, of which he was a member for some years. In 1879 he united with the Mennonite Brethren in Christ, of which church he is still an active member. In 1881 he gave his life to ministry and has faithfully served the church of his choice up to the present time. In October 1888 the general conference held in Berlin, Ont, appointed him editor of the "Gospel Banner," a position he still holds. C : Manilla, Abner, Nancy Ellen, Lorne, Annette.

VII. Rebecca Rosenberger, b in Waterloo co, Ont, Apr 19, 1863. S.

VII. Hannah Rosenberger, b in Wilmot twp, Waterloo co, June 23, 1865 ; m James Coleman Dec 21, 1886. P O Elmwood, Ont. Farmer ; Menn Br in Christ. C : (**VIII**) Rosetta Coleman, b Dec 31, 1887 ; Milton, b July 6, 1891 ; Gorden, b Oct 1, 1894.

VII. Christian Rosenberger, Jr, b in Waterloo co Aug 11, 1867 ; m Phidellia Reist, of Kossuth, Ont, January 2, 1894. P O New Dundee, Ont. Farmer ; Menn. C : (**VIII**) Benaiah Rosenberger, b Aug 26, 1896.

VII. Lucinda Rosenberger, b in Wilmot twp, Waterloo co, March 28, 1871 ; m Theodore Reist Dec 22, 1891. P O Kossuth, Ont. Farmer ; New Menn. C : (**VIII**) Wilmer Reist, b Jan 8, 1893. (**VIII**) Mabel Reist, b May 9, 1894. (**VIII**) Alton Reist, b June 23, 1895 ; d Nov 15, 1895. (**VIII**) Pearl Reist, b Nov 20, 1896.

Rev. A. S. Rosenberger, M. D.

VII. Noah Rosenberger, b in Waterloo Co , Ont. June 10, 1875, m Lizzie Schultz Nov 4, 1896. P O Elkton, Mich. Farmer, Menn. Br. in Christ.

VII. Minerva Rosenberger, b in Waterloo Co. Ont. July 19, 1878. P O New Dundee, Ont. S.

VI Sarah Rosenberger, b Apr 16, 1836, d July 10, 1880, aged 44 yr. 2 m. 24 d.

VI. Benjamin S. Rosenberger, b in Waterloo Co., Ont. July 1, 1838, m Nancy Shantz, daughter of Henry Shantz, Oct 11, 1859. P O New Dundee, Ont. Farmer, Menn. C: Lydia, Menno, Mary, Leah. Eli, Nancy, Benjamin. Sara. Osia, Edwin.

VII. Lydia Rosenberger, b June 4, 1860.

VII. Menno Rosenberger, b Sept 25, 1862, m Lucinda Stauffer Sept 8 1891. P O New Dundee, Ont. Farmer, Menn. Br. in Christ. C: (**VIII**) Annie Vera Rosenberger, Lorne Stanley Rosenberger.

VII. Mary Rosenberger, b Apr 12, 1865, m John H. Coleman Nov 4, 1891. P O Elmwood, Ont. Farmer, Menn. Br. in Christ. C: (**VIII**) Ina, Coleman, b Oct 2, 1894. (**VIII**) Verna Coleman, b Jan 27, 1897. (**VIII**) Nancy Coleman, b Apr 12, 1899. (**VIII**) Lydia Pearl Coleman, b Jan 21, 1901.

VII. Eli Rosenberger, b May 7, 1870, m Clara Snyder Feb 5, 1896. P O Brown City, Michigan. Farmer, Menn. Br. in Christ. C: (**VIII**) Mabel Rosenberger, b Feb 2, 1897. (**VIII**) Olive Rosenberger, b Apr 29, 1898. (**VIII**) Floyd Rosenberger, b Aug 31, 1901.

VII. Nancy Rosenberger, b Feb 21, 1873.

VII. Benjamin Rosenberger, b June 16, 1875.

VII. Sarah Ann Rosenberger, b Sept 10, 1877.

VII. Osia Rosenberger, b Aug 18, 1880.

VII. Edwin Rosenberger, b Aug 13, 1884.

VI. Isaac Rosenberger, b in Waterloo Co., Ont. Jan 2, 1842, m Elizabeth Shantz, Jan 24, 1865. P O Plattsville, Ont. Farmer, Menn. C: Hannah, Isaiah, Mary, Moses, Emory, Emaline, Titus, Elsie.

VII. Hannah Rosenberger, b in Waterloo Co., Ont. Dec 10, 1865, m Joshua M. Shantz Nov 3, 1891. P O Haysville, Ont. Farmer, Menn. C: (**VIII**)

Alberta Shantz, b Oct 2, 1898, d Mar 14, 1901.

VII. Isaiah Rosenberger, b Aug 15, 1867, m Persida Shantz. Farmer, Menn. C: (**VIII**) Bessie Rosenberger.

VII. Mary Ann Rosenberger, b Jan 24, 1870, d Feb 9, 1894, m Norman Shantz.

VII. Emaline Rosenberger, b Apr 20, 1872, m Norman Shantz. C: (**VIII**) Mary Ann Shantz.

VII. Moses Rosenberger, b Dec 11, 1874.

VII. Emory Rosenberger, b Jan 17, 1877.

VII. Titus Rosenberger, b July 18, 1879.

VII. Elsie Rosenberger, b July 8, 1883.

VI. Susanna Rosenberger, (b)——— d June 2, 1876, aged 32 yr. 6 mo. 24 d. S.

VI. Lydia Rosenberger, b May 27, 1845, m Levi S. Shantz Mar 28, 1865. P O Phillipsburg, Ont. Farmer, Menn. C: Abraham, Nancy, Isaiah, Wendell, Barbara, (d); Susanna, Lydia, Sarah, Emery, Noah, (d); Hannah, (d); Hiram, (d).

VII. Abraham Shantz, b Jan 8, 1866, m Mary Ann Wolf. Farmer, Luth. C: (**VIII**) Orfa, Laura, Theodore, Herbert, Hiram.

VII. Nancy Shantz, (twin to Abraham), b Jan 8, 1866, m Daniel Rudy. Wagon-maker, Menn. C: (**VIII**) Norman, (d); Clarence, Clayton, Aloin.

VII. Isaiah Shantz, b Apr 11, 1868, m Sarah Honderick. Merchant, Menn.

VII. Wendell Shantz, b Mar 1, 1870.

VII. Barbard Shautz, b Jan 27, 1872, (d).

VII. Susanna Shautz, b Aug 14, 1874.

VII. Lydia Shantz, b Jan 1, 1877, m Abraham Honderick. Farmer. C: (**VIII**) Earl Honderick, b Aug 26, 1897.

VII. Sarah Shantz, b Mar 9, 1879, (d).

VII. Emery Shantz, b Oct 20, 1881.

VII. Noah Shantz, b July 20, 1883, (d).

VII. Hannah Shantz, (twin), b July 20, 1883, (d).

VII. Hiram Shantz, b Mar 23, 1885, (d).

V. Jacob Rosenberger, b 1803, d at Guelph, Ont. May 3, 1891, m Lucinda Bigelow. She d at Hespler, Ont. in 1857. Mr. Rosenberger fell heir to a large amount of his father's property, but in later years lost nearly all of it. Farmer and Butcher, Methodist. C: Hettie, Elvira, Walter, Elizabeth.

VI. Hettie Anne Rosenberger, b in Preston, Ont. July 9, 1844, m Thomas Arthur Wesley Pearson Sept 19, 1873. Mr. Pearson was a native of Hull, London, England. He died after a long illness of ten years. P O Guelph, Ont. Ch. of England. C: Alice.

VII. Alice Maud Pearson, b Sept 30, 1874. P O Guelph, Ont. She is the head knitter in the largest wollen mill in the city. She is a great lover of nature, and books are her constant companions. She is an excellent reader and has good conversational powers, and is also passionately fond of music. She is a very prominent and popular worker in the Paisley St. Methodist church of Guelph, and was selected and sent as a delegate to the Epworth League Convention held in Toronto July 1897. Meth. S.

VI. Elvira Rosenberger, b Mar 4, 1846, d 1855.

VI. Walter Rosenberger, b Apr 1, 1849, d Apr 18, 1883, m Harriet Bolduc, of Hespler, Ont., (a French lady). C: George.

VII. George Rosenberger.

VI. Elizabeth Rosenberger, b 1851, m David Field, of Hespler, Ont. P O Guelph, Ont.

V. Barbara Rosenberger, b Jan 29, 1804, d Jan 30, 1885, m Daniel Rudy. He was b in Lancaster Co., Pa. Dec 4, 1796, d Dec 7, 1857. Went to Canada when a young man; settled near Doon, in Waterloo Co., Ont. C: George, Rebecca, Nancy, Daniel, Abraham, Christian, Henry, Benjamin, Samuel, Barbara, Jacob.

VI. George Rudy, b Sept 23, 1823, m Barbara Lichty, Mar 16, 1847. She was b Jan 2, 1825. P O Waterloo, Ont. Retired farmer. C: Nancy.

VII. Nancy Rudy, b Apr 7, 1850, m John Kunkle May 3, 1868. He was a native of Lehigh Co., Pa. They resided on her father's old homestead where she died Apr 14, 1887. Farmer. C: (**VIII**) Sarah Jane Kunkle, (d); Josiah, Cyrus,(d);

Alice, Barbara, Nancy, (d); John, (d); George,
(d); Alfred, Emma.

VI. Rebecca Rudy, b Oct 29, 1825, m Samuel
Shantz Mar 25, 1845, (his second wife). He was
b Jan 16, 1811, d Jan 18, 1895. Farmer near
Berlin, Ont., where he was the possessor of one of
the finest farms on the Petersburg road. Menn.
C: Daniel, Esther, Abraham, Moses, Emily,
Josiah, Nelson, Matilda, Israel, Allen, Louisa,
Simon.

VII. Daniel Shantz, b Jan 1, 1846, d Aug 4, 1848.

VII. Esther Shantz, b Dec 27, 1847, m Menno
Shoemaker Nov 29, 1870. He was b Mar 8, 1845.
P O Berlin, Ont. Carpenter, Methodist. C:
Samuel, Rebecca, Clara, Emma, Harvey.

VIII. Samuel Allen Shoemaker, b Jan 5, 1872, d
July 6, 1893.

VIII. Rebecca May Shoemaker, b Mar 6, 1874, m
John Williams July 11, 1899. Farmer. C: (**IX**)
Olive Esther Williams.

VIII. Clara Elma Shoemaker, b Apr 28, 1877. P
O Berlin, Ont. Methodist.

VIII. Emma Lourina Shoemaker, b Dec 24, 1880,
m Charles J.H. Massel Dec 26, 1900. P O Berlin,
Ont. Baker, Methodist. C: (**IX**). Harold Walter
Massel, b Oct 1901.

VIII. Harvey Edwin Shoemaker, b July 24, 1886.
P O Berlin, Ont., Cabinetmaker.

VII. Abraham Shantz, b May 2, 1850, d Jan 23,
1861.

VII. Moses R. Shantz, b Feb 13, 1852, m Rebecca
Rickhert Jan 20, 1874. She d Dec 25, 1881. C:
Sarah, Edwin, Lavina. Moses m second wife,
Caroline Lipps, Oct 8, 1882. She was b Oct 29,
1862. P O Berlin, Ont. Farmer. C: (**VIII**) Ella,
Wesley, Dora.

VII. Emily Shantz, b Feb 18, 1854, m Samuel C.
Bowman Dec 9, 1873. He was b Dec 23, 1852. P
O Brown City, Mich. Farmer, Menn. Br. in Christ.
C: Alice, Matilda, Anna, Isaiah, Ethel, Walter,
Nettie, Emily.

VIII. Matilda Bowman, b Feb 23, 1875. Res. St.

Nicholas Hotel, Springfield, Ill. S.
VIII. Anna Rebecca Bowman, b Jan 21, 1877.
Mission worker, Menn. Br. in Christ. Res. Port
Huron, Mich. S.
VIII. Isaiah Bowman, b Dec 24, 1878. Res. 94
Wendell St., Cambridge, Mass. School teacher. S.
VIII. Alice Bowman, b Sept 4, 1881. S.
VIII. Ethel Bowman, b July 11, 1885.
VIII. Walter Bowman, b Mar 9, 1889.
VIII. Nettie Bowman, b Feb 14, 1891.
VIII. Emily Margaret Bowman, b Aug 27, 1899.
VII. Josiah Shantz, b Feb 20, 1856, d Feb 5, 1861.
VII. Nelson Shantz, b Aug 2, 1858, d Jan 18, 1861.
VII.Matilda Shantz, b Oct 16, 1860, m Noah E.
Ely Feb 12, 1879. P O Petersburg, Ont. Farmer.
C: (**VIII**) Josiah, Louisa, Samuel, Edwin, Saman-
tha, Priscilla, Milton.
VII. Israel R. Shantz, b Aug 15, 1863, m Elizabeth
Schmidt. P O Berlin, Ont. Farmer. C: (**VIII**)
Soleda, Lloyd, Samuel, Orva.
VII. Allen R. Shantz, b in Waterloo Co., Ont.
Sept 2, 1865, m Louisa Detwiler Aug 10, 1888. P
O Garstairs Alta, Canada. Lumber Mer., Post-
master; and coal & implement dealer. C: (**VIII**)
Cornelia Violet Shantz, b June 21, 1889, d Oct 6,
1889. Roswell Jay Shantz, b May 17, 1899.
VII. Louisa Rebecca Shantz, b Oct 2, 1867, m
Benjamin E. Ely Mar 14, 1886. P O Berlin, Ont.
C: (**VIII**) Milford, Sylva.
VII. Simon R. Shantz, b Apr 28, 1871, m Annie E.
Knorr Aug 30, 1891. P O Louisa Bridge, Manitoba,
Canada. Employed by the Waterloo Mfg. Co. at
Winnipeg, Man., and also runs a retail butcher busi-
ness at that place. C: (**VIII**) Alberta Violet Shantz,
b Jan 8, 1893. (**VIII**) Edgar Shantz, b Apr 15, 1896,
d Mar 11, 1897. (**VIII**) Bessie Luella Shantz, b Apr.
28, 1898. (**VIII**) Herold Hugh Shantz, b Mar 31,
1902.
VI. Nancy Rudy, b Oct 14, 1827, d Feb 20, 1862, m
Aaron Ziegler Apr 11, 1854. He was b Dec 16,
1829, d Jan 13, 1885. C: Jacob, Barbara, Sarah.
VII. Jacob R. Ziegler, b Apr 10, 1856, m Catharine

Koenig. P O Chippewa Hill, Ont. Farmer. C:
(**VIII**) Addison, Lizzie, George.

VII. Barbara Ziegler, b Jan 21, 1858, m Aaron
Martin, Nov 27, 1892. P O Gorrie, Ont. Farmer,
Menn. No issue.

VII. Sarah Ziegler, b Oct 27, 1859, m Solomon
Lichty Jan 21, 1885. He was b Aug 4, 1861. P
O Waterloo, Ont. Farmer, Menn. C: (**VIII**) Noah
Lichty, b Sept 16, 1883. (**VIII**) Nancy Lichty, b
Dec 22, 1884. (**VIII**) Hettie Lichty, b May 6, 1887.
(**VIII**) John Lichty, b May 29, 1889. (**VIII**) Sidney
Lichty, b Dec 12, 1891. (**VIII**) A son still-born
Sept 23, 1896.

VI. Daniel Rudy, b July 27, 1830, d July 29, 1892,
m Mary Ann Detweiler. Farmer. C: David.

VII. David Rudy, b—, m Mary Ann Hewitt. P O
Tavistock, Ont. Farmer and auctioneer.

VI. Abraham Rudy, b Jan 2, 1833, m Nancy Shantz
Sept 12, 1854. She was b May 5, 1835, d Aug 12,
1857. C: Susanna, Elizabeth. Abraham m second
wife, Mary Snyder, Oct 15, 1858. She d Dec 2,
1897. C: Barbara, Angeline, Sophiana.

VII. Susanna Rudy, b in Waterloo twp. Ont. Cana-
da. July 10, 1855. m Martin M. Frey Mar 8, 1874.
P O Waterloo, Ont. Teamster, Menn. Br. in Christ.
C: Eliza, Abraham, Amanda, Edwin, Harvey, Elam,
Luetta, Elsie, Lloyd.

VIII. Eliza Ann Frey, b Jan 16, 1875, m Fred D.
Ruland July 10, 1901. P O Mayville, N. Y.

VIII. Abraham Frey, b Aug 19, 1876, d Dec 13,
1887.

VIII. Amanda Frey, b Mar 18, 1878.

VIII. Edwin Frey, b Feb 9, 1880.

VIII. Harvey Frey, b Apr 13, 1882.

VIII. Elam Frey, b Nov 18, 1884.

VIII. Luetta Frey, b Apr 10, 1887.

VIII. Elsie Frey, b Aug 5, 1890.

VIII. Lloyd Frey, b Sept 24, 1892.

VII. Eliza Rudy, b in Waterloo twp. Ont. Canada,
Aug 1, 1857, m John S. Becker Oct 17, 1875. P O
Elmwood, Ont. Farmer, Luth. C: (**VIII**) George
Becker, b Aug 3, 1876. Maggie Becker, b Oct 22,

1878. Herman Becker, b Jan 20, 1881. William Becker, b June 14, 1883. Abraham Becker, b Feb 11, 1885. Ida Becker, b Mar 3, 1887. Lucinda Becker, b Mar 13, 1889. Emanuel Becker, b Dec 28, 1891. Alexander Becker, b Feb 24, 1894. Edna Becker, b June 13, 1896.

VII. Barbara Rudy, b Aug 31, 1859, m Ezra S. Bauman Oct 15, 1878. P O Waterloo, Ont. Farmer, Menn. C: (**VIII**) Allan Bauman, b Nov 8, 1879. (**VIII**) Mary Ann Bauman, b Aug 17, 1882. (**VIII**) Sarah Bauman, b Feb 18, 1886. (**VIII**) Lizzie Bauman, b Mar 17, 1888. (**VIII**) Malinda Bauman, b Aug 16, 1893.

VII. Angeline Rudy, b Oct 18, 1860, d Feb 18, 1891, m John M. Brubacher, Oct 4, 1881. He was b Mar 8, 1859. Farmer, Menn. C: (**VIII**) Edwin Brubacher, b Oct 16, 1882. (**VIII**) Clara Brubacher, b June 11, 1885. (**VIII**) Abraham Brubacher, b Jan 8, 1888. (**VIII**) Luannah Brubacher, b Dec 22, 1891.

VII. Sophianna Rudy, b Feb 8, 1862, m Josiah S. Shantz Nov 25, 1884. P O Waterloo, Ont. Farmer, Menn. C: (**VIII**) Alvin Shantz, b Jan 30, 1886. Elvina Shantz, b Oct 5, 1890.

VI. Christian Rudy, b Jan 2, 1833, m Lydia Horst Jan 2, 1855. She was b Mar 17, 1838. P O St. Jacobs, Ont. Farmer, Menn. C: Leah, Amanda, Amos, Daniel, Emma, Veronica, Lydia, Christian, Josiah, Susanna, Barbara.

VII. Leah Rudy, b Aug 8, 1855, m Henry P. Martin Jan 31, 1875. He was b Aug 13, 1852. P O Winfield, Ont. Farmer, Menn. C: (**VIII**) Lydia Martin, b Jan 18, 1876. Menn. Menno Martin, b Sept 7, 1877. Menn. Josiah, Jeremiah, and Veronica, (triplets), b and d Nov 24, 1878. Christian Martin, b Feb 6, 1880. Amos Martin, b June 6, 1882, d Sept 1, 1883. Jonathan Martin, b Dec 30, 1884. Boy, still-born Aug 3, 1886. Girl, still-born May 28, 1888. Susanna Martin, b Aug 22, 1889. Mary Ann Martin, b Apr 10, 1892. Anna Martin, b Feb 17, 1894. Leah Martin, b Aug 29, 1897.

VII. Amanda Rudy, b May 14, 1857, d May 24, 1889, m Samuel Snyder May 31, 1887. He was b

Mar 13, 1856. P O Baden, Ont. Farmer, Menn·
C: (VIII) Menno Snider, b Sept 16, 1888.
VII. Amos Rudy, b Mar 25, 1859, d Feb 4, 1886,
m Anna Steiner Jan 24, 1884. She was b Aug 6,
1861, d July 10, 1891. C: (VIII) Isaiah Rudy, b
May 25, 1885.
VII. Daniel H. Rudy, b Apr 24, 1861, m Nancy
Shantz Jan 26, 1886. P O Blair, Ont. Carriage-
maker. Menn. C: (VIII) Norman Rudy, b Jan 4,
1887, d Apr 29, 1890. Clarence Rudy, b Sept 27,
1890. Clayton Rudy, b Nov 7, 1892. Alvin Rudy,
b Jan 15, 1895. Melvin Rudy, b Dec 27, 1897.
Levi Rudy b May 8, 1902.
VII. Emma Rudy, b Sept 1, 1863, m Jonathan
Martin Nov 12, 1887. He was b Aug 8, 1860. P
O Waterloo, Ont. Farmer, Menn. C: (VIII) Jo-
siah Martin, b Sept 28, 1883. Ephraim Martin, b
Feb 12, 1885. Irwin Martin, b Mar 23, 1887.
Hannah Martin, b Dec 15, 1888. Isaiah Martin, b
Oct 24, 1890. Malinda Martin, b Mar 5, 1892. Nor-
man Martin, b Feb 25, 1894. Alvina Martin, b
Mar 4, 1897. Milton Martin, b Aug 13, 1898.
VII. Veronica Rudy, b Oct 18, 1865, m Daniel
Ernst Apr 20, 1886. He was b Feb 3, 1865. P O
Waterloo, Ont. Farmer, Menn. C: (VIII) Josiah
Ernst, b Jan 13, 1887. Nelson Ernst, b Aug 30,
1888. Salinda Ernst, b June 14, 1890. Noah
Ernst, b Jan 19, 1892. Jonathan Ernst, b Dec 9,
1893. Barbara Ernst, b Jan 11, 1898.
VII. Lydia Rudy, b June 17, 1869. P O St. Jacobs,
Ont. Menn. S.
VII. Christian Rudy, b June 17, 1869, d Feb 6,
1871, (twin to Lydia).
VII. Josiah Rudy, b Sept 21, 1871, d Oct 4, 1885.
VII. Susanna Rudy, b July 28, 1874, d Mar 22,
1875.
VII. Barbara Rudy, b May 13, 1876. Menn. S.
VI. Henry Rudy, b in 1835, m Louisa Anna Meyer.
Resided in Illinois where he died. C: Joseph,
Elizabeth, Emily.
VI. Benjamin Rudy, b in Waterloo Co. Ont. Cana-
da, Oct 13, 1837, d Apr 23, 1890, m Mary Ann

Hoffman Nov 7, 1862. She was b Apr 20, 1844, in
Waterloo, Co. Ont. d Apr 27, 1894. Farmer,
Menn. C: William, Menno, Nancy, Sarah, Bar-
bara, Magdalena, Eleanor, Mary. Mary, Jeremiah,
Josiah, Hannah, Elias, Lucy.

VII. William Rudy, b Apr 24, 1864, m Rachel
Reist Dec 24, 1890. She was b Aug 17, 1862. P O
Waterloo, Ont. Farmer. C: (**VIII**) Mary Etta
Rudy, b Apr 28, 1892. Jacob R. Rudy, b Mar 9,
1894. Martha Ellen Rudy, b Jan 12, 1896. Rachel
Ann Rudy, b May 8, 1898. Sarah Ann Rudy,
(twin), b May 8, 1898.

VII. Menno Rudy, b Jan 16. 1866, d Jan 17, 1867.

VII. Nancy Rudy, b Sept 19, 1867. P O Jordan,
Ont. S.

VII. Sarah Ann Rudy, b in Waterloo Co. Ont.,
Dec 21, 1868, m Caleb Shelley Feb 28, 1899. P
O Berlin, Ont.

VII. Barbara Rudy, b Jan 19, 1870. P O
Strasburg, Ont. S.

VII. Magdalena Rudy, b July 31, 1872. P O
Baden, Ont. S.

VII. Eleanor Rudy, b Oct 6, 1874. P O
Waterloo, Ont.

VII. Mary Ann Rudy, b May 8, 1877, d
May 8, 1877.

VII. Mary Etta Rudy, (twin), b May 8, 1877,
d May 22, 1877.

VII. Jeremiah Rudy, b July 24, 1878. P O
Berlin, Ont. S.

VII. Josiah Rudy, (twin), b July 24, 1878.

VII. Hannah Rudy, b Mar 6, 1880.

VII. Elias Rudy, b June 13, 1882.

VII. Lucy Ann Rudy, b Nov 3, 1884.

VI. Samuel Rudy, b Mar 3, 1840, m Nancy Jones
1861. She was b Apr 22, 1845. P O Berlin, Ont.
Teamster. C: Joshua, Hannah, Jonas, Barbara,
Samuel, Emanuel, Moses, Addison, Albert.

VII. Joshua Rudy, b Mar 11, 1862, m Rebecca
Spaetz. P O Waterloo, Ont. Farmer. C: (**VIII**)
Noah, Amos, Israel, Aaron.

VII. Hannah Rudy, b July 6, 1863, m Alexander

Dingwall. P O Wellesley, Ont. Carder and Spinner. C: (**VIII**) Martha Valeria Dingwall. Harry Alexander Dingwall.

VII. Jonas Rudy, b Dec 21, 1864, m Louisa Thiele. P O Berlin, Ont. Cabinetmaker. (**VIII**) William, Anna, James.

VII. Barbara Rudy, b June 10, 1867, m Jacob Sauer. P O Berlin, Ont. Cabinetmaker and M'fg. of Parlor frames. C: Norman, Harold.

VII. Samuel Rudy, b Sept 20, 1868, m Lizzie Lantz. P O Waterloo, Ont. Employed in a furniture factory. C: (**VIII**) Lenora, Oscar.

VII. Emanuel Rudy, b Aug 21, 1870. P O Berlin, Ont.

VII. Moses Rudy, b Mar 18, 1875, d Mar 23, 1875.

VII. Addison Rudy, b Mar 11, 1876. P O Berlin, Ont.

VII. Albert L. Rudy, b Mar 26, 1888.

VII Barbara Rudy, b June 18, 1842, m Menno E. Shantz Sept 18, 1864. He was b Mar 11, 1841. P O Petersburg, Ont. Farmer. C: Nelson, Angeline, Gleason. William, Maria, Clara.

VII. Nelson Shantz, b June 11, 1865, m Barbara Snyder. P O Petersburg, Ont. Farmer. C: (**VIII**) Agnes, Arthur, Lorne, Cornelia.

VII. Angeline Shantz, b Oct 6, 1867, m Samuel Snyder Sept 20, 1893. P O New Dundee, Ont. Farmer. Menn. C: (**VIII**) Perly May, b Feb 7, 1895. Violet Snyder, b Nov 28, 1897. Rosetta Snyder, b Aug 15, 1902.

VII. Cleason Shantz, b July 28, 1870, m Maria Shantz Dec 19, 1894. P O Waterloo, Ont. Farmer. Menn. C: (**VIII**) Burnice Shantz, b Jan 21, 1896. Clinton Shantz, b Sept 18, 1897.

VII. William R. Shantz, b Apr 3, 1872. P O Petersburg, Ont.

VII. Maria Shantz, b May 28, 1876.

VII. Clara Shantz, b July 1, 1884.

VI. Jacob Rudy, b 1844, m—. P O St. Antonia, Texas.

V. Elizabeth Rosenberger, b—, m Henry Shaeffer. No issue.

V. Nancy Rosenberger, b—, m John Graham. Res. Dundas. Ont.

IV. Jacob Rosenberger, b in Bucks Co., Pa. about 1770, d of cholera in Sheffield, Ont. Canada, in 1834, m Polly Detweiler. She was b in Montg. Co. Pa. about 1780, d of cholera in 1834. Weaver and farmer. They first belonged to the Mennonite church, and afterwards to the German Baptists. They emigrated to Canada in 1822. C: John, Rebecca, Elizabeth, Jacob, Benjamin, Abraham, Henry, Joseph. Christian. Nancy, Mary. Susan.

V. John D. Rosenberger, b Feb 4, 1800, d Feb 8, 1884, m Nancy Harley Mar 28, 1830. She was b Oct 21, 1810, d Nov 25, 1871. Both born, lived, and died in Montg. Co. Pa. Farmer. C: Margaret, Sarah, Catharine, Mary, Elizabeth, Simeon, John, Lydia.

VI. Margaret Rosenberger, b Oct 23, 1830, m William Rahn. P O Graters Ford, Pa. C: Warren, Clara.

VII. Warren R. Rahn, b in Montg. Co. Pa. Nov 29, 1861, m Emma L. Lewis July 17, 1893. P O Ambler, Pa. Princ. of Schools, Luth. C: .**VIII**) Marguerite L. Rahn, b Oct 11, 1894. Janey L. and Jessie L. Rahn, b Jan 3, 1896. Clara Rosenberger Rahn, b Jan 30. 1899.

VII. Clara R. Rahn, b—. S.

VI. Sarah Rosenberger, b June 20, 1832, d June 5, 1880, m Aaron Reed. C: Annie, John, Clayton, Mary.

VII. Annie Reed, m Samuel Moore.

VII. John Reed. P O Neiffer, Pa.

VII. Clayton Reed.

VII. Mary Reed, m Harry Steimnetz.

VI Catherine Rosenberger, b Jan 15, 1834, m Wilson Thomas Nov 5, 1853. P O Limerick, Pa. Farmer. Ref. ch. C: John, Wilson.

VII. John H. Thomas, b Apr 12, 1858, m Sallie Kepler. Farmer, Ref. ch. C: (**VIII**) Laura K. Thomas, b Feb 24, 1885. Katie K. Thomas, b Feb 28, 1890.

VII. Wilson A. Thomas, b Dec 11, 1864, m Alice

E. Dickerson. Farmer. No issue, (1879).
VI. Mary Ann Rosenberger, b July 1, 1836, m
Abraham D. Alderfer. (See A. D. Alderfer Family).
VI. Elizabeth Rosenberger, b in Montg. Co. Pa.
June 31, 1839. m Jacob L. Wartman Oct 20, 1866.
P O Graters Ford, Pa. Farmer, Luth. C: Sarah,
Mary, Elizabeth.
VII. Sarah Ann Wartman, b in Upper Providence
twp. Montg. Co. Pa. July 16, 1869, m Abraham
U. Raun Oct 22, 1887. P O Graters Ford, Pa.
Farmer. C: (**VIII**) Raymond W. Raun, b Dec 21,
1891. Lizzie W. Raun, b Nov 25, 1893. Jennie
W. Raun, b June 16, 1897. Jacob Rosevelt Raun,
b June 29, 1900.
VII. Mary R. Wartman, b Nov 17, 1873, d Feb
13, - 1882.
VII. Elizabeth R. Wartman, b in Montg. Co. Pa.
Feb 28, 1875, m Maurice M. Kerr Apr 30, 1901.
Res. 442 Beech St. Pottstown, Pa.
VI. Simeon Rosenberger, b May 19, 1841, d May
15, 1880. m Lydia Taylor, (d). C: John, Laura.
VII. John Rosenberger. P O West Point, Pa.
VII. Laura Rosenberger, b—, m— Kepler; live
in Ohio.
VI. John Rosenberger, b Nov 17, 1842, m Lydia
Jane Bucher. P O Royers Ford, Pa. C: (**VII**)
John, Katie, Jennie, Mary, Martha, Arthur.
Florence.
VI. Lydia Rosenberger, b Apr 4, 1844, m Jonathan
Christman. P O Royers Ford, Pa. C: Lizzie.
John, Edward, Lydia, Bertha, Ida, Mamie.
VII. Lizzie Christman, b in Frederick twp. Montg.
Co. Pa. Mar 7, 1871, m Warren E. Peterman Apr
22, 1893. P O Royers Ford, Pa. Evangelical.
C: (**VIII**) Cora L. Peterman, b Jan 31, 1896.
Florence M. Peterman, b Feb 10, 1895. J. Lloyd
Peterman, b Dec 20, 1900.
VII. John Christman, b—, m—.
V. Rebecca Rosenberger, b Aug 16, 1801, d May
28, 1882, m Joseph Stauffer. He was b Aug 15,
1802, d Oct 13, 1880. Farmer near Waterloo,
Ont. C: Elizabeth, Susanna, Mary, Nancy, Levi.

VII. Elizabeth Stauffer, b Sept 19, 1823, d Oct 17, 1863, m John S. Bowman Mar 3, 1846. He was b May 12, 1822. C: Hiram, Jonathan, Mary, Angeline, Rebecca.

VII. Hiram Bowman, b—, m Elizabeth McNally.

VII. Jonathan Bowman, m Anna Bauman.

VII. Mary Ann Bowman, d--, m James Hannah.

VII. Angeline Bowman, m Albert Shoemaker. P O West Montrose, Ont. Farmer.

VII. Rebecca Bowman, b—, m William McNally. Farmer in Mich.

VII. Joseph Bowman, b—. S.

VI. Susanna Stauffer, b May 9, 1828, d Apr ?, 1862, m Moses Echelman. He was b July 26, 1824. P O Berlin, Ont. Farmer. C: Sarah, Mary, Joseph, Simon. Nancy.

VII. Sarah Echelman, b Mar 13, 1846, d Mar 10, 1850.

VII. Mary Ann Echelman, b Mar 15, 1848, m Menno B. Clemens, (d). P O Berlin, Ont. Farmer. C: (**VIII**) Austin Clemens, Edgar Clemens, Horace Clemens.

VII. Joseph Echelman, b June 8, 1850, d June 15, 1878, m Magdalena Clemens. C: (**VIII**) Oliver Echelman, (d).

VII. Simeon Echelman, M. D., D. D. S., L. D. S., b at Blair, Waterloo Co. Ont. Canada, Aug 31, 1852, m Annie Paulina de Bell Sinclair Dec 28, 1881. Res. 421 Franklin St. Buffalo, N. Y. Dentist, Baptist. C: (**VIII**) Carl Ferdinand Dormer Echelman b Oct 15, 1882. Leo Sinclair Echelman, b Dec 1, 1883.

VII. Nancy Jane Echelman, b Sept 5. 1859, d Sept 23, 1860.

VI. Mary Stauffer, b June 30, 1830, d May 5, 1897, m Jacob S. Bowman Sept 7, 1847. He was b Oct 14, 1824. P O New Dundee, Ont. Farmer. U. Br. in Christ. C: Noah, Menno, Polly, Levina, Joshua.

VII. Noah Bowman, b Aug 1, 1848, m Sarah Buckborough Apr 2, 1878. P O Haysville, Ont. Farmer, U. Br. in Christ. C: (**VIII**) Mervin B.

Bowman, b Nov 26, 1880. U. Br. in Christ.

VII. Menno Stauffer Bowman, b Aug 14. 1849, m
Edna Henry. P O Oshawa, Ont.

VII. Polly Bowman, b in Waterloo Co. Ont. Apr
5, 1851, m Elias Hallman Mar 5, 1872. P O
Washington, Ont. Farmer, U. Br. in Christ. C:
Jessie, Edwin, Lauretta, Minota.

VIII. Jessie Ann Hallman, b Dec 26, 1872, m Will-
iam Richmond Oct 4, 1893. P O Washington,
Ont. Farmer, U. Br. in Christ. C: (**IX**) Hilda
M. Dickie Richmond, b Mar 2, 1897.

VIII. Edwin Hallman, b Aug 10, 1876. P O
Washington. Ont. Farmer. S.

VIII. Lauretta Hallman, b Sept 7, 1881. U. Br.
in Christ.

VIII. Minota Hallman, b Feb 27, 1888.

VII. Livia Bowman, b in Woolwick twp. Water-
loo Co. Ont. Mar 21, 1853, m Dr. David H.
Waugh, July 27, 1875. Res. 6 East Ave. Roches-
ter, N. Y. Surgeon and Dentist, Presby. C: (**VIII**)
Dr. Ira Luman Waugh, b Mar 6, 1877, m Etta
Callia Byers Nov 26, 1902.

VIII. Lorne Emmerson W. Waugh, b Jan 7, 1879,
d Feb 1, 1881.

VIII. Samuel Austin Waugh, b Feb 27, 1881.

VIII. Lola Emmerilla Waugh, b Sept 1, 1883.

VII. Joshua Bowman, b Mar 21, 1855, d Dec
6, 1862.

VI. Nancy Stauffer, b Jan 15, 1834, m Jonas B.
Snyder July 16, 1850. He was b May 26, 1827.
Farmer. C: Joseph, Susanna, Levi, Angeline,
Alice.

VII. Joseph S. Snyder, b Mar 25, 1851, m Lucinda
Snyder Apr 14, 1874. P O Bloomingdale, Ont.
Farmer. C: Ervine, Herbert, Lillia, Alfred, Elmi-
na, Irene, Lucy, Ion Joseph, Elenor.

VII. Susanna S. Snyder, b Aug 13, 1852, m William Snyder June 18, 1884. He was b Aug 22,
1849. P O Bloomingdale, Ont. Farmer. C: Alton, Alva, Ivan, Ina. Farmer.

VII. Levi S. Snyder, b June 17, 1855, m Hannah
B. Clemens Feb 26, 1880. P O Bridgeport, Ont.

Levi C. Rosenberger.

Dr. E. H. Monk.

VII. Angeline Snyder, b Apr 5, 1860, m Amos Horst Feb 23. 1887. Farmer. No issue.

VII. Alice Amanda Snyder, b Oct 29, 1869, m Solomon Koch. P O Conestoga, Ont. Farmer. No issue.

VI. Levi Stauffer, b Sept 19, 1839, m Esther, daughter of John and Judith (Bingeman) Snider, Nov 27, 1859. P O Waterloo, Ont. Farmer, and owns two fine farms, one the homestead of his father. He has been manager of the North Waterloo Farmers Mutual Fire Insurance Company for upwards of fifteen years, and is one of the prominent members of the United Brethren church. C: Matilda, Lydia, Josiah, Clementina, Alfarata, Annetta, Mary, Alfiemenia, Jessie, Lorne.

VII. Matilda Joanna Stauffer, b Sept 3. 1861, m Alexander Wilson. P O Ellington, Mich. Farmer. C: Herbert, William, Clayton, Arthur, Clara.

VII. Lydia Ann Stauffer, b Dec 14, 1862, m Ezra S. Shantz. He d May 10, 1895. P O Haysville, Ont. Farmer. C: (**VIII**) Winnie, Susanna, Lorne, (d); Burton.

VII. Josiah Stauffer, b Sept 18, 1864, m Bella Wilson. Farmer. C: (**VIII**) Harley, Clarence, Mary.

VII. Clementina Stauffer, b Feb 10, 1866, m Ephraim Groff. Resides in Iowa. C: (**VIII**) Gertrude, Violet, Ephraim, Clarence, (d).

VII. Alfrata Stauffer, b Jan 30, 1868, m James Mitchell. Farmer. No issue.

VII. Annetta Rebecca Stauffer, b Aug 28. 1870, m Charles Moore. P O Unionville, Mich. Veterinary Surgeon. C: (**VIII**) Lorne Moore.

VII. Mary Jane Stauffer, b Sept 2, 1872.

VII. Alfiemenia Stauffer, b July 14, 1874

VII. Jessie Ann Judith Stauffer, b June 26, 1876.

VII. Lorne Levi Stauffer, b Mar 8, 1880.

V. Jacob Rosenberger, b in Bucks Co. Pa. Oct. 19, 1802, d at Corinth, Mich. Nov 12, 1881, m Hannah Panabecker. She was b in Penn. Apr 15, 1810, d at Blenheim, Waterloo Co. Ont. in 1848.

Farmer, Menn. C: John, Benjamin, David, Cornelius, Abraham, Nancy, Elizabeth, Jacob, Amos, Moses.

VI. John Rosenberger, m Lydia Colborn. C: Mary, Cornelius, John. John m second wife—Turner. P O Grand Rapids, Mich. C: Eva, Ida.

VII. Mary Ann Rosenberger, b—, d—, m Andrew White.

VII. Cornelius Rosenberger, b-,died in the army at Louisville, Ky.

VII. John Rosenberger, d young.

VII. Eva Rosenberger, m Arthur Seymour. P O Seattle, Washington. C: (**VIII**) Maud Seymour.

VII. Ida Rosenberger.

VII. Benjamin Rosenberger, b Feb 5, 1827, d Jan 3, 1896, m Mary Ann Shugart in 1848. P O Lisbon, Mich. Farmer, Disciple Ch. C: David, Elizabeth, Hannah, Henry, George, Mary, Emma.

VII. David Rosenberger, b--, m Rose Robine. P O Berlin, Mich. C: (**VIII**) Jennie, Myrtie, Lylie, Florence.

VII. Elizabeth Rosenberger, b in Kent Co. Mich. Jan 30, 1851, m Benton Thurston June 12, 1871. P O Lisbon, Mich. Farmer. C: (**VIII**) Viola Thurston, b Aug 14, 1873. Vinnie Thurston, b Aug 11, 1875. Earl Thurston, b Aug 17, 1877. Hazel Thurston, b May 30, 1882.

VII. Hannah Rosenberger, b in Kent Co. Mich. Mar 1853, d Feb 10, 1893, m Philip Burman in 1872. C: Mamie, Birnie, Jessie.

VII. Mamie Burman, b Nov 6, 1873, m Charles Whittier June 1894. Disciple Ch. C: (**IX**) Myrl Whittier. Lyle Whittier.

VIII. Birnie Burman, b June 11, 1877.

VIII. Jessie B. Burman, b Jan 31, 1881, d Nov 10, 1886.

VII. Henry Rosenberger, m Katie Miller. P O Lisbon, Mich. C: (**VIII**) Etta, Violet.

VII. George R. Rosenburg, b at Lisbon, Mich., m Mary E. Gates. P O Newaygo, Mich. Real Estate and Loan Agent. C: (**VIII**) Getty Rosenburg.

VII. Emma Rosenburg, b in Ottawa Co. Mich. Apr

4, 1869, m W. E. Matthews, M. D. Dec 27, 1893.
Res. 251 N. Lafayette St. Grand Rapids, Mich. Physician. C: (**VIII**) Gladys Evelyn Matthews, b Mar 1,
1900.

VII. Mary Rosenberger, b—, m Isaac Mrdeland. C:
(**VIII**) Lloyd, Clyde, Marvin, Vera.

VI. David Rosenberger, b in Canada Jan 1, 1830, d
in Texas Dec 10, 1892, m Mary Pine Mar 10, 1849.
She was b in Ont. Apr 6, 1831.   They lived some
time in Michigan, where he amased a fortune. He then
engaged in manufacturing of furniture, but lost all his
wealth by fire.   In 1873 he went to Kansas and engaged in farming. In 8876 he removed to Wise Co.
Texas; engaged in farming, and later built a mill at
Decater, costing $25000, which, eight years later,
was burned down   Notwithstanding these losses the
family are now in good shape financialy.   Spiritualists C: John, Frank, Alice, Gilbert, Walter, Oselia,
Charles, Mary.

VII. John H. Rosenburg, b 1850, d 1851.

VII. Francis Rosenburg, b at Grand Rapids,
Mich. Jan 19. 1852, m Emeline Meyers Jan 1878.
She d Nov 23, 1899. P O Decatur, Texas.
Farmer, Spiritualist. C: (**VIII**) Lee C. Rosenburg,
b July 4, 1879, m Manda Rawls. David A. Ros-
enburg, b Dec 1881. Willie W. Rosenburg, b Oct
6, 1883. Amos N. Rosenburg, d infant. Libbie
Rosenburg, b Dec 1886. May Rosenburg. Bert
Rosenburg. Rosa Rosenburg. Maggie Rosenburg.

VII. Alice Rosenburg, b in Kent Co: Mich. Oct 5,
1853, m Louis E. Pillars in Wise Co. Texas in 1880.
P O Alvord, Texas. Christian Science. No issue.

VII. Gilbert Rosenburg, b 1855, d infant 7 Mo.

VII. Walter Rosenburg, b in Kent Co. Mich. Mar 5,
1859, m Kate Meyers, Nov 21, 1880. P O Decatur,
Texas. Druggist, Spiritulist. C: (**VIII**) John W.
Rosenburg, b Aug 26, 1881. Thomas J. Rosenburg,
b Mar 23, 1884.   Roy H. Rosenburg, b Sept 21,
1887.

VII. Oselia Rosenburg, b in Kent Co. Mich. Apr
4, 1861, m Chas. F. Sharp Jan 19, 1882. P O
Sunset, Texas. Farmer, Meth. Ep.   C: (**VIII**)

Harry Edwin Sharp, b Nov 30, 1882, d Dec 16,
1882.   Cassie Evelyn Sharp, b Apr 5, 1884.
Meth. Ep. Charles Glen Sharp, b Aug 10, 1889, d
July 16, 1893. Edna Sharp, b Jan 17, 1895, d 1895.
VII. Charles LeRoy Rosenburg, b Mar 4, 1872, m
Eliza Wheelis in 1891. P O Decatur, Tex.   Far-
mer, Spiritualist. C: (**VIII**) Rubie Rosenburg, b
Nov 5, 1891.   Fred Leroy Rosenburg, b Sept 15,
1893.   David William Rosenburg, b June 27, 1896.
Clara Rosenburg, b June 1899.

VII. Mary Elizabeth Rosenburg, b at Council Grove,
Kans. May 31, 1875, m J. F. Booth Feb 24, 1893.
P O Decatur, Tex.   Farmer.   C: (**VIII**) Mary Ka-
tharine Booth, b Oct 6, 1894.

VII. Mary E. Rosenburg, b in Kansas May 31, 1874,
m James Booth Feb 1893.   Farmer in Texas.   C:
(**VIII**) Katie Booth.

VI. Cornelius Rosenberger, b in Canada Dec 12,
1831, d in Mich. 1888, m Susanna Colborn in 1854.
She d June 14, 1891.   Farmer, Meth. Ep. C: Mary,
Benjamin, Lydia, Moses, Anson, Ernest.

VII. Mary A. Rosenberg, b Oct 31, 1854, d Jan 24,
1879, m A. D. Williams in 1872.   Farmer, Meth.
Ep.   C: (**VIII**) Olive M. Williams, b Apr 12, 1875,
m Fred E. Mead.   Inez R. Williams, b and d in
1872.

VII. Benjamin Franklin Rosenberg, b at Gates, Mich.
Jan 26, 1858, m Ada Jane Johnson July 28, 1881.
P O Middleville, Mich.   Farmer.   C: (**VIII**) Ber-
tha Bell Rosenberg, b Oct 2, 1882.   S.

VII. Lydia Rosenberg, b Apr 7, 1860, m Charles
J. Dutcher Oct 18, 1882.   P O LaBarge, Mich.
Farmer, Meth. Ep.   C: (**VIII**) Guy T. Dutcher, b
Oct 11, 1883.   Maynard R. Dutcher, b Nov 27,
1895.

VII. Moses Rosenberg, b Apr 26, 1892, m Mary
Forbes July 20, 1887.   P O   Middleville, Mich.
Lumber Business.   C: (**VIII**) Claude C. Rosenberg,
b June 1, 1892.

VII. Anson C. Rosenberger, b in Gaines, Kent
Co. Mich. Oct 8, 1866, m Ada M. Bechtel at
Grand Rapids, Mich. Oct 17, 1888.   P O Brock,

Ind. Engaged in the Lumber Trade. C: (**VIII**) Eva Allene Rosenberger, b Apr 15, 1891. Glen Rosenberger, b July 21, 1892.

VII. Ernest Rosenberger, b Aug 26, 1879. S.

VI. Abraham Rosenberg, b near Berlin, Ont. Aug 11, 1834. m Nancy Hamacher Dec 18, 1859. P O Reed City, Mich. Lumbering, Spiritualist. C: Emma, Adeline, Rose, William, Carrie, Mina, Judson, Hudson.

VII Emma Rosenberg, b Sept 12, 1860, m Stanley Rayner Feb 16, 1896. P O Tomahawk, Wis. Miller, Spiritualists. No issue, 1898.

VII. Adeline Rosenberg, b Feb 1, 1861, d Oct 3, 1869.

VII. Rose Rosenberg, b Sept 27, 1863. m George M. Hardes Dec 23, 1882. P O Traverse City, Mich. Lumbering, Spiritualist. C: (**VIII**) Vernice Hardes, b Nov 17, 1883. Victor L. Hardes, b July 16, 1896

VII. William H. Rosenberg, b July 22, 1865. P O Reed City, Mich. Farmer. Spiritualist. S.

VII. Carrie Rosenberg, b May 1, 1868, m Henry B. Allen Jan 3, 1898. P O Reed City, Mich. He is a traveling Spiritualist Medium, formerly of Summerland. C: No issue, 1898.

VII. Mina Rosenberg, b Apr 1, 1870, in Reed City, Mich. Artist, Spiritualist. S.

VII. Judson H. Rosenberg, b Sept 7, 1872. P O Torch Lake, Mich. Miller, Spiritualist. S.

VII. Hudson T. Rosenberg, b June 14, 1874. P O Clyde, Mich. Telegraph Operator, Spiritualist. S.

VI. Nancy Rosenberger, b in Waterloo Co. Ont. Canada. Dec 10, 1836, m Levi S. Kinsey Jan 15, 1854. P O Caledonia, Kent Co. Mich. Farmer. C: Florence, Clara, Ella, Virginia, Amos.

VII. Florence Sylvia Kinsey, b in Kent Co. Mich. Feb 14, 1855, d Mar 29, 1879. Teacher.

VII. Clara Climena Kinsey, b in Kent Co. Mich. July 16, 1857, d Apr 19, 1881. Teacher.

VII. Ella Rosalia Kinsey, b in Kent Co. Mich. Jan 13, 1860. P O Caledonia, Mich.

VII. Virginia Kinsey, b in Kent Co. Mich. Jan 22, 1862, d Dec 4, 1885.

VII. Amos Kinsey, b Jan 25, 1870, d Feb 28, 1872.
VI. Elizabeth Rosenberger, b in Waterloo Co. Ont. Canada, Apr 10, 1839, d Mar 8, 1893, m Abraham Hoover Mar 10, 1869. Farmer. C: Jermina.
VII. Jermina Hoover, b in Kent Co. Mich. Aug 27, 1873, m William Dochowon Jan 22, 1892. P O Caledonia, Kent Co. Mich. Farmer. C: (**VIII**) Homer R. Dochowon, b Dec 4, 1894. Caroline E. Dochowon, b Oct 14, 1898. Dovess S. Dochowon, b Apr 9, 1901.

VI. Jacob P. Rosenberger, b at Dunfreis, Waterloo Co Ont. June 21, 1841, m Mary Rice Apr 1865. She d Mar 1872. He m second wife Salome Clemens, Oct 14, 1886. P O Caledonia. Kent Co. Mich. Lumber-dealer. Children by first wife: (**VII**) Florence Rosenberger, b June 8, 1867, d Mar 19, 1872. Ina Rosenberger, b Dec 25, 1870, d May 1874.

VI. Amos Rosenberger, b in Waterloo Co. Ont. Oct 4, 1844, d—, m Martha E. Millard Nov 11, 1864, in Ottawa, Mich. P O Reed City, Mich. Manufacturer, Whole-sale and Retail dealer in Lumber. C: William, Millard, Adela, Bert.

VII. William M. Rosenberger, b Sept 6, 1865, d May 11, 1883.
VII. Millard M. Rosenberger, b Mar 19, 1868, m Flora C. Goodale Oct 4, 1893. P O Reed City, Mich. Manufacturer and dealer in Lumber. C: (**VIII**) Eugene A. Rosenberger, b May 31, 1895. Ralph M. b June 30, 1901.
VII. Adela Rosenberger, (d).
VII. Bert A. Rosenberger, (d).

VI. Moses Resenburg, b in Canada, 1846, m Alice Williams 1869. P O Corinth, Mich. Farmer. C: (**VII**) Myrtle Rosenburg, m Owen S. Kinsey.

V. Elizabeth Resenberger, b Apr 7, 1806, d of cholera Aug 2, 1834, m John Bricker. He was b Feb 15, 1805, d May 20, 1871. Farmer near Roseville, Ont. C: Benjamin, Abraham, Christian, Nancy, Polly.

VI. Benjamin Bricker, b Dec 19, 1825, m Esther, daughter of George B. and Mary (Shoemaker)

Bechtel. She was b Mar 4, 1826. P O Roseville,
Ont. Farmer, and resides on the "Old Ben." Rosenberger Farm." C: Elizabeth, Susanna, Abraham, Maria, Anna, Amos, Elijah, Hannah, Benjamin, Noah, Menno, George, John.

VII. Elizabeth Bricker, b Apr 7, 1847, m Daniel
D.| Snyder.

VII. Susanna Bricker, b in Waterloo Co. Ont. Oct
29, 1848, m Abraham H. Bricker, Oct 5, 1869.
P O Yale, Mich. Farmer, Menn. Br. in Christ. C:
Alvin, Josiah, Rosanna, Edwin, Oscar, Hattie,
Orpah.

VIII. Alvin Bricker, b Aug 20, 1870, m Serena E.
Graybiel Feb 9, 1896. P O Brown City, Mich.
Farmer. C: (**IX**) Glenford Allen Bricker.

VIII. Josiah Bricker, b Apr 25, 1872, d Dec 25,
1880.

VIII. Rosanna Bricker, b Jan 30, 1874, m Rev. Ed-
ward F. Gill Mar 30, 1896. P O Clarksville, Mich.
Minister, Menn. Br. in Christ. C: (**IX**) Clayton S.
Gill.

VIII. Edwin Bricker, b Feb 20, 1876. m Effie May
Graybiel Dec 12, 1900. P O Yale, Mich. Farmer; Mrs. B. Menn. Br. in Christ.

VIII. Oscar Bricker, b Sept 26, 1880. S.

VIII. Hattie Bricker, b Mar 31, 1888. Menn. Br. in
Christ.

VIII. Orpah Bricker, b Aug 10, 1891, d Dec 14,
1895.

VII. Abraham Bricker, b Aug 28, 1850, d Apr 2,
1853.

VII. Maria Bricker, b Apr 15, 1852, m Henry
Graaf. P O Roseville, Ont. Farmer. C: (**VIII**)
Benjamin Bricker.

VII. Anna Bricker, b Feb 6, 1854, m Joseph Detweiler. P O Wolverton, Ont. Miller. C: (**VIII**)
Astor, ——, Joanna, Herbert, Bertha.

VII. Amos Bricker, b Sept 8, 1855, m Lydia Rosen-
berger Nov 27, 1883. P O Berlin, Ont. Implement
Agent. C: (**VIII**) Nettie Bricker, b Oct 2, 1884.
Wilton Bricker, b Aug 1885. Howard Bricker, b
Aug 15, 1886. Horace Bricker, (twin), b Aug 15,

1886, d Apr 10, 1900. Addie Bricker, b Nov 16, 1888.

VII. Elijah Bricker, b Jan 22, 1858, m Louisa Burkholder Oct 27, 1878. P O Yale, Mich. Farmer. C: (**VIII**) Ira Bricker, b June 19, 1881. Ora Bricker, b Feb 16, 1888, d 1888. Roy. Bricker, b Aug 16, 1887.

VII. Hannah Bricker, b Jan 6, 1860, m Ephraim B. Cassel Apr 5, 1881. P O New Hamburg, Ont. Farmer. Menn. C: (**VIII**) Allan B. Cassel, b May 7, 1889.

VII. Benjamin Bricker, b Nov 8, 1861, d Nov 25, 1861.

VII. Noah Bricker, b Oct 8, 1862, m Susanna Bock. P O Roseville, Ont.

VII. Menno Bricker, b Oct 17, 1864, m Regina Stepps. P O Roseville, Ont.

VII. George Bricker, b at Roseville, Ont. Sept 24, 1866, m Mary Ann Good Mar 13, 1889. P O Yale, Mich. Farmer. C: (**VIII**) Eden Bricker, b Jan 7, 1892. Ruth Bricker, b Mar 1, 1895.

VII. John Bricker, b May 17, 1869, m Christina Barton Mar 9, 1892. P O Roseville, Ont. Farmer U. B. Ch. C: (**VIII**) John Sanford Bricker, b June 3, 1896, d Feb 27, 1897. Phyllis Grace Bricker, b May 23, 1898. Mildred Esther Bricker, b Aug 19, 1891.

VI. Abraham Bricker, b—, d--, aged about 16 years.

VI. Christian Bricker, b—, d in infancy.

VI. Polly Bricker, b—, d in infancy.

V. Benjamin Rosenberger, b June 20, 1806, d Oct 18, 1880, m Sallie Strome, (d.) C: Christian, Lydia, Maria. Benjamin m second wife, Mary Woods. Farmer. C: Louisa, Menno.

VI. Christian Rosenberger. P O Freeport, Mich.

VI. Lydia Rosenberger, m Jacob Stauffer. P O Berlin, Ont.

VI. Maria Rosenberger.

VI. Louisa Rosenberger. m—.

VI. Menno Rosenberger, m—. C: Son.

VII. Benjamin Rosenberger. P O Middleville, Mich.

V. Abraham D. Rosenberger, b in Montg. Co. Pa,
Apr 2, 1808, d in Huron Co. Ont. Dec 11, 1893,
m Rebecca Eby Oct 4, 1834. She was b Apr 4, 1814,
d at Carlisle, Middlesex Co. Ont. Aug 29, 1879.
Farmer and Shoemaker, Methodist. C: William,
Simeon, Jeremiah, Isabella, Margaret, Catharine,
Abraham, Rebecca, Francis.

VI. William Rosenberger, b in Hulton Co. Ont.
Oct 14, 1836, m Elizabeth Dixon Sept 11, 1861.
She died Jan 1865. No issue. William m second
wife, Lucy Ann Miller, Mar 26, 1866. She died
Jan 16, 1881. C: Arthur, Dora. William m third
wife, Rachel Ann Groves, Sept 12, 1881. C: Mary.
P O Nappanee, Ind. Farmer, United Br. in
Christ.

VII. Arthur Rosenberger, b in Elkhart Co. Ind.
Jan 1, 1868, m Alice Read June 21, 1896. P O
Nappanee, Ind. Carpenter by trade. C: (**VIII**)
Howard William Rosenberger, b June 21, 1898.

VII. Zorah Rosenberger, b in Elkhart Co. Ind. Mar
21, 1875, m Harry L. Unger Apr 11, 1903. P O
Nappanee, Ind. Christ Scientist.

VII. Mary Berneice Rosenberger, b in Elkhart Co.
Ind. July 12, 1886. U. Br. Ch.

VI. Simeon Rosenberger, b at Beverly, Ont. Apr
22, 1839, m Anna Carter Jan 26, 1863. P O St.
Thomas, Ont. Car-builder, Methodist. C: Mary.

VII. Mary E. R. J. Rosenberger, b Oct 20, 1864,
m Thomas Dearden Sept 16, 1889. P O St. Thomas,
Ont. Conductor on M. C. R. Rail-road, Methodist,
No issue, (1897).

VI. Jeremiah Rosenberger, b in Elgin Co. Ont.
Apr 12, 1842, m Jane Darrach Apr 20, 1868. P
O Dayton, Ind. Miller, Methodist. C: (**VII**) Mar-
garet Alice Rosenberger, b Mar 29, 1869. Bertha
Jane Rosenberger, b May 25, 1871, d July 29, 1872.

VII. Edith Emily Rosenberger, b Feb 28, 1874, m
Charles E. Summers, of Chicago, Ill. June 8, 1897.

VII. John William Rosenberger, b July 31, 1876.
VII. Charles Rosenberger, b June 24, 1879, d July 7,
1879.

VI. Isabelle Rosenberger, b in Bayham twp. Ont.

Oct 9, 1843, m James Walker Feb 8, 1872. P O
Devon, Ont. Farmer. Meth. C: Robert, Abram,
Mary, Joseph, Pearl.

VII. Robert Eby Walker, b Feb 19, 1873, m Annie
Gertrude Crompton. P O Crediton, Ont. Butcher.

VII. Abram Ingram Walker, b May 21, 1876.

VII. Mary Rebecca Blanche Walker, b Oct 9, 1878.

VII. Joseph Henry Osmond Walker, b Nov 7, 1880.

VII. Pearl Gladius Belle Walker, b Jan 2, 1885.

VI. Margaret Rosenberger, b Jan 2, 1846, d 1846.

VI. Catharine A. Rosenberger, b Oct 16, 1848, in
Elgin Co. Ont. m Joseph Hutchinson Dec 16, 1883.
P O Falkirk, Ont. Farmer, Methodists. C: (**VII**)
Wilfred J. Hutchinson, b Mar 14, 1885, d Aug 27, 1886.
Cyrus Hutchinson, b Sept 21, 1887, d Mar 7, 1888.
Annie Belle Hutchinson, b Mar 18, 1889. Wesley
Homer Hutchinson, b Mar 7, 1891, died same day.

VI. Abraham E. Rosenberger, b in Middlesex Co.
Ont. Canada, Dec 25, 1852, m Annie Mc Alpine
Mar 18, 1878. She d Aug 11, 1883. C: Ethel,
Annie. Abraham m second wife, Mary Neil, July
18, 1885. Res. 136 Carling St. London, Ont.
Baker Confectioner, Member of Salvation Army.
C: Jennie, Edwin, Frederick, James.

VII. Ethel Ray Rosenberger, b Mar 17, 1880.

VII. Annie Elizabeth Rosenberger, b Aug 7, 1883,
d Aug 15, 1883.

VII. Jennie Louisa Rosenberger, b Apr 18, 1886, d
Aug 17, 1886.

VII. Edwin Neil Rosenberger, b Apr 12, 1888, d
Nov 25, 1888.

VII. Frederick Osmond Rosenberger, b Aug 20,
1889, d Oct 18, 1889.

VII. James Lloyd Rosenberger, b Mar 2, 1894.

VI. Rebecca Ann Rosenberger, b in McGillwary,
Ont. Feb 20, 1856, m George Humble Dec 12,
1876. P O Falkirk, Ont. Methodist. C: (**VII**)
John Alvin Humble, b Feb 18, 1878. Percy Melvin
Humble, b Feb 19, 1879. Ethel Rosella Humble,
b Apr 24, 1880. Edith Bell Humble, b Apr 18,
1882, d Sept 15, 1882.

VII. Whitfield Franklin Humble, b June 7, 1884.

VII. Howard Sherwood Humble, b Mar 16, 1890.

VII. Estella Isabelle Humble, b June 13, 1893.

VI. Francis Rosenberger, b in McGilvery twp. Ont. Canada, Dec 17, 1859, m Minnie Drader Apr 25, 1888. P O Copleston, Ont. Engineering, now a butcher|by·trade; Methodist. C: (**VII**) Arilla Edith Rosenberger, b July 18, 1889. Otta Bell Rosenberger, b Sept 27, 1891.

V. Henry Rosenberger, b about 1811, d of cholera in 1834, aged about 23 years.

V. Nancy Rosenberger, b May 7, 1812, m John Strome Mar 31, 1831. He was b in Lancaster Co. Pa. February 12, 1810, d near Fishers Mills, Ont. on the "Strome Homestead." Aug 19, 1865. C: Henry, Abram, David, Polly, John, Aaron, Elizabeth, Moses, Nancy, Amos, Isaiah, Elijah.

VI. Henry Strome b Nov 1, 1831, m Elizabeth Martin Aug 22, 1852. She was b Aug 2, 1834. P O Berlin, Ont. Builder and contractor. C: Hiram, Clara, Lucinda, Franklin, Almeda, John, Eliza, Amelia Abram, Mary, William.

VII. Hiram Strome, b Apr 27, 1853, d May 29, 1853.

VII. Clara Malissa Strome. b Apr 10, 1854, m Frederick Miller. Farmer. C: (**VIII**) Jeremiah, Frederick, Eliza.

VII. Lucinda Strome, b Feb 5, 1857, m Peter Schwindt. P O Elmira, Ont. Farmer. C: (**VIII**) Andrew, Mary, Charles, (d); Melvin, (d); Dora, Lillie, (d); Percival, (d); Edith.

VII. Franklin Strome, b Apr 24, 1859, m Helena Battenburg. P O Elmira, Ont. Carpenter. C: (**VIII**) Henry, Oscar, Florence, Harvey, Eliza, Franklin.

VII. Almeda Strome, b May 19, 1861, d Nov 15, 1887, m John Miles. No issue.

VII. John Henry Strome, b Oct 16, 1863. P O Newstadt, Grey Co. Ont. Clerk. S.

VII. Eliza Ann Strome, b Dec 6, 1865. P O Berlin, Ont. Dressmaker. S.

VII. Amelia Strome, b Apr 23, 1868, m Simon Brunk Sept 13, 1893. P O Berlin, Ont. Clothing

Merchant at Berlin, afterwards Mfg. of Boots and
Shoes at Port Elgin, in partner with T. Musselman
under the firm name of "The Star Shoe Co." Mr.
Brunk taking the road as traveling salesman for the
firm, which position he still holds. Meth. C:
(**VIII**) Pearl E. Brunk, b Oct 19, 1895. Ronald H.
Brunk, b Apr 15, 1897.

VII. Abram Lincoln Strome, b Apr 24, 1870.

VII. Mary Jane Strome, b Sept 23, 1872.

VII. William M. Strome, b May 20, 1874.

VI. Abram R. Strome, b Mar 21, 1833, m Esther
Martin May 15, 1855. She was b May 29, 1831.
P O Berlin, Ont. Contractor and builder. C:
Jeremiah, Menno, Almeda, Mary, Merritt, Christian.

VII. Jeremiah Strome, b Feb 27, 1856, d May
22, 1894, m Elizabeth Peppler. P O Berlin, Ont.
C: (**VIII**) Annie, Priscilla, Esther, Eva, George,
Clarence.

VII. Menno Strome, b Aug 3, 1857, m Anna Pep-
ler. P O Berlin, Ont. Agent for sewing machines, organs, etc. C: (**VIII**) Lewis, Charles, Arthur, Ella, Irene, Gertrude, Viola, Mabel, Menno.

VII. Almeda Strome, b June 10, 1859, d May
25, 1860,

VII. Mary Ann Strome, b Jan 13, 1861, d
same day.

VII. Merritt Strome, b Apr 8, 1862, d Apr
20, 1862.

VII. Christian Strome, b Dec 3, 1864, d next
day.

VI. David R. Strome, b in Canada, Oct 3, 1834,
m Martha S. Schader Jan 15, 1856. P O Elmira,
Ont. In early life he worked at the Carpenter
trade about Waterloo and later at Elmira. In
1870 he engaged in farming in Wellington Co.
until 1895 when he retired. Ev. Ass'n. C:
Melinda, Norman, Josiah, Annie, Alexander,
Noah, Urias, Simon, Amanda.

VII. Malinda Strome, b Apr 29, 1857, m John C.
Amy Feb 5, 1878. He was b May 6, 1855, d
Nov 27, 1893. P O Elmira, Ont. Farmer, Meth.
C: (**VIII**) Oliver Alvin Amy, b Jan 19, 1879.

Bertha Venetta Amy, b Sept 7, 1882.

VII. Norman S. Strome, b in Waterloo Co. Ont. Oct 31, 1858, m Isabella Anderson Jan 5, 1881. P O Floradale, Ont. Foreman in Planeing Mill. C: (**VIII**) James Ervin Strome, b Sept 12, 1883, d Sept 28, 1883. Emma Ethel Strome, b July 23, 1884, d Apr 26, 1886. Mortford Stanley Strome, b Apr 13, 1887. Edna Pearl Strome, b Mar 24, 1890. Lula Vira Strome, b Oct 2, 1895, d Jan 5, 1896.

VII. Josiah Strome, b Sept 4, 1860, d Oct 23, 1872.

VII. Annie Strome, b July 26, 1865, m Eber Stickney Nov 24, 1887. P O Creek-bank, Ont. Farmer, Methodists. C: (**VIII**) Annie May Stickney, b Nov 2, 1889. David Thomas Emerson Stickney, b Apr 7, 1895.

VII. Alexander Strome, b July 1, 1869, m Harriet Ann Stickney Feb 21, 1894. P O Floradale, Ont. Farmer, Methodists. C: (**VIII**) Etta Winifred Strome, b June 7, 1895. Ada Priscilla Strome, b Nov 24, 1897.

VII. Noah Strome, b Apr 16, 1871, m Phoebe Stickney Nov 13, 1895. P O Pentland, Ont. Farmer. Meth. No issue.

VII. Urias Strome, b Mar 29, 1874. P O Elmira, Ont. Teacher, Meth. S.

VII. Simon Strome, b Oct 13, 1876. P O Elmira, Ont. Tailor, Meth. S.

VII. Amanda Strome, b Nov 10, 1878, d Apr 19, 1880.

VI. Polly Strome, b—, d—, m John Stauffer. Lived in Oxford Co. Ont. where she died. The family has since removed to Mich. C: (**VII**) Priscilla, Flora, Jared, Martha, Anna, William, and one died infant.

VI. John Strome, b—, d aged about 16 years.

VI. Aaron R. Strome, b in Oxford Co. Ont. May 2, 1842, m Catharine Sand Jan 1, 1868. P O Floradale, Ont. Carpenter, Evangelical Ch. C: Milton, Levina, Sarah, Astor, Ezra, Aaron. Melvin, Thirly, Orrin, Annie.

VII. Milton Strome, b Sept 28, 1868, m Mary Wild-

fong. P O Berlin, Ont.   Milk-deliverer. C: **(VIII)**
John, Alvin, Reginald, Olive.
VII. Levina Strome, b Jan 31, 1871, m David Robert-
son.   P O Elmira, Ont.   Farmer, Evangelical.   C:
(**VIII**) Ella May Robertson.
VII. Sarah Etta Strome, b Dec 31, 1872, d Sept 21,
1878.
VII. Astor Strome, b Nov 3, 1875.
VII. Ezra Strome, b May 22, 1879.
VII. Aaron Erwin Strome, b Jan 16, 1882.
VII. Melvin Strome, b May 22, 1885.
VII. Thirly Menerva Strome, b June 6, 1888.
VII. Orrin Roy Strome, b Apr 29, 1890.
VII. Annie May Strome, b Apr 5, 1892.
VI. Elizabeth Strome, b—, d—, m Andrew Miltz,
(d).   C: (**VII**) Anna, John, William, (d).
VI. Moses Strome, b—, m Sarah Congo, (d).
Moses m second wife, Emma Stone. P O Linwood,
Ont.
VI. Nancy Strome, b in Oxford Co. Ont. Oct 2,
1847, m George Diebel Sept 9, 1874. P O Waterloo,
Ont.   Merchant and Mayor of Waterloo, Ont. Mrs.
D. Meth. C: Sylvia, Emma.
VII. Sylvia Florence Diebel, b Dec 27, 1875.   P O
Waterloo, Ont. Meth. S.
VII. Emma May Diebel, b Apr 4, 1878. P O Water-
loo, Ont. Meth. S.
VI. Amos Strome, b--, m Mary Freyvogee.   P O
Lakefield, Manitoba.   Merchant.
VI. Isaiah R. Strome, b in Blenheim twp. Oxford
Co. Ont. Canada, Oct 7, 1851, m Mary I. Peffers
Aug 16, 1882. P O Brandon, Man. Canada.   Dry
Goods Merchant, Presby. C: (**VII**) Jesse D. St-
rome, b Feb 23, 1884.   Bertha M. Strome, b Dec
14, 1886.   Ivan Roy Strome, b July 6, 1889.
Charles M. Strome, b Sept 12, 1891.   Velma Ruth
Strome, b June 22, 1897.
VI. Elijah Strome, m Agnes Vinson. P O Minto,
N. Dak.   Merchant. C: (**VII**) Rhoda Strome.
V. Joseph Rosenberger, b 1818, d 1834.
V. Christian D. Rosenberger, b in Bucks Co. Pa.
Feb 25, 1817, m Elizabeth Schlichter, (d).   C:

Mary, Elizabeth, Nancy, Hannah, Susannah,
John, Magdalena, Samuel, Lydia, Priscilla, Rosetta,
Margaret.   Christian m second wife, widow Hannah
Detweiler, (sister to his first wife).   P O Berlin,
Ont.   Retired farmer.

VI. Mary Rosenberger, b July 9, 1839, d 1860, m
John R. Hillgartner in 1858. He was b Feb 20, 1833.
Farmer and carpenter, U. Br. Ch. C: Hannah, Ed-
mund.

VII. Hannah Hillgartner, b in 1859, d in 1871.

VII. Edmund G. Hillgartner, b in Fullerton twp.
Waterloo Co. Ont. Aug 11, 1860, m Jennie Zeigh
Forsythe May 19, 1886.   P O Brantford, Ont.
Cong. C: (**VIII**) Eva Hillgartner, b Mar 13, 1887,
d Nov 11, 1887.

VI. Elizabeth Rosenberger, b Jan 29, 1841, d 1880,
m Jacob Lautenschlager. C: Malinda, Isaac, Lydia,
Rosetta, Albert, Annetta.

VII. Malinda Lautenschlager, b—.

VII. Issac Lautenschlager, b—, m Mary Ann Sch-
weitzer. C: (**VIII**) Stanton, Roy.

VI. Nany Rosenberger, b in Oxford Co. Ont. Feb 1,
1843, m Louis Adolph Dec 6, 1871. P O Wallace,
Ont. Farmer, Meth. C: (**VII**) Samuel Louis Adolph, b Jan 1, 1873. P O Listowel, Ont.   Hardware
Merchant, Meth. S. Johnny Adolph, b July 31,
1875, d same day. Austin Sinclair Adolph, July 21,
1877. Minnie Rosetta Adolph, b July 22, 1880, died
next day. Milton Asa Adolph, b Oct 4, 1882. Ella
Adolph, b Nov 3, 1883, d Jan 8, 1884.

VI. Hannah Rosenberger, b Feb 17, 1845, m John
Bricker. P O Fargo, Mich. Farmer. C: (**VII**)
Chester, Eusebius, Leander, Addison, Arthur, Mag-
gie, Hannah, Minerva.

VI. Susanna Rosenberger, b in Wilmot twp. Waterloo Co. Ont. May 20, 1847, m George W. Bell Jan 8,
1867. P O Yale, Mich. Farmer and auctioneer;
attends Meth. Ch. C: Annetta. Urias.

VII. Annetta Bell, b July 23, 1868, m R. G. Mc-
Laughlin July 15, 1890. P O Yale, Mich. Traveling salesman for Welt & Reidelsheimer Paper house,
of Detroit, Mich.   Mrs. McLaughlin when quite

young studied music and painting; is a good music-
ian and a fine artist; Presby. C: (**VIII**) Vera Bell
McLaughlin, b Mar 27, 1892. Danna Dee Mc-
Laughlin, b Nov 11. 1894.

VII. Urias George Bell, b Aug 13, 1870, d Jan
1, 1882.

VI. John Rosenberger, b July 17, 1849, d Oct
1849.

VI. Magdalena Rosenberger, b Aug 13, 1850, d
Aug 1, 1878, m John W. Groh. C: Lavina, Mary.

VII. Lavina Lauretta Groh, b in Waterloo Co. Canada, Oct 21, 1874, m George F. Dunckel Jan 3,
1893. P O Williamston, Mich. Farmer. C: (**VIII**)
Leroy Dale Dunckel, b Nov 27, 1893. Orville Edward Dunckel, b July 21, 1896. Claude Franklin
Dunckel, b Oct 14, 1900.

VII. Mary Elizabeth Groh, b in Waterloo Co. Ont.
July 5, 1877. P O Berlin, Ont. U. B. Ch. S.

VI. Rev. Samuel S Rosenberger, b in Wilmot,
Waterloo Co. Ont. Mar 5, 1853, m Phebe Jane Erb
Sept 21, 1875. P O Brown City, Mich. Farmer
and minister of the Free Will Baptist Church. C:
Joanna, Irvin, Maud, Isabelle, Hattie, Gordon,
Beaulah.

VII. Joanna May Rosenberger, b May 17, 1877, m
Simon Bechtel. P O Brown City, Mich. Farmer,
Menn. Br. in Christ.

VII. Irvin George Rosenberger, b Dec 9, 1878.

VII. Maud Rosenberger, b Sept 24, 1880, d same
day.

VII. Isabelle Rosenberger, b Oct 3, 1882.

VII. Hattie Rosenberger, b Oct 6, 1885.

VII. Gordon Rosenberger, b Nov 11, 1891.

VII. Beaulah Rosenberger, b Oct 18, 1895.

VI. Lydia Ann Rosenberger, b Mar 26, 1855, m
Amos Bricker Nov 27, 1883. P O Berlin, Ont.
(See Amos Bricker Family).

VI. Margaret Rosenberger, b at New Dundee, Ont.
May 10, 1857, m Rev. Isaac W. Groh Oct 12, 1880.
P O Sherkton, Ont. Minister United Brethren Ch.
C: (**VII**) Elma Groh, b Dec 10, 1881. U. Br. Ch.
Lottie Groh, b Jan 5, 1885, d Jan 1899. U. Br. Ch.

Alonzo C. Groh, b Feb 12, 1886, d Sept 25, 1886.
Claud W. Groh, b Nov 19, 1887, d Dec 2, 1887.
Clive L. Groh, b Nov 19, 1887, d Dec 6, 1887.
VI. Priscilla Rosenberger, b June 14, 1859, d May
8, 1891, m Simon Thaler. Farmer. C: (**VII**) Geo.
Horace Thaler, (d). Ella Sirene Thaler. Flossie
Irene Thaler. (d). Nettie Priscilla Thaler.
VI. Rosetta Rosenberger, b in Wilmot twp. Water-
loo Co. Ont. Jan 12, 1862, m Thomas Hummett Mar
8, 1893. P O Galt, Ont. Music-dealer, Meth. Ep.
No issue.
V. Mary Rosenberger, b—, m Benjamin Colburn,
(d). C: Nancy, John, Amos, Abram, Isaac. Mary
m second husband, Owin Dodge. P O Caledonia,
Mich.
VI. Nancy Colburn, m Isaac Stauffer.
VI. John Colburn, m Mary Frost.
VI. Amos Colburn, m Sarah Frost.
VI. Abram Colburn.
VI. Isaac Colburn.
V. Susanna Rosenberger, b Dec 14, 1821, d June
26, 1884, m Rev. Moses Erb in 1841. He was b Aug
6, 1821, d—. He was ordained to the ministry of
the Mennonite Ch. Apr 14, 1854, and faithfully serv-
ed the church until his death. C: Menno, Aaron,
Moses.
VI. Menno Erb, b Oct 16, 1842, m Lydia Bricker. P O
Berlin, Ont. Furniture dealer. C: (**VII**) Malinda, d;
Ephraim, Maggie, Archibald.
VI. Aaron Erb, b Jan 7, 1849, m Julia A. Unger. P
O Berlin, Ont. Traveling Salesman. C: (**VII**) Mil-
ton, Edna.
VI. Moses Erb, b 1856, d 1858.
IV. Anna Rosenberger, b about 1778, d 1841, m
Abraham Lapp. Menn. Deacon at Line Lexington,
Pa. Lived and died near Chalfont, Bucks Co. Pa.
Farmer. C: John, Joseph, Abraham, Jacob,
Elizabeth, Henry, Samuel.
V. John Lapp, b near White Hallville, (now Chal-
font), Bucks Co. Pa. Nov 14, 1803, d June 12,
1883, m Anna Wisler Oct 15, 1829. She was b in
Bedminster, Bucks Co. Pa. July 19, 1804, d at

Line Lexington, Pa. Mar 5, 1880. Farmer, Menn.
C: Abraham, Elizabeth, Samuel, Joseph, Anna,
John, Jonas, Maria, Henry, Catharine.

VI. Abraham Lapp, b Aug 30, 1830, d Sept 8,
1832.

VI. Elizabeth Lapp, b Nov 5, 1831, d Dec 14,
1888, m Abraham Moyer May 1856, (his second
wife). He was b Nov 14, 1820. d Nov 1879. Farmer, Menn. C: Jacob, John, Sallie, Mary, Abraham,
and two (d).

VII. Jacob L. Moyer, b Nov 15, 1858, m Susanna
Diehl Dec 23, 1884. P O Quakertown, Pa. Farmer.
Menn. C: (**VIII**) Lida Nora Moyer, b Nov 1, 1885.

VII. John L. Moyer, b Nov 5, 1862, m Annie M.
Ruth Jan 27, 1887. P O Line Lexington, Pa.
Farmer, Menn. C: (**VIII**) Harry Moyer, b Jan
17, 1890. Mabel Moyer, b Aug 10, 1893.

VII. Sallie L. Moyer, b in Bucks Co. Pa. July
21, 1865, m John B. Garges Oct 29, 1887. P O
Line Lexington, Pa. Farmer. Menn. No issue.

VII. Mary L. Moyer, b Mar 8, 1867, m Isaac M.
Swartley.

VII. Abraham L. Moyer, b Feb 4, 1871, d Aug
2, 1881.

VI. Samuel W. Lapp, b in Bucks Co. Pa. Sept
22, 1833, m Sarah Gross Oct 16, 1856. She was
b July 26, 1837. P O Ayr, Neb. Farmer. Deacon
of Mennonite Ch. C: John, Amanda, Anna,
Emma, William, Daniel, Samuel, Mahlon, Abraham, Sarah, George.

VII. John Lapp, b Oct 31, 1857, d Mar 18, 1860.

VII. Amanda Lapp, b Aug 4, 1859, d Aug 18,
1860.

VII. Anna Lapp, b May 17, 1861, m John T.
Hill Feb 9, 1879. P O Juniata, Neb. Menn.
C: (**VIII**) Altie Hill, b Jan 29, 1880. Charles Hill,
b Apr 29, 1882. Hazel Hill, b Feb 6, 1887.

VII. Emma Lapp, b Oct 15, 1863. d May 4, 1865.

VII. William Lapp, b Feb 11, 1866, d Mar 11,
1866.

VII. Rev. Daniel G. Lapp, b in Bucks Co. Pa. Apr
29, 1867, m Ida M. Good Feb 22, 1898. P O Rose-

land, Nebr. Farmer. He was ordained a minister of the Mennonite church in 1893. C: (**VIII**) Paul Andrew Lapp, b Dec 24, 1898. Titus Samuel Lapp, b Feb 25, 1901.

VII. Samuel G. Lapp, b in Bucks Co. Pa. Oct 4, 1869, m Kate Ebersole Jan 25, 1899. P O South English, Iowa. Farmer, and ordained minister of the Mennonite church Feb 1901, and Bishop Nov 1902. C: (**VIII**) Myron E. Lapp, b Oct 15, 1899. Ruth Lapp, b July 26, 1901.

VII. Rev. Mahlon G. Lapp, b in Bucks Co. Pa. Feb 4, 1872, m Sarah Hahn June 7, 1901. P O Damtari, Central Province, India. Missionary to India, Mennonite Church; ordained minister and Bishop in June 1901.

VII. Abraham G. Lapp, b Oct 18, 1874, d Jan 11, 1878.

VII. Sarah G. Lapp, b Apr 18, 1876, d Sept 1, 1880.

VII. George Jay Lapp, b in Adams Co. Neb. May 26, 1879. Teacher, Menn. S., (1903).

VI. Joseph W. Lapp, b Bucks Co. Pa. Oct 17, 1834, m Hannah B. Landis Jan 16, 1861. She was b in Bucks Co. Pa. Mar 16, 1838. P O Chalfont, Pa. Farmer, Menn. C: John, Abraham, William, Isaiah, Sallie, Joseph, Erwin, Elizabeth, Mary, Emma.

VII. John J. Lapp, b Nov 27, 1861, d June 12, 1881.

VII. Abraham L. Lapp, b Apr 20, 1864, d Sept 26, 1865.

VII. William L. Lapp, b May 27, 1866, m Amanda M. Biedler May 11, 1889. Farmer, Menn. C: (**VIII**) Laura Lapp, b Oct 1891.

VII. Isaiah L. Lapp, b Dec 8, 1867, m Kate Clemmer of Lansdale, Pa. Oct 1, 1892. P O Lansdale, Pa. Firebrick-maker, Menn. C: (**VIII**) Lester C. Lapp, b Dec 6, 1895.

VII. Sallie A. Lapp, b Aug 10, 1870, m Abraham G. Gross Feb 25, 1893. P O Fountainville, Pa. Farmer, Menn. C: (**VIII**) Nora L. Gross, b Feb 17, 1894. Hannah L. Gross, b Sept 6, 1895. Phares L.

Gross, b Dec 6, 1898.

VII. Joseph L. Lapp, b Mar 5, 1872, m Sallie S.
Walter Oct 5, 1897. Farmer, Menn. No issue,
(1899).

VII. Edwin L. Lapp, b July 9, 1873.

VII. Elizabeth L. Lapp, b May 12, 1876.

VII. Mary L. Lapp, b Dec 2, 1878.

VII. Emma L. Lapp, b Jan 30, 1881.

VI. Anna Lapp, b Aug 15, 1836, d May 19, 1862,
m Samuel Hiestand in 1856.   C: (**VII**) Emma
Hiestand, (d).   Mary, (d).

VI. John W. Lapp, b Nov 12, 1838, d Sept 27,
1875, m Barbara Barnes.   She was b in 1842, d Apr
9, 1890.   Farmer, Menn.   C: Daniel, Anna,
Fannie.

VII. Daniel B. Lapp, b Apr 26, 1864, d May 1,
1864.

VII. Anna M. Lapp, b Oct 14, 1865. m Wilson
K. Clemmer Dec 24, 1887. P O Jenkintown, Pa.
Painter and Decorator, Presby. C: (**VIII**) Horace
L. Clemmer, b Oct 8, 1888.   Mabel L. Clemmer,
b Oct 17, 1889.   Clarence L. Clemmer, b June 2,
1892, d July 24, 1892.   Abram L. Clemmer, b Dec
10, 1894.   Elizabeth Irene Clemmer, b May 19,
1897.   Mary L. Clemmer, b May 15, 1899, d Feb
7, 1900.   John L. Clemmer, b Oct 12, 1900.

VII. Fannie B. Lapp, b Dec 20, 1867, m Tobias
R. Clemmer.   P O Hatfield, Pa.

VI. Jonas Lapp, b Sept 6, 1840, d Dec 22, 1889,
m Anna Ruth.

VI. Maria Lapp, b in Bucks Co, Pa. Nov 5, 1842,
m Abraham M. High Jan 9. 1870.   He was b June
14, 1845.   P O Chalfont, Pa.   Farmer, Menn.   C:
William, Anna.

VII. William L. High, b Feb 20, 1871.

VII. Anna Lizzie High, b June 7, 1875.

VI. Henry W. Lapp, b in Bucks Co. Pa. May 4,
1844, m Lydia Gehman Dec 7, 1869.   P O Salina,
Kan.   Farmer, Menn.   C: Abraham, John, Lizzie,
Anna, Clemens, William.

VII. Abraham Lapp, b Oct 21, 1868, d Oct 24,
1872.

VII. John G. Lapp, b in Bucks Co. Pa. Feb 27, 1870, m Laura J. Nuss July 30, 1893. Res. 7018 Adams Ave. Parkside, Chicago, Ill. Medical Student, Ref. Ch.

VII. Lizzie Lapp, b in Pa. May 17, 1872. P O Salina, Kan. Teacher, Cong. Ch.

VII. Anna Lapp, b in Pa. Sept 29, 1874. P O Salina Kan. Teacher, Cong. Ch.

VII. Clemens Lapp, b Mar 27, 1877.

VII. William Henry Lapp, b Aug 23, 1882.

VI. Catharine Lapp, b at Whiteballville, (now Chalfont), Bucks Co. Pa. Feb 14, 1846, m Henry Leatherman Dec 9, 1871. He was b Jan 13, 1845. P O Line Lexington, Pa. Farmer, Menn. C: Anna, Abraham, Sallie, William, Henry, Franklin.

VII. Anna Leatherman, b May 28, 1873. S.

VII. Abraham Leatherman, b Sept 17, 1876.

VII. Sallie Leatherman, b Jan 24, 1879.

VII. William Leatherman, b Sept 5, 1882.

VII. Henry Leatherman, b July 20, 1884, d Sept 17, 1884.

VII. Franklin Leatherman, b Nov 12, 1885.

V. Joseph Lapp, b—, m Susanna Haldeman. Farmer, Menn. C: Abraham, Jacob, Mary, John, Joseph, Rachel, Susanna.

VI. Abraham Lapp, died aged 18 years.

VI. Jacob Lapp, (twin to Abraham), d aged 18 years.

VI. Mary Lapp, b July 3, 1834, (d); m William G. Overholt Feb 4, 1860. He was b May 4, 1832. P O Silverdale, Pa. Retired farmer, Menn. No issue.

VI. John H. Lapp, m Catharine Ruth, daughter of Michael Ruth. P O Chalfont, Pa. Retired farmer, Menn. C: Ann, William, Harvey, Reuben, John, Susan, ——, ——, (d).

VII. Ann Eliza Lapp, m John Detweiler. P O Tradesville, Pa.

VII. William Lapp. P O Chalfont, Pa.

VII. Harvey Lapp.

VII. Reuben Lapp.

VII. John Lapp. P O Fountainville, Pa.

VII. Susan Lapp, m— Houck.

VII. —Lapp.

VII. —Lapp, (d).

VI. Joseph H. Lapp, m Ann Eliza Clymer.   P O Chalfont, Pa. Farmer, Menn.   C: Mary, Infant, Fannie, Franklin, Susie, Annie, Ida, Debbie, Emma, Edith, Howard.

VII. Mary Lapp, m Ed. Hinkle.

VII. Infant.

VII. Fannie Lapp, (d); m Levi Shelly, P O Plumsteadville, Pa. Mrs S. Baptist. No issue.

VII. Fanklin Lapp, d infant.

VII. Susie Lapp, m William Texter.

VII. Annie Lapp.

VII. Ida Lapp.

VII. Debbie Lapp.

VII. Emma Lapp.

VII. Edith Lapp.

VII. Howard Lapp.

VI. Rachel Lapp, b in New Britain twp. Bucks Co. Pa. Jan 21, 1840, m Elias Shaddinger of Plumstead twp. Bucks Co. Pa. Nov 22, 1862.   P O Gardenville, Pa. Farmer. Menn. C: Susan, Priscilla, Mary, Millicent, Griffith, Samuel, Franklin.

VII. Susan Shaddinger, b Oct 30, 1863, m Emanuel Landis Oct 13, 1883.   He died Nov 7, 1895. Menn.   C: (**VIII**) Henry Landis, b July 16, 1885. Elmer Landis, b Sept 5, 1890.   Harvey Landis, b May 12, 1893.   John S. Landis, b Dec 30, 1895.

VII. Priscilla Shaddinger, b Nov 6, 1865, d Aug 6, 1870.

VII. Mary Shaddinger, b June 1, 1868, m Harvey H. Baum Nov 15, 1890.   P O Blooming Glen, Pa. Farmer, Menn.   C: (**VIII**) Charles S. Baum, b Mar 25, 1892.   Wilmer S. Baum, b May 22, 1893. Rachel S. Baum, b Jan 30, 1896.   Harold S. Baum, b Oct 24, 1897.   Bertha May Baum, b May 31, 1900.

VII. Millicent Shaddinger, b Oct 5, 1870, m Frank W. Hinkle Jan 7, 1893.   P O Plumsteadville, Pa. Tinsmith, Baptist.   C: F. Walter Hinkle, b July 21, 1894, d July 5, 1897.   Claude S. Hinkle, b Jan 20,

Henry Rosenberger, Sr., Homestead, Franconia Township, Montgomery County, Pa

1897.   Arthur S. Hinkle, b Jan 31, 1899.
VII. Griffith Shaddinger, b Apr 9, 1873.
VII. Samuel L. Shaddinger, b Sept 1, 1875, m Mary A. Melcher May 25, 1899. P O Plumsteadville, Pa.
VII. Franklin Shaddinger, b Apr 2, 1878.
VI. Susanna Lapp, m Eli D. Nice. P O Doylestown, Pa. Farmer, Menn. C: Mary, Joseph, William, Enos, Lizzie, Maggie, Susie, Eli, Jacob, John.
VII. Mary Nice, m Peter L. Hunsberger. (See Peter L. Hunsberger Family).
VII. Joseph Nice, d infant.
VII. William Nice. S.
VII. Enos Nice, m —— Worthington. P O Fountainville, Pa.
VII. Lizzie Nice, m Leidy Moore.
VII. Maggie Nice, m Henry Stout.
VII. Susie Nice, m —— Greable.
VII. Eli Nice. S.
VII. Jacob Nice. S.
VII. John Nice. S.
V. Abraham Lapp, m Sallie Godshall, (d). C: Sallie, Tobias,. Abraham m second wife, Anna, Myers. Farmer, Menn. No issue.
VI. Sallie Lapp, m Joseph Kulp. P O Bedminister, Pa. Farmer, Menn. C: Isaac, ——.
VII. Isaac L. Kulp, m Esther M. Bewighouse. P O Bedminister, Pa.
VII. —— Kulp. S.
VI. Tobias Lapp, (d), m Eliza Detwiler. Farmer, Menn. C: William, Ella.
VII. William Lapp.
VII. Ella Lapp, m —— Rosenberger. P O Line Lexington, Pa.
V. Jacob Lapp, b in New Britain twp Bucks Co. Pa. d in Hilltown, Bucks Co. Jan 17, 1895, m Esther Bergey. Carpenter, Menn. C: Katie, Henry, Mahlon, Amanda, Annie, —, Ephraim, Isaac, Abram.
VI. Katie Lapp, b 1851, d 1872.
VI. Henry Lapp, b Feb 20, 1853, m Susan L.

Swartz Sept 18, 1879. P O Fricks, Pa. Harness-
maker, Menn. C: (VII) Nelson, Stella, Agnes,
Esther, Martha, Walter.

VI. Mahlon Lapp, b 1856, d 1859.
VI. Amanda Lapp, b 1859, d 1865.
VI. — Lapp, m Henry Landis.
VI. Ephriam Lapp.
VI. Isaac Lapp.
VI. Abram Lapp.
VI. Annie Lapp, m—Hendrick.
V. Elizabeth Lapp, b—, d—, m David Rickert.
(See David Rickert Family).

V. Henry Lapp, b in Bucks Co. Pa. July 15,
1822, d Aug 27, 1890, m Barbara Wisler Feb 1852.
She was b Oct 15, 1832, d Sept 12, 1894. Farmer
near Doylestown, Pa. Menn. C: Abraham,
Joseph, Samuel.

VI. Abraham Lapp, b 1853, d Jan 5, 1854.
VI. Joseph Lapp, b Jan 16, 1855, m Sallie Gods-
halk Dec 8, 1877. P O Doylestown, Pa. Clerk,
Menn. C: (VII) Dillwyn Lapp, b Sept 19, 1883,
d next day.
VI. Samuel Lapp, b in Bucks Co. Pa. July 15,
1857, m Sallie Swartley Oct 5, 1878. P O Chal-
font, Pa. Farmer, Menn. C: Lizzie, Laura.
VII. Elizabeth H. Lapp, b Nov 2, 1881, m Howard
N. Wynn Dec 23, 1899. Driving a delivery wagon
in Phila. Pa. Baptist.
VII. Laura Lapp, b Mar 20, 1884. S.
V. Samuel Lapp, b—, d S.

IV. Susanna Rosenberger, b in Montg. Co. Pa. Jan
15, 1781, d in Canada Sept 9, 1846, m Rev. Jacob
Detweiler Dec 15, 1803. He was b in Bucks Co. Pa.
Nov 25, 1778, d Aug 8, 1858. He run a mill near
Line Lexington, Pa. at which place all has children
were born, except the youngest daughter. In 1823
they moved to Canada, where they bought a "bush"
farm which Mr. Detweiler cleared. Here he and his
wife died and are buried. They were members of the
old Mennonite church of which he was a minister.
C: John, Mary, Jacob, Susanna, Elizabeth, Benjamin,
Annie, Enoch, Abraham, Lydia.

V. John R. Detweiler, b Jan 1, 1805, d Oct 17, 1876, m Nancy Dodge in 1826. They resided at Port Elgin, Ont. C: Moses, Mary, Abraham, Nathaniel, Fannie, Elizabeth, Joseph, Abigail, George, John.

VI. Moses Detweiler, b Dec 21, 1826.

VI. Mary Ann Detweiler, b Oct 8, 1827, m Daniel Rudy. He d July 27, 1892. P O Tavistook, Ont. Farmer. C: **(VII)** David Rudy.

VI. Abraham Detweiler, b Jan 14, 1828. Res. New Orleans, La.

VI. Nathaniel Detweiler, b Mar 13, 1830, died young.

VI. Fannie Detweiler, b June 4, 1833, d Apr 17, 1857.

VI. Elizabeth Detweiler, b Dec 22, 1836, m Henry Burton. P O Port Elgin, Ont.

VI. Joseph Detweiler, b July 4, 1839. P O South Lyons, Mich.

VI. Abigail Detweiler, b Dec 22, 1844, m Benjamin Hilker.

VI. George Detweiler, b Feb 15, 1846.

VI. John Detweiler, b Dec 31, 1850. P O Harriston, Ont.

V. Mary Detweiler, b in Bucks Co. Pa. Sept 20, 1806, d near Roseville, Ont. July 4, 1874, m Samuel Snyder 1825. He was b in Franklin Co. Pa. Apr 29, 1801, d May 15, 1887. C: Susanna, Benjamin, Isaac, Nancy, Mary, Enoch, Elizabeth, Lydia, Sarah, Samuel, Daniel, Magdalena.

VI. Susanna Snyder, b Feb 1, 1826, d Oct 9, 1873, m Jacob S. Cressman Apr 27, 1847, He was b May 21, 1823, d June 13, 1877. Farmer. C: Mary, Nancy, Leah, Isaiah, Isaac, Magdalena, Susanna, Lydia, Emanuel, Emma, Jacob.

VII. Mary Cressman, b Oct 2, 1848, m Henry Bauer May 30, 1879. He was b Aug 28, 1855. P O New Dundee, Ont. Farmer, Menn. C: **(VIII)** Lillie May Bauer, b Oct 26, 1880. Austin Bauer, b June 30, 1883.

VII. Nancy Cressman, b Mar 9, 1850, d Jan 30, 1866.

VII. Leah Cressman, b May 23, 1851, m Menno
Rellinger Jan 1870. He was b Mar 7, 1847. P O
New Dundee, Ont. Laborer. C: Oliver, Jacob,
Herbert.

VII. Isaiah Cressman, b Feb 18, 1853, d July 5,
1853.

VII. Isaac Cressman, b June 18, 1854, d Sept 5,
1866.

VII. Magdalena Cressman, b July 23, 1855. P O
Hanover, Ont. S.

VII. Susanna Cressman, b Sept 10, 1858, m Joseph
Miehlhausen Jan 7, 1880. He was b Mar 2, 1858.
P O Walkerton, Ont. Wagon and Carriage builder.
C: (**VIII**) Clarence Miehlhausen. Allen Emanuel
Miehlhausen.

VII. Lydia Cressman, b Jan 9, 1860, m Peter Studer
Oct 17, 1883. He was b Jan 22, 1860. P O New
Dundee, Ont. Mr. Studer died Nov 26, 1893. No
issue.

VII. Emanuel S. Cressman, b Jan 8, 1865. P O
Hanover, Ont. Merchant, Presby. S.

VII. Emma Ann Cressman, b Feb 20, 1866, m Alexander Heller Oct. 26, 1887. He was b Mar 8, 1865.
They resided at Elmwood, Ont., where he had leased
roller flour mills. On the morning of May 10, 1892,
the boiler of the Mills exploded killing him instantly.
P O Hanover, Ont. C: (**VIII**) Leroy.

VII. Jacob Allen Cressman, b Jan 30, 1867, m Mar-
garet McNally of Hanover, Ont. Mar 13, 1894.
P O Hanover, Ont. In the mercantile business with
his brother Emanuel; Presby. C: (**VIII**) Alexander
Emanuel Cressman, b June 21, 1895. Rocksie
Merle Cressman, b Apr 13, 1897.

VI. Benjamin D. Snyder, b Aug 18, 1827, m Catharine Bechtel. She was b Sept 2, 1828. P O Peabody, Kan. Farmer. C: Mary, Ephraim, Angeline,
Elizabeth, Emeline, Isaiah, Jeremiah.

VII. Mary Ann Snyder, b Sept 15, 1850, d Aug
27, 1895, m Samuel Haug. Farmer in Oklahoma,
U. S.

VII. Ephriam Snyder, b 1852, d 1855.

VII. Angeline Snyder, b Feb 8, 1855, d May 12,

David Rosenblum.

Mrs. Rosenblum.

1895, m John W. Meyers Dec 26, 1872.   P O
Listowel, Ont. Merchant, Miller, Meth. C: (**VIII**)
Caleb Meyers, b Nov 9, 1873, d Sept 5, 1875.
Emaline Meyers, b Feb 21, 1875, d Sept 1875.
Josephus S. Meyers, b July 20, 1876. Alva Her-
vey Meyers, b July 14, 1878, d Apr 7, 1878.
Archie John Meyers, b July 13, 1880. Benjamin
Homer Meyers, b July 28, 1882.   Angeline Orilla
Meyers, b June 28, 1884.   Ida Alberta Meyers, b
Sept 21, 1886. Arthur Oswold Meyers, b Oct 14,
1888.   Lillian Olive Snyder Meyers, Nov 7, 1894.
VII. Elizabeth Snyder, b June 8, 1857, m Simon
Reid Aug 31, 1876. P O Strasburg, Ont.   Prin-
cipal of the Public school.   C: (**VIII**) Ella May
Reid, b Apr 14, 1877. Elthea Reid, b Oct 5, 1879.
Herbert Spencer Reid, b Apr 26, 1881, d Feb 21,
1883.   Albert Elmer Reid, b Dec 2, 1885. Hecter
Gordon Reid, b Feb 21, 1888.   Florence Reid, b
Nov 3, 1889. Sarah Olive Reid, b Aug 26, 1891,
d May 24, 1892. Alexander Roy Reid, b July 31,
1893.
VII. Emeline Snyder, b Mar 8, 1859, m Jacob
Dohner July 5, 1878. P O —, Kan.
VII. Isaiah B. Snyder, b Feb 27, 1861, d Feb 18,
1885.
VII. Jeremiah B. Snyder, b July 27, 1865, m Bessie
Donaldson. P O Waterloo, Oklahoma, U. S. Far-
mer.
VI. Isaac D. Snyder, b Oct 4, 1829, m Naucy Horst
Feb 7, 1857. She was b July 21, 1834. P O Blen-
heim, Ont. Farmer. C: Eli, Josiah, David, Sam-
uel, Matilda, Uriah.
VII. Eli H. Snyder, b Mar 18, 1855, d Oct 25, 1863.
VII. Josiah H. Snyder, b June 19, 1857, d June 22,
1881.
VII. David H. Snyder, b Oct 9, 1858, m Lucinda
Shantz Apr 6, 1887. P O New Dundee, Ont.
Farmer. C: (**VIII**) Ida Snyder, b Feb 7, 1888.
Mary Ann Snyder, b May 25, 1889. Allen Snyder,
b Apr 20, 1893, d July 14, 1894. Alvin Snyder,
b June 9, 1895. Elden Snyder, b Apr 21, 1897.
Eden Snyder, b Oct 30, 1898, d Oct 30, 1898.

VII. Samuel H. Snyder, b Oct 16, 1864, m Angeline
Shantz Sept 20, 1893.   P O New Dundee, Ont.
Farmer, Menn.   C: (**VIII**) Perley May Snyder, b
Feb 7, 1895.   Violet Snyder, b Nov 28, 1897.
VII. Matilda H. Snyder, b June 20, 1870. S.
VII. Uriah H. Snyder, b June 24, 1872. Farmer.
Single.
VI. Nancy Snyder, b June 3, 1831, m Benjamin S.
Martin Jan 25, 1859. He was b June 12, 1830. P
O Roseville, Ont.   Farmer.   C: Samuel, Isaiah,
Jesse, Amanda, Oliver, Malinda, Magdalena,
Enoch.
VII. Samuel S. Martin, b May 15, 1860, m Mary
Ann, daughter of Christian and Barbara (Oberer)
Loier. She was b Oct 4, 1862.
VII. Isaiah Martin, b June 29, 1862.
VII. Jesse Martin, b June 29, 1862.
VII. Amanda S. Martin, b in Wilmot twp. Ont.
Aug 19, 1864, m Elisha Schiedel at Roseville,
Ont. in 1884. P O Port Elgin, Ont. Capitalist,
Methodist. C: (**VIII**) Elmer James Schiedel, b in
1888.
VII. Oliver Martin, b Sept 28, 1866.
VII. Malinda Martin, b Nov 4, 1867.
VII. Magdalena Martin, b Sept 10, 1869, d Oct
19, 1869.
VII. Enoch Martin, b Oct 8, 1871.
VI. Mary Snyder, b June 29, 1833, m Abraham
Rudy. (See Abraham Rudy Family).
VI. Enoch D. Snyder, b Feb 28, 1835, m Sophia
Schwartz Oct 27, 1857. She d Apr 12, 1877.   C:
Lavina, Angeline, Susanna, Isaiah, Emanuel,
Ezra, Clara, Lydia.   Enoch m second wife,
Priscilla Scheifley, Feb 16, 1879. P O Roseville,
Ont. Farmer. C: Ira, Sophia, Ida, Amasa.
VII. Lavina Snyder, b July 25, 1858, d Oct
4, 1878.
VII. Angeline Snyder, b Oct 6, 1859, d Apr 12,
1870.
VII. Susanna Snyder, b Mar 6, 1861, d Jan 4,
1862.
VII. Isaiah Snyder, b Apr 15, 1863, m Caroline

Cress Aug 17, 1896. P O Roseville, Ont. Farmer.
C: (**VIII**) Cecil Snyder, b Oct 27, 1900. Carson
Snyder, b Mar 27, 1902.

VII. Emanuel Snyder, b June 29, 1867. S.

VII. Ezra Snyder, b Feb 12, 1870. S.

VII. Clara Snyder, b Aug 20, 1872, m Eli Rosenberger. (See Eli Rosenberger Family).

VII. Lydia A. Snyder, b Jan 31, 1874.

VII. Ira Snyder, b Dec 20, 1879.

VII. Sophia Snyder, b June 4, 1881.

VII. Ida Snyder, b Dec 4, 1882.

VII. Amasa Snyder, b Oct 2, 1884.

VI. Elizabeth Snyder, b Feb 4, 1837, m Jonas Good
Mar 6, 1860. P O New Hamburg, Ont. Farmer.
C: (**VII**) Eli, Daniel, (d); Samuel, Simeon, Abraham, Jeremiah, Almeda.

VI. Lydia Snyder, b Jan 20, 1839, m Henry B.
Shantz Oct 20, 1863. P O Berlin, Ont, Farmer. C:
(**VII**) Mary, Hannah, Daniel, Ananias, Lydia,
Alvinia, William, Edwin, Samuel, Minerva, (d).

VI. Sarah Snyder, b Jan 6, 1841, d in 1844.

VI. Samuel D. Snyder, b Mar 17, 1843, m Margaret Clemens June 13, 1865. P O Wardsville,
Ont. Farmer. C: Malinda, Emeline, (d); Isaac,
David, Sarah, Phaleria, Maggie, Alta.

VI. Daniel D. Snyder, b Feb 26, 1845, m Elizabeth
Bricker Mar 31, 1868. P O Roseville, Ont. Farmer. C: Lucinda, Elizabeth, Esther, Mary, Elsie,
Melvin, Susan.

VII. Lucinda Snyder, b Oct 1, 1869, m Albert
Stoltz. Farmer. No issue.

VII. Elizabeth Snyder, b July 8, 1871, m Albert
Becker. P O Roseville, Ont. Farmer. C: (**VIII**)
Alice Becker, Myrtle Becker.

VII. Esther Laoma Snyder, b July 16, 1873, d
May 19, 1874.

VII. Mary Salina Snyder, b May 18, 1875.

VII. Elsie Mina Snyder, b Dec 15, 1877, d Aug
22, 1888.

VII. Melvin Snyder, b Aug 19, 1880.

VII. Susan Snyder, b Apr 17, 1883, d June 19,
1883.

VI. Magdalena Snyder, b Mar 8, 1847, d Sept 29, 1862.

V. Jacob R. Detweiler, b in Bucks Co. Pa. Dec 15, 1807, d July 2, 1885, m Anna, daughter of Isaac and Anna (High) Wismer. She was b in 1808, d Nov 5, 1871. Farmer, Menn. C: Isaac, Daniel, Benjamin, John, Jacob, Barbara, Barbara, Susanna, Christian, Enoch, Annie, Mary.

VI. Christian Detweiler, b July 22, 1836. P O Roseville, Ont. S.

VI. Enoch W. Detweiler, b in Waterloo Co. Ont. Sept 8, 1839, m Victoria Willits Nov 27, 1860. P O Roseville, Ont. Farmer, United Brethren. C: Lavina, Rosetta, Alice, Barbara, Elsie, George, Effie.

VII. Lavina Detweiler, b Sept 26, 1861. P O Hamilton, Ont. S.

VII. Rosetta W. Detweiler, b Mar 20, 1865, m Emanuel Hilborn Apr 1886. P O Grand Valley, Ont. Miller, United Brethren. C: **(VIII)** Ada Hilborn, b Feb 18, 1888. Leslie Hilborn, b Nov 3, 1889.

VII. Alice Jane Detweiler, b June 1, 1867, m John W. Battler Apr 2, 1890. P O New Dundee, Ont. Farmer, United Brethren. No issue.

VII. Barbara Annie Detweiler, b Feb 18, 1869, m John McGurn. P O Salem, Ont. C: **(VIII)** Maggie Victoria McGurn.

VII. Elsie Electia Cecelia Detweiler, b Aug 2, 1873.

VII. George William Detweiler, b Sept 16, 1875.

VII. Effie Detweiler, b Feb 14, 1879.

VI. Anna W. Detweiler, b July 21, 1844, m Adam B. Cassel May 2, 1861. P O New Dundee, Ont. Farmer, United Brethren. C: Milton, Oliver, Lavina, John, Jacob.

VII. Milton D. Cassel, b May 17, 1862, d same day.

VII. Oliver D. Cassel, b June 16, 1863, m Barbara S. Geiger Aug 24, 1886. P O New Dundee, Ont. Spinner and carder in wool factory. C: **(VIII)** James Lloyd Cassel, b June 15, 1887. Hattie Melissa G. Cassel, b Jan 6, 1890.

VII. Lavina D. Cassel, b Nov 29, 1865, m Henry H.

Wagner Nov 15, 1891.   P O New Dundee, Ont.
Farmer, U. B. Ch.   C: (VIII) Cecil Maurice Wag-
ner, b Dec 22, 1893.
VII. John D. Cassel, b Sept 3, 1871.
VII. Jacob D. Cassel,(twin), b Sept 3, 1871.
VI. Mary Ann Detweiler, b Sept 12, 1850, m Albert
Willits Feb 2, 1872.   P O Wroxeter, Ont. Farmer.
C: Jemima, Barbara, Alberta, Jacob, Alfred, Nor-
man, Gordon.
V. Susanna Detweiler, b Aug 20, 1809, d July 2,
1874, m Jacob Wismer in 1825.   He was b in Bucks
Co. Pa.   June 1797, d in Huron Co. Ont. Feb
1875.   He became a cripple and made his living mak-
ing ox yokes, rakes, axe handles and shingles.
Menn.   C: Catharine, Levi, David.
VI. Catharine Wismer, b in Waterloo Co. Ont.
Jan 5, 1839.   m Henry Treffry June 11, 1855.   P
O Burnside Station, Manitoba.   Meth.   C: Susanna,
Phebe, Mary, Robert, Jacob, William, Margaret,
Emma, Jacob, Catharine, Lydia, George.
VII. Susanna Treffry, b June 29, 1856, m Solomon
Beck May 24, 1879.   P O Burnside Station, Man.
Farmer.   Ch. of England.   C: (VIII) James Beck,
b Apr 27, 1882.   Emma Beck, b Oct 21, 1887.   Eva
Beck, b Sept 6, 1889.   Phebe Beck, b Sept 5, 1892.
VII. Phebe Ann Treffry, b Jan 16, 1858, m Henry
Voss Jan 17, 1876.   P O Burnside Station, Man.
Farmer, Luth.   C: (VIII) Catharine Voss, b Aug
1878.   Henry Voss, b June 29, 1880.   Mary Voss,
b Dec 1, 1883.   Violet Voss, b Sept 6, 1885, d Nov
6, 1885.   Robert Voss, b Sept 21, 1887.   Norman
Voss, b Oct 24, 1888.
VII. Mary Ann Treffry, b Nov 2, 1859, m Thomas
Beck Aug 17, 1882.   P O Burnside Station, Man.
Ch. of England.   C: (VIII) William Beck, b Sept
20, 1883.   Charles Beck, b May 6, 1887.   Eliza
Beck, b Jan 13, 1889.
VII. Robert John Treffry, b Dec 25, 1861, m Cas-
iah Elizabeth Lee Oct 24, 1888.   P O Burnside
Station, Man.   Meth.   C: (VIII) Jorsa Treffry, b
Oct 23, 1889.   Robert Leslie Treffry, b June 6,
1892, d Mar 30, 1893.

VII. Jacob Treffry, b Mar 22, 1864, d Mar 25, 1864.

VII. William Henry Treffry, b Apr 12, 1865, m Anna May Kizer of Michigan, Jan 27, 1892. P O Burnside Station, Mass. Farmer, Meth. C: (**VIII**) Carrie May Treffry, b Jan 23, 1893. Myra Rose Treffry, b Jan 20, 1895. Leroy Morris Treffry, b Nov 15, 1897. Blanche Kizer Treffry, b July 19, 1901.

VII. Margaret Treffry, b July 28, 1867, m Frank E. Green Dec 25, 1889. Res. 90 Hallot St. Winnipeg, Man. Miller, Ch of England. C: (**VIII**) Mabel Catharine Green, b June 23, 1892. Ivy Green, b Sept 25, 1893.

VII. Emma Treffry, b Jan 12, 1871, m James Acheson Feb 9, 1888. P O Burnside Station, Man. C: (**VIII**) Arthur Acheson b Mar 9, 1889. Martha Mabel Acheson, b Mar 17, 1890. Alislnese Acheson, b May 6, 1891. Florence Irene Acheson, b Sept 9, 1893.

VII. Jacob Treffry, b July 13, 1873.

VII. Catharine Treffry, b July 13, 1873, m Frederick W. Green July 13, 1892. Res. Winnipeg, Man. Miller. C: (**VIII**) Islay C. Green, b Aug 7, 1893. d Sept 26, 1893.

VII. Lydia A. Treffry, b Apr 30, 1876. Meth.   S.

VII. George Treffry, b Apr 9, 1879.

VI. Levi Wismer, b in Canada Aug 10, 1840, m Mary J. Broderick. P O Redman, Mich. Millwright. C: (**VII**) Mary, William, Emma, Ella, Shadrach, Isaiah, Infant, Catharine, Infant, Levi.

VI. David Wismer, b 1842, d 1844.

V. Elizabeth Detweiler, b Oct 2, 1811, d Sept 7, 1840, m Benjamin Snyder Feb 27, 1831. He was b July 4, 1803, d May 25, 1892. He was a farmer and resided a little west of Roseville, Ontario, where he owned one of the finest tracts of land in Ontario. C: Susanna, Lydia, Sarah, Nancy, David, Eliza.

VI. Susanna Snyder, b Nov 28, 1831, d July 23, 1859, m John Musselman Mar 17, 1857. C: (**VII**) Benjamin Musselman.

VI. Lydia Snyder, b May 8, 1833, m Isaac E Bricker July 8, 1856. He was b Sept 24, 1835. P O

Blenheim, Ont. Farmer. C: Oliver, David, Harold, Benjamin, Peter, Sarah, Mary, Isaiah, Isaac, Lydia, Malinda, Anson.

VI. Sarah Snyder, b Dec 4, 1834, d June 17, 1863, m Daniel G. Bowman, Feb 24, 1861. P O Lakeport, Mich. Farmer. C: (**VII**) Sarah Bowman, b May 15, 1863, m Israel Cressman. P O New Dundee, Ont.

VI. Nancy Snyder, b Nov 28, 1836, m John Wismer Sept 23, 1856. He was b Aug 11, 1835. P O Blair, Ont. Farmer, Menn. C: Benjamin, John, David, Henry, Leah, Nancy, Isaiah.

VII. Benjamin S. Wismer, b June 10, 1857, m Catharine Kumpf Feb 10, 1879. P O Blair, Ont. Farmer, Menn. C: (**VIII**) Nancy Wismer, b Jan 20, 1880, d May 11, 1880. Sarah Wismer, b Sept 12, 1881, d Jan 27, 1891. Leah Wismer, b Aug 10, 1883, d Jan 21, 1891. Mary Wismer, b Nov 22, 1885. Catharine Wismer, b Dec 28, 1888.

VII. John Wismer, b Apr 1859, m Susanna Gehman May 12, 1885.

VII. David Wismer, b June 12, 1861, m Esther, Shantz Oct 1, 1889. P O Blair, Ont. Farmer, Menn. C: (**VIII**) David Elton Wismer, b Aug 11, 1890.

VII. Rev. Henry Wismer, b Mar 23, 1863, m Lucinda Miller Jan 3, 1888. Farmer until 1892, when he entered the ministry of the Mennonite Brethren in Christ. C: (**VIII**) Harold Wismer, b May 27, 1891. Russel Wismer, b Aug 12, 1893.

VII. Leah Wismer, b Jan 28, 1865, m John R. Naissmith Apr 21, 1891. P O Blair, Ont. Farmer. C: (**VIII**) John Wismer Naissmith, b Feb 3, 1893.

VII. Nancy Wismer, b May 27, 1867, m John A. Gehman Oct 25, 1887. P O Freeport, Ont. Farmer. Menn.

VII. Isaiah Wismer, b Aug 28, 1870.

VI. David D. Snyder, b Aug 30, 1838. S.

VI. Eliza Snyder, b Mar 19, 1840. S.

V. Benjamin Detweiler, b in Montg. Co. Pa. Nov 23, 1813, m Elizabeth Kennedy Oct 10, 1837. She was

a native of Inverness, Scotland, where she was born
June 7, 1820. Mr. Detweiler when 9 years of age
came with his parents to Canada. Soon after marriage they moved on a farm near Roseville, Ont.,
where they resided 20 years. After farming
several years near St Jacobs—they later located in
Berlin, Ont. Mr. D. Menn. Mrs. D. Br. in
Christ.   C: Noah, Menno, Isaac, Daniel, John,
Sarah, Phoebe, Rebecca, Samuel, Benjamin, Magdalena, Lavina.

VI. Rev. Noah Detweiler, b Mar 23, 1838, m
Veronica Bush Sept 4, 1860. P O Berlin, Ont. In
early life farmer.   After his conversion, when the
Mennonite Brethren in Christ church was formed, in
1874, he became one of its earliest ministers, and
has done a noble work for the Master wherever he
has labored.   C: Eliza, Levina, Jemima, Sarah,
Priscilla, Hannah, Josephine.

VII. Eliza Detweiler, b May 18, 1861, m Samuel
Shirk. Carpenter, Menn. Br. in Christ. C: (**VIII**)
Edna Shirk. Noah Shirk. Ethel Shirk. Oliver
Shirk, (d).

VII. Lavina Detweiler, b Nov 4, 1865, d Dec 22,
1866.

VII. Jemima Detweiler, b Nov 1, 1868, m Simeon S.
Hallman. P O Berlin, Ont. Carpenter; Mrs. H.
Menn. Br. in Christ.

VII. Sarah Detweiler, b Mar 20, 1871.

VII. Priscilla Detweiler, b Oct 17, 1873, d Jan 17,
1882.

VII. Hannah M. Detweiler, b Apr 21, 1876, d Jan 10,
1879.

VII. Josephine Detweiler, b Sept 15, 1879.

VI. Menno Detweiler, b Sept 6, 1840, m Margaret
Rupped. He d July 6, 1892. Carriage-builder. C:
Laura, Margaret, Eliza, John, Henry, George,
Annie.

VI. Isaac Detweiler, b Dec 11, 1841, m Catharine
Bush. P O Port Elgin, Ont. Saddler by trade.
C: Alexander, Albert, Charles, Lillian.

VI. Daniel K. Detweiler, b Apr 26, 1843, m Catharine Snyder. P O Wallaceville, Ont. Farmer.

C: (**VII**) John, George, Jacob, Eliza.

VI. John Detweiler, b Feb 15, 1845, m Margaret Dodee, (d). Blacksmith. C: (**VII**) William, Phoebe.

VI. Sarah Ann Detweiler, b Feb 15, 1847, m Frederick W. Welz Jan 28, 1873. P O Moorefield, Ont. Carriage-builder. Evangelical Church. C: Lydia, George, John, William, Lucinda, Edwin, Martha.

VII. Lydia Ann Welz, b Mar 27, 1875, in Perth Co. Ont. Canada, m Oren O. McPheeters Mar 15, 1894. P O Ravanna, Neb. Clerk in store, Methodist. C: (**VIII**) Ona May McPheeters, b Mar 14, 1895. Harry Albert McPheeters, b Feb 13, 1897.

VII. George Benjamin Welz, b in Grey Co. Ont. Aug 4, 1876. P O Brantford, Ont. Piano tuner, Evangelical Ch. S.

VII. John Henry Welz, b Sept 4, 1877, d Sept 18, 1877.

VII. William Franklin Welz, b Sept 25, 1878. P O Moorefield, Ont. Tailor, Evangelical Ch.

VII. Lucinda Welz, b Apr 19, 1880, d Aug 12, 1880.

VII. Edwin Frederick Welz, b Dec 22, 1881. P O Moorefield, Ont. Tailor, Evangelical Ch.

VII. Martha Welz, b May 4, 1885, Evangelical.

VI. Phœbe Ann Detweiler, b in Waterloo Co. Ont. Jan 23, 1849, m Michael Haug Nov 10, 1867. P O Berlin, Ont. Agent, Menn. Br. in Christ. C: Benjamin, Solomon, Elizabeth.

VII. Benjamin Mathias Haug, b May 7, 1870, d July 13, 1870.

VII. Solomon Leander Huag, b Aug 16, 1877, m Emma Mertz Feb 18, 1896. P O Berlin, Ont. Clerk in store, Methodist. C: (**VIII**) Harold Ross Haug.

VII. Elizabeth Lavina Haug, b July 7, 1882, d Oct 5, 1882.

VI. Rebecca Detweiler, b June 11, 1852, m Isaac Kolb in 1873. P O Berlin, Ont. C: Benjamin, Magdalena.

VII. Benjamin Leander Kolb, b Apr 21, 1874, m Kate VanMallsen May 2, 1896. Res. 137 Fifth St.

Grand Rapids, Mich.   Finisher in Furniture factory. Ref. Ch. C: (**VIII**) Wilhelmina Kolb, b Dec 4, 1896. Ralph Benjamin Kolb, b Aug 12, 1898.

VII. Magdalena E. Kolb, b Sept 11, 1877. Meth. S.

VI. Samuel Detweiler, b May 25, 1853, m Mary A. Williams. P O Brantford, Ont. Teamster. C: Pearley, Sylvia, Maggie, Annie, Clayton, (d); Lavina, etc.

VI. Benjamin Detweiler, b Apr 7, 1855, d S.

VI. Magdalena Detweiler, b Jan 23, 1857, m Benjamin M. Eby. P O Berlin, Ont.

VI. Lavina Detweiler, b Dec, 13, 1859. S.

V. Anna Detweiler, b Mar 8, 1816, d Feb 17, 1856, m John C. Shantz Jan 12, 1833. He was b Oct 23, 1807, d Apr 17, 1875. C: Benjamin, Mary, Abraham, Aaron, John, Enoch, Magdalena, Menno, Susanna, Lydia, Nancy, Sarah.

VI. Benjamin D. Shantz, b Aug 20, 1833, d Jan 15, 1889, m Elizabeth Nahrgang. She was b Dec 12, 1836, d June 4, 1894. They resided in Wadsworth, Mich. C: Nancy, Christopher, Mary, John, (d); Lydia, (d); Allen, Isaac, Isabella, Salome, Caroline, Minerva, Alice.

VI. Mary Ann Shantz, b Aug 24, 1834, m Joseph Nahrgang Dec 22, 1857. He was b July 26, 1834. P O New Hamburg, Ont. Farmer. C: Josiah, Barbara, (d); Ephraim, Mary, Menno, John, Nancy, Henry, Matilda, (d).

VI. Abraham D. Shantz, b Mar 6, 1836, m Mary Treffy Oct 4, 1856. She was b Oct 4, 1836, d June 5, 1864. C: Nancy, Eliza, Emma, Enoch. Abraham m second wife, Rosina Bachert, Sept 18, 1866. She was b Dec 9, 1838. P O Walkerton, Ont. Methodist, Wood-turner. C: David, Allen, Charles, Mary, Edythe, William, Albert, Clara.

VII. Nancy Shantz, b Aug 18, 1857, d Oct 31, 1857.

VII. Eliza Shantz, b Sept 18, 1858, d Nov 27, 1873.

VII. Emma Anna Shantz, b Nov 24, 1860, m David Glebe May 27, 1884. Farmer, Methodist. C: (**VIII**) Emma Nora Glebe, b June 14, 1886. Windom Glebe, b Aug 17, 1889.

VII. Enoch Shantz, b Oct 18, 1862, d Jan 27, 1881.
ᶠ **VII**. David Shantz, b July 21, 1867, m Annie M.
Brigden Mar 18, 1890.   Res. 715 43rd St. West
Chicago, Ill.   Wholesale and Retail Meat Market,
Methodist. C: (**VIII**) Charles Frederick Shantz, b
June 10, 1891. William Shantz, still-born. Gladys
Lilllian Shantz, b Dec 2, 1895.
VII. Allen B. Shantz, b Jan 21, 1869, m Margaret
F. Brierley July 6, 1898.   P O Caledonia, Ont.
Teacher, Meth.
VII. Charles B. Shantz, b July 27, 1870. Meth. S.
VII. Mary R. Shantz, b Sept 30, 1872. P O Walk-
erton, Ont. Meth. S.
VII. Edythe B. Shantz. b Sept 18, 1874. P O Walk-
erton, Ont. Teacher, Meth. S.
VII. William H. Shantz, b Nov 13, 1876, d Dec 14,
1878.
VII. Albert Shantz, b June 1878, d June 1878.
VII. Clara Shantz, b Aug 19, 1880, d Oct 1880.
VI. Aaron D. Shantz, b Sept 17, 1837, d June 21,
1846.
VI. John D. Shantz, b in Wilmot twp. Ont. Canada,
Oct 4, 1839, m Elizabeth Steiner Feb 13, 1866. She
was b Dec 12, 1840, d June 24, 1901. P O Baden, Ont.
Farmer, Menn. He was ordained deacon June 8,
1879. C: Steiner, Lydia, Ezra, Annie, Sarah,
Tobias, Elizabeth, John, Mary, Barbara.
VII. Steiner Shantz, b Oct 20, 1866. Resides in
Manitoba.
VII. Lydia Shantz, b Jan 24, 1868, d Jan 28, 1872.
VII. Ezra S. Shantz, b Sept 12, 1869, m Anna
Loucks Feb 19, 1892. P O Wakarusa, Ind. Farm-
er. Menn. C: (**VIII**) John Henry Shantz, b Oct 18,
1894. Catharine Elizabeth Shantz, b Mar 7, 1897.
Elmer Oszer Shantz, b Oct 14, 1898.
VII. Annie S. Shantz, b July 25, 1871. Menn. S.
VII. Sarah Shantz, b Jan 18, 1873. Menn. S.
VII. Tobias Shantz, b Oct 18, 1874. Menn. S.
VII. Elizabeth Shantz, b Aug 3, 1876. Menn. S.
VII. John Shantz, b Dec 18, 1879. Menn.
VII. Maryan Shantz, b Oct 7, 1881. Menn.
VII. Barbara S. Shantz, still-born, Nov 23, 1885.

VI. Enoch D. Shantz, b Aug 6, 1848, m Catharine Ruedich. She d--. C: John, William, Abraham, Josiah, Philip. Enoch m second wife, Angeline Shoemaker. P O Walkerton, Ont. C: Maude, Selina, Goodwin.

VI. Magdalena Shantz, b Mar 26, 1843. P O Breslau, Ont. S.

VI. Menno D. Shantz, b Nov 3, 1844, m Elizabeth Histand Dec 30, 1873. She was b Oct 6, 1846. P O Baden, Ont. Engineer in Grist mill. C: (**VII**) Harvey D. Shantz, b Nov 10, 1877, d June 22, 1878. Amanda May Shantz, b Apr 12, 1879. Catharine Elizabeth Shantz, b Mar 22, 1881, d Mar 19, 1895. Mary Ellen Shantz, b Oct 13, 1891.

VI. Susanna Shantz, b Mar 8, 1847, d Oct 27, 1886, m David Devitt Dec 15, 1879. P O Breslau, Ont. Farmer, Menn. C: Isaiah, Jeremiah.

VII. Isaiah Devitt, b Dec 26, 1881.

VII. Jeremiah Devitt, b Feb 24, 1886, d Sept 1, 1886.

VI. Lydia Shantz, b Apr 11, 1849, m Daniel Hostetler. P O Wyandotte, Ont. Farmer. C: Mary, Emma, Minerva, Maranda, Hannah, Rebecca, Ella.

VI. Nancy D. Shantz, b Mar 15, 1851, m John S. Shantz Jan 29, 1873. He was b Dec 4, 1846. P O Berlin, Ont. Farmer. C: Alvin, Susanna, Linnie, Anson, Annetta, Laurena.

VI. Sarah D. Shantz, b in Wilmot twp. Ont. June 3, 1853, m Isaac C. Shantz Feb 28, 1874. P O Breslau, Ont. Farmer, Menn. C: Norman, Edwin, Luanna, Mary, Edith, Sylvina, Sarah, Laura.

VII. Norman Shantz, b Jan 23, 1875, d Apr 28, 1890.

VII. Edwin Shantz, b Mar 28, 1876, m June 4, 1902. P O Breslau, Ont. Miller.

VII. Luanna Shantz, b Oct 15, 1878, m Simon Baer Sept 17, 1902. P O Manheim, Ont. Farmer.

VII. Mary A. Shantz, b Feb 9, 1882. S.

VII. Edith Shantz, b Feb 10, 1884. S.

VII. Sylvina Shantz, b July 7, 1887, d July 17, 1901.

VII. Sarah Shantz, b Aug 10, 1890, d Aug 13, 1890.

VII. Laura May Shantz, b Sept 12, 1892.

V. Rev. Enoch Detweiler, b in Bucks Co. Pa. Mar 7, 1818, d Sept 18, 1874, m Abigail Bechtel Jan 18, 1842. She was b in Montg. Co. Pa. Oct 8, 1821. In 1822 he came with his parents to Canada. When a young man he joined the Menn·mite church, and June 5, 1859, he was ordained to the ministry. In all his sermons he urged holiness of life. C: Mary, Jacob, George, Susanna, Leah, Aaron, Hannah, Noah, Daniel, Sarah.

VI. Mary Detweiler, b June 29, 1843, m Samuel Hoch. P O Blair, Ont., Farmer. C: (**VII**) Ezra, (d); Ephraim, Maggie, Maria, Almeda, (d); Eliza, Daniel.

VI. Rev. Jacob B. Detweiler, b Oct 6, 1844, m Harriet Shantz Mar 18, 1866. P O Didsbury, Alberta, N. W. T. Canada. Farmer, later employed in Button works, Berlin, Ont. In 1880 entered the ministry of Mennonite Brethren in Christ, served as pastor of Nottawasaga Mission until Mar 1883, then Berlin circuit two years, after which he was appointed Editor of Gospel Banner and Evangelium Banier by the General Conference for three years. After serving various other charges, in May, 1894, he moved to Didsbury, Alberta, N. W. T. Canada, where he is engaged in Mission work. His labors in the ministry have been eminently successful in bringing many souls to Christ. No issue.

VI. Rev. George B. Detweiler, b Jan 6, 1847, m Harriet Lyson of Royers Ford, Pa. Nov 27, 1870. P O Sherkton, Ont. When 18 he taught school, afterwards engaged in farming. Some years ago he was ordained to the ministry of the River Brethren church, in which calling he has proved to be very successful. C: Emma, Lyson, Henrietta, Irene, Abigail, George.

VII. Emma Detweiler, b Oct 12, 1870, m Frank Cushman Dec 25, 1893. P O Sherkton, Ont. Clerk.

VII. Lyson Detweiler, b June 6, 1872.

VII. Henrietta Detweiler, b May 14, 1874, m B. O. Saylor Dec 25, 1900. P O Sherkton, Ont. Farmer, Presby.

VII. Irene Detweiler, b Aug 12, 1878, d Oct 18, 1882.

VII. Anna Abigail Detweiler, b Mar 17, 1882.

VII. George Leslie Detweiler, b Apr 28, 1885.

VI. Susanna Detweiler, b Mar 22, 1849, m Abraham Kinzie Mar 8, 1868. P O Roseville, Ont. Farmer, Menn. C: Oliver, Henry, Ellen, Clara, Ira, Eden.

VII. Oliver Kinzie, b Mar 16, 1869, m Selena C. Bowman Mar 8, 1898. P O Blenheim, Ont. Commercial traveler, Meth. C: (**VIII**) Belle Beatrice Kinzie, b Sept 20, 1899.

VII. Henry Kinzie, b Mar 2, 1871. P O Roseville, Ont. Farmer.

VII. Ellen Kinzie, b Aug 14, 1874.

VII. Clara Kinzie, b June 24, 1876, m Norman B. Snyder Dec 25, 1895. P O Didsbury, Alberta, Canada. Farmer. C: (**VIII**) Olive Pearl Snyder, b May 28, 1897. Verdella Snyder, b Sept 10, 1901,

VII. Ira Kinzie, b June 24, 1879. Farmer.

VII. Enden Kinzie, b Mar 15, 1886. Traveler.

VI. Leah Detweiler, b Apr 28, 1851, d Oct 29, 1854.

VI. Aaron B. Detweiler, b May 24, 1853, m Elizabeth, daughter of John Z. and Magdalena (Schlichter) Detweiler. She was b May 26, 1853. P O Roseville, Ont. Farmer. C: (**VII**) Ida, John, Naomi, Norman, Orpha, Elma, Bessie.

VI. Hannah Detweiler, b Dec 17, 1855, m David Huber. P O Berlin, Ont. Photographer. C: Julian, Herbert, Idessa, Alberta.

VI. Noah B. Detweiler, b at Roseville, Ont. June 3, 1858, m Mary, daughter of Jacob Y. and Nancy (Brubaker) Shantz, Dec 14, 1880. She was b May 9, 1859. Res. Buffalo, N. Y. Engaged in the Button business. Christian Alliance. C: (**VII**) Eldon Detweiler, b May 10, 1885. Lenora Detweiler, b May 7, 1887. Lizzie Detweiler, b May 22, 1889. Ethel Detweiler, b Sept 3, 1890.

VI. Daniel B. Detweiler, b Apr 10, 1850, m Amanda Albright. She was b May 19, 1854, d Sept 11, 1893. P O Berlin, Ont. Agent for J. Y. Shantz & Son Button Co. C: (**VII**) Bertha May Detweiler.

Milton Detweiler.   George Franklin Detweiler.

VI. Sarah Detweiler, b Jan 17, 1866.   P O Berlin, Ont.   Resides with her brother, Daniel, and is single.

V. Abraham Detweiler, b July 25, 1820, d infant.

V. Lydia Detweiler, b Aug 22, 1824, m Philip Doerr Mar 2, 1856.   P O Marion, Kan.   Retired farmer. C: Jonathan, Mary, Catharine, Lydia.

VI. Jonathan Doerr, b July 13, 1857.

VI. Mary Doerr, b Aug 5, 1859.

VI. Catharine Doerr, b Apr 13, 1861.

VI. Lydia Doerr, b Aug 16, 1863.

DESCENDANTS OF GERTRUDE ROSENBER-GER, DAUGHTER OF BENJAMIN ROSENBERGER, SR.

III. Gertrude Rosenberger, m *Jacob Landis, Jr. of Franconia. Farmer and Miller, Menn. C: Magdalena, etc.

IV. Magdalena Landis, b about 1757, m Abraham Nice. He was b Jan 8, 1756, d Apr 28, 1818. Farmer and Miller, Menn. C: John, Abraham, Jacob, George, William, Philip, Joseph, Cathariue, Tobias, Henry.

V. John Nice, b 1777, m Catharine R. Price. C:

VI. Elizabeth Nice, b 1804, m John Hagey.

VI. Catharine Nice, b 1806, m Henry Shugard.

VI. Leana Nice, b 1808, m Wm. Jacobs.

VI. Abraham Nice, b 1810, m Mary Price.

VI. Ann Nice, b 1814, m Wm. Haney.

VI. John Nice, b 1816, m Salome Cressman.

VI. Rev. Wm. Nice, b 1822, m Sarah Hagey.

VI. Deborah Nice, b—, m John Jamison.

---

*Son of Jacob Landis, pioneer who settled in Franconia twp. where he purchased a tract of land on the Indian Creek containing 187 acres, Dec 26, 1727, from Derick Johnson. In 1734 Jacob Landis received a patent from the proprietary government for a tract of 150 acres northwest of Morwood. Here he built a mill, long known as Nice's, later Koffel's mill. The land containing 113 acres belonging to the farm with messuage, gristmill, dam, race, water right, ponds, and all belonging thereto were granted by Jacob Landis, Sr. and wife Mary to their son Jacob Landis Dec 28, 1772. On March 30, 1784, Jacob Landis, Jr. and wife, Gertrude, conveyed the farm of 101 acres and mill to Abraham Nice, who was married to Magdalena Landis.

DESCENDANTS OF ELIZABETH ROSENBER-
GER, DAUGHTER OF BENJAMIN
ROSENBERGER, SR.

III. Elizabeth Rosenberger, b Feb 7, 1748, d Aug 7, 1823, aged 75. 5, 28; m *John Alderfer, of Lower Salford. He was b Feb 8, 1745, d Dec 19, 1820, aged 75, 10, 11. C: Ann, Benjamin, Fred-. erick, Mary, Joseph, Abraham, Elizabeth, John.

IV. Ann Alderfer, b Mar 13, 1769, d May 17, 1861, aged 92, 2, 4, m †Henry Lederach. He was b Jan 8, 1765, d Sept 4, 1841. They lived on the Skippack road in Worcester township about a half mile above Wentz's church, where they owned a large farm. C: Elizabeth, Mary, Catharine, Ann, Susanna, Henry.

V. Elizabeth Lederach, b Jan 11, 1790, d Mar 26, 1876, m John C. Moyer. He was b Jan 11, 1790, d Feb 7, 1851. Farmer, Menn. C: Benjamin, Henry, Jacob, Joseph, Mary, Elizabeth, Katie, Sarah, Susanna.

VI. Benjamin Moyer, b Nov 16, 1815, m Hannah Appenzeller Mar 3, 1839. She was b Feb 6, 1812, d Oct 14, 1889. P O Souderton, Farmer and laborer, Mr. M. Menn., Mrs. M. Ref. Ch. C: Annie, Catharine, William.

VII. Annie Moyer, b Aug 4, 1840. S.

VII. Catharine Moyer, b Sept 29, 1843, m Levi Nace. P O Souderton, Pa. Cigar-maker; Mr. Nace, Luth; Mrs. Nace, Ref. Ch. C: Emma, Jacob, William, Hannah, Maria, Nora, Milton, Alfred, Infant, Alice.

---

*Son of Frederick Alderfer, who was b in the Palatinate, Germany, May 18, 1715; emigrated to America, arriving in the ship Samuel, Aug 11, 1732; was a redemptioner to Hans Klemmer who paid his passage over. Hans Klemmer died; Alderfer had served his full time, and in 1738, Frederick Alderfer married the widow Klemmer (Nee Anna Detweiler).

†Grandson of Pioneer Andrew Lederach.

VIII. Emma M. Nace, b Nov 10, 1865. Ref. Ch.
VIII. Jacob M. Nace, b June 22, 1867. Baker, Luth.
VIII. William M. Nace, b Oct 15, 1869, m Sallie K. Allebach. She d Dec 31, 1892. Teamster, Luth.
C: **(IX)** Melvin Nace, b July 12, 1890.
VIII. Hannah M. Nace, b July 24, 1871, m Samuel H. Freed. Luth. C: **(IX)** Estella Freed b July 12, 1891.
VIII. Maria M. Nace, b Dec 24, 1873, d June 9, 1874.
VIII. Elnora Nace, b Aug 14, 1875. Luth.
VIII. Milton Nace, b Feb 11, 1878.
VIII. Alfred Nace, b Jan 28, 1880.
VIII. Alice Nace, b Dec 4, 1882.
VII. William H. Moyer, b —, m Amanda Leidy, (d). C: Nelson, Harvey. William m second wife, Maria Heaney, (Nee Scholl). C: Ida, Miriam, Lavina, etc.
VI. Henry Moyer, d infant.
VI. Jacob Moyer, m Anna Benner. C: Hannah, Mary, Gideon, (d).
VI. Joseph Moyer, d 1871, m Barbara Barns. C: Milton, William.
VI. Mary Moyer, m Moses Kulp, (d). C: John, Elizabeth, Veronica, Anna, Mary, Amanda, Isaac.
VII. John M. Kulp, m Sarah Rosenberger. P O Dublin, Pa. C: Leidy, etc.
VII. Elizabeth Kulp, d Single.
VII. Veronica Kulp, m Henry Kulp. No issue.
VII. Anna Kulp, d Mar 11, 1875, m Rudolph H. Moyer. C: Emma, Allen, (d); Elizabeth, Ellen, Leidy, (d).
VII. Mary Ann Kulp, m Rudolph H. Moyer. No issue.
VII. Amanda Kulp, m Christian M. Hockman.
VII. Isaac Kulp, d infant.
VI. Elizabeth Moyer, (d); m John Clemens. C: Amos, (d), Susanna.
VI. Sarah Moyer, b —, d —, m Henry F. Myers.
VI. Susanna Moyer, d infant.
V. Mary Lederach, m John Bergey. C: Henry, Anna, Mary.

VI. Henry L. Bergey, d Aug 7, 1900, m Hannah Keyser.

VI. Anna L. Bergey, m Abraham Kriebel.

VI. Mary L. Bergey, d young.

V. Catharine Lederach, m Christian Dettera.

V. Ann Lederach, b—, d 1868, m David Kratz. Farmer, Menn. C: Henry, William.

V. Susanna Lederach, m Joseph Heebner. C: Henry, Enoch.

V. Henry Lederach, m Lydia Hendricks. No issue.

IV. Benjamin Alderfer, b Oct 3, 1771, d June 18, 1840, Elizabeth Shoemaker. She was b Oct 1, 1772, d Nov 17, 1840. C: Michael, John, Anna, Elizabeth.

V. Michael Alderfer, m Kate Ziegler. Farmer, Menn. C: Michael, Benjamin, Elizabeth, Anna.

VI. Michael Alderfer, d young.

VI. Benjamin Z. Alderfer, b June 5, 1831, d July 31, 1899, m Sarah Harley. He was one of the most prominent citizens of his township. He died from effects of injury received in the railroad wreck at Exeter, Pa. May 12, 1899. C: Clayton, Mrs. J. Horace Ziegler, Mrs. M. B. Rosenberger, Milton, Ella, (d).

VI. Elizabeth Alderfer, (d), m Christian Alleback.

VI. Anna Alderfer.

V. John S. Alderfer, m Hannah Grater. C: Abraham.

VI. Abraham Alderfer, m—— Freyer. P O Lederachville, Pa.

V. Anna Alderfer, b Sept 21, 1795, d Sept 12, 1884, m Isaac Kratz May 9, 1816. He was b Nov 19, 1791, d Jan 23, 1873. Farmer in Lower Salford. Menn. C: Benjamin, John, Mary, Michael, Isaac, Elizabeth, Annie.

VI. Benjamin A. Kratz, b Jan 12, 1817, d Sept 16, 1860. S.

VI. John Kratz, b Nov 9, 1819, m Margaret Oberholtzer Dec 3, 1848. P O Elroy, Pa. Farmer. C: Levi, Isaac, Lizzie, Mary.

VI. Mary K. Kratz, b Dec 14, 1821, m Dr. Henry Kratz Feb 11, 1844. He was b Mar 9, 1817, d Oct 13, 1889. Teacher, later farmer, Menn. C:

Michael, Isaac, William, Henry.

VI. Michael A. Kratz, b Dec 23, 1824, m Julian Klein Dec 9, 1847. P O Green Lane, Pa. Farmer and Miller. C: Annie, Lizzie, Morris, Katie.

VI. Isaac Kratz, b Sept 9, 1829, d Nov 28, 1871, m Catharine Klein Jan 12, 1851. Menn. C: Senorah, Sallie.

VI. Elizabeth Kratz, b June 27, 1835, m John K. Shutt Jan 1, 1859. P O Harleysville, Pa. Miller, Menn. C: Andora, Alonzo, Jacob.

VI. Annie Kratz, b Dec 21, 1830, m Henry Quillman Dec 14, 1859. He was b Dec 14, 1836, d Sept 30, 1875. C: Amelia, Warren, Anna. Annie m second husband, Jacob Kenton, (d). No issue.

V. Elizabeth Alderfer, b in Lower Salford, Montg. Co. Pa. Nov 16, 1798, m Rev. Abraham Hunsicker May 30, 1816. He was b in Skippack twp. Montg. Co. July 31, 1793, d at Collegeville, Pa. Jan 12, 1872. He was a grandson of Valentine Hunsicker, probably the progenitor of all of the name in Montg. Co., who came to American in 1717. and about 1720 settled in what was then called Van Bebber, since Skippack, and now East Perkiomen Township. The next generation in the direct line was Henry Hunsicker, who was a noted Mennonite Bishop, and preached 54 years. He was the parent of Rev. Abraham Hunsicker, the subject of this sketch. His ancestors being followers of Menno Simon, a plain unworldly sect, most of whom grew up to look upon a liberal education ''as of the world.'' Abraham Hunsicker enjoyed but the most limited educational advantages. When grown up he felt the disadvantages of the want of Scholastic training, and being of a strong natural endowment, early conceived the idea of reforming his religious brethren in reference to that subject. He was ordained a minister of the Mennonite church Jan 1, 1847, and soon after was elected a Bishop. About that time a Schism occurred in the Mennonite body, and Rev. Mr. Hunsicker was seperated from ''the old school.'' In 1851 a second divission took place, when he set about organizing a society. He issued a pamphlet

Hon. A. Henschen

entitled a "Statement of Facts and Summary of views on Morals and Religion as related with Suspension from the Mennonite meeting." A copy of said Pamphlet may be seen in the rooms of the Historical Society of Penna.

About the time of his ordination, (1847), as Bishop of the Mennonites in the district of Skippack Providence, and Methatchen, he conceived the idea in connection with his son Henry A. Hunsicker of founding a Boarding School to furnish his people better means of education. This was accomplished in 1848 by the erection of the extensive building now occupied by Ursinus College. In 1851, in conjunction with Prof. J. W. Sunderland he founded Montgomery Female Institute, afterward Pennsylvania Female College. These proceeding in the cause of education and other liberal views held by Mr. Hunsicker, led to division in the Mennonite body in the locality, and he proceeded at once to organize Trinity Christian Church. The church was built in 1853. Several years later another church was built at Skippackville. He was of a humane and practically benevolent nature and dispensed freely what he had to help the poor and labored long and hard to establish through the church a fund for the poor. Practical religion born of love and good will to all was preeminently his, and that which he labored to establish. He was an advocate of free Communion among Evangelical Sects, and set the example in the church to which he ministered. He wore the plain Mennonite garb while he lived, but was not prepossessed in its favor, holding the view that attire is a thing of religious liberty. He followed the teachings of the Divine Word as he understood them. He was of a mild and generous nature, and yet firm and uncompromising in what he regarded as vital; so he may be set down as one of the genuine reformers of our day. In person he was tall and stoutly built, weighing over two hundred pounds, with a face expressive of honesty, force and resolution; his forehead was massive and his temperament bilious—sanguine, indicating power and endurance, his complexion was

dark but ruddy: he enjoyed good health as a con-
sequence of a strong constitution, vivacious spirits
and temperate living; he was eminently social, finding
enjoyment in the company of young and old alike
and ever giving good advice and counsel to all.   Mrs.
Hunsicker was a great granddaughter of pioneer
Frederick Alderfer, who was born in the Palatinate,
Germany, May 18, 1715, and emigrated to America,
arriving Aug 11, 1832. Mrs. Hunsicker's 99th. birthday anniversary was celebrated at her home in Collegeville, Pa. on the 16th. of November 1897, by a
large gathering of her descendants.   She died in
1897, in her 100th. year.   C: Ann, Benjamin, Esther, Henry, Abraham, Elizabeth, Elias, Mary,
Kate, Horace.

VI. Ann Hunsicker, b July 5, 1817, d Dec 13, 1897,
m John B. Landis.   C: Elizabeth, Mary, Esther,
Hannah, Abraham, Horace, Annie, Elias, Kate,
Benjamin, Henry, Josephine, Lincoln.

VII. Elizabeth Landis, b 1838, m Daniel D. Bechtel.
C: Henry, John.

VII. Mary H. Landis, b 1840, m Samuel M. Markley Dec 1, 1859.   P O Trappe, Pa.   Farmer, Ger.
Bap.   C: Elias, John, Catharine, Jacob.

VII. Esther Landis. S.

VII. Hannah Landis, m Charles M. Hunsicker.   C:
Sheridan, Henry, ———, Annie, Clayton.

VII. Abraham H. Landis, m —— Hallman.

VII. J. Horace Landis, m Lizzie Kratz.

VII. Annie Landis, d young.

VII. Elias Landis, d young.

VII. Kate Landis, b at Graters Ford, Pa. Sept 15,
1850, m James A. Harley Jan 1, 1876.   Res. 1848,
N. 23rd St. Philadelphia, Pa.   Ger. Bap.   C: (**VIII**)
Elmer Lemuel Harley, b Apr 9, 1877, d Feb 24, 1880.
John Warren Harley, b May 26, 1879, d July 10,
1883.   Jacob Linwood Harley, b Dec 1, 1881. Salesman, Ger. Bap.   Clarence Wilbur Harley, b May 1,
1888.

VII. Bejamin Franklin Landis, b May 3, 1852, m
Lillie R. daughter of Charles Y. Heckler, Mar 20,
1877.   She d Mar 17, 1893, aged about 34 years.

Res. 2611. Neff St. Philadelphia, Pa. Foreman with
M. L. Shoemaker & Co., Fertilizers Oil, Meth. Ep.
C: (**VIII**) Benjamin Franklin Landis, b Feb 20, 1878.
Lillie Mabel Landis, b July 8, 1883.   Sarah Eva
Landis, b Apr 8, 1887, d Oct 21, 1887.
VII. Henry H. Landis, m —— Longacre. P O
Graters Ford, Pa.
VII. Josephine Landis, b June 9, 1860, m Peter C.
Fritz May 9, 188). P O Royersford, Pa. Hosiery
Mfg. Meth. Ep. No issue.
VII. A. Lincoln Landis, b—. S.
VI. Benjamin A. Hunsicker. b Nov 13, 1819, d
Mar 25, 1855, m Hannah Detweiler in 1841. C:
Elizabeth.
VII. Elizabeth B. Hunsicker, b Apr 23, 1843, d in
California, m Henry H. Grobb, (d). C: William.
Elizabeth m second husband, Mark D. Bechtel.
VIII. William Henry Grobb. Res. San Francisco,
Cal.
VI. Esther Hunsicker, b Jan 3. 1822, m Abraham
Detweiler, (d). C: Christian, Elizabeth.   Esther
m second husband, Gideon Fetterolf. He d 1894.
C: Abraham, Gideon, Curtin, Horace.
VII. Christian H. Detweiler, d aged 12 yrs.
VII. Elizabeth Detweiler, d young.
VII. Abraham D. Fetterolf, b June 4, 1850, m
Sallie E. Graybill May 23, 1872. She d in 1889.
C: Harry, Ada, Clement, Horace. Abraham m
second wife, Bertha, daughter of Rev. John R.
Kooken, 1901. P O Collegeville, Pa. In Coal &
Ice business in Phila. Ref. Ch. Mr. Fetterolf
completed his education at Freeland Seminary(now
Ursinus College) then under the principalship of his
brother, Dr. A. H. Fetterolf. At 16 years of age
he taught in the public schools of Berks and Montg.
counties for five years.   In 1871 he engaged in
mercantile pursuits in Philadelphia, being first employed as a lumber inspector, and subsequently, under
the firm of Fetterolf & Rosenberger, was engaged in
the flour and feed business on Market St.   He remained here in business until 1884.   From 1888 to
1890 he was a member of the firm of the Roberts

Machine Company, of Collegeville, Pa., taking charge of its finances and general business. Mr. Fetterolf has held a number of public positions. He has always been a staunch Republican, and has taken great interest in local and state elections. In 1882 he was elected Justice of the Peace for the township of Upper Providence, and re-elected in 1887, but later resigned to accept a County office. As Justice of the Peace, he enjoyed the confidence of the people, and did quite an extensive business. During the time he acted in many trust capacities, settling a large number of estates of decedents and assigned estates, in all which he displayed signal ability. He was Deputy Clerk of the Courts of Montgomery County from 1891 until he resigned to accept a more responsible position in the House of Representatives, at Harrisburg. In 1885 he made his first appearance in the House of Representatives in the position of Transcribing Clerk. His ability and faithfulness in this position was such that at the following session he was promoted to the position of Speaker's Clerk, and so served during the session of 1887. During the session of 1889 he was again promoted, this time to the position of Journal Clerk. During the session of 1891 he was filling his position as Clerk of the Courts, and therefore was not in Harrisburg. In 1893 Mr. Fetterolf again received an appointment in the House of Representatives for a still more responsible position, that of Resident Clerk, and later was elected Chief Clerk.

In 1892 Mr. Fetterolf was unanimously elected Chairman of the Republican County Committee of Montgomery Co. and conducted the campaign of that year and the following year so successfully as to elect the entire ticket with a single exception. In this position he developed great executive ability, and demonstrated his shrewdness as a political organizer. In 1893 he was appointed Secretary of the State Republican Committee, in which position he served two years and was elected for a third term. In this position he has performed valuable services for his party.

Mr. Fetterolf has been Secretary for the Perkio-

men Valley Mutual Fire Insurance Company since
July 1889. Ref. Ch. C:

VIII. Harry Fetterolf, d infant.

VIII. Ada Gertrude Fetterolf, d 1877. aged 4 yrs.

VIII. Clement G. Fetterolf, d Feb 20, 1899, aged
20 years.

VIII. Horace M. Fetterolf, b 1885. Student at University of Penna., (1905).

VII. Gideon Fetterolf, b and d 1860.

VII. Curtin Fetterolf, b Oct 15, 1860, m Maude
Kellum Nov 7, 1888.   She d Feb 21, 1891.   C:
Dorothy.   Curtin m second wife, Lella A. de la
Mesa Nov 19, 1895.   Res. New York City.   Freight
Agent of White Star Line and Red Star Line Steam-
ers.   Ger. Ref.   C: **(VIII)** Dorothy Fetterolf, b Feb
7, 1891.   Carlos Fetterolf, b Oct 17, 1896.

VII. Horace G. Fetterolf, b Feb 20, 1863, m Anna
S. Holdzkom Apr 10, 1888.   P O Ambler, Pa.
Cashier, Presby.   C: **(VIII)** Morton H. Fetterolf, b
June 9, 1889.   Mildred E. Fetterolf, b Sept 11, 1893.
Allen C. Fetterolf, b July 2, 1895.

VI. Rev. Henry A. Hunsicker, b in Montg. Co.
Pa. Nov 10, 1825, m Mary S. Weinberger Aug 23,
1849.   She was b Jan 31, 1830, d May 7, 1874.
C: Clement, Joseph, Abraham, Flora, Alvin.
Henry m second w fe, Annie C. Gotwals, May 11,
1876. Res. 902 Chelten Ave. Philadelphia, Penn.
C: Mary, Edna.

Mr. Hunsicker spent his boyhood days on his
father's farm, and had only the limited advantages
of the country schools of that time.   In 1835 Henry
Prizer opened a boarding school in the village of
Trappe.   He died in 1838 and was succeeded in the
school by Rev. Henry S. Rodenbough.   This was
Mr. Hunsicker's Alma Mater.   In 1848 he and his
father founded "Freeland Seminary," an educational
institution designed for young men and boys.   He at
once became the principal of the school, and three
years later the proprietor.   He continued as Principal of this school until 1865, when he leased the
school and property to A. H. Fetterolf, one of his
assistants, for five years.   During the time of his

lease to Prof. F. he sold the school property to Rev. J. H. A. Bomberger, D. D., of Philadelphia, who, in connection with other enterprising persons, obtained a charter and founded Ursinus College. In 1850 Mr. Hunsicker was ordained to the ministry of the New(Oberholtzer) Mennonite Church. On account of the liberal and progressive ideas in church work, a chism took place in 1851, which resulted in establishing an independent church known as Trinity Christians, of which Mr. Hunsicker was one of the founders, and for which he continued to preach until 1875. He later connected himself with Presbyterian church, and is now a member of the Moravian church; the changes in his church relations were made on account of change of location.

VII. Clement W. Hunsicker, b May 29, 1851, m Lydia Miller Mar 1873. She d Apr 1891. C: Mamie, Alice, Irma. Clement m second wife, Flora Smith May 29, 1895. No issue. Res. Denver, Colo. Real Estate Broker.

VIII. Mamie E. Hunsicker, b Dec 18, 1874, m George Fischer Oct 1892. P O Great Falls, Mon. C: (**IX**) Dorothy Fischer, b 1894.

VIII. Alice Hunsicker, d young.

VIII. Irma Rosalind, b Nov 1881. P O North Wales, Pa.

VII. Joseph Henry Hunsicker, b Aug 16, 1853, d Oct 16, 1880, m Fannie Rutherford in 1875. She d Mar 1881. C: (**VIII**) Alfred R. Hunsicker, b Apr 22, 1877. Aida Hunsicker, b Dec 20, 1879.

VII. Abraham Lincoln Hunsicker, b Apr 8, 1856, d Feb 23, 1874, from accidental shooting.

VII. Flora G. Hunsicker, b in Collegeville, Pa. Dec 20, 1858, m Dr. James H. Hamer May 15, 1879. P O Collegeville, Pa. Physician, Ger. Ref. C: (**VIII**) Bertha Hamer, b May 29, 1880. Fannie Hamer, b Nov 10, 1881. Carrie Hamer, b Aug 18, 1885, d May 13, 1892. James H. S. Hamer, b Nov 28, 1890. Caroline Cecelia Hamer, b Jan 16, 1893. Harold Hamer, b Sept 12, 1900. Ethel Hamer, b Aug 11, 1902.

VII. Alvin Hunsicker, b Sept 20, 1864, m Helen T.

Boice June 19, 1889. Res. New York. Secretary of Standard Oil Cloth Co. 320 Broadway, New York City. Presby. No issue.

VII. Mary Anna Hunsicker, b Sept 25, 1879. Res 902 Chelten Ave. Phila. Pa. S.

VII. Edna E. Hunsicker, l. July 6, 1882. Res. 902 Chelten Ave. Phila. Pa. S.

VI. Abraham Hunsicker, b Jan 8, 1829. d 1890, m Rachel Rittenhouse. C: Annie, Mary, Newton, Abraham, Alice, Susan.

VII. Annie Hunsicker, (d); m Newton Wanner. C: Grace, Lillie, Abraham, Herbert.

VII. Mary L. Hunsicker, (d); m Rev. Abraham B. Markley. C: Mary, Alice, Florence, and three d infants.

VII. Newton R. Hunsicker, (d); m Bessie D. Jones. C: Davis, Bertina, Garfield, (d); Rachel.

VII. Abraham R. Hunsicker, m—. C: Abraham.

VII. Alice Hunsicker, m Dr. John Niles. P O Carbondale, Pa. No issue.

VII. Susan Hunsicker, m Edward Laros.

VI. Elizabeth Hunsicker, b Aug 14, 1834, d—, m Rev. Francis R. S. Hunsicker, D. D. in 1853. He was a son of Henry D. and Catharine (Shoemaker) Hunsicker, and was b in Montg. Co. Pa. Mar 27, 1832. He worked on his father's farm until he was sixteen years old, when he taught Public School for two seasons, after which he was appointed assistant teacher in Common English in the Freeland Seminary—now Ursinus College—then under the Principalship of Rev. Henry A. Hunsicker. Here he spent about seven years, a close student and an enthusiastic teacher. He held the position of Professor of Mathematics and History and Vice Principal for several years, when he was called to Carversville, Pa. to organize the Excelsior Normal Institute. Here he was engaged in educational work from '59-'62 and '67-'84. He received the honorary degree of A. M. from LaFayette in 1869, and D. D. from Ursinus in 1883.

Dr. Hunsicker was ordained to the Gospel Ministery in the Trinity Christian (now Trinity

Reformed) Church at Collegeville, Pa. in 1857; was Pastor of the Reformed Mennonite church of Germantown. Pa. '62–-'66. In 1867 he united with the Presbytery of Philadelphia North. He was pastor of the Carversville and Plumsteadville Presbyterian churches, '70—'84. Pastor at Junction, N. J. '84—'87, and Lafayette, N. J. '87—'94, after which he retired from the active work of the ministery. His present residence is Carversville, Pa., where he resides retired. C: Emma, Katie, Lizzie, Hannah, Ettie, Claudia, Frank.

VII. Emma Hunsicker, b 1854, d 1858.

VII. Katie Hunsicker, b 1856, d 1859.

VII. Lizzie Hunsicker, b Jan 15, 1859, m Isaiah W. Closson in 1881. P O Carversville, Pa. Farmer; Mrs. C. Presby. C: (**VIII**) Newton Closson, b in 1885, d in 1892.

VII. Hannah Hunsicker, (twin), b in Montg. Co. Pa. Jan 15, 1859, m Winfield Scott Black Nov 2, 1881. P O Clinton, N. J. Merchant, Presby. No issue.

VII. Ettie Hunsicker, b 1862, m Willett D. Evans 1884. School-teacher, Presby. C: (**VIII**) Ava Gould Evans, b 1886. Francis H. Evans, b 1888.

VII. Claudia Hunsicker, b in Montg. Co. Pa. Aug 8, 1865, m William A. Reeves Apr 12, 1888. P O Clinton, N. J. Bank Teller, Presby. C: (**VIII**) Austin H. Reeves, b June 9. 1889. (**VIII**) Mabel Reeves, b Oct 10, 1890.

VII. Frank Hunsicker, b 1875, d in infancy.

VI. Elias A. Hunsicker, b in Montg. Co. Pa. Mar 28, 1834, m Susan F. Moyer Dec 25, 1855. Res. 1842 Master St. Phila. Pa. He was a grain merchant for 20 years opposite the Baltimore Depot, Broad St. Phila., at present, Life and Fire Insurance Agent; Presby. C: Ella, Clayton.

VII. Ella M. Hunsicker, b Feb 15, 1857. S.

VII. Clayton M. Hunsicker, b Mar 25. 1860, m Amelia Seigel, of Phila., Dec 5, 1893. Res. 2018 Master St. Phila. Pa. Life and Fire Insurance Agent. In 1891 he was elected to the Common Council of the Twenty-ninth Ward, and was re-

elected in 1895 to serve his third term. C: (**VII**)
Katharine S. Hunsicker, b Mar 7, 1895.
  VI. Mary A. Hunsicker. b in Montg. Co. Pa. Nov
6, 1836, m Rev. Jared T. Preston. He d 1877. P
O Collegeville. Pa. C: Cyrus, Frank, Lizzie.
  VII. Cyrus Preston, d young.
  VII. Frank Preston, m Lizzie Grater. C: Mary;
Frances, ——, (twins).
  VII. Lizzie Preston, b 1872, m Henry Spare. C:
(**VIII**) —— Spare.
  VI. Catharine Hunsicker, b Jan 9, 1840, m Rev.
Joseph H. Hendricks, D. D. Dec 21, 1858. He
was b in Montg. Co. Pa. Sept 21, 1834, d Nov
1905. P O Collegeville, Pa. Mr. Hendricks was
reared on his father's farm, and in the spring of
1851, entered Freeland Seminary, (now Ursinus
College), and in the fall of 1852, took charge of a
public school in Milford Square, Bucks County.
During the four consecutive winters he was a
teacher in the public schools; he attended Freeland
Seminary during the summer months. In February
1856 he was appointed to the position of assistant
teacher in Freeland Seminary, and in two years he
was promoted to teach the higher mathematics, and
wae made vice-principal of the instution. It was
while engaged in these duties that at a meeting of the
Christian Society, at Freeland, (now Ursinus College), held A. D. 1860, he was, according to the
usages of the church, of which he was a member,
elected on trial to the office of the ministery. He at
once began to attend the duties of his new position
in connection with his school work. On June 25,
1861, he was ordained to the office of minister of
the Gospel. The Christian Society materialized and
was incorporated in the Spring of 1855. The society
built for itself, in 1854, what was styled the
"Christian Meeting House," and the same was
opened in the spring of 1855 for public worship. In
February 1862, Mr. Hendricks was elected pastor of
the Christian Society, and was installed in April
1862. At this time the duties of this new office occupied so much of his time that he was compelled to

resign his position as teacher and vice-principal of
Freeland Seminary. The original Christian Society,
subsequently Trinity Church, began as an independ-
ent church in 1888, when it was received into formal
fellowship with the Reformed Church in the U. S.
The other appointments of the charge are: Trinity
Church, Skippackville; and Ironbridge Chapel,
Rahn Station.

Mr. Hendricks enjoyed the distinction of having
served the same charge longer than any other living
pastor in Montgomery Co. He officiated at upwards
1000 funerals. He was greatly beloved by his own
congregation and in much demand outside of his own
churches. He was a fluent and forcible preacher,
speaking entirely extempore, in a rapid, earnest and
convincing manner. In June 1881, Ursinus College
conferred on him the degree of M. A. and in June
1897, the degree of D. D. C: Lizzie, Ella, Bertha,
Abraham, Sallie.

VII. Lizzie Hendricks, b Feb 9, 1860, d Feb 29,
1860.

VII. Ella M. Hendricks, b Sept 4, 1861, m Freeland
G. Hobson Sept 15, 1881. P O Collegeville, Pa.
He was b at Collegeville, Pa. Oct 13, 1857, d Jan 10,
1906. He was educated in the public schools of Upper Providence twp subsequently took a full course
in and graduated from Ursinus College in 1876. He
then entered the law office of Jacob V. Gotwals, at
that time District Attorney of Montgomery Co., and
was admitted to the bar on Oct 1, 1880. He immediately opened an office in Norristown, where he
soon began to build up a lucrative practice, and
where he has remained ever since. He was an elo-
quent pleader, and was uniformly successful in the
trial of cases. In 1888 Mr. Hobson put on foot the
movement to organize the Norristown Title, Trust
and Safe Deposit Company, and was made its secretary, treasurer, and trust officer. He was also founder and publisher of the Montgomery County Law
Reporter and the author of the History of
Providence township, and was one of the contribu-
tors to Col. Bean's History of Montgomery County.

Mr. Hobson was a leader in the Patriotic Order Sons of America, and a member of camp 267 at Iron-bridge. In 1893 he was elected State President, and at the conclusion of his term at Erie, Pa. he was the happy recipient of a handsome cane made from the hull of the old flagship Lawrence. He was a prominent member of the Valley Forge Memorial Association and a director of Ursinus College, Collegeville, Pa. He was for eight years an elder of Trinity Reformed Church of Collegeville. He has been a delegate to the Classes, Synods, and General Synods of the Reformed Church in the United States, taking very active part in all these bodies. C: **(VIII)** Harold Hobson, b and d July 30, 1882. Frank H. Hobson, b Aug 19, 1883. Anna Mabel Hobson, b July 27, 1885. Katharine Hobson, b Apr 29, 1889.

VII. Bertha Hendricks, b June 24, 1864, m Rev. Charles E. Wehler Dec 18, 1889. P O Blue Bell, Pa. Both graduates of Ursinus College. She of the collegiate and he of the Theological Department. Pastor of Boehms Reformed Ch., Blue Bell, Pa. C: **(VIII)**. Catharine H. Wehler, b Aug 12, 1892.

VII. Abraham H. Hendricks, b Dec 21, 1866, m Ella T. Miller Oct 21, 1890. P O Collegeville, Pa. Graduated at Ursinus College, and subsequently studied Law and is now practicing at Norristown, Pa; Firm of Hendricks and Hobson, Trinity Christian Reformed Church. C: **(VIII)** Miraim Elizabeth Hendricks, b Jan 3, 1892.

VII. Sallie C. Hendricks, b July 17, 1873. Graduate of Ursinus College, Trinity Christian Reformed Church.

VI. Horace M. Hunsicker, b Feb 17, 1843, m Eliza Cosgrove. C: Rosaline, Alice, William.

VII. Rosaline Hunsicker, d aged 8 yrs.

VII. Alice Hunsicker; d young.

VII. William C. Hunsicker. Practicing Physician in Phila., Pa.

IV. Frederick Alderfer, b Nov 24, 1773, d Dec 9, 1854, aged 81 years, m Susanna Showalter. C: Elizabeth, Magdalena, John, Joseph. Frederick m second wife, Elizabeth Shutt, (widow), daughter of

David and Anna (Funk) Rosenberger. C: Barbara,
Frederick, Henry. Frederick m third wife, Anna
Frederick. C: Isaac.

V. Elizabeth Alderfer, b Jan 11, 1802, d Aug 12,
1878, m *David Kriebel Jan 14, 1819. He, was b
July 19, 1783, d July 1, 1842. Farmer, Schwenkfelders. C: Henry, Susanna, Magdalena, Septimus, Barbara, Hannah, Elizabeth.

VI. Henry Kriebel, b July 8, 1819, m Sarah Rahn.
C: Septimus, etc.

VI. Susanna A. Kriebel, b in Montg. Co. Pa. Mar
17, 1821, d Oct 17, 1895, m William S. Moyer July
11, 1847. He was b in Berks Co. Pa. Oct 13, 1824,
d Feb 10, 1896. P O Bally, Pa. Shoemaker; Mr.
M. Ev. Ass'n; Mrs. M. Menn. C: David, Septimus,
Daniel, Enos, William, Peter.

VII. David K. Moyer, b in Berks Co. Pa. Jan 8,
1848, m Mary A. Grove, daughter of George and
Nancy Grove, of Mt. Carroll, Ill. Feb 24, 1874.
She was b in Franklin Co. Pa. June 19, 1840, d in
Iowa Oct 23, 1878. P O Mt. Carroll, Ill. Cigarmaker; Ch. of Jesus Christ. C: (**VIII**) Grove Moyer,
b Apr 24, 1877. Otto B. and Warren O. Moyer,
(twins), b Oct 19, 1878. . David m second wife,
Josie M. Grove, (sister to his first wife), Jan 3,
1884. She was b Nov 24, 1848. No issue.

VII. Septimus K. Moyer, b June 10, 1849, d Aug
31, 1850.

VII. Daniel K. Moyer, b Mar 16, 1851, m Hannah,
daughter of Philip and Hannah Kriebel Mar 16,
1893. She was b in Montg. Co. Pa. Jan 4, 1854.
Res. 404 N. 7th St. Philadelphia, Pa. Driver and
Collector, Menn. No issue.

VII. Enos K. Moyer, b in Washington twp. Berks
Co. Pa. Nov 21, 1852. Res. 2558 Philadelphia St.
Phila. Pa. Carpenter. S.

VII. William K. Moyer, b Feb 25, 1855, d Feb 17,
1882, m Adelia Conrad Shiffert Nov 6, 1880. Painter. C: (**VIII**) Susan E. Moyer, b Feb 14, 1881.

VII. Peter K. Moyer, b in Washington twp. Berks

*Son of Andrew Kriebel, b Sept 17, 1748, d Apr 17, 1830, m
Susanna, daughter of Abraham Yeakel, May 16, 1771.

Co. Pa. June 9, 1859.   Res. 2558 Philadelphia St.
Phila. Pa. Clerk. S.
VI. Magdalena Kriebel, b Oct 21, 1822, m Isaac
Rahn.
VI. Septimus Kriebel, b Aug 3, 1825, d at North
Wales, Pa. Aug 12, 1898, m Susanna Schlotterer
Sept 23, 1851. She was b in Montg. Co. Pa. June
16, 1828. Merchant and Farmer, Schwenkfelders.
C: Henry, Emma, Franklin, Edwiu, William,
Mary, Septimus.
VII. Henry S. Kriebel, b in Montg. Co. Pa. Aug
7, 1852, m Lizzie A. Cassel July 22. 1871. P O
North Wales, Pa. Merchant and Farmer, Ref. Ch.
C: Septimus, Elias, Edna, Lizzie.
VIII. Septimus Kriebel, b Sept 23, 1874, m
Marion Lowery Oct 5, 1897. P O Charlotte, N. C.
Agt. for N. Y. Oil Firm, Ref. Ch. No issue, (1898).
VIII. Elias Wilbur Kriebel, b Dec 25, 1877. P O
North Wales, Pa. Ref. Ch. S.
VIII. Edna Kriebel, b Dec 6, 1883, d Dec 2, 1890.
VIII. Lizzie Irene Kriebel, b Sept 16, 1888.
VII. Emma Kriebel, b July 25, 1854. P O North
Wales, Pa. S.
VII. Franklin S. Kriebel, b July 14, 1857, m
Sallie A. Freed Nov 9, 1878. She was b Nov 9,
1859. P O North Wales, Pa. Member of firm E.
K. Freed & Co. Merchant Millers, Baptists. C:
(**VIII**) Russel Harper Kriebel, b. Dec 16, 1881.
Iona Freed Kriebel, b July 10, 1884, d Oct 17,
1884. Mabel Francis Kriebel, b Nov 18, 1886.
Irma F. Kriebel, b Feb 28, 1891.
VII. Edwin Kriebel, b Jan 27, 1860, d Apr 14, 1860.
VII. William Kriebel, b Feb 5, 1861, m Annie
Wright Nov 3, 1887.
VII. Mary Elizabeth Kriebel, b May 30, 1864.
P O North Wales, Pa. S.
VII. Septimus Kriebel, b Dec 26, 1866, m Mary
Mulholland June 28, 1893.
VI. Barbara Kriebel, b Sept 3, 1827, m Henry
Schultz. P O Clayton, Pa. C: Frank, etc.
VII. Frank K. Schultz. P O Clayton, Pa.
VI. Hannah Kriebel, b Jan 5, 1829, m John Stoudt.

VI. Elizabeth Kriebel, b Jan 18, 1832, m Jeremiah K. Meschter. C: Allen, etc.

V. Magdalena Alderfer, m Henry Landis.

V. John Alderfer, m——.

V. Joseph Alderfer, m——.

V. Barbara Alderfer, m Wm. Eisenberg.

V. Frederick Alderfer.

V. Henry Alderfer.

V. Isaac Alderfer.

IV. Mary Alderfer, b Feb 15, 1777, d June 1, 1857. Menn. S.

IV. Joseph Alderfer, b Oct 11, 1779, d Mar 6, 1863, m Hannah Kinsey. She d Sept 12, 1824, aged 48 years, 7 days. Farmer, Menn. C: Susanna, Mary, John, Jacob, Abraham, Hannah.

V. Susanna Alderfer, m Jacob Tyson. C: (**VI**) Joseph Tyson.

V. Mary Alderfer, b in 1806, d Feb 17, 1889, aged 83 years. Menn. S.

V. John Alderfer, b in Montg. Co. Pa. Sept 5, 1807, d Jan 10, 1884, m Eliza Detweiler Feb 1830. She was b Feb 1813, d June 28, 1889. Farmer, Menn. C: Mary, Elizabeth, Rebecca, Abraham, Daniel, John, Michael, Henry, Benjamin, Hannah, Clement.

VI. Mary D. Alderfer, b Dec 10, 1831, d Mar 30, 1853. S.

VI. Elizabeth D. Alderfer, b in Montg. Co. Pa., m Joseph B. Hunsberger of Chester Co. Pa. Jan 11, 1856. P O Yerkes, Pa. Farmer, Menn. C: John, Milton, Daniel, Ervin, Martin, Catharine, Franklin, William.

VII. John Hunsberger, b Jan 1, 1857, m Ursula Sherlie. P O Central City, Colo. Farmer. C: (**VIII**) Edna Hunsberger, b Mar 10, 1891. Fay Hunsicker, b Feb 18, 1893. Jay Hunsicker, b Nov 26, 1898.

VII. Milton Hunsberger, b Nov 2, 1858, d aged 13 years.

VII. Daniel Hunsberger, b Aug 31, 1860. He d at the age of 30 years, m Harriet Craton. C: (**VII**) Elizabeth Hunsberger. Arthur Hunsberger. Ervin

Hunsberger, b Feb 26, 1861, d aged 1 year.

VII. Jacob Martin Hunsberger, b Oct 3, 1863, m Emma Jones Jan 1, 1887. P O Creamery, Pa. Farmer, Menn. C: (**VIII**) George J. Hunsberger, b Dec 26, 1887. Joseph J. Hunsberger, b June 27, 1890. Roy Hunsberger, b Sept 30, 1892. Ada J. Hunsberger, b Sept 20, 1894. Susanna J. Hunsberger, b Dec 16, 1896,

VII. Catharine Hunsberger, b Nov 26, 1867, d aged 3 years.

VII. Franklin Hunsberger, b Feb 18, 1868, d aged 1 year.

VII. William Hunsberger, b Oct 4, 1872. P O Yerkes, Pa. S.

VI. Rebecca Alderfer, b in Montg. Co. Pa. Oct 13, 1835, d Aug 7, 1879, m William B. Fryer in 1857. He was b in Montg. Co. Pa. in 1834. Farmer, Luth. C: John, Benjamin, Harry.

VII. John A. Fryer, b in 1860.

VII. Benjamin A. Fryer, b Apr 24, 1863, m Laura Fisher Dec 26, 1882. She d Sept 18, 1889. No issue. He m second wife, Lovereen Clewell, in 1898. Res. Reading, Pa. Journalist, Ref. Ch.

VII. Harry A. Fryer, b in 1866, m Emma Allcock in 1893. P O Geneva, N. Y.

VI. Abraham D. Alderfer, b in Limerick twp. Montg. Co. Pa. Oct 3, 1837, m Mary Ann Rosenberger Apr 2, 1863. P O Royer's Ford, Pa. Steward Montg. Co. Alms House, Meth Ep. C: Annie, Elizabeth, Mary, Abraham.

VII. Annie Alderfer, b Oct 5, 1865, d Aug 27, 1867.

VII. Elizabeth Alderfer, b June 5, 1868, m Rev. A. P. Frantz June 10, 1896. P O Newlin, Pa. Minister of the Reformed Ch. C: (**VIII**) Mary A. Frantz, b Sept 17, 1897.

VII. Mary Alderfer, b Jan 12, 1871, d June 11, 1887.

VII. Abraham Alderfer, b Oct 18, 1872. P O Royer's Ford, Pa. Book-keeper and Stenographer for Diamond Glass Co. of Royer's Ford, Pa. S.

VI. Daniel D. Alderfer, m Sallie Fox.

VI. John D. Alderfer, b Sept 28, 1841, d Nov 2,

1897, m Annie Weikel. P O Trappe, Pa., C: Clement, Emma, John.

VI. Michael D. Alderfer, b Oct 9, 1842, d May 26, 1879, m Emma Hunsberger. No issue.

VI. Henry D. Alderfer, m Emma Rhoads. No issue.

VI. Benjamin D. Alderfer, b in Montg. Co. Pa. Mar 21, 1848, m Susan Frederick Feb 1, 1876. She died. C: J. Linwood. Benjamin m second wife, Mary Snovel, Sept 24, 1881. P O Souderton, Pa. Notary Public and general business Agt. Luth. No issue by 2nd marriage.

VII. J. Linwood Alderfer, b Aug 9, 1876. S.

VI. Hannah D. Alderfer, b in Montg. Co. Pa. Sept 4, 1850, m Rev, Henry Leisse Apr 8, 1873. P O Orwigsburg, Pa. Rev. Henry Leisse was b near Womelsdorf, Berks Co. Pa. Aug 16, 1844. He graduated from Ursinus College, at Collegeville, Pa. in June 1872, and immediately after was ordained and installed pastor of the Reformed Church of Orwigsburg, which he has faithfully and successfully served. C: (**VII**) Elizabeth Mary Leisse, b Sept 27, 1875, graduated from Orwigsburg High School in June 1893. Harry Ursinus Leisse, b Sept 14, 1877, graduated from the Orwigsburg High School, with first honors, in June 1894. He then entered Ursinus College, from which he graduated in June 1899. Augustus Leisse, b Jan 19, 1883. Katherine Valeria Leisse, b Nov 7, 1887. Ernest Leisse, b July 6, 1889.

VI. Clement D. Alderfer, b at Trappe, Montg. Co. Pa. Dec 9, 1853, m Emma S. Hunsberger Aug 10, 1880, (his brother Michael's widow). Res. 1711 Willington St. Phila. Pa. Collector and Real Estate business. Ref. Ch. No issue.

V. Jacob Alderfer, d Mar 1895, m Amelia R. Detweiler. She d in 1899. Farmer, Menn. C: Joseph, Henry, Mary, John, Elizabeth, Catharine, Sarah, Philip, Jacob, Garret, Samuel, Amanda.

VI. Joseph D. Alderfer, b Sept 22, 1833.

VI. Henry D. Alderfer, b Nov 29, 1834, d 1891, m Mary Hendrick. Ref. Ch. No issue.

VI. Mary D. Alderfer, b July 7, 1836, d young.

VI. John D. Alderfer, b Dec 24, 1837. P O Creamery, Pa.

VI. Elizabeth D. Alderfer, b Mar 3, 1840, d 1899, Jan 10, m Andrew B. Kriebel Sept 12, 1865. P O Kulpsville, Pa. Farmer, Schwenkfelders. C: Jacob, Anna, Howard, Henry, Andrew.

VII. Jacob A. Kriebel, b Jan 24, 1866, m Emma Jane Freyer. P O Klupsville, Pa. Farmer, Schwenkfelders. C: (**VIII**) William Kriebel, b Mar 16, 1890. Norman Kriebel, b June 28, 1893. Ralph Kriebel b July 13, 1896, d July 21, 1898.

VII. Anna A. Kriebel, b Aug 17, 1868, m Irwin L. Reiter Jan 13, 1894. P O Kulpsville, Pa. Farmer, Schwenkfelders. C: (**VIII**) Elizabeth K. Reiter, b May 17, 1897. Mary Reiter, b June 9, 1902.

VII. Howard A. Kriebel, b Feb 1, 1871, m Kate Landes. P O Klupsville, Pa.

VII. Henry A. Kriebel, b May 20, 1873, m Mary Moyer. P O Hoppenville, Pa.

VII. Andrew A. Kriebel, b Jan 10, 1879, m Ella Johnson.

VI. Catharine D. Alderfer, b Dec 27, 1841, m Jesse S. Whitman. P O Salford, Pa.

VI. Sarah D. Alderfer, b Aug 1844, m Josiah Markley. P O Skippackville, Pa.

VI. Philip D. Alderfer, b Sept 15, 1846, m Lizzie Ziegler. P O Akron, O.

VI. Jacob D. Alderfer, b Sept 18, 1848. Res. Denver, Colo.

VI. Garret D. Alderfer, b Oct 25, 1850, d 1895, m Susan Miller. Farmer, Menn.

VI. Samuel D. Alderfer, b Jan 10, 1853, d Mar 25, 1896, m Susanna Wismer Feb 17, 1877. Farmer, Menn. C: (**VII**) William Alderfer, (d), Jacob Alderfer. David Alderfer, (d).

VI. Amanda D. Alderfer, b Jan 6, 1855, d 1857.

V. Abraham Alderfer, m Catharine Rahn. C: Harrison, William, Isaac, Rachel, Jesse, Lizzie, Samuel, Sallie.

VI. Harrison Alderfer. P O Trappe, Pa.

VI. William Alderfer.

VI. Isaac Alderfer. P O Neiffers, Pa.

VI. Rachel Alderfer, b in Montg. Co. Pa. Oct 21, 1846, m Aaron Booz Nov 22, 1873. P O Royer's Ford, Pa. Carpenter, Luth. C: (**VII**) Anna Catharine Booz, b July 8, 1874. S. Edith May Booz, b May 23, 1882. S. Amanda M. Booz, b Apr 20, 1888.

VI. Jesse Alderfer.

VI. Lizzie Alderfer, m John Spreece.

VI. Samuel Alderfer.

VI. Sallie Alderfer, m Milton T. Miller.

V. Hannah Alderfer, m Philip Krieble. He d May 9, 1871, aged 55 years, 5 mo. 3d. C: Nathaniel, Elizabeth, Lavina, Susanna, Mary, Hannah, Amanda, John.

VI. Nathaniel Krieble, (d).

VI. Elizabeth Krieble, (d).

VI. Lavina Krieble, (d).

VI. Susanna Krieble. (d).

VI. Mary Krieble, m Noah C. Kratz. (See Noah C. Kratz Family).

VI. Hannah Krieble.

VI. Amanda Krieble, (d); m George Slotter.

VI. John Krieble, b—, m Sarah Grater. P O Creamery, Pa.

IV. Abraham Alderfer, b July 21, 1782, d May 27, 1865, aged 87 yrs. 10 mo. 6 da., m Susanna Shoemaker. She was b Mar 10, 1784, d Aug 31, 1823. C: Benjamin, Henry, Abraham, Susanna, Elizabeth. Abraham m second wife, Anna Keely. She was b Jan 12, 1804, d Nov 5, 1890. Farmer in Franconia twp. Menn. C: Jacob, John, Margaret.

V. Benjamin S. Alderfer, m Lana Nyce. C: Michael, Jonas, Abraham, Benjamin, Nancy, Susan.

VI. Michael N. Alderfer. P O Telford, Pa.

VI. Jonas N. Alderfer, (d); m Catharine Saylor. No issue.

VI. Abraham N. Alderfer. P O Rudy, Pa.

VI. Benjamin N. Alderfer.

VI. Nancy Alderfer, m Jacob S. Groff.

VI. Susan Alderfer, m Henry G. Metz.

V. Henry S. Alderfer, b in Montg. Co. 1811, d in

1876, m Sarah Swartley, daughter of Abraham Swartley. Farmer, Menn. C: Elizabeth, Abraham, Anna, Sarah, Samuel, Henry, Michael, Susan, Milton.

VI. Elizabeth S. Alderfer, b June 23, 1833, d Dec 30, 1898, m Abraham Gehman, (d). No living issue. She m second husband, Abraham F. Moyer. No issue.

VI. Abraham S. Alderfer, b Oct 29, 1835, d Jan 1, 1892, m Susan Hackman, (d). C: Edwin, Sallie.
VII. Edwin Alderfer. S.
VII. Sallie Alderfer, m Audrew Derstine. P O Sellersville, Pa.

VI. Anna S. Alderfer, b Nov 12, 1837, m Tobias K. Nyce. P O Souderton, Pa. C: Willa. John, Harvey, Katy, Ellen.

VI. Sarah S. Alderfer, b Feb 27, 1840. P O Souderton, Pa. Menn. S.

VI. Samuel S. Alderfer, b July 8, 1842, d Feb 3, 1843.

VI. Henry S. Alderfer, b Mar 14, 1844, m Sarah Detweiler Nov 20, 1869. P O Souderton, Pa. Hay Merchant, Menn. No issue.

VI. Michael S. Alderfer, b Oct 27, 1846, m Mary Orr. P O Sabetha, Kans.

VI. Susanna S. Alderfer, b Nov 21, 1849, d in 1852.
VI Milton S. Alderfer, b in Montg. Co. Pa. Mar 2, 1855, m Annie Swartley Jan 5, 1878. P O Souderton, Pa. Laborer, Menn. C: (**VII**) Harvey Alderfer, b Dec 25, 1878. Harry Alderfer, (twin), b Dec 25, 1878, d Dec 25, 1881. John Alderfer, b Apr 1, 1881. Ella Alderfer, b July 9, 1883. Wm. Alderfer, b Aug 24, 1885. Sadie Alderfer, b Sept 3, 1887.

V. Abraham S. Alderfer, b in Lower Salford twp. Montg. Co. Pa. Aug 1813, d Apr 11, 1896, m Hannah Bergey daughter of Rev. John Bergey about 1834 or 5. She was b in Lower Salford twp. Montg. Co. Pa. Feb 2, 1809, d Sept 1877. Farmer, Menn. C: William, John, Abram, Elizabeth, Ann, Susan, Mary, Catharine, Malinda, Deborah.

VI. William B. Alderfer, d infant.

VI. John B. Alderfer, b July 13, 1839, d Oct 10, 1887, m Catharine Heckler Jan 5. 1867. Farmer, Ref. Ch. C: Romanus, Rose, Malinda, William, Mary, Irwin.

VII. Romanus H. Alderfer, b Feb 2, 1868, m Lizzie M. Young Feb 1, 1890. P O Harleysville, Pa. Watch-maker, Ref. Ch. C: (**VIII**) Willis Y. Alderfer, b Sept 23, 1892. Katie Y. Alderfer, b July 8, 1899. Mary Y. Alderfer, b Sept 17, 1901.

VII. Rose Malinda H. Alderfer, b June 13, 1870, m Isaiah Musselman Sept 1889. P O Harleysville, Pa. Ref. Ch.

VII. William H. Alderfer, b Apr 10, 1872, m Abbie Kriebel. P O Mainland, Pa. Ref. Ch. No issue.

VII. Mary Jane H. Alderfer, b July 18, 1877. P O Mainland, Pa. Ref. Ch. S.

VII. Irwin H. Alderfer, b Dec 8, 1879. P O Mainland, Pa. Ref. Ch. S.

VI. Abraham B. Alderfer, m Lenah Alderfer. P O Mainland, Pa. C: Wilson, etc.

VI. Elizabeth Alderfer, m Jacob R. Shoemaker.

VI. Anna Alderfer, m Geo. H. Metz.

VI. Susanna Alderfer, m Michael Land's.

VI. Mary B. Alderfer, m Isaiah Hendricks.

VI. Catharine Alderfer, m Henry G. Barnes.

VI Malinda B. Alderfer, m Benjamin B. Nyce, (d); and second husband, Abraham C. Godshall.

VI. Deborah B. Alderfer, b Dec 19, 1854, m Sylvester H. Orr Nov 13, 1880. P O Skippack, Pa. Justice of the Peace, Insurance and Real Estate business; Ref. Ch. No issue.

V. Susanna Alderfer, b June 20, 1819, d Jan 31, 1889, m John K. Stauffer. He was b Mar 5, 1814, d Apr 29, 1875. Farmer, Menn. C: Catharine, Abraham, Anna, John, Susan.

VI. Catharine A. Stauffer, b May 24, 1840, m John G. Metz. P O Kulpsville, Pa. Farmer, Menn. C: Lizzie.

VII. Lizzie Metz, b Jan 26, 1868, m Isaac C. Kulp Feb 9, 1889. Farmer, Menn. C:(**VIII**) Abraham, John, Wilmer.

Jos. H. Rushmore, M.D.

VI. Abraham A. Stauffer, b Apr 29. 1842, m Jane Bossart. P O Schwenksville. Pa.   Farmer. Luth. C: John, Lizzie, Horace, Ella, Katie.

VII. John B. Stauffer, b Nov 4. 1866, m Emma M. Kaye.   P O Creamery, Pa.   Farmer, Luth. C: Alfred, Ella, Katie.

VII. Lizzie Stauffer, b Dec 1867, m Henry Tyson. P O Schwenksville, Pa.   Farmer, Menn.   Br. in Christ.   C: Olive, Abraham, George, Lizzie, Ruth. Carrie, (d); Henry.

VII. Horace B. Stauffer, m Jennie Grinley.   Farmer, Luth.   C: Charles, Ethel, Infant, (d).

VII. Ella Stauffer. S.

VII. Katie Stauffer.

VI. Anna A. Stauffer, b Sept 28, 1845, m Evan Koons.

VI. John A. Stauffer, b May 7, 1853, m Hannah Boyer June 22, 1877. She was b Dec 25, 1859. P O Skippack, Pa. Taylor, Luth. C: (**VII**) Maggie B. Stauffer, b July 22, 1877. Harvey B. Stauffer, b May 10, 1879. Susie B. Stauffer, b May 7, 1881. Annie B. Stauffer, b Mar 12, 1884. Louisa B. Stauffer, b Apr 8, 1887. John B. Stauffer, b Sept 17, 1889.

VI. Susan A. Stauffer, b Jan 31, 1858, m Reuben Reinford.   P O Schwenksville, Pa.

V. Jacob K. Alderfer, b in Montg. Co. Pa. d—, m Susanna Swartley.   C: Levi, Mary, Lavina, Anna, Susanna, Jacob, Lewis, John, Abraham, Lizzie, Philip.

VI. Levi S. Alderfer, b in Lower Salford twp. Montg. Co. Pa. Jan 13, 1849, m Sarah M. Landis of Franconia. P O Lederachville, Pa.   Farmer, Menn. C: Mary, Susan, Sallie, Harvey, Jonas, Annie, Levi, Abraham.

VII. Mary L. Alderfer, b Feb 17, 1872, m Alvin C. Alderfer, son of George D. Alderfer, Oct 25, 1890. P O Harleysville, Pa.   Had taught school for nine terms; is a director of the Sehwinksville National Bank, and of several other corporations. He is partner with M. C. Clemens, as present proprietors of the Harleysville Creamery, and have for the past

year conducted the same in a very successful and
business-like manner. Alvin C. Alderfer is also
Justice of the Peace, Surveyor, and engaged in the
Insurance business; Menn. C: (**VIII**) Bertha May
Alderfer, b May 8, 1891. Sadie Alderfer, b Dec
22, 1895. Mary Ellen Alderfer, b Dec 10, 1897.
Alma Alderfer, b Oct 18, 1901.

VII. Susan L. Alderfer, b Oct 18, 1874, m Abram
M. Landis. P O Lederachville, Pa.

VII. Sallie L. Alderfer, b Apr 2, 1877, m Joseph
H. Huldeman. P O Mainland, Pa.

VII. Harvey Alderfer, b Apr 6, 1879, m Lizzie
Loux. P O Franconia, Pa.

VII. Jonas Alderfer, b Nov 5, 1881.

VII. Annie Alderfer, b Dec 1, 1883.

VII. Levi Alderfer, b Oct 14, 1886.

VII. Abraham Alderfer, b Jan 10, 1897, d Jan 1897.

VI. Mary Ann S. Alderfer, b in Montg. Co. Pa. Jan
18, 1851, m Samuel R. Bergey Feb 1870. He was
b Jan 19, 1846, in Montg. Co. Pa. P O Telford, Pa.
Farmer. Menn. C: Susanna, Jonas, Katie, Lizzie.

VII. Susanna A. Bergey, b May 26, 1869, m Ulysses
K. Kratz. He was b Apr 15, 1871. P O Bergey,
Pa. C: (**VIII**) Mary Ann Kratz, b Aug 23, 1898.
Abraham Kratz, b Apr 23, 1900. Sallie Kratz, b
Oct 23, 1902.

VII. Jonas A. Bergey, b Jan 10, 1871, m Annie R.
Landes. She was b Sept 16, 1872. C: (**VIII**) Abra-
ham Bergey, b May 10, 1894. Samuel Bergey, b
Jan 16, 1897, d 1898. Wilmer Bergey, b July 4, 1902.

VII. Katie A. Bergey, b Jan 16, 1882, m Milton M.
Conver. He was b Nov 15, 1877. C: (**VIII**) Ella
May H. Conver, b Apr 15, 1898.

VII. Lizzie A. Bergey, b Feb 12, 1887.

VI. Lavina Alderfer, m George M. Clemens. P O
Lederachville, Pa.

VI. Anna S. Alderfer, m Isaac N. Clemens Nov 1,
1873. He was b Feb 27, 1852. P O Lederachville,
Pa. Farmer, Menn. C: (**VII**) Lizzie A. Clemens,
b Feb 12, 1875. Jacob A. Clemens, b Nov 1, 1876,
d Apr 27, 1877. Garret A. Clemens, b Jan 17,
1878, d Sept 21, 1878. Harvey A. Clemens, b Aug

23, 1879. Isaac A. Clemens, b July 30, 1881, d Aug 19, 1882, Susan Clemens, b Aug 1, 1883. Clayton Clemens, b Jan 26, 1886, d Sept 21, 1886. Allen Clemens, b Oct 9, 1887.

VI. Susan S. Alderfer, b in Montg. Co. Pa. Mar 9, 1855, m Abraham M. Price Nov 21, 1874. P O Harleysville, Pa. Farmer, Ger. Bap. C: Wilson, Sallie, Ida, Susan, Jacob, Abraham, Katie, Lizzie, Elmer, Joseph, Horace, Mamie, William, Mabel, Annie.

VII. Wilson A. Price, b Jan 1, 1876. P O Harleysville, Pa. School teacher, Ger. Bap. S.

VII. Sallie A. Price, b Mar 18, 1877. P O Harleysville, Pa. Ger. Bap. S.

VII. Ida Price, b June 20, 1878, m Rev. Emanuel N. Cassel May 15, 1897. P O Dillinger, Pa. Minister of the Menu. Br. in Christ Ch. C: (**VIII**) Lulu Cassel, b June 12, 1899.

VII. Susan Price, b Sept 7, 1877, d Aug 10, 1892.

VII. Jacob Price, b July 8, 1881, m Amanda H. Cassel Mar 23, 1902. Ger. Bap.

VII. Abraham Price, b Mar 2, 1883.

VII. Katie Price, b Oct 10, 1884.

VII. Lizzie Price, b Sept 16, 1886.

VII. Elmer Price, Aug 9, 1888, d July 24, 1889.

VII. Joseph A. Price, b Jan 28, 1890.

VII. Horace A. Price, b June 13, 1891.

VII. Mamie A. Price, b Nov 12, 1892.

VII. William A. Price, b Jan 15, 1894.

VII. Mabel A. Price, b July 28, 1896.

VII. Annie A. Price, b Apr 23, 1898.

VI. Jacob S. Alderfer, m Caroline Alderfer. C: (**VII**) Horace, Flora, Susan, Martha, Wilmer, Lizzie, Caroline, Mary.

VI. Lewis S. Alderfer, b in Montg. Co. Pa. Apr 14, 1860, m Mary E. G. Heebner Oct 1, 1881. P O Lansdale, Pa. Farmer, Menn. C: (**VII**) Alvin H. Alderfer, b Aug 14, 1884, and two died infants stillborn.

VI. John Alderfer, died single.

VI. Abraham L. S. Alderfer, b Sept 5, 1864, m Katie R. Bower. She was b Nov 7, 1870. P O

Lansdale, Pa. Farmer, Menn. C: (**VII**) Stella B.
Alderfer, b Apr 26, 1891.

VI. Lizzie S. Alderfer, b Sept 11, 1865, m John C.
Moyer. He was b Mar 22, 1860. P O Lederachville, Pa. Farmer, Menn. C: (**VII**) Susan A. Moyer, b Oct 19, 1885. Ella A. Moyer, b Oct 4, 1886.
Elmer A. Moyer, b May 30, 1889.

VI. Philip G. S. Alderfer, m Kate Moyer. P O
Lederachville, Pa.

V. Elizabeth Alderfer, b in Lower Salford, Montg.
Co. Pa. June 6, 1815, d in Lansdale, Pa. Sept 29,
1894, m Abraham G. Delp Dec 18, 1836. He was
b in Franconia twp. Montg. Co. Pa. Dec 18, 1813,
d in Lower Salford twp. Apr 5, 1893. Farmer.
Menn. C: Abraham.

VI. Abraham A. Delp, b in Lower Salford twp.
Montg. Co. Pa. Aug 23, 1842, m Mary Ann Wam-
pole Oct 13, 1864. P O Lansdale, Pa. Mr. Delp
commenced teaching school in 1860, and taught
three winters and one summer session in Franconia
twp. after which he taught ten winters in succession
in Lower Salford twp., and the Harleysville school
two summer terms. On Apr 11, 1871, he engaged
in the auctioneer business, calling his first sale on
that day, and has now called 3414 in a little over 26
years. About 15 years ago he was elected a manager of the Harleysville and Lederachville turn-pike
Road Co., and later on was promoted and appointed
President of the Board, which position he still holds.
About 1888 he was elected a director of the Lansdale
Trust and Safe Deposit Co., which position he also
holds at the present time. He also, in connection
with his other duties, carried on farming until Sept
18, 1894. Mrs. Delp, Luth. C: William, Howard,
Mary.

VII. William Warren Delp, b Sept 19, 1868, d Jan
20, 1877.

VII. Howard W. Delp, b Dec 18, 1869, m Lavina
Allebach Oct 12, 1892. P O Lansdale, Pa. He is a
graduate of Pierces College, Philadelphia. Book-
keeper for a whole-sale Clothing house in Phila.
Luth. C: (**VIII**) Luther Delp, b Nov 18, 1893.

VII. Mary Lizzie Delp, b June 12, 1871, d Aug 31, 1871.

V. Anna Alderfer, b Jan 31, 1818, d Dec 5, 1887. Single.

V. Catharine Alderfer, b Oct 1, 1821, d Mar 8, 1857, m Harman Godshall. C: Susanna.

VI. Susanna Godshall, m Aaron Frick. C: **(VII)** Charles G. Frick.

V. John K. Alderfer, b in Montg Co. Pa. Oct 28, 1827, d Feb 5, 1897, m Sarah Swartley. She was b Nov 11, 1830, d Feb 7, 1897. Both funerals were held on Thursday following their death, Feb 11, 1897, and both buried in one grave. Farmer, Menn. C: Amanda, Catharine, Frank, Philip, Abraham, John, Benjamin, Emeline, Reuben, Jacob, Henry.

VI. Amanda S. Alderfer, b Jan 30, 1850, m John N. Clemens Oct 27, 1867. He was b Apr 6, 1845. P O Harleysville, Pa. Farmer, Menn. C: Sallie, Lizzie, Allen, John, Ida, Garhart.

VII. Sallie A. Clemens, b Oct 22, 1868, d May 10, 1880.

VII. Lizzie A. Clemens, b July 27, 1870, m Edwin W. Krupp Feb 2, 1889. P O Franconia, Pa.

VII. Allen A. Clemens, b Mar 24, 1872, d Jan 24, 1874.

VII. John A. Clemens, b June 21, 1873. P O Harleysville, Pa.

VII. Ida A. Clemens, b Sept 1875, d Sept 2, 1877.

VII. Garhart Clemens, b Nov 18, 1881.

VI. Catharine S. Alderfer, b Mar 8, 1851, d June 14, 1851.

VI. Frank S. Alderfer, b Mar 6, 1852, m Amanda Shellenberger. Res. 1440 Franklin St. Phila. Pa. Clerk at Penna. R. R. Presby. C: **(VII)** Ida, Carrie, John, Dayton, (d).

VI. Philip S. Alderfer, b Sept 29, 1853, m Lizzie K. Moyer. P O Elroy, Pa. Farmer, Menn. C: Katie, Emma, John, Lizzie.

VI. Abraham S. Alderfer, (twin), b Sept 29, 1853, m Sarah Ann Moyer, daughter of Rev. Michael Moyer. She was b Nov 28, 1857. P O Harleysville, Pa. Farmer, Menn. C: **(VII)** Ella M. Alder-

fer, b Oct 10, 1876, d—.   Sallie M. Alderfer, b Aug
18, 1878. Martha M. Alderfer, b Feb 17, 1880. Alice
M. Alderfer, b Nov 12, 1882, d May 21, 1883. Harvey M. Alderfer, b Oct 26, 1884.

VI. John S Alderfer. b Feb 28, 1855, m Barbara
M. Landis. P O Franconia, Pa. Farmer, Menn.
No issue.

VI. Benjamin S. Alderfer, b May 15, 1858, d Sept
24, 1858.

VI Emeline S. Alderfer, b Dec 26, 1861, d Mar
20, 1862.

VI. Reuben S. Alderfer, b in Franconia twp. Montg.
Co. Pa. Dec 13, 1863, m Mary Z. Kulp Nov 29,
1884. P O Franconia, Pa. Farmer, Menn. C:
(**VII**) Henry K. Alderfer, b Mar 22, 1888. Katie
K. Alderfer, b Dec 24, 1898.

VI. Jacob S. Alderfer, b Sept 27, 1867, m Mary
D. Detweiler. P O Franconia, Pa. Farmer, Menn.
C: Mahlon, Carrie.

VI. Henry S. Alderfer, b Oct 28, 1871, d May 6,
1872.

V. Margaret K. Alderfer, (d.); m Peter B. Hunsberger. C: Abraham, Levi, Sarah.

VI. Abraham A. Hunsberger.

VI. Levi A. Hunsberger, (d); m Kate Godshall,
(d); C: Mary, etc.

VI. Sarah Hunsberger, d single.

IV. Elizabeth Alderfer, b Aug 12, 1785, d June
25, 1857. S.

IV. John Alderfer, b July 27, 1789, d Jan 10,
1864. S.

III. Henry Rosenberger. Lived in New Britain.
No trace found of any of his descendants.

DANIEL ROSENBERGER, OF HATFIELD.

II. Daniel Rosenberger, b in Europe, m Fronica—. He purchased a tract of land in Hatfield, lying along the county line near the hamlet of Hockertown, in 1740. His lands composed 359 acres, bought in two tracts and at different times. This large plantation bordered on the county line 1 mile, and ½ southwest. Within this tract are now the properties of David, Samuel and Henry Rosenberger; Milton Jenkins, John Landis, and Kile's tavern property. He purchased his first tract of land, 159 acres, in 1740, of Ebernezer Kinnersly, and was the upper or northwest side of his subsequent plantation. In 1769 he purchased 200 acres of George Krieble. This latter purchase took place only two years before his death, so that during nearly the whole of his life, he only possessed the smaller portion of the tract afterwards held by his posterity.

The larger portion of this latter purchase was conveyed by will to Isaac, the youngest son of Daniel Rosenberger.

Tradition says Daniel Rosenberger first settled near the county line where Samuel Rosenberger now lives, then he removed a short distance westward, where was the residence of Henry Rosenberger. Here he built a stone house in which he died. This upper part of his plantation was devised to his son David, who built a new house in 1780; the date stone may yet be seen in the cellar way of present dwelling, and bears the initials, "D. R. B.," standing for "David Rosen Berger." David Rosenberger bequeathed this property to his son, Henry Rosenberger. It then passed into the hands of Aaron Rosenberger, who sold it to Jacob Allebach, and in 1895, it was sold at Sheriff's sale to one Pennypacker.

No information has come down to us concerning the personality of Daniel Rosenberger. He was a Mennonite and worshiped at the church near Line Lexington, where his remains were buried. He made his will Aug 15, 1771, was witnessed by Valentine Ulrich, John Rosenberger, and Christian Funk, and was registered September 23, 1771. The 200 acres were conveyed to his son David, and 159 acres to Isaac. The widow who had the singular name of Fronica, was to receive £700 from her son David, showing that Daniel had become a comparatively wealthy man, for those days. C: David, Isaac, Ann, Mary.

DESCENDANTS OF DAVID ROSENBEGER,
SON OF DANIEL ROSENBERGER.

III. David Rosenberger, d in 1829, aged about 80 years, m Ann Funk, daughter of Rev. Christ'an and Barbara (Cassel) Funk, and grand-daughter of Bishop Henry Funk, of Franconia twp. Montg. Co. Pa. C: Christian, Elizabeth, Mary, Ann, Philip, David, Abraham, Daniel. David m 2nd wife, Barbara, daughter of John Detweiler. C: Susanna, John, Henry, Franey, Valentine.

The two hundred acres bequeathed to David Rosenberger was bounded on the northwest by the cross road, now a turnpike, running from the Co. line to Hatfield station. It comprised the Landis farm, those of Henry and Samuel Rosenberger; the lot of David Rosenberger and the tavern property. At the premises of Henry Rosenberger, his great grandson, he continued to reside during his life. David Rosenberger lived to be quite an old man—probably over 80 years of age. Besides the patrimony he received from his father in 1771, he also acquired a farm of 78 acres in Hilltown, which he willed to his daughter, Fronica. The homestead of 109 acres was conveyed to his son Henry, in 1821. Another farm of 78 acres, at present that of Samuel Rosenberger's, was conveyed to his son John by will. Farmer, Menn.

IV. Christian Rosenberger, b about 1773, d 1821, m Elizabeth Kraut. His name appears in the records in 1795, when he bought for £408 123 acres of the Kinsey estate in Upper Gwynedd, but which he sold two years later. In 1797 he bought 129 acres in Lower Providence, where he remained until his death. He was a wealthy man and an extensive landholder. His heirs, in 1826, sold a farm of 64 acres to John Stinson, also six houses and 300 acres

in Worcester and Providence, to various parties.
The land was near the Germantown and Perkiomen
Turnpike. Farmer, Menn. C: David, Jacob,
John, Ann, Barbara, Hettie, Marie, Christian.

V. Rev. *David Rosenberger, b May 5, 1795, d Aug
1844, m Mary Corner. She died June 1865.
Farmer in Columbiana Co. Ohio, and minister of the
Evangelical Association Church. C: Elizabeth,
John, Christian, Josiah, David, Mary, George.

VI. Elizabeth Rosenberry, b in Pa. Dec 30, 1817,
d near New Hampton, Mo. Jan 20, 1876, m Henry
Gilbert. He d July 30, 1843, aged 27 yrs. Stone
Mason, Meth. Ep. C: John, Mary, Simon, and
Susan. Elizabeth m second husband, Leonard
Hime. He d June 1853. Farmer, Luth. C: Ruth,
Rachel, Leonard. Elizabeth m third husband, Henry
Mottinger. He d at St. Joe., Mo. Oct 1864. Farmer,
Ev. Ass'n. C: Sarah, Milton.

VII. John W. Gilbert b in Columbiana Co, Ohio,
Jan 28, 1838, m Eva M. Rauch Dec 30, 1862. Res.
1419 Penna. Ave. Canton, Ohio. House-mover,
Christian Science. C: James, Perry, Irene, Edward,
Jennie, Charles, Bert, Esie, Grace, Eva.

VIII. James E. Gilbert, b Oct 17, 1863, m Annie
Rouch.

VIII. Perry Gilbert, b July 11, 1865, d Feb 16, 1884.

VIII. Irene Gilbert, b Aug 26, 1866, d Oct 15, 1888.

VIII. Edward Gilbert, b Oct 17, 1867, d Oct 16,
1886.

VIII. Jennie Gilbert, b Sept 3, 1869, m Atlata
Davis. P O Knox, Pa.

VIII. Charles Gilbert, b Jan 9, 1871, m Esner. P
O Canton, Ohio.

VIII. Bert Gilbert, b Sept 11, 1873, d Dec 26,
1894.

VIII. Esie Gilbert, b July 6, 1875.

VIII. Grace Gilbert, b Sept 9, 1877.

VIII. Eva Gilbert, b Apr 11, 1880, d Jan 14, 1882.

VII. Mary Ann Gilbert, b June 11, 1839, m William
Zerbe Feb 17, 1860. He was b in Berks Co. Pa. and
when 18 years of age he went to Starks Co. Ohio.

---

*The names were recorded in the old Family Bible—Rosenberry.

After marriage they moved to Harrison Co. Mo.
where they still reside. P O Martinsville, Mo.
Farmer; Mr. Z. Luth; Mrs. Z. Meth. Ep. C: John,
Ida, Flora, Viola, Ruth, Joseph, Henry, Sarah,
Leonard, Jessie, Isaac.

VIII. John Edwin Zerbe, b Oct 23, 1861, m Theressa
Congleton Feb 27, 1889. P O Martinsville, Mo.
Farmer, Meth. Ep. C: (**IX**) Mary Blanche Zerbe,
b July 9, 1891. Lewis Wm. Dean Zerbe b Aug 13,
1898.

VIII. Ida Jane Zerbe, b May 2, 1863, m Samuel
Hall Goucher Aug 7, 1878. P O Merriman, Neb.
Raising stock, horses and cattle. C: Nora, Floyd,
R. W., Zora, Ora, Meda, Leona.

IX. Nora Ellen Goucher, b May 3, 1881, m Wm.
Hatten, (d). P O Merriman, Neb. C: (**X**) Mary
Hatten, b Jan 21, 1896. Dell Hatten, b Apr 1, 1899.
Roy Hatten, b Jan 1, 1901.

IX. Floyd H. Goucher, b Oct 30, 1883.

IX. R. W. Goucher, b Sept 30, 1885.

IX. Zora Etta Goucher, b June 11, 1888.

IX. Ora Ocy Goucher, b Oct 17, 1892.

IX. Meda May Goucher, b Dec 7, 1896.

IX. Leona Goucher, b Dec 15, 1899.

IX. Luebart Goucher, b Feb 24, 1902.

VIII. Flora Ellen Zerbe, b at Alliance, Stark Co.
Ohio, Apr 12, 1865, m John M. Crotts Feb 28,
1895. Farmer; Mrs. Crotts, before and after marriage, has been engaged in teaching music. She has
been devoted to that work at least for six months in
every year for 15 years. She is also a member of the
"Great White Ribbon Band," of the Womans'
Christian Temperance Union. Meth. Ep. C: (**IX**)
Marian Izora Crotts, b Jan 25, 1898, d Feb 23,
1898.

VIII. Viola Josephine Zerbe, b in Harrison Co. Mo.
Nov 21, 1866, m Lewis Adams Mar 22, 1883. P O
Merriman, Neb. Running a Cattle Ranch. C: (**IX**)
William Earl Adams, b Jan 4, 1885. Ethel Alice
Adams, b July 19, 1887. Edgar Adams, b Feb 9,
1891. Infant (twin) stillborn Feb 9, 1891. Flora
Maud Adams, b Aug 8, 1895.

VIII. Ruth Ann Zerbe, b in Harrison Co. Mo. Sept 21, 1868, m William Casebolt Dec 24, 1885. P O Martinsville, Mo. Farmer.

VIII. Joseph Lawrence Zerbe, b July 16. 1870, d Aug 24, 1871.

VIII. Henry William Zerbe, b Mar 7, 1872. d May 25. 1893. Meth. Ep.

VIII. Sarah Elizabeth Zerbe, b June 9. 1874, m Lewis Brown Dec 24, 1890. P O Bethany, Mo. Farmer. C: (**IX**) Edith Brown, b Oct 9, 1891. Eldbridge Brown, b May 1894, d Aug 1895. Pearl Brown, b Jan 25, 1898.

VIII. Leonard Albertus Zerbe, b Oct 19, 1876, m Susie Burton Dec 23, 1897. P O Bethany, Mo. C: (**IX**) Inis Zerbe, b Nov 13, 1899.

VIII. Jessie W. Zerbe, b Jan 21. 1879, d Aug 3. 1890.

VIII. Isaac Franklin Zerbe, b Mar 21, 1881, m Bessie Howard, Oct 19, 1902. P O Martinsville, Mo. Farmer.

VII. Simon Gilbert, b 1841. At the age of 22 years he enlisted in the Union Army and was killed in battle Sept 13, 1865, having served three years from date of enlistment Sept 13, 1862.

VII. Susan Gillert, b in 1843, d in Mich. about 1889, m John McLease about 1865. No issue.

VII. Ruth Ann Hime, b in Stark Co. O. May 26, 1850, d July 29, 1897, m Alexander Barret Needles in Gentry Co. Mo. July 1871. Ruth Ann Hime moved with her mother to Gentry Co. Mo. in 1865, where she remained most of the time until her marriage; when she with her husband moved to Nodaway Co. Mo. in the fall of 1871. At the early age of 17 years she professed faith in Christ and united with the Methodist Episcopal Church, in which she remained a faithful member until death. P O Parnell City, Mo. Farmer, Meth. Ep. C: (**VIII**) Cora E. Needles, b Mar 8, 1872, d Mar 9, 1898. At the age of 15 she gave her heart to God, and joined the Meth Ep. Church. George W. Needles, b Sept 14. 1873, d July 11, 1874. William A. Needles, b Apr 8, 1875. P O Parnell City, Mo. S. Ada L. Needles, b Feb 22, 1877. P O Parnell City, Mo. At the age of 17 she was converted and joined the Free Methodist Church. S. Charles S. Needles, b Mar 27, 18;9, d July 11, 1881. Elizabeth Needles, b May 2, 1881. She gave her heart and life to Jesus at the age of 16, and united with the Methodist Episcopal Church. P O Parnell City, Mo. S. Sarah C. Needles, b Oct 27, 1882. She became a disciple of Jesus when 15 years of age, and joined the Methodist Episcopal Church. P O Parnell City, Mo. S. Alexander E. Needles, b Oct 19, 1884. John L. Needles, b May 3, 1886, d Sept 26, 1886. James M. Needles, b Dec 2, 1887. Infant, stillborn Aug 12, 1892.

VII. Rachel Alice Hime, b in Stark Co. O. June 11, 1852, m Edward William Dahlgren Dec 22, 1869. He was b in Galesburg, Ill. Mar 4, 1851, d at Omaha, Neb. Dec 20, 1896. He was of Swedish descent, his parents having emigrated from Sweden to America about 1845. His maternal grandfather was a noted personage and Lord in Sweden. P O Merriman, Neb. Ranchman, Meth. Ep. C: William, Lewis, Frank, Arthur. Alfred, Andrew, Grace, Cecil.

VIII. William Leonard Dahlgren, b Feb 11, 1871, m Laura Agnes McNemel Sept 6, 1891. She was b in Harrison Co. Mo. Oct 22, 1876. P O Merriman, Neb. Farmer, Meth. Ep. C; (**IX**) Winifred Tessa Dahlgren, b June 7, 1894. Leonard Dahlgren, b Jan 12, 1897. Leyes Dahlgren, b Aug 3, 1898. Loal Dahlgren, b Feb 14, 1899.

VIII. Lewis Edward Dahlgren, b Jan 6, 1873. P O Merriman, Neb. Farmer. Meth. Ep. S.

VIII. Frank Dahlgren, b Dec 6, 1875, d Mar 6, 1878, was burned to death.

VIII. Arthur Dahlgren, b Dec 12, 1880.

VIII. Alfred Dahlgren, b Aug 13, 1882.

VIII. Andrew Dahlgren, b Oct 7, 1884.

VIII. Grace May Dahlgren, b Dec 11, 1886.

VIII. Cecil Lee Dahlgren, b Dec 14, 1890, d Mar 10, 1897.

VII. Leonard A. Hime, b in Stark Co. O. Sept 14, 1853, m Martha I. Lovelace Feb 19, 1880. She d

Feb 27, 1887. C: Hattie, Ralph, Marguriett. Infant. Leonard m second wife, Martha E. Hunsicker, May 9, 1889. P O New Hampton, Mo. Farmer and stock-raiser, Meth. Ep. C: Lala.

VIII. Hattie Hime, b Nov 29, 1880. Meth. Ep. S.

VIII. Ralph Leroy Hime, b July 29, 1882. Meth. Ep.

VIII. Marguriett Ann Hime, b Feb 22, 1885. M. Ep.

VIII. Infant, stillborn Oct 16, 1883.

VIII. Lala Elizabeth Hime, b Oct 30, 1890.

VII Sarah Catharine Mottinger, b Oct 1856, m John Shultz Jan 1884. P O McFall, Mo.

VII. Milton H. Mottinger, b in Stark Co. O. May 4, 1859, m Elizabeth McKillen Sept 23, 1886. P O Albany, Mo. Farmer, Meth. Ep. No issue.

VI. John C. Rosenberger, b in Pa. Oct 15, 1819, d in Stark Co. O. Aug 30, 1891, m Sarah Ickes. She was b in Pa. Mar 9, 1821, d in Stark Co. O. Mar 25, 1896. Farmer, Ger. Bap. C: Lydia, Albert, Edward.

VII. Lydia Ann Rosenberger, b at New Franklin, Stark Co. O. Jan 5, 1847, m David Scott May 28, 1868. P O Alliance, O. Farmer, Ev. Ass'n. C: William, Cora.

VIII. William Edward Scott, b Dec 11, 1869, d Jan 14, 1871.

VIII. Cora Belle Scott, b Jan 19, 1874, m Benjamin W. Mather Aug 25, 1895. P O Homeworth, Ohio. Farmer. C: (**IX**) Lydia Margaret Mather, b Oct 30, 1898. Irene Mather, b Nov 14, 1899.

VII. Albert Rosenberger, b at New Franklin, Stark Co. Ohio, Oct 17, 1849, m Nancy Coyle Dec 1, 1889. P O Freeburgh, Ohio. Farmer, Luth. C: (**VIII**) Lydia Rosenberger, b Dec 5, 1879. Chancy Rosenberger, b Sept 19, 1885.

VII. Edward Rosenberger, b in Stark Co. O. May 10, 1852, m Ellen Irwin Mar 18, 1875. P O Paris, Ohio. Farmer, Ger. Bap. C: Ida, Homer, Frank.

VIII. Ida M. Rosenberger, b May 20, 1877, m Chas. E. Ruff Apr 7, 1895. P O Homeworth, Ohio. Farmer, Ger. Bap. C: (**IX**) Glenwood Ruff. Howard Ruff.

VIII. Homer F. Rosenberger, b Jan 20, 1882.

VIII. Frank W. Rosenberger, b 1886.
VI. Christian Rosenberger, (d); m Christena Gilbert.
VI. Josiah Rosenberger, (d); m Kate McGrayer.
No issue.
VI. David Rosenberger. No issue.
VI. Mary Ann Rosenberger, b Sept 4, 1830, d in
Ohio Oct 26, 1867, m Owen M. Snyder Apr 5, 1849.
He was b in Columbiana Co. O. Sept 4, 1824. C:
May, Oscar, Almeda, Anna, Howard, Samantha,
Frank, Foster, Mary.
VII. May Snyder, b at New Franklin, Stark Co. O.
in 1849, m Thomas Ross in 1875. P O St. Joseph,
Mo. Episcopal Ch. C: (**VIII**) Rubena Ross, b 1876.
Maggie May Ross, b 1878.
VII. Oscar Snyder, b Sept 8, 1851, d at Cadiff Mines,
Alabama, May 13, 1892. He was caught by falling
slate, from effects of which he died.
VII. Almeda Snyder, b in Columbiana Co. O. Sept
10, 1853, m Andrew Summers Apr 20, 1872. He
d Aug 15, 1885. P O North Gorgetown, O. Black-
smith, Ger. Bap. C: Ida, Lula, Howard, Anna,
Rachel, Alvie.
VIII. Ida May Summers, b Dec 29, 1873, d Oct 18,
1877.
VIII. Lula Belle Summers, b Apr 8, 1875, m B. S.
Heiss. Res. 33 Grant St. Cleveland, O. Jeweler.
C: (**IX**) Archibald Warburton Heiss.
VIII. Howard Ellsworth Summers, b Oct 19, 1876.
VIII. Anna Mary Summers, b Jan 19, 1878.
VIII. Rachel Christena Summers, b Oct 16, 1880.
VIII. Alvie Andrew Summers, b Dec 23, 1885.
VII. Ruth Anna Snyder, b Aug 17, 1855, m Frank
Gugelman Dec 24, 1874. He was b Aug 3, 1856.
P O Paris, O. C: (**VIII**) Foster O. Gugelman, b
July 13, 1875. Charles R. Gugelman, b Apr 2,
1877, d Oct 25, 1877. Vivian I. Gugelman, b Oct
11, 1878. Homer C. Gugelman, b July 13, 1880.
Harry E. Gugelman, b Jan 28, 1882. Mary B.
Gugelman, b Mar 10, 1884. Forest A. Gugelman,
b June 20, 1886. May E. Gugelman, b July 22,
1888. William A. Gugelman, b Dec 22, 1891.
Ruth A. Gugelman, b Apr 27, 1894. George H.

Gugelman, b Jan 22, 1897.

VII. Milton Howard Snyder, b May 16, 1857. Res. Boliver St. Cleveland, Ohio.   S.

VII. Samantha C. Snyder, b Aug 26, 1859, m Chas. Harraden May 2, 1880. Res. 3505 Oak Park Ave. Berwyn, Ill. Fire Underwriter, Baptist. C: (**VIII**) George J. Harraden, b Nov 11, 1881. Charles G. Harraden, b Oct 14, 1888. Maria I. Harraden, b Jan 8, 1902.

VII. Franklin S. Snyder, b Sept 25, 1862. P O Canton, Ohio.

VII. Mary Isabella Snyder, b Sept 26, 1864, m Charles McMacken. P O Salem, O. Ref. Ch. C: (**VIII**) Raymond McMacken, b May 9, 1883. Hazel McMacken, b Apr 25, 1885.

VII. Foster L. Snyder, b Aug 6, 1867.   P O Emporia, Kan.

VI. George W. Rosenberry, b in Pa. Sept 8, 1831, m Maria Bohecker Dec 22, 1853. P O Dayton, O. Conductor on the Penna. R. R. Mr. R. Meth. Ep. Mrs. R., Christian Ch. C: Viola, Judson, George, Charles, Minnie.

VII. Viola Josephine Rosenberry, b at Alliance, O. Dec 14, 1854, m Edwin L. Ogden May 27, 1873. P O Alliance, Ohio. C: Florence, Cassie, Grace, (d).

VII. Judson M. Rosenberry, b Aug 30, 1858, d Feb 10, 1859.

VII. George L. Rosenberry, b in Alliance, Ohio May 6, 1860, m Maggie E. Croft Dec 16, 1890. P O Alliance, Ohio. Employed in the tool room of the Morgan Engineering Co; Presby. C: (**VIII**) Harry Walter Rosenberry. Edwin C. Rosenberry. Bertha May Rosenberry.

VII. Charles S. Rosenberry, b in Alliance, O. 1863. Res. 17 Clifton St. Cleveland, Ohio. S.

VII. Minnie F. Rosenberry, b in Alliance, O. Oct 21, 1869. Res. Alliance, O.

V. Jacob Rosenberger, b Aug 19, 1797, d Apr 11, 1831, m Mary Detweiler Dec 12, 1820. She was b June 19, 1799, d about 1848. Lived in Lower Providence twp Montg. Co. Pa. Farmer, Menn. C: Susanna, John, Catharine, Elizabeth, Mary.

Jesse, Jacob, Benjamin.

VI. Susanna Rosenberry, b Jan 6, 1822.

VI. John Rosenberry, b and d Dec 28, 182:.

VI. Catharine Rosenberry, b Nov 16, 1823, d Apr 18, 1900, m Henry G. Delp Dec 7, 1845. He died Apr 19, 1884. Farmer, Menn. C: Emeline, Anna, Hannah.

VII. Emeline R. Delp, b Mar 24, 1847, d Aug 6, 1901, m Isaac B. Kulp Dec 13, 1867. C: Mary, Katie, Harry, Irwin, Emma, Frank.

VIII. Mary Ellen Kulp, m Charles Bechtel. P O Limerick, Pa. C: (IX) Clarence, Hannah, Henry, Elmer, Elsie.

VIII. Katie Kulp, m Henry Allebach. C: (IX) Iva, Wilmer, Ethel.

VIII. Harry Kulp, b May 15, 1873, m Etta Alderfer Dec 25, 189;. P O Harleysville, Pa. Farmer. C: (IX) Blanch A. Kulp, b Oct 23, 1898. Frank A. Kulp, b Oct 18, 1902.

VIII. Irwin Kulp, m Laura Ganghorn Dec 1902.

VIII. Emma D. Kulp, b Nov 27, 1880, m Isaiah B. Clymer Apr 22, 1902. Butcher, Menn. Res. Phila. Penna.

VIII. Frank D. Kulp, b Aug 26, 1886. Res. Phila. Pa. Machinist, Menn. S.

VII. Anna Elizabeth Delp, b July 18, 1850, d Apr 23, 1887, m Hiram Steltz Sept 1873. P O Potts-town, Pa. C: Katie, Henry, Sarah, Hiram.

VIII. Katie Laura Steltz, (d).

VIII. Henry Wilson Steltz, b Sept 20, 1875, m Emma Seasholtz May 5, 1900. P O New Hanover, Pa. Miller, Luth. C: (IX) Edna May Steltz, b Aug 24, 1900. Rufus Melvin Steltz, b July 28, 1901, d Sept 27, 1901. Harvey Elwood Steltz, b June 24, 1902.

VIII. Sarah Agnes Steltz, m Frank Hunsberger. P O Frederick, Pa.

VIII. Hiram Edwin Steltz. S.

VII. Hannah R. Delp, b Jan 21, 1857, m Henry K. Kratz Oct 16, 1880. P O Kulpsville, Pa. Farmer, Menn. No issue.

VI. Elizabeth Rosenberry, b Dec 15, 1824, m George

F. Shuler Feb 16, 1856. P O Sterling, Ill. Retired farmer. C: Ann, John, Emma, Mary.

VII. Ann Eliza Shuler, b Nov 30, 1856, m Ferris H. Landis Dec 23, 1875. P O Sterling, Ill. Farmer, Luth. C: (**VIII**) Frank Fred Landis, b Jan 6, 1877. Harvey Shuler Landis, b Oct 28, 1878, d Feb 14, 1896. Cora Elizabeth Landis, b Dec 5, 1880. Bertha May Landis, b Oct 2, 1882. Arthur Roy Landis, b Feb. 2, 1885. Ida Susan Landis, b Aug 8, 1886. Walter Emanuel Landis, b July 9, 1890, d Jan 14, 1892. John Irvin Landis, b Nov 15, 1891, d Jan 15, 1892. Verne Ruth Landis, b July 27, 1893. Martha Anna Landis, b June 11, 1896.

VII. John Franklin Shuler, b Apr 15, 1858, d Jan 30, 1861.

VII. Emma Shuler, b Apr 26, 1865. m Christian F. Miller Mar 5, 1895. P O Sterling, Ill. Farmer. C: (**VIII**) Elizabeth Ruth Miller, b Feb 5, 1896.

VII. Mary Shuler, b Apr 26, 1867. P O Sterling, Ill. S.

VI. Mary Rosenberry, b in Montg. Co. Pa. Dec 6, 1825, m Ephraim D. Hendricks in 1848. He was b in Montg. Co. Pa. 1824. P O Cawker City, Kan. Tailor, Menn. C: Allen, Benjamin, John, Charles.

VII. Allen R. Hendricks, b in Lancaster, Pa. Aug 29, 1849, m Susan Moyer Sept 23, 1873. She was b Apr 11, 1853. P O Sterling, Ill. Druggist. C: (**VIII**) Olive Logan Hendricks, b May 10, 1876. Leon Sumner Hendricks, b Mar 21, 1880, d Jan 25, 1883. Lester Blaine Hendricks, b Feb 8, 1886. Leroy Russel Hendricks, b May 8, 1890.

VII. Benjamin Franklin Hendricks, b in Lancaster Co. Pa. Mar 16, 1851, m Lillian Emma Peck Aug 29, 1876. P O Savanna, Ill. Superintendant of City Schools, Savanna, Ill. C: (**VIII**) Earl Leslie Hendricks, b Mar 7, 1880. Clyde Peck Hendricks, b Apr 6, 1884. Hazel Dell Hendricks, b May 14, 1888. Paul Merton Hendricks, b May 14, 1888, d June 14, 1890.

VII. John R. Hendricks, b at Sterling, Ill. May 9, 1855, m Mollie A. Swartley June 17, 1875. P O Smithville, Ark. Formerly teacher, present occupation medicine. C: (VIII) Eldon Beethoven Hendricks, b July 18, 1877. Milicent Mozart Hendricks, b May 19, 1880. Gretrude Haydn Hendricks, b Feb 29, 1884, d Nov 29, 1886. Myrtle Weber Hendricks, b Apr 19, 1889.

VII. Charles R. Hendricks, b Aug 29, 1859, m Emma Marzolf Mar 27, 1883. P O Cawker City, Kan. Farmer, Ref. Menn. C: (VIII) Clyde Hendricks, b 1884. Pearl Hendricks, b 1886. Mabel Hendricks, b 1888. Amy Hendricks, b 1891. Gertrude Hendricks, b 1893. Ruth Hendricks, b 1896.

VI. Jesse Rosenberger, b in Montg. Co. Pa. May 1, 1827, m Esther Heim June 2, 1850. She d Dec 12, 1871, in Wis. C: Amos, several d infants, and Jesse. Jesse m second wife, H. Jane Holcomb. P O Iola, Kan. Shoemaker, Farmer, Nurseryman, Baptists. C: Franklin.

VII. Amos Rosenberger, b May 29, 1852, m Ella Thurber. P O Kansas City, Mo. Instructor in a business college, at 1214 Main St.

VII. Jesse L. Rosenberger, b at Lake City, Minn.Jan 6, 1860. He graduated from the University of Rochester, (N. Y.) in 1888, receiving the degree of A. B. and afterwards that of A. M. In 1889 he graduated from the Chicago College of Law, and in 1891, received the degree of L. L. B. from Lake Forest University Oct 7, 1889, he was admitted to the bar of the State of Illinois. Since the latter date, he has been, and is still, practicing law in Chicago. He is also now publishing what is called "Rosenberger's Law Monthly," primarily a business man's law journal. He is also author of a volume of "Street Railway Law," and of one entitled "Law for Lumbermen; office 1005 Opera House Bldg. Chicago, Ill. Baptist. S.

VII. Franklin H. Rosenberger, d Aug 1, 1900. S.

VI. Jacob Rosenberry, b Aug 30, 1828, m Mary Schlichter. She d without issue. Jacob m second wife, Emma Schlichter. C: Frank, Mary, Jacob, Harry, Isaac. Jacob m third wife, Mary Barclay. P O Fagleysville, Pa. Farmer. C: William, Frederick, John, Maggie, Robert, Joseph.

VII. Frank Rosenberry, b Nov 1, 1858, m Mary Madden. Res. 2507 Tulip St. Phila. Pa. Salesman and Book-keeper; Mrs. R. Catholic. C: (**VIII**) Francis Rosenberry.

VII. Mary Rosenberry, b about 1860, d young.

VII. Jacob Rosenberry, b about 1862, m Lizzie. Moury. P O Neiffer. Pa. Farmer, Ger. Ref. C: (**VIII**) Emily. Sadie, Alonzo.

VII. Harry Rosenberry, b 1866. Res. 2507 Tulip St. Phila. Pa. Moterman. S.

VII. Isaac Rosenberry, b 1868, m —— Kehl. P O Pennsburg. Pa. Huckster, Luth. C: (**VIII**) Stella, Frances. Cassie, Henry.

VII. William Rosenberry, b June 30, 1871. P O Fagleysville. Pa. Farmer, Ref. Ch.

VII. Frederick Rosenberry, b May 7, 1873.

VII. John Rosenberry, b June 1875. Ref. Ch.

VII. Maggie Rosenberry, b Oct 20, 1877, d 1894.

VII. Robert Rosenberry.

VII. Joseph Rosenberry, b June 1883.

VI. Benjamin F. Rosenberry, b in Lower Providence twp. Montg. Co. Pa. Mar 5, 1830, m Angeline Wear at Canton, Ohio, Feb 4, 1851. P O Argos, Ind. C: Mary, Emma, Amanda, John, James.

VII. Mary Rosenberry, b in Stark Co. Ohio, Nov 2, 1851, m James H. Watson Feb 14, 1871. P O Argos, Ind. Meth. Ep. C: John.

VIII. John Hunter Watson, b Nov 4, 1871, m Amy Chapman. Res. 1318. West Monroe St. Chicago, Ill. Printer, Meth. Ep. C: (**IX**) J. Howard Watson, b Aug 8, 1893. Paul C. Watson, b Feb 15, 1896. Nina Winona Watson, b Aug 25, 1898.

VIII. Janette Watson, b July 3, 1873, d Mar 6, 1874.

VIII. Homer Watson, b Nov 27, 1877, m Clara Bucher. Res. 617 Prairie St. Elkhart, Ind. Printer.

VIII. B. F. Watson, b June, 1, 1882. P O Argos, Ind. Clerk, Meth. Ep.

VIII. Howard Watson, b Dec 27, 1886, d Jan 7, 1887.

VIII. Mildred Watson, b Apr 24, 1889, Meth. Ep.

VIII. Paul Watson, b Aug 24, 1893, d next day.
VII. Emma Rosenberry, b Mar 18, 1854, d—.
VII. Amanda Rosenberry, b in Stark Co. Ohio. June 13, 1856, m L. N. Shedd, (d), in 1878. P O Argos, Ind. Meth. Ep. C: (**VIII**) Louisa Gertrude Shedd, b Mar 14, 1880. Eva Angeline Shedd, b June 16, 1882. Amanda m second husband, J. C. Gordon, in 1892. Ex-School teacher.
VII. John Franklin Rosenberry, b Mar 5, 1858, d—.
VII. James Harvey Rosenberry, bMay 4, 1872, d—.
VII. Susan Rosenberger, d aged 13 years.
V. Rev. *John Rosenberger, b in Montg. Co. Pa. May 21, 1801, d in North Georgetown, Ohio, Mar 17, 1853, m Elizabeth Z., daughter of Jacob Hunsicker, of Skippack, Pa. Dec 26, 1824. She was b May 26, 1798, d in Osage City, Kansas Dec 24, 1887. Farmer and Minister, first of the Menn., and in after life of the Evangelical Association. At the annual session of the Conference of the Evangelical Association Church in Pa. in 1838, he was licensed to preach and was sent as an assistant to travel the Lancaster Circuit, and in 1839 as an assistant on the York Circuit. The work of the church at that time was more on the order of Missionary work, with much traveling, and constantly, every day preaching, with many hardships to endure, and small salaries. He having a wife and six children, his small capital sank $400. which forced him to locate in 1840, when he 'and his family moved to eastern Ohio, then a new country, where other members of his father's family had preceeded him. He bought a farm of 80 acres and supported his family by farming, still continuing to preach on Sunday the balance of his life, and died in 1853, honored by all that knew him. C: Jacob, Annie, Elizabeth. Sarah, Isaac, John, Barbara, David, Maria.
VI. JacobH. Rosenberg, M. D., b inLower Providence twp. Montg. Co. Pa. Oct 17, 1825, m Mary Ann Caudels, daughter of George and Elizabeth

*In 1858 he changed his namefrom Rosenberry to Rosenberger. In 1860 his children further changed the name to Rosenberg.

Altmen Caudels, Oct 31, 1847.   She was b Nov 17,
1828, d Sept 2, 1880.   Res. 1626 Burdette St. Omaha, Neb.

Dr. Rosenberg was converted Jan 9, 1837, and
joined the Evangelical Association.   In Aug 1843,
at the Ohio Conf. of the Ev. Ass'n. Church, he was
licensed to the "Local Ministry."   He taught district schools, and preached on Sundays.   In 1853,
'54, '55, the Pittsburg Conf. Ev. Ass'n. sent him to
travel as preacher on their circuits in Armstrong,
Jefferson, Clarion and Venango counties of Pa., and
1856 to 1864 the Ohio Conf. sent him to travel and
preach on the missions and circuits in the counties of
Wood, Lucas, Henry, Wyandott, Pickaway, Fair-
field, and Wayne, Ohio; and Lenawee and Monroe
counties, Michigan.   His voice for public speaking
finally failed totally and in 1864 he located and entered and graduated from the Eclectic Medical Institute
of Cincinnati, Ohio, in 1869, and has practiced medicine successfully from that time to the present,
(1900).

Dr. Jacob H. Rosenberg educated himself after
marriage by much planning and economy.   He reads
Greek, Latin and Hebrew, giving the translation
very readily and rapidly.   He is now a member of
the Methodist Episcopal Church.   C: Sarah, Frank,
Mary, Emeline.

VII. Sary Ann Rosenberg, b Nov 9, 1848, d Oct
8, 1849.

VII. Frank J. Rosenberg, M. D. b at Columbianna,
Ohio, Aug 16, 1850, m Anna M. Case, of Wyandott
Co. Ohio, Mar 17, 1873.   P O Lexington, Neb.
Mr. Rosenberg was educated in Upper Sandusky
High School and Northwestern Normal, Adrian, O.
He studied medicine and graduated at the E. M. I.
Cincinnati, Ohio, in 1873, and took Post Clinical
Course at Bellevue Hospital College, N. Y. in 1881,
and a P. G. course in the P. G. School of Medicine,
London, England, in 1891, and has since been en-
gaged in the practice of his profession.   Meth. Ep.
C: (**VIII**) Claud C. Rosenberg, b Apr 14, 1874.
Meth. Ep. S. Roy Paul Rosenberg, b Jan 14,

1878, d July 1891. Meth. Ep. Ralph E. Rosenberg, b May 24, 1881. Earl H. Rosenberg, b Sept 24, 1884. Meth. Ep. Bulah Vere Rosenberg, b Jan 29, 1890.

VII. Mary Elizabeth Rosenberg, b in Venango Co. Pa. Aug 20, 1855. In 1895 she entered the Eclectic Medical Institute of Cincinnati, Ohio, and graduated in 1897. She is now a regular practicing physicial, m Carl O. Nelson Jan 30, 1901. He was b in Sweden Sept 26, · 1861. Res. 1626 Burdette St. Omaha, Neb. His occupation is that of Painter and Decorator. He became a naturalized citizen of America in Oct 1901. Meth. Ep.

VII. Emeline Rosenberg, b June 9, 1860, d Aug 13, 1861.

VI. Annie Rosenberg, b Dec 26, 1826, d Jan 1887, m John Vanhorn Dec 1847.

VI. Elizabeth Rosenberg, b Dec 26, 1826, d Sept 26, 1827.

VI. Sarah Ann Rosenberg, b Mar 28, 1829, m Isaac Packer July 2, 1852. He d Jan 1884. Millwright, Meth. Ep. C: Rosetta, Webster, Frank, Mary, Jane, Laura, John.

VII. Rosetta A. Packer, b Dec 16, 1854, m Kimble Thomas. P O Turney, Mo. C: **(VIII)** Daniel Thomas, (d). Laura Thomas. Nellie Thomas. Perley Thomas. Maudie Thomas, (d). Earl Thomas.

VII. D. Webster Packer, b at Salem, Ohio, Sept 18, 1855. P O Platte City, Mo. Farmer and stock-raiser, Christain Ch. S.

VII. B. Frank Packer, b at LaSalle, Ill. Apr 24, 1859. P O Platte City, Mo. Farmer and Stock-raiser, Christian Ch. S.

VII. Mary Ann Packer, d 1860.

VII. Jane Packer, d 1864.

VII. Laura Packer, b in Leavenworth, Kan. Mar 1, 1863, m Levi S. Deever Oct 23, 1895. Res. 1301 Kansas Ave. Topeka, Kan. Farmer, United Br. Ch.

VII. John H. Packer, b Sept 12, 1870. Res. 1559 N 19th. St. Omaha, Neb. Electric Engineer, Meth. Ep. Single.

VI. Isaac H. Rosenberg, b Oct 31, 1831, d Mar 17, 1853.

VI. John H. Rosenberg, M. D. b Apr 5, 1833, d Feb 1889, m Elizabeth L. Dundore July 27, 1858. Physician and minister of the United Brethren Ch. No issue.

VI. Barbara Rosenberg, b Mar 24, 1835, in Montg. Co. Pa. d in Osage City, Kan. Nov 30, 1874, m Benjamin Packer Feb 24, 1853. He was b Oct 26, 1831, d near Alliance, Ohio, Nov 30, 1855. Carpenter and Millwright. Mr. Packer, Quaker; Mrs. Packer, Ev. Ass'n. and later U. B. in Christ. C: Edwin.

VII. Edwin B. Packer, M. D., b near Mt. Union, Ohio, May 27, 1855. He was but an infant six months old when his father died, and his mother then took him to his grandmother Elizabeth Rosenberg, who raised him, living at Bloomville, Napolion, Broken Swords, and Sycamore, Ohio, the first 12 years of his life; then, at the age of 12 years he went to Blairistown, Iowa, where he remained 3 years and attended school occasionally. At 15 he went to Kan. and worked a short time. In 1869 he made his home in Osage City, and followed his trade, that of a Carpenter, and also did some surveying for railroads, clerking and coal mining. In 1875 he attended Lane University, Lecompton, Kan. The years 1877, '78, '79, '80, were spent in teaching, employing his time at various things during vacation. He was married to Mary E. Ferris, of Lecompton, Kan. June 16, 1878. In 1880 he attended Medical Lectures from the Preceptorship of Dr. John H. Rosenberg, (d), and graduated in June 1882, and located in practice in Osage City on the 15 day of the same month, at which place he still lives and practices his profession; Presby. C: (**VIII**) Ada Packer, b June 4, 1879, d June 27, 1880. Pearl Packer, b Nov 18, 1880.

VI. David H. Rosenberg, M. D., b at Skippackville, Montg. Co. Pa. May 19, 1837, m Catharine Dundore May 19, 1859. P O Mascotte, Fla. Dr. Rosenberg spent most of his time in Seneca Co. Ohio, but afterwards, on account of his health, he removed to Florida, where he is now strong and hearty, with

abundance of various tropical fruits growing in his
groves, ripe fruit every day of the year and with his
practice as physician and Surgeon is joyful and happy. He was also a minister of the Ev. Ass'n. Ch.
but is now member of Meth. Ep. Ch. C: John,
Sarah, Joseph.

VII. John B. Rosenberg, M. D. b at Napoleon,
Henry Co. Ohio, Mar 25, 1863, m Clara Eckert Nov
18, 1896. P O Clermont, Fla. Physician, Unitar-
ian. No issue, (1897).

VII. Sara Lou Ella Rosenberg, b in Crawford Co.
Ohio, July 26, 1865, m Rev. John H. Martin Sept 7,
1890. P O Winter Park, Fla. He was b at Tiffin,
Ohio, Mar 13, 1867. Part of his boyhood was spent on
a farm. He was converted at the age of 14 years
under the labors of Rev. J. A. Hensel of the Ohio
Conference Evangelical Association. He spent several years in a shop where he learned wood carving,
cabinet making and the construction of wood-work in
all forms, and drafting. He then attended Heidelberg University at Tiffin, Ohio. In Sept 1890, he
went to Florida, taught school one year, and in Aug
1892, entered the ministry of the Methodist Episcopal church, and stationed at Winter Park, Florida,
where he is just (1898) completing a full term pas-
torate of five years. C: (**VIII**) Rosella Esther Martin, b Sept 1, 1891.

VII. Joseph Scudder Rosenberg, b at Bettsville,
Ohio, Jan 21, 1870, m Libbie Buhler. Superintendant Cigar Factory, 3rd St. Philadelphia, Pa. C:
(**VIII**) Russel Rosenberg. Joseph Rosenberg. Eva-
lyn Rosenberg.

VI. Maria Rosenberg, b Oct 11, 1840, d Oct 18,
1841.

V. Anna Rosenberger, b in Montg. Co. Pa. June 20,
1805, d in Hilltown, Bucks Co. Pa. Dec 7, 1893,
m Samuel D. Heckler. He was b in Montg. Co. Pa.
Oct 1, 1803, d in Hilltown, Bucks Co. Pa. May 1,
1884. Farmer, Ev. Ass'n. C: Ann, George, Elias, 2
Hetty, David, Jacob, Aaron, John, Samuel,
Frank, Amanda.

VI. Ann Eliza Heckler, b 1825, d 1848.

VI. George Heckler, b 182;, d 1857. S.

VI. Elias Heckler, b 1828, m Angeline Garber. She d Dec 3, 1856. No issue. Elias m second wife, Margaret Rebecca Gerhart. P O Fricks, Pa. Farmer, Evangelical Ch. C: Emma.

VII. Emma Heckler, b in Hilltown, Bucks Co. Pa. Dec 26, 1860, m John Van Ommeren June 6, 1878. He was b Dec 8, 1853, at Ingen Province Genlderland, Netherlands. P O Quakertown, Pa. Attorney at Law, Ref. Ch. C: (**VIII**) Henrietta VanOmmeren, b Oct 15, 1879, d Apr 3, 1886. Lottie Mabel VanOmmeren, b May 14, 1883.

VI. Hester Ann R. Heckler, b Feb 20, 1830, d at Ashbourne, Pa. July 1, 1886, m George W. Ma-Gargal, about 1861. He was b in Montg. Co. Pa. Res. Bethlehem, Pa. Builder; Mr. M. Baptist, Mrs. M. Meth. Ep. C: Samuel, Annie, Harvey, Emma, Hester.

VII. Samuel H. MaGargal, b in Rockhill twp. Bucks Co. Pa. Jan 4, 1863, m Laura L. Garner, of Leidytown, Pa. Sept 13, 1883. P O Ashbourne, Pa. Lumber business: Mrs. M. Baptist. C: (**VIII**) Shelden G. MaGargal, b Aug 10, 1888. Infant daughter, b Mar 4, 1900, d Mar 8, 1900.

VII. Annie L. MaGargal, b Sept 12, 1864, m Wm. A. Crouthamel Dec 25, 1884. P O. Soudertou, Pa. Tailor. C: (**VIII**) George M. Crouthamel, b July 8, 1886. Alvin H. Crouthamel, b Sept 15, 1888. William R. Crouthamel, b Dec 14, 1891.

VII. Harvey G. MaGargal, b Apr 1867, m Lizzie Myers. Res. 1304 Butler St. Phila. Pa. C: (**VIII**) Russell MaGargal, b Oct 1887. Earl MaGargal, b Nov 1888, d Dec 1891. Harvey MaGargal, b Oct 1891.

VII. Emma R. MaGargal, b 1871, m Frank Evans in 1892. P O Bridgeport, Conn.

VII. Hester J. MaGargal, b 1872, m John M. Hunsberger 1891. P O Souderton, Pa. C: (**VIII**) Harold, Lola, (d); —.

VI. David R. Heckler, b 1831, m Amanda Kimble. P O Hagersville, Pa. Farmer. C: Anna, Sarah.

VII. Anna M. Heckler, m John Harrison.

VII. Sarah J. Heckler.

VI. Jacob R. Heckler, b 1833. m Lydia Baringer. P O Perkasie, Pa. Retired farmer, Evangelical. C: Ellen, Pierson, Amelia, Leidy, Henry, Levi, Sinniah, Ida, Franklin, Alice, Emma.
VII. Ellen Jane Heckler, d Jan 18, 1890, m John B. Neff. No issue.
VII. Pierson Heckler, d infant.
VII, Amelia Heckler, m Joseph Hunsberger. P O Fricks, Pa. Farmer. C: (**VIII**) Irwin, (d); Ida, d 1893. Leidy, Lauraetta, Harvey, Ella, Howard.
VII. Leidy Heckler. P O Ambler, Pa.
VII. Henry B. Heckler, m Eliza A. Fiester.
VII. Levi Heckler, d infant.
VII. Sinniah Heckler, m Max Fuechsel.
VII. Ida Heckler. m Benjamin Hedrick.
VII. Franklin B. Heckler, m Sabina Proctor. P O Perkasie, Pa.
VII. Alice Heckler, m Roscoe Beisel.
VII. Emma Heckler, d Aug 11, 1896.
VI. Aaron R. Heckler, b Oct 28, 1835, m Sophia R. Rosenberger Dec 4, 1888. P O South Hatfield, Pa. Retired farmer, Ev. Ass'n. C: Annie, Emma, Sophia, Lizzie, Mary.
VII. Annie Amanda Heckler, b Aug 25, 1860, m Abraham K. Fretz Oct 15, 1881. P O Hatfield, Pa. Farmer, Ev. Ass'n. C: (**VIII**) Mary A. Fretz, b Sept 3, 1882. Aaron M. Fretz, b Feb 15, 1887. William Fretz. Sophia Fretz.
VII. Emma R. Heckler, b Oct 2, 1863, m Rev. S. K. Heebner Feb 15, 1888. He d at Lincoln City, Del. Oct 16, 1893. He graduated at the North Western College, Ill., also of Chicago Musical College, and at the New York Institute of Phrenology; minister of the Meth. Ep. Church. C: (**VIII**) Mabel Beatrice Heebner. John Wesley Heebner.
VII. Sophia Ida R. Heckler, b Nov 16, 1868, m Joseph W. Koffel. C: Sophia, Samuel, Joseph, Walter.
VII. Lizzie May D. Heckler, b Oct 3, 1870. Ev. Ass'n. S.
VII. Mary Ellen R. Heckler, b Jan 11, 1873, m Harry B. Godshall. P O Souderton, Pa.

VI. Samuel Heckler, b 1838, d 1841.

VI. John R. Heckler. b in Bucks Co, Pa, Nov 3, 1840, m Victoria S. Fluck Oct 12, 1861. P O Perkasie, Pa. Mr. Heckler has lived in Hilltown twp fifty years, and a part of the time he has been engaged in farming although beginning at the age of 17 years he taught school for four successive terms. Since coming to Perkasie, Pa. he has been engaged as local representative of agricultural implements and fertilizer companies. Ref. Ch. C: William, Calvin, Allen, Nari.

VII. William Franklin Heckler, d infant.

VII. Calvin F. Heckler, b June 12. 1864, m Anna Durner. P O Quakertown, Pa. He is a member of the Philadelphia Bar. Ref. Ch. No issue, (1897).

VII. Allen Henry Heckler, b Aug 6, 1866, m Lizzie Hunsberger, of Souderton, Pa. Carpenter in the employ of the Phila. and Reading R. R. Co. Ref. Ch.

VII. Nari F. Heckler, b Feb 4, 1873, m Lorene Fretz.

VI. Samuel R. Heckler, b 1842, m Rebecca Kimble. P O Lansdale, Pa. Farmer. United Ev. C: Sophia, Abel, Howard.

VII. Sophia Heckler, b Apr 15, 1867, m Frank W. Krupp Apr 15, 1889. P O Lansdale, Pa. Painter, United Ev. C: **(VIII)** Elvie Krupp, b Apr 4, 1890. Infant, stillborn 1891. Rebecca B. Krupp, b Oct 22, 1893.

VII. Abel Heckler, b Mar 9, 1869, m Amanda Kulp. P O Hatfield, Pa. Carpenter. U. Ev.

VII. Howard Heckler. S.

VI. Mary Amanda Heckler, b in Bucks Co. Pa. July 13, 1844, m Charles Massinger July 1, 1867. P O Chalfont, Pa. Charles Massinger was b in Kaiserlautern Rhinepfals, Bavaria, Aug 17, 1832, son of Jacob and Catharine Wenzel Massinger. He emigrated to America, landing in New York City July 4, 1850. He located in Hilltown twp. Bucks Co. Pa. where he engaged in farming until 1854, then from 1854 to 1865 he traveled over many parts of the United States, going as far west as the Rocky Mountains. In 1865 he revisted his native country. Prior to 1867 he was engaged at various times in gold mining operations at Pike's Peak, but in that year he returned to Bucks Co. Pa. and settled in New Britian twp. where he engaged in farming until his death which occurred Feb 24, 1900. He was financially successfully, and was the owner of several fine farms in Bucks Co. Meth. C: Charles, Eber, Wesley, Omray, William, Katie.

VII. Dr. Charles Jerome Massinger, b in Bucks Co. Pa. Aug 31, 1868, m Alfaretta, daughter of Capt. James and Mary Chester, of Goshen, N. J. June 4, 1891. P O Collingswood, N. J. Physician, Presby. C: (**VIII**) James Chester Massinger, b Oct 27, 1892. Charles Massinger, b Aug 30, 1895.

VII. Eber Massinger, b Jan 20, 1870, m Mary Arnold Snyder Apr 4, 1894. P O Phoenixville, Pa. Veterinary Surgeon, attends Meth. Ch. No issue.

VII. Dr. Wesley Massinger, b Aug 16, 1871. P O Chalfont, Pa. Physician.

VII. Dr. Omray Lester Massinger, b in Bucks Co. Pa. Nov 30, 1873. P O Bridgeport, Conn. Physician and Surgeon, Meth.

VII. William Massinger, b Oct 18, 1877. P O Chalfont, Pa.

VII. Katie Mabel Massinger, b Sept 11, 1880.

VI. Frank R. Heckler, b in Hilltown twp. Bucks Co. Pa. Oct 27, 1848, m Maggie H. Moyer Mar 4, 1871. P O Fricks, Pa. Farmer, U. Evangelical. C: Melvin, Ward, Mary.

VII. Melvin M. Heckler, b Mar 27, 1873. School teacher, U. Evangelical. S.

VII. Ward M. Heckler, b May 26, 1875, m Kate R. Hedrick. P O Fricks, Pa. Farmer. C: (**VIII**) Stanley H. Heckler.

VII. Mary Ellen Heckler, b Sept 17, 1881.

V. Barbara Rosenberry, b July 15, 1807, m James Owen. C: (**VI**) Owen, (d); Maria, (d); Aaron and Charles (twins), David.

V. Esther Rosenberger, b in Montg. Co. May 10, 1810, d in Phila. Pa. Sept 18, 1877, m Jacob Wismer. He was b Feb 23, 1799, d in Phila. Pa. Apr 19, 1871. Produce dealer. Mr. Wismer, Meth. Ep.

Mrs. Wismer, Reformed. C: Mary, Joseph, Ann, Barbara, Emma, Henry, Charles, Jacob, Esther, Allen, Franklin.

VI. Mary Ann Wismer, b in Phila. Jan 8, 1830, m Frederick Theilacker Feb 6, 1848. He was b in Wurtemburg, Germany, came to the United States when six years of age; d Feb 27, 1864. Meth. C: Charlotte, William, Christian, Anna, Esther, Mary, Samuel.

VII. Charlotte Theilacker, m Antone F. Miller. Res. 2715 Girard Ave. Phila. Pa. Cigar manufacturer. C: **(VIII)** Alice, Lottie, Frank.

VII. William J. Theilacker, b Feb 14, 1850, m—. C: Mary, William.

VII. Christian F. Theilacker, b Mar 12, 1851, d Mar 23, 1851.

VII. Anna E. Theilacker, b 1853, d 1854.

VII. Esther A. Theilacker, b 1854, d 1856.

VII. Mary E. Theilacker, b Nov 28, 1855, m Mahlon E. Foust. C: **(VIII)** Mattie Foust.

VII. Samuel S. Theilacker, b May 27, 1868.

VI. Joseph Wismer, d 1832.

VI. Anna E. Wismer, b 1833, d 1848.

VI. Barbara A. Wismer, b 1835, d 1838.

VI. Emma M. Wismer. b Jan 14, 1837, m Henry Fetters Jan 14, 1856. He d Aug 12, 1886. C: James, Esther, Charles, Wilhelmina, Milton, Jacob, Clifford, Walter, Mary, Ella.

VII. James Fetters, b Jan 16, 1857.

VII. Esther A. Fetters, b and d Aug 1858.

VII. Charles Fetters, b Sept 13, 1859.

VII. Wilhelmina Fetters, b Sept 25, 1862, m Chas. H. Royer Apr 20, 1889. C: **(VIII)** Wilhelmina, Mabel.

VII. Milton A. Fetters, b Feb 6, 1865, m Clara Spencer.

VII. Jacob W. Fetters. b Sept 27, 1868. Res. 1326 Palmer St. Phila. Pa. Salesman, Meth Ep.

VII. Clifford Fetters, b Oct 19, 1870. Meth Ep.

VII. Walter Fetters, b and d 1870.

VII. Mary E. Fetters, b Sept 20, 1892. Meth. Ep.

VII. Ella M. Fetters, b May 29, 1876.

VI. Henry Wismer, b Aug 21, 1839, d Apr 1874, m Kate Siveaney. C: Hester, Drusilla.

VI. Charles R. Wismer, b Nov 7, 1841, m Eliza Shuman Dec 1, 1867. Res. 2122 Marshall St. Phila. Pa. Clerk, Ref. Ch. C: (**VII**) Laura V. Wismer, b Nov 17, 1869, d July 10, 1888. Charles E. Wismer, b July 12, 1872.

VI. Allen Wismer, b 1844, d 1846.

VI. Jacob Wismer, b Jan 7, 1847, m Mary C. Sill July 28, 1870. Res. 1422 Savery St. Phila. Pa. C: (**VII**) Lillian, Amice.

VI. Esther Wismer, b 1847, d 1848.

VI. Franklin Wismer, b 1851, d 1856.

V. Maria Rosenberry, b Aug 17, 1812, d Nov 17, 1879, m Jacob Munk Aug 1842. He was b in Stutgart, Germany, d at Alliance, Ohio, in 1872. It is stated that he worked in printing office in early life, but later was a farmer. Ev. Ass'n. C: Elizabeth, Mary, Annie, Joseph, Ephraim, Edward, William.

VI. Elizabeth Munk, d in infancy.

VI. Mary A. Munk, b in Columbiana Co. O. Nov 25, 1844, m Valentine Lorentz Sept 19, 1878. P O Alliance, O. Farmer, Meth. Ep. C: Evangeline, Charles, Mary, Edward.

VII. Evangeline Lorentz, b Aug 22, 1879.

VII Charles V. Lorentz, b Oct 12, 1880, d Dec 19, 1882.

VII. Mary Estella Lorentz, b June 2, 1882.

VII. Edward Percival Lorentz, b July 22, 1884.

VI. Annie Munk, m Samuel C. Greenwalt. C: Elizabeth.

VII. Elizabeth Greenwalt, m Harry McKean. P O Yuma, Arizona.

VI. Joseph Amasa Munk, M. D., was born on a farm in Columbiana County, Ohio, November 19, 1847. At the age of five years his family moved to Salem, Ohio, and four years later to a farm near the village of Mt. Union, Ohio, where he spent several years of farm life in work and play and going to a district school.

During the late civil war the boys of his neigh-

borhood, feeling the patriotic spirit of their elders,
organized a company for military drill of which he
was elected captain. In the summer of 1864 he determined to join the Union army and after gaining
his father's consent enlisted in Co. I, 178th O. V. I.
and with his regiment was immediately assigned to
active duty in the field. He served as private through
several campaigns both east and west and in June
1865, at the close of the war and while yet under 18
years of age, received his discharge and was mustered out of the service.

After returning home he became a student of
Mount Union college and after attending school one
year he left college to study medicine with Dr. D. H.
Rosenberg at Bettsville, Ohio; and in 1869 graduated
from the Electric Medical Institute in Cincinnati,
Ohio.

He first located at Lindsey, Ohio, but soon decided to go west and located next in Chillicothe, Mo.
in 1871. Here he practiced medicine ten years; but
not being satisfied with his opportunities moved to
Topeka, Kansas, in 1881 and bought a partnership
with Dr. P. I. Mulvane. The firm of Drs. Mulvane
& Munk did a successful business during its eleven
years of partnership. In 1891 the firm dissolved by
mutual consent, the senior partner Dr. Mulvane
moving to Chicago where he retired from active
practice, and in 1892 Dr. Munk moved to Los Angeles, Califorina, where he has since lived.

During his early years of practice he spent his
leisure time finding out what else he could do believ-
ing that no man knows what all he can do until he
tries. His love of nature and natural science often
took him to the fields and woods. He studied taxa-
dermy and many mounted specimens of birds and
small animals ornamented his office. He devoted
some time to music and composed a number of songs
that were published in sheet form by John Church &
Co. of Cincinnati and glees, choruses and anthems
were contributed to books edited by Prof. H. S. Per-
kins and published by Lyon & Healy of Chicago.
After leaving Chillicothe he discontinued writing

music as his time was fully occupied by his profession.

In Topeka, as a diversion, he joined the Modoc Club a musical organization composed exclusively of men and limited to thirty members. The club was organized in 1876 and under the able leadership of its permanent president Major T. J. Anderson prospered greatly and is in a flourishing condition at the present time. The club is in demand at Grand Army gatherings and public meetings and has traveled and sung from Boston to San Fransisco.

Soon after moving to Topeka he became interested with his brothers in the range cattle business near Willcox, Arizona where they started a cattle ranch in 1882. In 1884 he made his first trip to Arizona and was so much impressed by what he saw that after returning home he tried to find out what had been written on that far away land. In his search for Arizona books he found a copy of Hinton's Handbook of Arizona which contained a list of a dozen or more other Arizona books, copies of all of these books were procured and since that time he has been a constant collector of Arizoniana. In 1900 he published his Arizona Bibliography which contains nearly 1,000 titles. During the past five years he has more than doubled his collection and expects soon to publish a second, revised and enlarged edition which will contain more than 2,000 titles.

During the past twenty years he has made frequent trips to Arizona and the southwest and regards Arizona as the greatest wonderland in America. He is familiar with ranch life, has visited its many natural wonders and prehistoric ruins and has studied its fascinating climate—all of which is described in his new book of Arizona Sketches that is just out.

He has been a regular contributor to current medical literature during the past thirty years and has written for the local press on hygiene and other health subjects. He has been a member of the Eclectic Medical societies of the several states in which he has lived and was elected Vice President of the National Eclectic Medical Association in 1876. He is the present Dean of the Los Angeles Eclectic Poli-

clinic, a post graduate school of medicine that was
opened last year.

He married Emma S. Beazell of Webster, Pa.
January 9th, 1873. One child was born, a daughter,
which died in infancy.

He is a republican in politics and Methodist
in religion.

VI. E. Henry Monk, M. D., b near Georgetown,
Ohio, Apr 12, 1849, m Lillian Hoag in 1874. P O
Nevada, Iowa. Dr. Monk was educated at Mt. Union
College, and graduated, taking his Degree of M. D.
at the American Medical College in St. Louis after
which he settled in Story Co. Iowa, in the practice
of Medicine. Soon after he reached the legal age for
admission to the rites of Masonry he entered Columbia Lodge 292; changing his residence to the county
seat, his membership was transferred to Nevada
Lodge, No 99, where he entered into full membership as a Master Mason June 7, 1873. He has been
an active member of that Lodge for more than 20
years and has perhaps vouches for as many petitioners
as has any other member. He has filled numerous
offices and ably performed his full share of work on
committees and on the floor. He holds membership
and office in three times three chapters where he fills
his chair promptly when not professionally absent.
He has held the office of Health offices for the past
ten years. Mrs. Munk is a graduate of Carthage
College, Ill., and is City Librarian. She is also a
linieal descendant of Elder William Brewster the
spiritual leader of the Plymouth Colony, Mass. 1820,
that came to America on the Mayflower, also of Rev.
John Robinson, pastor of the Pilgrims at Lyden,
Holland. She is a charter member of Abigal Adams
chapter of the "Daughters of the American Revolution," and eligible to membership in Society of Colo-
nial Dames. Meth. Ep. C: (VII) Grace Monk, b
Dec 23, 1875. P O Nevada, Iowa. School teacher.

VII. Edward Brewster Monk, b Dec 26, 1887.

VI. Edward Rosenberry Monk, the third son of
Jacob and Maria Munk, (nee Rosenberry.) was
born January 31st, 1851, in Columbiana County,

Ohio, and with the family a few years later removed to Alliance, Ohio. He received his earlier education in the Union schools, and later entered Mt. Union College.

During the time required to complete a classical course at college, he taught school at various places each winter term in order to obtain funds to carry him through the remaining terms of the college year. Notwithstanding the time thus taken from his college work in teaching, by applying himself continuously by night study while teaching and long hours of study while in college, he finished the four years course prescribed in the college curriculum to obtain a classical degree in the short time of three years, and was graduated during the month of July 1872, by obtaining the degree of Bachelor of Arts. At a later date the same college conferred upon him the degree of Master of Arts, he having pursued a Post Graduate course of study including law and the scinences. After spending a two months vacation in the eastern states, he entered the law department of the University of Michigan, located at Ann Arbor, Michigan, October first of the same year. But being in want of sufficient funds to complete the college course, he entered the law office of Judge Kent at Detroit, Mich., to prepare himself for the coming annual examination to be held by the Supreme Court of Michigan at the April Term, and by continuing what had now become almost a habit of studing long hours, continuing often into the small hours of the night, his preparation was duly completed.

The examination was held on the 29th day of April, 1873, at a session of the Michigan Supreme Court, composed of Chief Justice Christiancy, Thos. M. Cooley, author of Cooley's Blackstone, Judge Kent, a nephew of the Illustrious Chancellor Kent, and the author of Kent's Commentaries; and Judges Cambell and Walker, who together composed the Michigan Supreme Court, and who were all present and participated in the exhaustive quizzing of the applicants for admission to the Bar.

Mr. Monk passed a most satisfactory examination and was duly congratulated by this august body
of eminent men that composed the Michigan Supreme
Court, upon his success and thereupon ordered that
a license to practice in all the courts of the state as
an attorney, solicitor and counselor at law be issued
to him, he receiving his license to practice law just
seven months from the time that he commenced his
law course of study, and matriculation at the Mich.
University, an achievement that has seldom if ever
been surpassed.

Mr. Monk being again out of funds, and it requir-
ing funds to properly open a law office, he accepted
the position of Superintendent of Schools at Nevada,
Iowa, that fortunately was offered to him at this time.

Having conducted the schools with success
during the school year and having thus obtained the
funds required, he opened a law office at Des Moines,
Iowa, and being aided by the kind assistance of
Chief Justice C. C. Cole, of the Iowa Supreme
Court, the officers of the Citizens National Bank,
and other clients, he obtained at once quite an extensive law practice, and successfully conducted a
number of important suits in the various courts of
the state.

During the year 1877, a good opening offering.
he together with his brother, W. C. Monk, removed
to St. Louis, Mo., and opened law offices with the
object of making real estate and corporation law a
specialty. They continued in business together with
much success until 1882, when by over-application
his constitution was completely broken down, and
on the recommendation of his physician he proceeded
to seek the benefits of a milder climat, and out door
life in Arizona.

Arriving in Southern Arizona, he at once saw
an opening to obtain his object and in cooperation
with his brothers located a cattle ranch, gaining the
control of a large body of government land, by locating upon the land and building cabins and stocking
the same with cattle and horses, at the same time
locating and appropriating and developing all the

water consisting of springs that were to be found on the land and thus in time they secured control of a large tract of land, about twenty miles square, located near the railroad with good shipping facilities, and although they experienced considerable trouble with the rustlers (cattle thieves) and Indians, the business venture has been a success from the start. During the years of 1882 to 1884, the Apache Indians under Geronimo made a number of raids from San Carlos Reservation into Southeastern Arizona, and on into Mexico, and more than once passed by or through the Monk Cattle Range that the Monk Brothers had located near Bowie, Arizona. These Indians after fruitless effort on the part of Gen. Crook to stop their raiding through the country, such raids always resulting in the massacre of many ranchmen, miners and cowboys living in the territory, Gen. Miles, who succeeded Gen. Crook in command of the troops in Arizona after a long chase, finally succeeded in capturing the Apache Chief Geronimo and his followers and brought the whole band numbering about 300, composed of bucks, squaws and children, to Bowie Station on the S. P. R. R. from which point they were at once shipped by rail to Ft. Sill and other points located in the East, where the influence of civilization has to some extent enlightened and christianized the band. Since the removal of this band of Indians, no further trouble has been experienced from the Indians, although at the San Carlos Indian Agency and Reservation, there are now living not less than 6,000 or 7000 Indians who are still supported more or less by the United States Government.

But with the removal of these Indians our troubles were not yet ended, for within a few months numerous bands of Rustlers (cow and horse thieves) infested this border country between Arizona and Mexico, and many startling and unlawful incidents might be told of thier murders, train robberies and depredations and injuries inflicted upon the ranch men located near this border country joining Mexico, on the South.

During the years 1884, 5 and 6 the crimes com-
mitted in this section of the country by the Rustlers
had become so numerous and atrocious that the
cowmen, miners and freighters united together and
determined to inaugurate a reform in the administration of the laws. To accomplish this purpose, they
concluded to nominate a reform ticket to be voted
upon at the next election. At the head of this
ticket, Mr. Monk was nominated for the office of
County Judge, together with prominent cowmen
for Prosecuting Attorney and Sheriff. After a most
exciting canvass and election, the opposition ticket
was badly snowed under, and the Cowboy Judge and
his cowboy friends elected by a large majority.

From the time that Judge Monk entered upon
his duties as Judge of the roughest and toughest
section of Southern Arizona, the cow thieves and
Rustlers received all that was coming to them. Some
were killed by the sheriff and his deputies; some
were hung by the Vigilance Committee, and some
were sent to the penitentiary and law and order was
soon established in this section of the territory. He
served with much success during his term of office
and was re-elected for a second term, and at the ex-
piration of this time, Tombstone and Cochise Co.,
Arizona, was as peaceable and orderly as any section
located in the Eastern states.

During the year 1893, there being a vacancy in
the United States Land Office at Tucson, Arizona,
Judge Monk was appointed Receiver of the U. S.
Land Office at Tucson by President Cleveland, and
this office he held and filled with credit to himself
and the Government for the term of four years.
During his term of office many of the Government
Reservations upon which the various Army Posts and
Forts had been located and then abandoned were opened up for settlement both at private sale and public
auction. These Public Sales were sometimes conduct-
ed under adverse circumstances, as an instance might
be given the sale at Old Fort Grand Reservation. This
Reservation is located on both banks of the San Pedro
River, and on account of heavy and continued rains

the river overflowed its banks, and washed away all
the bridges crossing the river for many miles in each
direction from the old fort.   As it was impossible by
those wishing to bid orally that were on the opposite
side of the banks upon which the sale was held by
him the written bid of the would-be-purchaser was
carefully wrapped around a weight and this weight
was attached to a cord and sent across the river, and
the award to the highest bidder was returned in the
same manner to the successful man, and although
rather tedious work, most of the old fort was dispos-
ed of before the sale was ended.

At this time Gov. Hughes of Arizona, appointed
Judge Monk a Regent of University of Arizona, the
school being quite small and not very successful but
under the new administration and the employment of
new and efficient corps of professions, the University
within a few years increased so rapidly in efficiency
and attendance, that many new departments have
been established, new buildings have been erected,
and a fund sufficient provided to insure its continued
future success.

Under his appointment by the Commissioners of
the United States Land Office, as Disbursing Agent
of the Land Office, and his appointment as Civil Service Examiner for Arizona by the Government, together as manager of the Monk Bros. Ranch, as well as
his other duties pertaining to the Land Office and the
University, he had his time fully engaged, and in
fact, his health again having failed, he determined
to again make a change for his future field of labor,
and after visiting a number of places, and cities in the
West, he determined that Los Angeles was by far
the most prosperous and possessed all those attractions
most desirous to establish a permanent home.   Having determined to remove to Los Angeles, California,
before doing so, however Judge Monk concluded to
spend some months in seeing the Old World and in
June 1900, sailed from New York on the Steamship
Furst Bismark,   Hamburgh-American Line for
France; He landed as Cherbough and spent a few
days in Paris visiting the Exposition and greatly en-

joying the many and to him then strange sights and
attractions to be found in the one Paris of the world.

In succession he visited Switzerland, crossed the
Alps, twice, once by Simplon Pass, and once across
the Alps by way of the Trete Noire Pass, traveling
on and sailing over the Northern Lakes of Italy,
thence to Milan and along the Riviera to Monte Carlo,
visiting the Casino, the largest gambling halls in the
world, where by placing a five franc piece on the
Roulette table, he won fifty, and on the same day
and hour many players lost their all, and to these
life became a burden because they were never able
to redeem the fortune they had lost. For but a few
men or women (the women gamble the same as the
men) can say that they are the ''one who broke the
Bank at Monte Carlo.'' Thence he traveled down
the east coast of the Mediterranean from Genoa to
Rome, the old capitol of Italy, wherein are to be
found still standing the old walls and the Collsseum
of the old Roman Empire, thence south to Naples,
on to Pompeii and to the top of Mt. Vesuvius.
Thence across Italy to Florence to the famous Cam-
panile, thence over to Venice, the city built on a
thousand islands, with canals for streets and gon-
dolas to convey the people across the city, engaging
a gondola he passed the Bridge of Sighs that crosses
one of the canals; visiting the Grand Square of St.
Mark, St. Mark's Church, the wonder among the
churches of Europe, and other points of interest.
Thence he traveled north through Germany to Oberammergau where the famous Passion Play is seen
for a season every ten years.

The following extract, taken from the old parish
records of Oberammergau, will explain the origin of
the play in that village:

''In the year 1633 the pest raged so fearfully
that in the parish of Kohlgrub (three hours from
here) there were only two couples left, and a man
named Casper Schuchler, coming here to visit his
wife and child, fell by the roadside and was buried.

''From that day to the eve of Simon and
Jude, a period of three weeks, eighty-four people

died of the plague; accordingly, eighteen burghers, assembling from the village of Oberammergau, vowed that once in ten years they would present in living pictures the Passion of Jesus Christ. From that instant the plague ceased, and those who were ill instantly recovered.''

This vow has, with few exceptions when prevented by war, been faithfully observed every ten years.

Not less than 5000 strangers visit the town every week that the play lasts, during the summer months of the year and are amply repaid for the expense and inconvenience involved in making the journey.

After spending a very pleasant time in Munich, a typical city of Germany and the richest city in Germany in its various treasuries of art, he passed through Austria to Vienna and was present at the annual celebration of the Emperor's Birthday, and witnessed the grandest illumination of a city that has possibly ever taken place.

Thence he traveled north through the city of Dresden and in which reside not less than 50,000 people who speak the English language, although in the very midst of German culture. Thence on to Berlin the capital of Germany. He had often heard and read of linden Strassa (unter den linden) and imagined its immense big linden trees shading the street, but in fact, found a very scraggy and stunted lot of linden trees lining the streets for some distance, and the Strassa is far from being what could be called clean and attractive to visitors.

From Berlin he traveled west to Wiesbaden, a great German watering place. Then to Beibrick on the Rhine and passing down the Rhine on a fine saloon steamer for a twelve hour daylight ride down the River past Bingen on the Rhine on to Bonn, between which points the interest of the Rhine scenery surpassing that of Europe or America for varigated and attractive features.

Passing through Mayence to Heidelberg, the home of the famous old Heidelberg University, he proceeded to the city of Stuttgart, the capital of

Wirtemberg, the place of his father's nativity, with
the object in view to obtain whatever information
that he could discover as to his ancestors on his
father's side.

After a somewhat hasty and unsatisfactory in-
vestigation by inquiring of a number of persons
bearing the name of Monk or Munk residing in
Stuttgart and the village of Constadt, nearby, as to
facts relating to his ancestors, or any facts connected
with their early history.   He became satisfied that
in the earlier genealogy of the family. his great
grandfather emigrated from England to Germany,
changing the spelling of the name from the English
Monk to the German Moonk or Munk, the German
u having the same sound as the o or oo in the
English.   Acting upon the knowledge obtained, he
as well as other members of the family have changed
the spelling of the name from Munk to Monk, although it is even yet uncertain as to the correct
spelling of the name.

From this place Judge Monk proceeded to
Cologne, thence through Belgium to Brussels, and
to the battlefield of Waterloo; thence to Amsterdam
through Holland across the channel to England,
Scotland and Ireland, to South Hampton and thence
by the Steamship New York, American Line. back
to New York.

The following year finds the Judge taking a
winter's trip through Mexico, spending most of the
time in the City of Mexico, with short trips to Vera
Cruz and other points of interest in the country.
Then a summer trip through Alaska, to Sitka, passing by the Muir Glacier and climbing the Davidson
Glacier and on his return trip passing through
Juneau, to Skagaway, and White Pass, back to
San Francisco.   These with side trips to Yellowstone
Park, Yosemite Valley and the Grand Canon of the
Colorado. have provided him with the recreation
and rest that his health demanded, and with renewed
energy and strength he has located and opened a law
office in the City of Los Angeles, California, where
he has sufficient business to keep him well employed.

From the time the Judge reached the age of twenty-one he has been connected with the various secret orders, having joined the Knights of Pythias, the order of Elks and the various Masonic bodies. In Masonry he passed through the degrees of the Blue Lodge, the chapter, the council, the Commandry, and the Shriners, and is now a member of Los Angeles Commandry, and Malaikah Council of the Mystic Shrine of Los Angeles.

He is a member of Christ Episcopal Church of the city, a member of the Los Angeles Country Club, the Jonathan Club, and the California Club, each club being the owners of magnificent club rooms in the city, and thus providing the opportunity for many years denied him by his residence in Arizona, that of the association with highly cultivated and educated people, and to live in an atmosphere permeated with the latest knowledge of Art, Literature, Science and Religion, as well as the enjoyments pertaining to the social life of a city of two hundred thousand people, and blessed with the finest climate in the world.

VI. William C. Munk.

V. Christian Rosenberry, b Nov 21, 1818, m Amanda Leidy. (**VI**) Henrietta, Mary, Josephine, Napoleon, (d); Theodore, (d).

IV. Elizabeth Rosenberger, b Aug 17, 1775, d 1821, m David Shutt. C: Jacob, David, Mary, Nancy, Deborah. Elizabeth m second husband, Frederick Alderfer, Nov 5, 1807. C: Barbara, Frederick, Henry. (See Frederick Alderfer Family).

V. Jacob Shutt, m ———. C: Samuel, etc.

V. David Shutt, (d); m ———.

V. Mary Shutt, m — Keyser.

V. Nancy Shutt, m John Rosenberger. (See John Rosenberger Family).

V. Deborah Shutt, m Abraham Groff.

IV. Mary Rosenberger, b about 1777, m Christian Wismer. He was b Dec 17, 1767, d Oct 11, 1852. Farmer in Skippack twp. Montg. Co. Pa. Menn. C: Jacob, Abraham, Barbara, Henry, David, Elizabeth, Ann, Mary, Hannah, Christian.

V. Jacob Wismer, b June 10, 1795, d 1852, m Mary Detweiler. Farmer. C: Jacob, Christian, Isaac, Henry.

V. Rev. Abraham Wismer, b May 15, 1797, d Oct 15, 1877, m Susanna Kolb. She d 1855. Farmer, minister and Bishop of the Mennonite Church. C: Henry, Susanna, David, Abraham.

V. Barbara Wismer, b Aug 12, 1798, m John Conner; moved to Ohio, he died soon after. No issue. Barbara m 2nd time to Abraham Bean. No issue.

V. Henry Wismer, b Aug 13, 1800, d May 26, 1884, m Hannah Bean. She d 1824. C: John, Kate. Henry m second wife, Catharine Detweiler. C: Samuel, Christian, Mary, Anna, Eliza, Barbara, Lydia.

V. David Wismer, b Apr 5, 1802, d 1876, m Hannah Shutt. Farmer, River Brethren. C: Joseph, Maria, Sarah, Hannah, Daniel, Hester.

V. Elizabeth Wismer, b Apr 14, 1804, d S.

V. Ann Wismer, b June 14, 1808, m Michael Bean. Farmer, Menn. C: Henry.

V. Mary Wismer, b Apr 21, 1810, d S.

V. Hannah Wismer, b June 13, 1814, d small.

V. Christian Wismer, b Apr 13, 1817, (d); m Mary Cassel Dec 3, 1837. Farmer and deacon of the River Brethren Church at Silverdale, Bucks Co. Pa. C: Susanna, Sarah, Elizabeth, Jacob, Mary, Joel, David.*

IV. Ann Rosenberger, m Joseph Kulp. No issue.

IV. Philip Rosenberger, b in Hatfield, Pa. Nov 20, 1781, d Jan 1835, m Mary Landis Mar 29, 1808. She was b Mar 15, 1783, d near Trappe, Pa. in 1840. He removed to Lower Providence, where he bought property as early as 1811. He afterwards lived near the Perkiomen Bridge, on a farm of 91 acres bought of his father in 1815. Farmer, Menn. C: Samuel, Christian, Elizabeth, Maria, Philip.

V. Samuel L. Rosenberger, b in Lower Providence twp. Montg. Co. Pa. June 21, 1809, d at River Styx, Medina Co. Ohio July 2, 1871, m Sarah

*For complete history of Christian and Mary (Rosenberger) Wismer, see Wismer Family History.

Bertolet in 1836 or 37. She was b in Skippack, Montg. Co. Pa. in 1817. d at River Styx, Ohio, Oct 5. 1861, Farmer, New Menn. C: Philip, Jacob, Mary, Eliza, Sarah, Samuel, Hannah, Alvan, Abraham, Harvey.

VI. Philip Rosenberger, b 1838. d Mar 7, 1892, at Forest, Ont. Canada, m Carrie Kilhiner. Dentist. P O Forest, Ont. C: (**VII**) Elmer, b 1861. Alice, Ada, Frank, Daisey, d Mar 7, 1891.

VI. Jacob Rosenberger, b 1839, m--. P O Vermilion, Ind.

VI. Mary Rosenberger, b 1841. m W. Mapes. P O Fulton, Mich. No issue.

VI. Eliza Rosenberger, b in Medina Co. Ohio, Jan 12, 1842, m Henry Walton of St. Marys, Ont. Mar 23, 1865. He was an Englishman by birth, and d Mar 18, 1878. P O Kimball, Ont. Farmer, Episcopalian. C: Sarah, John, Mary, Samuel. William, Jeanette, Eliza.

VII. Sarah Walton, b at Downie, Ont. Feb 2, 1866; was a public school teacher eight years, m Robert Young, of Waubuno, Ont. Mar 1, 1892. P O Waubuno, Ont. Farmer, Presby; Mrs Young, Episcopalian. C: (**VIII**) William Walton Young, b Dec 10, 1892.

VII. John Harvey Walton, b June 1, 1867. Sailor, Episcopalian.

VII. Mary Walton, b June 14, 1869. Taught school three years, m William G. McBean Mar 27, 1889. P O Waubuno, Ont. Farmer, Mr. McB., Presby; Mrs. McB., Episcopalian. C:(**VIII**) Eleanor Walton, McBean, b Sept 10, 1890. Harry Wallace McBean, b May 11, 1892.

VII. Samuel Walton, b Feb 14, 1871. P O Kimball, Ont. Farmer, Presby.

VII. William Walton, b Dec 9, 1872. P O Kimball, Ont. Farmer.

VII. Jeannette Walton, b Oct 22, 1874. School Teacher. ·

VII. Eliza Walton, b June 2, 1877. Teacher.

VI. Sarah Rosenberger, b Dec 19, 1844, m Harrison H. Kindig. P O Fulton, Mich.

VI. Samuel C. Rosenberry, b in Medina Co. Ohio, Feb 27, 1846, m Mary Amelia Hitchcock Sept 30, 1866. P O Fulton, Mich. Farmer, Ref. Ch. C: Marvin, Alice, Bertha, Eva, Ada, Harry, Walter, David.

VII. Marvin Bristol Rosenberry, b at River Styx, Medina Co. Ohio, Feb 12, 1868, m Kate A. Land-fair, Sept 2, 1897. In October 1868 his parents removed to Wakeshma township, Kalamazoo Co. Michigan, where he worked on the farm in the summer time and attended school in the winter. At the age of 17 he entered the Michigan State Normal at Ypsilanti Oct 1, 1890. After having attended the State Normal School three years, and taught school two years, he then entered the Law Department of the University of Michigan graduating with the class of 1898; commenced practice of law at Wausau August 1893, and on Jan 1, 1895, formed a partnership, doing business at the present time as Bump, Kreutzer & Rosenberry, Wausau, Wisconsin. Epis. Ch. C: (**VIII**) Florence Amelia Rosenberry, b Nov 23, 1898, d July 25, 1902. Katharine Rosenberry, b Oct 10, 1901.

VII. Alice Emeline Rosenberry, b June 29, 1870. P O Fulton, Mich. Ref. Ch; m Herman Stofflet May 7, 1902.

VII. Bertha H. Rosenberry, b Sept 1, 1872, m Jason Harrison Mar 2, 1898. P O Vicksburg, Mich. Tinner, Mrs. H. Ref. Ch; C: (**VIII**) Aelen E. Harrison, b Feb 1899. Norma Harrison, b Jan 1902.

VII. Erva Rosenberry, b Apr 3, 1875, m Alfred L. Hitchcox May 13, 1899.

VII. Ada Estella Rosenberry, b Aug 19, 1877, m John H. Stofflet Nov 2, 1897. P O Vicksburg, Mich. Evangelical. C: (**VIII**) Mary Catharine Stofflet, b 1898. Anna Beryl Stofflet, b 1899.

VII. Harry Lloyd Rosenberry, b Jan 31, 1880, d Aug 25, 1900.

VII. Walter Samuel Rosenberry, b Aug 3, 1882. Teacher in Wisconsin.

VII. David Dudley Rosenberry, b Nov 7, 1884.

VI. Hannah Rosenberry, b in 1847, d in infancy.

VI. Henry Rosenberry, b in 1849, d in infancy.
VI. Alvan J. Rosenberry, M. D., b at River Styx,
Ohio, Oct 2, 1851, m Martha Petty Sept 25, 1878.
P O Oak Park, Ill. Physician, Presby. C: (**VII**)
Edith E. Rosenberry, b Aug 12, 1879. Bertolet P.
Rosenberry, b Sept 26, 1881. Alvan A. Rosen-
berry, b Dec 25, 1883.
VI. Abraham Bertelot Rosenberrb, M. D. b in
Montville twp. Medina Co. Ohio, Sept 12, 1854, m
Kate V. Walton, of Bloomington, Ill. Aug 5, 1880.
She d Nov 14, 1886, m second wife, Kate L. Board-
man, of Grand Falls, N. Dak. Mar 26, 1890. P O
Arbor Vitae, Wis.

Dr. Rosenberry lived on the farm in his native
place until 1871, when he went to Michigan, worked
on farms, went to school, taught school, and one
term boarded around the district—worked at carpenter trade in summer. In spring of 1875 he attended
Michigan State Normal School at Ypsilanti, also the
year '75 and '76; graduated from short course in
1876 and taught as principal of small graded school
at Port Sanilae, Mich. during the school year of
'76 and '77. In the fall of 1877 he returned to the
Michigan State Normal School and graduated May
30, 1878, from the full English course. He then
had charge of the graded school at Menominee, Michigan, three years, from 1878 to 1881. In the fall of
1881 he entered the second year of the Medical course
in the department of medicine and surgery at the
University of Michigan at Ann Arbor. In fall of
1882 he entered the senior class at Rush Medical
College, Chicago, and received the degree of M. D.
Feb 20, 1883. Practiced at Peshtigo, Wis. and
Sheboygan, Wis; then moved to Oconto, Wis. and
in Jan 1889 to Harrison, Wis. and Apr 1894 to
Arbor Vitae, Wis.

Dr. Rosenberry has been a member of the Ma-
sonic Order since 1881. He united with the Presby.
Church in 1876,—affiliated with the Congregational
Church in 1884. C: (**VII**) Kate Louise Rosenberry,
b Dec 25, 1890, d Aug 13, 1891. Ruth Bertolet
Rosenberry, b Jan 6, 1893. Elizabeth May Rosen-

berry, b Dec 18, 1896, d May 31, 1897. Louisa
Rosenberry, b Jan 12, 1899.

VI. Harvey Lyman Rosenberry, M. D., b at River
Styx, Medina Co. Ohio, Sept 14, 1857, m Lillie
Belle Fowler Aug 5, 1884. P O Wausau. Wis.
Dr. Rosenberry, resided on the old homestead
until the age of 14, then removed to Kalamazoo Co.
Michigan. At the age of 18 he entered the State
Agricultural College, worked his way through,
graduated Aug 16, 1881. He then entered the
office of Dr. J. F. Baldwin, Columbus, Ohio; attended one course of lectures at the Columbus Medical College and a second course at the Starling Medical College of the same city and graduated from the
later institution Feb 28, 1883. He then located at
Malaga and Miltonsburg, Ohio, removed from there
July 15, 1891, to Menominee, Michigan, and May
15, 1894, he removed to Wausau, Wisconsin, where
he has since resided and practiced his profession.
Presby. C: (**VII**) Amy Fowler Rosenberry, b Dec
19, 1885. Sarah Maria Rosenberry, b July 26,
1888. Ella May Rosenberry, b Aug 2, 1892.

V. Christian Rosenberger, b Aug 29, 1811, d aged
seventeen.

V. Elizabeth Rosenberger, b Oct 30, 1814, d Apr
25, 1879, m Henry Weikel. He was b in Montg.
Co. Pa. Jan 6, 1812, d Mar 12, 1895. Farmer.
Ref. Ch. C: John, Harriet, Emma, Harry.

VI. John R. Weikel, b in Montg. Co. Pa. Feb 12,
1846, m Mary Jennings Nov 25, 1871. P O Fair-
view Village, Pa. Farmer and Justice of the Peace.
C: (**VII**) Bessie J. Weikel, b Dec 24, 1872. Harry
Weikel b Mar 31, 1876, d Apr 23, 1876. Hattie J.
Weikel, b June 10, 1877. Edith J. Weikel, b July
17, 1882. J. Randal Weikel, b Oct 21, 1885. De-
Witt Clarence Weikel, b Mar 7, 1894.

VI. Harriet Weikel, b Nov 22, 1851, m Peter B.
Frank. P O Fairview Village, Pa. C: (**VII**) Harry,
Ida, Bertha.

VI. Emma Weikel, b Mar 22, 1854, d Nov 17, 1873.

VI. Harry Weikel, b Apr 24, 1856, d Aug 30,
1876.

V. Maria Rosenberger, b June 17, 1818, m John Yocum.

V. Philip L. Rosenberger, b in Montg. Co. Pa. June 20, 1820, m Mary Snell Oct 10, 1844. She was b Dec 25, 1819, d in 1892. P O Lower Providence, Pa. At the age of twelve years Mr. Rosenberger's father died, after which he lived part of the time with his mother until he was seventeen, then learned the plastering trade, after which he went west with his cousin Daniel Rosenberger, to Ohio, which was then considered the far west. After a few years stay, he came east and married, and with his wife returned to Ohio, where they remained a number of years, when they again came east, and soon after purchased where he now resides—continuing at his trade for a few years, after which he purchased more land and settled down to farming. Ger. Bap. C: Sarah, Mary, Melissa, Alice, Ida.

VI. Sarah Aleen Rosenberger, b in Tiffin, Ohio, July 13, 1845, m Theodore S. Dome June 16, 1868. He died July 3, 1879. C: William, Mary, Malissa, Walter. Sarah m second husband, H. Wilson Seibert, Feb 3, 1887. Res. 536 George St. Norristown, Pa. Miller, Ger. Bap. No issue.

VII. William G. Dome, b Mar 20, 1869, d Nov 11, 1871.

VII. Mary Edith Dome, b Mar 4, 1871. Res. 536 George St. Norristown, Pa. S.

VII. Malissa Jennie Dome, b Jan 24, 1873. Res. 536 George St. Norristown, Pa. S.

VII. Walter R. Dome, b Oct 25, 1875. Res. 536 George St. Norristown, Pa. S,

VI. Mary Eliza Rosenberger, b in Tiffin, Ohio, in 1847, m Philip Markley. P O Lower Providence, Pa. Farmer, Miller, Ger. Bap. C: (**VII**) Iva, Markley. Philip Markley.

VI. Malissa J. Rosenberger, b near Bloomville, O., in 1850, m Rev. A. R. Thompson, (d). P O Collegeville, Pa., was a minister of the Reformed Ch. C: (**VII**) Arthur, Royer, Warren, Ida, Lawrence, Eva, Ada, Albert.

VI. Alice C. Rosenberger, b 1852, m Abraham D.

Carrel, (d). Res. 212 E. Main St. Norristown, Pa.
Harrite. C: (**VII**) Pamella, Stuart.

VI. Ida E. Rosenberger, b in Montg. Co. 1862. S.

IV. David Rosenberger, b about 1784, (d); m Catharine Delp. He lived in Lower Providence on the farm adjoining Philip Rosenberger, where his father had built a house for him. He could not keep the place, and was sold out at auction. He once said; they sold me out so clean they took all but my Bible. He removed up along the Perkiomen and died there. Menn. C: Abraham, Adam, Elizabeth, Barbara, Daniel, Ann, Mary, Catharine, Philip.

V. Abraham Rosenberger, b in Bucks Co. Pa. Nov 23, 1805, d at the residence of his daughter, Mrs. Mary Coe, near Arcadia, Hancock Co. Ohio, Apr 20, 1889, m Sarah Gehman. She was b in Bucks Co. Pa. in 1807, d in Medina Co. Ohio, Mar 16, 1867. Farmer, Menn. C: Catharine, Samuel, Mary, Sarah.

VI. Catharine Rosenberger, b 1832, d Sept 4, 1848.

VI. Samuel Rosenberger, b Aug 26, 1835. P O Findley, O.

VI. Mary Rosenbeger, b in Montg. Co. Pa. Aug 23, 1838, m Ebenezer Coe Sept 24, 1857. P O Arcadia, Ohie. Farmer, Ger. Bap. C: Sarah, William, Mabel, John.

VII. Sarah Ellen Coe, b Nov 27, 1858, d Oct 10, 1891, m George Wise Nov 26, 1877. C: (**VIII**) Robert A. Wise. Mary E. Wise. Arthur J. Wise. Phebe Ellen Wise. Alma Bell Wise.

VII. William Coe, b Oct 20, 1862, m Eleanor Ring Nov 5, 1884, C: (**VIII**) Mary Eva Coe, b Mar 20, 1886, d Apr 7, 1886.

VII. Mabel Coe, b Feb 21, 1872, m John C. Fisher Dec 24, 1891. C: (**VIII**) Ralph D. Fisher.

VII. John Coe.

VI. Sarah Rosenberger, b 1845, d Mar 16, 1869, m Adam Martin Nov 9, 1865. C: (**VII**) Ida Martin. b Sept 3, 1868, d June 29, 1873.

V. Adam Rosenberger, b in Montg. Co. Pa. 1807, d at Salem Centre, Ind. Feb 14, 1875, m Mary Oberholtzer. Ger. Bap. later Menn. C: Rebecca,

Abraham, Daniel, Jacob, Sarah, Isaac, John.

VI. Rebecca Rosenberger, b May 21, 1836, d Dec 22, 1897. S.

VI. Abraham Rosenberger, b in Seneca Co. Ohio July 3, 1837, d Dec 12, 1865, m Catharine Eckard d at Spring Lake, O. She d at Fort Pierre, Dak. Sept 29, 1883. Carpenter, Meth. Ep. C: Mary, Samuel.

VII. Mary E. Rosenberger, b at Fremont, Ind. Nov 8, 1859, m George E. Brooks Feb 14, 1878. P O Pleasant Lake, Ind. Farmer. C: (**VIII**) Earl A. Brooks,b Nov 20, 1880, m Della Shrimplin Apr 26, 1902.

VIII. Lloyd E. Brooks, b Dec 23, 1882, d July 5, 1885. Clarence S. Brooks, b Jan 23, 1887. Hugh E. Brooks. b Oct 13, 1891. Esther I. Brooks, b Feb 8, 1897.

VII. Samuel E. Rosenberger, b at Orland, Ind. Mar 12, 1863, m Alice Easthan Mar 13, 1889. She was b in Lincoln Co. Ky. P O Butterfly, Neb. Farmer, C: (**VIII**) Meredith Almer Rosenberger, b in Leadville, Colo. Apr 5, 1890. Stella Rosenberger, b in Ashby, Ind. Jan 21, 1896.

VI. Daniel Rosenberger, b in Seneca Co. Ohio, Feb 27, 1839, d in Kent Co. Mich. Dec 26, 1889, m Julia, daughter of Ira and Mary J. Anway. at Kinderhook, Branch Co. Mich. May 6, 1866. P O Kent City, Mich. Mr. Rosenberger enlisted in Co. G. 30th. Ind. Inf. Sept 24, 1861, for three years; was discharged Sept 29, 1864, and re-enlisted in Co. K. 152nd Ind. Vol. Inf; was appointed Sergeant in Co. K. May 23, 1865, served until the close of the war and was discharged at Charleston, W. Va. Aug 30, 1865. He served as Justice of the Peace for eight successive years in Tyrone twp. Kent Co. Mich. C: Adam, Ira.

VII. Adam J. Rosenberger, b May 21, 1867, m Myrtie Stark Oct 20, 1895. He spent some time in the lumber woods, and on the rivers running logs, later engaged in farming. Wesleyan Meth. C: (**VIII**) Charles Allen Rosenberger. b Apr 27, 1897.

VII. Ira V. Rosenberger, b May 4, 1877. He

graduated in the common schools at the age of 16, receiving a teachers certificate. Farmer, Wesleyan Meth.

VI. Jacob C. Rosenberger, b at Arcadia, Ohio, Sept 11, 1841, m Elizabeth Eckard Oct 22, 1865. She was b—, d at Geneva, Nebraska, Sept 21, 1872. P O Pleasant Lake, Ind. Contractor and builder. C: Ella. Robert.

VII. Ella I. Rosenberger, b at Union Hill, Ind. Dec 18, 1866, m Charles E. Freese June 21, 1885. P O Woodstock, Ill. C: (**VIII**) Leo S. Freese, b Aug 2, 1889, at Grand Ledge, Mich. L. Fern Freese, b Mar 23, 1891, at Elkhart, Ind.

VII. Robert E. Rosenberger, b at Flint, Ind. June 18, 1869, m Alice Campbell June 16, 1897. P O Bay Shore, Mich. Clerk. C: (**VIII**) Howard Campbell Rosenberger, b June 16, 1898. Margaret E. Rosenberger, b Jan 31, 1900.

VI. Sarah Rosenberger, b 1843 d aged 9 months.

VI. Isaac Rosenberger, b Dec 28, 1845. P O Hart, Mich. S.

VI. John Rosenberger, b in Williams Co. Ohio, June 26, 1849, m Martha M. Warburton of Quincy, Mich. Nov 21, 1869. P O West Olive, Mich. C: Charles, Nellie, Mary, Jacob, Glen, Carl.

VII. Charles Lester Rosenberger, b May 13, 1871. Sailor.

VII. Nellie Virginia Rosenberger, b June 5, 1873, m Charles Anys. P O Port Sheldon, Mich. Machinist. C: (**VIII**) Virma E. Anys, b Sept 18, 1891. Harry J. Anys, b Aug 21, 1893, d Oct 14, 1894. Leroy Anys, b Feb 24, 1895. Clyde Anys, b Dec 26, 1896, d Apr 26, 1897.

VII. Mary Ethlyn Rosenberger, b July 17, 1875, m George Peabody of Oceana Co. Mich. Farmer. C: (**VIII**) Laura Edith Peabody, b Dec 8, 1894. Charles Warburton Peabody, b Sept 11, 1897.

VII. Jacob Clyde Rosenberger, b Feb 2, 1879.

VII. Glen Leroy Rosenberger, b Aug 26, 1881, d Apr 3, 1883.

VII. Carl Hendricks Rosenberger, b Nov 28, 1884.

VI. Mary Rosenberger, b in Williams Co. Ohio,

Jan 23, 1853, m Charles Young Dec 9, 1872.
Blacksmith. C: Angus, Alma, John, Rebecca,
Isaac. Mary m 2nd husband, Isaiah Rowe, Oct 8,
1889. P O Hart, Mich. Farmer, U. B. Ch. C:
Emma, Magdalena, Ezra, Amanda, Sarah.

VII. Angus Young, b Sept 19, 1874. P O Mars-
field, Wis.

VII. Alma Young, b Aug 31, 1877, m Albert
Butler. P O Tigris, Mich.

VII. John Young, b Sept 5, 1879; was a soldier,
troop E., 13th Cav. Fort Keogh. Mont.

VII. Rebecca Young, b Sept 8, 1883, m Charles
Baxter July 22, 1899. P O Ferry, Mich. Farmer.
C: **(VIII)** Albert W. Baxter, b Aug 3, 1900.
Charles W. Baxter, b Aug 15, 1901.

VII. Isaac Young, b Oct 18, 1884.

VII. Emma E. Rowe, b Aug 11, 1890.

VII. Magdalena Rowe, b and d Mar 15, 1892.

VII. Ezra T. Rowe, b Apr 25, 1893.

VII. Amanda Rowe, b and d Apr 5, 1895.

VII. Sarah Irene Rowe, b Sept 19, 1897.

V. Elizabeth Rosenberger, m Peter Roth. C: Elias,
David, Abraham, Nancy, Catharine.

V. Barbara Rosenberger, b Montg. Co. Pa. Feb 20,
1808, d at Telford, Pa. Jan 27, 1896, m Christian
B. Shelly. He was b in 1805, d at Milford Square,
Pa, Mar 31, 1883. Farmer and Weaver, Menn.
C: Reuben, Jonas, Lewis, John, Philip, Tobias,
Moses, Kate.

VI. Rueben Shelly, b Mar 31, 1838, d May 31,
1896, m Fannie Price. Ger. Bap. C: Louis, Mary,
Wallace, etc.

VII. Louis P. Shelly.

VII. Mary P. Shelly. Res. 4314 Terrace St. Phila.
Pa. S.

VII. Wallace P. Shelly.

VI. Jonas Shelly, b in Bucks Co. Pa. June 3, 1839,
m Susan Fretz Mar 30, 1861. P O Harbine, Neb.
Farmer, Meth. Ep. C: Charles, John, Elmer, Amanda, Henry, Milton, Anna.

VII. Charles Dayton Shelly, b Mar 24, 1862, d Feb
1, 1864.

VII. John Shelly, b Dec 24, 1863, d Feb 18, 1864.
VII. Elmer E. Shelly,   b Feb 9, 1865, d July 18, 1865.
VII. Amanda E. Shelly, b in Bucks Co. Pa. Mar 10, 1868, m Herman Ziegenhain in Jefferson Co. Neb. in 1885. Meth. Ep. C: (**VIII**) William Henry Ziegenhain, b Jan 6, 1887. Albert Ziegenhain, b Apr 8, 1889. Chester A. Ziegenhain, b Aug 12, 1890. Harry Earl Ziegenhain, b Sept 17, 1892. Leslie Ziegenhain, b Aug 14, 1894, d Oct 25, 1894. Zella Ziegenhain, b Jan 11, 1896.
VII. Henry F. Shelly, b Apr 26, 1874.
VII. Milton Shelly, b Jan 20, 1876.
VII. Anna Mary Shelly, b Apr 13, 1879, d Aug 18, 1880.
VI. Lewis R. Shelly, b Oct 20, 1840, d Dec 5, 1892, m Catharine Musselman, daughter of Samuel Musselman, Apr 8, 1865. She d Mar 23, 1897. Farmer, Menn. C: James, Ida, Lizzie, Harvey, Mamie.
VII. Rev. James M. Shelly, b Mar 3, 1866, m Laura L. Hoover, of New Holland, Lancaster Co. Pa. Aug 18, 1888. P O Steelton, Pa. Minister of the United Brethren church, and has served at the following places, viz: Hummelstown, 1889—'91; Florin, Lanc. Co. 1891—'94; Pottstown, Pa. 1894—'96; Steelton, Pa. 1896. C: (**VII**) Ivan Shelly, b June 30, 1889. Russel Shelly, b Aug 31, 1890. Ethel Shelly, b Sept 8, 1893.
VII. Ida M. Shelly, b June 13, 1868, m G. Frank Dieterly Sept 22, 1902. P O Milford Square, Pa. Farmer, Menn.
VII. Lizzie M. Shelly, b June 9, 1871, m John D. Hunsperger.   P O   Milford Square, Pa. Miller. C: Russel, Flossie, Frank.
VII. Harvey M. Shelly, b Feb 4, 1877.
VII. Mamie Shelly, b July 22, 1882.
VI. John R. Shelly, b in Milford twp. Bucks Co. Pa. Mar 15, 1842, m Susanna M., daughter of Henry M. Diehl of Herford, Bucks Co. Pa. Oct 6, 1866. Res. 4312 Terrace St. Manayunk, Phila. Pa. Mr. Shelly in early life learned Blacksmithing, afterwards

puddling and later on engaged in farming for some time. He then started in the Produce business at 4312 Terrace St. Manayunk, Phila. Pa., where he still resides. Menn. C:

VII. Henry D. Shelly, b Mar 17, 1868, d Nov 26, 1874.

VII. Katharine D. Shelly, b June 17, 1871. P O 4312 Terrace St. Manayunk, Pa. Dressmaker, Menn. S.

VII. Anna D. Shelly, b June 11, 1874, d Jan 20, 1880.

VII. Elizabeth D, Shelly, b Oct 3, 1875. Res. 4312 Terrace St. Manayunk, Pa. Stenographer, Menn. Single.

VII. George D. Shelly, b Oct 23, 1877. Res. 4312 Terrace St. Manayunk, Phila. Pa. Stenographer and Book-keeper, Menn. S.

VII. Susanna D. Shelly, b Oct 21, 1879, d Feb 4, 1882.

VII. Moses D. Shelly, b Oct 10, 1881, d Feb 12, 1882.

VII. Angeline D. Shelly, b Aug 2, 1883.

VI. Philip R. Shelly, m Lavina Shutt. P O Preston, Neb.

VI. Tobias R. Shelly, m Annie Berlin. P O Lansing, Kan. Engaged in Mdse. business, Meth. Ep. No issue.

VI. Moses R. Shelly, b at Milford Square, Pa. Sept 10, 1849, m Angeline Shellenberger Sept 6, 1873. P O Telford, Pa. Merchant, Ref. Ch. No issue.

VI. Kate R. Shelly, b at Milford Square, Bucks Co. Pa. Feb 21, 1851, m Charles Z. Moyer July 6, 1872. P O Hillegas, Pa. Farmer, Menn. C: Elmer, Lizzie, Henry, Martha, Moses, Tobias.

VII. Elmer S. Moyer, b July 5, 1873, d Feb 17, 1875.

VII. Lizzie S. Moyer, b Oct 25, 1874, d Dec 8, 1876.

VII. Henry S. Moyer, b Mar 25, 1877. P O Hillegas, Pa. Farmer, Menn. S.

VII. Martha S. Moyer, b Dec 24, 1880, m Oliver Stoudt Nov 6, 1897. P O Pleasant Run, Pa. C:

(**VIII**) Minnie Stoudt, b 1898.

VII. Moses Moyer, b Apr 14, 1887.

VII. Tobias Moyer, b Feb 26, 1890.

V. Rev. Daniel Rosenberger, b Aug 25, 1815, d Nov 1, 1876, m Elizabeth Sidel Hartsough Sept 1, 1839. She was b Dec 22, 1818, d at their home near West Independence, Hancock Co. Ohio, July 27, 1852. C: David, Isaac, Israel, Jemima, Abraham, Edward, Elhanon. Daniel m second wife, Hannah Boastater, May 29, 1853. Farmer and minister of the German Baptist Ch. C: Jacob. Alice.

VI. David Sidel Rosenberger, b Sept 10, 1840; enlisted in the army and was killed in the battle of Chickamagua Sept 20, 1863.

VI. Rev. Isaac J. Rosenberger, b near Tiffin, Ohio Apr 20, 1842, m Mary Ann Workman Mar 14, 1867. P O Covington, Ohio. Traveling Evangelist of the German Baptist Brethren Ch.

VI. Israel Hartsough Rosenberger, b at Tiffin, Seneca Co. Ohio, Apr 8, 1844, m Margaret Susan Ebersole Oct 10, 1867. P O Townwood, Ohio. In early life he taught school, and is at present engaged in farming. Ger. Bap. C: (**VII**) Frank D. Rosenberger, b Nov 6, 1869, In June 1891 he completed the commercial course at Mount Morris College, Mt. Morris, Ill. Soon after he obtained a position in the Bank at Leipsic, O.

VII. Elizabeth Rosenberger, b Apr 18, 1876. She graduated in the Normal English course with the class of '97 of Juniata College, Huntingdon, Pa.

VII. Ella Rosenberger, b Jan 13, 1878. She completed the High School course in the McComb, O. High School with the class of '97 and took a literary course at Juniata College.

VI. Jemima Rosenberger, b in Hancock Co. Ohio. Apr 25, 1846, m Rev. Joshua J. Workman in 1865. He d in 1889. P O Loudonville, Ohio. Minister, Ger. Bap. C: Edward, Ellis, William, Edith, Etta, Jesse, Grace, Eva, Morgan.

VII. Edward C. Workman, b 1866, d 1871.

VII. Ellis Workman, b 1868, m Sophia Coble. P O Loudonville, O. Farmer, Ger. Bap. and Luth.

C: (**VIII.**) Seth, Morton, Theresse.

VII. William T. Workman, b 1871, m Rosa Boner P O. Loudonville, O. Farmer, Ger. Bap. C: (**VIII**) Helen Pearl d.

VII. Edith M. Workman, b 1873, m Rev. H. M. Barwick. P. O. West Alexandria, O. Minister Ger. Bap.

VII. Etta Workman, b 1876. Jesse C. Workman, b 1879. Grace M. Workman, b 1880. Eva M. Workman, b 1883. Morgan J. Workman, b 1886.

VI. Dr. Abram S. Rosenberger, b in Hancock Co., Ohio, May 8, 1848. He assisted his father on the farm, helping to clear a portion of it, and attended the district school during the winter. When 18 years old he entered Oberlin College, Ohio, and in 1868 commenced the study of medicine at Findlay, O. He graduated from the Cleveland (Ohio) Homeopathic Hospital College, in 1870, commenced the practice of medicine in Carey, Wyandott county, O., in April of the same year and remained there until the fall of 1872, when he moved to Leipsic, Putnam county, O. Here he engaged in an extensive practice, having to do most of his traveling on horseback, the country being new and roads bad. In the spring of 1878 he removed to Covington, Miami Co., where he has since maintained a good practice. He m Sabrina Workman, of Loudonville, O. April 13, 1871. She d April 4, 1891. C: Charles, Bertha, Clarence. He m second wife, Elizabeth H. Delp, of Montg. Co. Pa., August 15, 1893.

Dr. Rosenberger was elected to the ministry of the German Baptist church in 1880 and serves the church as a minister as well as his professional work allows.

VII. Charles Lee Rosenberger, b Sept. 11, 1873. Teacher.

VII. Bertha Rosenberger, b Sept. 1, 1875.

VII. Clarence Rosenberger, b Feb. 11, 1885, d June 12, 1885.

VI. Rev. Edward Hartsough Rosenberger, b in Washington twp., Hancock Co. Ohio, Oct. 19, 1849,

m Jennie Wickham, Feb. 25, 1875, P. O. McComb,
O. Farmer and minister, German Baptist. C:
VII. Everett Rosenberger, b Dec. 21, 1875, d Aug.
21, 1876. (**VII**. Jesse Rosenberger, b Jan 24, 1879.
VII. Harvey Rosenberger, b May 19, 1882.
VII. Hetty Rosenberger, b Sept. 7, 1896.
VI. Elhanon Rosenberger, b Oct. 21, 1851, d Aug.
17, 1861.
VI. Jacob Boastater Rosenberger, b July 27, 1859,
m Anna Weaver. M second wife Florence Shell-
house, P. O. Ada, Ohio.
VI. Alice Mary Rosenberger, b in Hancock Co.,O.,
Dec. 30, 1863, m Nathan C. Butler, June 1, 1884.
Res. 628 St. Hanna St., Cleveland, O. Taught
school '81-'94. Finished classical course at Ohio
Normal University. Ada, Ohio. 1897, and began
the study of medicine at Cleveland Homeophathic
Medical College, graduated 1900. Ch of Christ.
V. Ann Rosenberger, M. Christian Hunsberger, C:
Elizabeth, Sarah, David, Mary, Kate, Ephraim.
VI. Elizabeth Hunsberger.
VI. Sarah Hunsberger, m Abraham Ziegler, C:
Ellen,— .
VII. Ellen Ziegler, m Irvin Moll, P.O.Lansdale,Pa.
VI. David R. Hunsberger, P. O. Hatfield, Pa.
VI. Mary Hunsberger, m Samuel Detweiler. No
issue. M second husband Isaac Oberholtzer.
VI. Kate Hunsberger.
VI. Ephraim Hunsberger.
V. Mary Rosenberger, b Apr. 14, 1820, m Peter O.
Stover, June 3, 1838. He d Feb. 1, 1892. Butcher.
Menns C: Catharine, John, Margaret, Adam, Bar-
bara, Joseph, Mary, Peter, David, Charles, Lydia,
William, Philip.
VI. Catharine Stover, b Mar. 10, 1839, d 1842.
VI. John Stover, b Oct. 12, 1840, d 1842.
VI. Margaret Stover, b May 27, 1842, m Joseph
Benner, Merchant, Menns C: Isaac, Peter, Joseph,
Maggie.
VI. Adam R. Stover,b Nov. 10, 1844, d June 3,1872,
m Sarah Hemsing. Soldier in Civil War. C: Amelia,
Uriah. Ellwood, Sallie.

VI. Barbara Stover, b Feb. 14,1846,m Enos Frederick, C: Enos.
VI. Joseph Stover, b Apr. 10, 1847, m Susan Matz in 1867. She d 1884, P. O. Malcomb, Ohio. Farmer. Ger. Bap. C: Mamie, Susan, David.
VI. Mary Stover, b July 3, 1849, m Albert Peterman C., Joseph. Harry, Alice.
VI. Peter Stover, b Nov. 1, 1851, m Sallie A. Allabach. Res. Phila. River Brethren C. Henry, arietta, William, Peter, Lizzie, Charles.
VI. David Stover, b Apr. 15, 1854, m Mary A. Schmidt, Res. Phila., Pa., Ger. Bap. C: Mary, John, deceased, Florence, Maggie, Rebecca, decd., Charles, Emma, David, Sarah deceased, Ellen.
VI. Charles Stover, b Mar.23, 1856, m——C: Bessie.
VI. Lydia Stover, d infant.
VI. William Stover, b 1859, d 1861.
VI. Philip R. Stover, b Mar. 3, 1861, m Sarah J. Shilling in 1882. Res. Ohio. C: Albert deceased, Mary, Charles deceased, John deceased, Chester.
V. Catharine Rosenberger, m Isaac Bilger.
V. Philip Rosenberger, was thrown from a colt, broke a leg from effects of which he died aged 15 years.
V. Elizabeth Rosenberger, b June 18, 1803, d Oct. 21, 1884, m Peter Roth. He was b July 31, 1788, d Jan. 5, 1856. Farmer in Bucks Co., Pa., Menn C: Elias. David, Abraham, Anna, Catharine, Daniel, Peter.
VI. Elias R. Roth, b in Bucks Co., Pa., Sept. 17, 1823, d Mar. 25, 1899, m Anna Fravel, Nov. 5, 1853. She was b near Bath, Pa., Jan. 27, 1826, d Nov. 14, 1884. Weaver and Farmer, River Brethren. C: William, Edward.
VII. Dr. William F.Roth, b near Telford, Pa., Oct. 23, 1856, m Hannah Detweiler, Aug. 23, 1877, P.O. Manheim, Pa. Practicing physician at Manheim, Lancaster, Co., Pa., where he conducts a private institute, making a specialty of the treatment and radical cure of cancer without the knife and allied growths. C: Emma. Elizabeth,Anna,Palmer,Stella, Wilbur, Dorothy, Wallace.

VIII. Emma L. Roth, b June 30, 1879, d Apr. 13, 1881.

VIII. Elizabeth Roth, b Mar.22, 1881, m Dr. Pius A. Noll, May 13, 1899, P.O. Manheim, Pa. Physician. C: **IX.** Richard Montgomery Noll, b Jan. 8, 1900. William Russell Noll, b Feb. 15, 1901. Minnie Catharine Noll, b Apr. 13, 1903.

VIII. Anna May Roth, b Sept. 28, 1882, m Henry Grebe. Residence 109 Dauphin St., Phila., Pa. C: **IX.** H. Wallace Grebe.

VIII. H. Palmer Roth, b Jan. 14, 1886.

VIII. Stella Roth, b Jan. 3, 1890.

VIII. Wilbur F. Roth, b Apr. 23, 1893.

VIII. Dorothy M. Roth, b Oct. 27, 1896.

VIII. Wallace O. Roth, b Dec. 5, 1900, d July 6, 1901.

VII. Edward Roth, b Oct. 25, 1861, d May 27, 1864.

VI. David R. Roth, b Apr 15, 1825, d Oct 10, 1901, m Matilda Harr, blacksmith, Menn. C: Francis, Elizabeth, Mary, Amanda, Milton.

VII. Francis Roth, d young.

VII. Elizabeth Roth, d young.

VII. Mary H. Roth, m Abraham Derstine, P.O. Telford, Pa.

VII. Amanda H. Roth, b 1864, m Chas Freed, Ger. Ref. C: Clayton, Roscoe.

VII. Milton H. Roth, m Sallie Benner.

VI. Abraham R. Roth, b July 4, 1827, d Apr 13, 1879, m Barbara A. Oberholtzer, Aug 9, 1856. Farmer, Menn. C: Henry, Isaiah, Abraham, Mahlon, Mary, Emeline, Harvey.

VII. Henry O. Roth, b June 10, 1857, d Feb 1861.

VII. Isaiah O. Roth, b Jan 29, 1860, m Kate Souder, P. O. Telford, Pa. C: Harry de'cd, Elsie dec'd, Erma, Edna.

VII. Abraham O. Roth, b Nov 19, 1861, m Kate Alderfer, June 16, 1882. Two days after marriage, he took his newly made wife to her parents, and as he was returning to his home he was caught by a wreck train and instantly killed.

VII. Mahlon O. Roth, b Dec 1, 1862, m Katie Derstine, P. O. Lansdale, Pa. C: (**VIII**) Andrew, Laura, Annie decd.

VII. Mary L. Roth, b Oct 19, 1870, m Edwin B:
Bergey, de'cd. C: Edwin dec'd. She m 2nd husband Abraham Ruth.

VII. Emeline O. Roth, b July 22, 1874, d Oct 1874.

VII. Harvey O. Roth, b Nov 25, 1875, d 1876.

VI. Anna R. Roth, b Mar 17, 1829, d Nov 22, 1856,
m Adam Kleinkauf C: (**VII**) Joseph Kleinkauf, b
Feb 22, 1857, d infant.

VI. Catharine R. Roth, b July 18, 1833, d May 31,
1899, m Isaac N. Billger, Oct 6, 1855. He was b
June 29, 1833, d Jan 21, 1902. Blacksmith, Luth.
C: Amanda, Allan, Lizzie, Katharine, Willie.

VII. Amanda R. Billger, b July 4, 1856, m William
Bradbury, Mar 11, 1876, Res. 4937 N. 5th St. Phila.
Pa. Weaver. C: Charles, Agnes.

VIII. Charles W. Bradbury, b July 13, 1877, d Jan
14, 1905. S.

VIII. Agnes M. Bradbury, b Feb 11, 1879, m Clinton E. Sauers, Aug 4, 1898. Painter. C: (**IX**)
Charles, Clinton, Mildred.

VII. Allan R. Billger, b Jan 23, 1858, was twice
married. No issue. Luth.

VII. Lizzie R. Billger, b Aug 14, 1861, d July 15,
1885, m Charles Vearling. C: Katie, Mamie.

VII. Katharine R. Billger, b Nov 25, 1865.

VII. Willie Billger, b Sept 17, 1869, d Apr 26, 1878.

VI. Daniel R. Roth, b Jan 31, 1835, d Feb 4, 1901,
m Catharine Ann Dorn, June 14, 1862. Farmer
and assessor of Franconia Twp., Montg., Co., for
19 years. Menno. C: Lizzie, Enos, Henry, William.

VII. Lizzie D. Roth, b Mar 24, 1863, m Samuel M.
Richards, June 4, 1902, P. O. Zieglerville, Pa.
Butcher. Luth. No issue.

VII. Enos D. Roth, b Feb 1, 1867, d may 19, 1871.

VII. Henry D. Roth, b July 27, 1870, P. O. Franconia, Pa. Poultryman.

VII. William D: Roth, b Mar 3, 1877, m Ida Delp,
P. O. Telford, Pa. Creameryman.

VI. Peter Roth, last known of him he was in Ohio,
married, but no issue.

IV. Abraham Rosenberger, b 1788, d aged about
80 yrs, m Margaret Detweiler, (sister to his father's

second wife.) He lived in Upper Providence Twp. Montg., C. The Mennonite church was built on one corner of his land. Farmer. Menno. C: David, Jesse, Hannah, Fannie, Margaret, Abraham, Joseph, Samuel, Mary, Henry, Barbara, Bettsy.

V. David Rosenberger, b Jan 7, 1809, d Dec 7, 1882, m Catharine Longacre, Dec 31, 1837. She was b in Montg. Co. Pa., Oct 19, 1813, d Dec 8, 1893. He inherited his father's farm which is now occupied by his son J. Warren Rosenberger. Farmer. Menno. C: Mary, Margaret, Hannah, Abraham, Davis, Joseph, Henry.

VI. Mary Rosenberger, b in Lower Providence Twp. Montg. Co. Pa., Dec 21, 1838, m Samuel H. Hallman, of Upper Providence Twp. Montg. Co. Pa., Jan 26, 1862. He was b July 15, 1836, P. O. Mont Clare, Pa. Carpenter. Wife Menno. C: Sallie, David, Katie, Fannie, Harry, Joseph, George.

VII. Sallie Hallman, b Feb 22, 1863, m Jonas R. Umstad, Jan 16, 1883, P. O. Mont Clare, Pa. Machinist. C: (**VIII.**) Angeline R. Umstead, b July 5, 1884, Harry U. Umstead, b Nov 8, 1885, Samuel H. Umstead, b June 28, 1887.

VII. David R. Hallman, b 1865, d 1872.

VII. Katie Hallman, b Oct 16, 1866, m William C. Rosenberger, Feb 13, 1890, P. O. Skippack, Pa. Mrs. R Ger. Bap. C: (**VIII**) Allen H. Rosenberry, b Dec 29, 1890, Edwin Rosenberry, b July 12, 1892. Winfield Rosenberry, b Apr 20, 1894, Mary H. Rosenberry, b May 4, 1896, William H. Rosenberry, b Mar 12, 1899, d 1900.

VII. Fannie Hallman, b Aug 16, 1868, m Alfred Nichols, mar 15, 1895, Res. 310 Righter St. Wissahickon, Pa. Printer. Ger, Bap. C: (**VIII**) Warren H. Nichols, b and d Aug 1896. Mary Nichols, b Sept 30, 1897. Alfred C. Nichols, b Dec 12, 1899.

VII. Harry R. Hallman, b Feb 1, 1872, m Mary Lindauer, Apr 16, 1896, P. O. Spring City, Pa. Slater. C: (**VIII**) Charles H. Hallman, b July 18, 1897, Robert H. Hallman, b Sept 9, 1901.

VII. Joseph Warren Hallman, b Jan 14, 1875, P. O. Mont Clare, Pa. Roll Turner.

VII. George J. Hallman, b July 8, 1877, m Florence
Speece, Mar 18, 1899. She was b Feb 4, 1889. P.
O. Port Providence. Pa. Carpenter. She Ger.
Bap. C: (**VIII**) Helen.

VI. Margaret Rosenberger, b Feb 21, 1841, d Feb
11, 1887, m Job Cox, P. O. Oaks, Pa. Farm laborer.
She Menno. C: Catharine, Mary.

VII. Catharine Cox, b in Montg. Co. Pa., July 29,
1867, m Benjamin H. Famous, Mar 13, 1889, P. O.
Port Providence, Pa. Farmer, Ger. Bap. C: (**VIII**)
Frank C. Famous, b June 1, 1890, d Apr 10, 1891.
Frances F. Famous, b Sept 21, 1892. Martha W.
Famous, b Aug 28, 1894.

VII. Mary Cox, b in Montg. Co. Pa., Jan 6, 1863, m
Abraham H. Jones, Dec 23, 1882, P.O. Yerkes, Pa.
Farmer. Menno. C: (**VIII**) Susie C. Jones, b Oct
3, 1884, Ger. Bap. S. Charles C. Jones, b July 17,
1886. Catharine C. Jones, b Aug 17, 1888. David
C. Jones, b Dec 2, 1890. Abraham C. Jones, b May
4, 1893.

VI. Hannah Rosenberger, b Oct 1, 1845, m Milton
V. Detweiler, in 1875. P. O. Oaks, Pa. Far-
mer, Ger. Ref. C: David, Frank, Joseph, Catharine,
Mary.

VII. David R. Detweiler, b Oct 30, 1875, d Feb 17,
1895. S.

VII. Frank R. Detweiler, b July 25, 1877. Bricklayer at Webster, Pa. Ref. ch. S.

VII. J. Warren Detweiler. b Aug 20, 1879, P. O.
Oaks, Pa. Farmer. Ref. Ch. S.

VII. Catharine R. Detweiler, b May 25, 1881, P O.
Oaks, Pa. Ref. Ch. S

VII. Mary Lizzie Detweiler, b Mar 7, 1883, d Oct 9,
1884.

VI. Abraham Rosenberger, b May 16, 1847, d 1849.

VII. Davis Rosenberger, b Oct 22, 1849, d Apr 4,
1873.

VI. Joseph Warren Rosenberger, b at Yerkes,
Montg. Co. Pa., Sept 19, 1852, m Ida F. Kratz,
daughter of Jonas and Elanora B. (Fryer) Kratz,
Feb 9, 1876, P. O. Yerkes, Pa. Formerly farmer
and owned the old homestead, of Abraham and

Margaret Rosenberger, his grandparents and which
he sold in 1900 to ——. He is now engaged as
clerk. Menno. C: (**VII**) Katharine K. Rosenberger, b June 15, 1881, P. O. Yerkes, Pa. Stenographer and Typewriter. S.

VI. Henry L. Rosenberger, b in Montg. Co. Pa.,
Aug 19, 1858, m Hannah R. Schwenk, Jan 5, 1884,
P. O. Kirkwood, Alachna, Co. Fla. Farmer.
Presby. C. (**VII**) Edith M. Rosenberger, b Feb 7,
1886, d May 10, 1886. Eugene D. Rosenberger, b
Feb 10, 1889. Lena Rosenberger, b Aug 15, 1893.
Bertha Rosenberger, b Apr 10, 1895.

V. Jesse Rosenberger, b— d— young.

V. Hannah Rosenberger, b Mar 9, 1813, m Jacob
Kulp, dec'd, Res. 312 Righter St. Wissahickon,
Phila. Pa. Carpenter, United Ev. Ch. C: Margaret,
Abraham.

VI. Margaret Kulp m Samuel Longacre, Res.
Righter St. Wissahickon, Pa. Carpenter, U. Ev.
Ch. C: Gilbert, Katie, Isaac, John, Harry, Infant,
Hiram.

VII. Gilbert Longacre, m Agnes Kenworthy, dec'd,
Res. Wissahickon, Pa. Printer, Bap. C: Horace,
Earl, Gilbert.

VII. Katie Longacre, dec'd.

VII. Isaac Longacre, dec'd.

VII. John Longacre, m ——, Res. Wissahickon,
Pa. Printer, Catholic. C: Gilbert, Margaret.

VII. Harry Longacre, d single.

VII. Hiram Longacre.

VI. Abraham Kulp, d aged 15 months.

V. Frances Rosenberger, m Christian S. Moyer,
1836. He d 1886. Farmer, Menno. C: David,
Abraham.

VI. David R. Moyer, b Jan 28, 1837, d Feb 7, 1876,
m Anna Clevenstine, 1861. Wheelwright, Meth.
Ep. C: Wilhelmina, Eliza, Samuel.

VII. Wilhelmina Moyer, b June 21, 1862, P. O.
Toronto, Ont. S.

VII. Eliza C. Moyer, b July 20, 1862, m H. Irvin
Moyer, Sept 29, 1887, P. O. Perkasie, Pa. Clerk,
Ger. Bap. C: (**VIII**.) Marion V. Moyer, b 1889.

Joseph N. Moyer, b 1892.

VII. Samuel A. Moyer, b Mar 20, 1869, P. O. Alburtus, Pa. S.

VI. Abraham R. Moyer, b 1840, d 1886, m Wilhelmina Snyder.

V. Margaret Rosenberger, m Abraham Hunsicker, P. O. Fairbanks, Fla. No issue.

V. Abraham Rosenberger, b 1818, d 1894, m Mary Yerkes. No issue. M 2nd wife Susan Peters. Ger. Bap. No issue.

V. Joseph Rosenberger, b— d 1897, m Sarah Adams. Stone mason. United Ev. C: Sarah, Josephine, Benjamin, Joanna, Amanda, Albert, Lizzie.

VI. Sarah Jane Rosenberger, d single.

VI. Josephine Rosenberger, d infant.

VI. Benjamin Franklin Rosenberger, b Apr 1853, m Annie Ashenfelter, Feb 6, 1875, Res. 1208 Atlantic St., Phila. Pa. Carpenter. U. Ev. C: Sarah, Abraham, Bertha, Annie, Henry, Ida, William, Clara, Minerva, Charles, Joseph.

VII. Sarah Stella Rosenberger, b 1875, m Thomas Richard, Aug 1893, Res. 3171 Germantown Ave. Phila. Pa. Huckster. Mr. R Catholic, Mrs. R U. Ev. C: (**VIII**) Stella May Richard.

VII. Abram Rosenberger, b Oct 14, 1877.

VII. Bertha Rosenberger, b Dec.

VII. Annie Jane Rosenberger, b Sept 4, 1882.

VII. Henry Franklin Rosenberger, b Sept 15, 1884.

VII. Ida May Rosenberger, b Sept 18, 1886.

VII. William Albert Rosenberger, b Dec 1888.

VII. Clara Rosenberger, b Jan 17, 1890, d Dec 1895.

VII. Minerva Rosenberger, b Feb 1, 1892, d May 1, 1893.

VII. Charles Fred Rosenberger, b Nov 28, 1893, d Mar 21, 1897.

VII. Joseph Rosenberger, b Dec 31, 1895.

VI. Joanna Rosenberger, b at Roxborough, Pa., June 12, 1855, m Henry R. Evans, Jan 16, 1875. He was b Jan 12, 1851, d Sept 7, 1887. Carpenter. C: Elva, Edna, Joanna. M second husband Samuel Baugh, Feb 17, 1893. He was b Aug 28, 1836. Res. 328 Hall St. Phœnixville, Pa. Employed in

Restaurant. No issue.

VII. Elva Maud Evans, b at Mingo, Pa., Oct 28, 1881, m Reuben Dibsdale, Aug 6, 1899, P. O. — C: (**VIII**) Samuel Reuben Dibsdale.

VI. Edna Mabel Evans, b Nov 27, 1885.

VI. Amanda Rosenberger, m Abraham Barlow, P. O. Phœnixville, Pa. Carpenter. C: Joseph, Sarah, Annie, Lydia, ——

VII. Joseph Barlow, d infant.

VII. Sarah Barlow, m William Sweeney. C: (**VIII**) Eva, Esther.

VII. Annie Barlow, S.

VII. Lydia Barlow, S.

VI. Albert A. Rosenberger, b Jan 5, 1862, m Ella A. Gerhart, Dec 5, 1885. P. O. Lansdale, Pa. Blacksmith. C: (**VII**) Jennie G. Rosenberger, b Mar 5, 1886, d Nov 2, 1901. Verna G. Rosenberger, b Oct 26, 1894. Violet G. Rosenberger, b——

VI. Lizzie Rosenberger, d infant.

V. Samuel D. Rosenberger, b in Montg. Co., Pa , June 15, 1819, d Feb 22, 1871, m Lydia Bickhart. She was b in Montg. Co., Pa., in 1833. Farmer. Methodist. C: Mary, Henry, Abraham, Hannah, Howard, Annie, Samuel.

VI. Mary B. Rosenberger, b Mar 20, 1855, m James B. Hause, Jan 1, 1879. He d Feb 12, 1897. Res. 413 Riley St. Roxborough, Phila. Pa. Luth. No issue.

VI. Henry B. Rosenberger, b in Upper Providence Twp. Montg. Co., Pa., Dec 25, 1856, m Hattie Kenworthy, Oct 9, 1887. Res. 366 Riley St. Roxborough, Phila. Pa. Gardner. Prot. Ep. C: (**VII**) Samuel Lewis Rosenberger, b July 18, 1888.

VII. Laura Rosenberger, b Nov 9, 1890.

VII. Walter Rosenberger, b May 4, 1893.

VI. Abraham B. Rosenberger, b Dec 17, 1857, d Sept 8, 1858.

VI. Hannah B. Rosenberger, b Aug 23, 1859, d June 20, 1875.

VI. Howard B. Rosenberger, b Oct 18, 1863, m Emma Rosenberger, Sept 27, 1898, Res. 2453 N. 31st St. Phila. Pa. Motorman. C: (**VII**) Ida Rosenber-

ger, b Aug 1 1902.
VI. Annie B. Rosenberger, b Mar 9, 1865, m Walter
Silverwood, Apr 17, 1888. Res. 462 Conarroe St.
Roxborough, Phila. Pa. Merchant. Meth. Ep.
C: (**VII**) Mary Emma Silverwood, b and d Apr 1889.
Myrtle Silverwood, b Mar 22, 1895. Helen Silver-
wood, b Aug 17, 1899
VI Samuel B. Rosenberger, b Nov 8, 1870. Res.
451 Krams Ave. Roxborough, Phila. Pa. Weaver.
Single.
V. Mary Ann Rosenberger, de'cd, m John Kepler.
Luth. C: Hannah, Abraham.
VI. Hannah Kepler, de'cd. m Wells Moore. C:
(**VII**) Lulu, Alice,
VI. Abraham Kepler, d young.
V. Henry Rosenberger, d young.
V. Barbara Rosenberger, d young.
V. Bettsey Rosenberger, d young.
IV. Daniel Rosenberger, d young.
IV. Susanna Rosenberger, b Jan 17, 1793, d Aug
22, 1876, m John Rickert, April 6, 1813. He was
b May 28, 1783, d Jan 7, 1867. Farmer in Bucks
Co., Pa. Menno. C: Barbara, David, Daniel,
Catharine, Henry, John, Fanny, Abraham, Tobias,
Valentine, Joseph.
V. Barbara Rickert, b 1814, d — , m William
Strouse. No issue.
V. David Rickert, b Sept 1, 1815, d — , m Eliza-
beth Lapp. Farmer. Menno. C: Mary, Susanna,
Abraham.
VI. Mary Rickert, m John Ruth, P. O. Line Lex-
ington, Pa. C: Allen.
VI Susanna Rickert, m Abraham H. Fretz, P. O.
Hatfield, Pa. Farmer. Menno. C: (**VII**) Sarah,
Ellen, dec'd, Ida, Emma, David, Susanna, Anna.
VI. Abraham Rickert, m Lydia Johnson. C: Jacob,
David, Harvey. Abraham m 2nd wife Sallie Ros-
enberger, P. O. Ashbourne, Pa.
VII. Jacob C. Rickert, m Sarah Krewson, P. O.
Ashbourne, Pa.
VII. David E. Rickert, d single.
VII. Harvey J. Rickert, P. O. Ashbourne Pa. S.

V. Daniel Rickert, b Jan 28, 1817, d — . M Amelia
Swartley. C: John, Henry, Sarah. Daniel m 2nd
wife, Catharine Shisler. Farmer. C: Daniel, &c.

VI. John Rickert, dec'd, m —— .

VI. Henry Rickert, dec'd, m —— .

VI. Sarah Rickert, m —— Deiterly.

VI. Daniel S. Rickert, P. O. Perkasie, Pa.

V. Catharine Rickert, b Apr 11, 1819, d — . M
Joseph Fretz, July 15, 1845. He was b in Bucks
Co., Pa., Dec 11, 1803; d Dec 4, 1880. Mr. Fretz
was a great grandson of the pioneer Christian Fretz,
of Tinicum Twp. Bucks Co., Pa. He was a farmer and owned and lived all his lifetime on a part of
the homestead purchased by his grandfather Abraham Fretz, in Bedminster Twp. now owned by his
son, Anthony R. and Quincy A. Fretz. Mr. Fretz
was a man of perhaps more than ordinary intelligence, a very observing man and a great reader.
Menno. C: Allen, Quincy, Joseph, Susan, Anthony,
Ella.

VI. Allen W. Fretz, b March 5, 1846, d — , m Mary
E. McFarland, July 3, 1870. She was b in Mon-
treal, Canada, Dec 8, 1845. Res. Easton, Pa.

VII. Rilla Alice Fretz, b Apr 9, 1871.

VII. J. Titus Fretz, b Feb 2, 1873.

VII. Wilson Shurtz Fretz, b June 19, 1875.

VII. Charles J. Fretz, b Mar 22, 1877.

VII. Delbert B. Fretz, b Dec 28, 1879.

VII. Merrill Linn Fretz, b Dec 17, 1881.

VII. Robert A. Fretz, b May 26, 1883.

VII. Mamie Fretz, b Feb 15, 1886, d May 8. 1887.

VI. Quincy A. Fretz, b in Bucks Co., Pa., July 18,
1847, m Catharine Yeakel, of Hilltown, Pa. She
was b May 27, 1847. P. O. Bedminster, Pa. Farmer. Menno. C: (**VII**) Alice Y. Fretz, d an infant.

VI. Joseph Titus Fretz, b May 5, 1849, d Apr 27,
1870, aged 20 y., 11 m., 22 d.

VI. Susan Fretz, b June 7, 1852, m Mahlon Essig,
of Arcadia, Hamilton Co., Ind., June 22, 1884, P.
O. Arcadia, Ind. Farmer. Mrs. Essig Menno. C:
VII. Infant daughter, born and died Apr 11, 1886.

VII. Emma Mabel Essig, b July 8. 1887.

VI. Anthony R. Fretz, b Feb 19, 1856, m Ella Barron, P. O. Bedminster, Pa. Farmer. C: (**VII**) Morris D. Fretz, b Mar 5, 1883. Chester A. Fretz, b Mar 26, 1885. Joseph E. Fretz, b Aug 6, 1886. Ada M. Fretz, b Oct 8, 1888. Jennie E. Fretz, b Nov 9, 1890. Lila E. Fretz, b Apr 30, 1892. R. Lloyd Fretz, b Nov 12, 1893. Alma B. Fretz, b June 7, 1896.

VI. Ella R. Fretz, b Oct 22, 1862. S.

V. Henry Rickert, dec'd, b in Bucks Co. Pa., Dec 1, 1821, m Mary Hendricks, Jan 1844. She was b in Bucks Co. Pa., Aug 15, 1824, P. O. Wadsworth, O. Farmer. Menno. C: Susan, Jacob, Allen, Maria, Amanda, John, Emma, Henry, Harvey.

VI. Susan Rickert, b in Bucks Co. Pa., Jan 14, 1845, m John S. Hartzell, Sept 16, 1871, P. O. Wadsworth, O. Luth. C: (**VII**) Nelson Hartzell, b July 16, 1872, P. O. Wadsworth, O. Wood worker. (**VII**) Lloyd J. Hartzell, b Oct 25, 1872, P. O. Wadsworth, O. Mechanic. Ref. Ch. (**VII**) Elmer Wallace Hartzell, b Sept 22, 1879, P. O. Wadsworth, O. Luth.

VI. Jacob H. Rickert, b in Bucks Co. Pa., Oct 23, 1846, m Adeline Frankenfield, Sept 26, 1874. She was b in Lehigh Co. Pa., Nov 7, 1850, P. O. Wadsworth, O. Drayman. Ref. Ch. C: (**VII**) Ida Mae Rickert, b Jan 17, 1876, P. O. Wadsworth, O. Music teacher. Ref. Ch. (**VII**) Della Mabel Rickert, b Sept 25, 1877, P. O. Wadsworth, O. Ref. Ch.

VI. Allen H. Rickert, b in Bucks Co. Pa., Dec 20, 1848, m Mary K. Friedt, P. O. Wadsworth, O. Farmer. Menno. C: (**VII**) William Henry Rickert, b May 6, 1875. Menno. Elizabeth Gertrude Rickert, b Apr 1, 1877. Menno. Laura Josephine Rickert, b Mar 27, 1887. Charles Allen Rickert, b Aug 12, 1893.

VI. Maria Rickert, b in Bucks Co. Pa., Mar 12, 1851, m Jeremiah Loehr, Nov 14, 1874, P. O. Blake, O. Farmer. Luth. C: (**VII**) Freddie R. Loehr, b Nov 4, 1876, d Apr 12, 1881. Nettie May Loehr, b Sept 17, 1879.

VI. Amanda Rickert, b in Bucks Co. Pa., Sept 20, 1853, m Martin G. Honder, Apr 9, 1881. He was b in Lancaster Co. Pa.. May 5, 1853. P. O. Wadsworth, O. Merchant. Menno. C: (**VII**) Charles H. Honder, b Feb 21, 1882. Clerk.

VII. Harvey C. Honder, b Mar 20. 1884.

VII. Freddie R. Honder, b Oct 9, 1890.

VI. John Rickert, b in Medina Co., Ohio, Jan 27, 1857, m Hannah M. Good, Mar 26, 1881, P. O. Wadsworth, O. Stationary engineer. M. E. Ch. C: (**VII**) Verna Rickert, b Jan 13, 1887. Meth Ep.

VI. Emma Rickert, b in Medina Co., O., 1860, m John B. Drissel, of Phila. Pa., Dec 25, 1895. He was b in Bucks Co. Pa , June 26, 1853, P. O. Wads.-worth, O. Carpenter. Mr. D. Luth. Mrs. D. Menno.

VI. Henry Rickert, b in Medina Co, O., May 17. 1862, d Oct 1, 1891, m Ida Fritz, June 1889. C: (**VII**) Hazel Rickert, b June 9, 1890.

VI.Harvey Rickert, b in Medina Co., O., Mar 3, 1865, m Lizzie Kindig, of River Styx, O., Nov 21, 1891, P. O. Wadsworth, O. Farmer. Menno. C: (**VII**) Ruth Rickert.

V. John Rickert, b in Bucks Co. Pa., Sept 11, 1823, d 1899, m Eliza Fretz, Nov 9, 1851, P. O Medina, O. Farmer. C: Sarah, Valentine, Mary, Abraham, John, Ella, Ida.

VI. Sarah Rickert, b June 30, 1863, d July 1853.

VI. Valentine F. Rickert, b in Ohio Sept 17, 1854, m Lewic Henry, Dec 12, 1879. She d 1887, P. O Medina, O. Farmer. C: (**VI**) James Rickert, b 1880. (**VII**) Clare Rickert, b 1882, d 1883. (**VII** Carl Rickert, b 1883. (**VII**) Lewie Rickert, b 1886, m 2nd wife Minnie Thompson, 1891. She d 1898. m 3rd wife Alice Bateman, 1901.

VI. Mary Susan Rickert, b Oct 13, 1857, m Reuben Yoder, Feb 25, 1882. P. O. Dixon, Ill. Farmer. C: (**VII**) Ida Yoder, b Mar 2, 1884, d 1901.

VI. Abraham F. Rickert, b Oct 18, 1859, m Addie Reece, Sept 26, 1890, P. O. Medina, O. C: (**VII**) Hazel Rickert, b Mar 17, 1892.

VII. George Rickert, b Oct 2. 1894.

VI. Sarah Rickert, b in Medina Co., O., Apr 18, 1862, m George McCleary, Mar 4, 1896. He d May 19, 1898, P. O. Dixon, Ill. Farmer.

VI. John Rickert, b May 10, 1864, d July 2, 1888.

VI. Ella K. Rickert b in Medina Co., O., Sept 30, 1867, m Sherman Hill, May 29, 1894, P. O. Medina, O   Farmer

VI Ida Eliza Rickert, b Mar 11, 1871, m Henry Steiner, Dec 19, 1895, P. O Sterling, O   Dealer in implements

V Fanny Rickert, b Nov 13, 1826, d—, m Henry Musselman   He was b in Bucks Co. Pa., July 27, 1821, d Dec 11, 1851   C: Catharine, Susan.

VI. Catharine Musselman, m —— Rothrock, P. O. Doylestown. Pa

VI Susan Musselman, m Charles Painter, P. O. Quakertown. Pa

V. Abraham Rickert, b Oct 19, 1828. M Elizabeth Smith, Dec 10, 1853, P. O. Plumsteadville, Pa   C: Jonas, Martha, Albert, Isaac, Daniel, David, Eli.

VI. Jonas S. Rickert. b Nov 16, 1854, d May 3, 1866.

VI. Martha S. Rickert, b July 12, 1856, m Reuben B. Detweiler, (his second wife) June 24, 1882, P. O. Buckingham, Pa.   Farmer.   Menno.   C: (**VII**) Theodore R. Detweiler, b July 12, 1883, Elizabeth R. Detweiler, b Oct 30, 1884, David R. Detweiler, b May 10, 1886, Valentine R. Detweiler, b June 8, 1887, Katie R. Detweiler, b Sept 7, 1888, d Feb 2, 1890, Charles R. Detweiler, b June 14, 1892, Clayton R. Detweiler, b Nov 26, 1894, Anna Mary Detweiler, b Jan 18, 1896, Harvey R. Detweiler, b Aug 5, 1897, Sallie R. Detweiler, b Aug 10, 1899.

VI. Albert S. Rickert, b June 20, 1859, d 1866.

VI. Isaac S. Rickert, b June 14, 1866, m Mary J. Sames, P. O. Souderton, Pa.

VI. Daniel S. Rickert, b Mar 26, 1867, m Tillie Sames, P. O. Souderton, Pa.

VI. David S. Rickert, b June 30, 1866, m Sallie Sames, Jan 20, 1894, P. O. Jenkintown. Laborer. Luth.   C: (**VII**) Maria S. Rickert, Dec 18, 1895, Russel S. Rickert, b Apr 14, 1898.

VI. Eli S. Rickert, b Apr 29, 1870, m Hildah M. Myers, Oct 17, 1891, P. O. Pipersville, Pa.   C: (**VII**) Raymond M. Rickert, b Nov 18, 1893, Abraham M. Rickert, b Nov 29, 1896.

V. Tobias Rickert, b Dec 24, 1830, d — , m Hester Landis, de'cd. Farmer. Menno. C: Lizzie, William, Susan, Franie, Mary.

VI. Lizzie Rickert, m —— Carty.
VI. William Rickert, —— .
VI. Susan Rickert, m —— Black.
VI. Franie Rickert, m —— Fry.
VI. Mary Rickert, m —— Pross.

V. Valentine Rickert, b July 13, 1832, d Sept 17, 1892, m Elizabeth Drissel, Jan 8, 1853. She was b Jan 19, 1833. Farmer in Bucks Co., Pa. Menno. C: Salome, John, Kate, Sallie, Susan, Allen, Lizzie, Clara, Valentine.

VI. Salome Rickert, b Jan 2, 1856, d 1862.
VI. John Quincy D. Rickert, b Mar 8, 1857, m Christiana Meyers. She was b Aug 21, 1858, P. O. Dublin, Pa. Farmer. Ger. Ref. C: (**VII**) William, Valentine, Quincy.
VI. Kate D. Rickert, b Nov 26, 1859, m William H. Meyers, P. O. Dublin, Pa. Farmer. Menno. C: (**VII**) Valentine, Lincoln, Isaac de'cd, Lizzie.
VI. Sallie D. Rickert, b. Nov. 20, 1861, m Jacob W. Meyers, 1880, P. O. Dublin, Pa. Carriage-builder. Menno. C: (**VII**) Frank, Lizzie, Clara, Emma.
VI. Susan D. Rickert, b Jan 21, 1864, m John K. Alderfer. Sept 19, 1885, P. O. Garisville, Pa. Farmer. Menno. C: (**VII**) Irwin, Lizzie, Mahlon.
VI. Allen D. Rickert, b Feb 21, 1866, m Katie H. Derstine, Feb 24, 1887, P. O. Milford Square, Pa. Farmer. Menno. C: (**VII**) Bertha D. Rickert, b Aug 14, 1890, Clara D. Rickert, b June 26, 1894, Joseph D. Rickert, b July 16, 1898.
VI. Lizzie D. Rickert, b May 19, 1868, m Henry H. Hartman, Dec 20, 1890, P. O. Milford Square, Pa. Blacksmith. Ref. Ch. C: (**VII**) Philip R. Hartman, b Apr 1892, d 1892.
VI. Clara D. Rickert, b July 14, 1870, m John F. Detweiler. Farmer. Menno. C: (**VII**) Anna, Ida, Lizzie.
VI. Valentine D. Rickert, b Aug 30, 1872, m Ella Bergey, P. O. Perkasie, Pa. Laborer. Ref. Ch. C: (**VII**) Allen B. Rickert.

V. Joseph R. Rickert, b in Bedminster Twp., Bucks Co., Pa., Jan 4, 1835, m Alice Jones, daughter of Joseph M. and Ann Grier Jones, Feb 1, 1862, P. O. Carversville, Pa. Harness maker and carriage trimmer. Presby. C: Luella, Anna.

VI. Luella Rickert, b Oct 25, 1863, P. O. Carversville, Pa. Dressmaker. Presby. S.

VI. Anna B. Rickert, b Sept 22, 1866, P. O. Carversville, Pa. Dressmaker Presby. S.

IV. John R senberger, b about 1798, d - -, m Sarah Detweiler. He was one of the executors of his father's will, and settled on part of the old homestead and lived and died there. Farmer. Menn. C: Martin, Bar.ara, David, Samuel, Joseph, Mary, Sarah.

V. Martin Rosenberger, b Feb 14, 1819, d in 1895, m Esther Bergey. Farmer. Menn. C: John, Mary, Benjamin, Lizzie, Frank, Sallie.

VI. John B. Rosenberger, b July 25, 1842, d May 5, 1895, M Mary G. Fetterolf in 1864, P. O. Lansdale, Pa. He was the founder of the Lansdale Republican and later conducted a news-store and restaurant in Lansdale, Pa. Luth. C: Rebecca, Frank, George, John, Jerome.

VII. Rebecca Rosenberger, b Aug 7, 1864, m William T. Ewing, July 5, 1883, P. O. Lansdale, Pa. Episcopal. C: (**VIII**) William T. Ewing, b July 20, 1884, Mary Winifred Ewing, b Mar 2,1887, Beatrice Ray Ewing, b Jan 5, 1891, Rebecca Claire Ewing, b Jan 15. 1896.

VII. Frank Rosenberger, b Nov 9, 1865, m Matilda G. Beck, Jan 22, 1895, Res 1436, Columbia St., Phila., Pa. Caterer.

VII. George F. Rosenberger.

VII. John F. Rosenberger, b July 5, 1871, m Linda Pennich, June 23, 1897. P. O. Lansdale, Pa. Stationer and bookseller. Ref. Ch.

VII. Jerome F. Rosenberger, b at Hatfield, Pa., May 9, 1874, m Ella T. Ziegler, Jan 2, 1893. She was b June 21, 1874, P. O. Lansdale, Pa. Employed on R. R. Luth. C: (**VIII**) Mary Rosenberger, b Apr 1, 1894, d Nov 10, 1895, Ella Rosenberger, b

Sept 27, 1895.

VI. Mary Rosenberger, d young.

VI. Benjamin Rosenberger, d single.

VI. Elizabeth Rosenberger, m Benjamin Ruth.

VI. Frank Rosenberger, de'cd, m ——. No issue.

VI. Sallie Rosenberger, m John B. Clemens. C: Esther, Martha, John.

VII. Esther Clemens, m —— Moyer.

V. Barbara Rosenberger, b Apr 1, 1820, m Henry B. Fretz, Oct 9, 1842. He d May 6,1903. Farmer. Menn. C: Sarah, Abraham, Susanna, Sylvester, Mary, James.

VI. Sarah Ann Fretz, b Nov 29, 1844, m James Garis, March 21, 1874. Luth. C: (**VII**) Pearson Garis, b and d 1875, Mary E. Garis, b 1881, d 1882, Warren Garis, b 1877, d 1898, Sylvester Gari.. l. March 19, 1883.

VI. Abraham J. Fretz, b Apr 9, 1847, m Mary Handle. She d Feb 1, 1873. C: Franklin,William. He m 2nd wife, Susan A. Yoder, Jan 24, 1874. She d Jan 21, 1891. C: Ephriam, Laura, Cora, Malinda, Martha, Bertha. He m 3rd wife, Mrs. Emeline J. (Newhart) Gilbert. Nov. 15, 1892, Res 2550, N 7th St., Phila., Pa. C: Barbara, Elnora.

VII. Franklin H. Fretz, b 1869, d 1895.

VII. William H. Fretz, b July 7, 1872, m Margaret Innis, Oct 21,1891. Presby. C: (**VIII**) William W. Fretz, b Dec 31, 1892, Charles H. Fretz, b Nov. 4, 1894, Robert I. Fretz, b Sept 10, 1896.

VII. Ephriam Y. Fretz, b Dec 22, 1874, m Susan H. Benner, Oct 27, 1898. C: (**VIII**) Abraham B. Fretz, b May 3, 1900, Walter B. Fretz, b Sept 10, 1901, Irma B. Fretz, b Dec 12,1903.

VII. Laura Y. Fretz, b Sept 21, 1876, d April 22, 1900, m Orlando L. Rice, March 14, 1899. C: (**VIII**) Orlando Rice, b and d April 19, 1900.

VII. Cora Y. Fretz, b Oct 12, 1877, d Feb 8, 1902, m John G. Bell, Sept 21, 1900. C: (**VIII**) Elsie,de'cd.

VII Malinda Y. Fretz b May 30, 1880, m Jacob A. Detweiler, Nov. 15, 1902.

VII. Martha Fretz, b Feb 23, 1883, d 1883.

VII. Bertha Fretz, b Nov 7, 1887, d 1888.

VII. Barbara N. Fretz, b April 26, 1894.

VII. Elnora N. Fretz.

VI. Susanna Fretz, b April 14, 1850, m Addison Reinhart, 1868. Farmer. Ger. Bap. C: (**VII**) Alice Reinhart, b April 17, 1869, m J. Y. Gross, Sept 13, 1892. C: (**VIII**) Ethel Gross, b 1894, Elnora Gross, b 1896, James A. Gross, b 1897, Cora Gross, b 1900, Russell Gross, b 1902.

VII. Erwin Reinhart, b 1871, d 1872.

VII. Nelson Reinhart, b Aug 24, 1872, m Kate McKargh.

VII. Clinton Reinhart, b Dec 12, 1874.

VII. Mabel Reinhart, b June 25, 1885.

VI. Sylvester R. Fretz, b Nov 5, 1854, d Oct 17, 1899, m Laura G. Yerger, Aug 23, 1882. C: (**VII**) Amanda N. Fretz, b Mar 25, 1884, d 1884. Arthur S. Fretz, Dec 26, 1886.

VI. Mary Amanda Fretz, b Aug 31, 1857, S.

VI. James H. Fretz, b Sept 10, 1862, d Nov 6, 1881.

V. David D. Rosenberger, b about 1833, d Apr 1876, m Elizabeth Rosenberger, about 1845. Farmer. Menn. C: John, Mary, Abner, Samuel, Katie, Maggie. M 2nd wife Catharine Clemmer and 3rd wife Lydia Bitting. No issue.

VI. John R. Rosenberger, b Sept 18, 1845, m Charlotte J. VanHorn, Dec 9, 1873, P. O. Meridan, Ill., R. R. Agent and Telegraph Operator. C: Faye, Floy.

VII. Faye Rosenberger, b at Pawpaw, Ill., Nov 17, 1874, m Albert L. Stevenson, Dec 10, 1895, P.O. Ohio, Ill. Barber. C: (**VIII**) Merton, Floyd Stevenson, b Oct 27, 1896. Hazel L. Stevenson, b——

VII. Georgia Floy Rosenberger, m B. S. Sweet, P. O. Kangley, Ill.

VI. Mary Rosenberger, b Feb 13, 1849, m Isaac Hager, 1860. Res. 1008 W Orleans St. Phila. Pa. Carpenter. Meth. Ep. C: Ella, Katie, Harvey, Jacob, Mary, Isaac.

VII. Ella N. Hagey, b 1872, m Frank Baird, P. O. Norristown, Pa. Car Inspector. Luth.

VII. Katie Hagey, b 1875. Luth.

VII. Harvey Hagey, b 1878. Meth. Ep.

VII. Jacob G. Hagey, b 1880. Meth. Ep.
VII. Mary Hagey, b 1884. Meth. Ep.
VII. Isaac Hagey, b 1886. Meth. Ep.
VI. Kate C. Rosenberger, b in Franconia Twp. Montg. Co., Pa., Apr 6, 1852, m Charles W. Keck, May 7, 1872. P. O. North Wales. Pa. Ger. Ref. Ch.   C: Wilson, Maggie, Edwin, Lillian, Charles, Bertha, Florence, Elsie, Abner.
VII. Wilson D. Keck, b Mar 1, 1873, in Bucks Co., Pa., P. O. North Wales. Carpenter. Baptist.
VII. Maggie Idella Keck, b Jan 7, 1875, d Mar 22, 1876.
VII. Edwin F. Keck, b at Hatfield, Pa., Apr 2, 1877, m Clara M. Lukens, July 2, 1896, P. O. North Wales, Pa. Cigarmaker. Meth. Ep. C: (**VIII**) Kathryn E. Keck.
VII. Lillian M. Keck, b Jan 26, 1879. Ref. Ch.
VII. Charles R. Keck, b Aug 9, 1881, d Nov 20, 1891.
VII. Bertha S. Keck, b July 29, 1883, d Oct 1, 1896.
VII. Floeanus R. Keck, b May 4, 1885.
VII. Elsie C. Keck, b Dec 14, 1889, d Nov 10, 1891.
VII. Abner W. Keck, b May 30, 1893.
VI. Margaret Rosenberger, m Theodore Hardenfelt, P. O. North Wales, Pa. C: Oscar, Vernon.
VI. Samuel Rosenberger, b 1858, m Lizzie Renner, P. O. Fountainville, Pa. Farmer.   C: (**VIII**) Oscar, Warren, Clarence, Pearl, Emma.
VI. Abner W. Rosenberger, b Sept 2. 1862, m Emma S. Kulp. Dec 13, 1885, P. O. Skippack, Pa. Merchant. Ref. Ch. No issue.
V. Samuel Rosenberger, dec'd, m Lana Wile, went to Illinois.   C: Sallie, Jennie, Elizabeth, &c
V. Joseph Rosenberger, b June 9, 1828, d Feb 21, 1885, m Mary Shutt, dec'd. No issue. M second wife Mary Nace. Laborer. Menn. C.
VI. James Rosenberger, b Sept 13, 1859, m Emma Gerhart, P. O. Sellersville, Pa. Cigarmaker. C: (**VII**) Stella Rosenberger.
V. Sarah Rosenberger, d aged 16 years.
IV. Henry Rosenberger, b in Montg. Co., 1800, d 1865, m Sallie Landis, in 1819. She was b in Bucks

Co., d 1860. He lived on the old homestead t'll near the close of his life, when he bought a ten acre-lot in Hilltown, where he died. Farmer. Menn's. C: George, David, Aaron, Josiah, Simon, Enos.

V. George Rosenberger, M. D., b Mar 3, 1823, d Mar 1894, m Lizzie Trively, from whom he was divorced. No issue. He m 2nd wife————. No issue. He was a surgeon in the army and after leaving the army he located near Quincy, Ill., where he died.

V. David Rosenberger, b 1825, m Mary Ann, dau. of Philip Swartley, in 1852. C: Lyman, Josiah, Monroe. Jeannetta, Jermina. David m 2nd wife Catharine Swartley, (nee Haldeman) P. O. Lansdale, Pa. Farmer. Ger. Bap.

VI. Lyman Rosenberger, b Jan 14, 1854, m Sallie Barndt, she d 1874. C: Sallie. Lyman m 2nd wife Lizzie Ann Clemens, Res. Harleysville, Pa. Creameryman for some years. C: Wellington, Harry, Stella.

VII. Sallie Rosenberger, b ————, Wellington Rosenberger, b Apr 18, 1877, Harry Rosenberger, b July 3, 1879, Stella Rosenberger, b Nov 17, 1880.

VI. Josiah Rosenberger, d infant.

VI. Monroe Rosenberger, d infant.

VI. Jeannetta Rosenberger, d infant.

VI. Jermina Rosenberger, b Feb 28, 1862, m Isaiah Rosenberger. (See Isaiah Rosenberger Family.)

V. Aaron Rosenberger, b 1827, m Mary Detweiler, dec'd P. O. Mase, Ariz. C: Henry, Reuben, Josiah, Mary, Lizzie.

VI. Henry D. Rosenberger, M. D., b in Hatfield, Montg. Co., Pa., Feb 8, 1852, m Mary A. Allebach, dau. of Jacob M. Allebach, of Skippack, Montg. Co., Dec 16, 1875, P. O. Manheim, Pa. Physician. One child, (**VI**) Emma E. Rosenberger, b in Bucks Co., Pa., Apr 17, 1877. She graduated in Hatfield Twp. Montg. Co. Pa., public school, being the first graduate from that district in the spring of 1893. She then took two years at North Wales Academy, North Wales, Pa., one year in Perkasie high school and two spring sessions at the State Normal School, Millersville, Pa. and is now teaching.

VI. Reuben D. Rosenberger, m Mary Scibrick, Res. Arizona.

VI. Josiah Rosenberger, P. O. Yates Center, Kan.

VI. Mary Rosenberger, m John Seibrick, P. O. Burlington, Iowa.

VI. Lizzie Rosenberger, m Newton Seals, P. O. Moscow, Idaho.

V. Josiah Rosenberger, b 1829, d 1850. S.

V. Simon Rosenberger, M. D., b Apr 1, 1831, m Catharine Hillegas, Oct 25, 1853. She d Aug 26, 1882. When about 19 years old he went to Philadelphia and learned the drug business and studied medicine, graduating in 1853. He practiced medicine in Frenchtown. N. J until 1861, removed to Phila and established the old and popular drug store, located at the corner Seventh & Germantown Ave., and soon thereafter became the most popular and successful physician in the northern portion of the city. In 1863 he was commissioned assistant Surgeon in the army in the 2nd P. V. Heavy Artillery. After leaving the army he again practiced in Philadelphia until 1886 he went to California locating at Pasadena where he died Dec 1899. Congressman. C: Emma, Edmund, William.

VI. Emma E. Rosenberger, b in Montg. Co., Pa., Oct 31, 1854, m Edward J. Paine, Oct 29, 1879, P. O. Carversville, Pa. Farmer. Ref. Ch. C: (**VII**) Fanny, E. Christian, Robert, William, Frederick.

VI. Edmund S. Rosenberger, M. D., b in Phila. Pa., Dec 9, 1856. He learned the drug business with his father and studied medicine, graduating in 1877. He engaged in the drug business in Philadelphia and practiced about 15 years. In the summer of 1892 he went to California and associated with his father in the drug business and practice of medicine in Pasadena. He m Olive B. Townsend. C: (**VII**) Earnest T. Rosenberger, dec'd.

VI. William D. Rosenberger, b at Frenchtown, N. J., Feb 18, 1861, m Esther E. Kolb, Dec 27, 1892. After quite extensive travels in every State and

Territory in the United States, also Cuba, Mexico, Van Couvers Island and Canada, crossing several states on horseback, going by steamboat on Mississippi from St. Paul to New Orleans - over the great lakes to Buffalo and Quebec, traveling over 15,000 miles by railroad, and enjoying a season of cow-boy life on the western plains, he returned, completed his studies, graduated from Baltimore College of Pharmacy, and about 1887 engaged in the drug business at the stand established by his father at the corner of Seventh and Germantown Ave., at which place he still contines. No issue.

V. Enos L. Rosenberger, b in Hatfield, Pa., m Elizabeth Detweiler. She was b in 1841, P. O. Hiawatha, Kansas. Hotel keeper. River Brethren. C: Marietta, Ellen, Sallie, Lillie, Ida, Bessie, Mamie.

VI. Marietta Rosenberger, d aged 12 yrs.

VI. Ellen Rosenberger, m George Haldeman, Res. 823 Cambria St., Phila., Pa. Contractor and builder. Baptists.

VI. Sallie Rosenberger. P. O. Hiawatha, Kansas. Baptist. S.

VI. Lillie Rosenberger, b in Montg. Co., Pa., Feb 2, 1868, m Benjamin F. Eyer, Sept., 1891, P. O. Manhattan, Kansas. Professor of Physics and Electrical Engineering at the State Agricultural College at Manhattan, Kansas. Baptists. C: (**VII**) daughter, b Nov 11, d Nov 25, 1892, Donald B. Eyer, b Jan 27, 1898, Helen F. Eyer, b Sept 27, 1901.

VI. Ida Rosenberger, m Prof. J. W. Sparklin, P. O. Hiawatha, Kansas. Professor of music.

VI. Bessie Rosenberger. P. O. Hiawatha, Kansas. Teacher in public schools. Baptist. S.

VI. Mamie Rosenberger. Teacher. Baptist. S.

V. Henry Rosenberger, d from effects of falling into a tub of hot soap, aged 5 yrs.

IV. Fronica Rosenberger, b Aug 15, 1801, d Sept 20, 1832, m Abraham Rosenberger, grandson of John Rosenberger. (II, Abraham Rosenberger family.)

IV. Valentine Rosenberger, d aged 15 years.

DESCENDANTS OF ISAAC ROSENBERGER,
SON OF DANIEL ROSENBERGER.

III. Isaac Rosenberger, b Nov 30, 1751, d July 30, 1830, m Christian, adopted daughter of Rev. John Funk. She d Mar 8, 1821. He was probably the youngest son of Daniel and received the lower portion of the plantation, comprising 159 acres, and as a consideration the amount of £20 and 18 shillings were paid. The tract is now most occupied by the fine farm of Milton Jenkins, comprising 135 acres.

Here, surrounded by shade trees, are excellent farm buildings of modern construction. The farm is watered by a creek, flowing southward, which joins the other branches of the Neshaminy south of Line Lexington. Near the present dwelling are two old houses, relics of the past, one of stone, the other of logs. The latter was built before the Revolution, or perhaps about 1772. It was the dwelling of Isaac Rosenberger. He afterwards erected a stone house and a barn adjoining. In 1810 he purchased 22 acres adjoining on the southern side, and had in all 170 acres. After his death the farm was sold to Martin Rosenberger, and by him conveyed in 1831 to Isaac Rosenberger, Jr. In 1855 the old homestead was sold to Milton Jenkins, the present owner. Farmer. Menn's. C: Henry, Jacob Isaac, Anna, Elizabeth.

IV. Henry Rosenberger, b Oct 1, 1775, d Sept 10, 1846, m Hannah Detweiler. She was b Dec 17, 1778, d May 2, 1857. Farmer. Menn's. C: Mary, Christiana, Hannah, Samuel, Sally, Jacob.

V. Mary Rosenberger, b about 1806, d 1866, m William Kratz. (See William Kratz family.)

V. Christiana Rosenberger, b Jan 12, 1808, d July 12, 1891, m Martin Rosenberger. (See Martin Rosenberger family.

V. Hannah Rosenberger, m —— Stutz. No issue.

V. Samuel Rosenberger, b 1812, d Oct 1843, m Annie Krout. She was b 1812, d June 22, 1839. Farmer. Menn's. C: Henry.

VI. Henry K. Rosenberger, b in Bucks Co. Pa., Dec 18, 1842, m Westanah Auble, Sept 11, 1864, at Wadsworth, Ohio. P. O. Needles, Cal. Farmer. Christian Ch. C: Andrew, Annie, Maggie, Clara, Thomas, Bessie.

VII. Andrew Fretz Rosenberger, b at Wadsworth, Ohio, Sept 30, 1865, m Mary Amelia Dynes, Nov 2, 1901. Res. 1708, Melrose St., Chicago, Ill. Mining and Mining Investments.

VII. Annie Rosenberger, b Mar 18, 1867, m George B. Galbraith, Aug 25, 1887. P. O. Jansen, Neb. Nurseryman. Christian Ch. C: (**VIII**) infant, b and d Apr 7, 1889, (**VIII**) Clarence J. Galbraith, b Apr 16, 1891, (**VIII**) Margaret Westanah Galbraith, b Mar 22, 1896.

VII. Maggie Rosenberger, b Apr 9, 1869, m Ora H. Hardy, Oct 10, 1895, P. O. Fairbury, Neb. Railroad employee. Christian Ch. C: (**VIII**) Lela B. Hardy, b Jan 31, 1899.

VII. Clara E. Rosenberger, b at Wadsworth, Ohio, Nov 16, 1877. Stenographer. Christian Ch.

VII. Thomas H. Rosenberger, b Bower, Neb., May 25, 1882. Mining Engineering.

VII. Bessie Rosenberger, b at Bower, Neb., May 5, 1885. Christian Ch.

V. Sallie Rosenberger, d June 11, 1844, m Martin Detweiler. Farmer. Menn's. C: infant, infant, Kate, Hannah, Susan, William, Samuel, Enos, Henry.

VI. Kate Detweiler, m Jacob Harr.

VI. Hannah Detweiler, m John Buckheimer, de'cd, m 2nd husband, Garret Landis.

VI. Susan Detweiler, m George Henry.

VI. William R. Detweiler, d single.

VI. Samuel R. Detweiler.

VI. Enos R. Detweiler.

VI. Henry R. Detweiler, b May 28, 1844, m Maggie Swartley, Jan 17, 1873, P. O. Chalfont, Pa. Laborer. C: (**VII**) Horace, Ella, Laura.

V. Jacob D. Rosenberger, b Nov 28, 1819,d Jan 21, 1892, m Eliza Swartley, Dec 23, 1843. Farmer in Bucks Co., Pa.; was quite wealthy. Ger. Bap. C: Henry, Albert, Mary, William, Sarah. Hannah, Jacob, Ann, Isaiah, Alphens, Amanda, Artemus, Susan.

VI. Henry Franklin Rosenberger, b Oct 5, 1844, m Amanda E. Kline, Sept 5, 1869, Res. Chew Street, Allentown, Pa., graduate Kutztown Normal School and has been a school teacher since 1863. C: Robert.

VII. Robert Fulton Kline Rosenberger, b July 1, 1884.

VI. Albert S. Rosenberger, b Nov 2, 1845, d 1846.

VI. Mary M. Rosenberger, b Feb 6, 1847, m Jacob B. Snyder, May 12, 1867.   He d Nov 10, 1868. C: Jacob M. Married 2nd husband Jacob Fellman, June 1871, P. O. Hatfield, Pa. Farmer. Ger. Bap. C: Carrie, Katie, Isaiah, Frank.

VII. Jacob R. Snyder, b Nov 1, 1868, m Ida Hetrick.

VII. Carrie Ida Fellman, b Dec 9, 1872, d Jan 29, 1873.

VII. Katie R. Fellman, b at Bridgetown, Bucks Co. Pa., Dec 24, 1873, m Frank W. Munzinger, Nov 14,1891,P.O. S. Hatfield,Pa. Farmer. G. Bap. C: (**VIII**) Mary Edna Munzinger, b Nov 17, 1892. (**VIII**) Samuel Munzinger, b Jan 21, 1895. (**VIII**) Rosa Ellen Munzinger, b Jan 7, 1897. (**VIII**) Howard Munzinger, b May 23, 1899. (**VIII**) Sara Elizabeth Munzinger, b Apr 20, 1901.

VII. Isaiah Fellman, b Mar 6, 1876, d Mar 3, 1887.

VII. Frank Fellman, b June 21, 1878, d Feb 10, 1887.

VI. William F. J. Rosenberger, b Nov 29, 1848, m Wilhelmina Shellenberger, Res. 1507 Cumberland St. Phila. Pa. Owns Farr farm near Reiff's corner. C: (**VII**) Wilson, d infant, Paul, d infant, Henry, Alvin.

VI. Sarah J. Rosenberger, b Nov 27, 1851, m John M. Kulp, P. O. Dublin, Pa. Farmer. C: Leidy, Mary.

Judge E. R. Monk, Clubman, of Los Angeles, Cal.

VII. Leidy R. Kulp. b Aug 1871, m Hannah Cope, P. O. Souderton, Pa. Farmer. Ref. Ch. Two children deceased.

VII. Mary Ellen R. Kulp, b July 23,1873, m Henry H. Mohr Wire fence builder. Menn's. C: (**VIII**) Sallie. Mary.

VI. Hannah E. Rosenberger. b Feb 17, 1853, m Aaron Moyer, July 12, 1881, P O. Harleysville, Pa. Farmer. Ger. Bap. C: (**VII**) Jacob, dec'd, Eliza. dec'd. Hannah, Aaron, Emma, Ellen.

VI. Jacob Rosenberger, b and d 1855.

VI. Ann Eliza Rosenberger, b Aug 4, 1856, m Jacob S. Rosenberger. (See Jacob S. Rosenberger Family.)

VI. Isaiah Rosenberger, b Apr 11, 1858, m Jermina Rosenberger, Res. Phila. Pa. No issue.

VI. Alphens Rosenberger. b June 5, 1861, d June 2, 1862.

VI. Amanda Rosenberger. b June 5, 1861, d June 12, 1862.

VI. Artemas Rosenberger, b May 10, 1863, m Mary Ann, dau. of Jos. G. Hendricks, Nov 22, 1884, P. O. Souderton, Pa. Farmer. C: (**VII**) Joseph Wesley Rosenberger. b Nov 5, 1885. Fannie E. Rosenberger,b May 1, 1888. Jacob H. Rosenberger, b Feb 2, 1891. Rufus W. Rosenberger, b Feb 18, 1893. Howard T. Rosenberger, b Nov 10, 1895.

VI. Susan Rosenberger, b May 16, 1866, m William D. Kratz, Jan 2, 1882, P. O. Silverdale, Pa. Farmer. Ger. Bap. C: (**VII**) Lucretia, dec'd, Jacob, Lavina, Henry, Artemas.

IV. Jacob Rosenberger. b about 1780, m Catharine Rickert. Farmer. Menn's. C: Daniel, Barbara, Christiana. Mary.

V. Daniel Rosenberger, m Elizabeth Stover, 1824. Farmer. Menn's. C: Joseph, Catharine, Leah, Henry, Amos, Samuel.

VI. Joseph Rosenberger, b 1825, d 1880, m Nancy Derstine, Farmer. C: Amanda, Amos, Titus.

VII. Amanda Rosenberger, m James Schock.

VII. Amos D. Rosenberger, b 1852, m Barbara D. Detweiler, she d Feb 19, 1898. C: Andrew, John,

William. Amos m 2nd wife Susan B. Frederick,
(nee Godshall) Nov 24, 1900, P. O. Silverdale, Pa.
Carpenter and farmer. Menn's.

VIII. Andrew D. Rosenterger, b Nov 9, 1875, m
Tillie D. Bechtel, May 25, 1895, Res. North Da-
kota. Carpenter. Menn's. C: (**IX**) Clarence D.
Rosenberger, b June 4, 1897. Cora Rosenberger, b—,
Paul Rosenberger, ——.

VIII. John D. Ro enberger, b 1880, m Lizzie Hunsicker, Jan 31, 1903, P. O. Silverdale, Pa.

VIII. William D. Rosenberger, b 1884.

VII. Titus D. Rosenberger, b in 1854, d 1890. m
Anna Moyer, P. O. Blooming Glen, Pa. C: (**VIII**)
Samuel M. Rosenberger, (**VIII**) William M. Rosen-
berger, (**VIII**) Anna M. Rosenberger, (**VIII**) Christian
M. Rosenberger dec'd.

VI. Catharine Rosenberger, b 1829, d 1872. S.

VI. Leah Rosenberger, b June 30, 1835, m Charles
D. Haldeman, in 1855, P. O. Hatfield, Pa. Farmer. Menn's. C: Harvey, Elizabeth, Isaiah.

VII. Harvey R. Haldeman, b Oct 5, 1857, m Sallie
Cope, Res. 2600 Jessup St. Phila. Pa. Expressman.
C (**VIII**) Charles Haldeman, b Oct 1, 1879. John
Haldeman, b Nov 2, 1887. Flora Idella Haldeman,
b Aug 3, 1889. Harvey Haldeman, b May 20, 1891.
Lillie Viola Haldeman, b Sept 20, 1893.

VII. Elizabeth Haldeman, b and d 1865.

VII. Isaiah R. Haldeman, b Feb 4, 1868, m Kate
C. Rosenberger, dec'd, Oct 5, 1890. C: Ella, Eva.
Isaiah m 2nd wife Anna Rosenberger. He attended public school until 14 years of age, when he entered the Lansdale, (Pa.) Reporter office to learn
the art of printing. Four years later, or after serving an apprenticeship, he was employed on the
Harleysville News (then in its infancy) at $1.50
and board per week, and later was promoted to
editor.

After being employed on that paper for over three
years he took a position as foreman on the Ambler
(Pa.) Gazette and later was employed on the Philadelphia Press, but lost his position by a strike of
the Typographical Union in that office one year

later. He was again employed in the Harleysville News office as foreman, the paper than being owned by the A. E. Dambly estate, of Skippack, Pa., and about one year later, on May 8, 1892 purchased the establishment from the estate. He was also founder of the Harleysville and Hatfield Beneficial and was elected treasurer of the former in 1894.

Mr. Haldeman is a self-made man in every sense that the word implies. He started in life with nothing but good health and plenty of ambition and he worked himself up by careful attention to every detail of business both as an employee and employer. He saved his money which he invested in a building and loan association until he possessed $300. This formed the nucleus capital with which he started in the newspaper business.

After entering the newspaper business he took an active part in local politics and his paper was the only one in Montgomery county that came out for Quay in his memorable fight for control of the State Republican organization at a time when the Senator's fight was a seemingly hopeless one.

Mr. Haldeman was elected an alternate delegate from the seventh Congressional District to the Republican National Convention held at St. Louis in 1896 and was appointed a member of the County Execu:ive Committee during the same campaign.

He is also a member of the Republican County Committee. C: (**VII**) Ella C. Haldeman, b Aug 8, 1892. Eva Haldeman, b July 22, 1895.

VI. Henry S. Rosenberger, b Oct 21, 1838, d in Philadelphia July 14, 1891, m Mary Ann Beidler, in 1861. She was b Oct 23, 1841, Res. Phila. Pa. Menn's. C: (**VII**) Allavesta E. Rosenberger, b Nov 7, 1862. Dressmaker. Meth. Ep.

(**VII**) Catharine Rosenberger, Nov 7, 1865. Seamstress. Meth. Ep.

(**VII**) Emma Rosenberger, b Sept 4, 1866, m Howard B. Rosenberger. (See Howard B. Rosenberger Family).

(**VII**) Minerva Rosenberger, b Apr 9, 1868. Seamstress. Meth. Ep.

(**VII**) Charles Henry Rosenberger, b Mar 14, 1877, d Jan 5, 1895.

(**VII**) Annie Rosenberger, b June 16, 1879, d Mar 1882.

(**VII**) Ida Rosenberger, b July 5, 1881. Address of all Cor. 12th and Diamond Sts. Phila. Pa.

VI. Amos Rosenberger, b—, d—.

VI. Samuel Rosenberger, b—, d—.

V. Barbara Rosenberger, b in Hatfield Township, Montg. Co. Pa., Dec 27, 1800, d Nov 30, 1842, m Rev. George Landis, mar 28, 1820. He was b in Richland Twp. Bucks Co. Pa., Dec 20, 1796, d Aug 28, 1881. Farmer and minister. He preached first at Flatland Mennonite church, and later at Perkasie, Pa. C: Jacob, Ephraim, George, John.

VI. Jacob Landis, b July 7, 1822, d 1894, m Susan Krout. Farmer. Menn's. C: John, Henry, Levi, Manuel, Mary, Susan. Jacob m second wife——. C: Ezra, Samuel, Lydia, Rosa

VI. Ephraim R. Landis, b in Haycock Twp. Bucks Co. Pa., Dec 13, 1824, m Catharine Rosenberger, Nov 5, 1854, P. O. Dublin, Pa. Farmer. Menn's. C: George, William, Mary, John, Reuben, Katie, Emma.

VII. George Landis, b Aug 23, 1855, d Nov 13, 1865.

VII. William R. Landis, b Feb 22, 1857, m Amanda Campbell. Dec 25, 1883. She was b Mar 17, 1862, P. O. Dublin, Pa. Farmer. C: (**VIII**) Willie H. Landis, b Sept 16, 1883. Elbert E. Landis, b Oct 26, 1886.

VII. Mary R. Landis, b Aug 17, 1859, m Abraham C. Moyer, Nov 20, 1879, P. O. Dublin, Pa. Farmer. Menn's. C: (**VIII**) Lillie L. Moyer, b Aug 14, 1881.

VII. John R. Landis, b Mar 22, 1862, d Aug 12, 1864.

VII. Reuben R. Landis, b Oct 12, 1864, m Lizzie M. Moyer, Jan 30, 1886, P. O. Dublin, Pa. Farmer. Menn's. C: (**VIII**) Elmer M. Landis, b Mar 11, 1887. Stella M. Landis, b Apr 22, 1889. Annie Landis, b Apr 12, 1892. Katie Landis, b Sept 16, 1894.

VII. Katie R. Landis, b in Bucks Co. Pa., June 16,

1867, m Franklin L. Alderfer, Jan 8, 1887. He was
b in Montg. Co. Pa., Oct 11, 1864, P. O. Dublin,
Pa. Farmer. Menn's. C: (VIII) Cora L. Alderfer,
b Jan 17, 1888, Horace L. Alderfer, b May 29, 1889.

VII. Emma R. Lan lis, b Jan 5, 1870, m Edward
Heacock, in 1887, P. O. Fountainville, Pa. Farmer.
Menn's. C: (VIII) Willis Heacock, b Feb 2, 1888.
Katie Heacock, b Sept 27,1889. Bessie Heacock, b
July 18, 1891. Mamie Heacock, b Nov 10, 1893.
Claude Heacock, b Aug 11, 1896, d Mar 11, 1897.
Warren Heacock, b Dec 30, 1897.

VI. George R. Landis, b in Bucks Co. Pa., Nov 2,
1828, m Barbara Moyer, daughter of William A.
and Sarah (Clemmer) Moyer, Nov 18,1860. She was
b Mar 1840, P. O. Dublin, Pa. Farmer. Menn's.
C: Sarah, Daniel, William, John, Samuel.

VII. Sarah Landis, b 1861, m Daniel O. Landis, in
1880, P. O. Silverdale, Pa. Farmer. C: (VIII)
Abraham, Barbara, Ida, Samuel.

VII. Daniel M. Landis, M. D. b in Milford Twp.
Bucks Co., Apr 17, 1864, m Lizzie Hedrick, in 1889.
In March 1881 he was sent to the Quakertown high
school. In the winter of 1882 he resided with his
uncle Dr. S. C. Moyer and attended the Lansdale
high school. His residence there no doubt had
something to do with his future profession. In the
fall of 1883 he began teaching and taught for three
successive winters. In the spring of 1884 he went
one course to the North Wales Academy. In the
summer of 1886 he took the study of medicine with
his uncle and in the fall of the year entered Hahne-
man Medical College, of Phila., where he graduated in April 1889 as doctor of medicine and doctor
of Homeopathic Medicine. He at once located at
Perkasie, where he is still practicing his profession.
Menn's. C: (VIII) Joycelin Landis, b May 2, 1892,
d July 16, 1892.

VII. William M. Landis, b July 4, 1869, m Salome
Detweiler, Nov 10, 1892, P. O. Garisville, Pa. Farmer.

VII. John M. Landis, b Sept 25, 1876, P.O. Dublin.

VII. Samuel M. Landis, b Nov 15, 1884.

VI. John Landis, b Mar 25, 1832, d 1876, m Deborah King.

V. Christiana Rosenberger, d Sept 25, 1875, m Dilman Kulp, Feb 13, 1829. He was b 1807, d 1882. Farmer. Menn's. C: Jacob, Isaac, Mary, Catharine, Elizabeth.

VI. Jacob R. Kulp, b Mar 14, 1831, m Mary Kulp, P. O. Hatfield, Pa. Farmer. C: Henry, Dilman, Amanda.

VI. Isaac R. Kulp, b Dec 4, 1832, m Mary Oberholtzer, Oct 4, 1857, P. O. Hatfield, Pa. Farmer. Menn's. C: Catharine, Christine, Dilman, Mary, Ellamina, Esther.

VII. Catharine Kulp, b Aug 31, 1860, d 1866.

VII. Christine Kulp, b Oct 9, 1863, m Henry S. Weirman, Jan 5, 1883. C: (**VIII**) Charles.

VII. Dilman Kulp, b Jan 13, 1866, m Clara J. Gerhart, May 28, 1887. Printer. Ger. Ref. C: (**VIII**) Elmer, Estella, &c.

VII. Mary L. Kulp, b 1867, d 1877.

VII. Ellamina Kulp, b and d June 1869.

VII. Esther Kulp, b Dec 18, 1871, d — .

VI. Mary Ann Kulp, b June 12, 1834, m Henry M. Kulp, 1859. Farmer. Menn's. C: (**VII**) Isaac K. Kulp, b Mar 21, 1865.

VI. Catharine Kulp, b Apr 13, 1836, d Aug 12, 1878, m Samuel G. Leidy, de'cd. C: Mary, Lydia.

VII. Mary A. Leidy, m VanBuren Lutz, de'cd. No issue. M 2nd husband, John A. Fluck. No issue.

VII. Lydia A. Leidy, m Frank Leidy.

VI. Elizabeth Kulp, b June 28, 1848, d Apr 22, 1885, m Charles E. Ball. No issue.

V. Mary Rosenberger, m Abraham Gehman. C: Jacob, Catharine, Annie, Elizabeth, Maria.

VI. Rev. Jacob R. Gehman, de'cd, m Maria Rosenberger.

VI. Catharine Gehman, —— .

VI. Annie Gehman, m Henry R. Swartley.

VI. Elizabeth Gehman —— .

VI. Maria Gehman —— .

IV. Isaac Rosenberger, Jr., b 1782, d May 1, 1853, m Susan Detweiler. She d 1847. Owned the later

Stong farm from 1806 to 1833, then removed to old ancestral home, now owned by Milton Jenkins. C: Magdalene, Martin, Mary, Isaac, Joseph, Sarah, Elizabeth, John, William. Isaac m 2nd wife, Elizabeth Benner. She d Dec 19, 1886. Farmer. Men n's.

V. Magdalena Rosenberger, d in infancy.

V. Martin D. Rosenberger, b in Montg.Co.,Pa.,May 24, 1805, d in Bucks Co., Pa., Jan 5, 1887, m Sarah Sellers, Aug 2, 1832. Farmer. Menn's. C: Susanna, Isaac, Mary, William, Franklin, Harvey. Martin m 2nd wife Elizabeth Geil, Apr 9, 1844. C: Aaron, Sarah, John.

VI. Susanna Rosenberger, b Oct 17, 1833, d — , m Daniel Stout. C: Martin, John, Edward, Frank, Lizzie, William.

VI. Isaac Rosenberger, b Oct 16, 1834, d Apr 17, 1836.

VI. Mary Ann Rosenberger, b Mar 24, 1836, m John McClintock, de'cd. C: (**VII**) Alexander, de'cd, Albertus, John, George, Martin, de'cd,Grant,dec'd, Charles, de'cd, Mary, de'cd, Lysander.

VI. William H. Rosenberger, b Nov 2, 1837, m Maria Maurer, P. O. Hilltown, Pa. C: Lizzie, Orvilla.

VII. Lizzie Rosenberger, b Aug 22, 1858.

VII. Orvilla Rosenberger, b July 5, 1871.

VI. Franklin B. Rosenberger, b Aug 20, 1840, m Wilhelmina Ruth, P. O. SanAntonio, Texas. C: (**VIII**) Ella, de'cd, Maggie, Lizzie.

VI. Harvey Rosenberger, b and d 1842.

VI. Aaron G. Rosenberger, b June 3, 1845, d Aug 6, 1845.

VI. Sarah Elizabeth Rosenberger, b July 2, 1847, m Abraham Rickert, Jan 8, 1889, P. O. Hilltown, Pa. Farmer. Menn's. No issue.

VI. John G. Rosenberger, b Jan 27, 1849, m Wilhelmina Beyer, Apr 12, 1873, P. O. Hilltown, Pa. Farmer. Menn's. C: Harvey, Laura, William.

VII. Harvey B. Rosenberger, b May 20, 1874.

VII. Laura Rosenberger, b June 1, 1876.

VII. William B. Rosenberger, b Dec 21, 1883.

V. Mary Rosenberger, b at Line Lexington, Pa.,

Jan 4, 1804, d June 12, 1864, m Michael Snyder, — .
He was b Jan 23, 1804, d Jan 29, 1867. Farmer.
Luth. C: Simon, Elizabeth, Isaac, William,
Susanna, Wilhelmina.

VI. Simon R. Snyder, d 1895, m ——. C: Martha,
Ella, Emerson, Maziere. M 2nd wife Sarah —— .

VII. Martha Snyder, m Edgar Hull, de'cd. C: (**VIII**)
Truman, Preston.

VII. Ella Snyder, m O. Eldridge.

VI. Elizabeth Snyder, m Thomas Landis, de'cd.
C: (**VII**) Clinton, Shepherd, Charles, Gerald, Alfred,
Toledo, Mary.

VII. Isaac R. Snyder, —— .

VI. William R. Snyder, b Feb 2, 1836. M Emily
L. Ruck, May 8, 1869, res 2326 N. 19th St., Phila.
C: Simon, Harriet, Flora, Susie, Wesley, Marion.

VII. Simon L. Snyder, b June 10, 1870, d Sept 22,
1872.

VII. Harriet L. Snyder, b Oct 26, 1872, Res. 2544
N. 16th St., Phila., Pa. S..

VII. Flora M. Snyder, b Oct 4, 1874, d Sept 14,
1879.

VII. Susie I. Snyder, b Dec 6, 1876, d Sept 16, 1879.

VII. Wesley A. Snyder, b Mar 24, 1882.

VII. Marion H. Snyder, b Feb 12, 1886.

VI. Susanna Snyder, m Oliver G. Morris, P. O. Line
Lexington, Pa. C: (**VII**) Charles, Norman, Mary.

VI. Wilhelmina Snyder, b June 24, 1844, m Jacob
C. Yost, May 7, 1864, P. O. Wayne, Pa. Presby.
C: Willard, Della.

VII. Willard S. Yost, b Apr 27, 1865.

VII. Della Irene Yost, b Nov 10, 1867.

V. Isaac D. Rosenberger, b Mar 10, 1814, d Dec 8,
1896, m Eve Shellenberger, Jan 8, 1837. She was
b July 23, 1817, d Jan 6, 1868. Farmer. Ref Ch.
C: Isaac, John, Elias, Levi, Mary, Noah. Isaac m
second wife, Jerusha Lefferds, Jan 22, 1870. He
was formerly a Justice of the Peace in Hatfield.

VI. Isaac S. Rosenberger, b near Hatfield, Montg.
Co., Pa., Nov 20, 1838, d July 25, 1899, m Sarah
Hargrave in 1864, daughter of John Hargrave, of
Doylestown, Pa. During his younger days he taught

school, later entered the foundry business as book-keeper for Abram Cox, of Philadelphia. On July 17, 1864, he enlisted in Co. B, 31st Reg P. H. Guards to protect the City and State. After his discharge he returned to Philadelphia and engaged in the grocery business. In 1866 he moved to Punxsutawney, Pa., and made his home, doing a very prosperous business in general merchandise in which he had been engaged until a short time before his death. He was an active member and work-er in the Cumberland Presbyterian Church from his advent in Punxsutawney, and was a member of the Masonic Fraternity for thirty-five years, originally of Girard Lodge, No. 214, of Philadelphia, and lat-erly of John W. Jenks Lodge, No. 35, of Punxsu-tawney, Pa. He was also a member of the Inde-pendent Order of Odd Fellows. Isaac S. Rosen-berger was a man of excellent qualities. He was honorable with his dealings with his fellow-men, loyal to his friends and a good neighbor. C: Mary, Ella, William, Charles, Noah, Levi, Anna, Watson.

VII. Mary Elizabeth Rosenberger, b Apr 9, 1865, m Lou Pantall, Aug 8, 1887, P. O. Punxsutawney, Pa. Cashier in Bank. Cum. Presby. No issue.

VII. Ella Eve Rosenberger, b Nov 2, 1866, m Isaac L. Smith, Aug 24, 1892, P. O. Punxsutawney, Pa. Cum Presby. No issue.

VII. William Isaac Rosenberger, b at Punxsutaw-ney, Jefferson Co., Pa., Oct 4, 1868, m Maude Stiver, Nov 4, 1903, P. O. Punxsutawney, Pa. When quite young he attended the public schools and clerked in his father's store until he was 17 years of age, when he entered the employ of the Coal and Iron Co. stores at Walston and was em-ployed by them for thirteen years. Tiring of the mercantile business he went into the lumber busi-ness with A. M. Armstrong and had a very success-ful business, Mr. Armstrong retiring from the Penna. field and Mr. Rosenberger succeeding. Mr. Rosenberger is a prominent member of the Knights of the Golden Eagle, being District Grand Chief of Jefferson Co., and a member of Mahoning Castle,

No. 266, for 17 years. No issue.

VII. Charles G. Rosenberger, b May 10, 1870, m Laura McCullough, Oct 19,1892,Res. 2015, N. 18th St., Phila., Pa. Clerk in grocery store.

VII. Noah N. Rosenberger, b Jan 9, 1874, m Ada Bley, Jan 9, 1896, Res. 7th and Fairmount Ave., Phila., Pa. Clerk in grocery store. C: (**VIII**) Elizabeth, Charles, Anna, Arthur.

VII. Levi L. Rosenberger, b Nov 11, 1876,m Sarah Hauck, P. O. Rossitter, Pa.

VII. Anna Paul Rosenberger, b Mar 12, 1879.

VII. Watson T. Rosenberger, b Sept 26, 1880, Res. Washington, D. C. Soldier in U. S. Army.

VI. John S. Rosenberger, (twin) b Nov 20, 1838, d Aug 4, 1855.

VI Elias S. Rosenberger, b Feb 1, 1840, d Apr 19, 1842.

VI. Levi A. Rosenberger, b Dec 29, 1842, m Amanda Crator. On July 15, 1895, as he was driving a horse and carriage to market in Philadelphia the girth on the horse became loose and the animal became frightened and started to run away. His son Walter who was with him jumped out and escaped injury, but Mr. Rosenberger was thrown violently to the pavement. He was taken to St. Mary's Hospital where he died in the evening. He served in the late civil war as a Sergeant in Co. D, 104 Regiment Pa. Vol. He was captured by the rebels in 1862 but after a short captivity was paroled and rejoined the regiment. He was selected to blow up the Magazine of Battery Gregg, a strong sand fort in the rear of Fort Wagner on Morris Island. He was the first President Survivors Association,104th Pa. Vol. and was very efficient in promoting its interests. C: Randle, Isabella, Walter.

VII. Randle C. Rosenberger, M. D. b Mar 4, 1873, m Etta Schoch, Sept 25, 1899, Res. 2330 N. 13th St. Phila. Pa. Physician.

VII. Isabella Rosenberger.

VII. Walter L. Rosenberger, b Nov 12, 1878, Res. Phila. Pa. Wholesale Drugs.

VI. Mary E. Rosenberger, b Aug 9, 1845, d Sept

14, 1873, m Charles Diehl.   C: Mary, Isaac.
VI. Noah N. Rosenberger, b June 4,18ᵢ2, m Amanda
Kellar, Sept 1875, Res. 2231 N. 30th St. Phila. Pa.
Manufacturer of cotton and Woolen goods. Ref.
Ch. C: (**VII**) Alverda C. Rosenberger, b May 21,
1876, (**VII**) Stewart K. Rosenberger, b Nov 29, 1882,
(**VII**) Estella K. Rosenberger, b Nov 29, 1887, (**VII**)
Russell K. Rosenberger, b Apr 24, 1895.
V. Elizabeth Rosenberger, b Mar 6, 1816, d Nov
17, 1893, m John Eckhart, Nov 27, 1836. He was
b June 28, 1314, d May 13, 1856. Farmer. Luth.
C: Susanna, Mary, Elmina, Ann, Oliver. Elizabeth
m 2nd husband Michael Snyder.
VI. Susanna Eckhart, b Apr 5, 1838, d Oct 20,
1896, m Leidy Scheip, Dec 25, 1855. P. O. Chal-
font. Pa. Merchant and farmer. Ref. Ch. C: Mary,
George, Ella, John, Infant.
VII. Mary E. Scheip, b May 19, 1858, d Feb 1859.
VII. George C. Scheip, b Dec 27, 185ᵣ, d Sept 1862.
VII Ella M Scheip, b Apr 26, 1867, d Nov 4, 1896,
m Erwin T. Johnson, M D , Mar 11, 1886   P. O.
Hilltown, Pa. Practicing physician. Ref. Ch. C:
(**VIII**) Susanna, Margaret, Raymond.
VII. John S. Scheip, b and d Jan 1868.
VI. Mary C. Eckhart. b June 14, 1840, d Apr 24,
1883, m Lee M. Fluck. P. O. Souderton, Pa. C:
Artemus. &c.
VI. Elmina Eckhart, b Aug 25, 1842, m Samuel G.
Kerns.   P. O. Chalfont, Pa.   Luth.   C: Franklin,
Willard, Oliver.
VII. Franklin P. Kerns, m Anna Toy.
VII. Willard Kerns, d young.
VII. Oliver P. Kerns.   S.
VI. Ann E. Eckhart, b Apr 4, 1868.   S.
VI. Oliver P. Eckhart, b Jan 27, 1852, d 1870.
V. Joseph Rosenberger, d Mar 31, 1877, m Mary
Ruth. She d July 21, 1881. Farmer and merchant.
He was prominently identified with township and
county affairs, yet in no sence of the word a poli-
tician. He was also a director of the Doylestown
Bank. Menn's. C: Henry, William, Susanna,
Emma. Anna, Isaac, Joel, Aaron, Elizabeth,Charles.

VI. Henry Rosenberger, b 1837, d 1846.

VI. William Rosenberger, deceased,

VI. Susanna Rosenberger, b Oct 4, 1839. 1906 m Reuben Alderfer, dec'd. Farmer, Menn's. C: Laura, Stanley.

VII. Laura Alderfer, m Samuel L. Rosenberger.

VII. Stanley Alderfer, d infant.

VI. Emma Rosenberger, b Aug 21, 1841, d 1886, m Abram Hunsberger, dec'd. No issue. She m 2nd husband William Souder. No issue.

VI. Anna M. Rosenberger, b Feb 12, 1844, m Mahlon H. Myers, Feb 13, 1864. P. O. Perkasic, Pa. Merchant. Ger. Ref. C: (**VII**) Emma L. Myers, b Nov 10, 1864, d Feb 28, 1869 A daughter stillborn 1870. A son stillborn 1873.

VI. Isaac R. Rosenbergerger, b July 15, 1846, m Harriet Brunner, daughter of William Brunner, of Chalfont, Pa., Dec 4, 1866. She was b Feb 16, 1848. Mr. Rosenberger spent his early life on his father's farm during the summer months and at the district school in the winter season, until he was 15 years of age. From that time until he arrived at the age of 21 years he performed such work as was necessary upon the farm, in the store and lumber yard. After that he worked a farm on his own account for himself and in 1872 he located at Colmar and engaged in the wholesale and retail flour, feed, coal, hay and phosphate business. Here he conducted business alone until 1881, when he admitted his brother, Charles R., as partner. In 1885 the Rosenberger Brothers extended their business by building a large warehouse at Doylestown and later at Buckingham, Northeast Penn Railroad, where they are engaged in the same trade as at Colmar. C: Mary, Harrington, Flora, Ella, Charles, William.

VII. Mary Alice Rosenberger, b Apr 12, 1868, d Sept 29, 1881.

VII. Harrington Rosenberger, b Oct 27, 1869. P. O. Colmar, Pa.

VII. Flora Estella Rosenberger, b June 4, 1871, d June 20, 1876,

VII. Ella Blanche Rosenberger, b Mar 4, 1873, m Wilsen D. Godshall. P. O. Lansdale, Pa. C: (**VIII**) Leon Godshall, b Apr 27, 1895.

VII. Charles Grant Rosenberger, b Dec 4, 1874. P. O. Colmar, Pa.

VII. William Rosenberger, b Sept 20, 1877.

VI. Joel Rosenberger, b May 24, 1848, m Sallie Moyer, Apr 30, 1872. She was b Jan 19, 1854. Res. 851 N. 5th St., Phila., Pa. Boarding House. Presby. C: (**VII**) Joseph M. Rosenberger, b Aug 17, 1873. (**VII**) Howard Norman Rosenberger, b May 5, 1877, d Aug 5, 1877. (**VII**) Rae Elizabeth Rosenterger, b Dec 22, 1878.

VI. Aaron Rosenberger, (twin) b May 24, 1848, d infant.

VI. Elizabeth Rosenberger, b Mar 10, 1850, m Edward Jones. P. O. Richboro, Pa. Merchant. Presby. C: (**VII**) Mary, Cora.

VI. Charles R. Rosenberger, b Feb 28, 1854, m Amanda Fluck. P O Colmar, Pa   Partner with his brother Isaac. C: (**VII**) Lizzie, Bertha, Elnora, Raymond, Grace, Blain, Daisy, Marie

V. Sarah Rosenberger, b —, d Sept 1871,m Jacob Ruth. He d in Phila., Nov 20, 1865. Farmer. Menn's. C: Aaron, Isaac, Susanna, Mary, Elizabeth, Henry, Sarah.

VI. Aaron Ruth, b Jan 11, 1829, d July 1, 1873, m Mary Jacquemin, 1857. She was b in Louisville, Ky., in 1840, d at Decatur, Ill., Aug 13, 1878. Merchant. Mr. Ruth Menn. Mrs. Ruth Catholic. C: Lillie, Sallie, Martineaux, Hettie,Joseph, Annie, Sadie.

VII. Lillie Ruth, b in 1858, d in 1887.

VII. Sallie Ruth, d young.

VII. Martineaux Ruth, d young.

VII. Hettie Ruth, d young.

VII. Joseph L. Ruth, b at Decatur, Ill., Oct 6, 1863, P. O. Tacony, Phila., Pa. Iron moulder. Free Thinker. S.

VII. Annie Ruth, b Dec 12, 1866, m H. W. Measell. Res. 82, First Place, Brooklyn, N. Y.

VII. Sadie Ruth, b May 16, 1869, P. O. Lexington,

Ky. Teacher. (Sister Alma) at St. Catharines Academy, Lexington, Ky. Catholic.

VI. Isaac Ruth, b in Bucks Co., Pa., Sept 30, 1831, m Missouri High, June 20, 1861, Res. 6819, Letter-ly St., Phila., Pa. Bricklayer. Episcopalian. C: Jacob, Harry, Morris, Samuel, Hannah, Frank.

VII. Jacob Ruth, b Nov 24, 1863, m Kate Young. She d June 2, 1893. Res. 1814 Letterly St., Phila., Pa. C: (**VIII**) Elmer A. Ruth, b June 23, 1886, Harry S. Ruth, b Oct 16, 1888, Jacob Wesley Ruth, b Dec 2, 1890.

VII. Harry Ruth, b July 12, 1865, d July 1, 1870.

VII. Morris Ruth, b Oct 4, 1868, m Mary Bradley. Res. 1814 Letterly St., Phila., Pa. C: (**VIII**) Kate Ruth, b Apr 9, 1891, Morris Ruth, b July 23, 1896.

VII. Samuel Ruth, b Jan 27, 1871, d Mar 1, 1871.

VII. Hannah Ruth, b Jan 27, 1873, m Charles C. Curry. Res. 3955 Lawrence St., Phila., Pa. C: (**VIII**) Charles C. Curry, b Jan 5, 1893, d Feb 11, 1893, Hannah Ruth Curry, b Jan 27, 1894, Esther M. Curry, b Aug 31, 1897.

VII. Frank Ruth, b Jan 1, 1879, Res. 1814 Letterly St., Phila., Pa.

VI. Susanna Ruth, b Apr 20, 1833, d Mar 7, 1871, m Charles Heller, May, 1854. C: Frank, Emma, Ellwood, Cornelius.

VII. Frank Heller, P. O. Tacony, Pa.

VII. Emma Heller, m —— Thompson.

VII. Elwood R. Heller, b Nov. 1, 1865, m Jennie T. Byers, Oct 20, 1896, Res. 834 N 26th St., Phila.,Pa. Stone cutter. Presby. C: (**VIII**) Elwood Heller, b Mar 23, 1897.

VII. Cornelius Heller.

VI. Mary A. Ruth, b Sept. 22, 1834, d Nov., 1857, m Joseph Swartley.

VI. Elizabeth Ruth, b Apr 13, 1837, d Oct 12, 1857, m Samuel W. Hines.

VI. Henry Ruth, b Sept 10, 1839, m Mary B. Challis, 1873, Res. 2216 N 10th Phila., Pa. No issue.

VI. Sarah Ruth, b Sept 10, 1841, d July 3, 1857.

V. William D. Rosenberger, dec'd., m Malinda Medary, dec'd. Merchant. Mr. Rosenberger Quaker.

C: (**VI**) William, others died infants.

V. John Decatur Rosenberger, b Dec 29, 1820, d Dec 29, 1881, m Elizabeth Johnson, dec'd. C: Ellwood. John m second wife Isabelle McCormick, June 12, 1864. Produce merchant. Presby. C: Alonza, Mary.

VI. Ellwood J. Rosenberger, b in Phila., Pa., Aug 29, 1854, m Martha S. Eckman, May 8, 1877, P. O. Munith, Mich. Employed by Grand Trunk R. R. Co. Meth Ep. C: (**VII**) Frank W. Rosenberger, b June 3, 1881, Marguerite A. Rosenberger, b Oct 1, 1883, Mary E. Rosenberger, b Aug 10, 1885, d Sept 10, 1899, Grace G. Rosenberger, b Oct 1, 1887.

VI. Alonzo Potter Rosenberger, b Sept 6, 1865, m Katharine Myers, Nov 4, 1896, P. O. Ogontz, Pa. President of the Whiting & Rosenberger Co., Phila., Pa. Prot. Ep. No issue.

VI. Mary E. Rosenberger, b Nov 17, 1874, P. O. Jacksonville, Fla. Prot. Ep. S

IV Anna Rosenberger, m —— Swenk. C: John, Isaac, Abraham, Elizabeth, Christiana

IV. Elizabeth Rosenberger, m Henry Wireman. C: Michael, Martin, Isaac, Sophia, Catharine, Christiana, Annie, Elizabeth.

V. Michael Wireman, m Catharine Wisler. C: Eliza, Henry, John, Martin, Isaac, Jacob, Abraham, Catharine, Sophia, Michael.

V. Martin Wireman, d s.

V. Isaac Wireman, m —— Delp. C: Sophia, Elizabeth. He m 2nd wife, Barbara Stauffer. C: Wm.

V. Sophia Wireman. S.

V. Catharine Wireman, b Apr 6, 1808, d Apr 28, 1877. M Peter Hines, Dec 13, 1827, b Dec 16, 1801, Feb 7, 1844. Farmer. Menn's. C: Eliza, Samuel, Henry, Joseph, Sophia, Mary.

VI. Eliza Hines, b Nov 3, 1828, P. O. Chalfont, Pa.

VI. Samuel W. Hines, b Aug 7, 1830, m Elizabeth Ruth, Apr 18, 1856. C: Clara. Samuel m 2nd wife, Susan Garner, Dec 31, 1864, P. O. Lansdale, Pa. Shoemaker. Baptists. C: Emma, Mary, Toleda, George, Thomas, Frank, Ada, Laura. Mr. Hines enlisted in the 4th Regiment, Company G, P. R. V. C., May 29, 1861, for the term of three years. He

was promoted to 5th sergeant, and participated in
the following battles, viz: Mechanicsville, June 26,
1862; Gaines Hill, June 27, 1872, Charles City, Cross
Roads, June 30,1862; Malvern Hill, July 1.1862; 2nd
Bull Run, Aug 2. 1862; South Mountain, Sept 14,
1862; Antietam, Sept 17,1862; Fredericksburg, Dec
13. 1862, and Floyds Mt., Western Virginia, May
1854. In none of the battles did he receive so much
as a scratch. He was mustered out of service June
17, 1864.

VII. Clara Hines, b Mar 20, 1857, d Oct 17, 1857.

VII. Emma Hines, b Apr 7, 1869,m J.H. Meredith,
P. O. Ivyland, Pa. Farmer. Baptists. No issue
(1899).

VII. Mary Hines, b Dec 11, 1870, m J. W. Boorse.
P. O. Lansdale, Pa. Clerk. Mrs. Boorse Baptist.
C:(**VIII**) Ella Boorse, b Oct 3, 1893, (**VIII**) Bertha
Boorse, b June 19, 1895, (**VIII**) Frank Boorse, b Dec
22, 1896, (**VIII**) Charles Vincent Boorse, b Sept 8,
1899.

VII. Toleda Hines, b Aug 2, 1874, m Philip S.
Fry, Res. 1231 Firth St., Phila., Pa. Clerk. Baptists. No issue (1899).

VII. George Meade Hines, b Dec 12, 1875, d Dec
23, 1875.

VII. Thomas Wesley M. Hines, b Nov 24, 1876, d
Aug 23, 1877.

VII. Frank Magilton Hines, b June 18, 1878.

VII. Ada Hines, b Dec 20, 1880.

VII. Laura G. Hines, b Oct 29, 1882, d July 7,1890.

VI. Henry W. Hines, b in Bucks Co., Pa., Aug 3,
1832, m Christiana Garner, Dec 13, 1856. She d
Oct 2, 1865. C: Edward, Watson, Estella, Willie.
Henry m 2nd wife, Priscilla Garges, May 18, 1872,
P. O. Chalfont, Pa. Wheelwright and undertaker.
Baptists. C: Albert.

VII. Edward G. Hines, b Nov 9, 1857, m Sallie
Barnard Benson, of Phila., Pa., June 9, 1886. Res.
916 N. 15th St., Phila., Pa. Traveling salesman.

VII. Estella Hines, b Oct 22, 1860, m Wilson W.
Delp, Nov. 5, 1891.

VII. Willie Hines, b May 2, 1865, d July — , 1865.

VII. Albert G. Hines. b Dec 23, 1875.

VI. Joseph Hines, b in Bucks Co., Oct 6, 1834, m Cordelia Garner, P. O. Lansdale, Pa.

VI. Sophia Hines, b in Bucks Co.,Pa., Jan 2, 1837, m George Shellenberger, of Hatfield Twp., Montg. Co., Pa., Dec 24, 1859. He was b Jan 31, 1839, d Oct 12, 1890. Ger. Ref. Ch. C: Leidy, Wilson, Amanda, Milton, Infant, Elmer, Laura, Emma.

VII. Leidy Shellenberger, b Aug 2, 1861, m Mary, daughter of Joseph Detweiler. Oct 11, 1884, P. O. Hatfield, Pa. Ger. Ref. C: (**VIII**) Frank Shellenberger, b Mar 10, 1885, Stella Shellenberger, b Feb 3, 1888, Arthur Shellenberger, b Dec 31, 1891, Joseph Shellenberger, b Jan 2, 1894, Emma Shellenberger, b Aug 26, 1895, Elmer D. Shellenberger, b Sept 12, 1898.

VII. Wilson Shellenberger, b July 7, 1863, P. O. Hatfield, Pa. Ger. Ref. S.

VII. Amanda Shellenberger, b June 29, 1866, P. O. Hatfield, Pa. Ger. Ref. S.

VII. Milton Shellenberger, b Jan 16, 1870, m Mary Ford, Oct 26, 1895, Res. Phila., Pa. Ger. Ref. No issue.

VII. Infant b and d 1873.

VII. Elmer Shellenberger, b June 1, 1874, P. O. Hatfield, Pa. Ger. Ref.

VII. Laura Shellenberger, b and d 1881.

VII. Emma Shellenberger, b Dec 4, 1878, P. O. Hatfield, Pa. Ger. Ref.

VI. Mary Hines, b Sept 18, 1839, d July 11, 1855.

V. Annie Wireman, m John Apple.

V. Christiana Wireman, m Francis Davis. C: (**VI**) Carmine, Angeline.

V. Elizabeth Wireman, m John McKinney. C: Rebecca, Elizabeth, Jacob, Mary and others.

DESCENDANTS OF ANN ROSENBERGER, DAUGHTER OF DANIEL ROSENBERGER, SR.

III. Ann Rosenberger, m Michael Kolb. C: Helena, Isaac, Barbara.
IV. Helena Kulp, m Michael Weierman. Res. Hatfield, Pa. C: (**V**) Elizabeth Weierman. (**V**) Magdalena Weierman.
IV. Isaac Kulp.
IV. Barbara Kulp, m Jacob Geisinger. C: (**V**) Henry Geisinger.
V. Michael Geisinger.

DESCENDANTS OF MARY ROSENBERGER, DAUGHTER OF DANIEL ROSENBERGER.

III. Mary Rosenberger, b about 1758, d Jan 23, 1805, m Valentine Kratz, son of John Valentine Kratz, who was of a noble and titled family, of Switzerland, that through persecution and exile lost their birthright. The family were driven to Alsace and later John Valentine Kratz emigrated to America, arriving on the ship "Friendship" October 16, 1727. (See Kratz History.)
IV. Ann Kratz, b Nov 17, 1778, d Oct 24, 1822. S.
IV. Daniel Kratz, m —- Geist. Lived near Rochester, N. Y., where he died without issue.
IV. Valentine Kratz, b Feb 5, 1783, d Oct 29, 1865, m —— Boyer, (widow, nee Christman). She d Oct 24, 1822. C: Jonas, Valentine, Mary, Ann, George. Valentine m 2nd wife, Mary Detweiler, (widow.) She d Mar 6, 1866. Farmer in Freder-

Isaac R. Rosenberger.

Isaiah S. Rosenberger.

ick Twp., Montg. Co.   Menn's. C: Jacob, Rebecca,
Daniel, Sarah, Esther, Hannah.

IV. Abraham Kratz, b Aug 25, 1785, d Feb 11,
1870, m Elizabeth Cassel. She d Nov 9, 1861. Farmer in Skippack Twp.   Menn's.   C: Mary, John,
Jacob, Lydia, Abraham, Daniel, Elizabeth, Catharine.

IV. John Kratz, b Apr 27, 1783, d Oct 21, 1820, m
Catharine Detweiler. She d Mar 8, 1864. Lived
in Skippack Twp. C: Henry, Jacob.

IV. Isaac Kratz, b Nov 13,1790, d July 13, 1868, m
Catharine Hunsicker. She d Aug 24. 1864. Far-
mer. Menn's. C: Valentine, William, Ann,
Margaret, Elizabeth, Catharine, Mary, Isaac.

IV David Kratz, b Mar 14, 1792, d Jan 27, 1872,
m Ann Lederach. She d Sept 6, 1868. Farmer.
Menn's. C: Henry, William.

IV. William Kratz, b 1793, d 1834, m Mary
Rosenberger, in 1820. She d 1866. Lived in Hill-
town, Bucks Co. Weaver, Menn's. C: Jesse,
Samuel, Henry, David, Sarah, Hannah.

V. Jesse Kratz, b Oct 8, 1821, m Susanna Heistand,
Oct 20, 1844. P. O. Perkasie, Pa. Farmer. Menn's.
C: Abraham, William, Mary, Lizze, Albert, David,
Henry, Susan, Jesse, Annie, Marcus.   He m 2nd
wise Catharine Freed. She d 1897.

V. Samuel R. Kratz, b Oct 18, 1824, m Elizabeth
Hunsberger, 1853. P. O. Hebron, Neb. Farmer.
Ger. Bap. C: William, Emma, Sarah, George,
Mary, Isaiah, Hannah, David, Elmer, Jacob,
Amanda, Eohriam, Anna, Samuel, Lydia, Cornelius.

V. Henry R. Kratz, b Feb 26, 1827, m Sarah Delp.
She d 1865. C: Mary, Clayton, William, Catharine.
He m 2nd wife Levina Fluck. Farmer, Hatfield,
Pa. Ger. Bap. C: Harry, Ella, Martha.

V. David Kratz, d young.

V. Sarah Kratz, b Sept 25, 1831, d Mar 29, 1877,
m Valentine Kratz 1852. He d —. Farmer. Menn's.
C: Mary, Allen, William, Abraham, Valentine,
Tobias, Henry, Sarah, Emma, Laura.

V. Hannah Kratz, d young.

IV. Jacob Kratz, b June 24, 1798, d Aug 25, 1881,

m Mary Stover. She was b 1830, d Feb 13, 1887,
Farmer on his father's farm. Menn's. C: John,
Rachel, Eli, Mary, David, Hannah. For complete
records of Valentine and Mary (Rosenberger)
Kratz, see Kratz Family History.

━●━◆━◆━●━O━◆━◆━◆━●

JOHN ROSENBERGER, SR., OF HATFIELD.

━●━◆━O━◆━◆

II. John Rosenberger, b 1724,d 1808. In "Fricks"
graveyard lies the body of Johannes Rosenberger,
b 1724, d 1808, aged 84 years. During his lifetime
he purchased many hundred acres of land. His
ambition was to give a farm to each of his children.
The site of Hatfield village and station was owned
by him. His lands extended from thence to the
Franconia line and even beyond. They covered an
extremely level territory, with extensive meadows.
In the northern end of Hatfield village and close to
the eastern side of the railroad are the modern
farm buildings formerly belonging to Enos Krieble.
Here was the site of the old homestead of John
Rosenberger. The old log house stood there until
1884 and was torn down and the old barn was destroyed by fire. At the upper road crossing of the
brook, on the western side, may be seen a depression or hole in the bank, about which trees of considerable size are growing. This was the site of a
grist mill, which was built before the Revolution.
The land on which it was built was purchashed by
him in 1769 and the mill built soon after. It was
the first mill erected in this region. It was torn
down by Peter Conver in 1820. The place where
stood the old mill is now on the premises of William
Delp. The lands of John Rosenberger was comprised of at least 308 acres purchased before the
Revolution and at later periods he purchased sev-

eral hundred more. The farms now owned by
Jacob Kulp, William Delp, Enos Krieble, John
Rosenberger, John Kindig, Jacoby Ott, J Wireman,
Abraham Gehman J. D. Gehman, besides smaller
lots of the village of Hatfield, belonged to John
Rosenberger. John Rosenberger was twice married,
his first wife's name was Barbara and his second
wife's name was Christiana, maiden names unknown.
He was a Mennonite and was one of the four trus-
tees to whom was deeded the lot where stands the
Line Lexington Mennonite Meetinghouse. C:
Martin, Abraham, John, Benjamin, Daniel, Henry,
Catharine.

DESCENDANTS OF MARTIN ROSENBERGER,
SON OF JOHN ROSENBERGER, SR.

III. Martin Rosenberger, b about 1753, d July 1781,
m Elizabeth ——. He became a miller and to him
his father sold 77 acres in 1776. He died when a
young man, leaving four minor children. He made
his will February 1781, in which the mill and plantation were ordered to be rented until his youngest
child was eighteen, then to be sold and proceeds
divided between the widow and four children. His
real estate was sold to Peter Conver in 1799. The
old mill property has been owned since 1874 by
William Delp. C: John, Elizabeth, Mary.

IV. John Rosenberger lived at Mt. Bethel, Pa.
IV. Elizabeth Rosenberger, ——.
IV. Mary Rosenberger, ——.
IV. —— Rosenberger, ——.

DESCENDANTS OF ABRAHAM ROSENBERGER, SON OF JOHN ROSENBERGER, SR.

●●●●●●●●

III. Abraham Rosenberger. M Margaret Morris. To Abraham was conveyed in 1794, 144½ acres in Franconia, which was another portion of land bought of the Clibborn Wilson estate by John Rosenberger in 1790. It is now the farm of John Loux. C: John, Mary, Anne, Elizabeth.

IV. John Rosenberger, b Sept 4, 1801, d Feb 17, 1848, m Elizabeth Swartz. She d Sept 15, 1828. C: Abraham, Mary, Jonathan. John m 2nd wife Elizabeth Eckhart. Farmer in Bucks County, Pa. Menn's. C: George, Sarah, Levi, Elizabeth, John.

V. Abraham Rosenberger, d infant.

V. Mary Rosenberger, d single.

V. Jonathan Rosenberger, b in Montg. Co. Pa., Dec 13, 1827, d Nov 18, 1902, m Fanny Hager. 1851. She d May 28, 1897. Merchant. Ref. Ch. C: Infant, Edwin, Harvey, Franklin.

VI. Edwin H. Rosenberger, b in Bucks Co. Pa., May 7, 1858, m Lillie Amelia Patton, Aug 21, 1880. Res. 2326 N. Hancock St., Phila. Pa. Reporter on the Philadelphia Evening Bulletin Staff. Methodist. C: (**VII**) Emerson Matthews Rosenberger, b Sept 20, 1884, Elva Sarah Rosenberger, b June 27, 1890, Mary Sadie Rosenberger, b Sept 24, 1893.

VI. Harvey Rosenberger, b Apr 7, 1861, d 1893, m Louisa T. Dietz. Ref. Ch. C: (**VII**) Laura Rosenberger, b June 7, 1889.

VI. Franklin H. Rosenberger, b 1853, d 1895, m Carrie Le Feber. C: (**VII**) Fanny dec'd, Marion.

V. George Rosenberger, b Feb 3, 1865. Res. Bethlehem, Pa.

V. Sarah Ann Rosenberger, b Mar 16, 1837, m Lewis Ahlum. P. O. Keller's Church, Pa.

V. Levi Rosenberger, b Jan 11, 1843, d 1844.

Laura I. Resenberger

V. Elizabeth Rosenberger, b May 16, 1845, d — , m Andrew Roth, dec'd.

V. John E. Rosenberger, b Apr 28, 1847, m Emma Hunsberger. P. O. Rich Hill, Pa.

IV. Mary Rosenberger, m Andrew Swartz. C: Jacob, Aaron, Morris, Peter, Mary, Lizzie.

V. Jacob Swartz, d — , m Hannah Delp. C: (**VI**) Milton, P. O. Line Lexington, Pa.

V. Aaron Swartz, d — , m . No issue.

V. Morris Swartz, m — .

V. Peter Swartz, d — , m Eliza Brunner.

V. Mary Swartz, d single.

V. Lizzie Swartz, m Isaiah Leidy, P. O. Line Lexington, Pa. C: Helen.

VI. Helen Leidy, m Philip C. Swartley.

IV. Anna Rosenberger, m Valentine Clemmer. C: Levi, Peggie, Abraham.

V. Levi Clemmer, d — , m Lavina Ott. No issue.

V. Peggie Clemmer, m Abraham Ruth. C: Wilhelmina, Valentine, etc.

VI. Wilhelmina Ruth, m Franklin B. Rosenberger.

VI. Valentine Ruth.

V. Abraham R. Clymer, m Katie Althouse, dec'd. C: — . — . He m 2nd wife, — , P. O Fricks, Pa. C: Kate.

VI. Kate Clymer, m Samuel Leatherman, P. O. Line Lexington, Pa. C: —

IV Elizabeth Rosenberger, m John Hunsicker, C: Mrs. Abraham, Witeman, Mrs. Henry Kooker.

DESCENDANTS OF JOHN ROSENBERGER, JR.
SON OF JOHN ROSENBERGER, SR.

III. John Rosenberger, Jr., b May 3, 1755, d Sept 18, 1832, m —— ——. Menn's. John Rosenberger, Jr., bought a farm in Hatfield, on the borders of Franconia, of Jacob Reed, in 1793. The next day after purchase he conveyed 50 acres to his brother Daniel. John Rosenberger was succeeded in ownership of his farm by his son Samuel. The farm is now owned by Abraham Gayman, a grandson of Samuel Rosenberger. This fine farm has a deep depression near the Franconia line, which is quite in contrast with the plain country of Hatfield. The banks are very steep and high and through it flows a rivulet westward to the Skippack. C: John, Samuel, Mary, Barbara.

IV. John Rosenberger, b in Hatfield, Pa., Apr 12, 1790, d Sept 12, 1873, m Mary Hockman, Jan 22, 1826, daughter of Henry and Barbara (Fretz) Hockman. She was b in Bucks Co., Feb 22, 1800, d Oct 11, 1845. Farmer. Menn's. C: Elizabeth, Catharine, Mary, John; Henry, Samuel, Abraham. Sarah, Nancy, William. John m 2nd wife, Catharine Oberholtzer, widow of John Swartz.

V. Elizabeth Rosenberger, b Jan 13, 1827, d —, m John Anders, dec'd. C: Henry, Josiah, Catharine, Nathaniel.

V. Catharine Rosenberger, b in Hilltown Twp., Bucks Co., Pa., July 28, 1828, m Ephriam R. Landis. (See Ephriam R. Landis family.)

V. Mary H. Rosenberger, b in Bucks Co., Pa., Oct 7, 1830, d Mar 1895, m David H. Anders, Dec 3, 1859, Res. Phila., Pa. Professor of Music. Presby. C: Horace.

VI. Horace R. Anders, b Skippack, Montg. Co., Pa., Sept 16, 1860, Res 2145 N Camac St., Phila.,

Pa. Teacher of music, piano and organ, also leader or bandmaster, and first sergeant of the band of the First Brigade, National Guards of Penna., and as such he is on duty on all great military occasions, going into camp for one week every year. His band is also engaged every year for a period of 12 to 15 weeks, giving concerts at Asbury Park or some other seaside resort or public park in or near Philadelphia. Presby. S.

⫪ Rev. John H. Rosenberger, b Jan 7, 1832, m Annie Clemmer, Nov 20,1856, Hatfield,Pa Farmer. He was ordained to the ministry of the Mennonite Church at Line Lexington, Oct 28, 1884. C: Mary, Lizzie, Sue, Harry, Emma, Kate, Ella, Levi, John, Annie.

VI. Mary C. Rosenberger, b Sept 12, 1857, m Wm. K. Godshall, Oct 13, 1877. C: (VII) Henry R. Godshall, b Jan 22, 1878, Annie E. Godshall, b Dec 22, 1879, John F. Godshall, b Aug 23, 1881, Wellington R. Godshall, b July 23, 1883, Edwin M. Godshall, b June 19, 1885, d Aug 27, 1886, Mamie R. Godshall, b Dec 7, 1886, Lavina Godshall, b Aug 1, 1888.

VI. Lizzie C. Rosenberger, b July 3, 1859, m Henry F. Hendricks, Oct 13, 1883, P. O. Beattie, Kans. Farmer. Ger. Bap. C: (VII) Mamie Hendricks, b May 8, 1878, Elmer Hendricks, b Dec 10, 1884, Raymond Hendricks, b Mar 11, 1887.

VI. Sue C. Rosenberger; b Mar 15, 1862,m John M. Myers, Dec 11, 1886, P. O. Silverdale, Pa. Farmer. Menn's. C: (VII) Ottomar R. Myers, b Feb 28, 1888, Titus R. Myers, b Jan 9, 1891, Edna R. Myers, b Sept 13, 1893, Mabel R. Myers b July 18, 1896, Ella R. Myers, b Dec 12, 1898.

VI Harry C. Rosenberger, b Aug 8, 1864, m Mary E. Lapp, May 8, 1887, P. O. Hilltown, Pa. Farmer. Menn's.

VI. Emma C. Rosenberger, b Oct 16, 1866, d Dec 23 1866.

VI. Kate C. Rosenberger, b Dec 8, 1867, d Sept 22, 1895, m I. R. Haldeman. (See I. R. Haldeman family.)

VI. Ella C. Rosenberger, b June 24, 1869, m Harry M. Heckler, P. O. Harleysville, Pa.

VI. Levi C. Rosenberger, b Apr 30, 1873, m Martha Lapp, P. O. Lansdale, Pa.

VI. John C. Rosenberger, b Feb 21, 1876.

VI. Annie C. Rosenberger, b Nov 30, 1878, m I R. Haldeman. (See I. R. Haldeman family.)

V. Rev. Henry H. Rosenberger, b Feb 23, 1834, d —, m Mary Frick, Oct 31, 1857. Farmer. He was ordained to the ministry of the Brethren church at Silverdale, Pa., 1877, and Bishop in 1886. C: John, Abraham, Frany, Kate, Sarah, William, Henry.

VI. John F. Rosenberger, b Aug 28, 1861, d Feb 26, 1863.

VI. Abraham F. Rosenberger, b Nov 28, 1863, d July 22, 1865.

VI. Frany Rosenberger, b Jan 3 1866, m John R. Kindig. C: (**VII**) Harvey R. Kindig, b and d 1886.

VI. Kate Rosenberger, b Sept 18, 1868, d July 19, 1873.

VI. Sarah Rosenberger, b Mar 3, 1871.

VI William F. Rosenberger, b June 6, 1874, m Sallie Henning, P. O. Kulpsville, Pa.

VI. Henry F. Rosenberger, b June 15, 1877.

V. Rev. Samuel H. Rosenberger, b Feb 11, 1836, m Elizabeth D. Stover, Nov 12, 1859. She d Sept 21, 1877. P. O. Hatfield, Pa. Farmer and minister of River Brethren Ch. C: Mary, Milton, James, John, Henry, Rachel, Catharine, Samuel.

VI. Mary Rosenberger, b Jan 4, 1861, d Feb 13, 1862.

VI. Milton Rosenberger, b Feb 8, 1863, m Clara McKennedy, Apr 20, 1886, P. O. White Cloud, Kans.

VI. James Rosenberger, b Oct 18, 1864, d Feb 27, 1878.

VI. John Rosenberger, b Aug 20, 1867, m Susan Kckert. C: (**VII**) Stella, Edna, Harry.

VI. Henry Rosenberger, b Nov 14, 1869.

VI. Rachel Rosenberger, b Dec 10, 1872, m John Ziegenfuss, 1892. P. O. Perkasie, Pa. Cigar Manufacturer. Luths. C: (**VII**) Irwin d young, Howard d young, J. Oliver, Norman.

VI. Catharine Rosenberger, b Mar 3, 1874, d Sept 19, 1875.

VI. Samuel Rosenberger, b May 14, 1875, m Mary Landes. P. O. Telford, Pa.

V. Abraham H. Rosenberger, b in Montg. Co. Pa., May 29, 1838, m Anna S. Kulp, Nov 29, 1868. C: (**VI**) John K. Rosenberger, b Nov 29, 1872, d July 29, 1873. Erwin K. Rosenberger, b Nov 29, 1872, d July 25, 1873, (twins.) Sallie K. Rosenberger, b June 18, 1874. Katie K. Rosenberger, Mar 17, 1879. Anna Mary K. Rosenberger, b May 28, 1882, Carrie K. Rosenberger, b Dec 29, 1884.

V. Sarah Ann Rosenberger, b June 23, 1840, m Enos Landes, Aug 30, 1876. P. O. Reserve, Kans. Farmer. Ger. Bap. C: (**VI**) William H. Landes, b June 25, 1878. Ellen J. Landes, b Dec 20, 1880. Mary E. Landes, b May 7, 1884.

V. Nancy Rosenberger, b Apr 7, 1842, d Feb 27, 1880.

V. William Rosenberger, b Aug 3, 1844, d 1845.

IV. Samuel Rosenberger, dec'd, m Mary Swartz. Farmer. Menn's. C: Elizabeth, Maria. John.

V. Elizabeth Rosenberger, dec'd, m David D. Rosenberger. (See David D. Rosenberger family.)

V. Maria Rosenberger, m Rev. Jacob Gehman, dec'd. C: Abraham, Catharine.

VI. Abraham R. Gehman, P. O. Hatfield, Pa.

VI. Catharine Gehman, m Enos Hackman, dec'd, P. O. Hatfield, Pa.

V. John S. Rosenberger, b in Montg. Co, Pa., July 25, 1824, d Oct 15, 1861, m Katharine Ruth, dec'd. No issue. John m 2nd wife, Margaret Gehman. She was b Sept 4, 1833, d Mar 31, 1860. Farmer. Menn's. C: Kate, Mary.

VI. Kate G. Rosenberger, b Sept 18, 1857, d Nov 6, 1883, m Jacob L. Reiff, Nov 17, 1877, P. O. Bechtelsville, Pa. C: (**VII**) Howard R. Reiff, b Dec 15, 1880, Jacob Reiff, b May 28, 1883, d Oct 3, 1883.

VI. Mary Ann Rosenberger, b in Montg. Co., Pa., July 30, 1859, m Henry K. Alderfer, Feb 9, 1878, P. O. Souderton, Pa. Farmer. Menn's. C: (**VII**)

Enos Alderfer, b Nov 28, 1878, John Alderfer, b
Feb 22, 1880, d July 7, 1880. Allen Alderfer, b
May 11, 1881. Lizzie Alderfer, b Mar 7,1884,Henry
Alderfer, b Jan 11, 1886, Hiram Alderfer, b April
28, 1888, Jacob Alderfer, b Oct 24, 1890, d Oct 19,
1891, Frank Alderfer, b Feb 3, 1895, Clara Alderfer, b Mar 5, 1898.

IV. Mary Rosenberger, m John Allebach. Farmer. Menn's. C: John, Samuel.

V. John Allebach, m ——. Probably no issue.

V. Samuel Allebach, m ——. Have issue.

IV. Barbara Rosenberger, m Samuel H. Detweiler.
Farmer. Menn's. C: Nancy, Elizabeth, John.

V. Nancy Detweiler, b —, m Jacob L. Moyer, P.
O. Souderton, Pa. Retired farmer. Menn's. C:
Samuel, Levi, Jacob, Mary, David, John, Amanda,
Mathias, Ephraim.

VI. Samuel D. Moyer, b Feb 9, 1846,m Mary M.
Moyer, P. O. Morwood, Pa. Menn's. C: (**VII**) Anna
M. Moyer, b Sept 27, 1874. Ella Moyer, b May
24, 1878. John M. Moyer, b Nov 7, 1881.

VI. Levi D. Moyer, b June 7, 1848, d Apr 16, 1855.

VI. Jacob D. Moyer, b Jan 27, 1851, m Mary B.
Auchey. She was b May 21, 1856, P. O. Hatfield,
Pa. Farmer. C: (**VII**) David A. Moyer, b Nov 18,
1880, d Mar 16, 1882. Anna Mary Moyer, b Aug
17, 1883. Ida Moyer, b May 8, 1887. Jacob Moyer,
b Sept 23, 1893.

VI. Mary D. Moyer, b Dec 2, 1852, m Noah M.
Moyer, Dec 5, 1874, P. O. Morwood, Pa. Farmer.
Menn's. C: (**VII**) Minerva Moyer, b July 26, 1876.
Erwin Moyer, b Apr 26, 1878. Barbara Moyer, b
Nov 11, 1882. Jacob Moyer, b Mar 23, 1884. Anna
Moyer, b Feb 13,1887. Mary Moyer,b Dec 16, 1889.
Flora and Laura Moyer, (twins) b Aug 1, 1893.

VI. David D. Moyer, b May 7, 1855, m Sarah Ann
Detweiler, Dec 20, 1879. She was b Apr 29, 1860,
P. O. Franconia, Pa. Menn's. C: (**VII**) Annie D.
Moyer, b Oct 12, 1882. Jacob D. Moyer, b June
20, 1885, d June 15, 1886. Henry D. Moyer, b Apr
15, 1887. Katy D. Moyer, b Sept 14, 1889, David
D. Moyer, b Mar 16, 1892. John D. Moyer, b Jan

31, 1895.

VI. John D. Moyer, b Feb 15, 1857, m Mary Ann
S. daughter of Daniel Detweiler, Dec 18, 1880. She
was b Apr 27, 1858, d Apr 10, 1891, P. O. Harleysville, Pa. Menn's.   C: (**VII**) Katie Ann D. Moyer,
b Oct 26, 1882. Vincent Moyer, b Oct 29, 1885.
Emma Moyer, b Mar 9, 1890.

VI. Amanda D. Moyer, b Nov 26, 1859, d Sept 9,
1860.

VI. Mathias D. Moyer, b Dec 17, 1862, d Mar 21,
1868.

VI. Ephriam D. Moyer, b Oct 10, 1865, d Mar 12,
1868.

V. Elizabeth R. Detweiler, b Sept 5, 1819, d Oct
31, 1852, m David H. Kulp, Jan 14, 1848.   He died
Nov 18, 1892. Farmer.   Menn's.   C: Samuel,
Sarah, John.

VI. Samuel D. Kulp, b Aug 4, 1849.

VI. Sarah Ann D. Kulp, b Apr 2, 1852, m Jacob H.
Kulp, Jan 11, 1879, P. O. Souderton, Pa.   Farmer.
Menn's.   C: (**VII**) Harvey K. Kulp, b May 28, 1881.
David K. Kulp, b May 10, 1884, d Apr 30, 1888.
Katie K. Kulp, b Apr 4, 1887, d Aug 24, 1887.

VI. John D. Kulp, b Oct 25, 1852, d Sept 21, 1853.

V. John R. Detweiler, P. O. Souderton, Pa.

DESCENDANTS OF BENJAMIN ROSENBERGER, SON OF JOHN ROSENBERGER, SR.

III. Benjamin Rosenberger, b in 1761, d in 1832, m —. To him was conveyed the homestead now owned by Abraham Moyer, and other lands. This was sold to him in 1794 in two lots of 57 and 68 acres. The first lot of the Moyer farm was part of the 109 acres obtained by patent in 1770. The 68 acres was below the line of the turnpike, and was part of the 95 acres sold by Alexander Foreman to John Rosenberger and confirmed to him by the executors of the Warner estate in 1759, and a later date owned and subdivided by Tobias Shull. Upon this he built the village of Hatfield. The remaining 27 acres had been sold to Martin Rosenberger. In 1831 Benjamin conveyed the homestead to his son Benjamin Rosenberger, Jr., for £1400, stipulating that he should have home and maintenance the remainder of his life. In 1833 the farm was sold to John Rosenberger, miller, of Hilltown. The subsequent transfers have been: 1856 to William S. Strunk; 1861 to Henry Rosenberger; 1866 to Tobias Hangey; 1872 to Enos Kriebel, then to —— Hoot, then to Abraham Moyer present owner. Menn's. C: Abraham, Isaac, Jacob, Benjamin, Nancy.

IV. Abraham Rosenberger, b July 1, 1792, d Aug 30, 1832, m Fronica Rosenberger, daughter of David Rosenberger. Farmer. Menn's. C: Barbara, Susanna, Benjamin, Jonas, Tobias.

V. Barbara Rosenberger, m Jacob Fry. Family in Ohio. Ger. Bap.

V. Susanna Rosenberger, b Dec 20, 1823, d Oct 11, 1838

V. Benjamin R. Rosenberger, b Mar 9, 1826, m Sarah Frick, Nov 9, 1845, Res. 2218 Marshall St., Phila., Pa. Laborer. Ger. Bap. C: Amanda,

John, Mary, Elizabeth, Willamina, Emma, Ida. Allen.

VI. Amanda Rosenberger, b Sept 19, 1847, Res. 2218 Marshall St., Phila. Pa. Ger. Bap. S.

VI. John F. Rosenberger, b Dec 16, 1849. Grocer in Phila., Pa. S.

VI. Mary Ann Rosenberger, b Aug 22, 1852. River Brethren. P. O. Scuderton Pa. S.

VI. Elizabeth Rosenberger, b Apr 11, 1855, m Oliver Althouse. P. O. Souderton. Pa. Hotel keeper. C: (**VII**) Laura, Stella.

VI. Willamina Rosenberger; b Feb 21, 1860, d infant.

VI. Emma Rosenberger, b Dec 15, 1862, m John Cope, Res 2218 Marshall St., Phila., Pa. Horse dealer. No issue.

VI. Ida Rosenberger, b Aug 6, 1864, d Jan 17,1886, m Lincoln Kaler. C: (**VII**) Viola Kaler, b Sept 20, 1884.

VI. Allen Rosenberger, b Aug 10, 1867, m Ada Parkley, Res 6533 Main St., Phila., Pa. Grocer.

VII. Clifford Allen Rosenberger, b July 24, 1896.

V. Tobias Rosenberger, b in Bucks Co,, Pa., Jan 24, 1829, m Barbara Wagner, Nov 1850. She was b Sept 25, 1829, d June 8, 1888, P. O. Hatfield, Pa. Retired farmer. Ger. Bap. C: Sarah,Jacob,Jonas, Mary.

VI Sarah Ann Rosenberger, b June 9, 1851, m Abraham W. Kulp, June 29, 1872, P. O. Hatfield. Pa Farmer. Ger. Bap. C: (**VII**) Maggie Kulp, b Nov 6, 1872, d Aug 2, 1873; Susan Kulp, b May 11, 1874, d May 13, 1874; Jacob Kulp, b June 3, 1875, d June 4, 1879; Mary Ellen Kulp, b Sept 10, 1877, Ger. Bap; Wilson Kulp, b Sept 25, 1879; Sarah Ann Kulp, b Oct 6, 1881; Amanda Kulp, b Aug 6, 1884; Barbara Elizabeth Kulp. b June 24, 1886; Isaac Tobias Kulp, b July 10, 1888; Maria Kulp. b Aug 20; 1890, d Aug 22, 1890; Emma Kulp, b Aug 4, 1895.

VI. Jacob W. Rosenberger, b Jan 27, 1853, m Amanda Kratz, Oct 13, 1883, P. O. S. Hatfield, Pa. Farmer. Ger. Bap. No issue.

VI. Jonas W. Rosenberger, b Feb 5, 1855, d Apr 8, 1890, m Leanna Scheetz, June 8, 1878. Employed on railroad and later at Snyder's Mill, where he was killed by the cars, while crossing the track with a plank. C: (**VII**) Katie Rosenberger, b Mar 17, 1880; William S. Rosenberger, b Dec 4, 1882, Mary Ellen - Rosenberger, b Aug 14, 1885; Jacob Rosenberger, b and d Mar 12, 1887; Sallie Amanda Rosenberger, b Mar 19, 1889.

VI. Mary Ellen Rosenberger, b Apr 15, 1858, m Rev. William B. Fretz, Nov 27, 1879, P. O. Hatfield, Pa. Tinsmith and minister. He was ordained to the ministry of the German Baptist Breth church at Hatfield, Pa., in 1889, where he has since served as one of the ministers. No issue.

V. Jonas Rosenberger, b in Bucks Co., Pa., Nov 15, 1831, m Elizabeth Gottshalk, Jan 1854. She was b May 23, 1836, Res. 2243 Germantown Ave., Phila.. Pa. Laborer. Moravian. C: Franklin, Davis, Irvin, Dillman.

VI. Franklin Rosenberger, b July 30,1855, m Sallie Pane, Res. 2433 Reese St., Phila., Pa- Employed in wood and willow ware store. Moravian. C: (**VII**) Mary Rosenberger.

VI. Davis Rosenberger, b Sept 23, 1857, d Mar 15, 1880, m Mary Kriebel. Farmer. No issue.

VI. Ervin Rosenberger, b Mar 5, 1861, m Emma Hatfield, Res. Phila., Pa. Employed in saw factory. C: (**VII**) Ada, Stella, Elmer, Viola, Ethel.

VI. Dillman Rosenberger, b Apr 20, 1869, m Isabella Smith, Nov 27, 1894, Res. 32 N. 13th St., Phila., Pa. Salesman in wholesale paper store. Moravian. No issue.

IV. Isaac Rosenberger, d Aug 1866, from effects of a fall from the barn floor into the yard below,breaking his neck. M Catharine Ruck. Farmer. Menn's. C: Ann, Benjamin, John, Mary, Catharine, Amos.

V. Ann Rosenberger, d — , m Joseph Landis. No issue.

V. Benjamin Rosenberger, b Aug 30, 1829, d Aug 7, 1891, m Sophia Derr, dec'd. Mrs. Rosenberger Menn. C: Emeline.

VI. Emeline Rosenberger, b Apr 11, 1856, m Wm. Fisher, P. O. Hatfield, Pa. C: (**VII**) Irwin Fisher, b Dec 11, 1875; Clarence Fisher, b Aug 24, 1884.

V. John Rosenberger, b Jan 10, 1833, m Mary Weaver, Sept 1855, Res. Phila., Pa. Carpenter. C: (**VI**) Edward Rosenberger, b 1856, d 1885. S.

V. Mary Rosenberger, d infant.

V. Catharine Rosenberger, d — , m William Reifinger. Wheelwright. C: Emma, Clarence.

VI. Emma Reifinger, m George Pierce, P. O. Royersford, Pa.

VI. Clara Reifinger, b July 9, 1871, m Samuel B. Meyers, Dec 29, 1892, P.O.Royersford, Pa. Presby. C: (**VII**) Catharine R. Meyers, b Aug 6, 1893; Verna P. Meyers, b Oct 8, 1896.

V. Amos Rosenberger, m Jennie Leister, P. O. Penllyn. Pa. Farmer. C: (**VI**) Wilbur, Alvin.

IV. Jacob Rosenberger, d single.

IV. Benjamin Rosenberger, b 1802, d 1874, m Susanna, daughter of Abraham and Anna (Clemmer) Gehman, 1828. She was b 1808, d 1892. Farmer. Menn's. C: Abraham, Benjamin, Henry.

V. Abraham Rosenberger, b 1828, d aged 22 years.

V. Benjamin G. Rosenberger, b in Montg. Co.,Pa., 1831, m Rachael, daughter of Abraham Benner, 1853, P. O. North Wales, Pa. Fruit grower. Menn's, C: Susanna, Sarah, Abraham, Elizabeth.

VI. Susanna Rosenberger, b 1854, d infant.

VI. Sarah Rosenberger, b 1856, m Joseph Bustard, P. O. Cedars, Pa. Farmer. C: (**VII**) Elizabeth, George, Arthur, Wellington, Benjamin, Mabel, Joseph dec'd, Sallie dec'd.

VI. Abraham B. Rosenberger, b July 26, 1860, Res. 447 Magnolia St. Phila. Pa. Teamster for P. & R. R. R. Co. Christian Ch. S.

VI. Elizabeth Rosenberger, b 1862, m John Weikel, P. O. North Wales, Pa. Engineer in feed and flour mill. Luth. Mrs. W. Meth. Ep. C: (**VII**) Esther, George, Anna, Sarah, Caroline.

V. Henry G. Rosenberger, b 1834, d infant.

IV. Nancy Rosenberger, m Abraham Wireman. Farmer. Menn's. C: Barbara, Nancy, Katie, John,

Abraham.

V.Barbara Wireman, dec'd. m Samuel Gehman, dec'd. Farmer. Menn's.

V. Nancy Wiremen, m Abram Ruth. Farmer. Menn's. C: Katie, Benjamin, Daniel, Anna.

VI. Katie Ruth, m Isaac Young, P. O. Hatfield, Pa. Bricklayer. Ger. Bap. C: Abram, Isaac, Lizzie, Fannie, Annie, Amelia, Milton, Martha, Mary, Sallie, Katie.

VII. Abraham Young, m Amanda Fosbenner, P. O. Line Lexington, Pa.

VII. Isaac Young, m ——, P. O. Schwenksville, Pa.

VII. Lizzie Young, m Abraham Snyder, P. O. Hatfield, Pa.

VII. Fannie Young, m Samuel Souder, P. O. Hatfield, Pa.

VII. Annie Young, m ——.

VII. Amelia Young. Single.

VII. Milton Young, deceased.

VII. Martha Young. Single.

VII. Mary Young. Single.

VII. Sallie Young.

VII. Katie Young.

VI. Benjamin Ruth, d—, m Elizabeth Rosenberger. C: Clayton, Esther.

VII. Clayton Ruth, m ——.

VII. Esther Ruth, m Jonas Landis.

VI. Daniel Ruth. Single. P. O. Hatfield, Pa.

VI. Anna Ruth, m Rev. Benjamin C. Krupp. He was b Mar 12, 1857. Minister of the Ev. Ass'n. Ch. C: (**VII**(Lillie Krupp, dec'd; Jennie Krupp, dec'd; Annie Krupp; Ruth Krupp.

V. Katie Wireman, m Philip Richenbach. Mason and hotel keeper. Mrs. R. Menn. C: Fannie, Mathias.

VI Fannie Richenbach, m Lewis Cowell, P. O. Lansdale, Pa.

VI. Mathias Richenbach, m ——, P. O. North Wales, Pa.

V. John Wireman, Sr. m Angeline Stillwagon, P. O. Hatfield, Pa. C: Henry, John, Annie, Charles.

VI. Henry S. Wireman, b —, m Christine Kulp,

Jan 5, 1883. She was b Oct 9, 1863, P. O. Hatfield, Pa. Produce merchant. C: (**VII**) Charles Wireman, b Nov 17, 1884.

VI. John Weierman, m Mary Schantz, dec'd, second wife Annie Price, P. O. Hatfield, Pa.

VI. Annie Weierman, m Amos Stettler. C: (**VII**) —— Stettler, d small.

VI. Charles Weierman, m ——- Sliffer. Res. 4th and Dauphin St. Phila. Pa.

V. Abraham Weierman, m Sybilla Wagner, Farmer. Menn's. C: Lizzie, Jacob, Samuel, ——, .

VI. Lizzie Weierman, m ——- .

VI. Jacob Weierman, P. O. Norristown, Pa.

VI. Samuel Weierman, dec'd, m Lizzie Hecker. Farmer. C: (**VII**) Susie, m ——-, (**VII**) Bertha, S.

VI. —— Weierman, died single.

VI. —— Weierman, died single.

DESCENDANTS OF DANIEL ROSENBERGER,
SON OF JOHN ROSENBERGER, SR.

III. Daniel Rosenberger, b in Montg. Co., about 1765, d 1830, m Sophia Wiereman. Farmer. Menn's. To Daniel was conveyed in 1790 for £ 400 two lots, one of 51½ acres, and one of 25 acres. The first was the upper portion of the 109 acres of his father's estate, obtained by patent in 1770. It is now the farm of Rev. John Rosenberger, a Mennonite preacher. His large and commodious house stands on the bank overlooking the meadow below, through which flows the brook, the water of which turned the old mill of his ancestors. The other, or smaller tract obtained by Daniel from his father, was in Franconia, bought in 1789 from the Clibborn Wilson estate. Farmer. Menn's. C: John, Martin, Jacob, Daniel, Elizabeth, Lena, Nancy, Barbara.

IV. John Rosenberger, b   , d   , m Beatrice Stover. No issue.

IV. Martin Rosenberger, b Sept 24, 1798, d Oct 19, 1866, m Christiana Rosenberger, daughter of Henry Rosenberger. Farmer. Ev. Ass'n. C: Hannah, Sophia, Jacob, Henry, Christiana, Daniel, Martin.

V. Hannah R. Rosenberger, b Feb 6, 1828, d Feb 23, 1854, m Charles Dreisbach.

V. Sophia R. Rosenberger, b Feb 3, 1831, m Aaron R. Heckler.

V. Jacob Rosenberger, b   1834, m Elizabeth Snyder, in 1861. P. O. Kulpsville, Pa. C: Mary, Oliver, Annie.

VI. Mary Rosenberger, b in 1863, m Oswin Pfleiger, in 1883. Res. Williams St. South Bethlehem, Pa. Employed in rolling mill. Luth. No issue.

VI. Oliver S. Rosenberger, b in 1875.

VI. Annie Rosenberger, b in 1877.

V. Henry R. Rosenberger, b , d young.

V. Christiana R. Rosenberger, b   , d   . Single.

V. Daniel R. Rosenberger, b in Montg. Co. Pa., Sept 1, 1844, m Sarah Hendricks, in 1866, P. O. Hatfield, Pa. Farmer. Ev. Meth. C: Annie, Josiah, Jacob, Daniel, Sallie, Mary.

VI. Annie Rosenberger, b Sept 13, 1867, m William Sturzebecker, P. O. Lansdale, Pa.

VI. Josiah Rosenberger, b in Franconia township, Montg. Co. Pa., Feb 12, 1870, P. O. Colmar, Pa. Carpenter. Methodist. S.

VI. Jacob Rosenberger, b in Hatfield Twp., May 13, 1875.

VI. Daniel Rosenberger, b Nov 19, 1877.

VI. Sallie Rosenberger, b June 14, 1879.

VI. Mary Rosenberger, b Aug 14, 1881.

V. Martin Rosenberger, b   , d   .

IV. Jacob W. Rosenberger, b in Montg. Co., Dec 6, 1809, d Jan 6, 1894, m Elizabeth Swartley, Nov 20, 1836. Mr. Rosenberger received a common school education. In early life he engaged in the manufacture of various articles of utility and ornament. For many years he was extensively engaged in the manufacture of wooden seives used by powder manufacturers to sift the powder. He later engaged in farming and on retiring from that vocation engaged in making brooms and all kinds of bric-a-brac for his grand children. He was of such a nature that he could not content himself without some useful employment, although afflicted with a peculiar ailment since his 35th year, since which time he had few hours in which he was entirely free from pain, or able to do hard work, yet notwithstanding all that, he was a remarkably well preserved man up to his old age. Menu's: C: Anna, Mary, Abraham, Daniel, Jacob, Elizabeth, Catharine, Sarah.

V. Anna Rosenberger, b Aug 9, 1837, d Nov 15, 1839.

V. Mary Rosenberger, b Apr 3, 1841, m Michael Swartley. (See Michael Swartly Family.)

V. Abraham S. Rosenberger, b in Hatfield Twp. Montg. Co. Pa., Aug 19, 1843, m Catharine C. Alle-

bach, Oct 3, 1868, P. O. Hatfield, Pa. Mr. Rosenberger was given a good education. On leaving
the township schools at the age of 15 years, he took
a course at Kulpsville Seminary for two winters.
He then took one term at the Carversville Normal
Institute and a short teachers preparatory course
at Pottstown under Robert Crinkshank. He then
went into the world to make his own way and for
ten successive terms taught school. In 1869 he
settled in Hatfield Twp. and in 1872 bought a farm
which he has since successfully conducted. Mr.
Rosenberger has always been a very active Repuli-
can and has held office of a local nature for many
years. He was a school director for one term and
in 1890 was a delagate to the Republican State Con-
vension at Harrisburg, Pa. A few years after settling in Hatfield township he was elected assessor
and filled that post for eighteen consecutive years.
In 1889, after serving 12 years as assessor he was
re-elected to this office for three years and received
every vote that was polled at that election.

His long term as assessor, has made Mr. Rosenberger acquainted with almost every man, woman
and child in the district, and familiar with every
lot of ground, its dimensions and ownership.

Mr. Rosenberger has been a very considerable
collector of books on a wide range of subjebts, and
possesses a good working library. He is a constant
reader and one of the intelligent and well informed
men of his community. He is a close student of
public questions, as well, and familiar with county,
state and national issues. Although he never served an apprenticeship in the mechanical arts, yet he
evinces marked inventive genius as an artisan. He has
invented, draughted and constructed many devices
and machines of merit which, however, he made no
efforts to have patented. Menn's. C: David, Mary,
Harvey, Jacob, Allen, Edwin, Erwin, Lizzie.

VI. David A. Rosenberger, b Aug 8, 1869, d Aug
16, 1869.

VI. Mary Ellen Rosenberger, b Apr 16, 1871. M
Fred H. Hunsberger, P. O. Souderton, Pa. Farm-

er. C: (**VII**) Alvin Merton Hunsberger, b Jan 5, 1899, d Aug 4, 1902.

VI. Harvey A. Rosenberger, b Sept 14, 1872. S.

VI. Jacob A. Rosenberger, b Aug 18, 1876, d Nov 24, 1881.

VI. Allen Rosenberger, b——.

VI. Edwin A. Rosenberger, b May 26, 1881, d Aug 12, 1882.

VI. Erwin A. Rosenberger, b July 27, 1886.

VI. Lizzie Martha Rosenberger, b Oct 4, 1887.

V. Daniel S. Rosenberger, b in Montg. Co. Pa., Jan 29, 1847, m Catharine, daughter of Rev. Abel Horning, Oct 16, 1869. She was b Feb 19, 1850, P.O. Earlington, Pa. Farmer. Menn's. C: Wallace, Lizzie, Mary, Katie, Abel, Emma, Jacob, Eva.

. Wallace H. Rosenberger, b Jan 25, 1873, m Addie D. Detweiler. P. O. Telford, Pa. Foreman in Telford Standard Hay Baling Co. C: (**VII**) Wilmer D. Rosenberger, b Feb 13, 1895. Maria D. Rosenberger, b May 13, 1897.

VI. Lizzie H. Rosenberger, b May 25, 1876, m Benjamin G. Alderfer. P. O. Telford, Pa. Miller. C: (**VII**) Noble A'derfer, b Feb 1, 1899.

VI. Mary H. Ro enberger, b Nov 26, 1877. S.

VI. Katie H. Rosenberger, b May 25, 1879.

VI. Abel H. Rosenl erger, b Sept 21, 1880.

VI. Emma H. Rosenberger, b June 21, 1883.

VI. Jacob H. Rosenberger, b May 28, 1886.

VI. Eva H. Rosenberger, b Feb 14, 1892.

V. Jacob S. Rosenberger, b Jan 30, 1850, m Anna G. Heebner, Dec 7, 1878. P. O. Souderton, Pa. Farmer. Menn's. C: (**VI**) Lilly H. Rosenberger, b Dec 17, 1879. Horace H. Rosenberger, b Sept 13, 1881. Raymond Rosenberger, b Apr 9, 1883. Jacob H. Rosenberger, b Aug 2, 1885. Edwin H. Fo enberger, b Feb 2, 1888. Annie H.Rosenberger, b Jan 5, 1890, d Apr 29, 1890. Clayton H. Rosenberger, b March 19, 1891. Mame H. Rosenberger, b Sept 6, 1893.

V. Elizabeth Rosenberger, b Nov 20, 1853, m Jonas Hunsberger, Dec 4, 1888. P.O. Kulpsville, Pa. Farmer. Menn's. C: (**VI**) Lizzie R. Rosenberger, b

May 24, 1890.   Edgar R. Rosenberger, b Nov 24, 1893, d 1893.

V. Catharine Rosenberger, b July 27, 1855, m Aaron L. Gehman, 1877.   P. O. New Britain, Pa.   Farmer.   Menn's.   C: (**VI**) Harvey Gehman, b 1879. Clarence Gehman, b 1881.   Allen Gehman, b 1888. Erwin Gehman, b 1891.

V. Sarah Ann Rosenberger, b Jan 30, 1858, d Feb 12, 1871.

IV. Daniel Rosenberger, b Mar 4, 1813, d Mar 17, 1896, m Mary Benner.   Cabinet maker.   No issue.

IV. Elizabeth Rosenberger, d aged 30 years, m John Frick.   He was b in 1801, d 1833.   Farmer. Menn's.   C: Sarah, Sophia, Levi.

V. Sarah Frick, b Feb 25, 1825, m Benjamin Rosenberger.   (See Benjamin Rosenberger family.)

V. Sophia Frick, b 1827, m Levi Godshall.   Oyster stand.   Mrs. Godshall Bap.   C: William, Minnie, Ida, Tillie, Lucinda, Levi.

VI. William Godshall.   S.

VI. Minnie Godshall, m Daniel Smith.

VI. Ida Godshall, m David Thomas.

VI. Tillie Godshall, m Harry Champion.

VI. Lucinda Godshall, m Harry Schimmel.

V. Levi Frick, d young.

IV. Magdalena Rosenberger, b in Montg. Co., Pa., May 7, 1805, d Apr 14, 1892, m Daniel Reeder, in 1829.   He was b in Bucks Co., Pa., Jan 9, 1809. Farmer.   Menn's.   C: Oliver, Sophia, Levi, William.

V. Oliver Reeder, b in Bucks Co., Pa., in 1836, m Matilda Cooper, in 1860, P. O. Fricks, Pa.   C: (**VI**) Charles Reeder, b —, d —, aged about 10 years; (**VI**) Rechina Reeder, b —, d —, aged about 7 years.

V. Sophia Reeder, b in Bucks Co., Pa., in 1839.   S.

V. Levi Reeder, b Aug 9, 1841, m Emma Ott, Oct 1865, P. O. Souderton, Pa.   Cigar maker.   Ref. Ch.   C: William, Sophia, Magdalena, Anna, Elnora, Emma.

VI. William F. Reeder, b June 12, 1866, m Maggie E. Wendel, Dec 1887, Res. 925 Richfield St., Phila., Pa.   Printer.   Ref. Ch.   C: (**VII**) Walter Reeder, b Apr 7, 1890.

Isaac S. Rosenberger.

VI. Sophia A. Reeder, b Apr 30, 1868, d June 25, 1881.

VI. Magdalena Reeder, b Apr 4, 1873, m Edward C. Hagey, Oct 30, 1894, P. O. Souderton, Pa. Harness maker. Ref.Ch. C: (**VII**) Stanley Hagey, b May 8, 1896, d 1896; Howard Hagey, b Aug 27, 1897, d May 12, 1898; LeRoy Hagey, b Nov 11, 1898; Lester Hagey, b Dec 5, 1899.

VI. Anna E. Reeder, b Mar 10, 1875, d Mar 19, 1891.

VI. Elnora Reeder, b Sept 2, 1878.

VI Emma O. Reeder, b Jan 31, 1884.

V. William Reeder, b —, 1844.

IV. Nancy Rosenberger, b Apr 12, 1816, d Aug 10, 1876, m George Gehman, Dec 22, 1839. He was b in Bucks Co., Pa., Nov 5. 1818, d Sept 19, 1893. Farmer. Menn's. C: William, Tobias, David.

William R. Gehman, b July 23, 1842, d Mar 25, 1903. m Eliza Freed, b Sept 10, 1841, P. O. Blooming Glen, Pa. Menn's. C: Salome, Harvey, Allen, George.

VI. Salome F. Gehman, b Mar 7, 1864, m William Yoder. Ref. Ch. C: (**VII**) Ella, Stella, Bertha; Walter, George, Russell, Elizabeth, Anna.

VI. Harvey F. Gehman, b Nov 9, 1865, d in 1869.

VI. Allen F. Gehman, b Mar 6, 1871, m Sue Der.tine, P. O. Blooming Glen, Pa. Ref. C: (**VII**) Florence.

VI. George F. Gehman, b Mar 15, 1874, m Anna Coleshreiver. P. O. Quakertown, Pa. Luth. C: (**VII**) Ella May Gehman, d in infancy.

V. Tobias R. Gehman, b in Montg. Co., Pa., Oct 14, 1846, m Maria M. Hedrich, Jan 7, 1871, P. O. Silverdale, Pa. Farmer. Mennonite Deacon at Blooming Glen, Pa. C: Dianna, Minerva. Emma. Sallie, Aquilla.

VI. Dianna H. Gehman, b Sept 16, 1874, m Jacob G. Musselman, Oct 15, 1898, P. O. Silverdale, Pa. Wheelwright. Menn's. C: (**VII**) Sadie G. Musselman, b July 1, 1901, d July 6, 1901.

VI. Minnie H. Gehman, b Sept 22, 1876, m Wilson G. Detweiler, Oct 16, 1897. He was b Apr 19,1871,

P. O.. Blooming Glen, Pa.   Laborer.   Menn's.   C:
(**VII**) Florence G. Detweiler, b Mar 31. 1900.
VI. Sallie H. Gehman, b Feb 26, 1882.
VI. Aquilla H. Gehman, b Dec 1, 1891.
V. David R. Gehman, b Feb 12, 1852, m Elizabeth
A. Detweiler in 1876. Menn's. C: Sallie, Laura,
Blanche.
VI. Sallie D. Gehman, b Nov 13, 1877.
VI. Laura D. Gehman, b Jan 16, 1882.
VI. Blanche D. Gehman, b Feb 20, 1897.
IV. Barbara Rosenberger, b — , d — , m Christian
Allebach. Farmer. Menn's. C: Susanna, David.
V. Susanna Allebach, b -- , m —— Schlotter,
dec'd. She m 2nd husband, Enos Derstine, P. O.
Telford, Pa.
V. David Allebach, dec'd.

———•◦•◦—•◦•◦—•

DESCENDANTS OF HENRY ROSENBERGER,
SON OF JOHN ROSENBERGER, SR.

—•◦•◦—•

III. Henry Rosenberger, b about 1751, d in 1824, m
Ann ——. To Henry was conveyed the farm now
owned by Jacoby Ott. formerly A. H. Rosenberger's.
He afterwards removed from Hatfield to Rockhill,
where he died in the spring of 1824. The Ott farm
was sold to a Shellenberger, perhaps as early as the
beginning of this century. In his will, registered
on May 15, 1824, he ordered his plantation sold. C:
John, Henry, Margaret, Elizabeth, Mary, Nancy,
Catharine, Daniel.
IV. John Rosenberger, b in Bucks Co., Mar 2,
1772, m Catharine Keiper. She was b Feb 7, 1771,
d June 14, 1859. Farmer. Menn's. C: Elizabeth,
Henry, Hannah, Sophia, Abraham, Nancy, Mary,
Catharine, ——.
V. Elizabeth Rosenberger, b June 9, 1794, d July
29, 1882, m Abraham Hunsberger. He was b Dec

16, 1789, d Dec 31, 1853. Farmer. Menn's. C:
Isaac, Kate, John, Nancy, Abraham, Jacob, Chris-
tian. Henry, Mary, Elizabeth.
VI. Isaac Hunsberger, d infant.
VI. Kate Hunsberger, b Mar 7, 1816,d Jan 19,1854,
m Henry Sweisford.   C: Mary, Elizabeth,Amanda,
Caroline, Kate, Emma.
VII. Mary Sweisford, m Samuel Faust.
VII. Elizabeth Sweisford, m John Shaner.
VII. Amanda Sweisford, m John Markley.
VII. Caroline Sweisford, b Feb 22, 1846, m Henry
Schwenk, June 13, 1868. P. O. Red Hill, Pa.
Farmer. Ref. Ch. C. (**VIII**) Sallie, Harry, Josiah.
VII. Kate Sweisford, m John Erb.
VII. Emma Sweisford, m George Streeper.
VI. John R. Hunsberger, b in Montg. Co., Pa.,
Aug 9, 1818, d there Sept 26, 1893, m Maria Ober-
holtzer, Oct 24, 1841. She was b in Washington
Twp., Pa., July 20, 1815, d Dec 22, 1851. Farmer.
Menn's. C: Isaac, Isabella, Amanda. John m 2nd
wife, Isabella Fox, Nov 4, 1854. She was b Oct 8,
1813, d July 18, 1896.
VII. Isaac O. Hunsberger, b in Montg. Co., Pa.,
July 11, 1844, m Sarah M. Gottshall. P. O. Fred-
erick, Pa. Farmer. Menn's. C: Henry, Lizzie,
William, Ephriam, Franklin, Maggie,John,Bertha.
VIII. John G. Hunsberger, b Nov 16, 1870, d Mar
18, 1871.
VIII. Lizzie G. Hunsberger, b in Mont. Co., Pa ,
Jan 11, 1873, m James Calvin Wood, 1890. P. O.
Finland, Pa. Farmer. Mr. Wood Ref. Ch.; Mrs.
Wood, Menn. C: (**IX**) Rufus H. Wood, b Jan 5,
1892; Irwin H. Wood, b Sept 2,1894; John H.Wood,
b Jan 21, 1895; Calvin H. Wood, b Aug 16, 1896;
Emma H. Wood, b Jan 28, 1898, d May 8, 1898;
Maggie H. Wood, b May 17, 1899·
VIII. William G. Hunsberger, b July 1, 1875, m
Katie M. Richard, Mar 24, 1900. P. O. Frederick,
Pa. Engineer. Menn's.
VIII. Ephriam G. Hunsberger, b Mar 31, 1877, m
Alice R. Grubb, Dec 19, 1896. P. O. Frederick,Pa.
Farmer. Menn's. C: (**IX**) Clarence Hunsberger, b

July 3, 1898; Charles Raymond G. Hunsberger, b Apr 14, 1902, d Sept 5, 1902.

VIII. Franklin G. Hunsberger, b Nov 7, 1878.

VIII. Maggie G. Hunsberger, b Jan 26, 1881, m Ammon R. DeLong. P. O. Spring Mount, Pa.

VIII. John G. Hunsberger, b Feb 26, 1883.

VIII. Bertha G. Hunsberger, b June 30, 1885.

VII. Isabella Hunsberger, b Nov 6, 1846, d Jan 12, 1847.

VII. Amanda O. Hunsberger, b in Montg. Co.,Pa., July 26, 1848, m Charles Benner. P. O. Frederick, Pa.

VI. Nancy Hunsberger, b in Montg. Co., Pa., Oct 18, 1819, m John C. Stauffer, Oct 20, 1848. P. O. Bechtelsville, Pa. Farmer and miller. Menn's. C: Edwin, Henry, Elizabeth, Sarah, Emma.

VII. Edwin H. Stauffer, b Mar 22, 1851, m Lavina Bechtel, July 10, 1875. P. O. Bechtelsville, Pa. Farmer. Menn's. C: Olivia, William.

VIII. Olivia Stauffer, b Apr 17, 1879, m Morris Grof, June 8, 1899. Res. Reading, Pa.

VIII. William Stauffer (twin) b Apr 17, 1879.

VII. Henry H. Stauffer, b Jan 22, 1853, m Minerva Oberholtzer, Oct 14, 1877. P. O. Bechtelsville, Pa. Miller and creameryman. Menn's. No issue.

VII. Elizabeth H. Stauffer, b Aug 28, 1856, m. July 28, 1885, William Conrad. P. O. Bechtelsville, Pa. Dealer in furniture and undertaker. Mr. Conrad Ref. Ch.; Mrs. Conrad Menn. C: (**VIII**) John Conrad, b Apr 2, 1887.

VII. Sarah H. Stauffer, b Aug 29, 1861, m William J. Ritter, July 28, 1881. He d at Pottstown, Pa., —. Landlord. C: (**VIII**) Elmer Ritter, b Feb. 1882; Florence Ritter, b Nov 2, 1885; Annie Effie Ritter, b June 8, 1891. Sarah m 2nd husband, John Baker, — . Res. 260 Walnut St., Pottstown, Pa. Supt. of Life Insurance Agency. Luth's.

VII. Emma H. Stauffer, b Sept 22, 1863, m Noah S. Borneman, dec'd., Apr 18, 1884. Res. 209 Swede St., Norristown, Pa. Dentist. Menn's. C: (**VIII**) Walter S. Borneman, b Sept 6, 1894, d — 1895; Annie S. Borneman, b Apr 20, 1897; May S., b Sept

10. 1901.

VI. Abraham Hunsberger, b in 1821, d 1889, m Catharine Bartolet, about 1844. She was b 1825, d 1889. Farmer. Menn's. C: Mary, Sarah, Samuel, Abraham, Kate. Henry,Lizzie, Ephriam, John, Amanda, Emma.

VII. Mary Hunsberger, b — 1848, d aged about 12 years.

VII. Sarah B. Hunsberger, b in 1848, d in 1887, m William B. Moyer, dec'd. Mr. Moyer Luth.; Mrs. Moyer Menn. C: William. Sarah m 2nd husband, ——- Clayton. C: Annie.

VIII. William Moyer, b in Montg. Co., Pa., Mar 8, 1868, m Sallie K. B. Fox, Aug 3, 1889, P. O. Frederick, Pa. Cigarmaker. Luths.: C: (**X**) Warren Ellsworth F. Moyer. b Jan 23, 1890; infant daughter stillborn Aug 28, 1899.

VIII. Annie H. Clayton, b — 1871, d Dec 29, 1898, m Jonas Rawn. C: (**IX**) Sallie Bardman Rawn, b May 16, 1888.

VII. Samuel Hunsberger, b Sept 23, 1850, m Rebecca Gottshall. P. O. Zieglersville, Pa.

VII. Abraham B. Hunsberger, b Dec 14, 1852, m Lucinda Kehs, Jan 16, 1875. P. O. Perkasie, Pa. Laborer. United Ev. Ch. C: (**VIII**) Katie K. Hunsberger. b in 1875, d Feb 4, 1883; Oliver K. Hunsberger. b Feb 24, 1877, d Feb 13, 1882; Abraham K. Hunsberger, b July 13, 1878, d Feb 5, 1883; Howard K. Hunsberger, b Apr 13, 1880, Mary Elizabeth K. Hunsberger. b Jan 19, 1882, d Feb 2, 1883; Miriam K. Hunsberger, b Feb 19, 1884, d May 13, 1886; Minnie Minerva K. Hunsberger. b Oct 26, 1886; Elsie K. Hunsberger, b Oct 28, 1888, d June 10, 1891; Raymond K. Hunsberger, b July 25, 1890; Edna Florence K. Hunsberger, b July 25, 1892; John Henry K. Hunsberger. b May 19, 1895, d Sept 5, 1896.

VII. Kate Hunsberger, b June 5, 1855, m Jonathan B. Gilbert, Dec 23, 1876. P. O. Frederick, Pa. Farmer. Menn's. C: Annie, Irwin, Katie, Elmer.

VIII. Annie Maria Gilbert, b Mar 1, 1878, m Wm. J. Little. C: (**IX**) Lloyd Little.

VIII. Irwin Gilbert, b July 26, 1879.
VIII. Katie Gilbert, b Aug 4, 1882.
VIII. Elmer Gilbert, b July 29, 1890.
VII. Henry B. Hunsberger, b Dec 8,1856, m Lizzie
B. Markely, Feb 14, 1880.   P. O. Royersford, Pa.
Laborer.   Menn's.   C: (**VIII**) Sarah Ella Hunsberg-
er, b Feb 8, 1881. Menn.; Horace Markley Huns-
berger, b Apr 8, 1886, Anna Laura Hunsberger, b
June 5, 1890.
VII. Lizzie Hunsberger, b 1859, m Benjamin Yern.
VII. Ephraim Hunsberger, b 1861, m Lizzie Neidig.
P. O. Richland Centre, Pa.
VII. John Hunsberger, b 1863, m Lizzie Tyson. P.
O. Schwenksville, Pa.
VII. Amanda Hunsberger, b 1865,m Henry Grubb.
P. O. Obelisk, Pa.
VII. Emma Hunsberger, b 1867, m Mahlon Fryer.
P. O. Anise. Pa.
VI. Rev. Christian R. Hunsberger, b in Montg.
Co. Pa., May 3, 1823, m Fanny D. Van Fossen,
Nov 22, 1846.   She was b Nov 6, 1824, d Apr 13,
1881. P. O. Creamery, Pa.   Farmer.   He was or-
dained to the Ministry in Upper Skippack Menno-
nite church 1878.   C: Elizabeth, John, Susan,
Katharine, Abraham, Hannah, Christian, Jacob,
Fannie, Henry, Mary, Emma, Isaac.
VII. Elizabeth Hunsberger, b Dec 18, 1847. S.
VII. John Hunsberger, b Apr 5, 1849, d June 5,
1851.
VII. Susan Hunsberger,b Feb 9,1851, m John May-
berry, Oct 2, 1897. P. O. Creamery, Pa. Laborer.
Menn's.
VII. Katharine Hunsberger, b in Montg. Co. Pa.,
Nov 22, 1852, m Henry A. Ruth, in 1874. P. O.
Creamery, Pa. Laborer. Menn's. C: (**VIII**) Sallie
H. Ruth, b July 9, 1875, d same day. Jacob H.
Ruth, b May 20, 1876, d May 21, 1876. Christian
H. Ruth, b July 10, 1877, d Aug 26, 1878. William
H. Ruth, stillborn Apr 2, 1880. Henry H. Ruth, b
June 2, 1881. Daniel H. Ruth, b Apr 16, 1883, d
Jan 12, 1885. Benjamin H. Ruth, b Nov 23, 1884.
Mary H. Ruth, b Sept 3, 1885. Abraham H. Ruth,

William L. Rosenberger.

b July 2, 1887. Lizzie H. Ruth, b Nov 28, 1888.
Melvin H. Ruth, b Aug 17, 1890. Harvey H. Ruth,
b Nov 19, 1891. John H. Ruth, b Nov 26, 1892.
Wilson H. Ruth, b July 21, 189 .

VII. Abraham V. Hunsberger, b in Montg. Co. Pa.,
Apr 30, 1854, m Hannah G. Bergey, Dec 15, 1877.
P. O. Creamery, Pa. Farmer. Menn's. C: (**VIII**)
Mary B. Hunsberger, b Feb 24, 1879. P. O. Cream-
ery, Pa. Brethern Church. S. Samuel B. Huns-
berger. b Feb 25, 1880. P. O. Kulpsville, Pa.
Katie B. Hunsberger, b July 29, 1881. Abraham
B. Hunsberger. b July 7, 1883, d July 14, 1883.
Lizzie B. Hunsberger, b Dec 23, 1884. Henry B.
Hunsberger, b Jan 12, 1888.

VII. Hannah Hunsberger, b Aug 2, 1855. P. O.
Creamery, Pa. Menn. S.

VII. Christian Hunsberger, b Jan 6, 1857, m Mary
Kulp, May 11, 1878. Res 530 W York St. Phila.
Pa. Piano mover. Menn's. C: Sallie, Mary, Lydia,
Harvey, Ella.

VIII. Sallie Hunsberger, b in Skippack Twp. Montg.
Co. Pa., Apr 25, 1879, m Howard R. George, Sept
28, 1898. Res 530 W York St. Phila. Pa.

VIII. Mary Hunsberger, b Jan 26, 1881. Res 530
W York St. Phila. Pa. S.

VIII. Lydia Hunsberger. b Mar 16, 1883. Res 530
W York St. Phila. Pa.

VIII. Harvey Hunsberger, b May 24, 1885.

VIII. Ella Hunsberger, b Feb 3, 1887.

VII. Jacob Hunsberger, b Feb 27, 1859, m Lizzie
Drey. Res Moore St. Norristown, Pa.

VII. Fannie Hunsberger. b Nov 20, 1860. Res 545
Swede St. Norristown, Pa. S.

VII. Henry Hunsberger, b Feb 4,1862, d June 1862.

VII. Mary Hunsberger, b Apr 11, 1863. P. O
Creamery, Pa. S.

VII. Emma Hunsberger, b in Montg. Co. Pa., Nov
18, 1865, m William Prizer, in 1887. P. O. Collegeville, Pa. Farmer. One child stillborn in 1895.

VII. Isaac Hunsberger, b Apr 5, 1868, d Sept 27,
1868.

VI. Henry Hunsberger, died infant.

VI. Mary Hunsberger, died infant.

VI. Elizabeth Hunsberger, b in Montg. Co. Pa., July 12, 1830, m Elias B. Brendlinger, Oct 13, 1850. He was b in Earl Twp. Berks Co. Pa., July 13, 1826, d in Montg. Co. Pa.. Aug 13. 1893. P. O. Frederick, Pa. Mr. B. Luth. Mrs. Menn. C: Mary, Jacob, Missouri, Samuel, Lizzie, Kate, Morris, Abraham, Emanuel.

VII. Mary A. Brendlinger, b in Montg. Co. Pa., July 16, 1851, m Amos B. Oberholtzer, Nov 16, 1872. P. O. Bechtelsville, Pa. Farmer. Luth. C: Elmer, Morris, Martha, Henry, Annie.

VIII. Elmer B. Oberholtzer, b Mar 31, 1874, m Cora T. Ehst, Feb 7, 1899. P. O. Bechtelsville, Pa. Farmer. Menn's.

VIII. Dr. Morris B. Oberholtzer, b Sept 15, 1875, m Lizzie Gotshall, Sept 5, 1898. P. O. Red Hill, Pa. Physician.

VIII. Martha B. Oberholtzer, b Dec 26, 1879, died Aug 16, 1880.

VIII. Henry B. Oberholtzer, b July 18, 1881, d Apr 16, 1883.

VIII. Annie B. Oberholtzer, b June 19, 1886.

VII. Jacob H. Brendlinger, b Apr 2, 1853.

VII. Missouri E. Brendlinger, b Dec 7, 1854, m A. J. Stetler. P. O. West Point, Pa. Luth.

VII. Emanuel H. Brendlinger, b Mar 21, 1857, m Lavina Leidy, Feb 28, 1880. Res Norristown, Pa. Luth. C: (**VIII**) Elizabeth Brendlinger, b Feb 1, 1881. Luth.; E. Leidy Brendlinger, b Sept 7, 1893.

VII. Samuel Brendlinger, b July 29, 1861. P. O. Perkiomenville. Pa. Luth.

VII. Lizzie H. Brendlinger, b Aug 17, 1863, m John F. Mensch, Sept 6, 1890. P. O. Obelisk, Pa. Farmer. Luths. C: (**VIII**) Mabel M. Mensch, b May 10, 1891: Elias B. Mensch, b Sept 7, 1893; William R. Mensch, b Jan 12, 1896; Clark Mensch, b June 30, 1898: Mary L. Mensch, b Aug 1, 1899.

VII. Kate H. Brendlinger, b Oct 28, 1865, d Apr 25, 1886, m Jacob Boyer, Mar 27, 1886. Luth. No issue.

VII. Morris H. Brendlinger, b Sept 13, 1867. Res

Norristown, Pa. Luth.

VII. Abraham H. Brendlinger, b Nov 17, 1868, m Kate E. Renninger, Aug 19, 1890. P. O. Obelisk, Pa. Farmer. Luths. C: (**VIII**) Alice M. R. Brendlinger, b Sept 19,1891; Katie L.R.Bendlinger, b Sept 27, 1892; Charles W. R. Brendlinger, b Oct 7, 1894.

V. Henry K. Rosenberger, b in Bucks Co., Dec 1800, d Sept 11, 1872, m Elizabeth Gerhart. C: Thomas, Isaac, John. Henry m 2nd wife Sarah Hartranft. She was b Dec 29, 1811, d Feb 21, 1889. Farmer. He Menn. wife Luth. C: Mary, Henry, Sarah, Lewis.

VI. Thomas G. Rosenberger, b in Bucks Co. Pa., July 2, 1826, m Rebecca Dillinger, Nov 18, 1851. P. O. Milford Square, Pa. Farmer. Luths. C: Daniel, Henry, Dianna, Sarah, Charles, Samuel, Thomas, Mary.

VII. Daniel Rosenberger, b Dec 12, 1853, m Noemma Shearer, 1875. P. O. Milford Square, Pa. Farmer. Luths.

VII. Henry Rosenberger, b Aug 15, 1856, m Mary Sarver, Dec 14, 1889. P. O. Quakertown, Pa. Teamster. Luth. C: (**VIII**) Florence Rosenberger, b June 12, 1891; William Jacob Rosenberger, b Aug 15, 1893.

VII. Dianna Rosenberger, b July 7, 1858, d Sept 12, 1860.

VII. Sarah Rosenberger, b Feb 4, 1860. P. O. Milford Square, Pa. Cigarmaker. Luth.

VII. Charles Rosenberger, b June 16, 1862, d Mar 28, 1865.

VII. Samuel Rosenberger, b Mar 11, 1865, m Alice Deily, Dec 27, 1888. Farmer. Luths.

VII. Thomas Rosenberger, b Nov 7, 1868, m Ida Backensto, Jan 9, 1897. P. O. Milford Square, Pa. Farmer. Luth.

VII Mary Rosenberger, b Mar 12, 1872, m Wilson O. Heaney, July 18, 1895. P. O. Milford Square, Pa. Cigarmaker. Luths. C: (**VII**) Esther Ruth Heaney, b Nov 12, 1896.

VI. Isaac G. Rosenberger, b in Bucks Co. Pa., July 7, 1829, m Hannah Bartholomew, 1857. P. O. Per-

kasie, Pa. Farmer. Reformed Church. C: Henry,
John, Annie. Isaac m 2nd wife, Maria Kinsey,
Sept 27, 1862. Three children deceased. Isaac m
3rd wife, Maria Kehs, June 10, 1871. No issue.
On August 26, 1905 Mr. Rosenberger while in the
act of pitching rye from the overhead in his barn
stepped on a board which broke and he fell to the
thresh floor below, receiving internal injuries from
which he died August 30, 1905.

VII. Henry B. Rosenberger, b Aug 27, 1857, m
Annie L. Kinsey. She was b July 3, 1858, d Feb
23, 1902. P. O. Perkasie, Pa. Cigarmaker. Ref.
Ch.   C: (**VIII**) Clara K. Rosenberger, b May 3, 1880,
d Nov 2, 1887; Mary Ellen Rosenberger, b May 7,
1883; William Henry Rosenberger, b June 13, 1887;
Ida Florence Rosenberger, b June 11, 1890; Emma
Irene Rosenberger, b Sept 6, 1894; Elmer Rosen-
berger, b May 27, 1900. Henry m 2nd wife, Annie
E. Lyle, Dec 19, 1904.

VII. John B. Rosenberger, b July 16, 1859, d ——.

VII. Annie B. Rosenberger, b in Bucks Co. Pa.,
Aug 16, 1860, m Isaac K. McCrork, Jan 29, 1881.
P. O. Sellersville, Pa. Carpenter. Ref. Church.
C: Elmore, Carrie, Miriam, daughter stillborn, Isaac.

VIII. Elmore R. McCrork, b Aug 11, 1881, m Estella
K. Fillman, Sept 13, 1902. She was b in Dublin,
Bucks Co. Pa., Aug 5, 1884. P. O. Sellersville.
Printer. Mr. C. Ref. Mrs. C. Luth.   C: (**IX**) Clyde
Alton McCrork, b Nov 27, 1906.

VIII. Carrie R. McCrork, b Dec 17, 1884; Miriam
Esther R. McCrork, b Jan 4, 1892, d Oct 5. 1896;
daughter stillborn, Jan 16, 1895; Isaac R. McCrork,
b Jan 10, 1898.

VI. John G. Rosenberger, b—, d—. Single.

VI. Mary A. Rosenberger, b in Bucks Co. Pa., Apr
1, 1840, m Aaron B. Schoch, Jan 24, 1874. P.O. Milford Square, Pa. Luths. C: (**VII**) Infant stillborn,
Apr 23, 1875.

VII. Howard R. Schoch, b Oct 15, 1876.

VI. Henry H. Rosenberger, b in Bucks Co. Pa.,
Dec 29, 1844, m Elvina M. Moyer, Oct 8, 1870. P.
O. Quakertown, Pa. Cigarmaker. Menn's.   C:

Seward, William, Daniel.

VII. Seward M. Rosenberger, b in Milford Square Bucks Co. Pa., Aug 9, 1872, m Emma Sell, daughter of William B. Sell, of Spinnerstown, in 1896. P. O. Quakertown, Pa.   When 12 years of age Mr. Rosenberger began working on a farm in the neighborhood, attending the public school of the village for five months in the year.   Being devoted to his books, he made the best of these short terms and at age of 16, was granted a teacher's provisional certificate.   At the beginning of the term of 1888-89, he started the work of teaching, taking charge of the public school at Geryville, Bucks Co. Pa.   The following two terms he taught at Spinnerstown, and then for three terms the Milford Square grammar school, all in Milford, Bucks County.   During these years he availed himself of the advantages which the Normal school of the district, located at West Chester offered, attending the spring sessions.   During the term of 1894-95, he had charge of the study room at the Normal, in the meantime pursuing his studies.   Entering the senior class next term, he graduated in the Elementary course.   Before completing the work of the course, he had been elected to the principalship of the schools of Quakertown Pa. and entering upon his duties at the opening of the term of 1895-1896.   He is devoted to the calling which claims him and is eminently successful in it.   He is actively identified with the various educational interests of this county, having served as vise president of the Annual Teacher's Institute and as president of the Principals Association of the county, besides doing work on important committees.   He has from his early years been deeply interested in religious activities.   While attending Normal sceool, he was active in the work of the Y. M. C. A.   At present he is a trustee of the Mennonite church at Quakertown and is active in Sunday school and Young People's Association work.   For two years he was assistant editor of the Mennonite, the organ of the church of his choice.   C: (**VIII**) Arthur Rosenberger, b Sept 6, 1898; Willard S.

Rosenberger, b May 10, 1890.

VII. William Henry Rosenberger, b Mar 24, 1877. Clerk. Menn.

VII. Daniel Webster Rosenberger, b Mar 3, 1884.

VI. Sarah Amanda Rosenberger, d unmarried.

VI. Lewis Rosenberger, d Jan 1898. S.

V. Abraham Rosenberger, b in Bucks Co. Pa., Nov 19, 1810, d Mar 8, 1875, m Mary Roth, Apr 19, 1835. She was b in Rockhill Twp., May 27, 1811. Farmer. Menn's. C: John, Henry, David, Abraham, Chatharine, Frank.

VI. John R. Rosenberger, b Feb 25, 1836, d Apr 24, 1858. S.

VI. Henry R. Rosenberger, b July 20, 1838, m Mary Loux, Apr 23, 1863. P. O. Milford Square, Pa. Farmer. Menn. C: Mahlon, Lizzie, Harvey, Emma, Mary, Clara, Annie, Menno, Ellen, Andrew.

VII. Mahlon Rosenberger, b Sept 9, 1864, m Emeline Shelly, Apr 14, 1888. P. O Spinnerstown, Pa. Farmer. Menn's. C: (**VIII**) Aaron S. Rosenberger, b Feb 23, 1889; Ida May Rosenberger, b Sept 8, 1890; Oscar S. Rosenberger, b Jan 30, 1892; Clayton S. Rosenberger, b Mar 2, 1894; Mabel S. Rosenberger, b Aug 25, 1895; Mary S. Rosenberger, b Aug 5, 1897.

VII. Lizzie Rosenberger, b in Bucks Co. Pa., Feb 20, 1886, m Aaron W. Sweinhart, Jan 10, 1891. P. O. Niantic, Pa. Farmer. Menn's. C: (**VIII**) Jennie R. Sweinhart, b Mar 8, 1892; Calvin R. Sweinhart, b July 5, 1894; Melvin R. Sweinhart, b March 25, 1897.

VII. Harvey L. Rosenberger, b in Bucks Co. Pa., June 22, 1867, m Ella Nora Renner, Feb 6, 1891. P. O. Telford, Pa. Farmer. Menn's. C: (**VIII**) Paul R. Rosenberger, b Feb 5, 1896.

VII. Emma Rosenberger, b in Bucks Co. Pa., Nov 4, 1868, m Oliver M. Keiser, June 4, 1892. P. O. Milford Square, Pa. Farmer. Menn's. C: (**VIII**) Elmer R. Keiser, b Apr 7, 1873; Austin R. Keiser, b Feb 22, 1897.

VII. Mary J. Rosenberger, b Aug 11, 1870, m John A. Roth, Jan 13, 1894. P. O. Milford Square, Pa.

Farmer. Menn's. C: (**VIII**) Florence R. Roth, b Jan 27, 1897.

VII. Clara Rosenberger, b in Bucks Co. Pa., Oct 16, 1872, m Samuel W. Bauman, Apr 8, 1893. P. O. Congo, Pa. Farmer. Menn's. C: (**VIII**) Emma R. Bauman, b Feb 26, 1894; Henry R. Bauman, b June 24, 1895; Harvey R. Bauman, b Feb 26, 1897.

VII. Annie Rosenberger, b in Bucks Co. Pa., Sept 29, 1874, m Eugene D. Roeder, Dec 19, 1896. P. O. Spinnerstown, Pa. Farmer. Menn's.

VII. Menno S. Rosenberger, b Mar 9, 1877.

VII. Ellen Rosenberger, b Oct 16, 1879.

VII. Andrew F. Rosenberger, b Feb 28, 1883.

VI. David R. Rosenberger, b Mar 7, 1842, m Sarah Bauman, Apr 3, 1870. P. O. Milford Square, Pa. Farmer and Miller. Menn's. C: (**VII**) Leo B. Rosenberger, b July 11, 1872; Jennie B. Rosenberger, b Sept 11, 1873; David B. Rosenberger, b Aug 3, 1877; Elmer B. Rosenberger, b Apr 3, 1879; Elmira B. Rosenberger, b Mar 3, 1882, d Oct 22, 1891.

VI. Abraham R. Rosenberger, b May 7, 1845, d Nov 10, 1869, m Elizabeth George, deceased. Farmer. Menn's. C: Emanuel, Abraham.

VII. Emanuel G. Rosenberger, b June 11, 1868, m Emma Imhof, Nov 29, 1897. P. O. Argus, Pa. After death of his father he was adopted by his Grandfather Abraham Rosenberger, who died several years later. He remained with his grandmother until 18, then served an apprenticeship as machinist, which he followed a short time. He then took a business course at Peirce Business College graduating in class 1890. Menn's.

VII. Abraham G. Rosenberger, b Feb 1870, m Bertha Sherm. in 1892. P. O. New Britain, Pa. Farmer. Luths. C: (**VIII**) Wilson S. Rosenberger, b Nov 13, 1892; Flora S. Rosenberger, b Oct 22, 1894; Melvin S. Rosenberger, b Nov 22, 1897.

VI. Catharine R. Rosenberger, b Apr 12, 1850, m John Miller, in 1878. P. O. Milford Square, Pa. Farmer. Menn's. C: (**VII**) Franklin R. Miller, b Oct 14, 1878, m Sallie Rosenberger, Dec 23, 1899. P. O. Milford Square, Pa. Luth.

VII. Alvin R. Miller, b May 15, 1880; Nelson R.
Miller, b Feb 22, 1887; Alice R. Miller, b Mar
1889; Freddie R. Miller, b Feb 10, 1891.
VI. Frank R. Rosenberger, b Mar 30, 1852, m
Emma Bergey, Mar 3, 1877. P. O. Milford Square,
Pa. Farmer. Menn's. C: (**VII**) Reno B. Rosen-
berger, b Apr 22, 1878. School teacher; James A.
Garfield Rosenberger, b July 16, 1881; John B.
Rosenberger, b June 23, 1883.
V. Hannah Rosenberger, m David Mumbauer. Ref.
Ch. C: Peter, Joseph, John, Henry, Hannah,
Angeline. P. O. Spinnerstown, Pa.
V. Sophia Rosenberger, m David Bealer. Luth.
C: Josiah, John, Henry, Malinda, Sarah.
V. Nancy Rosenberger, deceased, m Peter Kline,
deceased. Mr. K. Luth. Mrs. K. Men. C: Infant,
Infant, Edward, Josiah, Infant, Willoughby,Peter.
VI. Edward R. Kline, b Aug 8, 1832, d Aug 24,
1887, m Caroline Gerhart, July 8, 185e. She died
July 5. 1888. Carpenter and cigarmaker. He Luth.
She Ger. Ref. C: Oliver, Mary.
VII. Oliver Kline, b Feb 28, 1859, m Lydia Leidy,
Aug 7, 1878. P.O. Telford, Pa. Cigarmaker. Luth.
VII. Mary Kline, b Mar 23, 1865, m William H.
Shaw, Dec 25, 1888. P. O. Quakertown, Pa. Cigar-
marker. Luth.
VI. Josiah Kline, b 1837, —.
VI. Willoughby Kline. b 1841, d young.
VI. Peter R. Kline, b Jan 8, 1842, m Mary Ram-
bo, May 21, 1865. Res 2319 N 6th St. Phila. Pa.
Produce merchant. Menn's. C: Horace, Emma,
Laura, Clara, Mahlon, Paul, Mamie, Eva.
VII. Horace E. Kline, b Aug 2, 1865, m Laura
Morris. Res Phila. Pa. Clerk.
VII. Emma J. Kline, b Mar 12. 1867, m Charles O.
Kruger. Phila. Pa.
VII. Laura Kline, b Feb 28, d Nov 14, 1871.
VII. Clara Kline, b Jan 29. 1873, m John Shelly.
VII. Mahlon R. Kline, b Mar 30, 1877, m Ida Barto.
VII. Paul R. Kline, b Sept 19, 1880.
VII. Mamie R. Kline, b Sept 7, 1882.
VII. Eva R. Kline, b May 14, 1888.

V. Mary Rosenberger, deceased, m Christian Doll, deceased. Soldier in war of 1812. Farmer. Ref. Ch. C: Washington, Elizabeth, Mary, Jesse, Charles.

VI. Washington Doll, d, m Anna Musselman, d. C: deceased.

VI. Elizabeth Doll, b in Bucks Co., Nov 5, 1824, d June 7, 1892, m Samuel Diehl, Nov 23, 1845. She was a faithful wife and mother, cheerfully sharing the struggles of earlier years to secure the best opportunities for advancement of her children and by a firm faith in the redeeming love of our Heavenly Father, she exemplified her christian faith to the end. Samuel Diehl, before marriage was a shoemaker, but later engaged in teaching school, farming and keeping store. Res 709 Linden St. Allentown, Pa. Mr. D. Luth. Mrs. Ref. Ch. C: Tilghman, Mahlon, Leanna, Milton, Oliver.

VII. Tilghman Diehl, b in Bucks Co. Pa., May 21, 1847, m Rosina A. Schall, June 1873. Res Allentown, Pa. Mr. Diehl attended the public schools at Quakertown, Seidersville and Allentown until 14 years of age, when he was apprenticed to learn the printer s trade in the office of Rev. S. K. Brobst. He had hardly finished his apprenticeship when he was placed in charge of the accounts of the various publications of the establishment. At the same time he was called upon to read proof and assume other similar duties. In 1872 he was taken into partnership by Rev. Brobst and till the end of 1876 when the latter died, the firm title was S. K. Brobst & Co. The founder's son then became partner, the firm name changing to Brobst, Diehl & Co., this arrangement continuing several years, when the subject of this sketch by purchase became the sole owner of the establishment, which is now publishing three periodicals and a list of books of nearly 30 titles and also conducting a general book and stationary store. Luths. C: Edward, John, Samuel, Caroline.

VIII. Edward I. Diehl, b July 11, 1874, m Mary E. Snyder, Sept 17, 1896. He graduated from Allentown High School, had a position in his father's store for some years, then passed a civil service examination successfully and entered as clerk in the post office at Allentown, Pa.   C. (**IX**) Henry Diehl, b July 18, 1897.

VIII. John F. Diehl, b Aug 5, 1875, m Lillie Troxell, Oct 4, 1898.   P. O. Allentown, Pa.   Luths.

VIII. Samuel L. Diehl, b Dec 3, 1877.   Res Jenkintown. Pa.   Jeweler.   S.

VIII. M. Caroline Diehl, b Sept 12, 1879.   Graduated Allentown High School.   Res Allentown, Pa.   S.

VII. Mahlon Diehl, b Oct 30, 1848, d May 31, 1892, m Mrs. Mary L. Tavener (nee Booth) in 1886. After leaving school he learned the trade of machinist in an iron foundry at Allentown.   He later began the study of medicine with Dr. S. S. Apple, of Allentown, Pa., and later entered the Medical Department of the University of Pennsylvania from which he graduated in 1874.   He located at Jeddo, Luzerne Co. Pa., as company physician of a large coal mining district.   He later became physician at Leisenring, Fayette, Co. Pa., where he found a field of activity beyond his strength.   In 1886 he built a fine home and engaged in cattle raising in addition to the care of his large practice until he succumbed to an attack of pneumonia.   No issue.

VII. Leanna Diehl, b Mar 1851, m Henry J. Hornbeck, in 1869.   He d Sept 30, 1898.   Res 509 Linden St. Allentown, Pa.   Mr. Hornbeck enlisted during the Civil War in the 47th Pennsylvania Regiment and was advanced to be quartermaster Sergeant of the same, which position he held at its disbandment and for the greater part of his three years term, as such he participated in the varous marches and engagements of the regiment in Virginia, South Carolina, (battle of Pocotaligo); the Red River campaign in Louisiana, the period of guard duty at Key West.   After the close of the war he became accountant and book keeper for iron works at Allentown, Emaus and Fullerton successively in the latter position as chief his of department in the McKee and Fuller car wheel and foundry works.   Luths.

C: Mamie, Bessie, Harry.'

VIII. Mamie Hornbeck, b Mar 2, 1870, d May 2. 1877.

VIII. Bessie Hornbeck, b Oct 28, 1879. She is an honor graduate of the Allentown College for Women and counts among her accomplishments a gift for painting, which promises, if cultivated, fine artistic results.

VIII. Harry Hornbeck, b Aug 6, 1881. He attended the Allentown grammar school and is now bookkeeper in the Lehigh Trust and Safe Deposit Co.

VII. Milton Diehl, b Sept 7, 1852, d Mar 13, 1853.

VII. Oliver Diehl, M. D., b in Quakertown, Pa., June 21, 1856, m Sarah Hester Williams, Phila. Pa.. Oct 11, 1882. Res 6326 Burbridge St. Phila. Pa. While an infant his parents removed to Seidersville, Pa. and from there to Allentown, Pa. When six years old he entered the public schools at the latter place. At fourteen years of age he left school to enter the employ of the Lehigh Valley Railroad Co., at Allentown station. learning telegrapy and serving in various capacities in the offices of the Company until 1877 when he left the employ of the company to enter the Jefferson Medical College at Philadelphia, Pa. He had previously prepared himself for the course in medicine by devoting his spare moments to study and by taking advantage of opportunities offered by practitioners of Allentown to witness operations and to study cases of diseases. He was graduated from the Jefferson Medical College in the spring of 1879 and shortly afterwards secured an appointment as house physician at St. Mary's Hospital, Philadelphia, Pa., where he spent a year. After leaving this hospital he passed the examination for entrance into the Navy and was commissioned an Assistant Surgeon on July 6th, 1880. His first duty was on board the U. S. Receiving Ship "St. Louis," at League Island, Pa., from which he was transferred to the U. S. Receiving Ship "Franklin," at Norfolk, Va. He then served successfully at the Recruiting Rendezvous Phila.. again on the "St. Louis" and then at the

Naval Academy, Annapolis, Md., making the Summer practice cruise in 1883 on board the U. S. S. "Constellation." In July 1883 he was promoted to the rank of Passed Assistant Surgeon and in September 1883 was ordered to the U. S. S. "Quinnebaug" on the European Station, serving until 1886 when he was ordered home and to duty at the U. S. Naval Hospital, New York. From there he was transferred to the Naval Hospital and Home at Philadelphia, serving there for three years he was ordered in Jan 1890 to the U. S. S. "Baltimore" which vessel went into commission at Cramps Ship-Yard at Phila., where she had just been completed and was commanded by Capt. Winfield S. Schley (now Rear Admiral). However, on the way to Chile the "Baltimore" stopped at Montevideo for coal and it so happened that the Surgeon of the U. S. S. "Essex," then in that port was taken ill and was invalided home. Surgeon Diehl was ordered by cable to succeed him on the "Essex" and finished his cruise in that vessel on the South Atlantic station, coming home on her in the spring of 1893. He was then ordered to the Naval Hospital Philadelphia where he served until April 1897 when he was ordered to the Monitor "Terror" having in the meantime been promoted to the rank of Surgeon. The "Terror" was one of our ships serving in the late war with Spain. After the destruction of the "Maine" and while preparations were being made for the conflict which was now regarded as inevitable she was ordered to New York to protect that Port. In the latter end of March she was ordered to Key West and on the commencement of hostilities went to Havana and was stationed at Cardenas, Cuba, to maintain the eastern end of the blockade. Shortly after her arrival she captured as prizes the following Spanish vessels viz steamers "Guido" and "Bolivar," schooners "Tres Hermanas" and "Mascoto." From this point she went with Admiral Sampson's Squadron to the eastward in search of Cervera's Squadron and took part in the bombardment of San Juan, Porto Rico. After re-

turning to Key West she again did blockade duty
off Havana and other Cuban Ports and later on
joined General Miles' expedition to Porto Rico lying at Ponce and Guanica at which Ports she was
of valuable assistance to the Army in aiding the
landing of the troops and stores. In September
the "Terror" was ordered North and went into reserve at Norfolk, Va. Surgeon Diehl was then
ordered to the U. S. S. "Michigan" on the Northwestern Lakes where he is serving at the present
time. Luths. C: (**VIII**) Mary Winifred Diehl, b
September 16, 1887, d May 15, 1889; Oliver Roland
Diehl, b July 7, 1890.

VI. Mary Doll, b in Bucks Co. Pa., in 1830, d Apr
20, 1891, m Gotlieb Kraft, in 1856. He was b in
Saxony, Germany, Feb 18, 1810, d in Bucks Co.
Pa., Feb 3, 1876. Laborer. Mr. Kraft Luth, Mrs.
Ref. Ch. C: Lizzie, Herman, Frank, Annie, Lucy.

VII. Lizzie Kraft, b in Bucks Co. Pa., Oct 1, 1861,
m Charles Murray, Dec 6, 1884. P. O. Warring-
ton, Pa. Farmer. Baptists. C: (**VIII**) Mabel May
Murray, b May 29, 1887; Charles Roy Murray, b
Nov 17, 1893.

VII. Lucy Kraft, b in Bucks Co. Pa., June 13, 1866,
m Erwin H. Woodring, Nov 19, 1891. · P. O. Milford Square, Pa. Luths. No issue

VII. Frank Kraft.

VII. Annie Kraft, m —— Stauffer.

VII. Harman Kraft, b in Bucks Co. Pa., Jan 23,
1872, m Rosana E. Ford, Aug 3, 1893. P. O. Edi-
son, Pa. Luths. C: (**VIII**) Charles Walter Kraft,
b Aug 29,1894; Leo Franklin Kraft, b Feb 23, 1897.

VI. Jesse R. Doll, b in Bucks Co. Pa., Dec 20, 1831,
m Mary Bearns, Sept 27, 1851. P. O. Quakertown,
Pa. Plasterer. Ref. Ch. C: Sarah, Jesse.

VII. Sarah Jane Doll, b Oct 25, 1852, d Feb 28,
1873.

VII. Jesse B. Doll, b in Quakertown, Bucks Co. Pa.,
Sept 29, 1875. Res 1021 Spring Garden St. Phila.
treasurer and secretary of Maws Homo-Allo-Pathic
Chemical Co. Phila. Pa. Ref. Ch. Single.

VI. Charles R. Doll, b in Bucks Co. Pa., Aug 25,

1835, d Sept 23, 1898, m Elizabeth Swenk, dec'd,
Oct 31, 1857. C: Edwin, Elizabeth. Charles m
second wife Amanda Maugle, (nee Althouse) Jan
19, 1867. She was b Sept 8, 1839. P. O. Quakertown, Pa. Cigar Manufacturer. Ger. Ref. C:
Lillie, Charles, Mary, John.

VII. Edwin S. Doll, b Apr 4, 1860, d Jan 17, 1884.
VII. Elizabeth Doll, b Jan 15, 1866, d Feb 2, 1866.
VII. Lillie Estella Doll, b Mar 10, 1868. P. O.
Somerton, Pa. School teacher. Ger. Ref. S.
VII. Charles Monroe Doll, b in Bucks Co. Pa., Nov
1, 1869. P. O. Ashbourne, Pa. Station Agent.
VII. Mary Martha Doll, b June 4, 1871, d Oct 20,
1891.
VII. John Eugene Doll, b in Bucks Co. Pa., July 8,
1875. P. O. Somerton, Pa. Station Agent.

V. Catharine Rosenberger, m Samuel Keiper. Ref.
Ch. C: (**VI**) John, Sylvester, Solomon, dec'd. George
dec'd. P. O. Spinnerstown, Pa.

V. —— Rosenberger, m Joseph Balliet, moved to
Oil City, Pa., thence to some place in Missouri. C:
Josiah, Abraham, William, Loranda.

IV. Henry Rosenberger, b in Bucks Co. Pa., Dec
23, 1778, d Feb 1, 1869, aged 90 years, 1 month and
8 days, m Anna Derstine. She was b Dec 26, 1784, d
June 6, 1847. Farmer. Menn's. C: Catharine,
Samuel, Mary, Anna.

V. Catharine Rosenberger, b June 18, 1807, d July
31, 1893, m Samuel Ziegenfuss. He was b Jan 11,
1809, d Nov 11, 1894. Farmer. Luths. C: Sarah,
Lucyetta, Henry, Levina, Elias, Samuel, William.

VI. Sarah Ann Ziegenfuss, b Feb 22, 1834, m
Henry H. Freed, Oct 8, 1854. P. O. Richland
Centre, Pa. Carpenter. Luth. C: Samuel, Jonas,
Albanas, Amandus, Lucyetta, Wilson, Matilda,
Jacob, Sylvanus, William, Katie, Sallie, Isaac.

VII. Samuel Z. Freed, b Nov 10, 1856, m Lizzie
Nicholas. P. O. Doylestown, Pa. Lawyer. Luths.
C: (**VIII**) John, Henry.

VII Jonas Edwin Freed, Mar 2, 1858, m Annie
Frankenfield. Res 2449 Harold St. Phila. Pa. Clerk
P. & R. Railroad Co. Luths. C: (**VIII**) Harry.

Allison, Wilson.

VII. Albanas Z. Freed, b Aug 18, 1859, m Sallie Frederick. P. O. Richland Centre, Pa. Cigarmaker. Luths.

VII. Amandus Z. Freed, b Aug 30, 1861, d Mar 12. 1862.

VII. Lucyetta Z. Freed, b Mar 15, 1863, m John Hillegas. P. O. Church Hill, Pa. Farmer. Luth. C: (**VIII**) Jacob, Carrie.

VII. Wilson Z. Freed, b Oct 17, 1865, m Lillie Ann Hope. Res 143 Liberty St. N. Y. Telegraph Operator. Luth.

VII. Matilda Z. Freed, b Dec 24, 1866, m Amandus Stoneback. P. O. Richland Centre, Pa. Carpenter. Luths. C: (**VIII**) John, Florence, Annie, Miriam, Wilson.

VII. Jacob Z. Freed, b Nov 17, 1868, in Bucks Co. Pa. P. O. Richland Centre, Pa. Bricklayer. Luth.

VII. Sylvanus Z. Freed, b Nov 16, 1870, m Lydia Housekeeper. P. O. Richland Centre, Pa. Carpenter. Luth. C: (**VIII**) Albert, Carrie, Elmer, Harvey.

VII. William Z. Freed, b Jan 26, 1873. P. O. Richland Centre, Pa. Farmer. Luth.

VII. Katie Z. Freed, b Dec 10, 1874, m Elmer Weaver. P. O. Passer, Pa. Farmer. Ref. Ch. C: (**VIII**) Harlem Weaver.

VII. Sallie Z. Freed, b July 13, 1877. P. O. Perkasie. Pa. Luth.

VII. Isaac Z. Freed, b Aug 27, 1880. P.O. Richland Centre, Pa. Bricklayer. Luth.

VI. Lucyetta Ziegenfuss, b in Bucks Co.Pa.,Nov 16, 1835, m Lewin Deaterly, Oct 20, 1859. P. O. Line Lexington, Pa. Tailoring. Luths. C: Lizzie, Katie, Ida.

VII. Mary Elizabeth Deaterly, b in Dublin. Pa., Dec 18, 1891, m Eli Frankenfield, Nov 15, 1888. P. O. Line Lexington, Pa. Tailor. Luths. C: (**VIII**) Rodman Frankenfield, b May 16, 1890; Sadie Frankenfield, b July 30, 1892; Clara D. Frankenfield, b July 6, 1894.

VII. Katie Minerva Deaterly, b Nov 30, 1873, d

Feb 5, 1894.

VII. Ida Violetta Deaterly, b Aug 1, 1879.

VI. Henry R. Ziegenfuss, b in Bucks Co. Pa.. Aug 1, 1837, m Elmina O. Lynn, Feb 15, 1870. Res S. Bethlehem, Pa. Retired. Luth. C: Minnie.

VII. Minnie C. Ziegenfuss, b Dec 8, 1870, m W. H. Redline, Nov 6, 1890. Res 618 Ontario St, South Bethlehem, Pa. Merchant. Luths. C: (**VIII**) Edith E., Esther I., Infant deceased.

VI. William Ziegenfuss, b in Bucks Co. Pa., Jan 20, 1840, m Elizabeth Margaret Rothrock, Aug 16, 1870. Res 427 Pawnee St. S. Bethlehem, Pa. Carpenter. Luths. C: Jennie, Robert, Cora, Charles.

VII. Jennie Catharine Ziegenfuss, b July 9, 1871, m Howard S. Miller, Aug 13, 1892. Res 1004 Ferry St. Easton, Pa. Groceryman. Ref. Ch. C: (**VIII**) Dwight Everett Miller, b Aug 20, 1893; Luella Olga Miller, b Jan 17, 1895.

VII. Robert William Ziegenfuss, b Apr 15, 1873.

VII. Cora Levina Ziegenfuss, b Aug 8, 1880.

VII. Charles Samuel Ziegenfuss, b June 28, 1888.

VI. Levina Ziegenfuss, b in Bucks Co. Pa., Aug 15, 1842, m John S. Stover, Nov 3, 1866. He died Jan 31, 1891. Res 522 Alaska St. So. Bethlehem, Pa. Luths. C: (**VII**) Catharine Susan Stover, b Apr 9,1867,d July 4,1877; Ida Levina Stover, b Sept 29, 1868, d June 15, 1877; Samuel Addison Stover, b Apr 23, 1876, d June 10, 1877; Harry Arthur Stover, b in Bucks Co. Pa., Dec 5, 1878. Res 522 Alaska St. South Bethlehem, Pa. A foreman in Warren Silk Mills, So. Bethlehem, Pa.

VI. Rev Samuel A. Ziegenfuss, D. D., b near Quakertown, Bucks Co. Pa., Dec 12, 1844, m Mary E. Himmelwright, Oct 21, 1875. Dr. Ziegenfuss received his education in public schools and Quakertown Normal and Classical school, Pennsylvania College, Gettysburg and Muhlenberg College, Allentown, Pa., from which institution he graduated in 1870, and from the Lutheran Theological Seminary, Philadelphia in 1873. He was ordained to the office of ministry in the Lutheran church by the Ministerium of Pennsylvania in the same year, a few days after graduation from the Seminary. His first charge was at Sellersville Pa., where he labored successfully from June 1873 to Nov 1876, when he accepted a unanimous call from the Bath and Howertown charge in Northampton Co. Pa. He continued his labors in this charge until Jan 1892, when he followed an urgent call from St Michael's Lutheran church Germantown, Philadelphia, where he still labors. He has succeeded in building one of the finest Lutheran Churches in Philadelphia, the chancel arrangement being exceptionally well arranged. In all of his charges new church buildings were erected. He received the degree of D. D. from his Alma Mater in 1896. Dr. Ziegenfuss has filled many positions of honor and trust in the church. He is a member of the Board of Trustees of Muhlenberg College, and Secretary of the Board since 1886, member of the Board of Directors of the Theological Seminary of Philadelphia, and secretary of its executive committee. President of the Philadelphia English Conference, of Ministerium of Pennsylvania. Res 6671 Germantown Avenue, Philadelphia, Pa. No issue.

VI. Elias Ziegenfuss, b in Richland Twp. Bucks co, Pa. Dec 29, 1847, m Amelia D. Mohr, Oct 9, 1886, P. O. Richland Centre Pa, Cigarmaker, Luths.

V. Samuel Rosenberger, b in Bucks Co. Pa. Feb 27, 1809, d Mar 3, 1875, m Mary Licey, Nov 11, 1834. She was b in Bucks Co. Sept 15, 1813, d Nov 28, 1895. Weaver and farmer Bucks Co. Menn's. C: Anna, Christian, Marietta, John, Sarah, Alvin, Henry, Samuel, Mahlon.

VI. Anna Eliza Rosenberger, b Jan 31, 1836. C: Clara, Anna Eliza m Levi Means, Oct 9, 1875. P. O. Blooming Glen, Pa, Ger Ref. church.

VII. Clara Rosenberger, b Jan 1867. m Michael S. Althouse, b Jan 18, 1887. P. O. Blooming Glen Pa. C: (**VIII**.) Emerson Althouse, b Jan 22, 1888; Warren Althouse, b Mar 15, 1890; **Romanus Althouse**, b Feb 28, 1892; **Raymond Althouse**, b Jan 17, 1894.

VI. Christian L. Rosenberger, b Oct 27, 1838, m Magdalena Moyer, She was b in Bucks Co. Pa. Oct 1, 1843, d Apr 27, 1880. C: Anna, William, Elmer, Lizzie, Harvey, Samuel, Catharine. Christian m second wife Sarah Ann Fretz, in 1888. P. O. Zion Hill, Pa. Farmer. Menn's.

VII. Anna Mary Rosenberger, b Sept 14, 1866.

VII. William Henry Rosenberger, b Aug 9, 1868, m Alice Schlifer, in 1890. P. O. Centre Valley, Pa. Butcher. Menn. C: (**VIII**) Violet Rosenberger, b Feb 8, 1891; Mildred Rosenberger, b Mar 9, 1895.

VII. Elmer Rosenberger, b Jan 25, 1871, m Elemina Young. P. O. Zion Hill, Pa. Farmer. Menn's. C: (**VIII**) Henry Rosenberger, b Nov 23, 1889.

VII. Lizzie Rosenberger, b Apr 10, 1875.

VII. Harvey Rosenberger, b Aug 14, 1877.

VII. Samuel Rosenberger, b Feb 28, 1873, d Apr 21, 1873.

VII. Catharine Rosenberger, b Apr 4, 1880, d Sept 10, 1880.

VI. Marietta Rosenberger, b June 24, 1842, d Mar 17, 1883, m Levi L. Fretz.

(See Levi L. Fretz family.)

VI. John L. Rosenberger, b Sept 3, 1843, m Hester Gross, May 31, 1879. P. O. Richland Centre, Pa. Farmer. Menn's. C: (**VII**) Mamie dec'd, Laura dec'd, Lottie dec'd, Jennie.

VI. Sarah Rosenberger, b Apr 6, 1845, d Oct 16, 1870, m Jacob H. Myers, Nov 28, 1868. P. O. Dublin, Bucks county, Pa. Farmer. Mennonites. C: (**VII**) Rosella Myers, b in Bucks Co. Pa., Feb 12, 1870, m Elmer S. Umstead, Jan 25, 1890. P. O. Dublin, Pa. Farmer. Ger. Bap. C: (**VIII**) Laura Valeria Umstead, b Apr 26, 1891; Jacob Warren Umstead, b Dec 22, 1892; Aaron Linford Umstead, b Jan 23, 1895; Della Alberta Umstead, b Apr 1, 1897; Fietta Elizabeth Umstead, b Nov 6, 1899; Anna Mae Umstead, b May 19, 1901.

VI. Alvin L. Rosenberger, b Feb 25, 1847, married Amanda Smith. Milford Square, Pa. C: Mamie, Estella, Emma, Sallie.

VII. Mamie Rosenberger, m Milton Erdman.

VI. Henry L. Rosenberger, b in Bucks Co. Pa., Nov 26. 1849, m Katie S. Himmelwright, Dec 24, 1874. She was born June 27, 1854, d Nov 26, 1891. P. O. Spinnerstown, Pa. Farmer. Luths. C: (**VII**) Carrie Rosenberger, b Sept 1, 1875. Luth. S.; Peter Rosenberger, b June 7, 1878. Luth. S.; Elmer Rosenberger, b Sept 26, 1881. Luth.; Lillie Rosenberger, b Nov 2. 1885.

VI. Samuel L. Rosenberger. b in Bucks Co. Pa., Jan 24, 1853, m Laura R. Alderfer, Feb 11, 1883. P. O. Hilltown, Pa. Merchant. Menn's. C: (**VII**) Mabel A. Rosenberger, b Feb 11, 1884; Susie A. Rosenberger, b Dec 20, 1885; Florence A. Rosenberger, b July 8, 1892, d Nov 15, 1896; Anna Belle Rosenberger, b May 2. 1896.

VI. Mahlon L. Rosenberger. b Apr 1, 1857, d single.

V. Mary Rosenberger, m Peter Ziegenfuss. Farmer. Luths. C: Angeline, John, Mary, Amanda, Sophia, Peter, Sallie, Lizzie, Kate, Emma, William.

VI. Angeline Ziegenfuss, m Reuben Crouthamel. P. O. Schlichtersville, Pa. C: (**VII**) Henry, Peter, Ella, etc.

VI. John Ziegenfuss, d S.

VI. Mary Ziegenfuss, m Jonas Hillpot, dec'd. C: Peter, John, Savilla, Emma, Charles, dec'd.

VI. Amanda Ziegenfuss, m Aaron Dubbs. P. O. Trumbauersville, Pa. C: Henry, Emma, Cora, Charles, Carrie, Ella. John, etc.

VI. Sophia Ziegenfuss, m Milton Wolf, dec'd. C: James. Charles, Annie, Sophia. M 2nd husband Edward Carroll. C: Walter.

VI. Peter Ziegenfuss, b Apr 5, 1847, m Lizzie Althouse. Dec 20, 1866. She was b Jan 2, 1847. P. O. Silverdale, Pa. Farmer. Luth's. C: Thomas, Frank, Annie, William, Albert, Elmer, Laura, Lizzie.

VII. Thomas Ziegenfuss. b Feb 22, 1868, m Sallie Seiple. P. O. Sellersville, Pa. Artesian Welldriller. Luths. C: (**VIII**) Frank, Lillie, Thomas, Edwin.

VII. Frank Ziegenfuss, b Feb 4, 1870, died Dec 21, 1874.

VII. Anna Maria Ziegenfuss, b Jan 5, 1872, m
Charles B. Knight, Mar 5, 1891. P. O. South
Bethlehem, Pa. P. & R. conductor. Luth. C:
(**VIII**) Gertrude, Knight.

VII. William Henry, Ziegenfuss, b Nov 6, 1874, m
Ella Gilbert. P. O. Perkasie, Pa. Cigarmaker.
Luth. C: (**VIII**) Charles Ziegenfuss.

VII. Albert Ziegenfuss, b Apr 24, 1877, m Annie
Hettenbach. Feb 22, 1899. P. O. Sellersville, Pa.
Cigarmaker, Luth.

VII. Elmer A. Ziegenfuss, b May 24, 1879, d Mar
8, 1883.

VII. Laura Ziegenfuss, b May 18, 1882.

VII. Lizzie Ziegenfuss, b May 30, 1885.

VI. Sallie Ziegnfuss, b Sept 9, 1849, m Geo E.
Boyer, Oct 14, 1871. Res 708 Market St, Camden,
N. J. Painter. Luth. C: Walter, David, Laura,
Bertha, Sarah, George, Herbert, Mary, Lillie.

VII. Walter Curtis Boyer, b Dec 8, 1872, d Apr 17,
1875. David Arthur Boyer, b Nov 8, 1874, d Dec
30, 1878. Laura Amanda Boyer, b Feb 26, 1877,
m Samuel S. Conver, Oct 19, 1898. P. O. Lansdale, Pa. Architect. Ref. Ch.

VII. Bertha Lizzie Boyer, b Sept 24, 1879, m Herman W. Koehler, Mar 18, 1899. Six weeks after
marriage Mr. Koehler was killed by a train on N.
P. R. R. while delivering goods in a wagon along
with his brother and sister aged 5 and 9 years respectively. Baker. Luths.

VII. Sarah Ann Boyer, b Dec 29, 1881, d June 31,
1882; George Edgar Boyer, b June 16 1883; Herbert Boyer, b June 10 1884, d Jan 12, 1885; Mary
Emma Boyer, b Dec 11, 1887; Lillie Erma Boyer, b
Nov 14, 1890.

VI. Lizzie Ziegenfuss, m Alfred Moyer, dec'd. C:
Ervin, Lizzie, m 2nd husband Daniel Hoffman. P.
O. Richland Centre, Pa. Cigarmaker. Luth. No
issue

VII. Erwin Moyer, M———.

VI. Katie Ziegenfuss, dec'd, m Revere Heist. P.
O. Tylersport, Pa. Cigarmaker. Luth. No issue.

VI. Emma Ziegenfuss, d, m Daniel Hoffman. C:

(VII) Harry Hoffman. P. O. Richland Centre, Pa.

VI. William H. Ziegenfuss, d young.

V. Anna Rosenberger, m Reuben Cope. Removed to Iowa.

IV. Elizabeth Rosenberger, b ---, d ---, m Samuel Stauffer. C: Samuel, John, Henry, Abraham, William.

V. Samuel Stauffer, b --, d --, m ---. C: Isaac, etc.

VI. Isaac Stover. P. O. Lansdale, Pa.

V. John Stauffer, m ———. C: (VI) William Stauffer, P. O. Brick Tavern, Pa.

V. Henry Stauffer, m --. C: Henry and 5 daughters.

VI. Henry Stauffer, P. O. Zion Hill, Pa.

V. William Stauffer.

IV. Margaret Rosenberger, m John Freed. C: Joseph, Samuel.

V. Joseph Freed, m ———. C: Maria, Dr. --.

VI. Maria Freed, m Abraham Gerhart, dec'd. P. O. Perkasie, Pa. No issue.

VI. Dr. — Freed, V. S., P. O. Perkasie, Pa.

IV. Mary Rosenberger, m Jacob Coffel or (Hoffel).

IV. Catharine Rosenberger, m George Diehl. Potters. Menns. C: (V.) Henry, Samuel, dec'd, George, John dec'd, Joseph, Ann.

IV. Daniel Rosenberger, m ---. C: Henry. Samuel.

IV. Anna Rosenberger, b Oct 27, 1785, d June 9, 1867, m Michael Derstine. He was b July 11, 1776, d May 27, 1841. Farmer. Menns. C: Hannah, Catharine, Elizabeth, Abraham, Ann, Henry, Joseph.

V. Hannah Derstine, b Sept 22, 1808, d May 7, 1891, m, Jesse Springer. He d July 5, 1889. Farmer. Menn's. C: Deby, Abraham, Elizabeth, Franklin, Charles.

VI. Deby Ann Springer, b June 27, 1839, m David S. Angeny. Rosa, Frank, Lillie, Charles.

VII. Rosa Angeny, m John H. Miller.

VII. Frank Angeny, m Rosa Meyers, P. O. Lansdale, Pa.

VII. Lillie Angeny, m Abraham M. Hunsberger, P. O. Hilltown, Pa.

VII. Charles H. Angeny, P. O. Dublin, Pa. S.

VI. Abraham D. Springer. b Dec 16, 1842, m Mary E. Angeny, May 26, 1874. P. O. Hilltown,Pa. Blacksmithe. Presby. C: Ella, Harry, Laura.

VII. Ella M. Springer. m Ed. Crouthamel.

VII. Harry Springer,b Oct 9, 1878.

VII. Laura Springer, b Aug 11, 1880.

VI. Elizabeth Springer, Oct 1846, d 1863.

VI. Franklin Springer, b Jan 31, 1849, m Hannah Moyer, P. O. Hilltown, Pa.
C: (**VII**.) Ida Springer, m George Tice.

VII. Clara Springer.

VI. Charles H. Springer, b Sept 22, 1851, d Oct 3, 1891,m Maggie King.   C:(**VII**.) Elsie K. Springer.

V. Catharine Derstine, b in Bucks Co., Pa Feb 28, 1810, d Dec 12, 1874, m John Licey. Dec 6, 1831. He was b in Bucks Co, Pa , Sept 20, 1798, d at River Styx, Ohio, Nov 14, 1880. Farmer. Menn's. C: Alvan, Levi, Elizabeth, Kate, Margaret, Maria, Amanda, Sophia.

VI. Hon Alvan D. Licey, b in Bucks Co, Pa, Sept 13, 1832, m Martha Wilson, dec'd, Oct 19, 1857.

Hon Alvan D. Licey is a farmer and attorney at Law, was a merchant from his youth until Jan 1, 1864. In the spring of 1849 he removed from Dublin Bucks Co, Pa, with his parents, brothers and sisters to Wadsworth township, Medina Co, Ohio. Here he served as clerk in a store at River Styx, from September 1850 to April 1852. He then engaged as a clerk in a large Mercantile establishment at Akron, Ohio, remaining there until March 1856 when he entered the mercantile business on his own account at River Styx and continued in the business until January 1, 1864. He was selected Justice of the Peace for Guilford township in April 1857 and served 18 years.

He employed his leisure time in the study of law and was admitted at Columbus, Ohio by the Supreme Court in 1870 and has practiced law ever since in connection with his farm. He was a member of the State Board of Equalization in 1870 and 1871. In 1879 he received the nomination by the

Republican party as a candidate for Representative to the Ohio Legislature and was elected by the largest majority ever given any candidate in Medina county. He was renominated in 1881 and re-elected by an increased majority. His school life terminated at the age of 12 years. P. O. River Styx, Ohio, C: Desdemona, Ilzaide, John, Kate.

VII. Desdemona L. Licey, b in Medina Co. Ohio, Apr 19, 1859, m W. S. Rowley, M. D.   Res 27 Dunham ave,Cleveland, Ohio.

VII. Ilzaide D. Licey, b June 11, 1861, m Morton Shontz.   Res 104 Falor St. Akron, Ohio.   Plasterer and contractor.   C: (**VIII**) Alvan W. Shontz.

VII. John O. Licey, b Apr 11, 1864, m Adella Niswender.   P. O. Norfolk, Neb.   Attorney at Law.

VII. Kate D. Licey, b Aug 27, 1866, m Lester Beeman.   Res Cleveland, Ohio.   Chewing Gum Manufacturer.

VI. Levi S. Licey, b in Bucks Co. Pa., Feb 25, 1834, d at River Styx, Ohio, Feb 19, 1899, m Mary Koppelberger, Jan 1, 1863.   P. O. River Styx, Ohio.   Merchant.   He was in the service of the State of Ohio on Governor Brough's Staff, commissioned as a Lieutenant and did service in the State of Ohio only, during the latter part of the Civil War.   C: Dora.

VII. Dora Maude Licey, b Apr 12, 1867, m Jay Bissell.   P. O. Wadsworth, O. C: (**VIII**) Ula, Percey.

VI. Elizabeth Licey, b in Bucks Co. Pa., Apr 28, 1836, m Joshua Waltz, Aug 24, 1856.   P. O. Windfall, O.   Farmer.   Ger. Ref.   C: Manta, Alvan, Nelson, Famelia

VII. Manta Catharine Waltz, b June 13, 1857, d May 11, 1858.

VII. Alvan L. Waltz, M. D. b Oct 18, 1858, m Minnie Rose, 1888.   Res 526 Prospect St. Cleveland, O.   Physician.   Disciple Ch.   C: (**VIII**) Leon, Claude, Ray.

VII. Nelson R. Waltz, b Apr 14, 1860; m Delia Wiger.   P. O. Medina, O.   Employed in factory.   Disciple Ch.   C: **VIII.** Ernest, May.

VII. Famelia Waltz deceased.

VI. Catharine Ann Licey, b in Bucks Co. Pa., Oct 14, 1837, m Noah H. Kindig, Aug 1, 1858. P. O. Union City, Mich. Farmer. Cong. Ch. C: Milton, Charles, Ida, John, Romes, Melvin, Sadie.

VII. Milton Delfield Kindig, b May 22, 1859, m Cela Rockwell. P. O. Copemish, Mich. Employee of Manistee and Northeastern R. R. Cong. Ch. C: (**VIII**) Clemmie, Elsie, Ethel.

VII. Charles Hibbart Kindig, b Jan 18, 1862, d Dec 24, 1881.

VII. Ida Kindig, b Sept 30, 1863, m Charles Marshall. P. O. Hickory Corners, Mich. Farmer.

VII. John Licey Kindig, b Apr 15, 1866, m Ida Watkins. P. O. Athens, Mich. Employee of a large saw mill. C: (**VIII**) Mary, Noah

VII. Romeo Rettig Kindig, b Nov 28, 1868, m Millie Rickert. Res 8 Meridan St. Cleveland, O. Mechanic.

VII. Melvin Kindig, b Oct 18, 1877, d May 4, 1883.

VII. Sadie Kindig, b Nov 19, 1879, m Joseph B. Morris. P. O. Union City, Mich.

VI. Margaret Licey, b in Bucks Co. Pa., Feb 3, 1839, m Joseph Kriebel, May 2, 1861. P. O. Union City, Mich. Farmer. C: Nancy, Rufus, Millard, Myrta, Clyde, Frank, Alvan, Jennie.

VII. Nancy Kriebel, b Nov 1, 1861, m Nathaniel Fretz, Dec 29, 1886. P. O. Pratt, Kan. Teacher. Cong. Ch. C: (**VIII**) Earl, Daisy, Glen, Ada.

VII. Rufus S. Kriebel, b June 3, 1863, m Isabelle Bole, d July 27, 1892. C: (**VIII**) Hazel, Mabel, Fern dec'd, Bennie.

VII. Millard D. Kriebel, b June 16, 1865, m Nettie Moon. P. O. Union City, Mich. Carpenter. C: (**VIII**) Ruth, Blanche.

VII. Myrta Kriebel, b Dec 14, 1866, m Fremont Howard, dec'd. P. O. Union City, Mich. Farmer.

VII. Frank E. Kriebel, b July 5, 1871, m Jennie Guilford. P. O. Burlington, Mich. Farmer.

VII. Alvan C. Kriebel, b May 28, 1873, m Lizzie Norton. P. O. Union City, Mich. Railroading.

VII. Jennie Kriebel, b Feb 26, 1876, m C. DeWitt Parlin. P. O. Union City, Mich. Teaching.

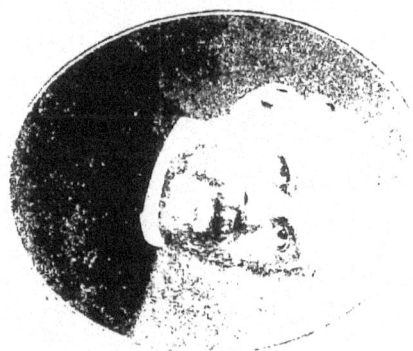

VI. Maria Licey, b in Bucks Co. Pa., Jan 1, 1843, m Charles H. Stevens, Aug 20, 1864. P. O. Kingsley, Pa. Farmer. Baptists. C: Rosabelle, Almon, Anna, Ralph.

VII. Rosabelle Stevens, b Feb 18, 1866, m Clarence Graves, Sept 30, 1890. P. O. Tompkinsville, Pa. Farmer. Baptists. C: (**VIII**) Charles Adelbert Graves, b Sept 3, 1892.

VII. Rev. Almon Odell Stevens, b Apr 21, 1868, m Laura B. Waters, May 6, 1896. P. O. Pontiac, Mich. Congregational Minister. C: (**VIII**) Ralph Waters, b Oct 7, 1897.

VIII. Anna Estella Stevens, b Aug 10, 1869. P. O. Kingsley, Pa. Baptist. Single.

VII. Ralph Henry Stevens, b Feb 5, 1872, m Sara A. Wilmarth, May 20, 1896. P. O. Cohoes, N. Y. Ass't. Supt. of the Metropolitan Life Insurance Co. Baptists.

VI. Amanda Licey, b in Bucks Co. Pa., Jan 18, 1845, m F. H. Lyons, in 1872. P. O. Poe, O. Farmer. C: (**VII**) Chloe N. Lyons, b July 17, 1872; John W. Lyons, b Nov 16, 1874: Dee F. Lyons, b Oct 30, 1876; Dora B. Lyons, b Sept 21, 1881; Ray Lyons, b Dec 18, 1882; Jennie Susan Lyons, b Apr 25, 1884; Lucy May Lyons, b Aug 18, 1886.

VI. Sophia Licey, b in Medina Co. O., Aug 5, 1852, m Frank P. Walling. P. O. Toledo, O. C: (**VII**) --.

V. Elizabeth Derstine, b — d July 9, 1882. S.

V. Abraham Derstine, b July 20, 1814, d —, m Nancy Fellman. C: Henry.

VI. Henry Derstine. P. O. Dublin, Pa.

V. Ann Derstine, b Dec 10, 1816, d Sept 18, 1878. S.

V. Henry Derstine, b in Bucks Co. Pa., Feb 10, 1819, m Susan Ziegler, Feb 16, 1849. P. O. Hatfield, Pa. Gentleman. Evangelical. C: Laura, Ida, Harry, Granville.

VI. Laura Ziegler Derstine, b in Bucks Co. Pa., Nov 16, 1850, m George W. Marter, Oct 2, 1873. Res 3713 Brown St. Phila. Pa. Mr. Marter was b in Philadelphia Oct 2, 1849. Attended the public schools of his native city. In July 1863 he enlisted among the emergency men for Gettysburg. When

16 years of age he left the school and went into business. Later entered the Hahnemann Medical College from which he graduated and practiced medicine for a number of years. His health failing from overwork, he turned his attention to the law, for which he had an especial liking. He is a member of the Philadelphia Bar and also of New York and entitled to practice at the Bar of the Supreme Court of the United States. He is a past officer of all branches of the Masonic order, up to and including Knights Templar. He is also a member and active worker in the Presbyterian church and Sunday school. C: (**VII**) Henry D. Marter, b May 27, 1877, d Nov 10, 1877; Leona M. Marter, b Apr 15, 1882, d Nov 14, 1885; Stanley Zane Marter, b Jan 19, 1886; Ethel Virginia Marter, b Sept 13, 1889.

VI. Ida Derstine, b May 20, 1856, m Dr. M. B. Dill. P. O. Perkasie, Pa. Physician. C: Gertrude, Nellie, Harry, Irwin, Ruth.

VI. Harry Derstine, d in infancy.

VI. Granville Lewis Derstine, d in infancy.

V. Joseph Derstine, m Sophia Schrauger. P. O. Hilltown, Pa. C: Susan.

VI. Susan Derstine, b —. Single

DESCENDANTS OF CATHARINE ROSENBERGER, DAU. OF JOHN ROSENBERGER, SR.

III. Catharine Rosenberger, b 1750, d May 1835, m Abraham Allebach about 1769. The latter obtained in 1776 from his father-in-law the farm east of Hatfield station now owned by Jacob Kulp. Here there is an old stone house, perhaps built by him. The farm was a long narrow strip extending from the Cowpath to Beaver Run comprising 101 acres. The farm was sold to Isaac Rosenberger in 1796.

Abraham Allebach died in middle life by yellow fever contracted while on a trip to Philadelphia in

1794. C: Abraham, John, Christianna, Benjamin, Mary, Sussanna, Lizzie, Barbara, Catharine.

IV. Abraham Allebach, b 1770, d —, m ——. C: Jesse, etc.

V. Jesse Allebach dec'd, m ——. C: Amos, etc.

VI. Amos O. Allebach, P. O. Lansdale, Pa.

IV. John Allebach,——.

IV. Christiana Allebach,——.

IV. Benjamin Allebach,——.

IV. Mary Allebach, m Jacob Cope. No issue. 2nd husband —— Brown. No issue.

IV. Susanna Allebach, m David Ruth. C: David.

V. David Ruth, 3117 Linden St. Phila.

IV. Lizzie Allebach, m Benjamin Rosenberger.

IV. Barbara Allebach, m John Wasser.

IV. Catharine Allebach, b Oct 15, 1784, d Aug 25, 1842, m Joshua Detweiler, Oct 5, 1803. He was b July 3, 1781, d July 21, 1841. Farmer, later sold medicine. Funkite, later Ger. Bap. C: John, Mary, Elizabeth, Sarah, Catharine, Jacob, Abraham, Susanna, Margaret, Anna.

V. John Detweiler, b 1805, d infant.

V. Mary Detweiler, b 1806, m Frederick Geisenhoffer. C: (**VI**) Jacob.

V. Elizabeth Detweiler, b 1808, d infant.

V. Sarah Detweiler, b 1810, m Frederick Hartman. No issue.

V. Catharine Detweiler, b 1812, d 1881, m John Jacob Leitenberger, 1837. C: John, Mary.

VI. John G. Leitenberger, b Feb 7, 1838, m Eva Mary Krauter. C: (**VII**) John, Frederick, Lewis, Catharine, Emma, Emanuel, Ernest, Eva.

VI. Mary C. Leitenberger, b June 27, 1842, m Fred J. Rentlinger, Sept 3, 1863. Res 412 Dickerson St. Phila. Pa. Engraver. Luth. C: (**VII**) John, Frederick, Anna, Charles, Mary, Emma, Bertha, Edward.

Rev. HENRY ROSENBERGER, of FRANCONIA.

●●●●●●●●●

II. Rev. Henry Rosenberger, b Dec 2, 1725, d 1809, m Barbara Oberholtzer in 1745. She was b 1726, d Feb 3, 1765. In 1745 Henry Rosenberger became the owner of the old homestead of his father Henry Rosenberger, Sr. in Franconia for which the son Henry paid £200. Henry Rosenberger also owned a farm in New Britain, Bucks Co., which he purchased from Christian Miller, deed bearing date of April 13, 1773, containing 100 acres for which he paid £600. This property he sold and conveyed to his son-in-law Mark Fretz, of New Britain, May 5, 1784. At this time (1784) Henry Rosenberger seems to have been a resident of Franconia, as the deed of Henry Rosenberger to Mark Fretz, reads "Henry Rosenberger, of Franconia Twp., etc. That he at one time lived in New Britain township where he owned other land, is certain. On Sept 26, 1774 he bought 29¾ acres of John Benner, situated at the Neshaminy Creek, adjoining lands of Thomas Barton and the said Henry Rosenberger and which he sold to John Redline, of New Britain township, July 13, 1790 for £175. At this time he must have lived in New Britain, as indenture to Redline reads "Henry Rosenberger, of New Britain township and Elizabeth being his second wife, maiden name unknown. No issue by her. April 15, 1774, "Henry Rosenberger, of New Britain township," bought of Theophules Reese, 140 acres, adjoining William Davis, Thomas Barton and David Morgan and sold it to Jacob Miller, April 6, 1795.

It is said that Henry Rosenberger lived in New Britain township about a mile N. E. from the Line Lexington Mennonite church, that his farm adjoined the township line of Hilltown on the N. W. and on the N. E. by a public road. His farm was for many years owned by George Scheip, who sold a part of it to Aaron S. Swartley.

Henry Rosenberger was a Mennonite minister and served as such at the Franconia Meetinghouse during the time of the Revolution. C: Gertrude, Anna, Abraham, Elizabeth, Barbara, Maria, Magdalena, Son. Daughter, Sarah.

III Gertrude Rosenberger, b May 4, 1746, d small.

DESCENDANTS OF ANNA ROSENBERGER, DAU. OF REV. HENRY ROSENBERGER.

III. Anna Rosenberger, b Feb 5, 1748, m Michael Leatherman. Menns. C: Henry, Jacob, Ann. She m 2nd husband John Loux, son of Peter Loux, who came to Bedminster in 1737, bought 170 acres of land on the Deep Run. He was b in Bucks Co. Dec 23, 1756, d May 1820. They lived and died in Plumstead Twp. on the farm owned by Enos F. Huns'erger. Mr. Loux Ref. Mrs. Loux Menn. C: John, Catharine, Peter, Abraham.

IV. Henry Leatherman, d 1815, m Elizabeth dau. of Mark Fretz, son of pioneer Christian Fretz, of Tinicum Twp. Bucks Co. Pa. See Fretz family history, 1797. She was b 1776, d 1867. Farmer. Menns. C: Abraham, John, Jacob, Henry, Catharine, Samuel.

IV. Jacob Leatherman, b 1778, m Elizabeth Overholt. Farmer. Menns. John, Anna, Abraham, Elizabeth, Jacob, Barbara, Joseph, Mary, Samuel. (See Overholt family history.

IV. Anna Leatherman, m John Delp. No issue.

IV. John Loux, b in Bucks Co. Pa., Oct 1782, m Susanna Delp, Apr 21, 1808. She was b Mar 7, 1787. Carpenter. Menns. C: George, Charles, Eliza, Magdalena, Sarah.

V. George W. Loux, b in Bucks Co. Pa., Feb 20, 1812, d in Monroe Co. Pa., Mar 18, 1880, m Catharine Algard, (nee Wagner) dec'd. C: Ephraim, Catharine. George m 2nd wife Sabina Kachline,

Feb 1849. She was b July 31, 1827. Ref. Ch: C:
William, Aaron, Delilah, Emma, Charles, Ellsworth, Reuben. In early life drove team from Easton to Philadelphia. He was employed as under-
steward of the Bucks County Almshouse for six
years, afterwhich he engaged in farming for some
years. In 1857 he rented a tannery at Jacobsburg,
Pa. and operated it until 1864, when he removed to
Effort, Monroe Co. Pa., where he bought a tannery
which he operated until his death. He was instrumental in building the first church (Reformed) at
Effort. One of his mottoes to his children was, "Do
not blemish the name of Loux, by your character,
but live an honest, industrious,sober, christian life."
Ref. Ch.

VI. Ephraim Loux, b in Bucks Co. Pa., Sept 23,
1843, m Sabina Trein, Oct 27, 1866. P.O. Nazareth,
Pa. Manufacturer of cigar boxes. Moravians. C:
Harrison, Charles. Anna, Mary, John, Edward,
Walter, Nellie.

VII. Harrison George Loux,b Nov 2, 1867.

VII. Charles William Loux, b Dec 4, 1868, m Helen
A. Giersch, July 20, 1890. Res. Pittsburg, Pa.
Clerk (Stenographer and type writer) Presby. C:
(**VIII**) Frances Willard Loux, b July 21, 1894; Neal
Dow Loux, b Nov 6, 1895; Wendell Phillips Loux,
b June 13, 1897.

VII. Anna L. Loux, b Feb 8, 1870, d 1893.

VII. Mary C. Loux, b July 26, 1871.

VII. John D Loux, b Jan 9, 1875, d 1896.

VII. Edward S. Loux, b Oct 29, 1879.

VII. Walter H. Loux, b May 7, 1881.

VII. Nellie M. Loux, b Oct 27, 1884.

VI. Catharine Loux, b June 20, 1845, m William
Shupp, Nov 16, 1867. P. O. Effort, Pa. Farmer.
Mr. S. Luth, Mrs. S. Ger. Ref. C: Emma, Louisa,
Oscar, Amos, Charles, Ida, David, William, Annie,
Edwin.

VII. Emma J. Shupp, b April 21, 1868, m Roger
W. Altemose, July 26, 1886. C: (**VIII**.) Alice, Edna
dec'd, Miles, Floyd.

VII. Louisa Shupp, b June 11, 1870, m Edwin Scr-

foss, Sept 4, 1886, P. O. Effort, Pa. Luths. C:
(**VIII.**) William, Nettie, Florence, Anna,
VII. Oscar Shupp, b May 19, 1872, d 1878.
VII. Amos Shupp, b Mar 22, 1874, m Lucetta Zaca-
rias, July 16, 1890. C: (**VIII.**) Annie, Floyd.
VII. Charles Shupp, b May 31, 1876.
VII. Ida S. Shupp, b Sept 21. 1878, m William Din-
stel, Nov 19, 1895. P. O. Effort, Pa.
VII. David F. Shupp, b Feb 21, 1881.
VII. William H. Shupp, b July 12, 1883.
VII. Annie A. Shupp, b Aug 25, 1885, d 1887.
VII. Edwin L. Shupp, b July 16, 1887.
VI. William K. Loux, b in Bucks Co; Pa., Feb 17,
1850, m Maragaret A. Moser, May 11, 1872, P. O.
Riegelsville, Pa. Tanner. Ref. Ch C: Daisy,
William, Lena, Raymond, Clara, Charles, Laura.
VII. Daisy G. Loux, b May 26, 1874, m Charles S.
Young, June 16, 1894. C: (**VIII.**) Floyd E. Young,
b Aug 6, 1895.
VII. William C. Loux, b Apr 16, 1876, d 1883.
VII. Lena M. Loux, b Apr 24, 1882.
VII. Raymond W. Loux, b Aug 27, 1884.
VII. Clara M. Loux, b Aug 23, 1886, d 1891.
VII. Charles A. Loux, b Apr 19, 1889.
VII. Laura G. Loux, b July 4, 1891.
VI. Aaron Loux, b in Bucks Co. Pa., Apr 6, 1854,
m Lucinda Everitt, Dec 28, 1878. P. O. Effort, Pa.
Ref. Ch. C: (**VII.**) Emma, Annie, Minnie.
VI. Delilah Loux, b Nov 8, 1864, m John Dailey,
C: (**VII.**) Helen Dailey.
VI. Emma Loux, b May 22, 1867, m John A. Dold,
Sept 6, 1886. P. O. 247 Mt. Vernon Ave, Camden,
N. J. In paid Fire Dept. Presby. C: (**VIII.**)
George T. Dold.
VI. Charles Loux, b Feb 2, 1861, d 1862.
VI. Ellsworth Loux, b Aug 19, 1869, d 1878.
VI. Reuben Loux, b June 22, 1872, m Mary Kelly.
Res. 247 Mt. Vernon Ave, Camden, N. J. Lo-
comotive fireman. C: (**VII.**) Pearl Loux, b Aug 18, '96.
V. Charles Loux, b Dec 29, 1815, m Frances West,
Sept 28, 1841. Infant.
V. Eliza Loux, b Aug 25, 1818, m Joseph M. Lan-

dis   Mrs. L. Menn.   C: Samuel, Peter, Catharine, Elizabeth, Sarah, Mary, Morris, Susan.

VI. Samuel Landis, b Sept 23, 1839.

VI. Peter L. Landis, b in Bucks Co, Pa., Sept 22, 1841, m Anna Culp, Feb 1866.   Hiawatha, Kansas. Removed to Elkhart, Ind, and from there to Brown Co, Kans in 1869 where they located on a farm of 160 acres.   They own 2 other farms, in all 40 acres of good land.   C: Alice, Eliza, Charles, Norman, Hester, Martha, Myron, Arthur.

VII. Alice I. Landis, b Nov 30, 1869, m Joseph H. Smith, Dec 25, 1888.   P. O. Robinson, Kans.   Farmer.   C: (**VIII.**) Charles, Grace, Anna, Walter, Edna.

VII. Eliza J. Landis, b June 20, 1872.

VII. Charles U. Landis, b Apr 18, 1876.

VII. Norman Landis, b May 20, 1878.

VII. Hester M. Landis, b July 7, 1880.

VII. Martha A. Landis, b Oct 2, 1882.

VII. Myron B. Landis, b Aug 27, 1885.

VII. Arthur Landis, b Sept 28, 1888.

VI. Catharine Landis, b Sept 16, 1843, m ---- Worthington.   P O. Dublin, Pa.

VI. Elizabeth Landis, b Oct 17, 1845, m----Rigel.

VI. Sarah Landis, b Dec 31, 1847, m----Cox.

VI. Mary Landis, b Sept 3, 1856, m John Bishop. P. O. Dublin, Pa.

VI. Morris Landis, b Jan 13, 1858, d----

VI. Susan Landis, b June 10, 1857, m Levi A. Ressler, Apr 6, 1876.   C: (**VII.**) Sarah, Christian, Magdalena, Eliza, Joseph, Noah, Levi.

V. Magdalena Loux, m----Ernst.   C: Sarah Rebecca, Susanna, John.

VI. Sarah Ernst, m----Morris, dec'd.

VI. Rebecca Ernst, S.

VI. Susanna Ernst, m Jerry Algard.   C: (**VII.**) Sallie, Ida, Mamie, Stella.

VI. John Ernst, dec'd, m----

V. Sarah Loux, b Dec 26, 1821, d June 21, 1879, m Christain Henning.   He d Mar 12, 1892.   No issue.

IV. Catharine Loux, m Isaac Delp.   C: John, George.

V. John L. Delp, b Jan 28, 1808, d June 17, 1875, m Anna Detweiler. She d Feb 26, 1879. Carriage builder. Mr. D. Baptist, Mrs. D. Menn. C: Abraham, George, Samuel.

VI. Abraham D. Delp, b July 26,1831,m Adeline R. Supplee, Nov 11, 1858. P. O. Bridgeport, Pa. Clerk. Baptist. C: Jennie, Catharine.

VII. Jennie S. Delp. Teacher. Baptist.

VII. Catharine A. Delp. Baptist.

VI. George Delp, single.

VI. Samuel D. Delp, m ——. C: Frank.

V. George Delp, b in Bucks Co., Nov 27, 1811, m Catharine Ruth. dec'd. C: Sarah. George m 2nd wife Catharine Gehman, Dec 20, 1835. She d 1879. Blacksmith. Menns. C: Mary, Catharine, Lavina, Samuel.

VI. Sarah Delp, b Feb 1, 1834, d 1865, m Henry R. Kratz.

VI. Mary A. Delp, b Nov 24, 1837, m Isaac K. Bergey, Sept 29, 1857. P. O. Blooming Glen, Pa. Shoemaker. Menns. C: James, Anna, Clayton, Minerva.

VII. James D. Bergey, b Apr 8, 1858, m Caroline Fretz, Apr 14, 1877. P. O. Blooming Glen, Pa. Blacksmith. C: (**VIII**) Mary, Ella.

VII. Anna C. Bergey, b Dec 26, 1861, m Henry Detweiler. Menns. C: (**VIII**) Cora, Elmer, Warren, Herbert.

VII Clayton D. Bergey, b Mar 31, 1878.

VII Minerva Bergey, b Sept 8, 1880, d 1885.

VI. Catharine Delp, b Mar 1, 1839, d ––, m Samuel Moyer. C: (**VII**) Lydia dec'd.

VI. Lavina Delp. b Mar 14, 1841, m Samuel Algard, dec'd. No issue.

VI. Samuel Delp, b Dec 9,1842, m Amanda Sampey dec'd. C: ——. He m 2nd wife Sarah Sampey. C: (**VII**) Ella.

IV. Peter Loux, b June 27, 1786, d July 24, 1871, m Rebecca Atherholt, Mar 6, 1814. She d Sept 28, 1834. C: John, Christian, Samuel, Anna. Peter m 2nd wife Anna Overholt, May 12, 1836. She was b May 15, 1801, d Sept 15, 1888. Farmer on old

Loux homestead Plumstead Twp. Menn. C: Mary.

V. John A. Loux, b Nov 19, 1815, d Jan 1, 1894, m Hannah Jaceby, May 30, 1841. She d Mar 19, 1844. C: Amanda. He m 2nd wife Rachel High, Feb 1, 1848. C: William, Emeline. In early life carpenter, later engaged in mercantile business at Dublin and later at Pipersville for some years, then retired to the farm. He also followed surveying many years, was County Auditor and was Justice of the Peace for over 45 years. Menn.

VI. Amanda Loux, m John F. Raus. C: (**VII**) Fannie Raus, b Feb 1, 1868, m --- .

VI. William Loux, d young.

VI. Emeline Loux, m Daniel L. Bennett.

V. Christian Loux, b Oct 15, 1817, d Jan 18, 1896, m Barbara Trumbower. C: (**VI**) Albert, Samuel. John, Hannah, Clinton, Mary.

V. Samuel Loux, b Oct 25, 1820, d 1847, m Mary Kidney. C: Oliver.

VI. Oliver K. Loux, b 1846, d 1893, m Sallie McAllister. C: (**VII**) Willie.

V. Anna Loux, b Oct 11, 1822, d Apr 21, 1833.

V. Mary Loux, b in Bucks Co. Pa., Mar 3, 1837, d 1899, m Enos F. Hunsberger, Nov 5, 1859. P. O. Plumsteadville, Pa. Farmer. Menns. C: Anna, Sarah, Emma, Peter, Harvey.

VI. Anna L. Hunsberger, b Feb 26, 1861, d Mar 29, 1863.

VI. Sarah L. Hunsberger, b Nov 11, 1862, died Apr 8, 1863.

VI. Emma L. Hunsberger, b June 12, 1864, m S. W. Gross, Oct 1888. P. O. Plumsteadville, Pa. Farmer. Menn's. No issue.

VI. Peter L Hunsberger, b Nov 9, 1869, m Mary Nice, Jan 19, 1893. P. O. Plumsteadville, Pa. Farmer. Menns. C: (**VII**) Walter Hunsberger, b Feb 1, 1894; Ruth Hunsberger, b Nov 28, 1895.

VI. Harvey D. Hunsberger, b Oct 8, 1873, m Annie F. Myers, Oct 5, 1895. P. O. Plumsteadville, Pa. Farmer. Menns. C: (**VII**) Willis Hunsberger, b June 30, 1896.

IV. Abraham Loux, b in Bucks Co. Pa., Apr 12,

1789, d Apr 11, 1867, m Mary Hofford, about 1814. She was b in Bucks Co. Pa., Jan 30, 1796, d Nov 24, 1864. Farmer and carpenter   Mrs. Loux Ref. Ch. C: Joseph, Rachel, Abraham, Charles, John, Oliver.

V. Joseph H. Loux, b 1816, d 1881, m Lydia Hockman. C:

VI. Aaron Loux, P. O. Dublin, Pa.

V. Rachel Loux, b 1817, d 1891. Single.

V. Abraham Loux, b 1822, d 1848. Single.

V. Charles Loux, b 1825, d 1893, m Margaret Sine.

V. John D. Loux, b Dec 28, 1839. P. O. Doylestown, Pa.   Superintendent of cemetery for twenty-five years.

V. Oliver Loux, b 1842, d 1844.

III. Abraham Rosenberger, b May 2, 1750, d young.

<hr>

DESCENDANTS OF ELIZABETH ROSENBERGER, DAU. OF HENRY ROSENBERGER.

III. Elizabeth Rosenberger, b Dec 19, 1752, d Jan 10, 1847, m Mark Fretz, son of pioneer John Fretz, of Bedminster, Bucks Co. Pa., May 11, 1773. He was b Dec 1750, d Feb 24, 1840. Lived in New Britain Twp. Bucks Co., on the place known as "Curley's Mill", which he purchased of his nephew John Fretz, of Warwick, in 1792. The tract consisted of 130 acres to which he added until he owned several hundred acres. Farmer and miller. He was a Mennonite and deacon at Line Lexington. C: Barbara, Maria, Elizabeth, Infant, Henry, Infant, Mark.

IV. Barbara Fretz, b Apr 21, 1775, d in Brazoria Co. Texas, June 10, 1840, m John Sliver. Brickmason. Meth. Ep. C: Elizabeth Sliver, b 1798, d 1840, m Rev. William Denyer. Meth. Ep.

IV. Maria Fretz, b Nov 16, 1778, d 1779.

IV. Elizabeth Fretz, b Jan 27, 1781, d Nov 6, 1849,

m Rev. John Geil, Apr 22, 1802. He was b Apr 9,
1778. Weaver by trade, later farmer in New
Britain. He was ordained to the ministry of the
Mennonite church at Line Lexington about 1810,
where he served for 55 years. C: Jacob, Barbara,
Elizabeth, Mark, Catharine, Mary, John, Anna,
Samuel.

IV. Daughter b 1785, buried Jan 6,1875.

IV. Henry Fretz, b June 24, 1787, d June 9, 1874,
m Elizabeth Beidler, May 14, 1809. She was b
Apr 10, 1787, d Dec 24, 1852. Lived on his father's
homestead in New Britain. Farmer and miller. C:
Susan, Christian, Eliza, Henry, Mark.

IV. Daughter b 1789, d unnamed.

IV. Mark Fretz, b Jan 9, 1799, d Sept 5, 1800.
For complete records of Mark and Elizabeth
(Rosenberger) Fretz, see Fretz family history.

DESCENDANTS OF BARBARA ROSENBER-GER, Dau. of Rev. HENRY ROSENBERGER, Jr.

III. Barbara Rosenberger, b Jan 6, 1755, d 1832, m
Daniel Rickert. Farmer. Menns. C: Henry, Daniel,
Abraham, Isaac, Leanna, Anna.

IV. Henry Rickert, m Barbara Wismer. She was
b Apr 15, 1785, d 1851. C: Daniel, Isaac, Samuel,
Catharine, Barbara, Frances, Henry, Jacob, Elizabeth.

V. Daniel Rickert, m——, No issue, m 2nd wife
——, c——.

V. Isaac Rickert, m——.

V. Samuel Rickert, d young.

V. Catharine Rickert, m Seneca Armitage. C:
Henry,etc.

V. Barbara Rickert, b 1806, d Aug 17, 1869, m
John Sherm. He was b Alsace France 1808, d June
18, 1889. Farmer. Luths. C: Elizabeth, Catharine, Mary, William, Sarah, Barbara, John, Mag-

dalena, Fannie, Noah, Abbie.
VI. Elizabeth Sherm, d young.
VI. Catharine Sherm, m Charles King, dec'd. Farmer. Luths. C: Mary, John, Sarah, Maggie, Ellen, Charles.
VII. Mary Ann King, m Geo. Slifer, dec'd, m 2nd husband George Willower.
VII. John F. King. P. O. Hilltown. Pa.
VII. Sarah E. King, b Dec 10, 1859, m Chas. S. Kletzing Sept 28, 1878. P. O. Hilltown, Pa. Farmer. Luths. C: (**VIII.**) Harvey K. Kletzing, b Aug 3, 1879. Luth. Willis K. Kletzing, b Jan 9, 1884.
VII. Maggie King, m Charles Springer.
VII. Ellen King, m Grier Shearer.
VII. Charles S. King, m Mary Benner,
VI. Mary Ann Sherm, m Enos Weiss. P. O. Schlichters, Pa. Carpenter. Farmer. Luth. C: William, Sallie, Irvin, Abbie.
VII. William Weiss, m Lizzie Eckert.
VII. Sallie Weiss, m Jacob Dettra.
VII. Irvin S. Weiss, b Sept 24, 1868, m Cora Z. Dubbs, Apr 16, 1892. P. O. Sellersville, Pa. Cigarmaker. Ref. ch. C: (**VIII**) Frank F. Weiss, b July 20, 1893, William R. Weiss, b Oct 18, 1894, d Aug 28, 1895, Bertha M. Weiss, b Mar 15, 1897.
VII. Abbie Weiss, m Amandus Wenhold.
VI. William H. Sherm, b in Bucks Co. Pa., Nov 30, 1839, m Elizabeth L. Barndt. Mar 31, 1866. · P. O. Chalfont. Pa. Mr. Sherm in early life taught school for eight years, after which he engaged in farming. He has also served as school director for fifteen years, was County Auditor three years from 1887 to 1890, township Auditor for three years, and judge of election. Luth's. C: Maggie, Alice, Neri, Hannah.
VII. Maggie B. Sherm, b June 21, 1867, m Frank S. Hartzell, Jan 28, 1888. P. O. Ashbourne, Pa. Milk dealer. Luth's. C: (**VIII**) Willie, Stanley, Frank, Lizzie, Neri
VII. Alice B. Sherm, b Dec 27, 1869, m Aaron S. Overpeck, Feb 11, 1892. P. O. Forest Grove, Pa.

Merchant. Luth's. C: (**VIII**) Lizzie.

VII. Neri B. Sherm, b Feb 26, 1872, d Dec 6, 1889.

VII. Hannah B. Sherm, b Nov 12, 1881.

VI. Sarah Sherm, b m Enos G. Detweiler, Oct 18, 1860. P. O. Chalfont, Pa. Farmer. Menn's. C: John, William, Anna, Enos, Irwin, Alfred, Phares, Emma, Elizabeth, Edwin.

VII. John F. Detweiler, b June 16, 1863, m Anna Eliza Lapp, Mar 26, 1885. She was b Dec 22, 1862. P. O. New Britain, Pa. Ger. Ref. C: (**VIII**) Clarence L. Detweiler, b Sept 9, 1886, Uriah L. Detweiler, b Oct 26, 1887, John R. Detweiler, b Apr 1, 1889, d Aug 17, 1889, Sarah L. Detweiler, b Aug 18, 1890.

VII. William H. Detweiler, b June 16, 1863, m Mary A. Weisel, May 6, 1886. P. O. New Britain, Pa. C: (**VIII**) Katie W. Detweiler, b Apr 30, 1887, Sallie W. Detweiler, b Oct 21, 1889.

VII. Anna Barbara Detweiler, b July 24, 1865, m Levi S. Moyer.

VII. Enos S. Detweiler, b Oct 3, 1869, d Apr 13, 1883.

VII. Irwin S. Detweiler, b Mar 5, 1872, m Anna Mary Swartley. P. O. Chalfont, Pa. Farmer. Ger. Ref. C: (**VIII**) Bertha dec'd.

VII. Alfred S. Detweiler Nov 5, 1873. S.

VII. Phares S. Detweiler, b Nov 26 1875, d July 11, 1876.

VII Emma B. Detweiler, b June 30, 1878, d Oct 30, 1878.

VII. S. Elizabeth Detweiler, b Sept 7, 1879.

VII. Edwin Detweiler, b Sept 14, 1880, d May 1, 1882.

VI. Barbara Sherm, m Eli Crouthamel. P. O. Hilltown, Pa. Farmer. Luth. C: Oscar, Emma, Warren.

VII. Emma Crouthamel, m Oscar Wismer.

VII. Oscar Crouthamel, m —. P. O. Hilltown, Pa.

VII. Warren Crouthamel, single.

VI. John Sherm, m Caroline Savacool. P. O. Chalfont, Pa. Farmer. Luth. C: Minerva, Harvey, Wilhelmina, Jacob, Martha, Frank, Lizzie, Willie.

VII. Minerva Sherm, m Henry Hedrick. P. O. Silverdale, Pa. Tailor. Luth. No issue.

VII. Harvey Sherm, single.

VII. Wilhelmina Sherm, m Samuel D. Campbell. P. O. Chalfont, Pa. Farmer. Luth.

VII. Jacob Sherm, m Crissie Moll. P. O. Perkasie, Pa. Cigarmaker.

VII. Martha Sherm, dec'd, m George Moll. P. O. Chalfont, Pa.

VIII. Harvey S. Moll.

VII Frank Sherm, single.

VII. Lizzie Sherm, single.

VII. Willie Sherm, single.

VI. Magdalena Sherm, b in Bucks Co. Pa., m Monroe L. Trumbore. P. O. Chalfont, Pa. Carpenter. Luth. C: Bertha, Clara.

VII. Bertha Trumbore, b Mar 23, 1872, m Abraham G. Rosenberger. P.O. Chalfont, Pa. Farmer. Luth. C: (**VIII**) Wilson, Flora.

VII. Clara Trumbore. P. O. Chalfont, Pa. Single.

VI. Fannie Sherm, b in Bucks Co. Pa., Feb 16, 1848, m Adam Leininger, in Boone Co. Iowa, Oct 20, 1868. P. O. Boone, Iowa. Farmer. Luth. C: John, Abbie, Emma, Mary, Fred, Minnie, Nellie, Fannie.

VII. John W. Leininger, b Aug 13, 1870, d Dec 18, 1882.

VII. Abbie C. M. Leininger, b Mar 26, 1872, m W. C. Granville, Oct 27, 1889. Res 214 Walnut St. E. Los Angeles, Cal. Wood and coal business. C: (**VIII**) William A. F. Granville, b in Iowa, Mar 7, 1890; Fannie M. L. Granville, b in Cal., Feb 13, 1892; Annie E. Granville, b in Cal., Aug 6, 1894, d Aug 27, 1894.

VII. Emma D. R. Leininger, b Sept 17, 1873, m Eric Ericson, Jan 6, 1895. P. O. Boone, Iowa. Company bridge builder. C: (**VIII**) Annie C. Ericson, b June 19, 1895; Carl O. Ericson, b Feb 9, 1897.

VII. Mary L. M. Leininger, b June 25, 1877, m Albert Mondt, July 14, 1895. P. O. Boone, Iowa. Buttermaker. C: (**VIII**) Fannie L. Mondt, b Feb 28, 1896, d next day.

VII. Fred Leininger, b Feb 20, 1879.

VII. Minnie A. K. Leininger, b Dec 18, 1880, m Harry G. Mondt, Apr 29, 1897. P. O. Boone, Iowa. Engineer.

VII. Nellie H. F. Leininger, b Oct 28, 1883.

VII. Fannie M. G. Leininger, b Aug 18, 1891, d Sept 29, 1891.

VI. Noah Sherm, d young.

VI. Abbie R. Sherm, b in Bucks Co. Pa., Sept 1, 1853, m Adam Martin, Nov 14, 1874   P. O. Chalfont, Pa.   Farmer.   Deacon Luth. Ch.   C: Infant d, Reuben, Flora, Alice, Bertha, Walter, Edward, Jennie.

VII. Reuben A. Martin, b May 1, 1880.

VII. Flora E. Martin, b Feb 13, 1882, m F. L. Brinker.

VII. Alice S. Martin, b Feb 18, 1884.

VII. Bertha M. Martin, b Apr 13, 1886.

VII. Walter S. Martin, b Dec 22, 1889.

VII. Edward H. Martin, b Jan 18,1892, June 1892.

VII. Jennie T. Martin, b Nov 30, 1895.

V. Franey Rickert, b—, d --, m — Delp. No issue. M 2nd husband Michael Hunsberger, dec'd. Farmer.   Luth.   C: Eliza, Emma.

VI. Eliza Hunsberger, m John Craw. Res Manayunk, Pa.   No issue.

VI. Emma Hunsberger, m John Rosenberger. P. O. Rich Hill, Pa.

V. Henry Rickert, m Mary Harmer. Res Germantown, Pa. Mason. Methodist. C: Mary, Samuel, Lizzie.

VI. Mary Rickert, m Andrew McFarland.

VI. Samuel Rickert, m ——. Res Germantown, Pa.

VI. Lizzie Rickert, m George Afflick. Res Germantown, Pa.

V. Jacob Rickert, dec'd, m Rachel Shaffer, dec'd. Mason contractor.   Baptists.   C: Mary, Eli, Eliza, Ellen, Fannie, Jacob.

VI. Mary Ann Rickert, dec'd, m William Smith. C: Bertha, Laura, Martha.

VII. Bertha Smith, m — Ellis.

VII. Laura Smith, m Charles Wisler.

VII. Martha Smith, m - ——.
VI. Eli Rickert. m ——.
VI. Eliza Rickert. Single.
VI. Ellen Rickert, m ——.
VI. Fannie Rickert. Single.
VI. Jacob Rickert. Single.
V. Elizabeth Rickert, m John Bircks. Res. 231
Haines St, Germantown, Phila, Pa. Retired Gard-
ner. Universalist. C: Rebecca, Louisa, Josephine,
Minerva, John, Lizzie.
VI. Rebecca Bircks, m ——. P. O. Louisville, Ky.
VI. Josephine Bircks, m Jacob Fretz dec'd. C: (**VII**)
James Garfield Fretz.
VI. John Bircks, m ——.
VI. Lizzie Bircks, d m ——.
V. John Rickert, m ——. C: William, Abbie.
V. William Rickert, m ——
VI. Abbie Rickert, d. Teacher. S.
IV. Daniel R. Rickert, b Nov 4, 1792, d Mar 7,
1869, m Elizabeth Kulp, June 23, 1818. She was b
in Bucks Co, Pa., Aug 21, 1793, d in 1864. Far-
mer. Menns. C: Isaac, Jacob, Daniel.
V. Isaac Rickert, b in Bucks Co, Pa., Apr 7, 1819,
m Anna G. Stauffer, Jan 9, 1858. P. O. Dublin,
Pa. Farmer. Menn's. C: Anna, Lizzie, Daniel,
Amanda, Sarah.
VI. Anna S. Rickert, died at birth.
VI. Lizze S. Rickert, b May 23, 1863. S.
VI. Daniel S. Rickert, b Sept 26, 1864, m Martha
B. Schwenk, Apr 9, 1898. P. O. Dublin, Pa. Far-
mer. Menns. C: (**VII**) Clayton S. Rickert, b Feb
8, 1899.
VI. Amanda S. Rickert, b Nov 26, 1867, m Henry
L. Wismer. P. O. Dublin, Pa. Farmer. Menn's.
C: (**VII**) Mabel, Edna.
VI. Sarah S. Rickert died at birth.
V. Jacob K. Rickert, b in Bucks Co, Pa., Feb 10,
1821, d m Mary M. Newhard, June 28, 1847. She
died Jan 26, 1858. C: Hiram, Daniel, Jacob, m
second wife Eliza A Hoffman, Aug 18, 1859. P.
O. Weissport, Pa. Farmer and Merchant. Ev.
Ass'n.

VI. Hiram Rickert, b May 22, 1848, m Ida Howe, in 1874. P. O. Weissport, Pa. Children: (**VII**) Harry Rickert, b Oct 27, 1875, Miles Rickert, b Mar 11, 1877.

VI. Daniel F. Rickert, b Sept 1, 1850, m Margaret Campbell, in 1879. P. O. Weissport, Pa. Painter. C: (**VII**) Robert R. Rickert, b Aug 15, 1886.

V. Daniel K. Rickert, b in Bucks Co. Pa., Sept 15, 1825, died — m Hannah Myers, Dec 21, 1851. She was b May 17, 1826. Farmer. Menn's. C: Aaron, Elizabeth, Lydia, Sophia, Susanna, Catharine.

VI. Aaron M. Rickert, b Jan 31, 1852, died — m Catharine M. Sell, in 1873. She was born in 1851. P. O. Dublin, Pa. Farmer. Menn's. C: (**VII**) Lillie Jane Rickert, b Feb 5, 1874.

VII. Hannah Louisa Rickert, b June 18, 1876.

VII. Daniel S. Rickert, b Nov 30, 1877.

VII. Barbara Ella Rickert, Feb 24, 1879.

VII. Peter Rickert, b July 28, 1880.

VII. Menno Rickert, b Oct 5, 1881.

VII. Katie May Rickert, b Nov 9, 1882.

VI. Elizabeth Rickert, b June 26, 1854, d May 6, 1855.

VI. Lydia A. Rickert, b Feb 13, 1856, d Oct 21, 1862.

VI. Sophia Rickert, b Aug 16, 1858, d Oct 27, 1862.

VI. Susanna Rickert, b Feb 8, 1865, d Jan 25, 1873.

VI. Catharine Rickert, b Aug 16, 1868, m William Powell in 1886.

IV. Abraham Rickert, d — , m Katie Ruth, (widow of his brother Isaac). Farmer. Menns. C: Kate, Magdalena.

V. Kate Rickert, b June 26, 1837, d Mar 14, 1868, m William M. Moyer P. O. Dublin, Pa. Farmer. Menns. C: Mary, Hannah, Sarah, Abraham, David.

VI. Mary Ann Moyer, b Feb 29, 1855, m William C. Moyer, Mar 9, 1876. P. O. Blooming Glen, Pa. Farmer. Menns. C: (**VII**) Elmer Moyer, b Dec 19, 1876; Della Moyer, b Mar 7, 1879; Eugene Moyer, b Apr 2, 1880; Clara Moyer, b Apr 22, 1884; Selena Moyer, b Aug 11, 1886; Norman Moyer, June 17,

1892.

VI. Hannah R. Moyer, b Apr 14, 1857, m Henry G. Moyer, Jan 20, 1877. P. O. Blooming Glen, Pa. Farmer. Menns. C: (**VII**) Annie Jeanetta Moyer, b Apr 7, 1887; Isaac Erwin Moyer, b May 2, 1881; William Oscar Moyer, b Apr 11, 1884; Henry Warren Moyer, b July 18, 1887; Sarah Elizabeth Moyer, b June 15, 1889; Mary Alice Moyer, b Sept 24, 1891.

VI. Sarah Elizabeth Moyer, b Sept 18, 1858.

VI. Abraham Moyer, b Nov 25, 1859, d Dec 26, 1887.

VI. David R. Moyer, b in Bucks Co. Pa., Mar 4, 1861, m Elizabeth, dau. of John Clymer, Mar 3, 1887. P. O. Dublin, Pa. Farmer. Menns. C: (**VII**) Sadie C. Moyer, b Oct 15, 1888; Ida H. Moyer, b Jan 17, 1892, d Feb 2, 1892.

V. Magdalena Rickert, b --, m William M. Moyer, (husband of her sister Kate) Apr 25, 1869. P. O. Dublin, Pa. Farmer. Menns. C: Catharine, Wilson, Samuel, William.

VI. Catharine Moyer, b Mar 9, 1870, m Tyrus M. Moyer. P. O. Blooming Glen, Pa.

VI. Wilson R. Moyer, b June 2, 1872.

VI. Samuel R. Moyer, b Nov 15, 1875.

VI. William Henry Moyer, b Sept 16, 1877.

IV Isaac Rickert, b May 9, 1797, d June 5, 1832, m Kate Ruth. Farmer. Menns. C: David, Abraham, Isaac, Daniel, Henry.

V. David Rickert, b in Bucks Co. Pa., --, d --, m Lavina Funk, dau. of Isaac and Mary (Bechtel) Funk, and widow of Jacob Swartz. Res 1250 Huntingdon St. Phila. Pa. Farmer. Menns. C: Isaac, Mary.

VI. Isaac F. Rickert, b in Bucks Co. Pa., m Lavina Fretz, daughter of Henry and Mary Fretz, dec'd. P. O. Dublin, Pa. Farmer. Menns. C: Clayton, William, Mary.

VII. D. Clayton Rickert, b Mar 28, 1874, m Catharine Lapp, daughter of Joseph Lapp, Nov 27, 1899. P. O. Dublin, Pa. Farmer. Baptists.

VII. William Henry Rickert, b Nov 15, 1877. Res

1250 Huntingdon St. Phila. Pa. Engraver.

VII. Mary E. Rickert, b Sept 25, 1889.

VI. Mary A. Rickert, b in Bucks Co. Pa., m Enos Fretz, Dec 3, 1873. He was b Jan 16, 1845. Res 1250 West Huntingdon St. Phila. Pa. Provision dealer. No issue.

V. Abraham Rickert, b in Bucks Co. Pa., d in Ohio, m Mary Ann Fretz, dec'd. Farmer in Medina Co. O. Menns. C: Allen, Catharine, Sarah, Henry, Levi, David, Abraham, Barbara, Amelia.

VI. Rev. Allen Rickert, b Dec 21, 1848, m Sarah Lehman, Jan 4, 1873. P. O. Columbiana, O. Farmer. Menn. Ordained minister Nov 13, 1892. C: (**VII**) Edwin, Lizzie, Edith, Harvey, Margaret, Isaiah.

VI. Catharine Rickert, b May 7, 1850. S.

VI. Sarah Rickert, b Nov 24, 1851. S.

VI. Henry F. Rickert, b Sept 10, 1853, m Sarah Markley, Nov 13, 1875. P. O. River Styx, O. Farmer. C: (**VII**) Uriah, Rilla, Clarence, Mary.

VI. Levi F. Rickert, b May 29, 1856, m Alice C. Custer, Oct 2, 1886. P. O. River Styx, O. Farmer. C: (**VII**) Mabel.

VI. David Rickert, b Aug 19, 1858, m Eva M. Heath, Jan 13, 1883. Carpenter. On June 12, 1891, while working on a new barn, he fell from the building into the basement fracturing his skull from which he died the next morning, C: (**VII**) Dick, Nellie

VI. Mary Rickert, b Jan 8, 1861, m David Gabel, Dec 21, 1882. 251 Marcey Ave. Cleveland, Ohio. Cong'l. C: (**VII**) Charles.

VI. Abraham Rickert, b Apr 3, 1863, m Eva M. Heath, (his brother David's widow.)

VI. Barbara Rickert, b Apr 3, 1870, m Abraham H. Rohrer, May 20, 1891. P. O. River Styx, Ohio. Farmer. C: (**VII**) Percy, Gladys, David.

VI. Amelia Rickert, b Apr 8, 1872, m Rome R. Kindig, Jan 12, 1895. 251 Marcey Ave. Cleveland, Ohio.

V. Rev. Isaac Rickert, dec'd, m Salome Gross. Farmer and minister of the Doylestown, Pa., Menno-

nite church.   C: Lizzie, Isaiah.

VI. Lizzie Rickert, m Harvey Myers, Jan 20, 1883. P. O. Gardenville, Pa. Farmer. Menns. C: (**VII**) Bertha, Isaac Laura, Ezra.

VI. Isaiah Rickert, m Emma Mack.

V. Daniel Rickert, b in Bucks Co. Pa., Feb 9, 1825, m Christina Hunker, Feb 5, 1846. She was b in Germany June 12, 1822, d May 23, 1888. Shoemaker, later farmer. Mrs. R Luth. C: John, Catharine, Isaac, Sarah, David, Emanuel, Daniel, Emma, Abraham.

VI. John Rickert, m — Kyle. P. O. Wadsworth, O.

VI. Catharine Rickert, m Park Pelton. P.O. Poe, O.

VI. Isaac H. Rickard, b in Westmoreland Co. Pa., Oct 16, 1848, m Caroline Jane Kennedy, Dec 30, 1875. She was b in Medina Co. O., May 8, 1856. P. O. Chippewa Lake, O. Manufacturer of drain tile, brick and hollow brick.   C: (**VII**) Inza Rickard, b Oct 15, 1876; Charley Emanuel Rickard, b Oct 12, 1878; Delbert Herman Rickard, b Aug 29, 1881; Edith Rickard, b Oct 6, 1883; Howard Isaac Rickard, b Nov 5, 1889; Clarence Don Rickard, b Feb 11, 1891; Stanley Boyd Rickard, b Dec 7, 1893.

VI. Sarah Rickert, b —, m Henry Koppes. P. O. Chippewa Lake, O.

VI. David Rickert, b —, m ———. P. O. Wadsworth, O.

VI. Emanuel H. Rickert, b in Medina Co. O., Nov 14, 1857, m Anna E. Williams, Sept 28, 1882. P.O. Dixon, Ill. Shipping Live stock. Luth. C: (**VII**) Clark W. Rickert, b July 14, 1885.

VI. Daniel Rickert, Jr., b —, m Lizzie Hoover. P. O. Wadsworth, O.

VI. Emma Rickert, m Jean Tinstman. P.O. Poe, O.

VI. Abraham Rickert, b —.   P. O. Wodsworth, O.

V. Henry Rickert, b Dec 22, 1829, m Elizabeth Hunsberger, Mar 27, 1853. She d Dec 18, 1888. P. O. Dublin, Pa. Farmer. Menn's. C: Mary, Catharine, Levi, Enos, Reuben, Rosa, Mahlon, Magdalena, Salome.

VI. Mary Ann Rickert, b Jan 6, 1854, d Apr 1886, m John H. Barnes. C: Lizzie, Bertha, Daniel.

VII. Lizzie Barnes, deceased.

VII. Bertha May Barnes.

VII. Daniel W. Barnes, m Laura Renner, Oct 1890. P. O. Fresno, Cal.

VI. Catharine Rickert, b Sept 21, 1855, d Feb 20, 1858.

VI. Levi Rickert, b July 18, 1857, d Mar 10, 1866.

VI. Enos Rickert, b Feb 2, 1859, d Apr 3, 1862.

VI. Reuben H. Rickert, b in Bucks Co. Pa., June 11, 1863, m Lavina Leatherman, (nee Heacock,) Feb 25, 1899. P. O. Dublin, Pa. Farmer. Menns.

VI. Rose Emma Rickert, b Sept 2, 1866, m Samuel Yoder, Nov 19, 1887. P. O. Blooming Glen, Pa. Farmer. Menns. C: (**VII**) Anna Valeria Yoder, b Sept 9, 1888; Florence May Yoder, b Jan 9, 1892; Norman Yoder, b Aug 20, 1895.

VI. Mahlon H. Rickert, b Mar 10, 1870, m Della E. Strohm, Feb 21, 1891. P. O. Dublin, Pa. Clerk. Ref. Ch. C: (**VII**) Jacob L. Rickert, b Dec 12, 1892; Mary G. Rickert, b June 27, 1894; Henry S. Rickert, b Nov 10, 1895; Alton G. Rickert, b Dec 6, 1896; Reuben James Rickert, b Mar 13, 1899.

VI. Magdalena Rickert, b Apr 8, 1873, m Bert Smith. P. O. Blooming Glen. Pa. Tailor. Menns. C: (**VII**) Walter Smith, b Mar 27, 1892.

VI. Salome Rickert, b Nov 21, 1875, m Harry H. Moyer, Oct 14, 1895. P. O. Elroy, Pa. Merchant. Menns. C: (**VII**) Eva R. Moyer, b Dec 14, 1897; Lloyd R. Moyer, b Mar 14, 1899.

IV. Leanna Rickert, m John Watts. No issue.

IV. Catharine Rickert, m Jacob Rosenberger.

III. Maria Rosenberger, b Aug 6, 1757, d Jan 14, 1778.

III. Magdalene Rosenberger, b Dec 18, 1759, d 1808, m John Schwardle.

(See John Schwardle Family.)

III. A son b 1761, d unnamed.

III. A daughter b 1762, d unnamed.

III. Sarah Rosenberger, b Jan 24, 1765, d Apr 6, 1849, m Philip Schwardle.

(See Philip Schwardle Family.)

FIRST ROSENBERGER FAMILY REUNION.

———o———

The first reunion of the Rosenberger family was held in Perkasie Park, Bucks County, Pa., on Thursday, August 10, 1899.

The weather in the early morning was rainy, and fears were entertained that the rain would interfere with the attendance. However, while o'er head the clouds hung dark and broken, it ceased to rain, and the descendants began to arrive, in vehicles of every description, from the surrounding districts of Bucks and Montgomery Counties, while the incoming trains brought hundreds more, until upwards of 1,500 descendants of the pioneer Henry Rosenberger were present. The arrangements of the reunion were in charge of a committee who had been engaged for some time in the work of preparation, and the exercises were signally successful.

Included in the gathering were representatives of the family from Bucks, Montgomery and Lehigh Counties, and Philadelphia, while several came from distant states in the West and Canada.

The exercises began at 10:30 a. m., when the chairman, Prof. Seward M. Rosenberger, of Quakertown, Pa., mounted the platform in the auditorium of the park and introduced Prof. Howard Freed, of Lansdale, Pa., as the first participant, who rendered a pleasing piano solo. This was followed by singing "All Hail the Power of Jesus' Name," and a fervent prayer was then offered by Rev. G. W. Hengen, of Perkasie, Pa., after which Prof. S. M. Rosenberger, of Quakertown, Pa., delivered the address of welcome, to which Rev. S. A. Ziegenfuss, D. D., of Germantown, Pa., responded in an appropriate address in which he cited his connection with the family and congratulated the committee on the success of the undertaking.

Miss Ella Geller, a promising young vocalist, of Lansdale, Pa., favored the audience with a vocal solo,

and Miss Stella Rosenberger, of Philadelphia, rendered
an excellent piano solo.

The memorial address, prepared by A. R. Place,
Esq., of Lansdale, Pa., was read by Dr. Daniel M. Landis, of Perkasie, Pa., Mr. Place, just having been treated
for an affection of the throat, his physician would not
permit him to use his voice. The address was one of
the best productions of the day.

The exercises of the forenoon were closed by singing that patriotic hymn, "America."

At 2 o'clock, the audience which had been considerably increased by later arrivals, again gathered in the
auditorium and the exercises for the afternoon were
opened by singing "Nearer My God to Thee," after
which a piano duet was rendered by Miss Stella Rosenberger and Howard Freed. The chairman then introduced Samuel Z. Freed, Esq., of Doylestown, Pa., who
delivered an address. He was followed by an address
by Prof. A. F. K. Krout, M. A., of Philadelphia. Misses
Mabel and Susie Rosenberger, of Hilltown, Pa., rendered
a piano duet, and J. V. Ommeren, Esq., of Quakertown,
Pa., addressed the audience briefly in the absence of F.
G. Hobson, Esq., of Collegeville, Pa., who was an-
nounced on the program as one of the speakers, but
failed to be present.

Miss Ella Geller sang another solo, after which the
historical address was delivered by Rev. A. J. Fretz, of
Milton, N. J.

At the close of the exercises the question of holding future reunions of the family came up for consideration, and it was moved and carried to hold a
reunion of the family every five years.

SECOND ROSENBERGER FAMILY REUNION.

———o———

The second reunion of the Rosenberger family was held on Thursday, August 11, 1904, when about 1,000 descendants of the pioneer Bishop Henry Rosenberger gathered in Perkasie Park, Bucks Co., Pa. The day did not open auspiciously, and the threatening skies kept many away. In the afternoon the large pavilion was well filled.

A short program was rendered in the forenoon. Prayer by Rev. S. A. Stopp, of Doylestown, Pa. Dr. D. M. Landis extended the welcome of the town and committee to the visiting relatives. Prof. S. M. Rosenberger responded to the words of welcome. James A. Rosenberger, of Milford Square, delivered an oration lauding the virtues of the ancestors, and emphasizing the need of cheerful devotion to duty and right. Miss Nora Rosenberger, of Perkasie, gave a touching reading, which was sympathetically received by the audience. Addresses in the afternoon were delivered by J. Ralphus Freed, Esq., of Doylestown, in the English language, and Frank R. Rosenberger, of Milford Square, in German. The addresses were replete with happy allusions and sparkling thoughts. A trio was rendered by W. B. Rosenberger's family and a number of instrumental selections were rendered by the Misses Susie and Mabel Rosenberger, of Hilltown. The musical renditions greatly delighted the audience. The historical sketch prepared by Rev. A. J. Fretz, the family historian, was read by the president of the Association. At a business session the officers of the Association were re-elected to serve the next reunion—1907. They are Prof. S. M. Rosenberger, President; I. R. Haldeman, Secretary; Frank Rosenberger, Treasurer; Dr. D. M. Landis, Isaac Rosenberger and Harvey Landis, Executive Committee.

VALEDICTION.

——o——

The gentle reminder of the editor that he has about
completed the manuscript for the Rosenberger Family
History, and that the last article in the form of a vale-
diction would therefore be expected without much
further delay, urges me to fulfill a promise which I
made some time ago, and which I have not forgotten.
Many of us have no doubt awaited the appearance of
this work with a great deal of interest. Various matters
have transpired within recent years to awaken our
expectations to a greater or less degree, so that any one
connected with the Rosenberger family, would, from
time to time, find his feelings agitated, his hopes excited
and his desires deepened, as these matters relating to
the history of the family took more definite shape.

The very first announcement from the Editor calling our attention to the fact that the publication of a
history of the pioneers and descendants of the Rosenberger family would be undertaken, could not fail to
awaken a responsive chord in the heart of every living
member who happens to be in any way connected with
the family. And every subsequent announcement of
the intended project, had the effect to increase our
interest and augment our sympathy in behalf of the
movement.

But this favorable regard reached its highest point,
(in our judgment) in the very successful ROSENBERGER
FAMILY REUNION, held at Perkasie Park in the summer
of 1899. Such an outpouring of people must certainly
have exceeded the most sanguine expectations of the
committee who arranged for the re-union, and demonstrated in no uncertain tones the attitude of the descendants to their family history.

The preparation and completion of such a history
is necessarily fraught with a great deal of labor, research

and patience. We are deeply sensible and fully appreciate the greatness and accuracy of the work done by the Editor in gathering, compiling and arranging the historical data of this family, tracing our lineage and making it possible for us to see the line of our particular descent from, and our relations to the parent stem. It is an intricate and yet withal an interesting study.

As we scan the pages of this volume, we learn a great many things that we had not known before. We gain a better insight into our family history, appreciate the more fully the noble deeds, the pioneer work, the glorious achievements, the arduous self-denials, the worthy examples and goodly heritage handed down to us by our fathers. Our eyes are opened and our hearts are impressed as we ponder the character of our ancestors in their integrity, uprightness, honesty and manly virtues. Such consideration and reflection cannot fail to incite us in constantly putting forth the greatest efforts to prove ourselves the worthy descendants of noble sires. What man hath done man can do. It would be idle folly, therefore, for any one to presume to rest on the laurels of his progenitors.

> "Let us, then, be up and doing,
> With a heart for any fate;
> Still achieving, still pursuing,
> Learn to labor and to wait."

While we may reasonably expect that all our kindred will make themselves the possessors of at least one copy of this valuable history, (for its price is certainly placed within the reach of each one) we, at the same time hope that they will not only give the volume a place on their library shelves, but will study its pages and acquaint themselves with its facts. The character of the work stamps it largely as a book of reference, one that needs to be consulted repeatedly, in order to be rightly understood and properly appreciated. Frequent recurrences to its pages, and a constant looking up of its events and names will fill the mind with a proper knowledge of our genealogy, and enable us to speak intelligently concerning the matters that are related to us so closely.

It is a work, therefore, not of passing value and present interest only, but one that grows upon us as time passes on, and will prove a treasure even to our succeeding generations.

I have already written enough and ought to say *farewell,* but before doing so finally, let me impress the thought: How will our lives compare with the lives of our forefathers ?   Will the world be the better because we have lived in it ?   Will our children and children's children rise up to call us blessed, because we have not lived in vain, and because we have made the best use of our talents, and have been faithful, devoted and true to our Divine Lord and Master ?   We thus leave a good example behind us and pass from the scenes of this life into the blessedness of the life beyond.   With these thoughts we lay our pen down as we write a last and an affectionate *farewell.*

REV. S. A. ZIEGENFUSS.

Germantown, Philadelphia, Pa.

July 30, 1900.

ERRATA.

Page 66 read Alvin Rudy, not Aloin.
" 66 " Barbara Shantz, not Barbard.
" 69 " Noah E. Eby, not Ely.
" 69 " Benjamin F. Eby, not Ely.
" 77 " Eschelman, not Echelman.
" 77 " VI. Elizabeth Stauffer, not VII.
" 74 " VI. Barbara Rudy, b. 1842, not VII.
" 78 " Ferman, not Farmer Snyder.
" 80 " VI. Benjaman Rosenberger, not VII.
" 80 " VIII. Mamie Burman. not VII.
" 80 " Rose Rabine, not Robine.
" 81 " W. B. Matthews, not W. E.
" 82 " Moses Rosenberg, b. 1862, not 1892.
" 82 " May Forbes, not Mary.
" 84 " Doress S. Dochowon, not Dovess.
" 91 " Montford S. Strome, not Mortford.
" 92 " Freyvogel, not Freyvogee.
" 97 " John L. Lapp, not John J.
" 106 " Matilda H. Snyder, b. June 10.
" 112 " Margaret Rupple, not Rupped.
" 116 " Enoch D. Shantz, b. 1841, not 1848.
" 123 " Henry D. Kratz, not Dr.
" 126 " Arrived August 11, 1732, not 1832.
" 138 " Fay and Jay Hunsberger, not Hunsicker.
" 138 " VIII. Elizabeth and Arthur Hunsberger, not
VII.
" 140 " Michael D. Alderfer, b. 1843, not 1842.
" 170 " Gelderland, not Genlderland.
" 173 " financially successful, not successfully.
" 175 " M. Kate Sweaney. not Siveany.
" 182 " Grant Reservation, not Grand.
" 183 " corps of professors, not professions.
" 205 " Menn's, not Menno.
" 207 " VI. David Rosenberger, not VII.
" 208 " Menn's, not Menno.
" 210 " VII. Edna M. Evans, not VI.
" 224 " M. Christiana, adopted daughter of Rev. John
Funk.

GENERAL INDEX.

BENJAMIN ROSENBERGER FAMILY,
OF HATFIELD, PA.

DANIEL ROSENBERGER FAMILY,

OF HATFIELD, PA.

JOHN ROSENBERGER, SR., FAMILY,
OF HATFIELD, PA.

0M

www.ingramcontent.com/pod-product-compliance
Lightning Source LLC
Chambersburg PA
CBHW071352290326
41932CB00045B/1541